On to Petersburg

ON TO PETERSBURG

Grant and Lee
JUNE 4–15, 1864

Gordon C. Rhea

LOUISIANA STATE UNIVERSITY PRESS

Baton Rouge

Published with the assistance of the V. Ray Cardozier Fund

Published by Louisiana State University Press
Copyright © 2017 by Louisiana State University Press
All rights reserved
Manufactured in the United States of America
First printing

Typefaces: Cochin, display; Times Roman, text
Printer and binder: McNaughton & Gunn

Library of Congress Cataloging-in-Publication Data
Names: Rhea, Gordon C., author.
Title: On to Petersburg : Grant and Lee, June 4–15, 1864 / Gordon C. Rhea.
Description: Baton Rouge : Louisiana State University Press, 2017. | Includes bibliographical
    references and index.
Identifiers: LCCN 2017009682 | ISBN 978-0-8071-6747-2 (cloth : alk. paper) | ISBN
    978-0-8071-6748-9 (pdf) | ISBN 978-0-8071-6749-6 (epub)
Subjects: LCSH: Overland Campaign, Va., 1864. | Grant, Ulysses S. (Ulysses Simpson),
    1822–1885—Military leadership. | Lee, Robert E. (Robert Edward), 1807–1870—Military
    leadership.
Classification: LCC E476.52 .R477 2017 | DDC 975.5/03—dc23
LC record available at https://lccn.loc.gov/2017009682

Contents

Illustrations

Preface

MORE THAN A CENTURY and a half has elapsed since the Army of the Potomac crossed the James River and the Union 18th Corps pressed toward Petersburg, aiming to sever the Army of Northern Virginia's main supply line. The six weeks of combat preceding this movement represents the most intense continuous bout of warfare the continent has ever witnessed. Each side's premier general—Ulysses S. Grant and Robert E. Lee—matched wits and endurance in a campaign of combat and maneuver from the Rapidan River to the James. Packed into those six horrific weeks were the Battles of the Wilderness, Spotsylvania Court House, the North Anna River, and Cold Harbor.

This book is the fifth and final volume in my series describing the contest of combat and maneuver between Grant and Lee that has come to be called the Overland Campaign. It begins with the aftermath of the bloody June 3 assault at Cold Harbor and follows the armies as Grant swings south toward Petersburg, aiming to cut Lee's supply lines and compel the Virginian to abandon his impregnable Cold Harbor defenses. Detailed are the final days at Cold Harbor, the Union army's movement to the James River, Lee's response, and the initial assault on Petersburg.

The popular name for Grant's offensive against Lee—the Overland Campaign—reflects a common misunderstanding of its objective. In 1862 Major General George B. McClellan attempted to capture the Confederate capital by transporting his army by ships to the gates of Richmond. Grant's 1864 offensive advanced across some sixty miles of Virginia countryside, passing near where McClellan had marched two years earlier. Critics have faulted Grant for incurring massive casualties to gain a position that McClellan had achieved with virtually no losses. This facile analysis, however, ignores that the two Union commanders had very different objectives. While McClellan was intent upon capturing Richmond, Grant's primary goal was not the capture of that city, but the destruction of Lee's army.

Historians generally treat the stalemate at Cold Harbor as ending the Overland Campaign. I take a contrary view and consider the initial assault on Petersburg on June 15, 1864, as the its last act and the Petersburg Campaign's opening salvo. Grant's withdrawal from Cold Harbor and his initial attempt to take the Cockade City was conceptually a continuation of his mobile operations to destroy Lee's army that had started with the crossing of the Rapidan more than a month before. June 15 terminated that campaign of maneuver; afterward the contending armies remained gridlocked in front of Petersburg for almost ten excruciating months.

The richness of Union sources and the comparative paucity of Confederate material unavoidably leads to an imbalance in telling the Overland Campaign's story. We simply know more about events in Grant's ranks than we do about those in Lee's. If I linger in Union camps more than in the Confederate, it is not because I consider one side more important or interesting than the other, but because I am led to do so by disparities in the availability of historical records.

I am indebted to a host of historians and archivists who helped me research and document the military operations discussed in this book. Two historians were especially helpful in reconstructing events during the armies' last days at Cold Harbor. Robert E. L. Krick of the Richmond National Battlefield Park walked much of the ground with me and introduced me to resources that I otherwise might have overlooked. Patrick S. Brady of Seattle, who has been researching and writing about Cold Harbor for these past several years, graciously shared his manuscript and guided me to numerous valuable sources. I am profoundly grateful for their assistance.

The executive director of Pamplin Historical Park, A. Wilson Greene, is the leading historian of the Petersburg Campaign. He has recently completed the first book of a multivolume study that when finished will stand as the authoritative word on the campaign. Mr. Greene not only shared with me his initial chapters dealing with the events preceding and including the battle on June 15 but also reviewed my chapters about the movement on Petersburg, saving me from several potentially embarrassing errors. I and the rest of the community of Civil War historians eagerly await the publication of Greene's series. I also thank Julia Steele, chief of resource management at Petersburg National Battlefield Park, as well as the rest of the park-service staff at the Petersburg facility.

Researcher and author Bryce A. Suderow expended prodigious efforts on my behalf researching Civil War–era newspapers and periodicals, locating reams of pertinent documents and letters, and patiently reviewing my manuscript. Mr. Suderow is a serious student of the Petersburg Campaign whose opinions I value highly, although I do not always agree with them. While he holds a more negative opinion of Grant's generalship, I enjoy our discussions and have learned much from them. I am similarly indebted to Joseph A. Rose, whose *Grant under Fire* contains a scathing criticism of the general's military acumen. Mr. Rose sent me material and critiqued some of my chapters. While we do not see eye-to-eye about Grant, his observations have challenged me to reexamine my own ideas. My current assessment of the Union general in chief appears in the epilogue and will, I trust, generate additional discussion of this fascinating topic.

Numerous historians, collectors, and archivists across the country have sent me material and reviewed portions of my evolving manuscript. Among them is Bobby Mueller, whose knowledge about the neglected portion of the Cold Harbor battlefield around Matadequin Creek assisted me in understanding the confused combat that occurred there. I also extend thanks to Alfred C. Young, whose recent *Lee's Army during the Overland Campaign* is the best modern attempt to calculate Confederate casualties. Mr. Young generously shared his data with me and estimated losses at my request for some engagements not discussed in his book.

As always, I was delighted when George F. Skoch agreed to prepare the maps for this book, as he did for my previous volumes. His ability to make troop movements comprehensible at a glance is truly phenomenal. I am also grateful to Paul R. Dotson, LSU Press's acquisition editor, who has supported this project from its inception, and to Kevin Brock, whose fine editing ensured that my sentences said what I meant them to say. Most importantly, I thank my wife, Catherine, who has supported and encouraged me in my writing projects over the past thirty years, and to my sons, Campbell and Carter, who grew up tramping the battlefields of the Overland Campaign with their dad.

ON TO PETERSBURG

I

MAY 5–JUNE 3, 1864

Grant and Lee Deadlock at Cold Harbor

"Cutting the toenails of our enemy."

THE ARMY OF THE POTOMAC'S grand offensive at Cold Harbor, launched at daybreak on June 3, 1864, had been a dismal failure. Nowhere did the blue-clad assailants gain ground. Lifeless heaps dotted the clearings in front of the Confederate fortifications, bodies stacked "like hogs in a pen," a southerner recalled, "some side by side, across each other, some two deep, while others with their legs lying across the head and body of their dead comrades." As the day warmed, "the fast decomposing dead sent over into our trenches a most sickening and nauseating stench," another Confederate remembered, "while the helpless and fly-infested wounded were left to die a most horrible death."[1]

Union survivors of the forlorn offensive, unable to retreat, sought cover behind barricades hastily constructed from dirt and corpses. "Troops yet clung tenaciously to the ground nearest the Confederate works, wherever so much as half-cover could be obtained," a Federal officer recalled. A northerner likened the killing field at Cold Harbor to a "boiling cauldron, from the incessant pattering and plowing of shot, which raised the dirt in geysers and spitting sands." It was "almost impossible to move and live," a New Englander added, "the lifting of a head or hand being the signal for volleys of musketry." A Connecticut man noted that "one of the poor fellows would hold up his hand and waive it feebly to plead for rescue, but after one or two had been brutally made a target by the enemy for doing so, these motions ceased and the blue overcoats lay still."[2]

Watching from the safety of the Confederate battlements, an Alabaman contemplated the tragedy before him. He had witnessed "many a field of carnage and blood, and imagined before reaching Cold Harbor that nothing could surpass the horrors and brutalities of cruel war," he reflected. "But this, the Battle of Cold Harbor, was the most horrible of any we had ever experienced."[3]

Under cover of darkness during the night of June 3–4, Federal commanders rectified their main line of entrenchments, pickets dug pits a few yards in advance, and reserves filled gaps in the fortifications. A few brave souls ventured into the no-man's land between the armies, responding to the groans of the wounded and the dying. "It was well nigh impossible to take a step without treading upon some human being, either living or dead," a northerner recounted. "Besides this obstruction, the ground was honeycombed with pits and holes where the men had burrowed for safety during the day's trial."[4]

A month earlier, Lieutenant General Ulysses S. Grant had inaugurated a campaign to defeat General Robert E. Lee's Army of Northern Virginia and bring the American Civil War to a close. Now, for the fourth time in as many weeks, the Confederates had fought Grant to an impasse. Sheltered behind an impregnable wall of earthworks, the flanks of their battlements anchored on marshy streams, Lee's rebels barred the way to Richmond. Why had the Union campaign, initiated with such grand prospects of quick victory, ground to a bloody stalemate? More importantly, how did the new Federal commander in chief plan to break the deadlock?

Eighteen sixty-four was an election year, and President Abraham Lincoln had sound reasons to question whether voters would award him a second term or remove him from office. The Army of the Potomac, led by Major General George G. Meade, had delivered a resounding rebuff to Lee at Gettysburg in the summer of 1863, but Union forces in the war's eastern theater had achieved little of note the rest of that year. Profound weariness, expressed in draft riots and antiwar pronouncements, gripped the northern populace. Unless Federal armies won victories this spring, the presidential race seemed destined to favor an opposition candidate willing to negotiate with the South.

Sharply aware of the need for military successes, Lincoln had summoned Grant to Washington. A midwesterner, the general had emerged as the northern military's rising star, delivering an impressive drumbeat of victories at Forts Henry and Donelson, Shiloh, Vicksburg, and Chattanooga. Hoping that Grant might work his magic in the East, Lincoln had arranged for his promotion to lieutenant general and placed him in charge of the nation's military might. Grant set as his objective the destruction of the Confederate armies, determining to "hammer continuously," as he put it, "against the armed force of the enemy and his resources until by mere attrition, if in no other way, there should be nothing left to [the rebels] but an equal submission with the loyal section of our common country to the constitution and laws of the land." Sealing perhaps the most compatible working relationship between president and general in chief the nation had seen, Lincoln promised Grant a free hand running the war and the troops and supplies he needed to win. The president's political fortunes, a New York newspaper noted, "not less than the great cause of the country, are in the hands of General Grant, and the failure of the General will be the overthrow of the President."[5]

On March 10, 1864, Grant jostled by train sixty miles down the Orange and Alexandria Railroad to Brandy Station, a siding north of Culpeper Court House that served as the Army of the Potomac's nerve center. His purpose was to meet with Meade, still the army's commander, to gauge whether he should appoint a new general to head the Union's premier fighting force in the East. Six years Grant's senior, Meade knew his standing in Washington was tenuous. "He has none of the dash and brilliancy which is necessary to popularity," a soldier commented. Accompanying the general in chief was Major General William F. "Baldy" Smith, who had impressed Grant during his recent campaigns in the West and a strong candidate to replace Meade. "It is rumored, and there are strong reasons for believing it true, that Baldy Smith is to replace Meade in command of this Army, backed by Grant," Meade's provost marshal, Marsena R. Patrick, reported in his diary. "This is producing much uneasiness in the minds of all who have the good of this Army at heart."[6]

To Grant's surprise, the hero of Gettysburg offered to step aside so that Grant could appoint someone of his own choosing. Impressed, he decided to retain Meade. Loosely defining their respective spheres of responsibility, Grant decreed that he would set broad strategic policy and coordinate the nation's far-flung armies, while Meade would command the Army of the Potomac. "My instructions for that army were all through him," Grant later wrote, "and were all general in their nature, leaving all the details and the execution to him."[7]

Throughout April, Grant labored to strengthen Meade's army. Soldiers on furlough returned to their commands, new recruits swelled the ranks, and garrison troops from the North's urban centers journeyed to the Virginia front. More men—the 9th Corps, commanded by Major General Ambrose E. Burnside—joined Meade's burgeoning monolith, which had grown by the first week of May to nearly 120,000 soldiers. Meade's quartermaster general, Brigadier General Rufus Ingalls, rightfully boasted that "probably no army on earth ever before was in better condition in every respect than was the Army of the Potomac."[8]

The army's command structure, however, was an unruly arrangement, and Grant's decision to accompany Meade guaranteed a collision between the two men's very different military temperaments. Willing to take risks and comfortable with improvising as events unfolded, Lincoln's new general in chief would find himself hobbled by a more deliberate subordinate whose caution often ran counter to his own bold plans. The addition of Burnside's 9th Corps multiplied the complications. The portly New Englander, boldly festooned with side-whiskers, had led the Army of the Potomac during its failed offensives around Fredericksburg in the bitter winter of 1862–63, and his commission as major general predated Meade's. Grant's awkward solution to this nightmare of military protocol was to let Burnside manage his corps as an independent command, with Grant coordinating Burnside's and Meade's movements.

Compounding the confusion was a recent reorganization of the Potomac army into three infantry corps headed by generals who had never before worked as a team. Major General Winfield S. Hancock, commanding the 2nd Corps, would spend much of the ensuing campaign in an ambulance, his mind clouded by drugs to dull the pain from a thigh wound received at Gettysburg; Major General John Sedgwick, heading the 6th Corps, was "steady and sure," a friend pegged him, but had difficulty adjusting to the fast-moving exercise envisioned by Grant and would soon fall victim to a sharpshooter's bullet; and Major General Gouverneur K. Warren, leading the 5th Corps, was brilliant but flawed by an annoying habit of openly second-guessing his superiors. New to the army and to Meade was Major General Philip H. Sheridan, Grant's subordinate from the West who now commanded the Cavalry Corps. Accustomed to speaking his mind, the hot-tempered son of Irish immigrants was soon ensnarled in a bitter feud with Meade over the proper role of the army's mounted arm.

In mid-January 1864, before coming to Virginia, Grant had outlined his initial thoughts for defeating Lee to Major General Henry W. Halleck, who then served in a largely administrative capacity as Lincoln's general in chief. The Union, Grant urged, should abandon its "previously attempted lines to Richmond" and instead concentrate on disrupting Lee's sources of supply. As he saw it, the spring campaign ought to begin with 60,000 troops advancing inland from Suffolk, Virginia; destroying the railroads around Weldon, North Carolina; and occupying Raleigh. "This would virtually force an evacuation of Virginia and indirectly of East Tennessee," Grant predicted, and would "draw the enemy from campaigns of their own choosing, and for which they are prepared, to new lines of operations never expected to become necessary."[9]

The Lincoln administration, Halleck cautioned, had vetted the idea of a major offensive in North Carolina and rejected that strategy. It was impossible to raise enough troops, he protested, without weakening the force protecting the nation's capital. "Uncover Washington and the Potomac River," Halleck warned, "and all the forces which Lee can collect will be moved north, and the popular sentiment will compel the Government to bring back the army in North Carolina to defend Washington, Baltimore, Harrisburg, and Philadelphia." He feared that any troops "sent south of James River cannot be brought back in time to oppose Lee, should he attempt a movement north, which I am satisfied would be his best policy." He also disfavored leaving one army to protect Washington and dispatching another to North Carolina, fearing that such a move might enable Lee to concentrate his entire force against either diminished Union force. The nation's military might, Halleck stressed, should be focused directly against the Army of Northern Virginia and not frittered away in subsidiary operations. "We have given too much attention to cutting the toe nails of our enemy instead of grasping his throat," he counseled. "These fundamental principles require, in my opinion, that all our available forces in the east should be concentrated against Lee's army," he wrote in conclusion. "We cannot take Richmond (at least with any military advantage), and we cannot operate advantageously on any point from the Atlantic coast till we destroy or disperse that army, and the nearer to Washington we can fight it the better for us."[10]

Duly chastened, Grant devised a strategy that employed his formidable edge in numbers and materiel to move directly against Lee while at the same time menacing the rebel army's source of supplies and ensuring Washington's safety. Even as Meade engaged Lee head-on, a second Union army, under Major General Franz Sigel, was to start south through the Shenandoah Valley to the west, depriving the Army of Northern Virginia of food and forage from the rich Valley farms and threatening the rebel army's western flank. Simultaneously the Army of the James, commanded by Major General Benjamin F. Butler, was to advance against Richmond from the south and sever Lee's supply lines. And in western Virginia, Brigadier General George Crook, commanding the Army of West Virginia, was to move on Dublin, cutting the critical Virginia and Tennessee Railroad. Battered in front by the huge Potomac army, denied sustenance by the Valley incursion, and harassed in rear by Butler, Lee would finally be brought to bay. Grant's plan was an intelligent exercise, carefully drawn to meet Halleck's requirements and to escalate the war in the East to a swift conclusion.

On April 1, 1864, Grant traveled to Fortress Monroe, at the confluence of the James and York Rivers, to confer with Butler about his role in the projected operations. Prolonged a day by a violent rainstorm, the conference ended with the generals seemingly in accord. When Meade started out against Lee from the north, Butler was to move partway up the James from the south, regroup, and continue along the river's southern bank against the Confederate capital.

"Richmond is to be your objective point," Grant stressed, "and that there is to be cooperation between your force and the Army of the Potomac, must be your guide." Two weeks later he reminded Butler to "seize upon City Point [partway up the James toward Richmond] and act from there, looking upon Richmond as your objective point."[11]

Questions swirled around Butler's competency to perform his assignment. He was, after all, a political appointee, and his battlefield experience was negligible. Partially compensating for Butler's deficiencies were the Army of the James's two corps commanders, "Baldy" Smith and Brigadier General Quincy A. Gillmore. Smith, who displayed "the air of a German officer—one of those uneasy, cross-grained ones," according to one of Meade's staffers, had performed so well during the Chattanooga campaign that Grant recommended him to War Secretary Edwin Stanton as "one of the clearest military heads in the army." Grant also recognized, however, that the short, portly general could be "obstinate" and was "likely to condemn whatever is not suggested by himself." Gillmore, a West Point graduate and engineer like Smith, had demonstrated talent in methodically overwhelming fixed fortifications but was "not known as an enterprising general or prompt to take advantage of opportunities." Grant would soon see his hopes for this operation dashed as Butler's ineptitude, Smith's tendency to argue with his superiors, and Gillmore's cautious streak combined to frustrate his plans.[12]

The elements of his offensive in place, Grant issued final instructions. His friend and trusted subordinate Major General William T. Sherman was to move against the main rebel army in the West to "break it up and get into the interior of the enemy's country as far as you can, inflicting all the damage you can against his war resources." Meade was to undertake the same role in the East, supported by Sigel and Butler. "Lee's army will be your objective point," Grant reminded the head of his chief combat force. "Wherever Lee goes, there you will go also."[13]

The Confederacy's president, Jefferson Davis, held a view of the strategic situation that was remarkably similar to Lincoln's vision. He too saw that the North's overwhelming edge in manpower and industry foreclosed the South from winning independence by military prowess. But by staving off Union victories, Confederate armies might nourish the budding northern peace movement and persuade the exhausted Union to let its defiant sister go. "Every bullet we can send is the best ballot that can be deposited against [Lincoln's] election," a Georgia newspaper reminded its readers. "The battlefields of 1864 will hold the polls of this momentous decision." Lieutenant General James

Longstreet, Lee's premier corps commander, was of similar mind. "If we can break up the enemy's arrangements early, and throw him back," predicted Longstreet, "he will not be able to recover his position nor his morale until after the Presidential election is over, and we shall then have a new President to treat with." [14]

The Confederacy's fate—in the eastern theater, at least—rested in the hands of Lee, whose victories during the past two years had made him a symbol of the rebellion's determined spirit. While the general had fared poorly when he ventured outside of the Old Dominion—as witnessed by the reverses at Antietam and Gettysburg—he had proven well-nigh invincible on his home turf. "General Robert E. Lee is regarded by his army as nearest approaching the character of the great and good [George] Washington than any man living," a Confederate wrote home. "He is the only man living in whom they would unreservedly trust all power for the preservation of their independence." [15]

Lee's aristocratic bearing seemed strikingly at odds with Grant's more plebian comportment. The two men, however, shared an aggressive military temperament. Like Grant, Lee was a master at conducting offensive operations and possessed an uncanny knack for turning seemingly impossible situations his way. The inventive Confederate's most brilliant successes had been against armies that outnumbered him better than two to one, coincidentally the same numerical advantage that the Army of the Potomac held over him this spring. Lee's victories during the previous two years, however, had exacted a painful toll in casualties, and replacements for fallen heroes were harder to find. Time would tell whether the Army of Northern Virginia could repel the Union armies converging in Virginia before Grant's multipronged juggernaut ground the rebel force into submission.

By the end of April, Lee commanded an army of nearly 64,000 soldiers. Facing an enemy almost twice as numerous and better supplied than his own force, he nonetheless held important advantages. Most of his soldiers were veterans, and new men were generally assigned to seasoned outfits where they could fight alongside experienced troops. Lee's warriors knew every road and path and displayed the élan of men defending their native soil. Each spring Union invaders had advanced on Richmond, and each spring the Army of Northern Virginia had driven them back, often against daunting odds. Reminiscing years later, one of Lee's former soldiers reflected, "The thought of being whipped never crossed my mind." [16]

The Army of Northern Virginia, like the Army of the Potomac, started the campaign with three infantry corps heads who exhibited mixed blends of talents and flaws. These included Longstreet, Lee's "War Horse," fresh from an unsuccessful independent foray in Tennessee and commanding the 1st Corps; Lieutenant General Richard S. Ewell, the eccentric, peg-legged 2nd Corps commander who seemed befuddled by Lee's deferential style of leadership; and Lieutenant General Ambrose P. Hill of the 3rd Corps, wracked by ill health and apparently overwhelmed by the responsibilities of high command. Closest to Lee was the flamboyant Major General James E. B. "Jeb" Stuart, heading the army's cavalry. After a month of fighting Grant, only one of these generals—Hill, or "Little Powell," as the soldiers called him—would remain in the field with Lee.

As April turned to May, it became clear that Grant meant to initiate a major offensive in the Old Dominion. Ever aggressive, Lee preferred to seize the initiative and attack, hoping that a Confederate victory might compel Lincoln to recall his forces to defend Washington. But the southern commander was unable to undertake offensive operations; food and fodder remained scarce, and he had no clue what route the Union leviathan on the northern bank of the Rapidan River or Butler's force south of Richmond might take. So Lee adopted a defensive strategy, resolving to assail the Army of the Potomac when it ventured across the river, sixty miles north of the Confederate capital. He was determined at all costs to avoid falling back to Richmond, for retreating would undermine his ability to maneuver, the trump card in his deck of military tricks. "If I am obliged to retire from this line," Lee famously predicted, referring to his hold on the country below the Rapidan, "either by flank movement of the enemy or want of supplies, great injury will befall us." [17]

Thus the stage was set for the Civil War's decisive campaign. In later years popular historians touted Gettysburg as the conflict's turning point. But by the spring of 1864, Lee had largely repaired his Gettysburg losses. Entrenched below the Rapidan, he faced the Army of the Potomac with slightly fewer men than he had taken into Pennsylvania the previous year. Supplies were thin, but Lee's lean veterans would lose no battles because of hunger or shortages of ammunition, and their morale remained high. "I don't have any fears but what we will give the Yanks the worst whipping they have got if they do attempt to take Richmond," a southerner penned his family. [18]

"Every day there is a fight."

The first week of May saw Meade, Butler, Sigel, and Crook on the march. Spearheading the grand Union offensive, the Army of the Potomac crossed the Rapidan River downstream from Lee and camped in a thickly forested region known as the Wilderness. Acting boldly, Lee seized the initiative and fought

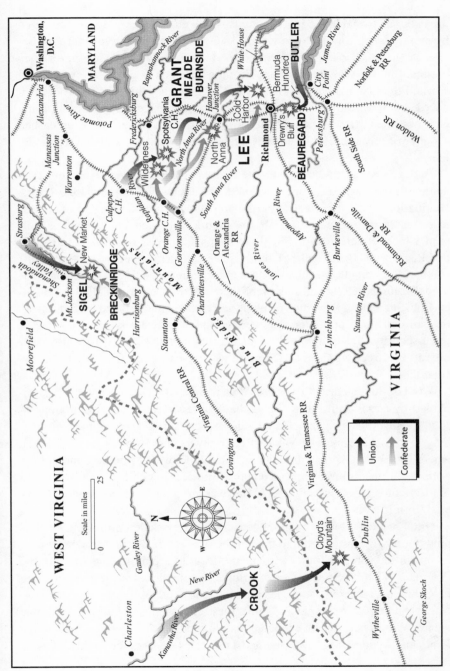

Movements from the Wilderness to Cold Harbor

the Federals to stalemate in a bloody two-day engagement. Meade countered by sidling south toward Spotsylvania Court House, aiming to interpose between Lee and Richmond and force the Confederates to fight him on open ground. But the Army of Northern Virginia reached the courthouse town first, blocked the Union advance, and crafted an imposing line of earthworks that once again thwarted the Federal commanders. Combat escalated at a dizzying pace over the next two weeks as Meade, under Grant's watchful eye, unleashed a welter of unsuccessful offensives intended to break Lee's Spotsylvania defenses.

Butler meanwhile advanced up the James River to Bermuda Hundred, a triangle of land formed by the junction of the James and Appomattox Rivers. Halting to construct protective earthworks, he ventured a flurry of uncoordinated and largely unsuccessful jabs toward the Richmond and Petersburg Railroad, which served as the principal supply line for Lee's army. On May 16 General Pierre G. T. Beauregard's Confederates defeated Butler at Drewry's Bluff south of Richmond, and Butler retired to his entrenched line at Bermuda Hundred. Beauregard followed and established a fortified position called the Howlett Line that fenced the Union army into Bermuda Hundred and barred it from the railroad. As Grant later observed, although Butler was "in a position of great security," his command was also "as completely shut off from further operation directly against Richmond as if it had been in a bottle tightly corked." [19]

Word of Butler's reverse reached Grant at Spotsylvania Court House accompanied by equally unsettling news that Confederates under Major General John C. Breckinridge had defeated Sigel at New Market, halting the Union offensive in the Shenandoah Valley. Better news came from western Virginia, where Crook defeated a Confederate force at Cloyd's Mountain and cut the critical rail line linking Tennessee and Virginia. But with Butler and Sigel out of the picture, the Army of the Potomac was left to defeat the Army of Northern Virginia alone.

Grant responded with more maneuvers, but Lee eluded him again by slipping twenty-five miles south to the North Anna River. While Meade pursued, Grant shifted some of Butler's troops northward to reinforce the Army of the Potomac. "The force under General Butler is not detaining ten thousand men in Richmond, and are not even keeping the road south of the city cut," the general in chief wrote Washington. "Under these circumstances I think it advisable to have all of it here except enough to have a foothold at City Point," where the James and Appomattox Rivers merged. Directions went out for "Baldy" Smith's

18th Corps, augmented by a division from Gillmore's 10th Corps, to leave Bermuda Hundred and unite with the Potomac army.[20]

Meade meanwhile managed to bring the 5th Corps over the North Anna River and threaten Lee's flank. The Confederate deftly responded by deploying the Army of Northern Virginia into a wedge-shaped formation, its apex touching the North Anna and each leg reaching back to anchor on strong natural features. The clever arrangement invited Union forces into an ambush: when the Federals advanced, the Confederate wedge would split their army in two, and Lee could spring his trap, concentrating to assail either part of the divided enemy force. Lee had suited the military maxim favoring interior lines to the North Anna's topography and given his smaller army an advantage over its more numerous adversary.[21]

On May 24 Grant stepped blindly into this snare. Lee, however, lay confined in his tent with dysentery and was unable to coordinate an attack. His cadre of talented corps commanders by this time numbered among the campaign's casualties. Longstreet had been severely wounded, Stuart was dead, Hill was chronically ill, and Ewell had become increasingly unreliable. With no dependable subordinate available to assume the army's reins, Lee let pass an opportunity to strike a telling offensive blow. By evening the Federals had discovered Lee's deception and began entrenching. For several days the hostile armies glowered at one another, pressed cheek by jowl south of the river. Grant, who had personally directed the North Anna operation, was sharply criticized by Meade's staffers, who considered the movement "not only badly conceived, but badly executed."[22]

Ever optimistic, Grant perceived a silver lining. "Lee's army is really whipped," he wired Washington. "A battle with them outside of intrenchments, cannot be had. Our men feel that they have gained morale over the enemy and attack with confidence. I may be mistaken but I feel that our success over Lee's Army is already insured."[23]

A short distance east of the armies, the North Anna joined other rivers to form the Pamunkey. Relying again on maneuver, Grant disengaged from Lee the night of May 26, crossed to the river's northern bank, and sidestep thirty miles southeast to passable crossings near Hanovertown. A quick dash across the Pamunkey, he reasoned, and the Confederate capital would fall, bringing the war to a rapid close. Not until morning did Lee discover Grant's departure, and the Army of Northern Virginia immediately marched to intercept the enemy. Sparks flew on May 28 as blue and gray cavalry collided south of the Pamunkey at Haw's Shop. The next day Lee spread his troops along Totopotomoy Creek, a sluggish stream that intersected Grant's direct route to Richmond. Union probes disclosed that the rebels were solidly ensconced behind earthworks lining the creek's southern bank, presenting Grant once again with the prospect of stalemate.

Federal fortunes brightened on May 30, however, when Warren's 5th Corps crossed the Totopotomoy downstream from Lee and advanced toward the vulnerable rebel flank. Recognizing an opportunity to overwhelm an isolated Union force, Lee directed Major General Jubal A. Early, who had replaced Ewell as commander of the 2nd Corps, to assail Warren with his own troops and those of Longstreet's corps, now commanded by Major General Richard H. Anderson. Anderson failed to make headway, however, and the attempt to turn Warren's flank ended in a bloody repulse for the rebels. The battle, named after nearby Bethesda Church, provided Grant further evidence that the grueling campaign had gutted the Army of Northern Virginia's offensive capacity.

Burnett's Tavern was a ramshackle wooden structure a handful of miles south of Totopotomoy Creek, nestled beside a star-shaped intersection called Old Cold Harbor. By seizing the road junction, Grant anticipated that he could gain an unobstructed route to Richmond and a chance to strike Lee's flank and rear. The arrival of Baldy Smith's 16,000 soldiers from Bermuda Hundred—they had traveled by ship down the James, rounded the Peninsula at Fort Monroe, and ascended the York and Pamunkey Rivers to White House Landing, within easy marching distance of Old Cold Harbor—gave him the necessary strength. Learning of Smith's arrival, Lee persuaded Beauregard to send him Major General Robert F. Hoke's division from the Richmond defenses, and cavalry battles sparked around Burnett's Tavern as Grant and Lee pumped additional soldiers toward the expanding front. On the morning of June 1, Anderson's lead elements attacked Sheridan's entrenched troopers at Old Cold Harbor only to be driven back by concentrated fire from the cavalrymen's repeating carbines. Retiring to a line established by Hoke's new arrivals, Anderson's men dug in, extending the rebel formation northward. Within hours the 6th Corps—now commanded by Major General Horatio R. Wright—tramped into Cold Harbor, and by late afternoon Smith's troops were entrenching next to Wright.

By the evening of June 1, Union and Confederate infantry faced off behind earthworks along a north–south axis. Anxious to maintain the initiative, Wright and Smith attacked. Funneling into a ravine, elements from both Union corps breached the rebel position, but nightfall prevented the Federals from exploiting their success. The results, however, were heartening to the men in blue.

Each side had lost about 2,000 soldiers, but the Federals were well situated to exploit their gains the next day.

Hoping to strike a killing blow, Grant hurried Hancock toward Cold Harbor. Dark roads and an ill-advised shortcut delayed Hancock's march, compelling Grant to postpone the attack until June 3. The delay proved fatal as Lee, alerted to Grant's intentions, gained time to shift soldiers from the far northern end of his line—Breckinridge's troops, recently arrived from the Shenandoah Valley, and much of Hill's corps—to the southern sector facing Cold Harbor. All day the rebels perfected their works in anticipation of a Union offensive.

Grant's decision to assail Lee's entrenched position at Cold Harbor the morning of June 3 was grounded in a sober appraisal. As the general in chief saw it, relentless pounding in the Wilderness and at Spotsylvania Court House had severely weakened the rebel army. Proof of Lee's disability lay not just in his failure to close his trap at the North Anna: the Virginian had also permitted Grant to cross the Pamunkey unopposed, had fumbled at Bethesda Church, and had almost been routed on June 1. Lee's army, it seemed, was a depleted force ripe for plucking. The Army of the Potomac, on the other hand, was as strong as ever, having been reinforced with fresh troops from Washington and by Smith's 18th Corps. Since Lee stood within seven miles of Richmond, his back to the Chickahominy River, a successful assault at this juncture seemed certain to wreck the Confederate army, capture its capital, and bring the war to a speedy conclusion.

Delaying made no sense, Grant reasoned—more time would only give the rebels a chance to bring up reinforcements, and more maneuvering would be difficult and uncertain in outcome. Besides, the Republican convention was scheduled to convene in a few days: what better gift could he offer President Lincoln than the destruction of Lee's army and the capture of Richmond? Aggressive by nature and accustomed to taking risks, Grant decided to attack. If the offensive worked, the rewards would be tremendous. If it failed, the consequence would simply be another reverse in a campaign filled with reverses, and he would try another tack. "It was a nice question of judgment," one of Grant's aides observed. "After discussing the question thoroughly with his principal officers, and weighing all the chances, he decided to attack Lee's army in its present position. He had succeeded in breaking the enemy's line at Chattanooga, Spotsylvania, and other places under circumstances which were not more favorable, and the results to be obtained now would be so great in case of success that it seemed wise to make the attempt."[24]

The plan called for an army-wide offensive across a six-mile front, a feat requiring careful planning. Meade, who was responsible for overseeing the details of the assault, was painfully remiss. Resentful of his subordinate position and thoroughly disapproving of Grant's hard-hitting tactics, the army commander expressed his discontent by doing little. The record reveals no steps to reconnoiter the ground, coordinate the army's elements, or tend to the things that diligent generals ordinarily do before sending troops against fortified lines. The victims of Grant and Meade's untidy and increasingly fractious command relationship would be the soldiers of the Army of the Potomac.

"The carnival of death."

Rain picked up after dark on June 2. Trenches sloshed with water, and cooking fires sputtered. Meade simply announced the time for the attack—4:30 A.M. on June 3—and left his corps commanders to cooperate as they saw fit. Concerted action was not in the cards. Matadequin Creek's swampy headwaters separated the Union army's southern wing—Hancock's, Wright's, and Smith's corps—from the northern two corps under Warren and Burnside, now clustered near Bethesda Church. Meade's deep resentment of Grant and regard for Smith as an interloper gave the Army of the Potomac the quality of a dysfunctional, bickering family; neither Meade nor Grant seemed capable of doing anything about it.

Lee's Confederates meanwhile labored to make their line as strong as any they had held since the Wilderness. "It is a rule that, when the rebels halt, the first day gives them a good rifle pit; the second, a regular infantry parapet with artillery in position; the third a parapet with abattis in front and entrenched batteries behind," Meade's staffer Lieutenant Colonel Theodore Lyman observed. This time Lee's men exceeded Lyman's prediction, in places completing three days' work in one.[25]

Mist swirled near daylight on June 3, obscuring objects more than a few yards ahead. The scene was chillingly familiar to Hancock's veterans on the southern end of the Union position. Three weeks before, on a foggy, rain-drenched morning very much like this one, they had lined up to charge Lee's fortifications at Spotsylvania Court House, and the results had been catastrophic. Now their superiors wanted them to repeat that performance. "I must confess that order was not received with much hilarity," one Federal related.[26]

A signal gun barked, and Hancock's soldiers lunged toward earthworks occupied by Hoke's and Breckinridge's Confederates. "A simple brute rush in open day on strong works," a participant described the attack. Another Union man recollected the Confederate response as a "veritable tempest," combining the "fury of the Wilderness musketry, with the thunders of the Gettysburg artillery superadded." In the enthusiasm of their initial attack, Hancock's troops managed to overrun a small salient in Breckinridge's line, but Hill's reserves drove them out, forcing them to seek shelter in a hollow where artillery fire whined over their heads "much as a charge of fine shot goes among a flock of blackbirds," a Union survivor wrote. Deadly musketry pinned the Federals in place, preventing them from moving forward or returning to their entrenchments. "The fire ran down our lines from left to right like the keys of a piano," a Confederate recalled, "and to the sharp crack of our rifles was added the roar of artillery as it joined them in the wild music of the hour—the carnival of death."[27]

Stepping into a clearing, other of Hancock's troops came under rebel artillery fire that "mowed down our lines as wheat falls before the reaper," as one northerner recounted. It was "terrible," another Yankee related, "to see our brave boys falling so rapidly and without a chance of success." A Federal remembered how the "air seemed completely filled with screaming, exploding shell and shot of all descriptions, and our soldiers were falling fast." Unable to advance or retreat, blue-clad figures scooped out makeshift entrenchments with their canteens. "It could not be called a battle," confessed a New Yorker. "It was simply a butchery, lasting only ten minutes."[28]

North of Cold Harbor Road, the soldiers of Wright's 6th Corps had held the same ground for two days and knew exactly what they faced. Many of them moved a short distance toward the rebels in their front—more of Hoke's men and Major General Joseph B. Kershaw's division of Anderson's corps—halted, and set to constructing new fortifications. Those who ventured farther met a predictable fate. "We advanced under a murderous fire in our front from the enemy's artillery [and] sharpshooters, and when within range of its main line of battle were simply slaughtered," a major reported. So timid was the Union advance in this sector that many rebels never realized that the enemy had attempted an attack. "It may sound incredible," one of Hoke's brigade commanders reminisced, "but it is nevertheless strictly true, that the writer of these Memoirs, situated near the center of the line along which this murderous repulse was given, and awake and vigilant of the progress of events, was not aware at the time of any serious assault having been given."[29]

Next to Wright, Baldy Smith's men found themselves in a brutal predicament. Determined to crack the rebel works, Smith had deployed his corps in two compact columns. Aiming at a ravine that penetrated the enemy position, he expected the weight of his attack to break the opposing line. Little did he imagine that the rebels facing him—more soldiers from Kershaw's division of the 1st Corps—had fashioned the ravine into a killing ground lined with rifle-men and artillery.

Smith's troops marched into a leaden storm. "Men bent down as they went forward, as if trying, as they were, to breast a tempest," a New Englander re-membered. "The files of men went down like rows of blocks or bricks pushed over by striking against each other." A southerner watched as a "destructive fire" annihilated the charging column. "I could see the dust fog out of a man's clothing in two or three places at once where as many balls would strike him at the same moment," he noted. It seemed to a frightened Union soldier that "all the powers of earth and hell [were] concentrated in the endeavor to sweep away every vestige of the Federal army." A Union cavalryman assigned to bring in prisoners and drive stragglers back to their units recalled June 3 as "one of the most horrible days in our whole experience. The piles of dead, the immense number of wounded, the ghastly spectacle of blood and suffering, can never be effaced from our minds."[30]

Meade urged his generals to renew the offensive, but none was willing to advance without support from the others. Finally the frustrated army com-mander directed Wright and Smith to attack independently, but to no avail. He also tried to push Burnside and Warren into the fracas, but coordination seemed impossible, and everyone had excuses. "After the failure [of the initial attacks]," an artillery officer wrote home, "there was still a more absurd order issued, for each commander to attack without reference to its neighbors, as they saw fit, an order which looked as if the commander, whoever he is, had either lost his head entirely, or wanted to shift responsibility off his own shoulders."[31]

Shortly before noon, Grant visited the battlefield. A newspaperman saw him and Meade conferring on a bare hill, gazing toward Richmond. "The small form with the slight stoop in the shoulders, sunken gray eyes, still reserved de-meanor, impassive face and chin as of a bull dog or close-set steel trap—that is Grant," he wrote. "The tall figure with the nervous, emphatic articulation and action and face as of antique parchment—that is Meade—and the antipo-des could not bring together a greater contrast."[32]

The situation was not auspicious. "Hancock gave the opinion that in his front the enemy was too strong to make any further assault promise success," Grant reported. "Wright thought he could gain the lines of the enemy, but it would require the cooperation of Hancock's and Smith's corps. Smith thought a lodgment possible, but was not sanguine; Burnside thought something could be done on his front, but Warren differed." Exasperated, Grant terminated the offensive.[33]

Fighting erupted sporadically throughout the afternoon. In the battlefield's northern sector, Warren and Burnside launched unsuccessful assaults against entrenchments held by Early's corps and elements from Hill's corps. "One line [of Federals] would fire and fall down, another step over, fire and fall down, each line getting nearer us, until they got within sixty or seventy five yards of some portions of our line," a rebel reported, "but finding themselves cut to pieces so badly, they fell back in a little disorder." Deadlocked before impenetrable earthworks, Warren's and Burnside's attacks ground to a standstill. Toward dark, in the battlefield's southern sector, the Confederates counterattacked without success. "And there the two armies slept," the aide Lyman wrote home, "almost within an easy stone-throw of each other; and the separating space ploughed by cannon-shot and clotted with the dead bodies that neither side dared to bury!"[34]

Grant's big offensive at Cold Harbor had been a disaster for the Federals. Meade had failed to achieve even a semblance of coordination; Hancock, reputedly the best Union field commander, had delivered a lackluster performance; Wright had never ventured anything resembling an attack; and Smith's charging columns had presented tightly massed targets that Confederate gunners had slaughtered with ease. The grand charge of the 2nd, 6th, and 18th Corps generated perhaps 3,500 Union casualties, with another 3,000-odd casualties occurring during the rest of the day on all fronts. Confederate losses were disproportionately smaller: 700 rebels were killed and wounded during the early morning attack, and about another 700 during the remainder of the day. Lieutenant Colonel Charles S. Venable, one of Lee's aides, aptly described Cold Harbor as "perhaps the easiest [victory] ever granted to Confederate arms by the folly of the Federal commanders."[35]

The campaign from the Wilderness to Cold Harbor had sapped the Army of the Potomac, which was scarcely recognizable as the same force that had marched to battle a month earlier. "A series of severe battles usually unsuccessful, or only half successes, closely connected by fierce skirmishes, and accompanied by weary marches and the heavy labor of building entrenchments, had enfeebled the muscles and unstrung the nerves of these hardy soldiers," Lyman observed. Casualties approached 55,000 men, and the terms of enlistment for more than thirty veteran regiments were fast expiring, threatening to rob the Army of the Potomac of its most experienced troops when it most needed them. "The quality of the loss is what made it almost disastrous, for the very best officers, and the bravest men were those who fell," a northern general observed. Replacements, it was true, were arriving at a rapid pace. A tally taken a few days after the big attack at Cold Harbor counted 48,265 soldiers who had joined the Army of the Potomac since early May. Including Smith's 16,000 men and subtracting 20,000 soldiers whose terms of enlistment had expired, Grant had some 110,000 troops at Cold Harbor, almost as many as had crossed the Rapidan with him a month earlier. But mere numbers were misleading, as the new troops were mostly greenhorns who augmented the army's size but not its expertise. "The army had lost thousands of its most capable officers and veteran soldiers," a northerner concluded, "who could not be replaced, and it no longer seemed to be the same army."[36]

Grant's persistent hammering—along with the prospect of even more combat—had also visibly eroded the army's morale. "It is fight! Fight! here day in and day out," a Massachusetts man wrote home. "Human patience cannot endure such wear and tear," an officer assigned to headquarters agreed, as did a surgeon. "I am heart-sick over it all," he wrote from Cold Harbor. "If the Confederates lost in each fight the same number as we, there would be more chance for us; but their loss is about one man to our five, from the fact that they never leave their earthworks, whereas our men are obliged to charge even when there is not the slightest chance of taking them." Colonel Wesley Brainerd, commanding the 50th New York Engineers, reported a "settled commotion which showed itself plainly in the faces of every officer and every man in the army, that [the soldiers killed at Cold Harbor] had been sacrificed for nothing."[37]

Grant's performance received mixed reviews. "I am disgusted with the generalship displayed," Brigadier General Emory Upton wrote his sister. "Thousands of lives might have been spared by the exercise of a little skill." Noted Colonel Charles S. Wainwright, commanding the 5th Corps's artillery: "Whoever was responsible for this extended mode of attack is getting no military credit, nor love of the men who are about used up by it." A private in the 17th Maine reported that "many soldiers expressed freely their scorn of Grant's alleged generalship, which consists of launching men against breastworks. It is well known," he added, "that one man behind works is as good as three outside the works."[38]

Some, however, saw a silver lining in Grant's persistence. "No matter what happened we moved forward," Charles E. Davis of the 13th Massachusetts recalled. "No backward steps were taken—an experience to which the Army of the Potomac had, heretofore, been unused to. The consequence was that the 'Old Man' (as General Grant was called) was always greeted with genuine enthusiasm, though he didn't seem to care much for it. It was wonderful how thoroughly this retiring, undemonstrative man had gained the confidence of the army." Davis asserted, "In spite of the hard work we had been having, the men were in good spirits, pleased that we were at last accomplishing something."[39]

"Grant is certainly a very extraordinary man," Charles Francis Adams Jr. wrote his father from the battlefield. "He does not look it and might pass well enough for a dumpy and slouchy little subaltern, very fond of smoking," who resembled "a very ordinary looking man, one who would attract attention neither in the one way or the other." The general sat well on a horse, "but in walking he leans forward and toddles." Yet Adams discerned in this unlikely figure a talented and thoughtful leader. "He handles those around him so quietly and well, he evidently has the facility of disposing of work and managing men, he is cool and quiet, almost stolid and as if stupid, in danger, and in a crisis he is one against whom all around, whether few in number or a great army as here, would instinctively lean. He is a man of the most exquisite judgment and tact." Adams summed up by observing, "The army has a head and confidence in that head."[40]

Everyone could agree that the debacle of June 3 dramatically underscored the flaws inherent in the unwieldy Federal command structure. Even the Potomac army's chief of staff, Major General Andrew A. Humphreys, who was perhaps Meade's strongest supporter, conceded that the divided command "was not calculated to produce the best results that [either] general singly was capable of bringing about." Writing home the day after the big Cold Harbor offensive, Meade questioned whether military history could "afford a parallel to the protracted and severe fighting which this army has sustained for the last thirty days." Grant, Meade observed, "has had his eyes opened, and is willing to admit now that Virginia and Lee's army is not Tennessee and Bragg's army." Meade's aides parroted their boss's skepticism. "I do think there has been too much assaulting, this campaign!" the staffer Lyman wrote in his journal. "The best officers and men are liable, by their greater gallantry, to be first disabled; and, of those that are left, the best become demoralized by the failures, and the loss of good leaders; so that, very soon, the men will no longer charge entrenchments and will only go forward when driven by their officers." Even Grant's inner circle expressed concern that the corrosive effect of head-on attacks had undermined morale. More productive, they agreed, were "the flanking and turning movements which brought the army from Spotsylvania to Cold Harbor, and which, if not yet successful in giving it a decided victory, were gradually pressing the enemy back upon his base and capital, without unusual delay or excessive loss."[41]

Brigadier General James H. Wilson, who had served on Grant's staff in the West and now commanded a cavalry division under Sheridan, visited army headquarters on June 4 and found Meade pacing in front of his tent, "flecking his top-boots nervously with his riding whip." The army commander greeted the cavalryman and voiced unease about the campaign. "Wilson, when is Grant

going to take Richmond?" Meade asked. "Whenever the generals and troops
in this theater all work together to that end," he replied, taking a swipe at the
erratic performance of Meade and his subordinates. Meade's emphasis on
"Grant" in posing his question underscored for Wilson the common perception
that the campaign was Grant's, not his. "At that juncture [Meade] was apparently willing Grant should have all the credit, along with all the responsibility,"
Wilson reflected.[42]

Speaking later with Grant, Wilson found the general "disappointed at his
failure to overwhelm Lee, and especially at the failure of his subordinates to
whom the details of carrying his general orders into effect were left, to select
proper points, form proper plans of attack, and, above all, to provide carefully
for the contingency of success." Grant's staffer Adam Badeau echoed his boss's
sentiment. "The result of [Grant] having a middleman was to make the whole
organization wooden," he wrote. "Meade severed the nerve between the gen-
eral-in-chef and the army. He was a non-conductor." Some aides recommended
that Grant consolidate the corps in Virginia into a single army and personally
supervise its operations. The general, however, insisted on keeping Meade as
the Potomac army's commander, explaining, "by tending to the details he re-
lieves me of much unnecessary work, and gives me more time to think and
mature my general plans."[43]

Despite his disparagement of Grant's heavy-handed tactics, Meade's overall
assessment of the campaign remained upbeat. Around eight o'clock on the
morning of June 4, he wrote his wife, Margaret, that the previous day's big battle had ended "without any decided results, we repulsing all attacks of the
enemy and they doing the same." Both sides were now entrenched, he added,
and were nursing losses the general considered about equal. "How long this
game is to be played it is impossible to tell," he concluded, "but in the long run,
we ought to succeed, because it is in our power more promptly to fill the gaps
in men and material which this constant fighting produces."[44]

Grant described the situation in a similar vein in a letter to his young daughter Nellie. "We have been fighting now for thirty days and have every prospect
of still more fighting to do before we get into Richmond," he assured the child.
"When we do get there I shall go home to see you and Ma, Fred, Buck, and
Jess."[45]

The Union army's staggering casualties notwithstanding, Grant's style of warfare offered a realistic possibility of success. Lee had stymied his opponent in
the Wilderness and at Spotsylvania Court House, the North Anna River, and
Cold Harbor, but the Union commander had held fast to his strategic objective,

treating these reverses as temporary roadblocks in his effort to destroy Lee's army and maneuvering for advantage after each stalemate. Each battle had whittled the Army of Northern Virginia, and each flanking march had diminished Lee's elbow room as the battlefield edged closer to Richmond. In conversations with Assistant War Secretary Charles A. Dana, who traveled with Grant's headquarters, the Union commander confessed frustration over his inability to get at Lee in open battle, "constantly revolving plans to turn Lee out of his entrenchments," as Grant added. He respected Lee's military acumen, Dana noted, although Dana thought that "the boldness with which he maneuvered in Lee's presence is proof that he was not overawed by Lee's prestige as a strategist and tactician." Grant, he wrote, recognized that the Virginian's "forte was as a defensive fighter, a quality displayed at Antietam and Fredericksburg, but [Grant] held no high opinion of his Chancellorsville operations, where he had recklessly laid himself open to ruin."[46]

As the magnitude of Grant's butcher bill registered on the northern populace, the casualties assumed a political dimension. How long would the public tolerate such losses? Grant, it was true, had forced Lee to the Confederate capital's very gates, but the southerner had eluded his death grip. Remarkably, although some newspaper editors raised an alarm, the general public seemed numb to the carnage. "Grant's attack last Friday (June 3rd), in which as he telegraphed, no decided advantage was gained, cost about 5,000 men; and so small is the number, in comparison with our average losses, that nobody thought much about it," a New York editorialist reported. "Once the nation was frozen with horror as it gazed upon the bloody ground of Bull Run, but today, so accustomed have we become to the contemplation of blood and long lists of slaughter, that we learn without emotion of 'affairs' in which double the number of men are slain than in any two of the pitched battles of last year's campaign."[47]

Meade's staffer Lyman later observed that the action at Cold Harbor "ended the attempt against Richmond itself, an attempt that had occupied the month of May." True to character, Grant was already considering his next move. The events of June 3 persuaded him that remaining at Cold Harbor offered no advantages. Entrenched behind imposing earthworks, the Army of Northern Virginia appeared invincible. The low-lying peninsula between the Pamunkey and the James was notorious for fevers and pestilence, a situation that the Potomac army's veterans who had fought on the same ground with Major General George B. McClellan two years before could readily confirm. "The season of the year was a sickly one," a 9th Corps man observed, "as it was now June, and the heat was excessive, and debilitating in the extreme." The commissary added quinine to whisky rations as a precaution against malaria, but disease remained commonplace.[48]

Prolonged stalemate threatened to undermine the army's morale—to say nothing of the effect that delay was having on the morale of the nation. Even if Union recruiters managed to "rake and scrape" reinforcements, as Grant colorfully put it, there were no assurances that a second big attack would reap any better rewards than the first had yielded. Bludgeoning was simply not the way to go. With a presidential election on the horizon, the political price of another costly reverse might well be catastrophic.

Lyman thought that the campaign had reached a "strategic crisis." During May, the Army of the Potomac had "advanced by a series of zig-zags," he later wrote, "nearer and nearer to Richmond; but now closer approach was barred, and a movement in the direction of either flank would be simply a march around Richmond as a center, while the enemy, on an inner circle, would constantly interpose his forces. In other words, the operation of flanking had come to an end, and the choice now lay between a direct attack and a new plan."[49]

A new plan it would be. The idea of cutting Lee's supply lines had been a central feature of Grant's proposal to Lincoln the previous January, and the present circumstances invited a variant of that theme. Their earthworks at Cold Harbor might be immune from attack, but the rebels had to eat, and their guns needed powder and bullets, all of which arrived along a network of transportation lines that converged on Richmond. If the Federals could sever the routes to the Confederate capital, Lee would have to abandon his Cold Harbor bastion, and Grant would finally gain a chance to assail the elusive rebels on open ground.

A glance at the map showed that war materiel reached Richmond from three sources—the Shenandoah Valley, Lynchburg, and most importantly Petersburg, known as the Cockade City. The Valley provided food and forage chiefly along the Virginia Central Railroad, which originated near Harrisonburg, climbed east across the Blue Ridge Mountains, and rolled past Charlottesville and Beaver Dam to Hanover Junction. There the Virginia Central crossed the Richmond, Fredericksburg, and Potomac Railroad, turned sharply south, and paralleled its tracks into Richmond. Breaking the Virginia Central west of Hanover Junction offered Grant an easy way to shut off the Valley's spigot.

Lynchburg, perched on hills along the James River some 130 miles west of Richmond, was also important to Lee's quartermasters. The town was a major transportation hub, where six turnpikes and three railroads converged, including the vital Virginia and Tennessee Railroad from East Tennessee. An effi-

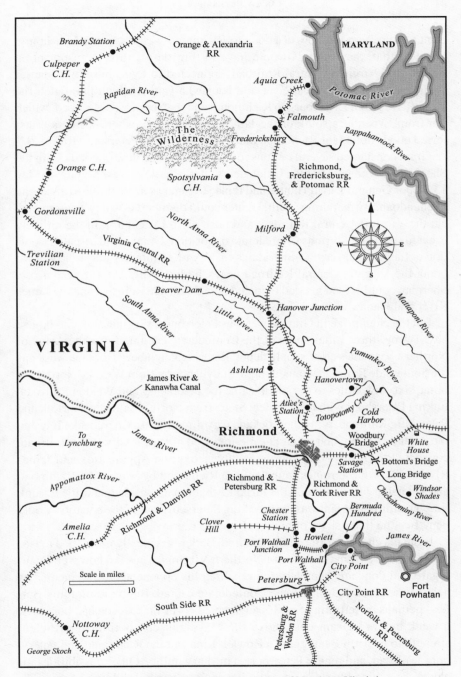

Supply routes to Richmond, Petersburg, and the Army of Northern Virginia

cient way to stem the flow of goods to Richmond was to capture Lynchburg. Short of that, the Federals would have to throttle off three transportation routes—the Virginia Central Railroad, connected to Lynchburg by a spur at Charlottesville; the James River and Kanawha Canal, which paralleled the James River from Lynchburg to Richmond; and the South Side Railroad, which ran from Lynchburg south of the James to Petersburg, where workers transferred goods bound for Richmond to the Richmond and Petersburg Railroad.[50]

Grant considered several options for neutralizing the flow of goods from the Shenandoah Valley. After the Union defeat at the Battle of New Market on May 15, Major General David Hunter had replaced Sigel as head of the Army of the Shenandoah. By marching south, Hunter could disrupt the Valley's commerce, cut the Virginia Central Railroad, and push on to Lynchburg. In the unlikely event his army met serious Confederate opposition, Grant could dispatch a portion of the Potomac army—Sheridan's cavalry or an infantry corps or two—to break the Virginia Central Railroad near Charlottesville. And if need arose, Sheridan could extend his raid to include the Southside Railroad and the James River and Kanawha Canal.

But the chief prize in Grant's eyes was Petersburg, Virginia's second largest city. Twenty-three miles south of the Confederate capital, it was the Army of Northern Virginia's chief supply depot. Entering Petersburg from the west was the South Side Railroad, connecting with Lynchburg; from Weldon, North Carolina, sixty-five miles to the south, came the Petersburg and Weldon Railroad, linking Petersburg with the Tar Heel State; from Norfolk came the Norfolk and Petersburg Railroad, tying the Cockade City directly with Chesapeake Bay and the Atlantic Ocean; and an eight-mile-long bed of tracks, City Point Railroad, connected it to City Point and the confluence of the Appomattox and James Rivers. All of those routes funneled into Richmond by way of the Richmond and Petersburg Railroad and the turnpike that ran alongside that critical trunk line. The military point was clear: taking Petersburg out of the equation would deny Lee the lion's share of his supplies.[51]

From his enclave at Bermuda Hundred, Butler was ideally positioned to isolate Petersburg from the Army of Northern Virginia. Thus far, however, Beauregard had done an exemplary job repelling his opponent's feeble incursions against the trunk railroad to the Confederate capital. But by reinforcing Butler—perhaps by returning Smith's augmented corps that Meade had borrowed a week before—Grant could give the Massachusetts politician sufficient strength to overrun Beauregard's Howlett Line, cut the Richmond and Petersburg Railroad, and render Petersburg a military nullity. Other possibilities included launching Sheridan on a mission against the vital rail line or going directly against Petersburg with Butler's reinforced army or with all or part of the Potomac army.

The Union high command remained divided over how best to wreck Lee's logistical lifelines. Meade agreed with cutting the railroads into Richmond and thought that Sheridan's cavalry should handle the assignment. Grant's aide Lieutenant Colonel Cyrus B. Comstock favored shifting the entire Army of the Potomac "up on RR's and destroy them thoroughly, abandoning temporarily White House if necessary and taking ten days' rations along." At least one of Meade's staffers thought that the army should march directly on Petersburg. "I have always advocated that [the present line of advance] was only a defensive one, and that the true line for decisive operations was on the south side of the James River," Major James Biddle wrote his wife. "They have made this the offensive line, and instead of sending all the spare force at the start to the James River, they send 26,000 men under Butler, who has had no experience in handling troops and who has shown great incompetency. This army has been fighting for 31 days—if Butler had cut the Petersburg and Danville roads, Lee could never have fought us as he has done, and by this time I believe we would have been in Richmond. I nevertheless do not feel discouraged," he added. "I am sanguine Richmond has to fall, it is only a question of time—but I think we might have accomplished the reduction of Richmond without such a severe loss."[52]

Halleck, ever fearful that Lee might attack Washington, lobbied for shifting the entire Potomac army north of Richmond. Such a move, he insisted, would enable Grant to cut the Virginia Central Railroad while interposing his army between Lee and the Federal capital. Halleck argued that his plan offered the added benefit of permitting Grant to draw supplies down the Richmond, Fredericksburg, and Potomac Railroad. The general in chief, however, was not interested in relying on rail lines for sustenance since rebel partisans could disrupt them at will. He had considered the limitations of railroads at the campaign's outset and had predicated his movement against Lee on a series of "flying depots" along Virginia's tidal rivers precisely to avoid the problems inherent in fixed supply lines. By rounding Lee's northern flank as Halleck suggested, Grant feared that he would leave the army's connection with the sea dangerously open to attack.[53]

For the time, then, Grant was content to wait. Having suspended the offensive at Cold Harbor, his immediate goal was to fix Lee in place while Hunter wrecked the Confederate supply lines in the Shenandoah Valley. As Meade's chief of staff Humphreys later recollected, Grant concluded that "further advances might be suspended for the present; that advances to advantageous po-

sitions should be made by regular approaches, after due reconnaissance; that
to aid the expedition under General Hunter it was necessary to detain all the
army then with Lee until Hunter got well on his way into Lynchburg." Humphreys noted that this latter objective "would be more effectively done by keeping the enemy out of the entrenchments of Richmond than by forcing him into
them."[54]

Grant also considered the advantages of swinging the Army of the Potomac
south and west of Richmond, a move that in one fell swoop promised to break
the Cold Harbor deadlock by turning Lee's southern flank, severing the rebel
army's supply lines from the south, and enabling Grant to protect his supply
routes to the sea. With supplies running short and the massive Union force
rounding his flank and threatening his rear, Lee would have no choice but to
abandon his Cold Harbor bastion and flee, enabling the Potomac army to pursue the rebels, catch them on open ground, and crush them.

Grant was still vague, however, about the maneuver's details. What route
should the army follow as it swung below Lee in its broad turning movement?
Should it cross the Chickahominy and bear west, advancing between that river
and the James as it drove for a junction with Butler at Bermuda Hundred and
a decisive attack against the Richmond and Petersburg Railroad? Or should it
undertake a more expansive turning movement, continuing across the James
and dashing toward Petersburg along roads south of the river? If Grant selected
the latter course, where precisely should the crossing occur? And what steps
should he take to prevent Lee from descending on Butler or attacking the Army
of the Potomac as it set off on its looping march?

Time was needed to answer these questions. Until then, the Army of the Potomac would remain at Cold Harbor, pinning Lee in place. Shortly after noon
on June 3, Grant formally cancelled the offensive along this front. "Hold our
most advanced positions and strengthen them," he instructed Meade, recom-
mending that the army commander contract his lines slightly southward to
make them more compact and resistant to Confederate attacks. Any advances,
he added, should be made by "regular approaches," the goal being to immobi-
lize Lee until Grant could finalize his plans. The time for assaults had ended,
and the campaign would start a new phase. Henceforth, the Army of the Potomac would begin "all along the lines, digging up to the enemy's works." As
Grant explained his objective, "it is necessary that we should detain all the
army now with Lee until [Hunter] gets well on his way to Lynchburg."[55]

That evening Meade proposed acquiring locomotives and cars to use on the
York River Railroad, which ran through the Federal army's supply base at
White House Landing. Grant suggested waiting and tipped his hand about the

timetable for his next maneuver. "The wagons now at White House will give us supplies to about the 15th," he replied, "and before that I hope our base will be changed to the James River."[56]

Southerners rightly proclaimed the Battles of the Wilderness, Spotsylvania Court House, the North Anna River, and Cold Harbor victories, and morale in Lee's army was understandably high. Before the campaign, Confederate wags suggested that Grant's initials—U. S.—stood for "Up the Spout." Now a Confederate staffer concluded that the initials really meant "Unfortunate Strategist." Grant, he wrote, was the "worse used up Yankee commander that we have ever combated." A brigadier from South Carolina assured his mother that he saw no reason "to fear Grant anymore." The general's "fury is expended," he predicted, "and his troops too."[57]

But winning battles against Grant had cost the Army of Northern Virginia almost 33,000 soldiers. Measured against the respective sizes of the armies at the beginning of the campaign, Lee had sustained a greater percentage of subtractions than Grant had suffered. Indeed, the number of men that he had lost from May 5 through June 3 approximated fully half the number of troops who had marched with him into the Wilderness. The South's dwindling manpower pool made it difficult to replace these losses. Several units, it is true, had reinforced Lee's army—the additions included Hoke's, Breckinridge's, and Pickett's divisions; Brigadier General Joseph Finegan's brigade of Florida infantry; a cavalry brigade under Brigadier General Matthew C. Butler; and a handful of additional regiments—approximately 30,000 reinforcements altogether, almost replacing the number of men lost. But the Confederate manpower barrel had been scraped clean. And with Stuart dead, Longstreet seriously wounded, Ewell on assignment to Richmond, and Hill increasingly sick, Lee's high command was in shambles. The Army of Northern Virginia could ill afford more victories whose net effect was to accelerate its demise.[58]

The rigors of campaigning had taken a visible toll on Lee. The general worked until well after midnight and, according to an aide, was awake by 3:00 A.M. During the North Anna operations, Lee had contracted dysentery that incapacitated him with violent intestinal distress and diarrhea. He was still weak at Cold Harbor and traveled in a carriage. The general, his staffer Walter H. Taylor related in a letter to his fiancée, "has remained more quiet and directs movements from a distance." While Taylor lauded Lee's style of delegating responsibility to subordinates, he regretted the absence of "capable lieutenants" to execute the general's wishes.[59]

Despite its triumph at Cold Harbor, the Army of Northern Virginia was precariously situated. Richmond stood seven miles in its rear, and the army was too depleted to undertake new offensives. Judicious use of earthworks kept Lee's men in the game, as did their proximity to the capital, which vastly improved the quantity and quality of food and supplies. "As to endurance and fighting qualities," a Union man accurately observed, "the two armies are about equal, all things being considered, and the enemy's lack of numbers is compensated for by the fact of their acting on the defensive."[60]

Lee was acutely aware of his predicament. He wanted to avoid entrapment in Richmond's fortifications, where he would forfeit his ability to maneuver. Yet here he was, pinned into earthworks with the Confederate capital only a handful of miles behind him. But so long as Grant repeated his frontal attacks, Lee was confident that he could hold on. "If they continue to fight us behind our breastworks we will whip them every time," a South Carolinian wrote home, in a boast that reflected the army's sentiment.[61]

Grant's invariable pattern of maneuvering after each stalemate, however, suggested to Lee that further Union attacks modeled after the June 3 offensive were unlikely. If past were prologue, Grant was planning another turning movement. The storm gathering in the Shenandoah Valley was especially disturbing. Lee had markedly reduced Confederate troop levels in the Valley after Sigel's defeat at New Market, summoning Breckinridge with two Virginia brigades to reinforce the Army of Northern Virginia. If Hunter swept through the Shenandoah and headed toward either Lynchburg or Richmond, Lee's Cold Harbor position would become untenable. The time might soon arrive when Breckinridge's troops—and perhaps even more soldiers—would be needed in the Valley, presenting Lee with the dilemma of weakening his army in front of Grant to resist Hunter.

Lee also understood that Butler, positioned between Petersburg and Richmond and abutting the critical railroad connecting the two cities, posed a serious threat to the Army of Northern Virginia's lifeline. From Bermuda Hundred, Butler might move against Petersburg, advance toward Richmond, or simply cut the railroad between them, in either event forcing Lee to detach troops to protect the capital and undermining his ability to hold Grant at bay.

Not a few southerners feared that Lee had met his match. "The game going on upon the military chessboard between Lee and Grant has been striking and grand, surpassing anything I have heretofore witnessed, and conducted on both sides with consummate mastery of the art of war," concluded John Tyler, a Virginian of impeccable pedigree who accompanied Lee's headquarters throughout the campaign. "It is admitted that Lee has at last met with a foeman who matches his steel, although he may not be worthy of it," he reported. "Each guards himself perfectly and gives his blow with a precise eye and cool and sanguinary nerve." The Union commander, thought Tyler, was a "scientific Goth resembling Alaric, destroying the country as he goes, and delivering the people over to starvation." But it would be dangerous to underestimate this foe. "From first to last Grant has shown great skill and prudence combined with remorseless persistency and brutality," was the southern aristocrat's grudging conclusion.[62]

Lee could only await his opponent's next move. Forfeiting the initiative ran counter to the Virginian's martial instincts, but Grant once again had left him no choice but to dance to the Union commander's tune. Judging from Grant's past performances, Lee would soon learn what the new refrain might be.

II

JUNE 4, 1864

The Army of the Potomac Tries Advancing
by Regular Approaches

"Entrenched like moles."

AT THE CLOSE OF COMBAT on June 3, the Army of the Potomac's labyrinth of earthworks at Cold Harbor traced a six-mile line that resembled an upside-down L, its upright main body extending vertically along a north–south axis, and its shorter horizontal limb reaching east. The main set of entrenchments, manned by Hancock's, Wright's, and Smith's corps, began a mile north of the Chickahominy River near Barker's Mill, followed Dispatch Station Road to Burnett's Tavern at the Old Cold Harbor intersection, and wound north past Beulah Church to end on high ground near Daniel Woody's home. Farther north, separated from the army's main body by a boggy tangle of streams and marshy hollows forming the headwaters of Matadequin Creek, stood the Union force's upper wing—made up of Warren's and Burnside's troops—which reached north, grazed Bethesda Church, and arched sharply east to form the northern arm.

Interposed firmly between the Army of the Potomac and Richmond, the Army of Northern Virginia held a line that clasped tightly against the outer perimeter of the Federal entrenchments. Lee had fastened the southern end of his fortifications on high ground known as Turkey Hill, where one of Hill's divisions under Major General Cadmus M. Wilcox kept watch over the Chickahominy lowlands. More Confederates—Breckinridge's and Hoke's Divisions, supported by another of Hill's divisions under Brigadier General William Mahone—continued the rebel fortifications north along high ground, facing Hancock and Wright. A short distance above Cold Harbor Road, Anderson's corps picked up the line, bringing the Confederate works past Mr. Allison's house and the Matadequin lowlands. Early's corps started where Anderson's ended and continued the Confederate line north to Shady Grove Road, where it angled sharply east to conform to the bend in Warren and Burnside's burrowings. Another of Hill's divisions—this one under Major General Henry Heth—anchored the far rebel terminus near the Bowles farm on Shady Grove Road.

Lee's force was stretched thin—the Confederate excavations extended at least a mile longer than their Federal counterparts and contained half as many soldiers—but rebel engineers exploited the terrain with skill. In most sectors the defenders held elevated positions and confronted their foes across cleared fields of fire. Rivers protected the Army of Northern Virginia's flanks—Totopotomoy Creek on the left and the Chickahominy River on the right—and supplies from Richmond were conveniently close at hand. If Grant wanted to resume the fight at Cold Harbor, Lee was ideally positioned to oblige him.

Renewing the offensive on these bloodied fields, however, did not figure in Grant's immediate agenda. The Union commander's first item of business this hot and rainy June 4 was to give Meade and his generals an opportunity to take stock of the previous day's losses and strengthen their deployments in case Lee decided to counterattack. For the time being, Grant's objective was to push the Union entrenchments forward in increments—"regular approaches," to use Meade's turn of phrase—and to assault only where conditions appeared favorable. To assist in this painstaking task, the Potomac army's acting chief engineer, Major Nathaniel Michler, directed Major James St. Clair Morton to take charge of excavations on the 9th Corps's front, Lieutenant Charles W. Howell and a company of engineers to construct batteries and covered ways for the 6th Corps, and Lieutenant Ranald S. Mackenzie and another engineering company to perform the same services for the 2nd Corps.[1]

The men of both armies depended on earthworks for survival, and by daylight on June 4, entrenchments honeycombed the battlefield. "At present we are digging like beavers," a Union soldier declared. In one sector successive Federal regiments had thrown up seven parallel lines of dirt, one behind the other, that reminded an observer of "gigantic furrows turned up by some enormous plough-share and awaiting the harrow." Remarked a soldier: "Our men were entrenched like moles, with clay."[2]

The Army of the Potomac's southern wing—Hancock's, Wright's, and Smith's corps—had borne the brunt of the June 3 offensive, and circumstances there were especially grim. Hancock's 2nd Corps, holding the line's southernmost flank, was the cream of the Federal force, and Meade had consistently relied on these troops to spearhead his offensive operations. The price had been high. Since crossing the Rapidan, Hancock had lost scores of officers and about 13,000 soldiers—an average of 400 men a day. The charge on June 3 was the last straw, costing the corps another 2,500 casualties—most in Brigadier

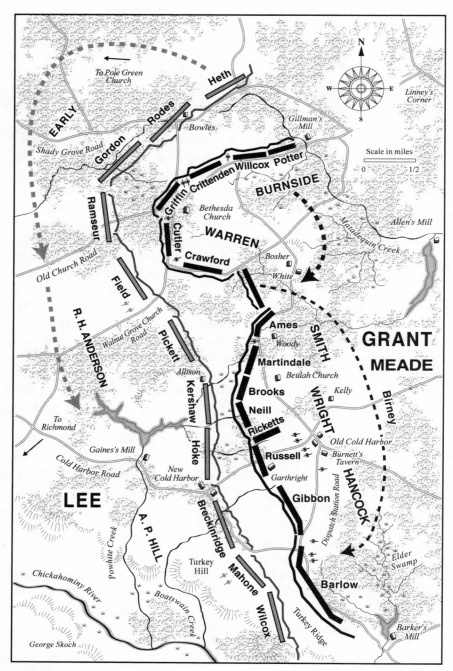

Operations on June 4

Generals Francis C. Barlow's and John Gibbon's divisions—and further diminishing its fragile cadre of talented officers. "The Second Corps here received a mortal blow, and never again was the same body of men," Hancock's chief of staff, Lieutenant Colonel Charles H. Morgan, sadly concluded. "The confidence of the troops in their leaders had been severely shaken," added a 2nd Corps aide, Lieutenant Colonel Francis A. Walker. "They had again and again been ordered to attacks which the very privates in the ranks knew to be hopeless from the start; they had seen the fatal policy of 'assaults along the line' persisted in even after the most ghastly failures; and they had almost ceased to expect victory when they went into battle." Reflecting on this dismal state of affairs, Walker expressed his heartfelt belief that Cold Harbor wrote "the epitaph of the Second Corps." Hancock later termed the fighting on June 3 "a blow to the corps from which it did not soon recover."[3]

Hancock's health had been visibly declining, but the general was still considered "the right hand corps commander of this army," as a surgeon observed, "one who is always where he is wanted at the critical moment and who punishes the enemy severely when he goes monkeying around with the 2nd Corps." Hancock expected the Confederates to attack on the morning of June 4 and at daybreak dispatched his staff to inspect the battle line. Major General David B. Birney's division was off on an independent assignment more than a mile away, plugging the gap between the army's two wings at Matadequin Creek, which left only Barlow's and Gibbon's divisions to man the mile and a half of entrenchments allotted to the 2nd Corps. Blue and gray skirmishers exchanged constant musketry, but the anticipated assault never came. Around ten in the morning, rebel artillery opened a "terrific fire" on Barlow, and Union batteries replied for half an hour before the rumble died away, "leaving nothing but the crack of the sharpshooters' rifles," one of Hancock's generals recorded in his diary. At two o'clock in the afternoon, 2nd Corps artillery blistered the adjacent Confederate positions with a flurry of shells that elicited a "brisk" response from the enemy. Some rebel ordnance reached as far east as Hancock's headquarters, located on high ground near the Old Cold Harbor intersection. "A short time ago a shot went through the kitchen tent, knocking our mess tabled to splinters," one of Hancock's aides wrote home. "The General sits on his camp stool in front of his tent watching the shelling as if it were a sham affair, instead of a very serious one."[4]

Although the Confederates shied from undertaking a concerted offensive, Hancock's casualties mounted throughout the day at an alarming pace. Especially hard hit was Barlow's division, securing the 2nd Corps's southern flank. Anchoring the left-most terminus of Barlow's line was Colonel Nelson A.

Miles's brigade, its left two regiments "re-fused," or bent back, and its largest regiment, the 5th New Hampshire, posted in the rear to recuperate from its recent mauling in the June 3 attack. Supporting Miles's troops was the Irish Brigade, famed for its performances at Antietam and Chancellorsville. Although that unit had participated only slightly in the June 3 assault, its commander, Colonel Richard Byrnes, had been seriously wounded—he would survive for a week and die in his native New York. The outfit was now led by Irish-born Colonel Patrick Kelly of the 88th New York.[5]

Miles's and Kelly's soldiers huddled in the depression cut by Dispatch Station Road and in trenches carved into rising ground east of the roadway. Facing them were Virginians from Brigadier General Gabriel C. Wharton's brigade of Breckinridge's Division and North Carolinians under Colonel John D. Barry of Wilcox's Division. Protected behind earthworks lining Turkey Ridge, the Confederates unleashed a veritable blizzard of lead into the Federals huddled below them, peppering Miles's re-fused regiments—the 26th Michigan and 140th Pennsylvania—in their left flank and front. "This was the worst place the army was ever in," a Pennsylvanian later claimed. "The sharpshooters of the enemy could pick our men off a half a mile in rear of our line, and the only safe place was close to or under the protection of our works." To show a head above the ramparts, a Federal added, spelled "instant death." The only water was a brackish brew brought back in canteens from nearby Alder Swamp. Food had to be cooked in the rear and carried to the front under cover of darkness.[6]

The situation immediately north of Miles and Kelly was equally miserable for the Federals. Here Colonel John R. Brooke's brigade had attacked the sharp salient in Breckinridge's line on June 3, achieving a brief breakthrough before suffering a brutal repulse. Brooke had been wounded during the attack and his replacement, Colonel Orlando H. Morris, had been killed, leaving command of the brigade in the able hands of the 7th New York Heavy Artillery's Colonel Lewis O. Morris. On June 4, pockets of Morris's men remained west of Dispatch Station Road, where they pressed tightly against a steep bluff below the rebel fortifications. Supporting them was the all–New York brigade of Colonel Clinton D. MacDougall, another Irish-born commander. "We are so close under the enemy's guns that they can do us no harm, firing entirely over us," Colonel James A. Beaver of the 148th Pennsylvania scrawled on a cartridge pack that provided the paper for a letter to his mother.[7]

Early on June 4, crack shots from Berdan's Sharpshooters joined Morris and MacDougall to help dampen the Confederate musketry, while mortars from the 2nd Corps concentrated on the rebels crammed into the hilltop salient. Brigadier General John Echols's brigade of Virginians and Marylanders was still there, buttressed by Brigadier General Finegan's Floridians of Mahone's Division. Judging from southern accounts, the augmented Union firepower proved effective. "Everybody that goes after water or ammunition does so at the risk of his life," a rebel stationed across from Morris observed in his diary, adding: "While I write the bullets are whizzing over my head at the rate of about 20 per minute." Union gunners, a Floridian noted, fired with "mathematical precision and deadly slaughter of our men." A shell exploding behind the Confederate breastworks lifted "men and muskets out of the trenches, killing and wounding many soldiers." Breckinridge himself became a victim of accurate Union mortar fire. As the Kentuckian rode behind his lines, a shell exploded nearby, causing his horse to rear and fall on him.[8]

Midmorning, Morris gave his division commander a tour of his brigade's entrenchments. After examining a point near the salient where the Union and Confederate lines closely converged, Barlow suggested that the colonel direct his troops to dig a tunnel into the hillside and ignite an explosive charge beneath Lieutenant Colonel David G. McIntosh's Confederate battalion, positioned on the ridge above them. Edging farther to the right, Barlow and Morris reached a gap in the Union fortifications. Making himself as small as possible, the general dashed safely across the exposed area. Morris, however, wanted to maintain "dignity of deportment" in front of his troops and strolled leisurely into the void. A rebel sharpshooter fired at the inviting target, hitting the colonel in the left shoulder and shattering his spine. The stricken officer was brought to a hospital in the rear, where he died. "He was a stranger to fear," a New York newspaper reported, "and died gloriously in the field in the face of the rebel foe." Colonel Beaver was appointed to take Morris's place, becoming the brigade's fourth commander in two days.[9]

North of Breckinridge's salient, the ridgeline descended gently into open fields that stretched three-quarters of a mile north to Cold Harbor Road. Boatswain Creek and its tributaries afforded the Confederates of Hoke's Division strong defensive positions, with Brigadier General James G. Martin's North Carolina brigade reaching north from Breckinridge's flank and Brigadier General Alfred H. Colquitt's Georgia troops carrying the Confederate line to Cold Harbor Road.

Gibbon's division, which extended north from Barlow to a juncture with the 6th Corps near Cold Harbor Road, had been badly cut up during the June 3 offensive. Charging in tandem with Barlow on his left, Colonel Thomas A. Smyth's brigade and Brigadier General Joshua T. Owen's Philadelphia Brigade had come under intense fire from Martin's Tar Heels on Boatswain Creek's opposite bank. Veterans of such affairs, the Federals had retired a short distance and thrown up breastworks of timber "and whatever came first to hand and could be made available," a participant wrote. During the night, Smyth advanced skirmishers, spaced five feet apart and armed with shovels, toward Martin's stronghold. "I had trenches dug from one hole to another," related New Jersey sergeant George A. Bowen, "making a continuous line along our front and also dug a 'covered way' back to our lines of battle so we could go in and out after water." By morning on the fourth, Owen's and Martin's earthworks were no more than twenty yards apart, so close that one Union officer "could distinctly hear [the Confederates] talking and giving commands." Most distressing were the constant calls for water by injured men pinned between the lines. "We can plainly hear the cries and groans of our friends as they lie out in our front but we cannot reach them," Sergeant Bowen scrawled in his diary. "War is a terrible thing."[10]

Conditions were also bleak on the northern end of Gibbon's line, where the brigades of Brigadier General Robert O. Tyler and Colonel H. Boyd McKeen had charged across open ground under massed artillery fire and musketry from Colquitt's Georgians. Tyler had been killed, as had McKeen and his successor, Colonel Frank A. Haskell. "Dead and wounded lay from our lines right up to the rebel works; but at the rebel works they are almost heaped in places," a New Yorker observed, noting that "every stump and tree and molehill is a shelter and every man is working himself into the ground." By sunrise on June 4, Tyler's and McKeen's survivors, like Smyth's and Owen's to their left, had merged their advance outposts with networks of ditches and parapets. "It was very irregular, running forward in places to within thirty yards of the enemy, and then receding in a way to leave many of those salients where the Confederates were able to pour in a cross fire upon [the Union soldiers] with infantry and artillery," an officer recalled. During the morning, the 1st Company, Massachusetts Sharpshooters, arrived to help counter the rebel marksmen. Taking advantage of cover offered by their own sharpshooters, the front-line Federals dug feverishly with bayonets and water dippers to construct walls that were ultimately eight feet tall and twelve feet thick, replete with traverses to protect against enfilading fire. A Massachusetts man thought that the edifices, when viewed from the rear, resembled rows of gigantic horse stalls. In their enthusiasm some Wisconsin soldiers heaped earthworks so high they were unable to fire over the top at the enemy.[11]

The ground in front of Tyler's works sloped gently toward the Confederates, an accident of terrain that made it virtually impossible for Federals caught between the lines to reach their main works behind them. "We remained in the hot sun," a New Yorker remembered, "so close to the enemy as to be unable to get to the rear for water or any necessaries of life without a volley of musketry after us. Sharp skirmishing was a frequent occurrence on any part of the line," he added, "and no man could stand erect one single moment without forming a target for the enemy's guns."[12]

Visiting army headquarters near Old Cold Harbor during the morning, Gibbon was coaxed into conducting a party of visitors, including General Grant's brother Orvil and the California newspaper reporter Frank M. Pixley, on a tour of the front. What started as a civilized ride quickly degenerated into a mad scramble as rebel sharpshooters focused on the approaching gaggle of stovepipe hats. Pixley executed a frantic dash back to headquarters, "hatless and with hair streaming in the wind, riding at full speed, leaning forward on his horse and, as [witnesses] expressed it, going a good deal faster to the rear than the horse," Gibbon later recounted. When Confederate artillery found the range, the rest of the party dove into a depressed section of Dispatch Station Road, where exploding shells showered them with dirt. "You never saw such a demoralized set in your life as they were," Gibbon wrote his wife, "nor a more gratified one when, during a lull in the fire, I proposed we should leave our advanced position."[13]

Wright's 6th Corps occupied the same territory that it had held since making the late-evening assault on June 1. The soldiers shared an understandably dim view of headquarters' penchant for attacking fortified rebel positions. "No men stand wholesale murder better than ours," one of Wright's aides bitterly wrote home, noting that "the commanding Generals are in the habit of putting them in when adequate results are not obtained." Wary of the Confederate earthworks' strength, the 6th Corps's soldiers had orchestrated a tepid performance during the grand attack of June 3. Along most of their line, they had simply advanced a short distance, halted, and dug new fortifications.[14]

The Confederate works across from Wright were truly unassailable. Poised along a low ridge and extending from below Cold Harbor Road to a wooded ravine later dubbed Bloody Run were three of Hoke's brigades under Brigadier Generals Colquitt, Johnson Hagood, and Thomas L. Clingman. Brigades drawn from the Confederate 1st Corps—those of Brigadier Generals Eppa Hunton, John Gregg, George T. "Tige" Anderson, and William T. Wofford— held low ground to another creek known locally as Muddy Run, where the terrain rose sharply to a plateau dominated by Evander Law's Alabama troops and a strong stand of 1st Corps artillery. As Wright's soldiers had learned on June 3, a charge into this horseshoe-shaped formation stood no chance of success.

The 6th Corps's line was compressed into a relatively narrow front of about 700 yards that ranged from Hancock's right flank near Cold Harbor Road to the headwaters of Muddy Run. Wright's largest division, commanded by Brigadier General David A. Russell, held the corps's southern sector. Two of Russell's brigades—Colonel William H. Penrose's six New Jersey regiments and Colonel Nelson Cross's brigade drawn from New York and Pennsylvania—stood immediately south of Cold Harbor Road, adjacent to the right end of Gibbon's division. Roughly handled during the evening assault on June 1, these brigades had remained stationary during June 3 as Gibbon's men charged past. "Their destruction seemed like that of the host of Sennacherib, so complete and so sudden," a New Jersey man recalled of Gibbon's inevitable repulse. When the dust settled, the 10th New Jersey advanced to a knoll in front of Penrose's main position and scraped out a trench to the right end of Gibbon's line. "First, a man crawling on his face threw up a little dirt to follow him," a witness recalled. "Behind him others followed, until a respectable pit was made, joining our left. We could see the bullets fall in the loose dirt thrown up, but the work was not stopped." Charles R. Paul of Penrose's staff estimated that the New Jersey troops pushed their foremost works to within seventy-five yards of the Confederate line. "We cannot go much farther without being on top of them," he wrote in his diary.[15]

Penrose and Cross spent June 4 strengthening their fortifications and losing soldiers with disconcerting regularity to Confederate sharpshooters. "The men had to hug the works, as the fire was close and active," a Pennsylvanian wrote. "Men who at sunrise helped to bury a comrade, felt that they might need others to perform the same office for them before the day closed," the 15th New Jersey's chaplain recounted. "One man was helping a wounded friend, when he received three bullets himself." Perhaps the only happy soldiers in Penrose's works were those of the 1st and 3rd New Jersey; their terms of enlistment having expired, they retired from the front and started back to Trenton. Their members who reenlisted were temporarily assigned to the 4th and 15th New Jersey.[16]

Russell's other two brigades, under Brigadier Generals Henry L. Eustis and Emory Upton, had burrowed north of Cold Harbor Road, Eustis's left flank touching the roadway across from Hagood's South Carolinians and Upton's line continuing north to a point near Bloody Run, facing Clingman's North Carolina brigade. Arrayed behind three successive rows of works, Eustis's soldiers hunkered low. "The rebs couldn't hurt us much and we couldn't hurt them much for they were entrenched as well as we were," John C. Arnold of the 49th Pennsylvania wrote home, "but the bullets were whistling all the time."[17]

While Eustis's troops turned the earth and squeezed off occasional potshots at Hagood's neighboring rebels, Wright pondered the vexing problem of what to do with their brigade commander. A West Point graduate and Harvard University engineering professor, Eustis's hard drinking and rumored opium use had stirred his subordinates to revolt, especially after the general disappeared for three days during the fighting at Cold Harbor. Still new to corps command, Wright was loath to sanction Eustis, but the drumbeat of complaints left him no alternative. "I am directed by the Lieutenant General to prefer charges against you for your conduct at Cold Harbor," Wright informed the former academic, putting the matter as tactfully as he could. "This I am unwilling to do, but can only avoid it by receiving your immediate resignation." Thanking Wright for his "kindness," Eustis replied that he had sent his resignation to Grant and was looking forward to resuming his scholarly pursuits at Cambridge. He was ultimately relieved on June 12, and temporary command of the brigade went to Lieutenant Colonel Gideon Clark of the 119th Pennsylvania, who had handled Eustis's job during his extended absence.[18]

Upton's brigade, on Eustis's right, faced no such leadership crisis. "If any person has ever earned a star for bravery and hard fighting it is Colonel Upton," an officer in the 121st New York wrote home. Upton's bravery, however, had exacted a high price. "The poorly interred corpses of our men within our line, and the dead lying between the lines had now become decomposed and putrid, and made an awful stench," one of Upton's warriors recalled. "The water was very poor and a long way off, and many of the men complained of being sick." In places only a few yards separated Upton's works from those of the Confederates, enticing a 2nd Connecticut Heavy Artillerist to crawl out and seize a Confederate flag dangling over the rebel entrenchments. "Reaching up with his hand he caught hold of the coveted bunting and began to pull it towards him," a newsman reported. "The rebels on the other side, not daring to raise their heads, caught hold of the staff, and there was a trial of strength between them and our friend from the land of wooden nutmegs." The enterprising Federal soldier won the tug-of-war but was wary of crossing the short interval to safety with his trophy in tow. Instead, he waited until nightfall to sneak back to the Union lines.[19]

Immediately north of Russell, Brigadier General James B. Ricketts's division occupied the headwaters of Bloody Run and its forested banks. Confronting Hunton's all-Virginia brigade from Major General George E. Pickett's division, Ricketts's outfit had been seriously damaged in the assaults of June 1 and 3 and its leadership decimated. Ricketts's left wing was led by Lieutenant Caldwell K. Hall, the third man to head the brigade in as many days, and its right wing was composed of a brigade under Colonel John W. Horn, who had been commanding for a single day.[20]

Brigadier General Thomas H. Neill's division settled in on Ricketts's right along a relatively flat field that continued north toward Muddy Run. Arrayed from left to right were Brigadier General Lewis A. Grant's Vermont brigade, Brigadier General Frank Wheaton's predominantly Pennsylvania brigade, Colonel Oliver Edwards's brigade drawn mainly from Massachusetts, and Colonel Daniel D. Bidwell's brigade from Maine, New York, and Pennsylvania. Facing Neill's troops across a flat, sandy plain were Gregg's Texas and Arkansas brigade and "Tige" Anderson's brigade of Georgians. Topography and a bend in the lines put the 1st Company, Richmond Howitzers, posted on high ground above Muddy Run, in an ideal position to enfilade Neill's entrenchments. To block the Virginians' cannon fire, Neill ordered new works dug closer to the front and traverses run at right angles to the shells' trajectory. Work proceeded slowly, and not until June 7 would Neill deem his troops "tolerably protected" from the rebel ordnance.[21]

In places Neill's fortifications were so close to the Confederate works, one of Wheaton's soldiers recalled, "that our men on the front line did not dare to appear on the breastworks, except in the darkness of the night, and almost any movement brought forth a storm of shells." An officer in Edwards's brigade noted that the "whole camp became one vast system of burrows." Responsible for covering a relatively narrow sector, each of Neill's brigades manned its front line with a single regiment, which remained in place for twenty-four hours, "then is relieved for 48 hours and goes about a half mile to the rear to straighten up, wash up, sleep and cleanup arms," Lieutenant Colonel Samuel E. Pingree of the 3rd Vermont wrote his cousin.[22]

June 4 brought vigorous shelling along Wright's front—"at daybreak are saluted by Parrot guns and Minnie balls," a Federal recorded, adding that "as they are doing no harm, we are firing but little, and only at their workmen." The digging revealed unusual treasures, including a multifaceted Fresnel lens originally constructed for a lighthouse. Manufactured in Paris and valued at $3,000, the lens stimulated hearty speculation over how it got to Cold Harbor. Some soldiers guessed that the Confederates must have pilfered it from a lighthouse. Others surmised that an ignorant official must have sent it to Cold Harbor on the assumption that the landlocked crossroads was really by the ocean. "The joke is apparent," a newsman remarked, "when it is remembered that Cold Harbor is not a harbor, and is fifteen miles from navigable water."[23]

As the day advanced, Wright's soldiers laced the ground to the rear with a complex maze of earthworks and trenches. "The whole plain occupied by our army was dug over," a surgeon wrote of the scene. "General officers had their tents erected in deep excavations surrounded by embankments of earth, and special duty men had each prepared for themselves burrows in the ground, many of which were creditable specimens of engineering. One was reminded, in riding over the plain, of the colonies of prairie dogs with their burrows and mounds." Recounted a soldier: "Some of us dug holes in the sand and spread our shelter tents over them so that we are safe while in there, although the tents suffer, some being punched full of holes." Despite these precautions, the 6th Corps's chief surgeon estimated that on Wright's front an average of six men were wounded each hour, or about two hundred a day.[24]

Charles A. Page of the *New York Tribune* recorded a vivid image of conditions along the 6th Corps's line. "Imagine it," he began. "Men work all day, and never once stand upright; load the pieces upon their hands and knees, extending the rammers out of the embrasures, while others ply shovels to replace the earth knocked away by hostile projectiles. Here, where the bushes have been allowed to stand in the embankment, if you will rise up cautiously and peer through, you shall see the shoveled earth as it is thrown up and falls upon [the Confederate] line 200 yards away. You must be wary, and you must drop to your knees when you see a puff of smoke, for they suspect some one is looking through that clump of bushes." Getting to the rear, the newsman warned, required stooping low and running. "More than a hundred men have run across there today," he reported. "Every one has been fired at and only three have been struck."[25]

Immediately north of Wright, Smith's 18th Corps persevered through a miserable ordeal that had begun on June 3 with its attack against Kershaw's entrenched line. The Union assault's main axis had followed swampy Muddy Run. South of the run and adjacent to Wright's corps, Brigadier General William T. H. Brooks's division, led by Brigadier General Gilman Marston's brigade of four New York regiments, had suffered a bloody repulse, leaving Colonel Guy V. Henry's brigade to hold an advanced line of abandoned rebel rifle pits. Expecting that he would be ordered to renew the attack, Brooks had shifted his remaining brigade under Brigadier General Hiram Burnham—augmented by the 21st Connecticut from Henry's brigade—into an assault column next to Wright. Late in the day, when word arrived that Grant had cancelled the offensive, Burnham moved his troops to a more sheltered position covering the ravine cut by Muddy Run.[26]

On Brooks's right were Brigadier General John H. Martindale's two brigades under Brigadier General George J. Stannard and Colonel Griffin A. Stedman. Pinned under fire from Kershaw's Confederates, Martindale's troops had excavated a jagged line of ditches stitched together from Muddy Run north across the adjacent Allison family field. Their works and those of the rebels were "scarcely a rifle shot apart," a Union man recalled, "and the exposure of a hand or head, upon either side, is pretty sure to result in a furlough of thirty days or eternity." A Federal survivor described how he and his companion piled bodies and logs into barricades and threw sand "upon the whole—anything to keep the rebel bullets back." Confederate shells exploding in these "horrid heaps," he confided, created "a scene better imagined than described."[27]

Stretching north from Martindale and angling eastward past Beulah Church was Brigadier General Charles Devens Jr.'s division, loaned to Smith from the 10th Corps. Too ill to command, Devens spent June 3 on a stretcher while two of his brigades, Colonel William B. Barton's predominantly New York outfit and the late Colonel Jeremiah C. Drake's brigade, now under Colonel Zina H. Robinson, watched the slaughter of Brooks's and Martindale's men from the safety of their entrenchments. Late in the day Smith relieved Devens and replaced him with Brigadier General Adelbert Ames, whose brigade had been guarding the Union supply base at White House Landing.

After dark on the third, Burnham forwarded several regiments from reserve to relieve Henry's frontline troops. "Rough breastworks [were] begun along our front, which was straightened and proper connections made with [our] right[,] left[,] and rear," a soldier in the 21st Connecticut recalled. "Skirmish pits were dug for the pickets a few lines in advance, and the reserves took the place of labor in the trenches," he wrote. "The musicians and the ambulance corps with stretchers groped cautiously about, responding to the groans of the wounded and the dying. Staff officers crawled warily to and fro, seeking to trace their path to the various headquarters with orders for the night and the morrow. It was well neigh impossible to take a step without treading upon some human being, either living or dead."[28]

In Martindale's sector dead and dying soldiers lay close to the Confederate works and in the narrow strip of land between the pickets. "We knew that many a brave soul was wrestling with a terrible death alone," a Connecticut man reminisced. "It made us heartsick that we could afford no relief, but it was sure destruction to venture one foot beyond our cover." Despite the danger, Union troops crept into the no-man's land all night to rescue the unfortunates. A party of forty soldiers from the 12th New Hampshire crawled among the corpses "listening, for they could make no call, for some deep sigh or low moan that would tell them where amid the surrounding gloom of night and death they might find one [still alive]," a man from the regiment recounted. Another search party rescued a wounded lieutenant by tunneling to where he lay, pulling him into the excavation, and dragging him back.[29]

While details braved Confederate sharpshooters to search for injured men, the rest of Smith's soldiers labored to strengthen their entrenchments. Stedman's brigade moved its front line forward several yards and threw up a tolerable set of earthworks. Sprawled across Muddy Run, Burnham's brigade found itself dangerously exposed to fire from Law's Confederates posted on high ground in front of them. So intense was the Alabama firepower that the 13th New Hampshire's flag staff was "split, smashed, and splintered" until it could no longer hold the regiment's flag. The flag bearer tied two planks from a cracker box to the staff as splints, cinched them tight with the strap from his knapsack, and kept the colors flying. Some of Burnham's troops, separated by Muddy Run, communicated by throwing messages tied to sticks and rocks across the ravine.[30]

Stannard's headquarters were on the right of his line "in a bigger pit, where one may stand upright under the canvas cover made necessary by the absence of trees," a Massachusetts man recalled. "Here he welcomed the medical staff, pending the efforts of the pioneers, who were set to dig a hole for their special accommodation."[31]

Smith's field hospitals overflowed with injured men. "Our surgeons worked nobly, looking like so many butchers," a soldier in the 81st New York recalled. "Many were bareheaded, with sleeves rolled up to their armpits, some of them spotted all over with blood; they really looked horrifying." The medical staff was overwhelmed. "I have seen more than a thousand of our men, within the past twenty-four hours, torn, mangled, smashed, disemboweled—every conceivable wound you can imagine—lying about our 18th Corps hospital, exposed to the rain without shelter, a scene of awful suffering," wrote Assistant Surgeon Sullivan of the 18th Corps hospital staff. The more serious cases were taken back to White House Landing for treatment at the main field hospital or loaded on ships bound for Washington. "I walked about half-way to the landing when I got into an ambulance," an injured color guard related. "There were hundreds of others just like myself, hobbling along down to the landing, some with their arms slung up and others holding on to their legs. I will never forget the sight when I was carried aboard the steamer at the Landing; the deck was simply covered with the wounded, some with their legs off and others with their arms off."[32]

Sunrise on June 4 revealed an "extremely irregular" 18th Corps line, a Union man noted. "Each division having entrenched its own front just where it paused in its charge, the line was full of salient angles, in shape something like the letter W," he wrote. The uneven front, however, worked in some instances to the Federals' advantage, as it made the position "very strong for defense," the soldier observed, "since it gave us a cross fire covering our front."[33]

Early in the morning, Ames's brigade, now commanded by Colonel Louis Bell, escorted a wagon train of ammunition and supplies from the Union depot at White House Landing to the front. Smith immediately shuttled the newcomers to the battle lines, where they received a brutal initiation into warfare Virginia style. "We had not gained our position in front of the woods, before the enemy began a brief musketry firing, which a reply from us tended to increase, and which was kept up almost without interruption during our nine days' stay at that point," one of Bell's soldiers reported. A compatriot agreed that the "crash and roar of artillery, the rattling of musketry, the bright glare of flashing guns, the deep yell and cheer of the charge along the line, filled the air with the din of battle almost without interruption."[34]

The men of the 18th Corps kept digging until the Allison family farm, a New Englander related, was "ribbed across with sand-heaps, behind which the reserves lay down to rest and smoke their pipes, and write letters home, and criticize the battle of yesterday, and to speculate upon what 'Old Grant' would do next." The earthworks, one of Stannard's men later explained, "were commenced by men crouching to escape the direct fire of the enemy at close range; that the bayonet for pick, and the tin plate for shovel were the chief and, in many cases, the only tools; that, even after three nights, with their comparative ease and safety of work, had intervened, wounds and death could only be escaped by constant vigilance."[35]

Soldiers from the 13th New Hampshire and 118th New York of Burnham's brigade moved into Henry's front line, relieving Henry's exhausted troops, and Burnham's 8th Connecticut, which had been spared the previous day's fighting, replaced the 2nd New Hampshire of Stedman's brigade, affording those troops much needed rest. The Connecticut men "immediately commenced and finished during the day a line of breastworks," Captain Charles M. Coit of the regiment reported, "our left connecting with the line being erected by the 13th New Hampshire." In the evening Marston's brigade returned to the front and relieved Burnham, setting a pattern in which each brigade rotated to the front every three days.[36]

"Like a thief in the night."

Compared to the constant din of musketry and artillery fire on Hancock's, Wright's, and Smith's fronts, the country north of Matadequin Creek seemed eerily quiet the morning of June 4. Most of Warren's 5th Corps, its headquarters near Bethesda Church, faced west, firmly installed in earthworks across from Major Generals Stephen D. Ramseur's and John B. Gordon's divisions of Early's 2nd Corps. Near Shady Grove Road Warren's line bent sharply east to form the upper extension of the Union formation's upside-down L, with Brigadier General Charles Griffin's division—opposed by Major General Robert E. Rodes's division of Early's corps—paralleling the roadway and connecting with the 9th Corps on its right. Burnside's men continued the Federal entrenchments east to the vicinity of the Bowles farm, where they faced Heth's Confederates.

A half-mile gap crisscrossed by marshy tributaries feeding into Matadequin Creek separated Burnside and Warren from the Union army's southern wing. Birney's division occupied this boggy, brush-choked interval but was manifestly insufficient to fend off a concerted enemy assault should Lee decide to launch one there. Facing Birney on high ground were Confederate earthworks occupied by Pickett's Division of Anderson's 1st Corps. The consequences of a successful rebel foray in the Matadequin Creek sector threatened disaster for the Federals, for it would sever Warren's and Burnside's corps—fully a third of Meade's troops—from the rest of the Union force.

To Meade's dismay, Warren and Burnside seemed incapable of cooperating. Warren could be difficult under the best of circumstances, and a month of squabbling with Burnside and his superiors had honed the wiry New Yorker's temper to a simmering rage. Even inconsequential infractions seemed to set him off. On the night of June 3, the precipitating event was an aide's failure to prepare Warren's tent to his liking. "I have heard Meade in one of his towering passions," a witness to the tirade recalled, "but I never heard anything which could begin to equal the awful oaths poured out tonight [by Warren]; they fairly made my hair stand on end with their profaneness, while I was filled with wonder at the ingenuity of invention and desperate blackguardism they displayed."[37]

Congenial Burnside offered a convenient target for Warren's barbs. Grant had ended Burnside's quasi-independent status during the North Anna operations by placing him under Meade, but the Rhode Islander continued to exercise an independent streak, and the rest of the army never seemed willing to accord the 9th Corps equal status. Soldiers referred to the outfit as "Burnside's Traveling Menagerie," a nod to the "wandering nature of its service" in different theaters during the war. "There is an immense amount of galloping to and fro all the time, and two or three men with stars on their shoulders are always around Burnside," Warren's artillery chief sarcastically—and unfairly—observed, "but from the start the corps has done nothing; it has been put in very little, and when sent forward always stuck at the first impediment." Burnside and his aides were painfully aware of their lackluster standing. "We have been bullyragged round so," wrote Burnside staffer Captain Daniel R. Larned, "and the corps spoken of as a superfluity—and no end to the insults and taunts we have received."[38]

Grant recognized the weakness in his defenses created by the Matadequin and, on the afternoon of June 3, suggested to Meade that he "contract" the Union formation from the right "if practicable." Meade had duly notified Warren and Burnside to tighten their positions during the night of June 3–4. Fearing a Confederate counterattack, they chose instead to stay put and strengthen their fortifications.[39]

Little did the Union commanders suspect that Lee's generals harbored concerns that mirrored their own fears of an enemy attack. After all, Rodes's and Heth's Divisions protruded dangerously east from the main Confederate formation, making it almost impossible for Early to reinforce them if Warren and Burnside resumed the offensive. Worried about their safety, Early ordered the two divisions back to the main Confederate north–south line. Under cover of darkness, Rodes retired next to Gordon's Division, resting his left near Hundley's Corner on Shady Grove Road. Around midnight Heth's troops also withdrew, bivouacked for a while behind Rodes, and after breakfast marched on to Gaines's Mill, where they passed General Lee stretched out in the grass, sleeping with a saddle for a pillow. They camped near the mill in a field littered with sardine cans left over from a Union encampment dating from McClellan's campaign in 1862. There they composed a reserve behind the center of the Confederate position.[40]

His corps now compressed into a more defensible line on the army's northern flank, Early wrote Lee his assessment of the situation. He doubted that the Federals intended any offensives in his sector and concluded that the "whole object of the enemy is, I think, to protect his flank." As for his part, Early promised to "keep a look out, and if I get a chance to strike the enemy on the flank I will do so."[41]

Shortly after daybreak on June 4, Warren's division commander Griffin—"a brave man and a good fighter and does not drink more than his share," a Pennsylvanian who served under him observed—dispatched skirmishers from the 22nd Massachusetts and 62nd Pennsylvania of Colonel Jacob B. Sweitzer's brigade to probe north across Shady Grove Road in search of the missing rebels. Gingerly approaching the looming entrenchments formerly occupied by Rodes, Sweitzer's soldiers found them empty. A Union man counted twenty-two dead artillery horses behind the vacant earthworks, a tribute to the northern gunners' accuracy during the previous day's fight. Warren duly informed headquarters that the Confederates appeared to have fallen back and that he intended to "push up" to find out where they had gone.[42]

Burnside's skirmishers, on Griffin's right, also felt northward and verified that Heth's Confederates had likewise left for parts unknown. "Like a thief in the night, the Johnnies had stolen away," a Yankee observed. "The sight within their works was sickening," a Rhode Island man recalled. "Ninety-eight dead artillery horses were counted on our brigade front, and a little to the rear were twenty buried and unburied soldiers, one of whom was a colonel." A hundred yards behind Heth's former line, the Federals found a woman who had taken refuge in the cellar of her log house. When the Yankees looted her sweet potato supply in the basement, she retreated to the main floor, braced herself across the doorway, and screamed for help. Pandemonium erupted when a soldier dug up a box containing $4,000 in coins. "He very generously divided it with his company," a newsman reported, "and that company has since been 'matching' quarters and half-dollars as though they were pennies."[43]

Strolling through a field of corpses, James Madison Stone of the 21st Massachusetts spied a Confederate shot through the body but still alive. "He was lying flat on his back and appeared to be unable to move, gazing up into the sky, his eyes were restless and rolling," Stone noted. When the Yankee offered to help, the man replied, "I wish you would turn me over on to my side so I can see the sun rise." After facing him toward the sun, Stone left to fetch a canteen of water. "When I got back fifteen minutes later the poor fellow was dead," he wrote. "He had fallen asleep to awake, I trust, to a more glorious sunrise."[44]

Relying on Warren's and Burnside's reports, Union headquarters concluded that the Confederates had indeed abandoned the Shady Grove Road sector, ending the threat to the northern flank. Ever cautious, Meade suspected that Early's disappearance signaled that the rebels were planning either to "mass for an attack somewhere on us, or they are withdrawing beyond the Chickahominy." Rejecting Warren's suggestion to go on the offensive, Meade characteristically decided instead to strengthen his existing line to fend off a possible enemy attack. Doing so, he concluded, required further contracting the army's formation, shoring up its flanks, and closing the half-mile gap where Matadequin Creek divided its two wings.[45]

Near eight o'clock that morning, Meade issued instructions designed to put the Army of the Potomac on a sound defensive footing. As soon as practicable, Birney was to abandon the marshy interval between the army's wings and join Hancock near Old Cold Harbor, reuniting the 2nd Corps's far-flung elements. To fill the vacancy left by Birney's departure, Warren was to slide the 5th Corps

southward, anchoring his right near Old Church Road and extending his left
across the open swampland to cement a junction with Smith's right flank near
Daniel Woody's house. As Warren reached left, Burnside was to leave his position at Bethesda Church and march south to Cold Harbor Road, where he
would serve as a reserve. Sheridan was to post cavalrymen on both ends of the
infantry line, one division operating out of Old Church to watch the army's
northern flank, another division picketing the Union left flank along the Chickahominy River, and a third division remaining "in reserve at some convenient
point."[46]

Orders went out right away directing Warren and Burnside to initiate their
part of the deployment. Both generals, Meade admonished, were to "get ready
for receiving attack as soon as possible." Smith, however, failed to receive notice of the headquarters directives and was at the Woody farm when he encountered Birney and learned that the division commander expected to be relieved.
"Under these circumstances I suppose [Birney] will scarcely feel disposed to
get his men to work on his line," Smith wrote headquarters in consternation.
"If he is to be relieved, other troops should be sent to fill his place that immediate steps may be taken to complete our defenses, now in a backward state,
which need cooperation of both commands." Shortly after 9:00 A.M., headquarters informed Smith that Warren had been ordered to replace Birney and forwarded Smith's message as a reminder.[47]

Eager to gain concrete intelligence about the battlefield's northern region,
Warren directed staff officer Major Washington A. Roebling to reconnoiter the
sector. A laconic engineer, Roebling "stoop[ed] a great deal," Meade's aide
Lyman remarked, "when riding has stirrups so long that the tips of his toes can
just touch them, and, as he wears no boots, the bottoms of his pantaloons are
always torn and ragged." More to the point, Roebling "goes poking around in
the most dangerous places, looking for the position of the enemy, and always
with an air of indifference."[48]

The major executed his assignment to perfection. "The [rebels] had retired
west on the Shady Grove Road, but not very far, as we soon struck their pickets," he reported. "Opposite the right of [Brigadier General Lysander] Cutler,
out the pike and all along the west of Bethesda Church they were still in force,"
Roebling added. Passing this latest intelligence on to headquarters—Early's
rebels remained in strength across from the 5th Corps's main north–south
line—Warren recommended that the quickest way to relieve Birney was for
Burnside, who now had no enemy troops facing him, to send part of his corps
directly south into the Matadequin gap.

Conceding the wisdom of Warren's suggestion, headquarters changed its plans: Warren was now to stay put, holding any surplus troops in readiness, while Burnside marched cross-country and relieved Birney. On receiving these new instructions, the 9th Corps commander directed his divisions under Brigadier Generals Robert B. Potter and Orlando B. Willcox to start south immediately to fill the void created by Birney's departure. Brigadier General Thomas L. Crittenden's division, which had performed poorly during recent fighting, was to remain with Warren until nightfall and then rejoin Potter and Willcox as a reserve.[49]

The change in plan, however, engendered further confusion. Humphreys, who as Meade's chief of staff had primary responsibility for coordinating the movements of the various corps, was unaccountably left out of the loop and learned of the new deployments only after they were underway. "I do not know why this arrangement is made unless to relieve Birney more quickly," he telegraphed Meade, who had ridden over to Wright's headquarters to examine the 6th Corps's situation. "This is the first intimation that I have had of Burnside's going into Birney's place," Humphreys complained, adding that substituting the 9th Corps for the 5th Corps "might interfere with the ulterior changes, should it go on." The movement, however, was well advanced by the time his protest reached headquarters, and Meade decided to leave matters as they stood.[50]

While the Army of the Potomac's infantry tightened into a more compact and defensible alignment, Sheridan's cavalry deployed to protect the flanks. Four weeks of campaigning had done nothing to improve relations between Meade and the strong-willed upstart imposed on him by Grant. Friction between the two generals had come to a boil during the movement to Spotsylvania Court House, with Meade accusing the thirty-three-year-old son of Irish immigrants of failing at every turn. Grant had backed Sheridan, humiliating the army commander so deeply that he considered resigning. He was deterred from that drastic step, he informed his wife, only because he could not find a way to honorably step down from his position.[51]

Unleashed by Grant, Sheridan on May 9 took the army's cavalry toward Richmond, intending to draw out Jeb Stuart and defeat him in a pitched battle near the Confederate capital. He did exactly that on May 11, trouncing the rebel mounted force near a hostelry called Yellow Tavern and mortally wounding Stuart. Since then, Sheridan's riders had screened the Union advance across the Pamunkey and had fought blistering engagements against their Confederate counterparts at Haw's Shop, Matadequin Creek, Hanover Court House, and Ashland. Morale in the Union mounted arm had soared, enhancing Sheridan's standing and casting Meade increasingly in the cavalryman's shadow.

Stuart's death had left the Army of Northern Virginia's cavalry without a head. Chief contender for the position was Major General Wade Hampton, a forty-six-year-old South Carolina planter with an intuitive knack for combat. Hampton's competition was Major General Fitzhugh Lee, a West Point graduate, former Indian fighter, and perhaps most importantly, Robert E. Lee's nephew. Fitz Lee, as he was called, had displayed commendable talent in slowing the Union advance to Spotsylvania Court House but had faltered since then, most notably by failing to hold a critical river crossing following the battle at Yellow Tavern and unsuccessfully attacking a garrison of black troops at Wilson's Wharf on May 24, for which he was "censured bitterly." Heading a third Confederate cavalry division was General Lee's son, Major General William H. F. "Rooney" Lee, recently returned to the army after imprisonment in the North. "Until further ordered," General Lee had directed, "the three divisions of cavalry serving with this army will constitute separate commands and will report directly to and receive orders from these headquarters of the army."[52]

The job of safeguarding the Army of the Potomac's northern flank lay with James Wilson, a twenty-six-year-old novice who had spent most of the war as an aide to Grant and as chief of the Cavalry Bureau, a desk job that had nothing to do with combat. "In personal appearance he is not remarkable, but he is the best horseman in the army—and rides a little bay devil of a horse to the admiration of his command and the astonishment of all pedestrians," a newspaper correspondent effused. Not everyone, however, held Wilson in high esteem. "The officer commanding our division is worse than a boy of 15 years," a trooper from Indiana wrote home of the general. "He knows nothing but it would not do for anyone to know I said so." It was Wilson's good fortune that his two brigade heads—Colonels McIntosh and George H. Chapman, both former midshipmen—were commanders of proven talent.[53]

On June 3, during Meade's futile assaults at Cold Harbor, Wilson had swept behind the Confederate army, first routing Brigadier General Thomas L. Rosser's mounted brigade at Haw's Shop, then descending across Totopotomoy Creek to threaten the rear of Heth's entrenched line. Unable to connect with Burnside, Wilson at nightfall withdrew to the creek's north bank. McIntosh's brigade—consisting of the 1st Connecticut, 3rd New Jersey, 2nd Ohio, 18th Pennsylvania, and 2nd and 5th New York—had camped near Haw's Shop, supporting Captain Dunbar R. Ransom's horse artillery. Backed by Lieutenant

Frank S. French's battery, Chapman's smaller brigade—it contained at this juncture only the 3rd Indiana, 8th New York, and 1st Vermont—covered the road from Hanovertown to Old Church. By midnight Wilson's troopers had encamped "with pickets properly posted," Wilson later noted, "and our exhausted and hungry men and horses again at rest."[54]

Humphreys congratulated Wilson on the "very successful execution" of his assignment and suggested that the cavalryman harass Heth's rear the next day "with increased force." Sheridan, he added, was under orders to reinforce Wilson with another mounted division—Brigadier General Alfred T. A. Torbert's outfit, brought up from guard duty along the Chickahominy River. "You will not, of course, delay any attack you may intend to make until the reinforcements join you," Humphreys stressed, "if you feel strong enough to make it without them."[55]

Wilson, however, did not feel sufficiently strong to start a fight alone. Early on June 4 he notified headquarters that Heth had withdrawn—an observation confirmed by Warren and Burnside—and that his own division was in no condition to pursue. "My horses have been without forage some thirty hours; my men out of rations over a day, and being hard at work with the enemy ever since crossing the Pamunkey," he wrote, adding: "Most of my horses have been saddled over forty-eight hours, and my command needs rest." Responding in jest, Grant sent Wilson a sample of Hosford's prepared rations that he had recently received, proposing that the Union troopers try the dried food for a few days and report back. Examining the sample, Wilson found "three dessicated, condensed, black meat biscuits, very much the size and color of a cake of shoe-blacking, and three half-pound packages of cracked wheat which had been toasted and slightly sweetened." Humoring Grant, he ordered ten thousand of the rations, which he thankfully never received. "The next time I met the general," he later wrote, "we had a pleasant chat about the rations and my requisition for a supply of the same. The joke was on him and not on me."[56]

After their drubbing by Wilson at Haw's Shop, Rosser's Confederates retired west to Atlee's Station, on the Virginia Central Railroad. Camped within supporting distance of Rosser were two other cavalry brigades—a North Carolina outfit, formerly under Brigadier General James Gordon and now commanded by Colonel John A. Baker, and a brigade formerly under Brigadier General Peirce M. B. Young and now under Colonel Gilbert J. Wright.

Around 10:00 A.M. on June 4, Rosser, accompanied by Colonel Elijah V. White's battalion, "The Comanches," reconnoitered toward Haw's Shop "with the purpose of gaining information." On reaching a sector of McIntosh's entrenched line manned by the 2nd Ohio Cavalry, Rosser instructed White to at-

tack. "The order was promptly obeyed without dismounting," a Comanche recalled, "and the Yankees fled precipitously from the rather novel scene of
horsemen leaping their works, and using both steel and ball in their curious
evolution." The incident had its light moment—"Rosser's cheers for the Comanches were joined in by the whole command," a southerner remembered—
but McIntosh ultimately pumped in reinforcements who "handsomely repulsed" White's troopers and recovered the captured works. With an extended
picket line to man, Wilson remained "very uneasy."[57]

While Wilson spent an anxious day sparring with Rosser, Sheridan's other
two cavalry divisions—those of Torbert and Brigadier General David McM.
Gregg—kept watch along the Chickahominy. Gregg's troopers patrolled three
miles of river from Hancock's southern flank to Bottom's Bridge, opposed by
Fitzhugh Lee's cavalry, and Torbert's division patrolled downriver to the Richmond and York River Railroad bridge, faced by Butler's Brigade of Hampton's
Division. The assignment along the boggy bottomland was noteworthy, a South
Carolina man recalled, for "some disagreeable picketing at night and (what was
worse) countless hordes of mosquitoes on all sides." Many of Butler's South
Carolinians had fought McClellan's Federals on this same ground two years
earlier. "Here, as elsewhere along the route, the hurried nature of McClellan's
retreat was evidenced by the debris still visible," a man in the Charleston Light
Dragoons observed. "Rusty canteens, cartridge-boxes and other leather accoutrements, now partially decayed; pieces of uniforms and blankets discolored
by long exposure to the weather; fragments of rubber cloths and similar re-
minders were strewn plentifully along the roads." John Cummings of the 5th
South Carolina Cavalry wrote home that the "bones of two dead Yankees that
were never found to be buried are lying near here."[58]

General Lee viewed the Federal cavalry buildup along the Chickahominy
with apprehension. As early as June 1, when Grant had first concentrated toward Cold Harbor, Lee had suspected the Federal commander of planning a
major move southward. "General Grant appears to be gradually approaching
the York River Railroad," he had written Beauregard on the first, "whether with
a view of touching the James River or not I cannot ascertain." Even though Lee
was still recuperating from his bout of dysentery, he visited the cavalry posts
along the river, "reconnoitering personally the enemy's position," according to
a witness.[59]

To help block a Union move across the Chickahominy, Lee lobbied Rich-
mond for some of Beauregard's forces idling in front of Butler at Bermuda
Hundred, in particular Brigadier General Matthew W. Ransom's newly arrived
North Carolina brigade, commanded during Ransom's convalescence by Col-

onel Paul F. Faison of the 56th North Carolina. Grudgingly agreeing to send these troops if necessary, Beauregard reminded Richmond that the brigade constituted "one-third of my force and will be only one twenty-fifth of Lee's."[60]

On June 3, as Union cavalry activity intensified along the Chickahominy, Beauregard received instructions to send the brigade to Bottom's Bridge "without delay." He protested that he had already given Lee Hoke's entire division, leaving him only 7,000 soldiers to man the Howlett Line. Ransom's departure, Beauregard argued, might make it "impossible to prevent the [enemy] from destroying the communications between Richmond and Petersburg, nay, from capturing Petersburg, which could not be retaken without great sacrifice of life." He would have no choice, the general predicted, but to abandon the Bermuda Hundred line and operate out of Port Walthall Junction. His arguments, however, fell on deaf ears, and the North Carolinians departed for the Chickahominy at daylight on June 4. A regiment from Brigadier General James Dearing's cavalry filled Ransom's vacancy in the Howlett Line, and Beauregard gamely promised to "endeavor still to hold our lines at Bermuda Hundred Neck." Reaching the Chickahominy late in the day, Ransom's troops, accompanied by the Washington Artillery, constructed earthworks along the river's southern bank near the Richmond and York River Railroad bridge. Fitzhugh Lee's horse artillery, augmented by the Richmond defense battalion under Lieutenant Colonel John C. Pemberton, stood guard at Bottom's Bridge.[61]

While Confederate reinforcements marched to the Chickahominy, Gregg's and Torbert's Federals traded potshots across the river with Fitzhugh Lee's and Butler's horsemen. "In the afternoon the rebels sent a few shells into our camp, 'boots and saddle' sounded, and we routed out in a hurry," an Ohio man noted. A cavalryman in the 1st New Jersey expressed surprise at the "remarkable accuracy" of Whitworth rounds fired by these gunners posted three miles away at Savage Station, on the Richmond and York River Railroad. But the only Union casualties were two injured horses and a very frightened soldier. "Striking the ground at a little distance," a witness recounted, a rebel projectile "ricocheted towards him, and the first intimation of its proximity which his comrades received was from seeing him seize his frying pan and dodge, as the shot struck where he had been sitting. Notwithstanding the imminence of the danger, he did not spill a particle of the gravy in his pan."[62]

Alert for signs that Grant might be starting across the Chickahominy, two of Butler's mounted regiments investigated reports of enemy activity farther downstream at Long Bridge. The rumors proved false—the ruckus was probably caused by Torbert pulling out to join Wilson and by Gregg extending to take up the slack created by his departure—but Confederate headquarters re-

mained suspicious. "R. E. Lee of opinion that the enemy may be moving down
the Chickahominy with a view of crossing lower down," Fitzhugh Lee's chief
of staff recorded in the division's diary.[63]

"Like angry meteors escaped from their orbits."

Midmorning on June 4, Meade and his staff rode from their headquarters at
the Kelly family farm to tour the Union army's entrenchments. The aide Lyman
was not impressed. "Of all the wastes I have seen, this was the most dreary,"
he later wrote. "Fancy a baking sun to begin with; then a foreground of abandoned breastworks; and on one side Kelly's wretched house; in the front an
open plain trampled fetlock-deep into fine white dust, and dotted with caissons,
regiments of weary soldiers, and dead horses killed in the previous cavalry
fight. On the sides in the distance were pine woods, some red with fires that
had run through them, some gray with the clouds of dust that rose high in
the air."[64]

Stopping at Hancock's headquarters near the Old Cold Harbor intersection,
the officers exchanged a few words with the ailing Pennsylvanian and with
General Wright, who was there as well. The visit, Lyman recalled, was "enliv-
ened by a battery in close proximity, which was firing furiously." Then the entourage rode off to find Smith. They located the 18th Corps's headquarters near
Daniel Woody's house around noon and paused for lunch. Smith feted his visitors with champagne and other luxuries and induced them to linger for several
hours, talking and smoking—"whether it was the lunch, or deep military problems, I know not, but General Meade remained there smoking for what seemed
to me an unnecessarily long time," Lyman wrote. The aide whiled away the
time watching cannonballs crash through trees and bounce across clearings
where troops had pitched their tents. "You ought to see them skip!" he wrote
home later that day. "It would be odd, if it were not so dangerous. When they
have gone some distance and are going slower, you can see them very plainly,
provided you are in front of, or behind them. They pass with a great whish, hit
the ground, make a great hop, and so go skip, skip, skip, till they get exhausted,
and then tumble—flouf—raising a puff of sand."[65]

While the army's top brass feasted, Burnside's soldiers filed into the earthworks that Birney's men were leaving. Willcox's division arrived first and snug-
gled tightly against the northern end of Smith's line, reaching north to a bog
formed by a sluggish tributary of Matadequin Creek. During the initial deployment, Colonel John F. Hartranft's brigade manned the front line and Colonel

Benjamin C. Christ's brigade formed in reserve. Potter's division picked up the 9th Corps's line on the far side of the marsh and extended northeast to another finger of the Matadequin, Colonel Simon G. Griffin's brigade deploying next to Willcox and Colonel John I. Curtin's brigade reaching to the right. Skirmishers drawn predominantly from the 48th Pennsylvania continued the formation in a northeastward cant across a third stream—known locally as Sandy Hill Creek—and on to a knoll occupied by the homes of the Bosher and Tucker families. Thus oriented, Potter's troops faced generally north, protecting the upper Union flank, now re-fused. Although skirmishers constituted much of this line, Burnside expected Crittenden's division to arrive during the night and mass in reserve east of the Woody place, backstopping Potter's thinly held formation. "We were brought up within easy rifle shot of the enemy," a New Hampshire man recalled, "and part of us went to digging and throwing up works, while others kept an eye on the rebels, and gave them shot for shot." It was damp and rainy and miserable.[66]

Midafternoon, Burnside arrived from Bethesda Church to arrange with Smith the junction of his corps's left flank with the right end of Smith's line. The sound of festivities greeted him at the camp. Meade and his staff were still there and appeared miffed that the 9th Corps commander's appearance might quell the jovial mood. Burnside, it appears, had been instrumental in trying to get Smith and his division commander Brooks, who was also in attendance at the lunch, relieved after the Battle of Fredericksburg in December 1862. According to Burnside's aide Larned, the 9th Corps commander "didn't care a fig" about the earlier tiff, but Smith and Brooks were still steaming over the slight. "They don't speak now," was how Lyman described the standoff between Burnside and the two generals from the 18th Corps, "and we enjoyed the military icicle in great perfection!"[67]

As Burnside's troops settled into Birney's stretch of line, that division marched south, passing through Cold Harbor and along Dispatch Station Road to form in reserve behind Gibbon. The 9th Corps soldiers taking their place were disgusted to find that the 2nd Corps men had "left their rubbish" in the abandoned entrenchments. Pickets prepared rifle pits far in advance of the main line to sound the alarm in case the rebels attacked. "Being within easy musket range of the enemy, we could not show our heads without receiving a warning note from the Johnnies in the shape of a Minnie ball," a Federal related, "and every few minutes they would send over some of their twelve and twenty-four pound shells to remind us that they were there, and had the tools to work with."[68]

Burnside's departure left Warren to protect the Union army's northern flank, and the 5th Corps was having a busy time of it. "The sharpshooting was fearfully annoying: one did not dare to expose oneself a moment," a Wisconsin man remembered. "The warning cry, 'Grab a root' (which means, lie down) was sounded every few moments. If we could see the smoke from the rifle we could drop under cover before the bullet could reach us." The only way to leave the front was to dodge from tree to tree or to crawl. "Not a man could expose his person above the earthworks without a dozen bullets 'zipping' at him from a watchful foe," a Union man explained.[69]

With Burnside gone, Warren became increasingly apprehensive about his exposed position and fired off a stream of alarmist dispatches to headquarters. "I do not exaggerate in stating my line to be between 4 and 5 miles long," he warned, although the actual length of his works was at most two miles. The 5th Corps was now deployed with Brigadier General Samuel W. Crawford's division forming Warren's left, the division's left touching Burnside's right a short distance north of Matadequin Creek. Cutler's division extended north of Crawford to Old Church Road, and Griffin's division angled the line eastward, generally following Old Church Road through Bethesda Church and on toward Linney's Corner. Reminding his division heads of the "very great length of our line, our isolated position, and the facility which the woods afford the enemy for massing against our center," Warren cautioned them to remain alert.[70]

That evening Meade's headquarters issued a batch of orders designed to keep pressure on Lee. Warren was to push Crawford and Cutler as close as possible against Early's entrenchments to prevent the rebels from secretly withdrawing more troops from the northern end of their line. "It is impracticable to do anything tonight," the 5th Corps commander snapped back, "as no arrangements have been made for doing so, and not contemplating it, I allowed my engineers to go back this evening after rations." Crawford's division, Warren suggested, could advance "at a jump without regular approaches, but it must be done in conjunction with an advance [by Burnside] on my left, which must be all arranged before hand, otherwise I might find my advanced position by daylight flanked by the enemy." The 5th Corps staff settled down for another night within uncomfortable range of their boss' tantrums and Early's artillery. "We have a collection of fifty cannon shot lying under the tree where our headquarters are," Warren's aide Roebling wrote home. "They all fell within a hundred feet of our tree [and] don't include the shells that have burst around us."[71]

Headquarters also reminded the other corps heads to advance their front lines during the night by "regular approaches." Hancock instructed his troops to push out "as far as possible toward the enemy," while Wright ordered his division chiefs to fortify their picket line, "making it a continuous line of entrenchments, to be occupied before daylight by your first line of battle, connected to the rear by zigzags." The campaign of maneuver was beginning to look suspiciously like a siege. "It is the days of Vicksburg over again," a newsman remarked. "The skirmishing lines are hardly forty yards apart, and each line is not much more than that in advance of the line of earthworks."[72]

The night was rainy and overcast, conditions that made a series of relatively minor Confederate probes along the Union position seem like fearsome assaults. "It was one of those nights when the soldier feels like early wrapping himself up in his blanket to rest; and it was a fitting night for the enemy, ever watchful and sagacious, to make a furious attack upon our lines," a soldier in the 5th Corps related. The rebels were quick to exploit the darkness, and isolated little battles erupted along the skirmish lines, provoking outbursts of musketry and cannon fire from the main entrenchments that put the pickets stationed between the armies in fear for their lives. "Deeper than midnight thunder peeled forth the cannon," a soldier recalled, "while the burning shells, coursing through the air, looked like angry meteors escaped from their orbits."[73]

Confederate artillery pumped a vigorous fusillade into Neill's division, on the right of the 6th Corps's line. Union batteries replied, "and for half an hour there was nothing to be heard but the steady roll of musketry, and the zip of the balls as they flew over our heads," a northerner wrote home. But the eruption, like its predecessors, proved relatively harmless. "After the affair was over," another Federal recalled, "I could not learn of a single man on our side that was injured, and I think the rebels fared equally as well."[74]

The uproar inspired one of Brooks's soldiers to reflect on the terror of night attacks. "Dreadful though the encounter may be by daylight, it is in some of its features a thousand times more hideous in the dark," he wrote. "First we had a startling volley from the pickets; then a few seconds later the crack, crack, of the aroused skirmish line, and then, chiming in to punctuate each message of death, the sharp twang of a Parrot Gun from the rear, or the belch of a howitzer with its load of grape or canister at close quarters. Then came the thickening roar of the combat, till its sound resembled the simmering noise of a rapidly puffing locomotive, only a thousand fold louder. Then we heard the long fiendish yell, at which we all involuntarily exclaimed, 'the Johnnies are charging!' and next the defiant Union cheer in response, which told of their repulse. Add to this the dreadful indescribable glare of flashing gun powder, and the consciousness that after each flash a missile is winging its way toward you, and the moment's suspense—especially where cannon are served at the rate of forty rounds a minute—to conjecture where and whom the balls will strike."[75]

Despite the shelling, Neill's men inched their lines forward. "We were in good musket range of the enemy and our safety as we went from one work to another depended upon the enemy's not knowing where we were," a soldier in the 1st Vermont recorded in his diary. "As soon as we got into our places a detail was made to work on another breastwork in front of that." The Confederates were less than a hundred yards away, the soldier recounted, and although the men worked quietly, "still occasionally a bullet would come whistling over fired by some suspicious picket."[76]

Musketry and artillery fire was also intense along Hancock's line. "After sunset and a fog had settled down, the rebels made another night attack but were repulsed as before," Luther Rose recorded in his diary. "Shells from them coming again uncomfortably close." Gibbon surmised that "no cause could be assigned to the firing when it broke out except the nervousness existing in the two armies, though some of it was undoubtedly caused by parties from our lines attempting, in the darkness, to bring in our wounded, the lines being so close together that scarcely any movement could take place without being heard by the enemy."[77]

While his troops shivered through the "dismal drizzle" and cursed their generals for forbidding campfires, Burnside tried to coordinate with Smith, who was still smoldering over ancient affronts at Fredericksburg. After dark the two generals rode together in stony silence to examine the ground where the 9th Corps was taking up its new position. Smith, it developed, now wanted Burnside to form in advance of the post Birney had vacated and to relieve part of Ames's division situated north of the swamp. To facilitate the transition, Burnside assigned his aide Major James St. Claire Morton to work with Smith. The prickly general, however, continued to find fault and unilaterally withdrew Ames's troops from north of the swamp without alerting Morton. To help Smith protect his sector, headquarters assigned him two fresh heavy artillery regiments that had arrived that morning—the 10th New York and 2nd Pennsylvania, some six thousand men in all.[78]

His equanimity shaken by Smith's open hostility, Burnside unburdened himself to his aide Larned. "It seems to me that patience ceased to be a virtue on the part of the general and he has let it slip once or twice that he was 'perfectly disgusted'—but still he submits," the staffer wrote home. Burnside, however, soon regained his composure. "They can't hurt me," he assured Larned after a few deep breaths. "These things will all react on themselves." Watching Smith and Burnside's sniping from afar only confirmed Roebling's impression that "if the 9th and 18th Corps only had live commanders like the other three, we could expect to do something, whereas now we positively have to act on the defensive half the time."[79]

Eager for action, Grant proposed that Meade direct his gunners to open on the rebels after midnight "to wake up the whole of the enemy's camp and keep them on the watch until daylight." Meade replied that he could fire his batteries as suggested but noted that "whilst it keeps the enemy 'awake,' their reply, which they will undoubtedly make, will keep our people awake, and, in addition, it will interfere with the approaches I have ordered to be made tonight." Acceding to his objection, Grant agreed to postpone the midnight artillery barrage if it would disrupt any operations. Translating all of this into an order, Meade's chief of staff Humphreys instructed each corps head that he was authorized to fire on every rebel battery bearing on him after midnight "and keep up the fire until daylight, if in his judgment the firing will not, by a retaliating fire from the enemy, cause as great annoyance and loss to our troops as to theirs, and if it will not interfere with the advance of the positions by regular approaches ordered for tonight." Needless to say, the corps commanders decided unanimously against the plan.[80]

That evening Assistant War Secretary Dana visited Wilson to investigate matters on the army's northern flank. "He remained for dinner and seemed to find the Hosford's prepared rations somewhat palatable, though hardly suitable for a steady diet," the general later wrote. "I had succeeded in adding hardtack, coffee, and bacon to the meal, all of which he found agreeable additions to what General Grant had contributed. It was a laughable episode, which well emphasized the conditions about us."[81]

Humphreys relished a few hours of rest. "For three nights previous to last night I had not two hours sleep for each night, and that broken," he wrote home. "I hate the very sight of a dispatch, and especially one from the telegraph office, from which they pour in like an overwhelming flood." The pestered general unburdened himself in a letter to his wife. "All day long wherever one may be, it is 'dispatch for General H.,' and then General H. must reply to it. Think of it! Some seventy or eighty one day, and quite as many written not only in reply but giving orders. I don't know what the effect will be, whether to make me the most patient or the most impatient of men."[82]

Lee felt confident that he had taken the precautions necessary for the Army of Northern Virginia to repel another frontal attack. "It is a matter of great importance when the enemy is bringing against us all the men he can possibly get," he wrote in a circular distributed after the June 3 assault, "that all our

fighting material in the army should be armed and equipped, and on duty with
their companies and regiments." Officers were instructed to inspect and mod-
ify their lines as needed, to ensure that their troops had enough food and ammunition, and to keep a third of their soldiers in the earthworks "alert against
night or early morning attacks."[83]

A glaring weakness in the Confederate defenses was the salient where Barlow's Federals had routed Breckinridge's Virginians during the June 3 attack.
Finegan's Florida troops had constructed new earthworks across the base of
Breckinridge's salient and occupied the new position until the night of June 4,
when Brigadier General Ambrose R. Wright's brigade relieved them. "After 48
hours in the advance entrenchments with scarce anything to eat or a drop of
water," a Floridian wrote a friend, "now we have plenty of water, an abundance
of supplies, and some rest." The next night a fatigue party from Mahone's Division tore down the old works. "Many dead Yankees were to be seen lying
about," a Virginian recalled, "and I saw one wounded whom I helped get out
of a ditch."[84]

Intelligence from the battlefield's northern sector continued to feed Lee's
suspicion that Grant intended to dash across the Chickahominy. Late in the day
Early's scouts reported that Wilson's cavalry pickets ranged from the Bowles
property to the Via farm and north across Totopotomoy Creek all the way to
Haw's Shop. "I think enemy's right rests at Bethesda, thrown back and strongly
entrenched," Early wrote Lee in an accurate assessment of the situation. "All
quiet in front except occasional sharpshooting." By 7:00 P.M. Early had received confirmation that Warren's Federals now occupied the entrenchments
that Rodes and Heth had abandoned the previous day. "This shows conclu-
sively," he advised Lee, "there is no movement to our left, and renders it probable that [Grant] will endeavor to continue to mass on our right" toward the
Chickahominy River. Circumstances might even favor a Confederate offensive,
Early suggested. "If the enemy attacks your right in the morning," the aggressive corps commander recommended, "I propose to withdraw Rodes to the
[Old Church] Road and attack his right, if I can do so to advantage."[85]

That evening Lee penned a dispatch to Richmond voicing his belief that a
sweeping Union maneuver southward was imminent. "I apprehend from the
quietude the enemy has preserved today that he is preparing to leave us tonight,
and I fear will cross the Chickahominy," the general wrote. "In that event the
best course for us to pursue . . . would be to move down and attack him with
our whole force, provided we could catch him in the act of crossing."[86]

Lee could do little, however, to prepare for Grant's likely maneuver. Shifting soldiers south of the Chickahominy at this juncture would dangerously

weaken the Cold Harbor defensive line and invite an attack. And an offensive such as Early recommended seemed premature: if Warren and Burnside were strongly entrenched, an assault would accomplish nothing. For the time, Lee saw little choice but to rely on his cavalry to sound an alarm if the enemy attempted to shift south and hope to catch the Army of the Potomac while it straddled the Chickahominy. To facilitate a rapid response, Lee directed his engineers to repair the causeway to the Woodbury-Alexander Bridge, a major crossing immediately behind his army's southern flank.[87]

But for another day at least, the initiative would remain with Grant.

III

JUNE 5–6, 1864

Grant Devises a New Plan and Jockeys for Position

"All cannot be accomplished that I had designed."

LEE AND EARLY WERE NOT alone in suspecting that Grant was planning another offensive. The Army of the Potomac's troops were confident that an important movement was afoot. "Our present position requires either a big fight
or a big flank," Lewis H. Steiner, the Sanitary Commission's chief inspector,
wrote home from the Cold Harbor front. Charles Francis Adams Jr., who fre-
quented Grant's headquarters, was struck by how preoccupied the general had
become. "I never noticed this before," Adams wrote his father the day after the
big attack at Cold Harbor. "Formerly he always had a disengaged expression
in his face; lately he has had an intent, abstracted look, and as he and Meade
sit around on our march I see Grant stroking his beard, puffing at his cigar and
whittling at small sticks, but with so abstracted an air that I see well that they
are with him merely aides to reflection. In fact as he gets down near Richmond
and approaches the solution of his problem, he has need to keep up a devil of
a thinking."[1]

Grant had matured his thinking about the general parameters of his next
move by the afternoon of June 4. He did not share the details with Washington
until the next day, however, when he sent a lengthy dispatch to Halleck. "A full
survey of all the ground satisfies me that it would not be practicable to hold a
line northeast of Richmond that would protect the Fredericksburg railroad, to
enable us to use it for supplying the army," he began, dismissing Halleck's favored supply route at the outset. "To do so," he warned, "would give us a long
vulnerable line of road to protect, exhausting much of our strength in guarding
it, and would leave open to the enemy all of his lines of communication on the
south side of the James."[2]

Since the beginning of the campaign, Grant asserted, his objective had been to "beat Lee's army, if possible, north of Richmond, then after destroying his lines of communication north of the James River to transfer the army to the south side and besiege Lee in Richmond, or follow him south if he should retreat." Achieving that goal, however, had eluded him. Echoing an observation he had voiced during the North Anna stalemate, Grant chided the Confederates for acting "purely on the defensive, behind breastworks, or feebly on the offensive immediately in front of them, and where in case of repulse they can instantly retire behind them." The soldiers of both armies, he felt, seemed to agree "that the rebels can protect themselves only by strong intrenchments, while our army is not only confident of protecting itself without intrenchments, but that it can beat and drive the enemy wherever and whenever he can be found without this protection."[3]

Grant now understood that Lee's defensive skills called for a new response. "Without a greater sacrifice of human life than I am willing to make, all cannot be accomplished that I had designed outside of the City," he wrote. The time had come once again to maneuver.[4]

"I have therefore resolved upon the following plan," the general in chief announced. "I will continue to hold substantially the ground occupied by the Army of the Potomac, taking advantage of any favorable circumstance that may present itself, until the cavalry can be sent west to destroy the Virginia Central Railroad from Beaver Dam for some twenty-five or thirty miles west." Once Sheridan had completed this mission, Grant intended to shift the Army of the Potomac across the James River, either by first crossing the Chickahominy and marching to Bermuda Hundred or by crossing several miles downstream near where the Chickahominy flowed into the James. "To provide for this last, and most probable, contingency," he suggested to Halleck, "six or more ferryboats of the largest size ought to be immediately approved."

"The object of crossing the James," Meade's chief of staff Humphreys later explained, was "to destroy the lines of supply to the Confederate depot, Richmond, on the south side of the James as close to that city as practicable, after those on the north side of the river had been rendered useless." After capturing the rail hub at Petersburg, the Potomac army was to swing north, turning Beauregard's entrenchments in front of Butler and pressing on to Richmond. Lee, the Union planners expected, would have no choice but to abandon the capital and retreat toward Danville or Lynchburg.[5]

Taken together, Grant expected Sheridan's foray and Meade's operation to sever Lee's sources of supply except for the James River Canal. That latter objective, he concluded, was best left to the Army of the Shenandoah. Grant had high hopes for Hunter and had already informed Meade that an important pur-

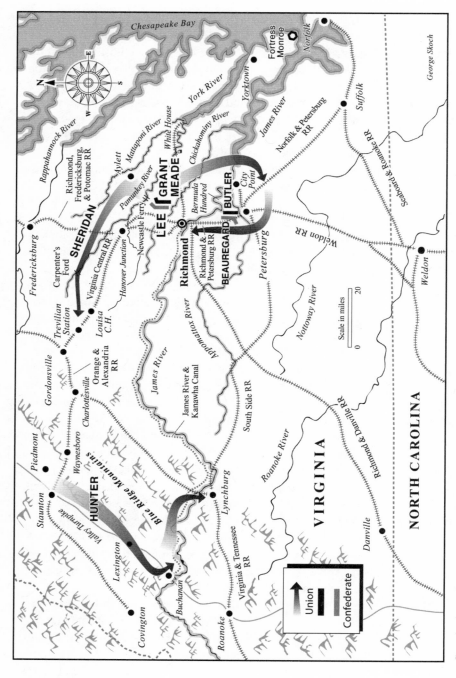

Grant's planned new turning movement

pose for lingering at Cold Harbor was to keep Lee from detaching troops against Hunter until he had gotten "well on his way to Lynchburg." In the event the Shenandoah army failed to reach Lynchburg, Grant looked to Sheridan to destroy the canal.[6]

Sheridan's mounted foray against the Virginia Central Railroad was a critical component of the overall plan. The purpose of this expedition, Grant wrote, was to "effectually break up the railroad connection between Richmond and the Shenandoah Valley and Lynchburg." Rebel workmen, he observed, had become adept at repairing railroads, and he wanted Sheridan's handiwork to last. "It is desirable that every rail on the road destroyed should be so bent or twisted as to make it impossible to repair the road without supplying new rails," he stressed. When the cavalry's work was done, Sheridan was to return to the Army of the Potomac, accompanied by Hunter if feasible. "If it is found practicable," the general in chief added, "whilst the cavalry is at the most westerly point reached by it, to detach a brigade or more to go over to the James River and destroy the canal, it will be a service well repaying for three or four days' detention."[7]

Although Grant was committed to swinging the Army of the Potomac boldly across the James, he had yet to formulate the precise route for the maneuver. The obstacles were formidable. The hostile armies were closely entwined at Cold Harbor, which diminished the prospects of stealing away without alerting Lee. Grant had engineered impressive withdrawals from the Wilderness and from the North Anna River, but the Confederates were wise to his tricks and remained alert for signs of movement. The first stage of disengagement was especially dicey, for it required crossing the Chickahominy under the enemy's very nose. If Lee caught the Union army astride the boggy stream, he could inflict serious injury. Moreover, once the Federals evacuated Cold Harbor, Lee would be free to maneuver, perhaps marching to Bermuda Hundred and overwhelming Butler before Meade could come to his assistance.

Transporting the massive Union force with its guns and wagons across the James River posed unique logistical challenges. Where, for example, was the best point to cross? The stretch of river from Richmond to Howlett's, where Butler's Bermuda Hundred fortifications were anchored, was largely controlled by the Confederates. Union gunboats and Butler's riverside forts protected the waterway from Howlett's to the sea, but that lower section of river was half a mile wide in places and vacillated in depth as much as four feet with the tide. Grant asked Halleck to send him six ferries, but whether they could carry enough men and supplies to evacuate the army before the Confederates rallied and attacked was an open question. A pontoon bridge was also an option, but constructing a floating span across the powerful tidal stream would tax the skills of the army's most experienced engineers.[8]

Grant's aide Adam Badeau considered the prospective movement across the James the riskiest operation the general had yet ventured. "He was to withdraw an army from within forty yards of the enemy's line, and to march through the difficult swamps of the Chickahominy bottom, to positions where that stream could be crossed without interruption from the rebels," the staffer later observed; "then, to advance to the James, a great and tidal river, at a point seven hundred yards across; to effect a passage with all the munitions and supplies of a hundred thousand soldiers, changing his base, at the same time, from White House to City Point, a hundred and fifty miles apart [by river]; to effect a combination of Meade's force with that of [Butler's Army of the James]; and, finally, advance, with his double army, against Petersburg." The dangers were many. "Not only was the movement liable to interruption by Lee on the northern side," Badeau noted, "but Grant's long and circuitous route would compel him to be several days on the march, while the distance from Richmond to Petersburg is only twenty miles, and Lee's camp was within five or six hours of the Army of the James."[9]

Grant agreed that the movement was "hazardous," especially since the Potomac army's departure would unleash the Army of Northern Virginia. "Lee, if he did not choose to follow me, might, with his shorter distance to travel and his bridges over the Chickahominy and the James, move rapidly on Butler and crush him before the army with me could come to his relief," he later wrote. "Then too he might spare troops enough to send against Hunter who was approaching Lynchburg, living upon the country he passed through, and without ammunition further than what he carried with him."[10]

Other options were open to Grant. An obvious course was to detach part of his force at Cold Harbor—the 18th Corps, perhaps accompanied by a corps from the Army of the Potomac—and send it to Bermuda Hundred. Butler would then be strong enough to overrun the Howlett Line, sever the Petersburg and Richmond Railroad, and take Petersburg at his leisure free from hindrance by Lee, whom Meade's main body would keep pinned at Cold Harbor. Existing records do not indicate if Grant, Meade, or their staffs considered reinforcing Butler while retaining most of the Potomac army at Cold Harbor. What we do know is that by the morning of June 5, Grant had committed to a wholesale evacuation of Cold Harbor and a rapid swing across the James River, fully understanding the hazards such an operation entailed. The details were yet to be decided. But by Grant's estimate, the turning movement offered a likelihood of victory that fairly compensated for the dangers of leaving Lee temporarily untended. "The move had to be made," he later insisted.[11]

"All this army have got to be very expert diggers."

Bickering among the Army of the Potomac's generals resumed early on Sunday, June 5. Shortly after midnight Warren learned that McIntosh's brigade of Wilson's cavalry division, which he assumed was watching his right flank on Old Church Road, was in fact two miles away at Linney's Corner, leaving a dangerous breach in the Union defenses. Fault for the mix-up lay in equal measure with Burnside, Warren, and Wilson. Burnside had never told Wilson that the 9th Corps was departing for the Matadequin, Warren had neglected to extend his line to occupy the ground abandoned by Burnside, and Wilson had failed to notice that he had lost contact with the infantry flank. When Warren learned that the cavalry had not kept apace with adjustments in the infantry line, he fired off a blistering note to headquarters. "I am not capable of maintaining any position whatever, if that is all the cooperation I am to have," he seethed, noting that his assumption that Wilson was patrolling nearby had given him "false assurances of being timely warned of the enemy's flank movements."[12]

Humphreys forwarded Warren's complaint to Sheridan and reminded both generals that headquarters expected "communication to be maintained between the cavalry commander on the right and the commander of the infantry corps on that flank, so that they will be mutually advised of every change that takes place in the position of each other." On receiving what he took to be a reprimand, Wilson wrote Warren to explain the dilemma that he faced. His picket line, he began, was more than four miles long, and he had received inconsistent instructions to cover the supply depot at White House, watch the army's flank, and give timely warning of enemy movements in that quarter. "So much for general instructions," he continued, "but permit me to observe, general, that till the receipt of your note, I had no information of your being on the right. My pickets and patrols are directed to connect and keep up direct communication with the right flank of the infantry line, and will do so as long as possible, but the infantry should not rely too much upon me for close connections, since I have so much country not only to watch but to guard from attacks of cavalry."[13]

Disposed from earlier run-ins with Warren to think the worst of him, Sher-

idan leaped to Wilson's defense by complaining to Meade about "the withdrawal of some army corps without any notification to the cavalry." Infantry
commanders, he lectured, were "quick to give the alarm when their flanks are
uncovered, but manifest inexcusable stupidity about the safety of cavalry
flanks." Humphreys returned a firm reply. Wilson, he reminded Sheridan, had
no excuse for losing contact with Warren; and while infantry commanders
should communicate with cavalry guarding their flanks, it was often not practicable for them to do so. "A close and constant communication should be kept
up between the cavalry and the infantry on the flanks" was his bottom line.[14]

Wilson remained puzzled by the dustup. "A communication received from
Warren through McIntosh saying his flank was uncovered, our pickets two
miles apart," he scrawled in his diary that evening. "Don't understand it or
meaning of last night's operation."[15]

Smith and Burnside's uneasy partnership also spawned an outpouring of
prickly missives. At 2:00 a.m. Burnside wrote Meade about his difficulties with
the 18th Corps commander and sought approval to relieve Smith's northernmost elements. Potter's and Wilcox's divisions, he explained, had filled the
works vacated by Birney, and a portion of Crittenden's division stood ready to
relieve part of Smith's corps. "I shall put a force there at daybreak, unless otherwise ordered," advised Burnside. "Am I right?" An hour and a half later,
Meade assured the skittish general, "Everything is satisfactory."[16]

Smith, however, continued to fault Burnside. "If you would put your left
where you said you would, it would shorten your present line and therefore be
more easily held," he complained in a note drafted shortly before dawn. "I cannot afford to straddle that swamp, for I cannot communicate with sufficient facility. Ask for the chief engineer of the army to come," Smith suggested, "and
settle the matter if you do not like the plan to which you agreed yesterday."
After conferring with an aide, Burnside conceded Smith's point and adopted a
conciliatory tone. "I have seen Major Morton and am quite satisfied with the
arrangement," he assured Smith. "You are quite right in not wishing to straddle the swamp."[17]

Headquarters' inquiry into how the infantry heads were faring with their
"regular approaches" toward the Confederate earthworks yielded disappointing responses. Barlow and Gibbon were now connected by a rifle pit, Hancock
reported, "and some 15 or 20 yards nearer the enemy than the one now held."
Warren advised that "affairs remain the same as last evening" and that he had
been "unable to make any advance during the night." Examining the 5th
Corps's front, Warren's artillery chief, Wainwright, noted that "siege operations" were advancing "so slowly, indeed, that their progress is invisible." For

his part, Wright credited Neill with an overnight advance of about forty yards, Ricketts with constructing works on the line his skirmishers had previously held, and Russell with "very little progress, except the establishing of new positions for guns." Burnside was still fine tuning his deployments and at 10:30 A.M. reported that his works in front of Smith's old fortifications north of the swamp were almost finished. His troops were also constructing a new line, he added, a hundred yards in front of Birney's former position, "which will place us on a ridge that commands the enemy's skirmish pits and enable us to push our approaches with greater facility." Grant and Meade rode out to inspect the 9th Corps's postings and became "dusty as mummies," a witness remembered, as they passed along roads "filled with tramping troops and grinding trains." [18]

Hancock's chief preoccupation this Sabbath involved Hill's Confederates on Turkey Hill, who reached well past his own left flank. "I understand that General Wright's line is very short, and that he has many troops in reserve, and that General Burnside has a division in reserve, and that General Smith has reserves," Hancock wrote headquarters. Pointing out that he faced both Hill and Breckinridge and that he had no reserves, the corps commander asked whether Wright could relieve part of Gibbon's line, which would free up 2nd Corps troops that Hancock could then shift to the southern end of his formation. This suggestion, Meade responded, was not "practicable." The 2nd Corps commander would simply have to make do with his forces at hand. [19]

Around three in the afternoon, Confederate artillery found the range of Hancock's headquarters once again, forcing the general and his aides to hastily evacuate. Captain Alexander M. McCune of Hancock's staff was mounting his horse when a projectile took his leg off at the knee. According to Lieutenant Colonel Walker, the incident deeply affected the general, who expressed regret at having located his headquarters in "unnecessary close proximity to the line of battle." [20]

While Meade's generals wrangled, their soldiers kept digging. "I have never seen such extensive works constructed with such magical rapidity, or that pressed so hard to the enemy's," a newspaperman reported. "Nor are they simply straight ditch and embankment. They are intricate, zig-zagged lines within lines, lines protecting flanks of lines, lines built to enfilade an opposing line, lines within which lies a battery which must keep silent. A maze and labyrinth of works within works, and works without works, each laid out with some definite design either of defense or offense." [21]

A New Englander described the routine. "Every night the engineers and pioneers are sent out in front of the advance pits, and throw up new ones, which are occupied by strong skirmish lines, and the next night a new pit is built," he wrote. "The rebels are continually sending bullets and a few shells and solid shot over us, and we are obliged to keep low, to avoid being hit. We have pits facing all ways except the rear, and there are traverses in every pit, a few yards apart, to protect us against cross-fires." He found it amusing to see men dart about, instinctively hunched over. "They think they had rather bend their backs a little, than to stop rebel bullets."[22]

Conditions in the no-man's land between the opposing works reminded Grant's aide Lieutenant Colonel Horace Porter of the horrors he had witnessed at Spotsylvania Court House. "The bodies of the dead were festering in the sun, while the wounded were dying a torturing death from starvation, thirst, and loss of blood," he recounted. Attempts to adjust the picket lines invariably stirred up heavy firing, and nervous troops interpreted the slightest movement as presaging an attack. "The men on the advanced lines had to lie close to the ground in narrow trenches, with little water for drinking purposes, except that obtained from surface drainage," Porter remembered. "They were subjected to the broiling heat by day and the chilling winds and fogs at night, and had to eat the rations that could be got them under the greatest imaginable discomfort." Recollected a Union soldier: "We have had to go into many places where it seemed that no man could look and live." It was strange, he reflected, "how men can become so accustomed to death and danger that they will acknowledge neither, and walk among whizzing bullets as though they were bees."[23]

Tunneling reached a feverish pace in Barlow's sector as soldiers of Company A, U.S. Engineer Battalion, assisted by troops from the 148th Pennsylvania, worked to run a mine into the steep bluff in front of the abandoned angle in Breckinridge's former line. Approaches to the tunneling site were prepared on June 5, and the next day engineers set to digging the shaft. David McIntosh, whose Confederate battalion was stationed above the mine, learned of the project and tried to disrupt the engineers. "I planted a howitzer a little in our rear, where the ground fell off, with its trail stuck in a pit, and fired shells with light charges, mortar fashion, into the enemy's works," McIntosh later wrote. Some shells landed near the mine's mouth, but the digging continued.[24]

Along Gibbon's front, Confederate fire swept the ground, preventing soldiers caught between the lines from going back for food or water. Several troops survived by constructing a small fort. Ranald Mackenzie, heading the 2nd Corps's engineering effort, decided to visit the outpost and invited fellow engineer Wesley Brainerd to join him in a two-hundred-foot dash to the isolated citadel. "Good bye, Brainerd!" Mackenzie shouted as he sprinted into the clearing. Bullets spit up puffs of dust, but the engineer made it to the fort, weaving around corpses that covered the ground.

Cursing, Brainerd followed his friend into the field—"the wicked whistling of the wind about me forced home to my consciousness the fact that hundreds of unseen bullets, meant for me, were searching for their victim," he later wrote—and soon lay gasping for breath next to Mackenzie. Looking around, he saw thick dirt walls with holes for muskets a few feet from the top. Two ragged yellow scars of dirt, one in front of him and one in his rear—the main Confederate and Union entrenchments—stretched north and south into the distance. Smoke billowed from the earthworks, musketry rattled without interruption, but not a living soul was visible. "Groups of bodies lay scattered along to the far distance," Brainerd remembered. "Silent and motionless they lay in all conceivable shapes and positions." Nearby was a form that he identified as Colonel Peter A. Porter of the 8th New York Heavy Artillery, shot down during the charge on June 3. "I knew him by his uniform and stout person, bloated and disfigured though he was, his arms uplifted, his legs stretched out, his blackened face with white foam oozing from his mouth, turned upward toward the blazing, scorching June sun," Brainerd wrote. "Around him in different stages of decomposition lay the bodies of the brave men who had died in the vain effort to recover his dead body. It was indeed a sickening, harrowing spectacle." Darting back, Brainerd and Mackenzie were greeted with cheers from their friends behind the main Union line.[25]

A mile north, in the 18th Corps's sector, the 21st Connecticut relieved the 98th New York of Marston's brigade from the front line next to Muddy Run. "Since June the 1st we had lived among the dead, and breathed the putrid air," Captain William Kreutzer of the 98th New York observed. "There, for the first, we had an opportunity to eat, to sleep, to wash in running water, to change our raiment and feel clean." In anticipation of the withdrawal, Captain Kreutzer arranged for rations for his 350-odd soldiers. He also asked the commissary for bread, rice, coffee, sugar, and beef for himself and his staff. "We also gave them an order on our old friend of the Christian Commission, Rev. Mr. Harris, for a bottle of *spiritus vini Gallici,* or brandy," Kreutzer recounted.

After the 98th had fallen back, its officers gathered in a trench under a stand of trees "to eat the first rational meal in five days," the captain remembered. Boards from bread boxes served as tables and plates. "While arranging and adjusting our tables, a solid shot passed so near that several of us felt its breath," Kreutzer wrote. "At the same time, to the right a few rods, a shell exploded in the headquarters of General Brooks, wounded one of his staff, and killed an

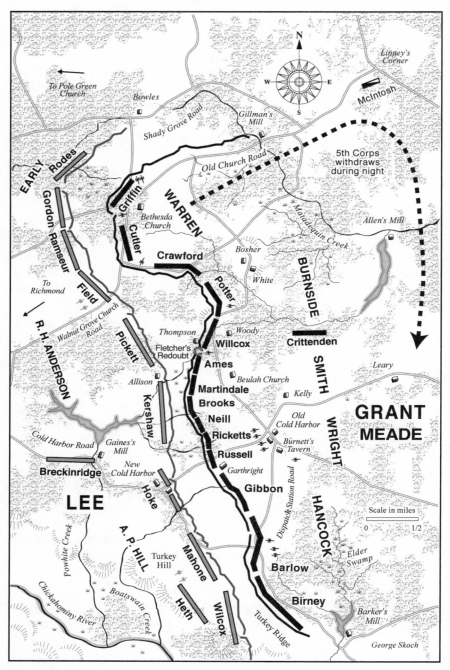

Operations on June 5

orderly and his horse." Spying Colonel Aaron F. Stevens of the 13th New Hampshire, Kreutzer invited him to the feast. Stevens sat down, placed a board in his lap, examined the bottle of brandy, poured a glass, took a sip, and turned to Kreutzer. "Captain, where did you get that?" he inquired. "I haven't had anything do me so much good in my life. Its five days since I've had anything to eat or drink but hardtack, and this miserable brook water." Presently Colonel E. M. Cullen of the 96th New York wandered by. "Pardon us, Colonel, for not sending for you," Kreutzer called out: "We thought you were supplied. We have *spiritus vini Gallici,* prepared by the doctors. Will you take a glass with us?" "With pleasure," Cullen replied as he joined the group and broke into song.[26]

Near noon Meade's headquarters issued a fistful of orders designed to shift the army's center of gravity south to facilitate the projected move across the Chickahominy. Warren, Humphreys instructed, was to withdraw the 5th Corps from the army's right flank near Bethesda Church, march to the Leary Farm a mile or so east of Cold Harbor, and "remain in reserve, prepared to move wherever required." Warren's departure would leave Burnside on the line's northern end. Meade wanted the 9th Corps to keep its left united with Smith's right and to orient the rest of its line more easterly along the Matadequin, forming a new re-fused flank for the army. Smith was to adjust his right to accommodate Burnside's shift, while at the other end of the Union line, Hancock was to reach south to the Chickahominy. While the army's infantry slid south, Sheridan was to concentrate Torbert's and Gregg's divisions near Newcastle Ferry on the Pamunkey in preparation for their rail-wrecking foray against the Virginia Central. Wilson's mounted division was to remain behind, McIntosh's brigade picketing off Burnside's right to the Pamunkey and Chapman's brigade patrolling the Chickahominy downstream from Hancock.[27]

Inspecting the proposed 9th Corps line during the rainy afternoon, Burnside and his chief engineer Charles Morton concluded that Meade's proposed deployment would never work. For one thing, the assigned position ran three and a half miles, stretching Burnside's troops too thin. More importantly, much of the terrain was marshy, and the line would pass in front of Matadequin Creek, leaving the men unable to retreat if attacked. Deferring to Burnside's judgment, headquarters agreed that the general could construct his main fortifications south of the creek and "throw back your right to [the Bosher family farm] and extend a line of skirmisher's beyond." Wilson's cavalry was to pick up where the pickets left off, and Brigadier General Edward Ferrero's 9th Corps's division of black troops was to congregate at Old Church, nailing down the new right end of the Union flank.

Once Burnside had rearranged his corps, his three white divisions would redefine the Army of the Potomac's northern terminus, abandoning to the rebels the ground north and west of the Matadequin formerly occupied by Warren and drawing a strong defensive position south of the creek's spider web of tributaries. Willcox's division—Hartranft's brigade now on the left and Christ's on the right—was to press tightly against Smith's right, facing Pickett's Confederates, while Potter's division was to continue the Union line northeastward toward high ground at the Bosher place. Warren's corps, camped in the Leary fields, would be close enough to pitch in if the Confederates attempted to overrun the screen of 9th Corps pickets and McIntosh's cavalrymen east of the Bosher farm.[28]

The 5th Corps's projected movement to its reserve position at Leary's farm required careful coordination between Warren and Burnside. An immediate sticking point involved the withdrawal of Colonel Nathan T. Dushane's Maryland Brigade of Crawford's division, located on the southern end of the 5th Corps's line and separated from its companion brigades by a boggy finger of Matadequin Creek. "Preparatory of movements ordered for tonight, I would like to have you replace [Dushane's] brigade on the left of my line so that I can have my troops a little more in hand," Warren requested of the 9th Corps commander. Burnside, however, was busy examining his new position and did not receive this request for several hours. His answer, when it came, did not please the New Yorker. He had been directed to post a new line extending more than three miles, Burnside explained, which made it "impossible" for him to relieve the Marylanders. Warren's response was to unilaterally withdraw the brigade, leaving only skirmishers in its place, and to advise Burnside after the fact to "look out" for that part of the 5th Corps's former territory.[29]

By nightfall Burnside's troops had taken up their new post. On the 9th Corps's left, workers drawn from Willcox's division and supervised by artillerist Captain Jacob Roemer labored to construct a massive fort at the junction with Smith's corps. Named Fletcher's Redoubt after a 9th Corps engineer, Lieutenant Nelson Fletcher, killed on May 24 at the North Anna River, the edifice commanded high ground south of the swamp near Widow Thompson's home. Even Burnside's detractors seemed pleased with the fort. "Burnside's men are great at throwing dirt," was the studied opinion of Warren's artillery commander, a regular critic of the 9th Corps. "All this army have got to be very expert diggers, being able to do a full day's work with no other tools than a tin plate and their bayonet; but the Ninth Corps far surpasses all others that I have seen both in the height and number of their breastworks."[30]

While Burnside entrenched, Warren prepared to march to the Leary farm. The route from Bethesda Church followed rutted wagon trails, and work parties fanned ahead to make repairs. Hoping to confirm the precise location of Early's rebels before his troops set out, Warren directed Colonel Sweitzer to reconnoiter west along Shady Grove Road. At 3:30 P.M. the brigade commander launched a reconnaissance with the 22nd Massachusetts and 4th Michigan, supported by the dismounted 21st Pennsylvania Cavalry. Deploying as skirmishers, the Massachusetts and Michigan soldiers passed through the Union picket line, immediately struck Confederates, drove them back, and after a running fight reached Early's fortified line at Hundley's Corner, confirming that the rebels were still where they had been the previous day.[31]

Before leaving for Leary's, Warren presided over an unusual ceremony. During the fighting on June 2 and 3, he had situated his headquarters by an oak tree on a knoll with a clear view of the battlefield. Some forty solid shot and unexploded shells had landed within a hundred yards of the tree, and the general directed workers to bury the ordnance in a pit dug to resemble a grave. "Altogether it was a jolly funeral," a participant recalled. "Several drums were heard, and several funeral notes—bugle notes, halting a battery that was going into position hard by." Gazing into the pit, Warren smiled "as an unrelenting man might smile upon the tomb of a mortal foe," the witness reflected.[32]

At sunset Brigadier General Romeyn B. Ayres's brigade of Griffin's 5th Corps division made a vigorous demonstration along Warren's front to conceal the movement from Early's scouts, and the 5th Corps slipped away without interference. Crawford's division, on Warren's southern flank, marched first, followed by Cutler's and Griffin's divisions. The night was dark and rainy, the road was muddy, and bands of stragglers slowed the pace to an agonizing crawl. "A line of small fires were built back through those woods," a Pennsylvanian remembered, "and a man standing at each fire to direct the men." An officer at Warren's headquarters noted "the coming and going of division and brigade officers and, as it seemed to me, a continuous torrent of profane swearing of the most emphatic kind." The general grew especially agitated at the slow progress because he wanted to be out of Bethesda Church before daylight. "Warren was exhausting the West Point vocabulary," a witness recounted.[33]

Returning to his headquarters from a visit with Meade, Burnside read telegraphs by the light of a candle perched on a cracker box. Wind blew out the flame and felled a tree across the telegraph line, breaking it and throwing the

general and his staff into darkness until aides screwed up enough courage to
venture outside and repair the broken wire. "It was after midnight, cold and
rainy," the aide Captain Larned wrote in his journal, "and we slept in wet, disagreeable beds." When rebel shells snapped a flagpole and drilled a hole
through a tent, staffers extinguished their campfires to render them less visible
to Confederate artillerists. Relentless shelling, however, forced them to move
to an old house populated by two women, two children, and a man who begged
bread from the general and his entourage. The new location was scarcely safer,
a point underscored when a stray shell perforated Larned's tent and hit a water
pail next to an officer. Over the next few days, rebels would shell the 9th
Corps's high command out of its headquarters five times.[34]

Oblivious to Burnside's nighttime ordeal, Warren's troops threaded through
Bethesda Church and passed the eastern end of Allen's Mill Pond, following a
narrow trail that came out near the Leary family home. "It was as dark as it
could possibly be and raining a drizzling rain when orders came to be ready
to get out of there and not to make the least noise," a marcher recollected. The
trek could not have exceeded five miles, but the soldiers complained all the
way. "I was plodding along, stepping into human excrement without number,
tired, my shoulders lame, toes underneath bloody and sore, boots all out, body
lice upon me, my face dirty and sticky," another wrote. "I stopped once to get
a drink, but the water was covered with the slime and filth of the drainage of
the 5th Corps, and I was not much refreshed."[35]

The excursion did nothing to improve Warren's mood. "An army on one of
these dark night marches is little better than the crowd that walks the street, as
far as organization is concerned," the general observed. "The men never march
well," he added, "except on a retreat when they are all hurried forward with the
common instinct of fear."[36]

Birney's division of Hancock's corps meanwhile initiated its own nighttime
excursion. Under Meade's plan, Birney was to leave Colonel William R. Brewster's brigade in reserve and proceed with the rest of his division south along
Dispatch Station Road. Deploying south of Barlow, he would extend the 2nd
Corps's line past Barker's Mill to a point near the Chickahominy. The troops
started after dark, hoping to avoid detection, but their commotion was too loud
for Hill's Confederates to miss. "The pickets became alarmed and fired; then
the artillery on both sides took it up, and the stillness of the Sabbath evening
was broken by an artillery duel," a marcher recalled. "The fiery balls flew over
us and through the pines, bursting around us to an extent that one unaccus-
tomed to these scenes would naturally suppose that one half of our army would
be destroyed." A soldier from Maine proclaimed it a "miracle we weren't gob-

bled, wandering around in the dark, with Johnny Reb all around us." As it was, several Union soldiers fell into "malodorous pits"—probably graves—while dodging the artillery fire. Despite the fuss, Birney's troops reached their destination and began erecting earthworks parallel to Dispatch Station Road, incorporating entrenchments dug during McClellan's campaign. "This country is one vast graveyard," one of Birney's brigadiers concluded. "Graves everywhere, marking the track of the army on the march and in battles." Birney reported that he occupied "the heights to left of [a] mill, with a battery of light twelves, and my remaining brigade covering the approaches from the Chickahominy." Pickets patrolled Dispatch Station Road to the Tyler property, where they connected with Union cavalry.[37]

Aided by "dense mist," the Confederates launched probing forays all night, making life miserable for the Federals. The first attack occurred around 8:30 P.M., when skirmishers from Clingman's brigade crept close to Upton's entrenchments and made a dash to overwhelm the defenders. "The firing commenced directly in front of us and run [sic] rapidly to the left as far as the Second Corps, where the engagement was the hottest," Dwight Kilbourn of the 2nd Connecticut Heavy Artillery jotted in his diary. "Our boys replied," a man in the 5th Maine added, "pouring in a steady shower of lead, the artillery opened on both sides, and for a half hour or more the roar was deafening, with shot and shell flying over and among us."[38]

A short distance south, Lieutenant Henry Lee of the 126th New York had just eaten dinner and was preparing to lie down when he heard what sounded like a band playing music. "It was musketry ten feet from us," he wrote his mother a few days later. "It ran down the line and soon was in front of us. Just then over came a spherical case shot and burst about ten feet from us. Well then, you ought to see us dive into the works." Solid shot and canister pelted Barlow's line for half an hour, but the expected assault never came. "We could have mowed them down awful," Lieutenant Lee concluded.[39]

Farther south, some of Mahone's soldiers tested Smyth's position, crawling up to the Union pickets on their hands and knees under cover of an "impenetrable fog." Smyth's main line blazed away at the phantom-like shapes. "They advanced several times, their lines being cut to pieces, and each attempt to reach our works failed," a newspaperman reported. "Their loss must have been fearful, as our men shot them at short range, while our batteries swept them down in masses." Confederates across from Owen's brigade "tried to creep up in the darkness and use the bayonet," Joseph R. C. Ward of the 106th Pennsylvania reported. "They were allowed to get very near, when a few volleys hastened their retreat."[40]

No sooner had that commotion ended than another skirmish, accompanied by artillery fire, erupted in front of Russell's division. "These night attacks have got to be so frequent that they cease to create an alarm, for the whole army is always on duty, ready at any moment to meet any emergency," a Union man observed. "It is a pyrotechnic display of gigantic proportions." Assistant War Secretary Dana reported that "the firing lasted for twenty minutes, and was very loud, but it was all about nothing, and no harm was done." Reflected a man in the 2nd Corps: "They seem to have a great grudge against this corps and hurl a heavy force against it at night to break through the lines. As yet they have not catched our brave boys a napping and have not succeeded."[41]

Around 9:00 P.M., elements of Early's 2nd Corps attempted to occupy rifle pits in front of Warren's works. They had just reached the pits, a soldier in the Stonewall Brigade reported, when the enemy "saw us and poured over a shower of rifle balls." The attempt failed, the Confederate related, because "the left part of our line had to advance in an open field and when the Yankees saw them coming, they thought that they were attacking the works and started firing at them, which gradually went along the whole line."[42]

Despite interruptions, Wright's soldiers connected and improved their advanced works, enabling Russell's division to occupy ground previously held by rebel sharpshooters. South of Cold Harbor Road, Gibbon's troops heaped more dirt in front of their rifle pits and connected their main entrenchments with the 6th Corps's works on their right. Owen's and Smyth's brigades, comprising Gibbon's left wing, hooked their picket lines together and in places pushed forward twenty feet. Where the ground was too hard to dig, Gibbon called for sandbags and gabions. Barlow made little progress as enemy marksmen kept up a "sharp fire," and his sector, the general reported, was "so near [the Confederate] work that scarcely anything more can be done at night than by day." Stedman's 18th Corps division reported tolerable success in advancing its fortifications. "This was done so close upon the rebel pickets that serious trouble was expected, but the work was done so quickly and quietly, not a word being spoken above a whisper, that only two men of the [2nd New Hampshire] and one of the 12th [New Hampshire] were wounded," a soldier reported. "This was thought to be rare good luck given the dangerous situation. It seemed as if Grant, having failed to drive the enemy out of his lines was now trying to crowd him out."[43]

Also during the night, Sheridan worked to assemble a strong mounted force for his raid to cut the Virginia Central Railroad. Torbert's division, which had shifted from the Chickahominy River to Haw's Shop, withdrew through Linney's Corner and Old Church to New Castle Ferry on the Pamunkey. As soon as Chapman's brigade of Wilson's division was in place along the Chickahominy, Gregg's division started north to rendezvous with Torbert. "The cavalry division [Wilson's] which Sheridan leaves behind here will have to cover both our flanks," Dana informed Washington, "but the task will be made easy by the new position of Ninth Corps on our right, while on left Second Corps is to extend its pickets down the Chickahominy, and thus relieve some of the cavalry heretofore employed in that direction."[44]

Around 9:00 that evening, the *Boston Evening Journal* newsman writing as "Carleton" visited Meade's headquarters. A fire illuminated the general's tent, and Meade was pacing back and forth, staring sometimes at the ground and other times at flashes that lit the sky. "There are Smith's batteries; those are Russell's," the general estimated. "It is going all right. I should like to have them try it every day and every night." An aide brought a dispatch from Hancock, and Meade read it aloud: "The firing commenced on the right, ran down the line, and was pretty severe in front of my line, but they have done us very little damage."

Riding to Grant's headquarters, Carleton met the general in chief sitting by a campfire with his staff. Grant held a half-consumed cigar in one hand and the *Richmond Examiner* in the other and read aloud the newspaper's criticism of his campaign "in the utmost good humor," Carleton noted. The reporter remarked on the general's ability to remain cool even in the midst of crisis. "Gen Grant is imperturbable," he wrote, "quite as much as any man I ever saw."

Retiring to his tent, Carleton reflected that combat at Cold Harbor had settled into a predictable rhythm. "There was a slow cannonade in the morning, which gradually died away, but the infantry took it up, and so the Sabbath hours have been far from peaceful," he wrote. Sunset "is the usual hour for the ripple of musketry along the lines, and several nights we have had it—the rebels choosing it for attacking our advanced forces." Then once darkness fully set in, the night assaults began in earnest. "There it comes, one, two, three, a dozen, a hundred shots, a toll, deep, heavy, prolonged, like the rush of a mighty torrent suddenly let loose. How it deepens! It is like the ripping of the mower, swinging his scythe in ripened grain, dried and scorched by the summer heat. The great reaper is out there upon that field, stalking unseen between the trenches, walking in darkness, bordered with lightning flashes, showering it with leaden rain, making it the Valley of the shadow of Death!"

"How little you know of the reality," Carleton scrawled on his notepad. "I hear it, but have little conception of what is taking place. I shall realize it more fully in the morning when the ambulances come in with the wounded. But to be there, in it, a part of it—with blood at fever heat—with the air full of strange, terrifying noises—hissings, screechings, howlings of balls, bullets, and deafening explosions—all darkness, excepting the blinding flashes and sheets of flame! The altar of our country drips with blood. It is a Sabbath evening sacrifice, pure and precious, freely offered. Fathers and mothers have given the firstlings of their flocks with thanks that they had them to give; they have given the best, they have given all. Patriotism is not dead."[45]

"It would be hazardous to attack."

Lee received little information on June 5 shedding fresh light on Grant's plans. Late in the day Captain Page of Early's staff ventured across Totopotomoy Creek at Pole Green Church and confirmed that no Union infantry remained north of the stream. "I am satisfied," Early reported, "that the enemy's right is at Bethesda, thrown back along and parallel to the road from Bethesda to Gillman's Mill." So far as he could ascertain, the Federals had no offensive designs in his sector. "In the morning I will test the enemy's strength at Bethesda," he promised, noting that it was "too late now." Lee personally inspected Fitzhugh Lee's line along the Chickahominy and confirmed that the Union presence there involved only cavalry. While Meade's contraction of the Union formation suggested that the Federals planned to move south, enemy infantry had yet to reach the Chickahominy. For the time being, Lee saw no choice but to wait for Grant to show his hand.[46]

June 6 brought news of developments in the Shenandoah Valley that dramatically altered the balance of military affairs. Exhibiting more energy and skill than Sigel had ever displayed, Hunter on June 5 defeated Breckinridge's successor, Brigadier General William E. "Grumble" Jones, at the Battle of Piedmont, killing Jones and opening the way for a Union drive south. The next day—June 6—Hunter's troops marched into Staunton, underscoring the magnitude of this new threat. The Valley was again in play, and a powerful Union army was free to ravage the countryside, depriving Lee of critical supplies and introducing a new variable into the military equation at Cold Harbor. Unless Jones's force could be reconstituted, there was little to prevent Hunter from marching south to the supply hub at Lynchburg or even swinging east to threaten Charlottesville and Richmond. He seemed poised to undermine Lee's ability to hold on at Cold Harbor.

Word of Jones's misfortune at Piedmont was followed by news that the defeated force's new commander, Brigadier General John C. Vaughn, was retreating south to Waynesboro. "Staunton is at [Hunter's] mercy—a great disaster,"

Robert Garlick Hill Kean of the Confederate War Bureau lamented. Lee was unfamiliar with Vaughn and voiced concern that "some good officer should be sent into the Valley at once to take command there." His first choice was Breckinridge, whom he believed possessed the stature and energy to "do what is practicable in rousing the inhabitants and defending the country." The Kentuckian was still recovering from his recent injury but expressed confidence that he would soon be available for duty.[47]

Writing President Davis, Lee stressed the link between the Shenandoah Valley and Cold Harbor. "It is apparent that if Grant cannot be successfully resisted here, we cannot hold the Valley," the Confederate commander warned. "If he is defeated, it can be recovered. But unless a sufficient force can be had in that country to restrain the movements of the enemy, he will do us great evil." Breckinridge, he urged, should return to the Valley with the troops he had brought to the Army of Northern Virginia. Lee needed every man he could get to oppose Grant, but he judged the threat in the Valley serious enough to justify pulling soldiers from the Cold Harbor defenses to defeat Hunter.[48]

Lee remained uncertain about Grant's next move but suspected that the Federal commander intended to slip south across the Chickahominy. "The enemy is now moving in my front," he informed Davis. "He is withdrawing from our left, but I have not yet been able to discover what is his purpose or intention. I fear he may have, during the night thrown a force across the Chickahominy below us." Prisoners captured in front of Early and Anderson claimed that Gillmore's entire 10th Corps from the Army of the James had joined Grant, leaving only black troops and cavalry to guard the Bermuda Hundred lines. While the information was incorrect—only a small portion of Gillmore's command accompanied Smith's 18th Corps to Cold Harbor—Lee had no way of judging its accuracy. "Their statements must always be taken with hesitation," he cautioned Davis, "but the officers who examined them say that they were apparently telling what they believed to be true."[49]

News of Hunter's victory breathed immediacy into Grant's plan for Sheridan and Hunter to join forces and disrupt Lee's supply lines. "General Sheridan leaves here tomorrow morning with instructions to proceed to Charlottesville Va. and to commence there the destruction of the Virginia Central Railroad, destroying this way as much as possible," the general in chief penned in a dispatch to Hunter. Noting that he had initially wanted Hunter to capture Lynchburg, Grant reported that he had refined his thinking. "That point is of so much importance to the enemy," he wrote, "that in attempting to get it, such resistance may be met as to defeat your getting on to the road or canal at all." To him, transportation routes were the real objectives. If the Army of the

Shenandoah reached Lynchburg, Hunter was authorized to capture the city or instead press on to the Virginia Central Railroad's spur there, then "move eastward along the line of the road, destroying it completely and thoroughly until you join Sheridan." If the later scenario came to pass, Sheridan could add the James River Canal to his agenda. "Lose no opportunity to destroy the canal," Grant urged in closing.[50]

As preparations for his new offensive gained momentum, Grant focused on finding the optimal point for the Army of the Potomac to cross the James. An attractive option involved slicing southwest below Lee's army to a point near Malvern Hill, crossing the river to Bermuda Hundred, and combining with Butler. The downside was that the Potomac army would be vulnerable to an attack by Lee as it rounded his army's southern flank. A safer plan, Grant decided, was to cross the James farther downriver, where Union cavalry and infantry could screen the movement and prevent an ambush during the crossing.[51]

Charles City Court House seemed the perfect staging area. Several possible crossing points, including Wilcox's Landing, were nearby, and Union-held Fort Powhatan controlled the southern shore. "The vicinity of Malvern Hill would have afforded better bridging places of the James than at Wilcox's Landing, and the routes to Butler's intrenchments, and to Petersburg, would have been ten or fifteen miles shorter than those by way of Wilcox's Landing," Humphreys later noted, "but the crossing near Malvern, as well as the preparations for it, would have been under the observation of the enemy, and exposed to interruption."[52]

Concluding that he needed more information, Grant summoned his aides Comstock and Porter and instructed them to reconnoiter potential James River crossings. The two men were perfectly suited for the mission, as they had served with McClellan in 1862 and were familiar with the terrain. The army was about to begin its movement to the James, Grant explained, and he wanted the officers to "select the best point on the river for the crossing, taking into consideration the necessity of choosing a place which will give the Army of the Potomac as short a line of march as practicable, and which will at the same time be far enough down-stream to allow for a sufficient distance between it and the present position of Lee's army to prevent the chances of our being attacked successfully while in the act of crossing." The river's width, Grant observed, was important, as was the "character of the country by which it will have to be approached." He added that he planned to send Smith's corps by boat to Butler at Bermuda Hundred. The aides were to "explain the contemplated movement fully to General Butler, and see that the necessary preparations are made by him to render his position secure against any attack from Lee's forces while the Army of the Potomac is making its movement."[53]

After the staffers had left, Grant penned a note to Butler. "An expedition under General Hunter is now on its way up the Shenandoah Valley, and a large cavalry force will leave here tomorrow under General Sheridan to join him, for purpose of utterly destroying the enemy's lines of communication on the north side of James River," he wrote. "When this is done it is my intention to transfer all the force now with me to the south side." His aides, Grant continued, would visit Butler "to see what preparations are necessary to secure the rapid crossing of the river, and to learn if your position will be secure during the time the enemy would necessarily be able to spare a large force to operate with against you before reinforcements could reach you."[54]

The campaign across the James was about to begin.

June 6 dawned clear and sparkling. "A bright day of summer bathed in sunshine and cooler with bracing air," a Pennsylvanian effused, "succeeding a yesterday of drizzling rain and heavy atmosphere." The Potomac army's infantry spent this glorious Monday completing the movements that Meade had initiated the previous day. Apprehensive that Early's Confederates might attack when they discovered the 5th Corps withdrawing, Warren had remained at Bethesda Church to see the last of his men off to the Leary farm. The rebels made lots of racket—"a considerable demonstration by yelling and firing," the general reported—but they never seriously threatened the departure. Griffin's division, bringing up the rear, cleared Bethesda Church near sunrise, and the last of the pickets—Colonel Ellis Spear's 20th Maine—slipped away shortly afterward. "A low fog had risen in the woods and this favored us," Spear remarked as his pickets departed. The tail of Warren's column straggled into Leary's fields exhausted and, by their commander's estimation, "unfitted today to do the work they may be called upon."[55]

Burnside completed his preparations during the night to safeguard the army's northern flank. By sunrise on the sixth, Willcox's division had latched onto Smith's right flank at Fletcher's Redoubt; Potter had reached northeastward toward the home of the White family, a quarter-mile or so south of the Bosher place; and two regiments had formed a skirmish line from Potter's right to Allen's Mill Pond. Soldiers from the 35th Massachusetts, which had been designated as Potter's engineering regiment, constructed a bridge and road from Burnside's headquarters south of the Matadequin uphill to the White property. Elements from Brigadier General Joseph J. Bartlett's brigade of Griffin's 5th Corps division camped south of the mill pond and linked Potter's right with the left of Wilson's cavalry line. Crittenden's division formed a reserve behind Potter, its left near Daniel Woody's house and its right running east.[56]

Midmorning, soldiers from Willcox's division spied scattered clusters of troops filtering south through the woods in front of them. They suspected the figures were rebels preparing to attack until they noticed blue uniforms. A soldier on the 9th Corps's ramparts raised a flag, and clusters of men darted across the cleared field of fire and into the Union lines. They were 5th Corps pickets whom Warren had unintentionally abandoned when the rest of his troops left for Leary's farm. "They were between our lines and those of the enemy, and would soon have been captured had we not discovered them and called them in, for the rebels were following them up, and succeeded in shooting some of them before they reached our lines," a New Hampshire man related. "They said some very hard things about their commanders for leaving them out on the picket line and not notifying them that the corps was going to withdraw during the night—and it was about as mean a trick as could have been played on them."[57]

On the far southern end of the Union formation, Hancock inspected Birney's deployment toward the Chickahominy—three brigades extended along Dispatch Station Road to Barker's Mill, another brigade stood on high ground beyond the mill, and pickets covered the remaining half mile to the river. He was surprised to discover that rebel pickets lined the Union side of the river almost to Bottom's Bridge. A deserter claimed that the Confederates were building a new bridge and intended to attack Birney.[58]

Despite this prediction, no attacks of substance interrupted the morning, although sharpshooters seemed unusually active along the entire Union front. Rebel marksmen in Potter's sector shot at anyone who showed his head, and the engineer Morton foolishly ignored advice to stay low. He was setting his compass on top of the breastworks when a Minié ball hit a nearby pine tree, spattering his face with bark. "At this, he jumped," an onlooker recorded, "and hastily gathering up his kit, stepped to the rear, with another shot whizzing after him which made him duck his head, while the boys were all laughing."[59]

Warren's troops enjoyed a reprieve from trench warfare as they pitched camp in fields around the Leary place. "The men are thoroughly exhausted and prostrate," a surgeon wrote, adding that many soldiers fell asleep where they halted. "We had been a sorry and woe-begone looking lot," a man reported, "and this opportunity was hailed as a blessing by all." Sprits soared when baggage wagons arrived and brought the road-worn troops their first opportunity since the beginning of the campaign to change into fresh clothes. "The cleaning operation is one that must have become fearfully needed by the line officers and men of the infantry," Warren's artillery chief observed. "What with the mud and dust which they have alternately been called up to march through and sleep in, and the fact that for a week at a time they have stood or lain in line of battle, night and day, the amount of dirt accumulated must be great." Soldiers waded into Allen's Mill Pond to bathe, wrote letters home, and "lounged deliciously" out of range of enemy artillery fire. "The day also marks a slicking up time," a Bay Stater reported, "the camp being policed and the quartermaster deals out much needed wearing apparel."[60]

Warren used the lull in combat to reorganize the 5th Corps. Griffin was to remain in charge of the 1st Division, which retained Bartlett's and Sweitzer's brigades and added a brigade of Pennsylvanians that had begun the campaign under Colonel Roy Stone and was now under Colonel Joshua L. Chamberlain. Ayres, formerly heading a brigade in Griffin's division, was elevated to lead the 2nd Division, constituted of his own brigade of regular troops (now under Colonel Edgar M. Gregory), Colonel Dushane's Maryland Brigade, and the Heavy Artillery Brigade under Colonel J. Howard Kitching. Crawford still commanded the 3rd Division, consisting of Colonel James Carle's two regiments of Pennsylvania Reserves (the 190th and 191st Pennsylvania) and the brigades of Colonels Peter Lyle and James L. Bates. Cutler continued in command of the 4th Division, reduced now to the Iron Brigade under Colonel William W. Robinson and Colonel J. William Hofmann's brigade.[61]

The 5th Corps's veterans felt confident that the respite would soon end. "The rebs don't seem to feel satisfied at our coming so near [Richmond], and there will be desperate fighting until we get well fortified, which is going rapidly on, and our lines come very near together now," predicted Sergeant James W. Lathe of the 9th New Hampshire. He then went on to explain why he felt as he did. "Spades have been trumps all the way," he wrote, "but now every rod of it must be dug through, until our big guns can vomit their overloaded stomachs into the doomed city." The Confederates, he concluded, "are nearly or quite ruined—but still they fight as only demons can, and but for our great numbers they would drive us from their soil."[62]

Both armies settled into a dismal existence of unbearable heat, unrelenting insects, incessant shelling, and whirring bullets from sharpshooters. Localized skirmishes rather than grand offensives had come to characterize life at Cold Harbor. "Some of our boys say that one of these skirmishes would have been called a 'battle' twelve months ago," a Richmond newspaper observed. "There was far less maneuvering at Cold Harbor after the first efforts than during the long struggle at Spotsylvania," Dana remarked. "We were merely waiting for the proper moment to withdraw to the James." A Union journalist confirmed that the fighting was "mainly confined to skirmishing, with an occasional artillery duel to enliven the monotony of life in the trenches so the casualties of the week [following the offensive of June 3] are consequently small, smaller than for any corresponding period since crossing the Rapidan."[63]

The soldiers' misery "was extreme, exposed as they were to a hot sun, constantly under a searching fire, short of water, and surrounded by the scantily buried dead," Lyman observed. A northerner confirmed that he could not lift his head "for an instant without receiving rebel bullets, and we keep the enemy down also, by shooting through holes made under logs laid along on top of the parapet." At night, he noted, "the men sleep on their arms, practically in line of battle, and with their clothing all on—ready at a moment's call to spring up and fire." A soldier in Owen's brigade remarked that the opposing earthworks were "so close together that each could hear the other talking." A newsman seconded that he could hear "the rebels ask each other for tobacco, for water, etc. They must be very strict," he surmised, "as their officers have the rolls of companies called as many as twelve times each day to see if any man shuns his duty. Their punishment in such cases must be severe, and is doubtless an application of some method found in the slave code."[64]

The situation, a Union officer feared, was "fast becoming a serious one in respect to the exposure of the men to disease as well as danger. The great strain upon the nervous system," he wrote, "together with lack of food and water, want of sleep and rest, and exposure to the extreme heat and noxious vapors, were already beginning to have their baneful effect upon the men, and without some change, would soon become more dangerous to the Federal army than rebel bullets." Constant musketry and cannon fire told on even experienced campaigners like Grant. "War will get to be so common with me if this thing continues much longer," the general wrote his wife, Julia, "that I will not be able to sleep after a while unless there is an occasional gun shot near me during the night."[65]

Everyone remarked on the stench. "Exceedingly offensive," a man in the 6th Corps reported, "and there was fear of its breeding infection if the stay was continued much longer. Shallow graves received the dead within our lines, who were at last all covered, though by scores they lay in full sight for days, bloated and blackened. Dead horses, swelled to bursting, were left where they had been shot down, objects of aversion to sight and smell."[66]

"You would scarcely know any of us," James McGinnis summed things up for his family. "We live like beasts, lying in the dirt anywhere we can find rest, covered with dust which rises in clouds whenever we move." Arthur B. Wyman warned his sister that he had "not grown any better looking and am just as ragged and dirty as need be. My pants I cut off just below the knees as they were filled with mud and weighed too much so I must look like an overgrown turkey," he added. "My lovely hat is filled with holes and covered with a compound of mud and grease. Perhaps it would look better if I did not use it for a holder to my coffee pot."[67]

Danger and death were commonplace. At Barker's Mill Pond one of Birney's brigadiers watched a Confederate artillery round land in a party of men bathing and washing their clothes. "The boys just looked around and continued to bathe and wash as though nothing had happened," he wrote home. "Such is war. So accustomed do we become to such scenes that we can brave danger to an extent almost incredible." Three miles north an officer eating lunch inspected a piece of bark and discovered that it was really a skull fragment covered with hair, blood, and maggots. "They're at dinner, too," he remarked as he finished his meal. "Thus does soldiering make the stomachs of men imperturbable." A newspaperman riding behind Hancock's and Wright's lines was surprised at how immune the soldiers had become to their exposure to death. "In the third line of breastworks, where shells were liable to alight any moment, and in the second, where musket balls were intruding themselves constantly, men were writing letters, playing cards, cooking meals or eating them, doing anything and everything that men would do anywhere else, and doing it with a sang froid that was delightful."[68]

And then there were the lice. "Doubtless they crossed over from the other side, as it was generally believed they had an overproduction," one of Hancock's warriors surmised. "The Western boys called them sand bugs, as they were supposed to generate from grains of sand and sweat, the soldiers being the incubator. They were no respecter of persons, but treated all alike," he reported. "From the general commanding to the eighth corporal and private, all were attacked, the mule only escaping. The average amount allotted to each man, officer, and private alike nine hundred ninety and nine to the square inch. The souls of the murdered ones entered into the new crop, and after three days of maturity, they with redoubled energy and vigor, worked without ceasing."[69]

Everyone agreed that life behind earthworks had become intolerable. "The men of our brigade suffered very much from the heat, in their exposed position; with no shelter of any kind except such as they could rig up behind the works of sand that seemed to attract and retain the heat," a Pennsylvanian complained. St. Claire A. Mulholland of the 116th Pennsylvania observed that the "continuous strain constant marching, fighting, want of sleep, absence of food and water, sleeping, when a chance offered, on the ground without even the slight protection of a shelter tent, sometimes in a drenching rain, and most times catching an hour's sleep under the broiling sun—all this was beginning to tell on the strongest constitutions, and even affecting the minds." Another soldier expressed doubt that he could "stand it in the trenches much longer, deprived of sleep and rest." Voicing the common sentiment, John J. B. Adams of the 19th Massachusetts wrote, "The mental strain was unspeakable."[70]

Looking on the bright side, Lieutenant Colonel Lyman later found "one thing for which we had reason to bless the rebels." Confederate authorities had asked the inhabitants to store plenty of ice during the winter, and icehouses were packed. "It was usually about three inches thick and of poor quality, but it was ice," Lyman effused. "One man had snow as they do in Naples—travelled man, possibly."[71]

Alerted to a spike in malingering, Grant instructed Brigadier General John J. Abercrombie at White House Landing to keep a lookout for stragglers, adding that he wanted "all stragglers who go to the rear apprehended and sent back under guard." If commissioned officers were caught shirking their duties, their buttons and shoulder straps were to be "publicly cut from their coats, and send them with their hands bound here for trial." A correspondent for a Detroit newspaper reported that soldiers routinely shot themselves in the second finger of their right hand in hopes of being sent back to Washington. "It is customary in ordinary cases to put the patient under chloroform," he recounted, "but as a punishment to the coward the surgeons now perform the amputation of wounded fingers without any anesthetic." Barlow tied stragglers and skulkers in a clearing exposed to rebel shelling. One prisoner was severely wounded, and the remainder badly frightened.[72]

Conditions were somewhat more tolerable for the Confederates, and the victory of June 3 and Grant's inability to renew offensive operations buoyed southern spirits. Richmond's proximity ensured a steady supply of food. "We draw rations every two days and get sugar, coffee, onions, sometimes 1/2 lb meat per day and bread in abundance," a soldier in Heth's Division observed. "The army are living better now than at any time in my knowledge since the war commenced." Another Confederate reported that he and his messmates "are now getting plenty to eat," noting that his daily ration of a pound of cornmeal and half a pound of bacon "will satisfy any common man." A North Carolinian proclaimed the army in "excellent spirits," a sentiment seconded by a South Carolinian, who reported that the troops were "in good cheer, are well fed, nearly equal in numbers to the enemy and confident of their ability to whip them."[73]

Morale in Confederate camps was indeed high. "From present appearances," an assistant surgeon in the 8th Alabama wrote home, "Lee intends to let Grant exhaust himself in attacks on our breastworks, when having gotten his men pretty much demoralized, will then assume the offensive, vigorously, and drive him back to his Abolition den." Writing his mother and sisters, a Tar Heel surmised, "Mr. Grant is going to try to dig to Richmond, but if he don't mind, Mr. Lee will hatch up a plan that will make him dig some other way besides Richmond." Summing things up, Colonel John Bratton concluded that Grant's recent bloody reverse was likely responsible for the "comparatively quiet season today" and expressed hope that it had "produced a greater affect on the spirits of the masses." The rest of the campaign, Bratton predicted, would be long and tedious. "Grant hangs on like a bulldog and will, doubtless, be more shy about attacking our works hereafter and go Yankee-like to ditching."[74]

The campaign's relentless pace, however, was also grinding down the southerners. "We are now experiencing the greatest hardships of the war, for over 30 days past there has been more or less fighting either a general battle or skirmishing with pickets, and it appears that the war is becoming more destructive," a soldier wrote his family. "One third of our men have to sit up at our works every night to watch the enemy. This is equal to losing every third night from rest and sleep all the while. This is very severe on the men and the losing of sleep will destroy the constitution of men as soon as almost anything." A Floridian noted that while he and his comrades "had plenty to eat today," they were still "crowded in a ditch and no chance to sleep," and most of them were sick. "Rebecca," he concluded, "I must say to you that it is a hard life and no telling when one may be killed. I can't say it was any worse than I expected, [but] I don't think I can stand it very long."[75]

Writing his mother and sisters, Captain A. B. Mulligan of the 5th Carolina Cavalry admitted that he did not "think it possible for men to undergo so much exposure without breaking down." He and his companions "take rain, and sunshine and are getting so that we can lie down in a mud hole and sleep about as well as we used to in our beds." He admitted, "We who are just from North and South Carolina have just begun to realize the war."

The Confederate 1st Corps's artillery chief, Edward P. Alexander, later pronounced the experience at Cold Harbor the "greatest hardship that the [Army of Northern Virginia] ever endured." Many agreed with him. "Thousands of men cramped up in a narrow trench, unable to go out, or to get up, or to stretch or to stand without danger to life and limb," a southerner wrote; "unable to lie down, or to sleep, for lack of room and pressure of peril; night alarms, day attacks, hunger, thirst, supreme weariness, squalor, vermin, filth, disgusting odors everywhere; the weary night succeeded by the yet more weary day; the first glance over the way, at day dawn, bringing the sharpshooter's bullet singing past your ear or smashing through your skull, a man's life often exacted as the price of a cup of water from the spring." The terrain behind the 3rd Corps's line was "perfectly honeycombed with holes in which the men ensconce themselves," a soldier wrote. "Besides these there are numberless trenches leading from one rifle pit to another, and back towards the rear. It is a queer looking arrangement but certainly a most comfortable one, for though the two lines of battle are so near each other and firing is quite constant, very few of our men are hit."[76]

In places, Federal marksmen proved every bit as deadly as their rebel counterparts. "The Yankee sharpshooters are within 75 yards of our first line and are picking off everybody that exposes himself," an Alabaman in Mahone's Division wrote. "It places us in a very uncomfortable position, as we have to remain in the trenches all the time. We have no zigzags, and everybody that goes after water or ammunition does so at the risk of his life." An artillerist in Captain Basil C. Manly's battery concluded that "if Mr. Grant ever takes Richmond, he must make a decided improvement on his style of fighting. His sharp shooters do much more execution than all of his 'charges.' His sharp shooters can strike anything from the size of a quarter dollar up to a man. Some of our boys put a tin cup on the breastworks yesterday, and in less than a minute they put three holes through it."[77]

Union mortars were also troublesome. "They have done but little serious damage," a Confederate remarked, "but I assure you that they are very demoralizing." One of Mahone's surgeons blamed Yankee artillery for his wobbly handwriting. "The Yanks are shelling us," he reported in a letter home. "We are all squatting behind the breastworks, and every time a shell whizzes close overhead, my neighbors at either elbow give a dodge, and thus jog my hand."[78]

The Confederates facing Smith were especially hard pressed. Kershaw's headquarters, which served as the sector's nerve center, had been cut into a hillside near the Allison house and capped by a wall of logs faced with earth. The general, one of his soldiers wrote, "might have found a safer place, but none nearer the point of peril and the working point of everything." Although the site was well protected, the approaches were exposed to enemy snipers and artillery. One of Lee's staff officers, Colonel Charles S. Venable, declared Kershaw's headquarters the "worst place he was ever sent to."[79]

The death of the popular captain Edward S. McCarthy of the 1st Company,

Richmond Howitzers, served as a stark reminder of how lethal Union marksmen could be. In a momentary lapse of caution, McCarthy mounted the battlements near the Allison house to survey the Federal position across the field. "One moment, I saw him standing there," a soldier in the battery recalled. "The next instant, I heard a sharp crash, the familiar sound of a bullet striking, and McCarthy was lying, flat on his back, and motionless." A bullet had passed through the captain's brain, killing him.[80]

At 10:30 A.M. on June 6, Meade canvassed his corps commanders about whether an assault was practicable. Hancock answered that he was "averse" to attacking, "simply because my men have been so constantly out at the front, lying in the trenches all the time for three days, and are so fatigued that I fear they have not the dash necessary to carry them through the obstacles of a second line." His cadre of experienced officers had been decimated, he continued, and the rebels had used every day to strengthen their works. His division heads concurred, putting the case against renewing the offensive in even stronger language. "The men feel just at present a great horror and dread of attacking earthworks again," stressed the normally aggressive Barlow, "and the unusual loss of officers, which leaves regiments in command of lieutenants, and brigades in command of inexperienced officers, leaves us in a very unfavorable position for such enterprises." Barlow thought that an offensive might have succeeded if it had been ventured on June 2, as Grant had initially ordered, but now that the enemy had gained four days to prepare, he considered it "hazardous to attack." Gibbon added that the rebels had posted batteries to control the approaches to their works and his division was so close to the enemy that he could not mass his soldiers for a charge.[81]

The other corps heads were equally pessimistic. Wright observed that the Confederates had "worked industriously" to bolster their works during the night, pronounced an attack "impracticable," and claimed that he was supported by "the unanimous judgment of the division commanders." For his part, Smith saw no opportunity to attack "from any point in my front" until Burnside got his batteries into place and silenced the Confederate guns that controlled his line. Doing that, of course, hinged on Burnside's ability to complete Fletcher's Redoubt, where he intended to concentrate his artillery. "We have been as hard at work at the redoubts as the rebel sharpshooters would allow," the 9th Corps leader reported when queried about his progress.[82]

With his subordinates united against another offensive, Meade suggested that they continue pushing their entrenchments closer to the enemy and con-

struct batteries to support their own and neighboring troops. The army's quartermaster, he reminded them, would furnish forage sacks and sandbags wherever needed.[83]

During the afternoon, Alexander A. Yard of the 3rd New Jersey Cavalry
accompanied Wilson to Grant's headquarters. "He is a fine looking man with
a large head and thick neck," Yard remarked of the general in chief. "The first
impression is that of stubborn bulldog obstinacy." Meade, Warren, and Brigadier General John A. Rawlins of Grant's staff were present as well. The mas-
sively bearded Rawlins made quite an impression on Yard. "Were all the generals together, I would pick out Rawlins as the leader," he confided to his
diary.[84]

While Meade and his generals counseled against attacking, Lee and his subordinates searched for opportunities to go on the offensive. Not long after
dawn, Early's scouts confirmed that Warren had left and that Burnside had
contracted his line behind the Matadequin. By 6:30 A.M. Anderson, on Early's
right, had also learned that Crawford's division of Warren's corps had vacated
its entrenchments in front of Major General Charles W. Field's division, which
was posted across Walnut Church Road. "We were aroused early this morning," a Georgian wrote in his diary, "sent out pickets as usual and when daylight came all the Yankees were gone except pickets and stragglers, who were
captured." Uncertain about what the Federals intended, Anderson issued a circular to his division heads. "It is probable that the enemy is engaged in a movement from our front which we must follow with the utmost promptitude," he
advised. "As soon as you shall discover indications of his withdrawal from your
front, make your preparations to move at once and hold yourself in readiness
for orders. We fear that he moved last night, and we have already lost much
time in detecting it."[85]

On receiving Early's intelligence, Lee sensed an opportunity to strike. He
urged Early to attack Burnside's re-fused right flank and Anderson to arrange
a "systematic advance" with Early "from which good results might be obtained." Here was a rare opportunity to catch a portion of Grant's force outside
of its entrenchments and on the move.[86]

Lee's plan was sound, but his choice of commanders to execute it was unfortunate. Early's hallmark was aggressiveness, a trait he had displayed while
commanding the 3rd Corps during Hill's illness at Spotsylvania Court House
and again on May 30 at Bethesda Church. But he could be "haughty and dis-
dainful," a contemporary noted, and was often indisposed "to act upon sug-
gestions submitted by subordinates." First Corps staffer G. Moxley Sorrel

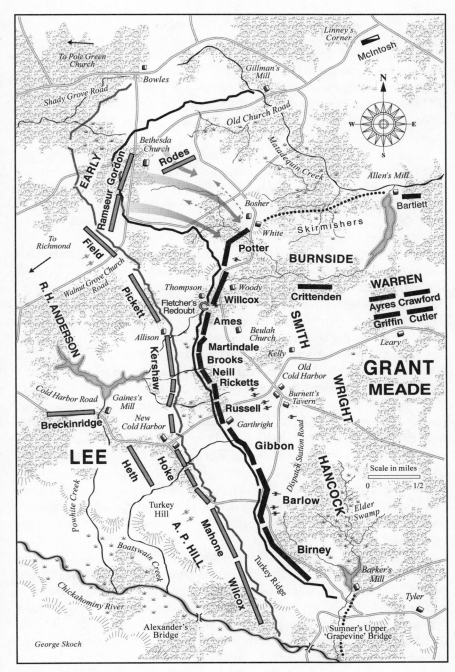

Operations on June 6

thought that the general, while "a most enterprising, resourceful officer, was much given to forced reconnaissances [which] seemed to me unnecessary and wasted men by death and wounds. Their intention was to ascertain accurately the positive strength and morale of the enemy, and generally a brigade was told off for the service. It appeared to me that the information could be gathered by scouts and picked men without sacrificing the ranks, but General Early thought differently."[87]

Anderson, on the other hand, was a genial soul, but he too seemed incapable of acting in concert with other generals. He had failed to execute his portion of the joint maneuver with Early at Bethesda Church and had botched an advance on June 1 that Lee had expected him to coordinate with Hoke. Considering Early's and Anderson's recent performances, the prospects for success appeared slim.

The Confederate offensive, however, started off with promise. The objective was to determine whether the Federals were withdrawing and, if so, to attack while they were on the move. Acting on Lee's directive, Anderson alerted his division commanders to attack "with the utmost promptitude," and Early dispatched patrols to ferret out Burnside's new line. At 10:30 A.M. Early reported with confidence that no Federals remained in front of either his corps or Anderson's left-most division (Field's), which linked with his right. So far as he could tell, Burnside's skirmishers extended from a point in front of Pickett's Division to Matadequin Creek and beyond in the direction of Old Church. In short, the Union line's contraction had left Early's entire corps unopposed and free to maneuver. "As the last message from you stated that no movement is reported to our right," the Virginian wrote Lee, "it has occurred to me that perhaps the enemy has moved back his right to induce us to uncover the Mechanicsville [Old Church] Road, and I do not deem it prudent, therefore, to advance farther until I ascertain something definite of the enemy's movements, which I am endeavoring to do." The country in front of his corps, he added, was "very rough and difficult, and rendered more so by an intricate system of works made by the enemy."[88]

At 1:30 P.M. Early confirmed that Burnside's line was configured as he had suspected. "I am going to try and strike at the enemy on the other side of Matadequin and run down toward Beulah Church," he wrote Lee. "The movement will be a difficult one, as I find the enemy has everywhere the most intricate system of breast-works, facing every way and making a perfect labyrinth, and that it is almost a matter of impossibility to strike him on the right flank, as he always has a fortified position for it to rest on." Informing President Davis of the impending offensive, Lee promised to "make every effort to strike" at

Grant but expressed concern that the Federal general's "usual precautions will prevent [this] unless I undertake to assault his fortifications which I desire to avoid if possible."[89]

Early launched his offensive at 4:00 P.M., pivoting his corps on its right flank to form a new line "almost parallel" to Old Church Road, with Rodes's Division on the left, Gordon's in the middle, and Ramseur's on the right. When the movement was complete, the 2nd Corps "formed a line," a correspondent from Richmond reported, "perpendicular to our center [where Early's right joined Anderson's left], which meantime had stood fast."[90]

Pushing south, Early's right-most division under Ramseur crossed three sets of abandoned Union earthworks and struck unexpectedly on Potter's left-most brigade under Simon Griffin, which held its ground. Gordon's Division, in the center of Early's line, slammed into Curtin's brigade on Potter's right, and additional elements swept onto the White family's cleared knoll, which was occupied by pickets from the 48th Pennsylvania. The troops from the Keystone State fell back but managed to hold on to a farm road south of the hill. Meanwhile Rodes's Division, forming the left of Early's formation, halted after reaching Old Church Road, then continued south, expecting to hit the extreme right of Burnside's position.[91]

With the high ground at White's farm in Gordon's hands, two Confederate batteries rolled up and began dropping shells into Potter's line and Crittenden's reserve position near Daniel Woody's home. Firing in concert with Ramseur's pieces to the west, Gordon's gunners caught Burnside's soldiers in a crossfire. "The shells shrieked and yelled," a 9th Corps man recalled, "but beyond making a great noise resulted in very little damage." Projectiles carried as far as 6th Corps headquarters, causing "much stampeding of wagons, bands, hospital men and other noncombatants," an aide reported. Among the wounded was Solon Carter of the 36th Massachusetts, whose foot was torn off by a shell.[92]

Fearing that a major Confederate offensive was in the works, Burnside petitioned headquarters for assistance. It was now a little after 5:00 P.M. Confederates were pressing the right of his line and had driven in Potter's pickets, Burnside reported, but Warren's staffer Roebling concluded that the Rhode Islander was exaggerating the threat. "Gen. Burnside called on us for assistance," the major later wrote; "went down to see; did not think he needed it." Chief of Staff Humphreys nonetheless directed Warren to prepare to support Burnside with a division, and the 5th Corps commander put Crawford's troops on alert. The 1st Michigan and 83rd Pennsylvania advanced from the Leary farm to Allen's Mill, a short distance east of the fighting, ready to assist, their left connecting with Potter's pickets and their right with Wilson's cavalrymen.[93]

Gordon, however, was reluctant to press his attack, which he deemed "exceedingly hazardous." Early concurred and as evening advanced cancelled the attack and pulled Ramseur and Gordon back to Bethesda Church. Rodes's Division, which never managed to fully engage the enemy, retired to Old Church Road. "A good many straggling Yankees were captured," a captain in the 12th Alabama recalled, "and reported the enemy moving to their left, and say their men are destitute of shoes, deficient on rations, and very tired of fighting." As they prepared camp, Confederates examined the earthworks formerly held by the 5th and 9th Corps. "These savages have stripped the widow and the orphan of their last mouthfuls of food, and sacked their houses through mere wantonness," a Richmond newspaper reported. "Their abandoned trenches are full of beds and bedding, besides many articles of household furniture willfully destroyed and left there."[94]

"Whenever the enemy moves, Old Jube [as the men called Jubal Early] will not be satisfied until he finds out where he has gone, so he keeps us on the run until he find him," a soldier in the Stonewall Brigade wrote. "He doesn't know that I have no shoes and but little breeches, torn from pockets to bottom."[95]

As night fell and firing sputtered to a close, Early blamed Anderson for the offensive's lackluster results. "General Anderson was to have cooperated with me by moving down the other side of the Matadequin," he later wrote, "but the division sent for that purpose did not reach the position from which I started until near night, and I was therefore compelled to retire, as my position was too much exposed." A soldier in Ramseur's Division echoed Early's complaint, noting that troops from the 2nd Corps had "moved in rear of the enemy's right flank but for want of cooperation on the part of [Anderson's] supporting column, we had to fall back to our former position." The attempted flanking movement "did not amount to much," concluded Brigadier General Bryan Grimes, commanding one of Rodes's brigades. The Confederates captured about fifty Union soldiers, who offered wildly divergent speculations about Grant's plans. Some reported that Grant had "fallen back to the White House to get the protection of his gunboats," a newsman wrote, while others thought that the Union army was "moving towards James River, in order to go to the Southside."[96]

Fighting flared sporadically into the night. At 8:00 P.M. some of Kershaw's troops made a "furious onset" against Barton's 18th Corps brigade, which adjoined the 9th Corps near Fletcher's Redoubt. "Our artillery swept their whole line with grape and canister doing much damage," James H. Clark of the 115th New York wrote. "After the enemy were repulsed our boys sent over cheers of defiance, and the different corps and division bands played the pleasant strains of victory, which do not please the Johnnies, so they undertook to shell the musicians out."[97]

Wright reported Confederates moving across his front in Hancock's direction, and around 9:00 P.M., a hand-picked force of a hundred or so Mississippians from Brigadier General Nathaniel Harris's brigade, reinforced by Mahone's skirmishers, attacked Barlow's skirmish line to "feel the enemy," as Harris later described their mission. "Went nearly to the breastworks and found them still in force," a Confederate reported. "Tremendous discharges of musketry, and the awful blasts of Coehorn mortars continued fifteen or twenty minutes longer," a newsman wrote, "and then like a tornado breaking into fitful squalls and then clearing into fine weather, this tempest of war broke into detached volleys, and finally ceased altogether." More than half of the Confederates involved in the foray were killed or wounded, including several men from the 48th Mississippi, and nine were captured.[98]

Near midnight some of Gordon's troops returned to Potter's sector of Burnside's line and launched a final assault with "much determination," according to a soldier from Maine. "The firing was heavy and rapid while it lasted, but the attack was soon repelled, and the charging column driven back to the works from whence they had advanced." As the offensive wound down, Confederate gunners on the White farm retired, and the 48th Pennsylvania reoccupied the hill, along with a working party that dug rifle pits to better secure the position.[99]

A late-night rumor circulated among Barlow's soldiers that headquarters was contemplating another charge against the rebel works at dawn. "It will be a difficult task to perform, and many must fall in the task, but we will do our duty like young heroes," Lieutenant Cornelius L. Moore of the 57th New York wrote in his diary. "We have handed each other the directions of our friends at home, so that the fortunate ones that escape may make them aware of the fate of the unfortunate ones that fall."[100]

Comfortable that it had averted Early and Anderson's threat to the army's northern flank, Union headquarters continued laying the groundwork for the trek to the James. At 11:00 P.M. Warren directed Cutler and Griffin to start for the Chickahominy four hours hence. "Their duty," he explained, "will be to guard the crossings of the river and picket its banks from the left of the Second Corps to below the railroad bridge, holding the last point in some force." On arriving, they were to drive the rebels from the river's northern bank, link with Birney's division, and hold themselves ready "to support General Hancock's left flank as far as practicable." Once the 5th Corps troops were in place, Chapman's cavalry brigade was to shift downstream and patrol below the railroad bridge.[101]

Writing to his wife that night, Grant gave a sober assessment of the task before him. "This is likely to prove a very tedious job I have on hand, but I feel confident of ultimate success," he wrote. "The enemy keeps himself behind strong entrenchments all the time and seems determined to hold on to the last."[102]

Meade also wrote home and likewise articulated a frank picture of the military situation. "Up to this time our success has consisted only in compelling the enemy to draw in towards Richmond," he explained. "Our failure has been that we have not been able to overcome, destroy or bag his army." The final battles, he predicted, would take place near the Confederate capital. "The enemy have the advantages of position, fortifications, and being concentrated in their center," he observed. "We shall have to move slowly and cautiously," he added, "but I am in hopes, with reasonable luck, we will be able to succeed."[103]

IV

JUNE 7, 1864

Grant and Lee Agree on a Truce

"There was never such an army of demons collected before."

TUESDAY, JUNE 7, OPENED clear and bright, offering promise that the rain was really over. Shortly after sunrise, Grant's staffers Comstock and Porter rode to White House Landing and boarded a steamer. Their destination was Fortress Monroe, the first leg on their mission to identify the Army of the Potomac's route across the James.

That same morning, a short distance upstream from White House Landing, Sheridan's mounted divisions under Torbert and Gregg set off on their foray to destroy the Virginia Central Railroad. "Quartermaster's and commissary officers swarmed over the cavalry's camp," a trooper recalled, "stocking a caravan of supply wagons and replenishing haversacks, forage bags, and cartridge boxes." Each rider carried forty rounds of ammunition and three days' rations—intended to last for five days—and two days' worth of grain for his horse, affixed to the saddle pommel. Wagons hauled reserve ammunition to the tune of sixty rounds per man and enough canvas boats to build a small pontoon bridge. Brigade and regimental commanders left behind anyone whose horse could not withstand a severe ten-day march. "All were warned," a New Jersey man recalled, "that they need not expect to find themselves near any depot or resting place until the expiration of that period."[1]

At 5:00 A.M. Sheridan's riders broke camp near Newcastle Ferry, Gregg in the lead, followed by Torbert and trailed by a brigade of horse artillery containing some twenty guns. More than 9,000 men strong, the procession crossed the Pamunkey on a pontoon bridge and started north. Wilson's division remained behind, Chapman's brigade watching the army's southern flank along the Chickahominy and McIntosh's brigade covering Grant's northern flank from Allen's Mill Pond to the Pamunkey.[2]

After crossing into King William County, Sheridan intended to skim along the Mattaponi River's southern bank near Aylett's and Dunkirk, veer west alongside the North Anna River's northern bank, cross at Carpenter's Ford, and strike the Virginia Central Railroad near Trevilian Station. From there the blue-clad troopers were to work east along the rail line, tearing up tracks to Louisa Court House, then turn west, ride past Gordonsville to Cobham Station, and begin wrecking the tracks toward Charlottesville, where they hoped to unite with the Army of the Shenandoah. "The success of the last part of this program," Sheridan observed, "would of course depend on the location of General Hunter when I should arrive in the region where it would be practicable for us to communicate with each other."[3]

The riders made tolerable speed until the day warmed, at which time men and mounts began to flag from dust and heat. Foraging parties fanning out from the main column aroused the populace's ire. "Heard that Sheridan's command crossed at Newcastle into King William," a Virginian wrote in her diary. "We see them passing all day with sheep, hogs, veal and fowls; with quarters of mutton and beef hung to poles which they carry between them. Certainly there was never such an army of demons collected before," she railed, "outside the infernal regions."[4]

Yet another contingent—this one composed of Confederates—also started a journey the morning of June 7. The previous day Lee had gauged Hunter's threat to the Valley and Lynchburg to be so serious that he had decided to send Breckinridge's two brigades to intercept the Union force. He was reluctant to lose a division from his army, but Grant's shortening of his infantry line at Cold Harbor made it possible for Lee to compress his line as well, thereby reducing the number of troops needed to hold the Army of the Potomac at bay. Breckinridge was still incapacitated by his battlefield injury, so Lee put the division's senior brigade commander, Gabriel Wharton, in charge until the Kentuckian healed. Leaving their encampment near Gaines's Mill, Breckinridge's nearly 2,100 soldiers marched to Richmond and boarded railcars for the first leg of their journey back to the Valley.

Before daylight on June 7, half of Warren's 5th Corps—Griffin's and Cutler's divisions—set off from Leary's farm toward the Chickahominy River, "feeling like new men, having had a splendid rest during the night." The rest of the 5th Corps—Ayres's and Crawford's divisions—remained in their camps south of Allen's Mill Pond supporting Burnside's line along Matadequin Creek. Warren remained headquartered at the Leary place, described by the artillerist Charles Wainwright as "a wretched spot, being right at the corner of two roads where trains are all the time passing, and covering them with dust." The 5th Corps's commander, the colonel observed, "appears to have sunk into a sort of lethargic sulk, sleeps a great part of the time, and says nothing to anyone. I think at times that these fits of his must be the result of a sort of insanity; indeed, that is perhaps the most charitable way of accounting for them. He has not got along well at Meade's headquarters lately, though I know nothing as to wherein the trouble has lain." The army's provost marshal, Marsena Patrick, seconded Wainwright's negative assessment, proclaiming Warren "a very loathsome, profane ungentlemanly & disgusting puppy in power."[5]

The Chickahominy was a sluggish stream that flowed through a wide, marshy floodplain on a meandering course southeast to the James. Several fords and bridge sites, most of them well known to Union and Confederate engineers thanks to McClellan's campaign, provided the Army of the Potomac opportunities to cross. Where Hancock's north–south line hit the Chickahominy, it bent sharply east, following the southern bank. Birney's pickets extended from Barker's Mill downriver to Sumner's Upper Bridge, known also as Grapevine Bridge. A mile and a quarter farther downstream was the site of Sumner's Lower Bridge, and two miles farther on stood the remains of the Richmond and York River Railroad bridge—the tracks passed through Dispatch Station a mile or so east of the river and through Savage's Station two miles to the west. A mile downstream from the railroad bridge was Bottom's Bridge, where the stage road from Richmond to Williamsburg crossed. Long Bridge was another three miles downriver, and Jones's, or Forge, Bridge another five or so miles farther on.

On reaching Sumner's Lower Bridge, Griffin sent skirmishers under Captain Luther S. Bent to purge the northern bank of rebels, connected his pickets with Birney on his right, and extended his division downriver. He had completed his junction with the 2nd Corps by 1:00 P.M., and Birney conformed his pickets with Griffin's to create a tolerable line along the river, which interposed an "impassable swamp" between them and the Confederates. Cutler posted Colonel Hofmann's brigade at the railroad bridge and the Iron Brigade at Bottom's Bridge. Chapman's troopers continued the Union line downriver past Long Bridge to the hamlet of Windsor Shades. Confederate resistance was minimal, prompting Warren to inquire whether he should try to cross in force. The query reached Grant, who cautioned that the 5th Corps should simply "hold the crossing to prevent the enemy coming to this side." Putting a river between Warren and the rest of the army seemed like a risky proposition.[6]

Posted at Sumner's Lower Bridge on the upriver end of the 5th Corps's position, soldiers from the 118th Pennsylvania befriended men from the 35th

North Carolina on the southern bank and traded coffee for tobacco. "Lone fishermen sat upon either end of the bridge," a soldier from the Keystone State remembered, "dangling their lines resultlessly and chatting complacently." A Union officer watched while his troops fished with improvised tackle. "The Confederates were similarly engaged on the opposite bank," he reported, noting that these informal truces "were always faithfully observed; notice of intention to fire was invariably given." Swimming, however, never caught on. "Had we been muskrats, frogs, water snakes or blood suckers, we might have had some sport in those murky waters of the Chickahominy," a soldier reflected, "but being neither, nor yet ducks or geese, we were denied the luxury of that liquid element, though I think a few did try it and when they came out they had to have the bloodsuckers scraped from them."[7]

The terrain was hauntingly familiar to many 5th Corps soldiers who had occupied the same campsites in 1862. "So here we are on the classic grounds of the Chickahominy," artillerist David F. Ritchie wrote home. "Two years have sped by. Now, like a benighted traveler, we emerge from the Wilderness to find ourselves walking in the same path we left but an hour ago. The Army of the Potomac occupies ground near that held by McClellan in 1862, but it occupies the country in a totally different manner. There is fire, energy and action in the army now. It fights and marches in downright earnest."[8]

The Union soldiers welcomed the quiet river duty but were rightly concerned about contracting fevers. "We now found ourselves, at a sickly season of the year, in the deadly swamps of the Chickahominy," a warrior from Maine wrote. "The sun glared down on us like a globe of fire, as he rolled through the brazen sky," he recounted. "The air was filled with malaria and death. Sickness, as well as battle, was doing fearful work in our ranks." A Pennsylvanian complained that the Chickahominy appeared "blacker than Old Tea Pond" and expressed thanks for his daily ration of whiskey and quinine.[9]

Skirmishing flared around the Richmond and York River Railroad bridge. Assigned to control the crossing, Colonel Hofmann maneuvered his brigade through woods to a point half a mile north of the river, constructed a screen of brush across the railroad to conceal his presence, and stationed troops on each side of the tracks. Skirmishers from the 18th Massachusetts drove a small but stubborn force of Ransom's North Carolinians across the river at the cost of five men wounded, then retired a quarter mile east of the bridge and posted pickets along the bank. Confederates tried to destroy the brush screen with artillery fire from across the river, and as the cannonade heated, Hofmann prepared a barricade manned by sharpshooters using telescopic sights. Elements from the 147th New York crossed the Chickahominy on logs—"running across the swamp like squirrels," a captain in the regiment recalled—and engaged the rebels on the southern shore, who fired bullets that a Federal claimed exploded when they hit. Finding themselves dangerously isolated from the rest of the regiment, the New Yorkers retired north of the stream. Dispatch Station, near the railroad bridge, defined the far eastern end of the Union line.[10]

In response to the growing Union presence along the Chickahominy, Ransom's troops concentrated several artillery pieces opposite the Richmond and York River Railroad bridge. Especially effective was a sixty-four-pounder mounted on a railway car lined with four-inch metal plates. "The gun could traverse only a small angle, for fear of kicking the machine off the track," a Union man noted, "so that the few shots fired from it were calculated rather to excite curiosity than to inspire dread." One shell, however, wounded seven Federals and, according to an officer in the 146th New York, drove an old woman who lived nearby "crazy with fright." A newsman reported that the ordnance "threw some 6-inch shells over our men, which elicited considerable criticism from those happening to make narrow escapes."[11]

Writing his fiancé, Emily, that evening, Warren's aide Washington Roebling quipped that "Griffin went down to the Chickahominy today where he met the 'Richmond clerks' who saluted him kindly with a battery; the next thing we will see are the female guards; they have sufficient patriotism to come out if that is all that is required." According to the major's sources, "we did capture a full-fledged artillery woman who was working regularly at the piece. She was very independent and saucy, as most Southern ladies are."[12]

Suspecting that the 5th Corps's appearance was a prelude to Grant's anticipated move across the Chickahominy, Lee directed Matthew Butler's brigade of South Carolina cavalrymen to picket the roads downriver from Savage Station southeast to White Oak Swamp and Frazier's Farm. "Our moving about so much is owing entirely to the movement of the enemy," an officer in the 4th South Carolina Cavalry wrote home. "We must confront him wherever he goes." Grant "is virtually whipped," he surmised. "I think he is at a loss to know what to do."[13]

Early on June 7 Meade asked his corps commanders to update him on developments in their sectors. Hancock reported that Birney, on the 2nd Corps's left, was still consolidating his position and expected to advance near his center, where the Confederate line angled to the Chickahominy. Barlow had been "working along steadily, but necessarily slowly, owing to the close proximity he is to the enemy," Hancock noted, and his troops had gained no more than six yards. Barlow abandoned the idea of an early morning charge after his

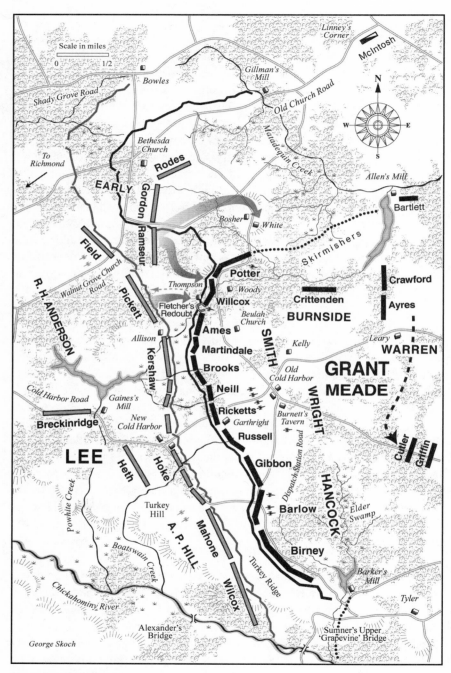

Operations on June 7

colonels "voted it a useless sacrifice of life." The mine, however, was progressing nicely and now ran nearly forty yards into the hillside. Gibbon, on Hancock's right, had taken only feeble steps forward because of harassing fire from pickets and sharpshooters. Many 2nd Corps troops had become so cautious, Hancock reported, that they had constructed breastworks that were too elevated for them to shoot over. An order went out from corps headquarters directing brigade commanders to erect platforms "so that the troops might be high enough to deliver an effective fire horizontally over the works." [14]

Wright also had little progress to report. "There are no changes discernible in the enemy's force or position in my front," he related, adding that most of his recent earthmoving had involved strengthening fortifications and running lines to the rear. "All is quiet along my front, except skirmish fire," Smith agreed. [15]

Clearly the strategy of overwhelming Lee with "regular approaches" was not working. Progress could be measured in single-digit yards, and nowhere had excavating increased the prospects of a successful attack. Now that Sheridan's mission to cut the Virginia Central Railroad was underway, the idea of digging Lee out of his entrenched position seemed obsolete. That afternoon Union headquarters put a formal end to its policy of advancing by regular approaches. "The major-general commanding," a circular stated, "directs that corps commanders suspend pushing their works up to the enemy, limiting their operations to completing those necessary for their security that have been commenced." [16]

The Confederate high command, however, had no intention of biding its time. While the Federals settled into their earthen hutches, Lee contemplated a new round of attacks modeled after Early and Anderson's unsuccessful offensive on June 6. Lee never clearly articulated his objective, but it is likely that he still hoped to launch a limited offensive against an isolated potion of the Union force. The previous day's inconclusive operation had done nothing to improve relations between Early and Anderson, however, and the two generals differed over what further offensive operations could accomplish. Early envisioned a joint assault by his and Anderson's corps: "We were to divert [Burnside's] attention to the flank while Anderson made a direct attack upon their front," was how one of Old Jube's staffers explained the plan. Anderson, however, had in mind a limited exploratory operation aimed, a brigade commander observed, "in finding out exactly [the enemy's] new position." [17]

Fighting on Early's remote eastern flank started shortly after sunrise, when a detail from the 45th Pennsylvania stumbled into Confederate pickets near a log house. "We gave them a volley and I can shut my eyes now and see those fellows grab their guns and skedaddle into the house," Private Allen D. Albert of the Keystone State reminisced. Then a bugle sounded, and a Confederate battle line materialized, marching toward the Pennsylvanians at the double-quick. "No two of us agree exactly as to what occurred after that," Albert admitted. "To try to hold our ground was to be surrounded and gobbled up. My recollection is that we gave them a volley or two and then it was a case of everyone for himself and the Devil (in a gray uniform) take the hind most." The Pennsylvanians managed to get away with only a few men wounded or captured. "It was a foolhardy undertaking all around and the great wonder is that we were not captured," Albert concluded.[18]

Midmorning, Ramseur's Division marched south across Anderson's front, passing Field's Division and part of Pickett's. Ramseur had been ill for several days—"Bread and meat and (frequently) muddy water has given me a slight diarrhea," he wrote his wife on June 7—but he remained as aggressive as ever. Charging toward Burnside, his skirmishers overran workers from the 60th Ohio of Christ's brigade on the right of Willcox's division and occupied 150 yards of Union rifle pits. They captured several Federals and a haul of entrenching tools but failed to break through to Christ's main fortifications. Prominent in the attack was Colonel William G. Lewis's North Carolina brigade, spurred on by Ramseur himself. Marshy, heavily wooded terrain confounded the Confederates, and by noon Christ had repelled the attack and reestablished his picket line. As Early later put it, Ramseur found his way blocked by a "ravine and swamp" that "prevented any further advance."[19]

Firefights flickered through the dank Matadequin lowlands on Willcox's and Potter's fronts. The marshy low ground, cut by streams, presented difficult terrain, and attacker and defender flailed about in the creek's bogs. "Men are sent forward of the pits from five to thirty rods, according to circumstance, enough to cover the regiments at a distance of five or six steps apart," a New Hampshire man wrote of the disorienting deep-woods combat. "They are to keep behind trees, or whatever they can cover themselves with, or dig a small pit and get into it. The rebs do the same thing, and the two lines of videttes or skirmishers keep firing at each other at every chance, and the bullets come over to see us quite often. When an advance is made the skirmishers have to run in, after holding their ground as long as possible. Many are taken prisoner, on both sides, in this way."[20]

Early failed to penetrate the main fortifications, but Burnside became increasingly concerned. Rebels were pressing both ends of his line, and his scouts reported a substantial enemy force marching toward high ground at White's farm. Expecting another attack in that quarter, the 9th Corps commander alerted Humphreys, who directed Warren to hold Ayres's and Crawford's divisions in readiness at the Leary farm. Burnside, Meade's chief of staff cautioned, was to call on Warren for reinforcements only if "it is apparent your own troops can no longer maintain your line." Burnside detached Brigadier General James H. Ledlie's brigade from Crittenden's reserve line and ordered it to Allen's Mill, east of the White place, and later added the 37th Massachusetts. Notifying headquarters of his action, Burnside suggested that Warren post Ayres in advance of Allen's Mill and hold Crawford subject to his call. Headquarters, however, instructed the Rhode Islander to garrison Allen's Mill with 9th Corps troops and reminded him to avoid asking Warren for reinforcements unless "absolutely necessary" to prevent the rebels from driving him from his works.[21]

At 12:45 P.M. Potter reported that Christ had largely recovered his advance line and that his connection with Willcox was "strong" and "ought to hold." Christ's rifle pits on the White knoll were almost completed, he noted, and the colonel expected to haul guns onto the hill as soon as he had finished corduroying the Matadequin crossing.[22]

Just when it appeared that the rebels had quieted, Anderson went on the offensive, no doubt goaded by Early's criticisms. The result was a disjointed, unsupported attack. Spearheading the 1st Corps assault were Pickett's Virginians, who broke from the woods into the cleared zone in front of Fletcher's Redoubt. The massive fort's three batteries, supported by Hartranft's Michiganders, broke the attack with ease, and the rebels pulled back into the woods.

Captain Roemer, commanding in the redoubt, decided to entice Pickett's troops back into the clearing by making them think that Confederate artillery had silenced his batteries. He ordered Captain Joseph W. B. Wright on the right side of the redoubt and Captain Adelbert B. Twitchell on the left to slacken their fire, then to cease altogether. Five minutes later Lieutenant Heasley, commanding the 34th New York Battery in the fort's center, stopped shooting, and the Union guns all fell silent. Ignorant of Roemer's intentions, Hartranft's men sarcastically remarked that "Roemer's three batteries are going to hell this time, sure."

In fact, Roemer's gunners were waiting for the rebels to return to the clearing. "I gave orders that all three batteries should fire at the signal, which was to be one shot from the 34th New York, and all should aim at the feet of the charging column," recollected Roemer. "Soon the rebel yell was heard in the woods in our front, and this notified us that the expected charge had begun." At the captain's command, fourteen Union pieces roared in unison, repelling the Confederate onslaught. "Then I gave the order, 'One more by battery fire at their backs,'" Roemer wrote, "which fire drove them back faster than at a double quick." According to the captain, an elated Willcox galloped into the redoubt and announced, "Roemer, you old rat, this is the best trick you have played yet."[23]

While Pickett sparred with Roemer and Hartranft, Ramseur shifted east and renewed his offensive, this time against Potter. Supported by artillery, the North Carolinian's soldiers overran the pickets in front of Simon Griffin's brigade. Since Griffin's entrenchments angled east from Willcox's line, much of the rebel cannon fire passed over his men and landed in Willcox's rear. Early later observed that this artillery took "the enemy's position in flank and reverse, so as to favor a movement from Anderson's front, which had been ordered but was not made."[24]

Early's criticism of Anderson was unfair. Lieutenant Colonel Frank Huger, commanding a battalion of 1st Corps artillery, had positioned Captain Osmond B. Taylor's Virginia battery on Pickett's front where it could "enfilade the enemy's line, with a view of assisting Genl. Early's attack." Anderson's aide Lieutenant Colonel Sorrell related that while Early probed the enemy position, "Pickett's skirmishers were supporting and cooperating with him," referring to that general's attempts to capture Fletcher's Redoubt.[25]

Hoping to capture White's farm near the 9th Corps's vulnerable eastern flank, elements from Ramseur's Division pounced on the 48th Pennsylvania's picket line. "The enemy made a sudden rush from the woods on the right of the hill," Potter alerted Burnside, "drove in my skirmishers, and rushed in simultaneously on the rifle pit I was building, from which, in the confusion, the men fell back and the enemy now hold." An officer in Christ's 36th Massachusetts recalled that Confederates "captured a portion of the working party, consisting of details from the 45th Pennsylvania and 58th Massachusetts." Caught by surprise, the commanding officer ran away, and according to Potter, the musketry became "pretty sharp."[26]

Before Potter could organize a force to recapture the position, Ramseur brought up artillery—apparently Lieutenant Charles B. Griffin's battery, along with the 2nd Company, Richmond Howitzers—and began shelling that portion of the Union line. Potter thought that the firing did little damage "except to horses around my headquarters." A newsman covering the attack witnessed an impressive display of "shot and shell screaming over the treetops in front of Burnside's position, then dropping into the breastworks that concealed and sheltered his men." According to the reporter, soldiers fell "to the earth in order to escape the murderous missiles but the shells fell among them and burst in the air above them, and in this way a large number were injured." Expecting an assault to follow, the Federals huddled against their breastworks, muskets at the ready. When the charging Confederates reached within fifty yards of the entrenchments, Potter's troops opened "with terrible effect," according to a witness, breaking the assault. Burnside tried to organize a counterattack but called it off because of an army-wide truce to recover wounded men and bury the dead that began at 6:00 P.M. According to Potter, the Confederates on White's hill "paid no attention whatever to the flag of truce, working hard all the time, and opening a very heavy fire on our lines, as soon as our fire was slackened." The 2nd New York Mounted Rifles from Colonel Marshall's Provisional Brigade—"mostly made up of new men and officers, about one-eighth being old men," Potter noted—tried to advance but failed to make headway. Concluding that the high ground was "almost unapproachable," Potter cancelled the offensive.[27]

Fighting in the darkening woods, Ramseur's Virginians took cover behind trees, firing at Federals a hundred yards away in a patch of low pines. "We could see the flash of their guns, but could not see them," a Confederate recounted. "We remained cornered up and nearly scared to death until dark when we were ordered to fall back. The Yanks gave a loud yell when they saw us go. They were no gladder than we were."[28]

During the afternoon, a skirmisher in the 45th Pennsylvania found a note signed by a Confederate lieutenant of engineers. A local resident named Jane Bowles, it seems, had gone to Old Church in search of crackers, taken a close look at the Union position, and reported her observations to the lieutenant, revealing the location of Ferrero's 9th Corps division of black troops and the Union picket line's configuration. When Humphreys learned that Bowles had relayed military intelligence to the enemy, he ordered Burnside to arrest her for questioning. An interrogation of the very pregnant farm woman and her fourteen-year-old daughter, also named Jane, persuaded the provost marshal that the Bowles ladies were "ignorant and simple-minded people" who exhibited not "the slightest evidence of any intent on their part." He recommended headquarters return them home, which presumably was done.[29]

That night Potter pushed skirmishers onto White's hill and prepared to try again to take the high ground. Early, however, decided the hill was not worth holding and pulled Ramseur back, forfeiting the position to the Federals. Near sunup on June 8, Potter's soldiers occupied Ramseur's vacant rifle pits and collected entrenching tools that the rebels had abandoned. Burnside ordered Curtin's brigade to occupy the eminence, with the 2nd New York Mounted Rifles securing the right flank.[30]

Early's excursion of June 7 had accomplished nothing more substantial than

had his abortive venture across the same ground the previous day. Lee referred
to the operation as "unimportant," involving only "slight skirmishing." "We
drove in their skirmishers to the main line of entrenchments, capturing about
40 prisoners," reported the *Richmond Sentinel* on the action. One of Early's
captains complained that Anderson had "failed to come up to the mark, and
thus our demonstrations were fruitless except in the capture of a few prisoners."

Early had no doubt about why the operation had failed. "I met with no cooperation from your force except the artillery, which opened on my request,"
he wrote the 1st Corps commander. "I could not find either General Pickett or
yourself on the line. Your skirmishers did not move forward to connect with
mine, and after continuing the fight until nightfall, I withdrew, as I could do no
good without cooperation, and my left and rear were exposed to attack, if the
enemy should be enterprising."[31]

Anderson had no patience with Early's carping and sent a blistering note in
reply. "I am sorry to see that a consciousness of the folly, which you repeated
on yesterday, of sacrificing some eighty or [one] hundred of your men to obtain
a little information, which added nothing to what was already known, has put
you in a bad humor," he began. "If you mean by cooperation, committing equal
folly with yourself, I grant that I did not cooperate; but if you mean that I did
not proceed to carry out the instructions of General Lee, your statement is
false. Your opinion as to the best point for attacking the enemy, and the manner of conducting the attack, is very obligingly given. I have not, however, a
high appreciation of your judgment, and I decline to be guided by it." Pickett,
who also had no use for Early, complained to Anderson that he was "continually getting messages from General Early to do things which may be right or
may not be, as I very much doubt whether he knows what he wants." Strife
among its generals plagued not only the Army of the Potomac, but the Army
of Northern of Virginia as well.[32]

"We came back to our old place, built a fire, and cooked supper," one of
Ramseur's soldiers wrote. "We lay down and went to sleep, thus ending another
attempt of Old Jube to feel the Yanks, and today it was pretty rough on both
sides."[33]

The significance of the June 7 foray would not become obvious until later.
It was the last infantry attack that either side ventured at Cold Harbor.[34]

Early's and Anderson's forays made no impression on Grant. "Nothing of importance since morning," Assistant War Secretary Dana reported from Cold

Harbor. "Rebels made attack upon Burnside, but it was of no consequence."[35]

During the afternoon, Thomas Crittenden resigned from his position as division commander. The Kentuckian had commanded a corps in the west and, according to an aide, "ranked every officer in the Army of the Potomac except Grant and Burnside and felt sore about it." Dana suspected that Crittenden might have experienced "mental trouble for some time because his division is small, and also belongs to a corps containing negro troops." His replacement, astoundingly, was James Ledlie, the inebriated brigade commander who had decimated his unit during the North Anna operations by assailing virtually impregnable Confederate fortifications at Ox Ford. "He is brave to rashness in a fight, but apt to lose his head, and on the whole I shouldn't have much confidence in him," an officer related. Ledlie was to cause serious mischief in the days ahead.[36]

Southerners expressed different opinions about Grant's probable next move. Clearly the Union commander's retraction of his northern flank and the 5th Corps's appearance along the Chickahominy meant that he was shifting the Union army's center of gravity southward. The big mystery was what he meant to do next. "He may be making for the Southside, or he may intend to strengthen his lines and mass his troops for another and a desperate final effort," a correspondent from Richmond speculated. "It is said, as I close this, however, that he is moving more to our right." On Mahone's front a Union prisoner reported that Grant's destination was Malvern Hill near the James. "I have thought it my duty to report this to you for what it may be worth," Colonel David A. Weisiger noted in passing the intelligence on to Mahone.[37]

From his headquarters at Dunlop's farm north of Petersburg, Beauregard discerned a disturbing pattern. "Should Grant have left Lee's front," he wrote the authorities in Richmond, "he doubtless intends operations against Richmond along James River, probably on south side. Petersburg being nearly defenseless would be captured before it could be reinforced." To guard against that eventuality, Beauregard urged that Hoke's Division and Ransom's Brigade, both of which had recently reinforced the Army of Northern Virginia, be returned to him "at once."[38]

John Tyler, who accompanied Lee's staff throughout the campaign, recorded the thinking at army headquarters. Grant, he observed, "has commenced again sliding his right down past his left, doubtless in order to reach Bottom's Bridge and Long Bridge, with the intention of crossing to the Richmond side. Lee, accordingly, is throwing down his left. On both sides," Tyler reported, "I apprehend the lines will be contracted and massed, and a desper-

ate encounter take place in the course of the movement." Noting Hunter's recent victory in the Valley, Tyler predicted with uncanny accuracy that Grant
meant to cross the James River, cut the Confederate supply lines through Petersburg, and compel Lee's surrender through starvation. "Should he succeed
in getting over the James and in forming his lines across our railroads on the
south side," wrote Tyler, "our situation will be at least uncomfortable, if not
alarming."[39]

"Humanity would dictate that some provision should be made."

Across much of the Cold Harbor front, the gap between opposing lines measured in the tens of yards. Anyone who ventured into the killing zone was immediately shot, and wounded soldiers languished beside decomposing corpses.
Baking under a relentless midsummer sun and tormented by flies and insects,
the invalids had neither food nor water. Any movement drew fire from sharpshooters. "We became indifferent to the noise and bloodshed and privation of
the horrible scenes," a Confederate confessed, "but we could not be indifferent
to the stench arising from the unburied dead."[40]

Precisely how many injured men occupied the no-man's land between the
armies remained unclear. The day following the June 3 assault, the Army of
the Potomac's medical director estimated at eight hundred fifty the number of
Federal wounded "who are yet on the field under fire of sharpshooters, and who
cannot be brought off." Not all of the invalids, however, wore blue uniforms.
The Confederates made several counterattacks late on the third, leaving well
over a hundred Floridians and North Carolinians in the field. More soldiers
found themselves trapped in no-man's land while trying to rescue their comrades or during forays ventured during the next three days. Roughly speaking,
by June 7, perhaps a thousand wounded men dotted the clearings, the vast majority of them dressed in blue.[41]

Moved by their comrades' suffering, Union soldiers attempted heroic res-
cues under cover of night. On Gibbon's front, two daring escapades involved
attempts to recover the bodies of colonels killed during the June 3 offensive.
Concealed by darkness and a rainstorm, soldiers from the 8th New York Heavy
Artillery crawled out to Colonel Porter's corpse, lying near Colquitt's fortifications immediately south of Cold Harbor Road. Tying a rope through the dead
officer's sword belt, they pulled his remains back to a hollow and brought the
body into their lines. Union sharpshooters also discovered the body of Colonel
McKeen, who had been killed in the same attack, and retrieved his papers and

watch. After dark a detail dragged his body back, losing two men killed in the process.[42]

The question of how to recover injured men trapped between the lines was a novelty for the armies in Virginia. Until Grant's appearance, battles in the Old Dominion had generally lasted only a few days, ending when one side abandoned the field and left its wounded to the care of the victor. When the armies remained close together, local commanders sometimes declared informal truces in discrete sectors. After the Battle of Fredericksburg, for example, a Federal corps commander proposed an armistice to collect wounded troops. His Confederate counterpart—Lieutenant General Thomas J. "Stonewall" Jackson—insisted on a written application, and the Union general agreed. This brief ceasefire, however, governed only a portion of the field; nothing had been done to establish a formal procedure, and the army chiefs never sought army-wide truces.

The same practice carried into the spring campaign of 1864. During the three weeks that Grant and Lee fought at the Wilderness, Spotsylvania Court House, and the North Anna River, neither commander had asked for a truce to remove wounded men from the battleground. Some negotiations had taken place after the Battle of the Wilderness, when Meade petitioned for the return of several hundred wounded prisoners. The Confederate authorities had refused, insisting that a "flag of truce be sent by order of Lieutenant-General Grant before their delivery can be effected." Grant in turn sent a request over his name, but that was rejected because it was not addressed directly to General Lee.[43]

The largest concentration of wounded soldiers at Cold Harbor lay in front of Hancock's corps, and around noon on June 5—more than forty-eight hours after the deadly assault—the 2nd Corps commander raised the matter with headquarters. "Can any arrangement be made by which the wounded in front of Barlow can be removed?" he inquired of Meade. "I understand men wounded on the 3rd are still lying there." Meade forwarded the message to Grant, writing across the bottom, "Is it possible to ask, under flag of truce, for permission to remove the wounded now lying between our lines, and which the enemy's sharpshooters prevent me bringing off?" Wounded men, he added, were still in front of the 2nd, 6th, and 18th Corps.[44]

Hancock's message struck a responsive chord in Grant, who the previous year had launched attacks against Confederate fortifications at Vicksburg that left many Union dead and wounded on the battlefield. Despite entreaties from one of his generals, Grant had done nothing. Finally the stench of decaying bodies drove the Confederate commander, Lieutenant General John C. Pemberton, to propose a cessation of hostilities for two and a half hours "in the name of humanity . . . that you may be enabled to remove your dead and dying men." Grant accepted the proposal and sent out burial parties that evening.[45]

Perhaps regretting that he had not acted with greater dispatch at Vicksburg, the general in chief now suggested to Meade that a flag "might be sent proposing to suspend firing where the wounded are, until each party get their own." Meade, however, refused to accept the responsibility. "Any communication by flag of truce will have to come from you," he insisted, "as the enemy do not recognize me as in command whilst you are present."[46]

Grant bit the bullet and penned a proposal to Lee, taking the initiative to open negotiations toward a truce. "It is reported to me that there are wounded men, probably of both armies, now lying exposed and suffering between the lines occupied respectively by the two armies," he began. "Humanity would dictate that some provision should be made to provide against such hardships. I would propose, therefore, that hereafter when no battle is raging either party be authorized to send to any point between the pickets or skirmish lines, unarmed men bearing litters to pick up their dead or wounded without being fired upon by either party. Any other method equally fair to both parties you may propose for meeting the end desired, will be accepted by me."[47]

Meade dispatched Lieutenant Colonel Lyman with Grant's note, suggesting that his aide cross to the enemy lines under a flag of truce at a place of Hancock's selection. Lyman had served on the Pennsylvanian's staff for almost a year, but this was the first that he had heard of flags of truce, and his ideas about such matters, he later wrote, were "chiefly medieval and were associated with a herald wearing a tabard." Wanting to dress appropriately, Lyman donned a sash, white gloves, and all the finery he could scrounge. Unable to find a bugler, he settled for a cavalry sergeant to accompany him on his mission.[48]

Lyman located Hancock near the Cold Harbor intersection. "Well, colonel," the general cautioned, "you can't carry [a message] out on my front, it's too hot there. Your best way is to go to the left, where there are only pickets, and the officers there will get it out." Hancock directed his aide Major William G. Mitchell to get Lyman a white flag and whiskey to placate the rebels. The liquor Mitchell found right away, but the white flag proved problematic. Resisting the temptation to raid Hancock's supply of clean white shirts, Mitchell ripped up a white pillowcase, tied it to a pole, and handed Lyman the makeshift banner.

Heading south along Dispatch Station Road, Lyman and his sergeant acquired a guide in the person of Colonel Charles E. Hapgood of the 5th New Hampshire, a tall, sinewy officer with bullet holes through his hat, trousers, and scabbard. A short ride took them to the headquarters of Miles's brigade at the Union line's southern end. Continuing into a stand of pines, Lyman found Lieutenant Colonel John S. Hammell of the 66th New York. "Do you know where you are going?" Hammell cautioned the staff officer and his companions. "There have been two field officers killed just here."

Riding on, the trio reached a field. "Now," cautioned Hapgood as he pointed across the clearing, "those tallest trees are full of their sharpshooters; if we strike into the field fifty yards above here, they will fire; but just below, they can't see."

Their white flag flapping, Lyman and his entourage galloped across the opening into the far woods and approached an assemblage of Confederates. "It looked exactly like a scene in an opera," Lyman wrote home later that day. "There was never anything that so resembled something got up for stage effect. The sun was near setting, and in the heavy oak woods, the light already began to fade. On the road stood a couple of Rebel officers, each in his gray overcoat, and, just behind, were grouped some twenty soldiers—the most gypsy-looking fellows imaginable; in their blue-gray jackets and slouched hats; each with his rusty musket and well-filled cartridge box."

Lyman introduced himself to Major Thomas L. Wooten of the 18th North Carolina's sharpshooters, who was obviously in charge. The major's dignified bearing impressed the New Englander. "To see us all together," Lyman wrote, "you would suppose we had met to go out shooting, or something of that kind." Wooten explained that Grant's dispatch would be received if in proper form and promised to bring back an answer in a few hours. There was nothing to do but wait, so the Yankees and Wooten's men—soldiers from Colonel Barry's brigade of Tar Heels—sat down together in a cleared glen.[49]

As the hours dragged by, Lyman's wait became increasingly unpleasant, made especially so by the stench of dead horses killed in a savage cavalry battle three days earlier. Around 8:30 P.M., musketry picked up close by, and firing rippled along the opposing lines. Lyman conjured up visions of the Yankees and rebels around him panicking and blazing away at one another, himself and the sergeant in the middle. "The officers sprung to their feet and ran down the lines, to again caution the men," Lyman observed with relief, "so nobody fired; and there we sat and listened to the volleys and the cannonading, that opened very heavily."

Sometime after ten, Major Wooten went to investigate the delay. An hour later a rebel lieutenant appeared and advised Lyman to go back; Lee's reply, when it came, would be passed through the picket lines. After shaking hands with the Confederates, Lyman and his sergeant crossed to their own lines and returned to Meade's headquarters. The army commander was relieved to see them. "Hullo, Lyman," he called out. "I thought perhaps the rebs had gobbled you during that attack."

Lee's written response reached Grant's headquarters early on June 6. The Confederate commander agreed with the spirit of the proposal to suspend hostilities to remove dead and wounded men from between the lines but had problems with the suggested procedure. Allowing litter bearers to wander into sectors where fighting had temporarily quieted struck him as a bad idea. "I fear that such an arrangement will lead to misunderstanding and difficulty," Lee protested, and he suggested a different course that he judged less risky. "I propose, therefore, instead," wrote Lee, "that when either party desires to remove their dead or wounded, a flag of truce be sent, as is customary. It will always afford me pleasure to comply with such a request as far as circumstances will permit."[50]

Understanding Lee's letter as insisting only that the rebel commander wanted a flag of truce to accompany the litter bearers, Grant drafted a reply that he thought met these demands. He intended, he wrote, to "send immediately, as you propose, to collect the dead and wounded between the lines of the two armies, and will also instruct that you be allowed to do the same. I propose that the time for doing this be between the hours of 12 M and 3 P.M. today. I will direct all parties going out to bear a white flag, and not to attempt to go beyond where we have dead or wounded, and not beyond or on ground occupied by your troops." Assuming that the matter was now settled, Meade notified his corps commanders at 9:00 A.M. of the timetable and instructed them to make arrangements to comply.[51]

Grant, however, had misunderstood Lee's proposal. The rebel commander wanted a general army-wide armistice, not informal local truces that he feared might spawn confusion. His initial jotting had been imprecise, and Lee conceded as much in a note that he shot off to Grant after receiving the Union commander's latest missive. "I have the honor to acknowledge the receipt of your letter of this date and regret to find that I did not make myself understood in my communication of yesterday," he explained in a message that made its way across the lines a few hours later. "I intended to say that I could not consent to the burial of the dead and the removal of the wounded between the armies in the way you propose, but that when either party desire such permission it shall be asked for by flag of truce in the usual way. Until I receive a proposition from you on the subject to which I can accede with propriety, I have directed any parties you may send under white flags as mentioned in your letter to be turned back."[52]

Grant was in no mood to dicker over details. Lee's reference to a flag of truce "in the usual way" was perplexing as there was no "usual way," but Grant had no objection to his apparent insistence on a general armistice. "The knowledge that wounded men are now suffering from want of attention, between the two armies, compels me to ask a suspension of hostilities for sufficient time to collect them in, say two hours," he wrote in response. "Permit me to say that the hours you may fix upon for this will be agreeable to me, and the same privilege will be extended to such parties as you may wish to send out on the same duty, without further application."[53]

While their generals tried to reach agreement, the soldiers of both armies concluded that a ceasefire was imminent and took it upon themselves to arrange informal truces. Colquitt's Georgians agreed to suspend hostilities for a few hours so Barlow's troops could begin the burial process. The 19th Maine's historian reported several such agreements between the men of his regiment and the rebels facing them. When Birney learned that a picket officer had sanctioned a truce, he arrested the man, complaining that his carelessness had afforded the enemy a peek at the Union position. "By tacit understanding our pickets have ceased firing on each other," Birney informed headquarters. "I have forbidden all intercourse of an irregular character."[54]

Other generals issued injunctions similar to Birney's, but the soldiers frequently ignored them. "Our picket lines are but a few rods apart," a Union officer wrote, "and have, just in our front, agreed not to fire upon each other except in case of an advance. Some of our boys are trading with them coffee for tobacco—you see that General Orders have very little influence over a picket line."[55]

During the afternoon of June 6, one of Baldy Smith's subordinates reported that the enemy "ceased firing and stood upon their works and our men did likewise, supposing a cessation of hostilities was going on according to the request of the commanding general of the army." Smith paid a visit and described what he saw. "An informal agreement had been made with the enemy troops in their front to stop picket firing," he wrote headquarters. "As this was very much in accordance with my own ideas, I expressed a wish that this state of affairs would extend all along my lines, as my men in the rear lines were suffering severely from such firing."[56]

Informal truces also occurred in the 6th Corps's sector. During the afternoon, Wright reported Yankees and rebels bringing in their wounded, "both parties refraining from firing as if by tacit consent." Neill, commanding one of Wright's divisions, apparently sent out a flag of truce on his own responsibility, but the Confederates refused to recognize his overture because it did not emanate from corps headquarters. In another mix-up a rebel burial party, acting under the mistaken belief that a truce had been declared, went out to locate the body of Lieutenant Colonel John R. Murchison of the 8th North Carolina, killed on June 1. Union pickets captured the rebels and brought them back as prisoners.[57]

Although the commanding generals finally reached agreement by the afternoon of June 6 on a procedure for removing the dead and wounded, transmitting messages across the lines delayed Lee's reply until 7:00 P.M. "I regret that your letter of this date asking a suspension of hostilities to enable you to remove your wounded from between the two armies was received at so late an hour as to make it impossible to give the necessary directions so as to enable you to effect your purpose by daylight," the rebel commander explained. "In order that the suffering of the wounded may not be further protracted, I have ordered that any parties you may send out for the purpose between the hours of 8 and 10 P.M. today shall not be molested, and will avail myself of the privilege extended to those from this army to collect any of its wounded that may remain upon the field. I will direct our skirmishers to be drawn close to our lines between the hours indicated, with the understanding that at the expiration of the time they be allowed to resume their positions without molestation, and that during the interval all military movements be suspended."[58]

This latest letter, however, did not reach the Union outposts until after ten o'clock that night. By then the new deadline set by Lee had passed, and the long-suffering invalids faced another agonizing night in no-man's land. A Richmond newspaper put a predictable spin on events. "Grant is too much of a bull dog to send in a flag of truce, according to the customary mode of civilized warfare" observed the *Dispatch,* "since it would be a painful acknowledgment of defeat."[59]

At 10:30 on the morning of June 7, Grant again wrote Lee. "I regret that your note of 7:00 P.M. yesterday should have been received at the nearest corps headquarters to where it was delivered after the hour that had been given for the removal of the dead and wounded had expired," he began. "10:45 was the hour at which it was received at corps headquarters, and between 11 and 12 it reached my headquarters. As a consequence it was not understood by the troops of this army that there was a cessation of hostilities for the purpose of collecting the dead and wounded, and none were collected."

Grant also addressed the question of the captured Tar Heels. "Two officers and six men of the 8th and [51st] North Carolina regiments, who were out in search of the bodies of officers of their respective regiments, were captured and brought into our lines owing to the want of understanding," he explained. "I regret this, but will state that as soon as I learned the fact I directed that they should not be held as prisoners, but must be returned to their commands. These officers and men having been carelessly brought through our lines to the rear, I have not determined whether they will be sent back the way they came or whether they will be sent by some other route. Regretting that all my efforts for alleviating the sufferings of wounded men left upon the battlefield have been rendered nugatory, I remain, U. S. Grant."[60]

Conspicuously missing from Grant's exposition was a request to set another time for the truce. Lee, however, took the initiative in a message sent at two o'clock that afternoon. "Your note of 10:30 A.M. today has just been received," he wrote. "I regret that my letter to you of 7 P.M. yesterday should have been too late in reaching you to effect the removal of the wounded. I am willing, if you desire it, to devote the hours between 6 and 8 this afternoon to accomplish that object upon the same terms and conditions as set forth in my letter of 7 P.M. yesterday. If this will answer your purpose, and you will send parties from your lines at the hour designated with white flags, I will direct that they be recognized and be permitted to collect the dead and wounded."

"I will also notify the officers on my lines," Lee continued, "that they will be permitted to collect any of our men that may be on the field. I request you will notify me as soon as practicable if this arrangement is agreeable to you. Lieutenant McAllister, Corporal Martin, and two privates of the Eighth North Carolina regiment, and Lieutenant Hartman, Corpl. T. Kinlow, and Privates Bass and Grey were sent last night, between the hours of 8 and 10 P.M., for the purpose of recovering the body of Colonel Murchison, and as they have not yet returned, I presume they are the men mentioned in your letter. I request that they be returned to our lines."[61]

Although Grant and Lee had at last reached agreement on a truce, news of the accord was slow to reach the soldiers. "Everything pretty quiet today until a few minutes ago (4 P.M.), when artillery fighting began on our left being in progress now," one of Colonel Weisiger's Virginians noted. "The customary skirmishing however has been uninterrupted."[62]

On receiving Lee's latest letter—it was now after 5:00 P.M.—Grant forwarded it to Meade. "I will notify General Lee that hostilities will cease from 6 to 8 for the purposes mentioned," he wrote, instructing Meade to "send the officers and men referred to as you deem best." Army staff immediately informed corps commanders of the agreement and directed them to "send out, under a white flag, medical officers with stretcher-bearers to bring in the dead and wounded. No other officers or men will be permitted to leave the lines, and

no intercourse of any kind will be held with the enemy, and the medical officers and attendants will be enjoined not to converse upon any subject connected with the military operations or likely to give information to the
enemy."[63]

Grant then penned a reply to Lee. "Your note of this date just received," he
observed. "It will be impossible for me to communicate the fact of the truce
by the hour named by you (6 P.M.), but I will avail myself of your offer at the
earliest possible moment, which I hope will not be much after that hour. The
officers and men taken last evening are the same mentioned in your note and
will be returned."[64]

Two days of negotiations, marred by miscommunications and delayed trans-
missions, had finally yielded a procedure for a truce and a workable timeframe.
In later years writers criticized Grant as heartless and Lee as too formal. Hancock's aide Charles Morgan recollected that "it was understood at the time that
the delay was caused by something akin to points of etiquette, General Grant
proposing a flag as a mutual accommodation, and General Lee replying that
he had no dead or wounded not attended to, but offering to Grant a truce if
General Grant desired it to attend to his own." Grant's aide Adam Badeau
blamed the holdup on Lee and sarcastically inquired in his *Military History of
Ulysses S. Grant* whether the Confederate commander's "military reputation
gained sufficiently to compensate for the sufferings he deliberately and unnecessarily prolonged." The debate also rocked the staid halls of the Military Historical Society of Massachusetts, where historian John C. Ropes chastised
Grant for the "horrible neglect of our wounded men," and Colonel Thomas L.
Livermore took up Grant's defense, maintaining that the general had negoti-
ated in good faith and that delays in transmitting correspondence "must be laid
to the inevitable difficulties incident to the passage of hostile lines, the long
distances, the movements of the commanders, and the barrier which darkness
raises." Accusations against Grant more recently surfaced in Shelby Foote's
historical novel *The Civil War—A Narrative,* in which Foote accused the general of making a "sacrifice of brave men for no apparent purpose except to salve
his rankled pride." Reviewing the novelist's work, a student of the campaign
pronounced it "an example of the limited scholarship and misrepresentation on
this subject that has gone unchallenged and should not be allowed to continue."[65]

Grant's modern biographer, Brooks D. Simpson, probably got it right when
he concluded that "neither general deliberately sought to prolong the human
suffering between the lines, and confusion, misunderstanding, and delays in

communication contributed to the tragedy." There was certainly ample blame to go around. It was the Confederates, after all, who were ruthlessly killing wounded soldiers and anyone who tried to save them, and Lee made no effort to stop the wanton slaughter. Of all the generals involved in the affair, Grant looks best. As soon as Meade alerted him to the problem, he immediately offered Lee a plan and announced his readiness to accept a reasonable counter-proposal. He and Lee consumed June 6 with a flurry of exchanges that were unduly protracted, not because of stubbornness, but because of honest misunderstandings and the difficulties of sending messages across active battle lines. Lee wrote a response that was genuinely ambiguous, and Grant misunderstood the letter as requiring only that a white flag accompany each localized truce. Lee set the Union commander straight, apologized for his imprecise language, and explained more clearly his concern that the ceasefire be army-wide. Grant again readily accepted this proposal, but impediments in transmission cost another day. Most of June 7 was frittered away finding an acceptable time for recovery parties to begin their grisly work.[66]

The formal truce began soon after 6:00 P.M. on June 7. "There was little time for ceremony," a surgeon in the 23rd Massachusetts recalled. "Carrying a ramrod, to which had been fixed a sheet of lint, I climbed over the works. On the neutral ground, I met a Mississippi major, who speedily assured me—it needed little demonstration—that all our men not already dead, had been made prisoners by the enemy." In another sector of the field, a soldier from Vermont watched two men from each side start from their respective works. "Our flag consisted of a white handkerchief fixed flag-like to a little staff—theirs, a white handkerchief simply held up in the hand," he later wrote. "I could not help wishing, as the two flags approached each other, that the good men of both sections might come together and, by reason, put an end to this fraternal slaughter."[67]

A chaplain in the 15th New Jersey watched in awe as soldiers from both armies clambered onto their earthworks in plain sight of one another. "The Rebels who came with the flag were good natured and ready to talk with us," an officer from Rhode Island discovered with relief. "Enemies met as friends," remembered a man from Vermont. "There was no boasting, no bandying of words—the event was too solemn for jokes between those who had fought with such stern bravery for so long." A Confederate had similar recollections. "Over the breastworks went Rebel and Yank, and met between the lines, and commenced laughing and talking, and you would have thought that old friends had met after a long separation," he related. "Some were talking earnestly together, some swapping coffee for tobacco, some were wrestling, some boxing, others trading knives." A Georgian in Colquitt's Brigade "got a little black handle, three bladed [knife], not much account."[68]

One of the first questions that the Confederates asked the Federals as they mingled between the lines was their prediction of who would win the approaching presidential nomination at the Baltimore convention. "On this subject they appeared especially anxious," a northerner noted, "frequently repeating the question."[69]

Lyman strolled into the killing fields and found himself next to a grave holding ten bodies. A crowd had gathered, and the Confederates were inquiring who would be the next president. When a Union man spoke up in favor of Lincoln, a southerner denounced him as an abolitionist. "A general fisticuff ensued," wrote Lyman, "only stopped by the officers rushing in."[70]

A 6th Corps surgeon could scarcely believe his eyes. "It was a strange sight," he wrote. "Five minutes previously it was worth a man's life to be seen upon the defenses, but now hundreds and thousands of both parties swarmed over the neutral ground, conversing in the most kindly and friendly manner." Officers exchanged greetings as stretcher bearers hauled off corpses and wounded men. "No one[,] to see officers and men of these contending armies in so close and friendly intercourse[,] would have supposed that their business here was for no other purpose than the slaughter of their fellow man," the surgeon recounted in wonder.[71]

The show of camaraderie, however, could not diminish the scene's horror. Constant shelling had gouged the ground so thoroughly that it looked ploughed. A foul odor—"the most unearthly stench that ever assailed the nostrils of mortal man," a witness remembered—caused squeamish soldiers to vomit. The corpses were in terrible condition; General Gibbon later noted that bodies had dissolved into a "mass of corruption very offensive to everybody, friends and enemy, in the vicinity." One of Hancock's aides described the dead "in a horrible state of putrefaction." In places burial parties dug trenches and deposited remains in common graves. "I went into the field but I could not recognize any of the boys," recalled a man from the 8th New York Heavy Artillery. "They all looked alike—black and bloated." Several New Yorkers searched for the remains of a man they had watched fitfully lifting his arm for the past two days. "When his body was recovered," recalled a Federal, "his arm was found to be riddled by balls put through it when he raised it."[72]

"I hope and pray it may never be my fortune to behold such a sight again," a Union man penned home. "The ground was strewn with our dead, but they were in such awful condition, it was impossible to recognize anyone except by their clothes, or papers found on them. They were all as black as the blackest negro you ever saw, and were covered with maggots, and a most sickening stench arose from their remains which it was almost impossible to endure." Somebody "supplied the working parties with whiskey," a New Englander remembered. "One could hardly blame even the abuse of stimulants under such circumstances." A Confederate in Colquitt's Brigade reported that the Federals "just threw dirt on their dead as they lay."[73]

No one kept count of how many wounded men were still alive. Assistant Secretary of War Dana wrote two days later that only two injured soldiers were recovered, along with 432 dead. He must have been mistaken, as numerous firsthand reports from various parts of the field document the removal of living soldiers. Those who were brought back had terrible tales to tell. One survivor related that he had been shot in the thigh during the big attack on June 3, and that he had been shot again each successive day, receiving a total of six wounds. "During all that time he had not a drop of water except what he obtained sucking the moisture from the dewy grass at night, or spreading his blanket on the ground to receive the dew and afterwards applying it to his mouth."[74]

Soldiers from both armies eagerly sought to recover the bodies of officers who had led the fateful charge. An officer in the 164th New York located the remains of his popular colonel, James P. McMahon, near the Confederate earthworks. The corpse was so badly decomposed that the colonel's brother buried it behind Union lines instead of sending it home. Confederates found the body of Captain C. Seton Fleming, who had led a forlorn charge against Barlow's entrenchments the evening of June 3, and buried him near the battlefield as well. Fleming's personal papers and ring were given to a surgeon from his home state of Florida. "His remains are lying in rather a pretty place, among fine trees," the surgeon wrote, adding that he had erected a headboard at the gravesite and promised to have the spot enclosed with rails.[75]

Meade had not forgotten the North Carolina prisoners and instructed Wright to see that they were returned. The 6th Corps commander, however, was reluctant to send the captives back, suspecting that their purported mission was a "fraud to get information of the strength of our position."[76]

The task of returning the wayward Tar Heels fell to Wright's aide Colonel Thomas W. Hyde. It was night when Hyde received the assignment, and the truce had expired. Understandably concerned that he might get shot in the dark, the colonel decided to try his luck in front of Russell's division, which was arrayed in fortified entrenchments connected with zigzags that reached close to the enemy line, minimizing the distance he and his wards had to cross. Working his way to the foremost entrenchment, Hyde found himself among Penrose's

New Jersey troops, lying down and trading lively fire with Confederates two hundred yards away. "Indeed the same thing was going on for some three miles," Hyde reminisced, "and it would have been impossible for anything to live between those rows of breastworks."[77]

Hoping to calm the rebels, Hyde asked Penrose to direct his men to stop shooting. The colonel complied, and after a while the rebel firing subsided. Climbing over the works, Hyde, accompanied by Penrose, strode toward the Confederates. Midway Hyde called out, "I want to see the commander of the rebel line." Penrose quickly interjected, "Say Confederate, for God's sake," and the staffer repeated his call with the correction.

"What do you want?" a southern voice piped up from close by, and Hyde explained his mission. "Wait till we communicate with General Lee," the man answered and promptly disappeared. "I own it was rather trying to the human nerves," Hyde later wrote his mother, "but Penrose and I held a lively conversation on everything else in whispers, though every dark prominence near was a body and its worms, and we were forced to hold our noses to prevent nausea."[78]

Seizing an opportune moment to return to his own fortifications, Penrose left Hyde to ponder his situation alone. "The thought came to me what it meant waiting there," he later reminisced. "If any irresponsible party fired his gun, it would all commence again just as it was going on to the right and left in vistas as far as I could see, and then there was no chance whatever for me. So I crouched in a half-filled grave and waited, despite the stench and horror of it all."[79]

Hyde waited for what seemed an hour, watching shadows shift in the darkness and listening to low murmurs from the rebel pits. Two forms finally materialized from the blackness and identified themselves as a Mississippi colonel and his adjutant. After receiving permission to bring the prisoners across, Hyde went back for the Tar Heels, who were so frightened the shooting might resume that they had to be forced over the Union works. After safely delivering his wards, the colonel chatted with the Confederates and returned to his own lines, "highly delighted that the thing was over, for the chances were decidedly against success."[80]

"He said it was the talk of the camp."

Despite the harmonious façade that Grant and Meade presented to the world, the Pennsylvanian's resentment over his subordinate position continued to fester. Unable to openly express his hurt over the constant praise that the press lavished on the general in chief, Meade found an outlet in his letters home. "Do not be deceived about the situation of affairs by the foolish dispatches in the papers," he warned Margaret from his camp at Cold Harbor. "Up to this time our success has consisted only in compelling the enemy to draw in toward Richmond; our failure has been that we have not been able to overcome, destroy or bag his army." The press's slavish devotion to Grant at the expense of his own reputation, Meade fumed, was simply a cross he and his family would have to endure in silence. "I fully enter into all your feelings of annoyance at the manner in which I have been treated," he assured Margaret, "but I do not see that I can do anything but bear patiently till it pleases good to let the truth be known and set matters right." By his reckoning, Grant had been a failure. "To tell the truth," he assured Margaret, "[Grant] has greatly disappointed me, and since this campaign I really begin to think I am something of a general."[81]

On this hot, sultry June 7, Meade's suppressed anger erupted in a display that set the army buzzing. Thumbing through the June 2 edition of the *Philadelphia Inquirer*—the newspaper that his family and friends back home were reading—the general came across an article by Edward Cropsey that set him boiling. The piece started off favorably enough, praising Meade for the army's "great movements" since crossing the Rapidan. The bad part came toward the end. On the night of the second day of fighting in the Wilderness, Cropsey wrote, Meade "was on the point of committing a great blunder unwittingly, but his devotion to his country made him loath to lose her army on what he deemed a last chance." Grant, the story continued, "assumed the responsibility and we are still 'On to Richmond.'" As Cropsey saw it, "History will record that on one eventful night during the present campaign Grant's presence saved the army and the nation too."[82]

Puzzled by this recounting—Meade read the passage to mean that "Grant saved the nation, when I desired to destroy it"—the high-strung Pennsylvanian summoned the newspaperman to his tent and asked him to explain the episode alluded to in his piece. Cropsey answered that he was referring to Meade's insistence that Grant withdraw the Army of the Potomac across the Rapidan after the Battle of the Wilderness. Grant, the reporter observed, had resisted his arguments and thus saved the nation from a disgraceful retreat. "I asked his authority," Meade wrote Margaret two days later. "He said it was the talk of the camp."[83]

Cropsey became the lightning rod for Meade's rage. "I told him it was a base and wicked lie," the general wrote home, "and that I would make an example of him, which should not only serve to deter others from committing like offense, but would give publicity to his lie and the truth." Before taking action against Cropsey, Meade consulted Grant, who advised him that the reporter hailed from a respectable Illinois family. Discussing his treachery, however, only stoked Meade's anger. "His wrath knew no bounds," recollected Grant's aide Porter, who was present for the interview. Dana joined Grant in attempting to calm the army commander, pointing out that the story was incredible and promising to help lay it to rest. Meade, however, could not be assuaged.[84]

The aggrieved general asked Provost Marshal Patrick to help him devise a fitting punishment. Meade could not have selected a worse advisor. Patrick despised the press and recommended a penalty that was very public and very humiliating. The next day he arrested Cropsey and had him mounted on the "sorriest looking mule to be found," facing backward toward the animal's rump. A placard blazoned with his name and stating "Libeler of the Press" hung around his neck, and he paraded through the ranks for hours, preceded by a mounted guard detailed from the 3rd Pennsylvania Cavalry, a bugler, and a drum corps playing the "Rogues March." Lest anyone miss the point, Meade's headquarters issued a general order denouncing the newsman—called "Crapsey" in the official pronouncement, for reasons that can only be imagined. The reporter, Meade railed, had made a "libelous statement on the commanding general of this army calculated to impair the confidence of the army in their commanding officer, and which statement Crapsey has acknowledged to have been false, and to have been based on some idle camp rumor." The order concluded with strong language that Patrick hoped would show Cropsey and "his Tribe" that Meade meant business. "The commanding general trusts that this example will deter others from committing like offenses," the order stated, "and he takes this occasion to notify the representatives of the public press that, whilst he is ready at all times to extend to them every facility for acquiring facts and giving circulation to the truth, he will not hesitate to punish with the utmost vigor all instances like the above where individuals take advantages of the privileges accorded to them to circulate false hood and thus impair the confidence which the general public and the army should have in their generals and other officers."[85]

Meade reveled in Cropsey's punishment, writing home that it had been carried out "much to the delight of the whole army, for the race of newspaper correspondents is universally despised by the soldiers." Some officers who shared Meade's sentiments, however, warned against offending the press. "I fear the general will hurt himself by this, for these newspaper fellows stick very close by one another when an outsider attacks them," wrote Warren's opinionated artillery chief, Colonel Wainwright. "But I rejoice seeing one of the rascals shown up, for they make more trouble than their heads are worth, with their lying accounts of affairs in the army; raising false hopes among the people, and almost always giving false ideas as to the merits of an officer."[86]

That evening Hancock and Gibbon visited Meade and found him, as Gibbon remembered, "laboring under great excitement." The Cropsey affair, it quickly became apparent, was only a symptom of the larger problem inherent in Meade's subordination to Grant. The general, Gibbon perceived, felt "shackled and sensible of the fact that he is deprived of that independence and untram-meled authority so necessary to every army commander." Meade, Gibbon con-cluded, was a man "of a peculiarly excitable disposition and his sensibility was such that he very quickly felt any lack of deference to himself or respect for his position. We did everything we could to sooth him," he wrote, "and when he had become a little more calm, he said he would not have expressed himself quite so freely except to officers of that army whom he regarded as the two best friends he had in it."[87]

Sylvanus Cadwallader, a war correspondent and intimate of Grant, dis-cussed the Cropsey affair with some of the general in chief's aides. The staff, he recalled, was divided in its opinion over Meade's handling of the matter, with professional military men applauding his actions and those from a civil-ian background less rabid. For his part, Cadwallader thought that Meade had overreacted and would come to regret the harsh and demeaning punishment. This prediction bore out over the ensuing days as the press closed ranks against the general. "Every newspaper correspondent in the Army of the Potomac, and in Washington City, had first an implied, and afterwards an express under-standing, to ignore General Meade in every possible way and manner," Cad-wallader observed. If a general order was issued over Meade's signature, his name was removed from it before it was printed. As far as the newspaper-read-ing public knew, the general had disappeared from the war. Not even Provost Marshal Patrick could have devised a punishment more excruciating to a man of Meade's pride.[88]

To help salve Meade's wounded dignity, Dana sent Secretary of War Stan-ton a telegram praising the army commander's martial skills and deriding Cropsey's report. "General Meade is very much troubled at the report that after the Battle of the Wilderness, he counseled retreat," Dana wrote, adding that the report was untrue. "He has not shown any weakness of the sort since mov-ing from Culpeper, nor once intimated a doubt as to the successful issue of the campaign." Stanton's reply was all that Meade could have wished. "Please say to General Meade that the lying report alluded to in your telegram was not even for a moment believed by the President or myself," the secretary wrote. "We

have the most perfect confidence in him. He could not wish a more exalted estimation of his ability, his firmness, and every quality of a commanding general than is entertained for him."[89]

Stanton's gushing response might have been "pure hypocrisy," as a student
of the exchange later concluded, but Meade seems to have fallen for it. He sent
a copy of the message to Margaret and related that he had recently learned that
Stanton was getting his information about the campaign from Dana, not from
Grant as he had initially suspected. This was important, Meade explained, because the secretary's dispatches had never alluded to his name, only to Grant's,
and he had supposed that Grant was behind the slight. "I was glad to hear this,"
he confided in Margaret, "because it removed from my mind a prejudice I had
imbibed, on the supposition that Mr. Stanton was quoting Grant."[90]

An unintended consequence of Meade's war against Cropsey was to em-
bolden Burnside, who was having problems of his own with unruly newsmen.
Burnside's quarrel was with William Swinton, who had already crossed him
in 1863 by criticizing his lackluster performance at Fredericksburg. Swinton's
latest transgression was an article he wrote for the *New York Times* describing
Burnside's offensive on June 3 as nothing more than furious cannonading
"doomed to disappointment." Forwarding a copy of the offending article to
headquarters, the Rhode Islander on June 11 informed Meade that the reporter
had committed "a libel upon the Ninth Corps, as well as upon myself" and that
the piece referenced confidential dispatches that Swinton could have obtained
only through surreptitious means. "I beg that this man immediately receive the
justice which was so justly meted out to another libeler of the press a day or so
since," Burnside requested, referring to Cropsey, "or that I be allowed to arrest
and punish him myself." On learning of the draconian measure the 9th Corps
commander had in mind, Meade sought Grant's advice. "General Meade came
to my headquarters," Grant related of the incident, "saying that General Burnside had arrested Swinton, who at some previous time had given great offense,
and had ordered him to be shot that afternoon." The general, who already had
his suspicions about Swinton, found Burnside's proposed remedy excessively
harsh. Instead of executing the newsman, Grant expelled him from the army.[91]

Lieutenant General Ulysses S. Grant and staff at Cold Harbor. *Library of Congress*

Major General William F. "Baldy" Smith and staff at Cold Harbor. *Library of Congress*

Burnett's Tavern at Old Cold Harbor. *Library of Congress*

Hancock's soldiers preparing earthworks at Cold Harbor. *Library of Congress*

Major General Andrew A. Humphreys at the Chickahominy River. *Library of Congress*

Union soldiers crossing Long Bridge over the Chickahominy River. *Library of Congress*

Willcox Landing on the James River. *Library of Congress*

Grant, Hancock, and their aides watching the 2nd Corps cross the James River at Willcox Landing. *Library of Congress*

The pontoon bridge across the James River. *Library of Congress*

U.S. Colored Troops with the captured Confederate gun at Baylor's Farm. Leslie's Illustrated Weekly

The 18th Corps storming the Dimmock Line. *Library of Congress*

V

JUNE 8–10, 1864

Petersburg Steps to Center Stage

"Good feeling generally."

THE TRUCE WAS SLATED to expire at 8:00 P.M. on the seventh, but the soldiers of both armies were reluctant to see it end. After Colonel Hyde returned the captured Tar Heels, Penrose's New Jersey men and Colquitt's Georgians agreed to extend the reprieve. When the sun rose on June 8, they continued to lounge on top of their rifle pits and stride about brazenly upright. "About seven o'clock in the morning, some of the Confederates opposite us waved newspapers, and some of our men went out and made exchanges, shaking hands most cordially and parting with good wishes for each other's welfare," a New Jersey soldier remembered. "There were shots above and below us, but none on our front all day." North of Cold Harbor Road, Upton's troops noted with satisfaction that Clingman's skirmishers and sharpshooters held their fire and, in keeping with the newfound mood of goodwill, "exchanged papers with our friends across the way."[1]

South of the 6th Corps, similar accommodations gave Gibbon's quarter a welcome respite. Hoke's and Mahone's Confederates agreed that if the Federals would refrain from firing on them, they would return the courtesy until a general engagement was declared. "It was rather a singular sight to see the rebels and our men mixed up and conversing together, as though they were the best of friends instead of mortal enemies," a soldier in the 8th New York Heavy Artillery wrote home. Shortly before noon, he noted, the battlefield remained "as quiet as though the two armies were a hundred miles apart, instead of being only a few yards, and the rebels stand upon their breastworks and talk to us, and several exchanges of papers have taken place this morning." It was, he concluded, very much "like Sunday at home."[2]

Also in Gibbon's sector, Adjutant John Russell Winterbotham of the 155th

New York, Corcoran Legion, was delighted to hear the Confederates across from him promise, "We won't fire on you if you don't on us." Curious to get a closer look at the enemy fortifications, Winterbotham sauntered across the cleared interval between the lines. "On [their earthworks] floated their red battle flag with its hateful Cross which put me in mind of the British, while opposite on our [works] was the glorious old Star Spangled Banner," he wrote home a few days later. "They were throwing up dirt in their works and we were doing the same, while those who were not on duty with the shovels sat looking serenely at each other and seemed the best of friends instead of deadly enemies."[3]

Nearby, soldiers in the 106th Pennsylvania continued the armistice well into the morning, bathing in Boatswain Creek alongside Tar Heels from Martin's Brigade. "It seemed very odd to see these men mingling with each other, laughing and joking and very friendly, that only a short time before were watching for an opportunity and trying their best to kill each other, and would so soon be trying it again," a Pennsylvanian reflected.[4]

Word of friendly relations between the opposing lines provoked strong reprimands from Meade, who worried that the rebels would seize the opportunity to spy on Union defenses. "No communications will be had with the enemy unless specially authorized from these or superior headquarters, or except so far as may be necessary to properly receive a flag of truce coming from the enemy's lines," the army commander directed. "All other communication is strictly prohibited, whether by means of conversation, signals, or otherwise, or by interchange of newspapers or commodities. Corps commanders will see that the unauthorized intercourse with the enemy, which it is known has from time to time taken place, notwithstanding the reiterated orders upon the subject, is no longer tolerated."[5]

As lunchtime approached, one of Martin's officers instructed his men to hurry into their works and gave the Yankees across from them five minutes' notice to do the same. Soon after, the rattle of musketry broke the quiet around Boatswain Creek. The truce was over, and the Battle of Cold Harbor started up again. A man in the 2nd U.S. Sharpshooters of Birney's division summarized the situation in a letter to his mother. "Yesterday our lines met, shook hands, traded some, drank out of the same canteen, then went back to their works and went to shooting at each other again. That is what I call rough business. Friends one minute and enemies the next, but such is war."[6]

The truce of June 7 and the rosy afterglow the next morning never took root along Matedequin Creek's swampy lowlands in the battlefield's northern sector. "The enemy in my front did not respect the flag of truce," Burnside informed headquarters. "My medical director was fired upon as he advanced with a white flag, and a continual fire kept up by the enemy during the whole period covered by the flag."[7]

The 9th Corps, holding the re-fused northern end of the Union line, greeted sunrise on June 8 with apprehension. Early's and Anderson's Confederates had been insistently probing their position for the past two days, and there were no signs that the rebels intended to let up. "Please send notes to Generals Willcox, Potter, and Ledlie," Burnside directed his aide Captain Larned at 8:00 A.M., "saying that the attacks [of June 7] upon our lines may have been for purpose of reconnoitering." A stronger rebel offensive, he surmised, was likely in the making, and he issued a stern caution: "Please have everybody on the alert."[8]

Around noon, Potter, whose division was responsible for safeguarding the high ground around the White home, became convinced that a Confederate attack was imminent. "Unless I have men enough to fill my line at once I shall be driven from that hill just as certain as the enemy attack me, and the indications now are that the enemy are preparing to attack my right again," he wrote Burnside. "Some of my men have been on the skirmish line forty-eight hours without being relieved," he added, "and my whole force has been at work all night every night since they have been here, and are getting used up." To help with the impending crisis, he proposed that Ledlie's division relieve his 48th Pennsylvania and connect with his line to extend it to the right. If the position could not be secured by 3:00, Potter predicted, "We will have trouble."[9]

By five o'clock that evening, Potter began to breathe more easily. "My line extends from a short distance north of Widow Thompson's to a branch of the Matadequin (which rises near Bethesda Church and runs along the line formerly held by the Fifth Corps), where the right rests on the creek and swamp west by southwest of Bosher's," he wrote headquarters. Colonel Ebenezer W. Peirce's brigade of Ledlie's division, 530 men strong, had relieved the 48th Pennsylvania and now connected with the rest of Ledlie's troops. Potter pronounced his line "very strong" and promised to post artillery by dark. "I think I have a position that can't be turned or taken unless the other divisions give way," he announced in satisfaction, "and which I don't much think will be attacked."[10]

At 8:00 P.M. Confederates south of Cold Harbor Road opposite Hancock opened a blistering fire, "so severe, and kept up so long, as very naturally to produce the impression that the enemy was making a most desperate and determined assault on our left wing," a newsman wrote. The rebels in front of Owen's brigade shot from their rifle pits, apparently to deter the Federals from augmenting their earthworks. On the southern end of Hancock's line, Colonel

Smyth reported that Confederates had crawled on their hands and knees almost to his entrenchments. His men drove them back in a noisy episode that lasted about forty-five minutes. "Inquiry subsequently elicited that although an attack had been made," a correspondent reported, "its magnitude was slight in proportion to the amount of powder exploded and the clamor made."[11]

In some sectors the spirit of June 7's brief armistice lingered. South Carolina troops in front of the 141st Pennsylvania "were very friendly, talking and trading with our men as if they had never been enemies," Captain Joseph Atkinson observed. "At a point between our lines I found five of them and five of our men sitting together and talking in a very friendly manner, a thing positively forbidden." As the Union officer approached, a Confederate greeted him with, "Good-morning, captain!" Atkinson ordered his men back to their posts and the rebels back to theirs, but one southerner refused to leave, brandishing his gun and explaining that he had been posted there. "I concluded to let him alone and went back to my own lines," the captain wrote.[12]

In his headquarters tent near Gaines's Mill, Lee struggled to make sense of Grant's unusual quiescence. The aggressive Union commander seemed certain to resume offensive operations, but where he aimed to strike was still not clear. Hunches in Richmond's newspapers ran the gamut from a Union offensive against the railroads north of the city to the more likely possibility of a sweeping maneuver to the south, although whether the bluecoats meant to stage such an expedition from the ten-mile stretch of land between the Chickahominy and the James or from a point south of the James was anyone's guess. Feeling better after the bout of dysentery that had disabled him during the operations at the North Anna River, Lee rode on his horse, Traveler, a soft felt hat shielding his eyes from the summer sun.[13]

Little new information offering reliable keys to Grant's thinking reached Lee on June 8. The most important development was news that Sheridan had left with two cavalry divisions, heading toward the Virginia Central Railroad. Wade Hampton, whose scouts discovered Sheridan's departure early on June 8, suspected that the cavalryman intended to strike Gordonsville or Charlottesville, destroy the railroad, and unite with Hunter. Plans were laid for Hampton to lead two Confederates cavalry divisions—his own and Fitzhugh Lee's— to intercept the Federal horsemen. Remaining behind at Cold Harbor would be Rooney Lee's cavalry division. Brigadier General John R. Chambliss's brigade of three Virginia regiments was to patrol the country off the northern end of the Confederate entrenchments. The task of guarding the Chickahominy fell to Ransom's infantry brigade, a recently constituted cavalry brigade under Brigadier General Martin W. Gary, and a brigade of three North Carolina cavalry regiments, formerly under Gordon and Baker, now under Colonel Rufus Barringer.[14]

During the afternoon of June 8, Hampton concentrated his and Fitzhugh Lee's divisions at Mechanicsville in preparation for the expedition against Sheridan. On reaching Mechanicsville, the men of the 4th South Carolina—from Butler's Brigade, which had been performing onerous picket duty along the Chickahominy—expressed astonishment at "many a comfortable tent and ration-wagon and fat horse of the Quartermasters." The cavalrymen engaged in "much interested discussion and speculation that evening as to where the command was about to move, for it was understood that it was to march early the next morning, and five days' rations had been issued," a trooper recalled. Clearly a raid or expedition was in the making, perhaps to Washington or Baltimore. "But no one doubted that there would be, at all events, plenty of 'music' of a certain kind," a Charlestonian noted.[15]

The departure of Butler's cavalry from the Chickahominy left Lee uneasy, for it weakened the very sector where he expected Grant to initiate his next move. At 7:00 A.M. on June 8, Ransom reported "no indication of a considerable force in my front" near Bottom's Bridge, which seemed inconsistent with a Federal shift south. A few hours later, however, Confederate scouts on the James River's lower reaches spotted steamers towing barges loaded with pontoons chugging upstream to Bermuda Hundred and returning empty. "This may indicate future operations of Grant," Beauregard suggested, although he did not venture a guess concerning what those operations might be. The *Richmond Dispatch* surmised that "the latest intelligence from the front represents that Grant is still moving toward our right, and the impression still prevails that he is endeavoring to make his way to James River."[16]

That evening President Davis visited Bottom's Bridge and spoke with General Lee's son Custis, who expressed satisfaction with the Confederate defensive preparations and concurred with Ransom's observation that the enemy did not appear to be in force on the Chickahominy's north bank. Davis also conferred with Ransom, who confirmed that he had learned "nothing important" during the day.[17]

In his evening report Lee informed Secretary of War Seddon that the enemy "has been unusually quiet today along the whole extent of his lines, and nothing of importance has occurred." The big news, in his estimation, involved Sheridan. "Two divisions of cavalry under Genl Sheridan are reported to have crossed the Pamukey yesterday at New Castle Ferry and to have encamped last night at Dunkirk and Aylett's on the Mattapony. They were accompanied by artillery, ambulances, wagons, and beef cattle."[18]

Lee had already concentrated all the cavalry he could spare to go after Sheridan. He was also hatching a plan to keep things lively in the battlefield's northern sector, much as Burnside and his division commander Potter had feared. On the off-chance that Grant might continue contracting his northern flank, Lee wanted Anderson to remain alert for an opportunity to attack at the first sign that the 9th Corps was slipping away. On the evening of June 8, Anderson directed Pickett, who was in close contact with Willcox's 9th Corps division near Fletcher's Redoubt, to "push on at once and drive after the enemy" if the opportunity presented. Field's Division, temporarily commanded by Brigadier General John Gregg, was to follow Pickett with his "whole strength and vigor," and Kershaw was to jump in with his division "rapidly after the enemy's line shall have been broken." At eleven that night Anderson ordered fifty rounds of ammunition dispensed to each of his men.[19]

"General Beauregard reports the enemy moving upon Petersburg."

The 1st Corps's offensive, initially slated for two o'clock on the morning of June 9, was cancelled when pickets confirmed that Burnside had not budged. "Enemy still in force in front," Anderson's aide Lieutenant Colonel Sorrell noted in his journal. Captain Page of Early's staff reconnoitered Burnside's deployment along Matadequin Creek and also found the enemy firmly entrenched. The Federals had erected new fortifications along the heights at Bosher's farm, he reported, and had extended videttes past the Barker place to Gilman's Mill and perhaps beyond. Concluding that an attack would be futile, Lee decided to withdraw Early's troops from the northern end of the Confederate line, where they were no longer needed, and shift them into reserve near Gaines's Mill, where they could help counter the expected Union incursion across the Chickahominy. As Early's corps retired, Anderson's northernmost divisions under Pickett and Field moved into the position vacated by the 2nd Corps, extending north to the Dickerson family farm on Shady Grove Road.[20]

Early on the morning of June 9, Hampton's and Fitzhugh Lee's cavalry divisions rode out of Mechanicsville on their expedition to intercept Sheridan. "We pushed along all day by roads apparently almost unused," a trooper recalled, "across woods and fields occasionally." Their pace was deliberate as they moved north along Telegraph Road past Yellow Tavern and on to Ashland, which they reached about noon. From there they continued to the Virginia Central Railroad, where they turned west to Bumpass and Fredericks Hall Stations. Sheridan, Fitzhugh Lee informed General Lee that afternoon, had reached Chilesburg. "Prisoners taken from him say that he is going to assist Hunter to join Grant."[21]

Back at Cold Harbor, Rooney Lee wrote General Lee as he rode out to examine his picket line. "Everything quiet here this morning so far," the cavalry division leader assured his father. "Scouts are out north of the Chickahominy, and, as I wrote you, Chambliss moved to the left last night." Word soon arrived that Chambliss had set up headquarters on the northern end of the Confederate line, near where the road to Hanover Court House intersected the road to Haw's Shop. There were no signs of activity on Grant's part.[22]

Lee took advantage of the lull in hostilities to update President Davis on developments. Referencing his previous evening's report to Secretary of War Seddon, the general explained that he had "received no definite information as to [Sheridan's] purpose, but conjecture that his object is to cooperate with Gen Hunter, and endeavor to reach the James, breaking the railroads et cetera as he passes, and probably to descend on the south side of that river." In order to thwart Sheridan's designs, Lee had "directed Gens. Hampton and Fitz Lee with their divisions to proceed in the direction of Hanover Junction, and thence, if the information they receive justifies it, along the Central R.R., keeping the enemy on their right, and shape their course according to his."[23]

As for Grant, Lee was certain that the Union commander had some mischief in mind, although he could not predict exactly what his opponent's next ploy might be. "The pause in the operations of Genl. Grant induces me to believe that he is awaiting the effect of movements in some other quarter to make us change our position," he posited, "and renders the suggestion I make with reference to the intention and destination of Gen Sheridan more probable." Lee noted that the *Philadelphia Inquirer* reported that Major General John Pope was coming from the West to reinforce Grant and that a citizen in the Shenandoah Valley reported rumors that two or three thousand troops under Pope were arriving to join Hunter. "There may therefore be some probability in the story," he advised.[24]

Responding to Lee's letter, Davis expressed concern about Sheridan's departure. "The indications are that Grant, despairing of a direct attack, is now seeking to embarrass you by flank movements," he advised the army commander, agreeing that "if our cavalry, concentrated, could meet that of the enemy, it would have moral as well as physical effects, which are desirable."[25]

The big news, however, involved Petersburg. "General Beauregard reports the enemy moving upon Petersburg," the president informed Lee, "but our scouts give no information as to the arrival of troops from below, and if none have come I can't believe the attack to be of much force." Had a portion of the Army of the Potomac slipped away without Lee's knowledge? Or had Butler, in an uncharacteristic display of energy, launched an offensive himself from Bermuda Hundred?

Surprisingly the culprit was Butler. Grant had alerted the Boston lawyer-turned-general on June 6 that he intended to advance the Potomac army across the James River against Petersburg, and the appearance of aides Porter and Comstock at Bermuda Hundred on June 8 confirmed to Butler that the general in chief's plans were well advanced. Recognizing that his opportunity to reap glory for cutting the rebel supply line at Petersburg was about to pass, Butler decided to act immediately. Beauregard's Howlett Line across Bermuda Hundred's neck still appeared impregnable, but reports from Union scouts and rebel prisoners indicated that Petersburg itself was only lightly defended. Hoke's Division and Ransom's Brigade had joined Lee at Cold Harbor, leaving only a skeleton force under Brigadier General Henry A. Wise to protect the town. Wise's troops consisted of some 1,200 regular infantry, cavalry, artillery, and a hodge-podge of local militia made up of boys under seventeen, men between fifty and fifty-five, conscripts who had been exempted from regular service because of physical disabilities, and prisoners from the local jail.[26]

Forming an arc with one end anchored on the Appomattox River above Petersburg and the other end touching the river below town, the town's defenses drew a continuous line of fortifications connected by entrenchments. Completed in 1863 under the supervision of Captain Charles Dimmock, the defensive perimeter contained fifty-five numbered batteries extending across some ten miles of earthworks. By June 1864 much of the Dimmock Line had fallen into disrepair, with portions so eroded that they afforded Wise's ragtag force scant protection.

Butler had only limited troops to spare for a foray to Petersburg—Smith was at Cold Harbor with the 18th Corps and part of Gillmore's 10th Corps, and Gillmore was stretched thin manning the Bermuda Hundred defenses—but the expeditionary force of some 4,500 men that he cobbled together was more than adequate to do the job. Gillmore himself was to lead the infantry component, composed of five regiments under Colonel Joseph R. Hawley and two regiments of U.S. Colored Troops commanded by Brigadier General Edward W. Hinks. Accompanying them were three cavalry regiments under Brigadier General August V. Kautz.[27]

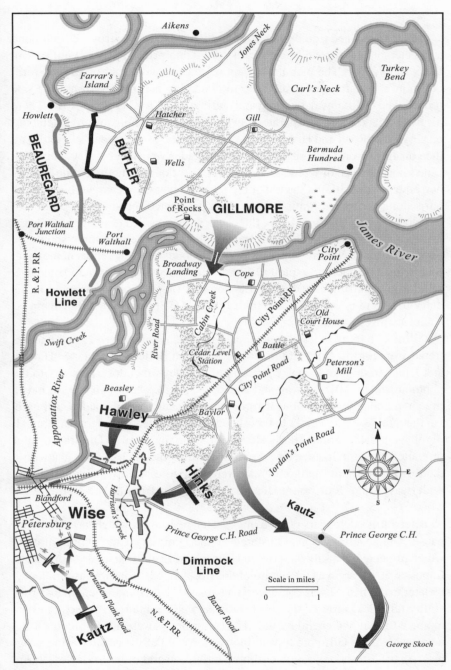

Gillmore attacks Petersburg, June 9

Butler envisioned a quick attack against Petersburg to destroy the Richmond and Petersburg Railroad bridge across the Appomattox River, a vital link in Lee's supply line. The plan underwent several revisions, but in its final form Gillmore's infantry was to advance in two columns, starting from the Cope property near Broadway Landing and cutting across to City Point Road. There his two brigades were to separate, Hawley's troops marching toward Petersburg on City Point Road and Hinks's men continuing across to Jordan's Point Road, then turning toward Petersburg. The two brigades were to strike the Dimmock Line's northern sector within supporting distance of one another while Kautz's horsemen swung around the arc of the rebel defenses and charged into Petersburg along Jerusalem Plank Road, which penetrated the southern portion of the works; riding through town, the cavalrymen were to destroy the railroad bridge and then withdraw. If all went as planned, the entire force should be back to Bermuda Hundred by nightfall, ready to man their defenses in the event Beauregard decided to exploit Gillmore's absence and launch an offensive. "Butler just starting expedition," Lieutenant Colonel Comstock noted in his diary the evening of June 8, "3000 infy under Gillmore and 1500 cav under Kautz against Petersburg."[28]

Gillmore's foray quickly degenerated into a comedy of errors that was extreme, even for the Army of the James. Although Butler had expected Hawley and Hinks to unite at Cope's by midnight, Hawley's men lost their way to the pontoon bridges at Broadway and ended up slogging "through the swamps a mile in rear of your lines," the army commander later complained to Gillmore, "in the mud reaching nearly to their knees, and fatigued with being kept up all night wandering about like sheep without a shepherd." The fiasco later prompted Butler to inquire how the troops could possibly have "got lost within their own lines." Not until 3:00 A.M. were Gillmore's units finally united and underway. Some four hours later they arrived in front of the Confederate works.[29]

Petersburg's defenders offered unexpected resistance, which gave Gillmore pause. The general was also flustered by the Dimmock Line's configuration, which projected in a salient between Hawley and Hinks that made cooperation impossible. "As soon as the nature of the works in our front was ascertained," he later explained, "I was convinced that an assault on them would in all probability fail, and I ordered the two positions to be maintained, expecting every moment to hear of General Kautz." The two generals were not communicating, however, leaving Gillmore to wait in vain for word of the cavalry arm's progress. As the afternoon passed, Gillmore retired several miles to Baylor's farm, waited a bit, and then marched back to Bermuda Hundred.[30]

While Gillmore dithered, Kautz pressed toward Jerusalem Plank Road. Headquarters, however, had underestimated the distance, and the horsemen did not reach their destination until almost noon. Opposing them was a scratch force of militia under Major Fletcher H. Archer, whose 3rd Battalion, Virginia Reserves, was composed of men, as Archer later explained, "with heads silvered o'er with the frost of advancing years, while others could barely boast of the down upon the cheek." Archer's 125 novices stood little chance against Kautz's 1,300 troopers.[31]

Over the next few hours, Kautz frittered away his advantage. The defenders stymied the Federals' opening charges and provoked an extended artillery duel. Cautiously deploying his horsemen, Kautz ventured a concerted attack that overran the threadbare Confederate position. Archer's stubborn resistance, however, had bought the defenders two precious hours. During that interval, Beauregard, alerted to Petersburg's peril, dispatched Brigadier General James Dearing's 4th North Carolina Cavalry and Captain Edward Graham's Petersburg Battery from the Howlett Line. Clattering across the Appomattox bridge, the Confederate reinforcements tore through downtown Petersburg, heading toward the ruptured works. Civilians filled the streets, but Dearing and Graham brooked no delay. "Damn the women," Graham shouted as some of Petersburg's ladies ventured into the road. "Run over them if they don't get out of the way!"[32]

In the nick of time, Graham's guns crested high ground at Reservoir Hill and opened on Kautz's approaching Federals. Then Dearing's cavalry appeared and, under the protection of Graham's artillery, drove Kautz's men back. Having heard nothing from Gillmore and concerned over the appearance of veteran Confederate reinforcements, Kautz decided to withdraw. "So ended a tragicomic succession of events that probably constituted the sorriest performance ever turned in by the Army of the James," a historian of Butler's army aptly concluded. "The litany of errors was appalling: an unconscionable lack of cooperation among the attack forces, no resolution on the part of any commander involved, a general disregard for the importance of speed and surprise, a chronic hesitancy to commit troops although ordered to do so, and a disregard of secondary objectives once the primary goal had been declared unattainable."[33]

Credit, of course, was also due to Petersburg's defenders. The town's old men and young boys had fought valiantly, fending off Kautz's veterans until reinforcements could arrive. "The salvation of the city of Petersburg is undoubtedly due in the first place to the brave militia of the city," observed Brigadier General Raleigh E. Colston, who had played a part in the town's deliverance, "for, had they retreated five or ten minutes sooner, the artillery, which was first to check the enemy's advance, instead of meeting them at the heights, on the south side of the city, would have been intercepted before they could cross the bridge, and the city would probably have remained in the enemy's hands."[34]

For Lee, June 9 was a day of alarms over Gillmore and Kautz's foray against Petersburg, punctuated by Beauregard's insistent demands to President Davis's military advisor, General Braxton Bragg, that the units he had grudgingly dispatched to the Army of Northern Virginia in its time of need—Hoke's Division and Ransom's Brigade—be returned to him immediately. "Without the troops sent to General Lee I will have to elect between abandoning lines on Bermuda Neck and those of Petersburg," Beauregard warned as the action heated during the morning. At 1:00 P.M., on learning that Kautz's troopers were advancing into town, the Louisianan asserted that he could not "reinforce [Petersburg's] line without abandoning lines on Bermuda Hundred Neck and probably be cut off from Drewry's Bluff and Richmond." Two hours later he advised that "delay in sending reinforcements will be fatal to [Petersburg] and to Richmond for its supplies."[35]

Lee responded: "No troops have left Genl Grant's army to my knowledge, and none could have crossed James River without being discovered. I think it very improbable that he would weaken himself under existing circumstances." Noting that only a "small force" threatened Petersburg, he stressed the impracticality of forwarding the reinforcements Beauregard demanded. Hoke's soldiers, after all, were holding the center of the Confederate line at Cold Harbor, and Ransom was on the Chickahominy's southern bank protecting batteries. "I know no necessity for the removal of these troops," Lee observed, "but if directed will send them."[36]

Casting about for reinforcements, Beauregard also asked that Brigadier General Archibald Gracie's brigade at Chaffin's Bluff be dispatched to him. Eight miles downriver from Richmond and across the James from Drewry's Bluff, Chaffin's Bluff was important not only as a critical cog in the capital's defenses but also as the site of a pontoon bridge across the river on the route connecting Petersburg and the Army of Northern Virginia. Lee objected to Gracie's departure but in response to Bragg's directions ordered Ransom to return to Beauregard, retracing the route through Chaffin's Bluff that he had taken a few days earlier. "If not necessary please countermand order," Lee implored Bragg.[37]

President Davis reconsidered and at 4:00 P.M. notified Beauregard that it was impossible to send aid "in time to save city by ordering troops to you from [other] commands. Even if they must be replaced, you should draw from Major General Johnson [whose division was holding the Howlett Line] the requisite assistance, concealing the movement so that their place may be supplied before their absence is discovered." In other words Hoke and Ransom would remain with Lee, and Beauregard would simply have to do his best with the troops already at hand.[38]

That night authorities in Richmond informed Lee that the Federals had relinquished their fleeting hold on Petersburg. But even this news failed to calm Beauregard. "The result of this reconnaissance will soon invite another attack," he predicted and insisted that "Gracie's brigade should be sent, as first ordered." Bragg, however, was reluctant to weaken Lee and informed the Virginian that "the order for Gracie to go over has been revoked, but he [is] to keep in readiness to move at moment's warning."[39]

After the immediate alarms had quieted, Beauregard sent Bragg his "views hastily thrown on paper." Grant, he wrote, "clearly seeks to move around Lee's forces, by an advance upon his left [southern] flank, in the direction of the James River, with a view to operate between that river and the Chickahominy, and in case of meeting with no adequate resistance to plant himself on both sides of the former, throwing across it a pontoon bridge, as close to Chaffin's Bluff as circumstances may permit, and failing in this scheme, he may continue his rotary motion around Richmond, and attack by concentrating the whole of his army on the south side of the James River, using the fortified position at Bermuda Hundred Neck as a base for his operations." To plug the gap between the Howlett Line and Petersburg, Beauregard renewed his request for the return of Hoke's Division.[40]

Major General Daniel H. Hill, serving as a volunteer aide-de-camp, commiserated with Beauregard. The only way that Beauregard could bring the authorities to their senses, Hill urged, was to stress that he lacked sufficient troops to guard both Bermuda Hundred and Petersburg and thus was withdrawing his entire force to the Cockade City. "It is arrant nonsense for Lee to say that Grant can't make a night march without his knowing it," Hill observed. "Has not Grant slipped around him four times already? Did not Burnside retire from Fredericksburg, and Hooker from the Wilderness, without his knowing it?" Based on this history, he concluded that Grant could easily slip 20,000 troops across the James undetected. "What then is to become of Petersburg?" he asked. "Its loss surely involves that of Richmond—perhaps of the Confederacy." Beauregard responded that while he concurred with Hill's views, he had already communicated them to the government and considered it "useless again to do so, as it would produce no good results." He had resigned himself to doing his best to hold both the Petersburg and Howlett defenses with the scant force available to him.[41]

Lee did not share Beauregard and Hill's worry that Grant might steal past the Army of Northern Virginia and attack Petersburg. He remained uncertain, however, about precisely what Grant meant to do, and his daily reports to Richmond reflected that uncertainty. "The enemy have been quiet today—apparently engaged in strengthening his entrenchments," Lee wrote on the evening of June 9. To buttress Confederate defenses along the Chickahominy's southern bank, he directed elements from Heth's Division, including the 52nd and 55th North Carolina, to join Ransom at Bottom's Bridge.[42]

"Was ever such strange warfare known before?"

For the soldiers of both armies entrenched at Cold Harbor, June 9 and 10 were two more interminable days of boredom and death. "There is nothing of interest to report from my front this morning," Wright wrote headquarters at 9:00 A.M., an observation seconded by Smith. Burnside sensed a "slight increase in the picket firing" on Potter's segment of line, "owing to the enemy's desire to trouble his working parties," but all remained still along the rest of the 9th Corps's entrenchments. Chapman, whose cavalry patrolled the Chickahominy, had pickets as far downriver as Jones's Bridge, where they saw no signs of Confederates. Late in the day Hancock's forward observers reported a Confederate column marching toward the Chickahominy, but the rebels did not venture to attack.[43]

"We are still lying idle," Warren's staffer Major Roebling wrote to his wife, Emily. "In a few days more the feeling for a move will rise again. We ought to move in any case," he added, "because we are in the dustiest place in America, right at a crossroads where the sand is a foot deep and all the army trains have to pass. Every morning we have to be shoveled out." An officer in the 1st Vermont Heavy Artillery echoed Roebling's sentiment. "How much longer we are to lie here front to front with the enemy is uncertain," he wrote home. "I think Grant is sick of charging the rifle pits."[44]

Circumstances that the generals considered uneventful were viewed very differently by their soldiers, who endured a numbing existence in which death could strike any moment. "We cannot show our heads for an instant without receiving rebel bullets; and we keep the enemy down also, by shooting through holes made under logs laid along on top of the parapet," a New Hampshire man wrote of conditions along the 18th Corps's front. "Troops can move from front to rear, or return, only at night. The covert way is now a deep trench covered with logs and earth for protection while going back and forth. Our trench is about five feet deep and more than that in width. The main earth-work is about twelve feet high, and ten or twelve feet thick. At night the men sleep on their arms, practically in line of battle, and with their clothing all on—ready at a moment's call to spring up and fire."[45]

Another northerner reported that "while behind breastworks, every man has his harness on; and half stand in readiness at a time, while the others lie down in their places like big dogs, wet or dry, with rifle at hand, and try to sleep. How do you suppose our clothes look, after lying in rifle pits, digging, or crawling on our belly, or lying flat on the plowed ground, during thunder showers and sunshine?" he wrote home. "Not very clean—no chance to wash a garment since Bristow Station on the 1st of May. L–i–c–e is no name for the gray-backed vermin that flourish on our wasting bodies; might as well call them man-eaters."[46]

A soldier from Maine expressed a similar sentiment. "We had thought the fire to which we were subjected while lying in the trenches after the battle of Spotsylvania, sufficiently harassing, but it was scarcely to be compared in degree of annoyance to that to which we were now exposed," he recalled. "There was little or no cessation in the work of the sharpshooters during all the time we continued in the lines at Cold Harbor. Men who had passed unharmed through the Wilderness and Spotsylvania were now stricken down in the trenches by the bullet of a concealed marksman."[47]

A rebel sharpshooter on Birney's front became so annoying that a captain and half a dozen men volunteered to catch him. Hiding in underbrush, they detected a shot fired from the fork of a tree. "The captain and his men rushed to the tree, when on looking up, they saw an old gray-haired civilian, of the Confederate school, seated on a board which had been ingeniously placed at the forks of the elm, so that in his murderous work he had not been perceived by the pickets," a Federal reported. "His wife came out from the house and begged that her husband might be permitted to come down in safety. The only response of the captain to this entreaty was a peremptory order to his men to fire. They did so, and the body of the old man, perforated by balls, shot through the air to the earth."[48]

Men of both armies relied on ingenuity to survive. Enterprising artillerists fired at one another from howitzers mounted on skids, dropping projectiles behind opposing earthworks. Private John R. Zimmerman of the 17th Virginia described how this was done. "These mortars are simply 12 pound field pieces with the trail of the gun sunk in the ground and so giving the gun an elevation of about 45 degrees, the upper part of the gun resting on a stout cross piece or bar of timber on two stout forked and so used as mortars." Major George Washington Whitman of the 51st New York devised a new way to construct earthworks. "I got a lot of empty cracker boxes and stationed the men about ten feet apart, gave each man a box, and made him crawl out on the line, lay down behind the box, fill it with earth, and then I took each one another box so that in a very few minutes the men had first rate protection and could work without much danger."[49]

The 15th New Jersey's chaplain, Alanson A. Haines, penned a vivid description of those last days at Cold Harbor. "The space of ground occupied by the works at Cold Harbor was becoming exceedingly offensive, and there was fear of its breeding infection if the stay was continued much longer," he wrote. "Shallow graves received the dead within our lines, who were at last all covered, though by scores they lay in full sight for days, bloated and blackened. Dead horses, swelled to bursting, were left where they had been shot down, objects of aversion to sight and smell." Men huddled behind mounds of dirt, baking under the intense summer sun by day and shivering through the cool of the night. Until the army pulled out on the evening of June 12, "we were still in the front line, expending powder and lead," the chaplain recollected.[50]

"It is fight! fight! here day in day out, the booming of cannon and rattle of musketry ringing in our ears," Joseph H. Pierce of the 36th Massachusetts wrote a friend. "Julie, this is terrible business," he explained. "Thousands of men seeking every means in their power to destroy one another. Sometimes I think that God should put a stop to it. But here we go into it just as cooly and with as much calculation as a man would go with any kind of business."[51]

Even Lee's Confederates felt the strain. "I do want Grant to make his best efforts on Richmond and then if he fails I want him to retire and let our army have some rest," a Georgian wrote his mother. "I think he is certainly one of the most inhuman wretches now living. He is willing to make any sacrifice in blood that will gain him laurels. He would willingly sacrifice one half his army if by doing so he would be enabled to capture Richmond. I think that he will make a grander failure than McClellan."[52]

A *New York Times* reporter concluded that the extended sojourn at Cold Harbor had spawned unexpected camaraderie among opposing soldiers crouching behind mounds of earth. The men of both armies were "utterly weary of loading and firing," he noted, particularly since nothing seemed to be accomplished by it. Shooting had slackened, officers had become lax, and "a tacit and magnetic spell influences with equal power our men and their mortal enemies."

Adventuresome spirits would peer over the works and call out, "How are you Johnny?" "How are you Yank." Someone would shout, "Won't you shoot?" And the reply would come back, "No." "Well, we won't," a voice would call in response, and soon the parapets were swarming with men.

"Out jump the fellows from the rifle pits," the newsman reported, "and putting down their guns, stretched their cramped forms upon the grass. Sharp-shooters covertly slide down from their perches and loll around in utter abandon. Trade is quickly opened, and all sorts of commodities are exchanged. The men have keen pleasure in their singular armistice, bantering each other sharply, and several overstepping the half-way line which separates their respective fortifications."

Suddenly someone would cry out: "Run back, Johnnys," or "Run Back, Yanks, we're going to shoot." And the hostilities would begin again. "It is always understood, however," noted the reporter, "that the first shot shall be aimed high and the veriest dawdler gets back to shelter safely. While this fraternal scene is being enacted on one part of the line, the battle rages hotly on other portions of the extended front which measures by miles."

Mused the newsman: "Was ever such strange warfare known before?"[53]

Meade had devoted June 8 to inspecting Burnside's lines as well as Wilson's cavalry, which was quartered east of Old Church at Marlbourne, the plantation owned by arch-secessionist Edmund Ruffin. The army commander devoted June 9 to examining the center and left of his entrenched positions. His first stop was Hancock's headquarters, located well back from the front in response to the shelling that had killed the 2nd Corps's provost officer a few days earlier. "There was no serious amount of military talk between the two commanders," Lieutenant Colonel Lyman noted, who seemed chiefly occupied in "rallying each other about a sword which was to be raffled for in Philadelphia, and for which they were the chief candidates." Hancock finally agreed to relinquish his claim to the sword if Meade would have his cook prepare a batch of his coveted fresh bread.[54]

After bantering with Hancock, Meade and his staff rode to the Union line's southern terminus. Birney's right rested on Barker's Mill Pond, and from there the line jogged southeast to a point in front of Dispatch Station. "Here was the classic ground of the Chickahominy Swamps, so destructive to the health of McClellan's army," Lyman observed. "From near the Mill Pond I could look across the heavy growth of trees that marked the course of the stream and see the Dudley house, a mile to the west of which was the Trent house where McClellan had his headquarters. Not far from the Mill Pond the land becomes very flat; indeed, Sumner's old headquarters, now occupied by Griffin, were in a house situated in a dry bog."

Continuing toward Dispatch Station, Meade's party trudged past St. James's Church—Lyman thought the building resembled "a second-rate country school house"—and struck the railroad. High ground near the station looked south across an open bog, past the railroad bridge, and along the tracks on the southern side of the river. Knots of rebel infantry filled distant clearings on the rail line. Lyman had hoped to see the Confederate railroad monitor, but the mounted artillery piece had been withdrawn.[55]

Near sundown rebel batteries on Turkey Ridge opened on Hancock's work parties, Union artillery responded, and the sector was treated to a "lively cannonade and skirmish fire," a correspondent to the *Richmond Sentinel* reported. "The hostile lines of work at this point approach within 125 yards of each other and the skirmishing is almost incessant," he noted, "each side assisting the skirmishers with a shell as opportunity offers." A New Englander in Burnside's corps remarked that night attacks had become routine. "There has been a change in programme, our fighting now is mostly done at night," he wrote his wife, Cynthia. "The battle commences about dusk and lasts the greater part of the night; the battle is going on now while I write with desperation. Perhaps in a few moments I'll have to pack up and move. We have just had one of our men struck by a shell within three feet of where I stood. The Johnny's have got a good range of us and mean to give us fits."[56]

An aide at Meade's headquarters summed up the prevailing mood in Union camps. "Nothing very exciting today," he wrote in his diary. "One would not think two hostile armies facing each other were in existence to be at the different headquarters these lovely evenings and hear bands playing national airs and sentimental pieces for the amusement of officers and men. Nevertheless it is so, and tomorrow morning we may hear the clash of arms instead of the sweet music we have been favored with of late."[57]

From his tent at Confederate 1st Corps headquarters, engineer Charles Minor Blackford enjoyed the sound of singing from the nearby McRae house. A local lady warbled "all the Scottish airs and many songs from Byron and Moore," he wrote home to his wife. "Mother would enjoy her singing greatly. I had been eating raw onions and thought my breath too strong to join the party, but the flavor of the onions made the music sound sweeter as it was wafted over the soft evening breeze."[58]

Lieutenant Colonel Alexander, commanding the 1st Corps artillery, pondered the apparent absence of activity behind the Union earthworks. "We are rather at a loss to know what Grant means by lying so quiet," he wrote his wife, "and I wish he would do something for I am very tired of stooping and crawling thro the trenches every day in the hot sun, with Minnie balls shaving the parapet above, and soldiers crowding the ground beneath."[59]

The big news that reached the armies entrenched in the sandy soil around Cold Harbor involved the National Union Party's convention in Baltimore. On June 8 Lincoln was nominated to run for a second term. The next day the president wrote a letter thanking the delegates with his accustomed humility. "I have not permitted myself, gentlemen, to conclude that I am the best man in the country; but I am reminded, in this connection, of a story of an old Dutch farmer, who remarked to a companion once that 'it was not best to swap horses when crossing streams.'"[60]

The Army of the Potomac's troops in large measure viewed Lincoln's nomination as guaranteeing that the North would pursue the war to a successful conclusion. "I want this war ended before my time is out," a soldier from Massachusetts wrote home. "I see by the papers that they have nominated Lincoln again. I am glad of it and hope he will have a chance to finish up the job he has begun."[61]

That evening Butler congratulated Secretary of War Stanton on Lincoln's renomination. "I trust it will give quiet to the country and strength to the cause," he assured the war secretary.[62]

On the morning of June 10—"fair and warm, most beautiful weather," a soldier recorded—Lee informed War Secretary Seddon that he was still "unable to determine" Sheridan's destination. He had initially thought that the Union cavalrymen planned "to cooperate with the forces under General Hunter in the Valley, and there is nothing as yet in their movements inconsistent with that idea." Lee also surmised that Sheridan "may intend to strike for the James River above Richmond, and cross to the south side to destroy the Danville road." Stressing the importance of "being on our guard against such an attempt," he suggested that "parties should be held in readiness to burn the bridges over the river upon [Sheridan's] approach." Lee promised to keep Seddon advised "as far as I can of the enemy's movements, and should he turn toward the river our cavalry under General Hampton will endeavor to protect the bridges, and if unable to do so, will aid the parties charged with burning them." In closing, he reminded Seddon that "no effort should be spared to provide against such interruption of our transportation as the enemy's superiority in cavalry many enable him to effect."[63]

In the meantime Lee urged Rooney Lee's meager cavalry force to continue probing Grant's lines. White House Landing, the Potomac army's supply depot

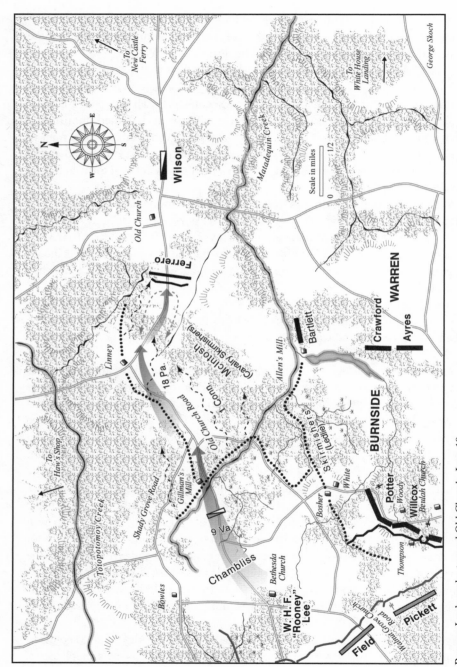

Rooney Lee's probe toward Old Church, June 10

on the Pamunkey, was shielded from Confederate view by Ferrero's division of U.S. Colored Troops, which occupied entrenchments at Old Church on the road to the landing. Pickets from McIntosh's cavalry brigade stretched west from Ferrero's bastion to Allen's Mill, on the right end of Burnside's fortified line. Colonel George O. Marcy's 1st Connecticut Cavalry comprised the left of McIntosh's pickets, next to Burnside, and Colonel William P. Brinton's 18th Pennsylvania Calvary occupied the sector from Marcy's right to the Linney family home, near where Shady Grove Road and Bethesda Church Road merged to form Old Church Road. Much of the picket line, a Pennsylvanian recorded, wound through pine woods.[64]

Chambliss, whose Confederate cavalry brigade was stationed in the battle-field's northern sector, endeavored to "force the enemy's line of pickets, which were so posted that our scouts couldn't enter to find out what force occupied Old Church and its vicinity." Shortly after noon, Colonel Richard L. T. Beale directed two companies of his 9th Virginia Cavalry to attack the Federal pickets. Two more companies were to sweep alongside to cover the adjoining roadways, while three squadrons remained in reserve in case things went awry. Beale's horsemen thrashed through a stand of woods toward Colonel Brinton's pickets on Old Church Road but were brought up short by "strands of barbed wire, the first we had seen in military use, which ran into the woods with only a narrow space left between two small pine trees sufficient to admit one horse at a time," a Confederate later wrote. Plunging through the opening, Beale's troopers surprised the Pennsylvanians just as they were finishing lunch near the Linney place. "While men and horses were eating a bite and everything seemed perfectly safe, a dash was made by the enemy's cavalry," was how the Pennsylvanian W. A Rogers recollected the attack. "Like magic they seemed to come from all sides with their infernal yell. Haversacks and nose-bags flew in all directions as the rebs came charging into us."[65]

Lieutenant Henry A. Blough, commanding a company of Pennsylvanians, sat propped against a tree when the Virginians appeared. The lieutenant's horse, Mouse, his nose-bag filled with oats, bolted, and Blough ran after him. "It was laughable to see Blough frantically trying to catch that horse, and the Johnnies trying to catch him too," an observer recounted. Realizing his peril, Blough crawled into a thicket. Captain Joseph Backus of the 1st Connecticut tried to rally his men but was killed in the roadway, and fighting degenerated into face-to-face struggles as the Union pickets retired toward the protection of Ferrero's earthworks at Old Church. An officer in the 9th Virginia Cavalry won his countrymen's praise by swinging his saber down on a Federal's head, "splitting his skull in twain."[66]

"In our run [along] the road and through the thick, hot dust, Yanks and Johnnies got so promiscuously mixed up that many came inside the breastworks and were captured," a Federal recounted. "One big fellow galloped alongside the writer and asked, 'What side you belong?' My answer, 'your side,' seemed to satisfy him." Shot through the wrist, the Confederate "was unable to check his spirited steed, and so dashed on and into the breastworks and was made a prisoner," a southerner reported.[67]

The Confederate attack faltered when the rest of McIntosh's brigade and two of Ferrero's regiments jumped into the fray. Unable to dislodge the Federals, Beale's horsemen retreated west along Old Church Road. The Union men followed in hot pursuit, several of them attempting to cut off the rebels by angling in on side roads. "We were reinforced by our brigade, and immediately started back on the gallop, putting the Johnnies to flight and again occupying the pines, from which Lieut. Blough came forth," Rogers of the 18th Pennsylvania recalled. "From this time on," he noted, "bridles remained on horses' heads instead of nose-bags."[68]

Passing the Linney yard, a Confederate officer spied Captain Backus's body stripped of clothing. "I glanced at his nearly nude body with a sense of shame for that small part of our men whose aim in battle seemed to be rather for the pockets of the enemy's dead than the armed persons of the living, and whose bravery was less noticeable than their brutality," he wrote years later.[69]

Ferrero's African American troops won accolades. At the beginning of the campaign, there had been "great prejudice against the Negroes as soldiers," Colonel Zenas R. Bliss of the 9th Corps noted, "and in the regular army it was stronger than anywhere else." Although headquarters attempted to keep Ferrero's soldiers out of combat, the black troops had earned grudging admiration by repelling Rosser's Confederate cavalry at Spotsylvania Court House. Their performance on June 10 enhanced their standing. A man in the 18th Pennsylvania wrote that the rebels "were stopped by the negroes in the breastworks and then were driven back by our cavalry." Ferrero's troops had "fortified themselves with strong and beautifully constructed earthworks," a New York cavalryman agreed, adding, "They are fine appearing soldiers."[70]

At 2:30 P.M. Wilson reported that the Confederate foray had been repulsed and that "the line at present is again reestablished as it has been." Chambliss's aggressive display, however, was troubling. Were the Confederates planning to attack the Union supply depot at White House? Anxious to get answers, headquarters directed Wilson to "make a reconnaissance in force early tomorrow morning and ascertain what force of the enemy is in your front.[71]

While McIntosh and Chambliss waged their heated skirmish in the battlefield's northern sector, the Chickahominy front remained relatively peaceful. Other than routine rebel troop movements and a work party digging entrench- ments near Bottom's Bridge, Captain Benjamin F. Fisher, a Union signal offi- cer, noted no enemy activity south of the river. Deserters from Ransom's Bri- gade confirmed that the unit's five North Carolina regiments formed the extreme right of the Confederate infantry line below the Chickahominy, with Hoke's infantry on their left and Butler's cavalry in support. They had erected "slight works" three-quarters of a mile south of the river, a captive explained, "but have taken no position that they expect to hold." A prisoner reported ru- mors that Major General Butler was pressing toward Petersburg and that Ran- som's troops expected to be dispatched to help defend the town. "The feeling of the troops in their brigade is not very buoyant," he admitted, "and it is gen- erally thought the force for the protection of Richmond is altogether too small."[72]

That evening Lee wrote Seddon that the Army of the Potomac remained stationary, although skirmishing had been "somewhat more active and system- atic than during the last two days." Beauregard, on the other hand, remained convinced that Butler intended to renew his offensive against Petersburg. Shortly after ten o'clock that night, he reported that a "considerable column of the enemy's infantry has crossed this evening to the south side of the Appo- mattox, indicating another attack on Petersburg." Unless he received immedi- ate reinforcements, Beauregard warned Bragg, "we shall lose that city or our lines in front of Bermuda Landing." Instructions went out to Gracie at Drew- ry's Bluff to march "by the shortest and quickest route" to the Howlett Line.[73]

"Everything will be sent forward as soon as you direct."

During the week following the big attack at Cold Harbor, while the Army of the Potomac and the Army of Northern Virginia sparred like two boxers searching for openings, Grant pushed forward with his plans to shift his army south. He was still uncertain of the precise route—as late as June 12 Assistant War Secretary Dana would write that the general was considering crossing the James either at Bermuda Hundred if unopposed by Lee or from a point oppo- site Fort Powhatan if the rebels blocked the way to Bermuda Hundred—but uncertainty over details did not prevent him from laying the logistical ground- work for the move. Depending on which site his aides Comstock and Porter recommended, he would need boats aplenty and most likely pontoons, string- ers, and planking for a floating bridge. Assistance from the navy was critical as gunboats were necessary to keep enemy ships from disrupting the crossing. Union engineers would have to prepare fallback positions for use during the army's withdrawal in case the Confederates pursued, and decisions had to be made about whether to repair or destroy the Richmond and York River Railroad, whose tracks ran east from Richmond, crossed the Chickahominy, and passed through White House Landing. Traversing the countryside where the armies would be marching, the rail line could move supplies to Grant's soldiers or, depending on circumstances, might be used by Lee in support of a pursuit. To provide a seamless transition of provisions, arms, and medical services to the Potomac army's marching columns as they neared Petersburg, the supply base at White House Landing would have to be closed, its hospital wards and prisoners shipped north, and a new base established on the James, most likely at City Point. Last but not least, Grant had to ensure that the armies and services implicated in the massive movement coordinated seamlessly.[74]

To assist in the operation, Halleck dispatched Brigadier General John G. Barnard to serve as chief engineer of the armies in the field. A rough-looking character—Lyman described him as a "railroad looking man with a long beard, whose clothes would be improved by a brush"—Barnard had become intimately acquainted with the region two years earlier as part of McClellan's engineering staff. "I know of no one who has a more thorough knowledge of all the passes of the Chickahominy and of the approaches to Richmond," Halleck urged. Secretary of War Stanton, however, was uncomfortable with the appointment. "I hope General Grant will not put too much confidence in Barnard," he warned Dana. "I have no confidence in his judgment on practical military affairs and believe that he is in large degree responsible for McClellan's blunders." The army would remain safe, Stanton wrote, so long as Grant made his own decisions, "but trust in Barnard is dangerous."[75]

One of Barnard's first assignments was to find ways to reduce the risk of attack as the army withdrew from Cold Harbor. Disengaging frontline troops from earthworks that pressed closely against the enemy was always a perilous undertaking. Thus far in the campaign—after the Battles of the Wilderness, Spotsylvania Court House, and the North Anna River—the Army of the Potomac had managed to slip away from Lee undetected. The challenge was whether the Union juggernaut could repeat that difficult stunt.

Grant's evolving plan required his troops to withdraw under cover of darkness while a skeleton force remained behind to create the illusion that the army was still entrenched. "To prepare for the withdrawal of the army from its present position, which will take place in a few days, a direct line from the present right to left should be marked out and partially fortified," Grant instructed, suggesting that the fallback position could be manned by the two 5th Corps divisions near the Leary place and by elements from other corps as they evacuated the front line. On June 8 Barnard surveyed an interior line a short distance behind the existing works to serve as a buffer when the army moved out. The next day the Potomac army's acting chief engineer, Major Nathaniel Michler, put the finishing touches on plans for a new set of earthworks that dropped south from Allen's Mill Pond, passed in front of Old Cold Harbor, and anchored on the northern end of Elder Swamp above Barker's Mill. The purpose of the fortifications, Michler later wrote, was "to enable the troops to retire from the immediate front of the enemy without being molested, and to cover the movement off toward the east and along the east bank of the Chickahominy."

On the morning of June 10, Wright and Hancock detailed troops to dig the reserve line of earthworks. Hancock's soldiers prepared the segment running from Elder Swamp to Old Cold Harbor, and Wright's men finished the portion north to Allen's Mill Pond. They completed the project the next morning, though only after "plenty of bickering between Majors Duane and Michler on one side and Generals Hancock and Wright on the other; the latter insisting that those engineers had laid out their entrenchments in a most exposed manner, while the former maintained that the line was quite a gem of fortification."[76]

Grant also considered how best to deal with the Richmond and York River Railroad. During the fighting at Cold Harbor, Union engineers had worked to repair the rail line. Meade, it appears, thought that the railroad might be useful as the campaign progressed and sent a work party to repair the tracks without consulting Grant, who recalled the laborers when he learned of these actions. "He has never intended to use that road," Dana informed Stanton on learning of the general's displeasure, "and does not wish to leave its iron to be employed by the enemy in restoring his own broken communications." On June 7 Grant dispatched an aide, Captain Ely Parker, to make sure that workers removed the rails and loaded them on steamers at White House Landing for transport north. "I shall not want to use the railroad at all for supplying the army," he informed Brigadier General Abercrombie, who was managing affairs at White House, "but will destroy it so that the enemy cannot use the iron for the purpose of relaying other roads." Another aide, Brigadier General Rawlins, oversaw the removal, starting with the Chickahominy railroad bridge and proceeding by stages to the landing. By June 12 Abercrombie was able to report that the railroad had been destroyed and its iron and rolling stock sent to Washington as ordered.[77]

An important feature of the movement to the James involved supplying the army as it marched south. Grant had predicated his campaign against Lee on "flying depots" established along Virginia's tidal rivers. Ships would load with provisions in Alexandria and Washington, traverse the Potomac River and Chesapeake Bay to the temporary depot nearest the army, and unload their cargo for wagons to deliver to the army. During the Wilderness and Spotsylvania operations, supplies had reached the army through Belle Plain, on Potomac Creek; the army's move to the North Anna prompted a southward shift of the depot to Port Royal, on the Rappahannock; and the move to the Cold Harbor region was responsible for the current depot at White House Landing, on the Pamunkey. When the army continued to the James, Grant wanted a new depot at City Point, where the James and Appomattox Rivers merge. The place was already firmly in Butler's hands and ideally situated to support a strike against either Petersburg or Richmond.

The timing involved in changing supply bases was critical. White House Landing could not be closed until the Army of the Potomac had left, and City Point had to be functional by the time the army arrived a few days later. The shift would have to occur in phases. Under Abercrombie's direction, White House had become a bustling little city. Wharves jutted into the Pamunkey, where stevedores unloaded provisions, fodder, ammunition, and other necessities from the Alexandria warehouses. New troops arrived there as well and camped until receiving their assignments to the front. Tents crowding around the ruins of the old Custis plantation home—the structure had burned during the 1862 campaign—served as the army's main hospital, and a steady stream of maimed soldiers flowed back from there to Alexandria and Washington. More than 13,000 troops passed through the hospital at White House from June 1 until the army left for Petersburg. Rebel prisoners were also held at the landing, awaiting transport to prisons in the North.[78]

Concerned about the security of the invalids and supplies remaining behind when the army moved south, Grant requested his inspector general, Colonel Edward Schriver, to investigate conditions at White House Landing. Schriver found the depot's "permanent garrison" of nearly 1,400 officers and men "well disposed for the defense of the post." Five redoubts connected by rifle trenches and a small interior line for a reserve force persuaded him that "any attempt the enemy might make on the depot might be easily resisted with the present arrangement." Supplies were abundant, officers were attentive to their duties, and "order is everywhere observed." In sum, White House Landing would be secure when the army moved south, permitting the continued evacuation of wounded men and prisoners.[79]

To expedite this process, the quartermaster at White House Landing, Captain Perley P. Pitkin, requested five steamers and five tugs in addition to the boats he already had. "We also have 2,500 wounded yet to be removed," he added in his missive to Washington. "Please send me the necessary transportation, if possible." Pitkin also advised that he was forwarding a thousand captives by steamer to the prison at Port Lookout.[80]

The 18th Corps's journey by river to Bermuda Hundred presented another thorny set of problems. First was the question of where the troops should disembark. Brigadier General Ingalls, the Potomac army's quartermaster, recommended sending Smith's men back to Bermuda Hundred along the same water route they had used to join the army. Meade thought that Smith's troops should march to Coles Ferry on the Chickahominy and board ships there, a water route shorter than that from White House Landing that would "cause the operation to be greatly hastened." Grant, however, decided that the long march from Cold Harbor to Coles Landing, combined with the "uncertainty of being able to embark so large a number of men there," favored Smith's departing from White House Landing as Ingalls suggested.[81]

Whatever Smith's point of embarkation might be, transports were needed. The ships that had brought his troops to White House ten days earlier had already left, transporting property, wounded men, and prisoners to Washington. Ingalls suggested that Meade instruct the quartermaster at Fortress Monroe— the large Union fortification and supply depot at Port Comfort, where the York and James Rivers join—to assemble suitable transports, arrange for their delivery, and "be at the time and place designated, in person, to superintend the transportation."[82]

On June 9 Grant advised Meade that the movement to the James would "take place in a few days." He also directed that any newly arrived troops still at White House be sent to City Point and that any troop ships that might arrive in the future be sent on to Bermuda Hundred without disembarking. Wounded men were forwarded north "steadily and rapidly," according to the Medical Director's Office, and hospital tents were dismantled and packed for transport as soon as their occupants had left.[83]

The logistics of crossing the Army of the Potomac over the Chickahominy and James Rivers promised to be complex. Lieutenant Colonel Ira Spaulding's 50th New York Engineers carried enough pontoons and materials to construct whatever bridges might be needed. The regiment's 1st Battalion, under Major Wesley Brainerd and assigned to the 2nd Corps, had fourteen pontoons; Major Edmund O. Beers's 2nd Battalion, attached to the 6th Corps, had thirteen pontoons; Major George W. Ford's 3rd Battalion, with the 5th Corps, had thirteen pontoons; and Spaulding's Reserve Battalion had two pontoon bridges under Captains William Folwell and Martin Van Brocklin, each with twelve canvass boats. Reporting to Major James C. Duane, the Potomac army's chief engineer, Spaulding thus far in the campaign had supervised the construction of thirty-eight pontoon bridges across the Rapidan, the North Anna, the Pamunkey, and a host of lesser streams, spanning an aggregate of 6,458 feet. By Spaulding's assessment the Chickahominy appeared no more problematical than its predecessors.[84]

The James, however, presented a daunting obstacle. Grant was counting on Comstock and Porter to identify the ideal location for a pontoon bridge, but precisely how wide the river would be was unknown. Assembling a pontoon bridge might well require more material than was readily at hand. One solution was to dismantle the pontoon bridges across the Chickahominy when the troops moved on and reassemble them at the James. That process, however, risked delay, and the pontoons might still be insufficient, depending on the site the aides recommended. On June 4 Meade had queried Brigadier General Henry W. Benham, heading the Potomac army's Volunteer Engineer Brigade at Fortress Monroe, for an accounting of bridge material available there. Benham replied that he had sent almost 1,500 feet of pontoon bridging to Bermuda Hundred, that he was awaiting 460 more feet from the Port Royal and White House sites, and that he had on hand at Fortress Monroe fifteen canvas pontoon boats. Another 1,200 feet of bridging had been forwarded from New York via Washington, he added, and was on its way to Bermuda Hundred by order of Major General Halleck. "There is no more bridging of any consequence now at the depot, and I expect no more at present," he advised.[85]

Surprised by Benham's response, Meade made it clear that the engineer was to "collect at Fortress Monroe all the bridging material at your command, including that just sent to Washington from New York, and that you hold the same by readiness to be moved at very short notice." In the event that he received contrary orders from a superior authority—presumably Grant or Halleck—he was to promptly notify Meade.[86]

For reasons that are not clear from surviving accounts, the material from New York ended up at Bermuda Hundred instead of Fortress Monroe. Grant, however, still wanted the bridging concentrated at Port Comfort. Pursuant to his instructions, Butler on June 10 forwarded most of his pontoons to the fortress, where they arrived on June 12. Captain James L. Robbins of the 50th New York Engineers, charged with transporting the pontoons, reported on hand at Fortress Monroe "155 French pontoons, 1,000 long balks, 2,000 chesses, 144 anchors, 100 claw balks, 8 trestles complete, cables and lashings for 2,600 feet bridging, 68 pontoon trucks, 1 army forge, 3 tool wagons, [and] 2 chests carpenter's tools (large size)." To ensure sufficient planking, Grant requested Halleck to "order the saw mill at Fort Monroe to saw all the 2-inch lumber they can, and place it on board barges, subject to my order."[87]

Grant recognized that part of the Potomac army might have to cross the James on boats, depending on the route he ultimately chose. Brigadier General Montgomery C. Meigs, the quartermaster general in Washington, assured the general in chief that he would hold all the ferryboats he could find near Fortress Monroe subject to Grant's orders. "Many of the side-wheel boats in the Quartermaster's Department will also answer all purposes of ferry boats," Halleck wrote, adding that "the barges will also be excellent for teams and stores, and can be towed by the tugs. Everything will be sent forward as soon as you direct."[88]

Grant also looked to the U.S. Navy for support. The idea of a joint operation between land and water forces was not new to Grant, who had relied on gunboats for his victories in Mississippi and Tennessee. The navy had already played a supporting role in Butler's operations along the James. Acting Rear Admiral Samuel Phillips Lee, commanding the North Atlantic Blockading Squadron, had provided gunboats and transports for Butler's advance to Bermuda Hundred and had helped barricade the James after the general's repulse at Drewry's Bluff, clearing the river of rebel torpedoes and keeping a few gunboats on watch downriver from Howlett's.[89]

Because Butler was already on the James and had a working relationship with Admiral Lee, Grant left him to coordinate the naval effort to keep the river below the Howlett Line free from rebel gunboats. Delegating that responsibility, however, proved to be a mistake, as relations between Lee and Butler had become increasingly strained. The rift apparently started when the general urged the admiral to dispatch gunboats to protect the vulnerable end of his entrenched line resting on the James. Lee, however, insisted that Butler first silence the Confederate batteries near the riverbank. Then toward the end of May, he informed Butler that three Confederate gunboats armed with torpedoes and nine fire rafts were rumored to be preparing to attack down the James. Butler forwarded five schooners for sinking in the river as obstructions and directed his quartermaster to collect rocks for ballast. Lee, however, interpreted this proposal as an affront to his sailors' courage and balked. Writing Butler that he could not sink obstructions in the river without first receiving authorization for the cost, Lee revealed the real reason for his obstinacy to Secretary of the Navy Gideon Welles: "The Navy is not accustomed to putting down obstructions before it, and the act might be construed as implying an admission of superiority of resources on the part of the enemy." Butler promised the admiral that the War Department would foot the bill and assured him that obstructing the river did not reflect poorly on the navy's courage. "I am aware of the delicacy naval gentlemen feel in depending upon anything but their ships in a contest with the enemy, and if it was a contest with the enemy's ships alone, I certainly would not advise the obstructions, even at the great risk of losing the river," he wrote Lee, "but in a contest against such unchristian modes of warfare as fire-rafts, and torpedo boats, I think all questions of delicacy should be waived by the paramount consideration of protection for the lives of the men and the safety of the very valuable vessels of the squadron."[90]

On June 7, the schooners still afloat, Admiral Lee forwarded his correspondence with General Butler to Secretary Welles and sought guidance. He had four ironclads on hand, he reported—one was due to leave shortly—which was "better than was originally expected." Although he had yet to hear definitively from Grant, Richmond's newspapers predicted that the Army of the Potomac was preparing to cross the James and operate against Richmond from the south. "I understand it would be of vital importance to the success of the campaign that the river should be held secure against the casualties of a novel naval engagement," he observed, referring to rebel torpedoes and fire boats, and expressed concern about the consequences "should the novel plans of the enemy succeed in crippling the monitor force." He was also worried that the James was too narrow and shallow near Howlett's for his ironclads to maneuver to advantage. All in all, Lee was inclined "to obstruct the shoaler parts of this reach so as to prevent the convenient approach of the enemy's smaller torpedo vessels and limit his approach to the channel way, which is narrow and under the control of the monitor fire."[91]

The admiral, however, still did nothing—the anticipated threat had yet to materialize, and he was still protective of the navy's reputation. "The necessity of holding our position here is an overwhelming military one," Butler reminded Lee on receiving word of his decision to wait, "but how you are to hold yours on the river is, of course, wholly for you to determine." The admiral agreed that his and the general's common objective was to protect the James "beyond peradventure for the great military purposes of General Grant and yourself" and that if Confederate gunboats penetrated downriver, the Army of the Potomac's crossing would be seriously imperiled. Once again the admiral looked to Welles, who deftly passed the buck back to Lee. "Action in this matter is left to the discretion of the admiral of the squadron," the secretary responded, "in whom the Department has confidence." Lee then tried to transfer responsibility to Butler, writing the general that obstructing the river "must be your operation, not mine." Butler's return volley was not unexpected: "The vessels are wholly at your service," he reminded Lee, "upon your good judgment, and not mine, must rest their use." The channel remained unobstructed.[92]

By evening on June 10, however, Grant felt satisfied that the elements necessary to execute his grand maneuver were falling into place. The devil, however, still lurked in the details. Two days hence he intended to launch the most audacious venture of his military career, crossing Virginia's queen river, severing the Army of Northern Virginia's main supply artery, and then engaging the Confederate force when it abandoned its entrenchments. Grant and his generals could only speculate about the Army of Northern Virginia's response as the Union force marched away from Cold Harbor. The lieutenant general was a master at improvising, as he had demonstrated multiple times over the previous month. But now he was juggling a host of cooperating elements—the Army of the Potomac, the Army of the James, the navy, and various engineers. Were they capable of delivering the flexibility that his plan demanded? Could their commanders adjust to the inevitable changes that would occur as the campaign progressed?

Most importantly, had Grant communicated his vision of operations to the various cooperating elements with sufficient precision to ensure that they moved toward a common objective? The next five days would tell.

VI

JUNE 11–12, 1864

Grant Plans His Next Maneuver

"Everything is progressing favorably but slowly."

CONCERNED THAT THE CONFEDERATES might be planning mischief in the Cold Harbor battlefield's northern sector, Meade had directed Wilson to venture a "reconnaissance in force" early on Saturday morning, June 11. At 4:30 A.M. McIntosh's cavalry brigade, supported by two regiments of Ferrero's U.S. Colored Troops, left the Old Church fortifications to reconnoiter Shady Grove and Bethesda Church Roads. On reaching the Linney place, McIntosh divided his mounted force into two segments. Lieutenant Colonel Brinton rode west out Shady Grove Road with the 18th Pennsylvania and the 2nd Ohio Cavalry, while McIntosh proceeded southwest along Bethesda Church Road with the 5th and 2nd New York Cavalry.[1]

Just beyond Gilman's Mill, McIntosh's wing slammed into Chambliss's cavalry pickets and drove them back, passing over arms and accoutrements abandoned by the fleeing Confederates. Advancing through Bethesda Church, the Union force pressed on for another half mile. Ahead loomed fortifications made from logs heaped with earth and "swarming with men"—the northern section of Lee's entrenched line, manned by Hunton's Brigade of the 1st Corps. In full view behind the rebel works were tents, camps, and troops marshaling to repel the interlopers. Severely outnumbered, McIntosh judged caution the better part of valor and called off the reconnaissance.[2]

Brinton's wing meanwhile advanced out Shady Grove Road, driving Chambliss's pickets past the Bowles house to the main Confederate works about a mile north of where McIntosh encountered Hunton's rebels. Georgians of Colonel Dudley M. DuBose's brigade manned this sector of line and braced for action as their pickets came running back. "Our boys behaved gallantly in the charge, some of them urging their horses over the fortifications," a New Yorker recalled. "A few of them never returned." Like McIntosh to the south, after testing the Confederate defenses, Brinton fell back before superior numbers and returned to Old Church. Wilson reported his losses at four or five men killed and six or eight men wounded. Prisoners included a soldier from the 1st South Carolina of Colonel John Bratton's brigade, 1st Corps. While the foray accomplished little, it at least clarified for the Federals the upper contours of Lee's entrenched position.[3]

The opposing battle lines saw little action the rest of the day. Some of the cavalrymen involved in McIntosh's excursion bivouacked on the Ruffin plantation near Old Church. "There we found an ice-house pretty well filled," an officer later reminisced. "The enemy had thrown some dead mules in, to prevent our enjoying the great luxury, but their plan did not work. The carcasses were soon taken out, and the way the ice disappeared was sufficient proof that its flavor had not been impaired." Baldy Smith reported, "All quiet on my front"; Colonel Christ, commanding a brigade in Burnside's corps, sensed "less firing by the enemy's picket this morning than formerly." Writing to Congressman Elihu Washburne, Grant aide Lieutenant Colonel W. R. Rowley noted that "even the pickets have quit shooting at each other and there is nothing other than the occasional boom of a piece of artillery." He predicted, however, that "this will not last long."[4]

Grant's and Meade's staffs labored all weekend hammering out details of the impending movement south. Managing the broad sweep of the campaign was the general in chief's job, which included coordinating Meade, Sheridan, Hunter, Butler, and the naval forces necessary to keep Confederate ironclads out of the James River. The task of plotting the precise routes of the various infantry corps as they streamed from Cold Harbor belonged to Meade, and the scrivener of those details was the Army of the Potomac's chief of staff, Brigadier General Humphreys, whose hand was evident in the carefully crafted final product. "It was in drawing orders for such complicated movements as these," Charles Dana later wrote, "along different roads and by different crossings, that the ability of General Humphreys was displayed."[5]

"Everything is progressing favorably but slowly," Grant advised his friend and mentor Washburne. "All the fight, except defensive and behind breast works, is taken out of Lee's army," he promised, echoing a refrain that had guided his actions since leaving the North Anna. "Unless my next move brings on a battle," he predicted, "the balance of the campaign will settle down to a siege."[6]

On Saturday the eleventh, Grant crystallized his grand plan for the move-

ment across the James. Aides Comstock and Porter, he began in a dispatch to
Meade, had not yet returned from their mission to ascertain the best crossing
point below Bermuda Hundred. "It is now getting so late," Grant concluded,
"that all preparations may be made for the move tomorrow night without waiting longer." In sum, the Union army was to withdraw from its Cold Harbor entrenchments in secrecy the night of June 12 and head for the James. The trick
was to conceal the departure behind an impenetrable screen of cavalry and infantry and dash across the Chickahominy before Lee could react. The Federal
army had successfully executed disengagements of comparable difficulty after
impasses in the Wilderness, at Spotsylvania Court House, and at the North
Anna. This time, however, Lee expected precisely the maneuver that Grant had
in mind and had posted cavalry along the Chickahominy to sound the alarm
the moment the Union force set off. For the gambit to succeed, Union planners
had to anticipate a host of contingencies, and the Army of the Potomac had to
move with clocklike efficiency, a feat that it had rarely achieved.

In broad outline, Grant wanted the Potomac army to steal from Cold Harbor and strike out for the James in four coordinated columns. Warren's corps
was to cross the Chickahominy at Long Bridge and head west on Long Bridge
Road, blocking Lee's approaches south of the Chickahominy and screening the
army's movement from the rebels. One of the remaining corps—to be designated by Meade—was to follow Warren across Long Bridge, while the other
two corps crossed the Chickahominy nine miles downriver at Jones's Bridge.
A third column, composed of Smith's corps, was to slide east to the Pamunkey,
board transports at White House Landing, and travel by the Pamunkey, York,
and James Rivers back to Bermuda Hundred. A fourth column with the army's
wagon trains was to proceed east of the infantry and cross the Chickahominy
downriver from Jones's Bridge. The movement's goal was to unite the entire
army in the vicinity of Charles City Court House, where it would cross the
James on ferries and a pontoon bridge.[7]

Grant sent a companion message to Benjamin Butler. Comstock had not yet
returned, he began, "so that I cannot make instructions as definite as I would
wish, but the time between this and Sunday night [June 12] being so short in
which to get word to you, I must do the best I can." The 18th Corps, Grant explained, was returning to Bermuda Hundred with 15,300 men, and the Army
of the Potomac was marching cross-country and would strike the James at the
"most practicable crossing below City Point." Smith, he assured Butler, would
reach Bermuda Hundred "as soon as the enemy could going by the way of
Richmond," and the balance of the army "will not be more than one day behind, unless detained by the whole of Lee's army, in which case you will be
strong enough."

For his part, Butler was to "explore all means" of assisting Meade's crossing of the James. "I wish you to direct the proper staff officers, your chief engineer and chief quartermaster, to commence at once the collection of all the means in their reach for crossing the army on its arrival," Grant ordered. "If there is a point below City Point where a pontoon bridge can be thrown, have at it."

By Grant's calculation Smith would reach Bermuda Hundred well before the Army of the Potomac could cross the James. The 18th Corps's return would dramatically shift the balance of power in front of Petersburg and afford the Army of the James a sterling opportunity to capture the town, especially if it could attack before Lee understood Grant's game and rushed to reinforce Beauregard. Gillmore's venture on the ninth was a sobering reminder of the Army of the James's fatal penchant for muffing good prospects, but Smith had impressed Grant as an officer of talent, and he alerted Butler to the opportunity. "Expecting the arrival of the Eighteenth Corps by Monday night [June 13], if you deem it practicable from the force you now have to seize and hold Petersburg, you may prepare to start on arrival of troops to hold your present lines." With the fiasco of June 9 doubtless in mind, Grant cautioned that he did "not want Petersburg visited, however, unless it is held, nor an attempt to take it unless you feel a reasonable degree of confidence of success."[8]

In sum, if all went according to plan, Grant expected two days of rapid maneuver to see Smith rejoining Butler while the Army of the Potomac crossed the James. When the 18th Corps reached Bermuda Hundred, it would be several miles closer to Petersburg than was Meade and ideally positioned for a swift and unexpected assault against the city. As Grant later described his thinking, Smith's rapid deployment "was for the express purpose of securing Petersburg before the enemy, becoming aware of our intention, could reinforce the place."[9]

In some respects Grant's contemplated movement mimicked the swings south that the Army of the Potomac had executed after the fighting earlier in the campaign, all undertaken in a manner that protected the army's supply lines. Lieutenant Colonel Lyman later noted that Grant's signature maneuver was "usually, though incorrectly, described as moving by the flank, whereas it always broke by the right to march to the left. That is to say, the right wing marched to the left, in rear of the centre; and the centre followed in rear of the left wing which stood fast and at the proper moment moved after the rest, as a rear guard." It went without saying, he observed, "that any attempt to move directly by the flank would have at once invited an attack of the most dangerous description."[10]

Thomas Livermore, reviewing Grant's strategy several years later, considered the general's decision to cross the James a dramatic change in the campaign's strategic course. "It is useless and needless for the admirers of General Grant to say that his movement across the James was a continuation of the Wilderness campaign, for in fact, when he began the movement, he abandoned the attempt to reach Richmond or to draw out the enemy by menacing Richmond, and he abandoned his direct attack upon Lee's army," he observed. "His new campaign was against its lines of supply, with, of course, the ultimate objective of destroying or capturing that army in its attempt to reach that line." More recently, the historian Mark Grimsley, in a thoughtful analysis of the Overland Campaign, agreed in large measure with Livermore. Grant's new plan, Grimsley concluded, "was a different concept than the one underlying the campaign just ended. The Overland campaign had been intended to destroy Lee's army in the open field. The new offensive, presently dubbed the Petersburg campaign, would do so by choking off the lifeblood of supplies on which the Army of Northern Virginia depended." [11]

In point of fact, Grant's plan for breaking the impasse at Cold Harbor had much in common with the campaign's pattern thus far as well as elements that were new. The general in chief had shifted the Union army south by its left flank to break stalemates after the Wilderness, Spotsylvania Court House, and North Anna River operations, and he was prepared to follow a similar course to force Lee from his Cold Harbor bastion. But the maneuver would have a new objective. This time Grant would not attempt to interpose between Lee and the Confederate capital. Instead, he would aim to capture Petersburg and cut the supply line to both Richmond and Lee's army. Once Petersburg was in Union hands, Lee would have no choice but to abandon his Cold Harbor fortifications and seek a new source of supplies, most likely fleeing west toward Lynchburg. Grant would follow, pouncing on the retreating rebels stripped of their protective earthworks.

A Richmond newspaper's accusation that Grant was "enamoured of his left flank" prompted a rejoinder from the Union war correspondent Charles A. Page: "And a very good and fruitful thing to be enamoured of, the paper might have added." He continued, "No mistress fickle and false has the left flank been, but a handmaiden faithful and true to her lord and master." [12]

This, then, was Grant's overall plan. The details, including precisely where the Potomac army would cross the James and which units would cooperate in the offensive against Petersburg, were to be decided once the withdrawal was underway and Lee's response became evident. Grant was comfortable that his maneuver would ideally position Butler, Smith, and Meade to slice Lee's supply lines and turn the Army of Northern Virginia out of its strong earthworks. Exactly how to administer the coup de grace depended on Grant's ability to

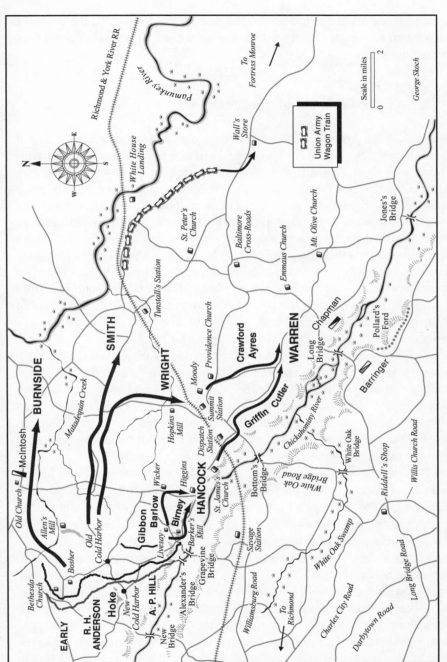

Union withdrawal from Cold Harbor, June 12

communicate his vision to his subordinate commanders and on the ability of those men to execute Grant's vision. The next three days would deliver very mixed answers.

"Wrought up to an intensity of thought and action that he seldom displayed."

Positioning the Army of the Potomac for the big move required a great deal of preliminary jockeying. Warren's corps, slated to lead the advance, was still divided, with Griffin's and Cutler's divisions patrolling the Chickahominy near Hancock while Ayres's and Crawford's divisions encamped several miles away at Leary's farm, east of Cold Harbor. On the evening of June 10, headquarters directed Warren to shift Ayres and Crawford south of the Richmond and York River Railroad to a Mr. Moody's property, near Summit Station, bringing those divisions closer to the other 5th Corps divisions and within easy marching distance of Long Bridge, where they were slated to cross the Chickahominy. To avoid detection, Ayres and Crawford were to take a roundabout path from Leary's farm southeast to Parsley's Mill, then on through Prospect Church to Moody's place. Ayres was to lead, followed by Crawford and the 5th Corps's reserve artillery, pontoon trains, and ambulances.[13]

Warren executed the initial phase of his move at 4:00 A.M. on the eleventh. By evening Ayres's and Crawford's troops sprawled across Moody's yard and onto the grounds of nearby Providence Church. "My command is all in camp as ordered," Warren informed Meade at 6:30 that evening. "I picket all around my camp to prevent my men from straying out or spies from getting through our lines as far as I am able." Major Roebling agreed that "great care was taken that our movement should not become known to the enemy."[14]

The next day—June 12—Warren issued orders to his division heads initiating the big march. Promptly at 6:00 P.M., Ayres and the artillery attached to his division were to start south from Moody's, followed by Crawford and the 5th Corps's reserve artillery under Colonel Wainwright. Simultaneously, upstream on the Chickahominy, Griffin and Cutler were to set off "without the observation of the enemy," taking Dispatch Station Road and subsidiary routes past St. James's Church, Ratcliff's Old Tavern, Ruckle's, and White Hall. Inaccurate maps had hampered Union movements during the campaign, and Warren worried about the quality of those available for this operation. "I send you the best map I have, but may have a better one this evening" he informed Griffin, "and also a guide to conduct your column after crossing the railroad; but make the best arrangements you can to get along with them." Warren reminded him to move "as promptly as you can, keeping well closed up," as Hancock would be coming behind him. If all went according to plan, the 5th Corps's two columns, one from the north and the other from the west, would unite at Long Bridge behind Chapman's cavalry brigade by midnight on the twelfth.[15]

Warren harbored second thoughts about whether Long Bridge was a suitable place to cross the Chickahominy. Federal pickets reported that Barringer's North Carolina cavalrymen and elements from Ransom's Brigade picketed the far bank, making it a "bad place to force a passage." Pollard's Ford, a few miles downriver, seemed free of Confederates, which prompted the general to suggest that Chapman cross some of his cavalry at Pollard's, then swoop back up the far bank and drive the Confederates from Long Bridge.[16]

Warren was expected to coordinate his advance with Hancock, whose 2nd Corps comprised the other component of the army's first column. In anticipation of evacuating Cold Harbor, Hancock slid his command a short distance south during the night of June 10–11 as did Wright, whose 6th Corps troops replaced the stretch of line adjacent to Cold Harbor Road vacated by Hancock's northern elements. The 2nd Corps men relieved by Wright's replacements were ecstatic over the development, for the Confederates had placed small brass howitzers in a hollow behind their lines that regularly lobbed shells into the Union works. "This made our position very uncomfortable to say the least," a Pennsylvanian recounted, "as night and day these unwelcome visitors would drop among us." Engineers surveyed a four-mile road "practicable for a column" running from Washington Livesay's house near the southern end of Elder Swamp east to the Wicker farm, where it struck a major road that fed into Dispatch Station Road near the Higgins farm. This new trail, Hancock reasoned, would speed his evacuation by affording him two routes to the rear.[17]

The assignment of cutting the new road fell to the engineer Wesley Brainerd, who began work the morning of June 12. "Arriving with axes," he recalled, "my men struck into the woods, felling trees as we advanced." By nightfall they had completed a track through the forest wide enough for artillery. Passing over to Dispatch Station Road, Brainerd met Hancock's chief of staff, Lieutenant Colonel Morgan, who informed him that the general was "much pleased with the road we had made," Brainerd reminisced.[18]

Midmorning on June 12, Hancock met with his division commanders to review the details of the withdrawal scheduled to take place that evening. The plans were thorough. At 8:30 P.M. Gibbon, on the northern end of Hancock's battle line, was to evacuate his entrenchments and retire to the new set of reserve works between Old Cold Harbor and Elder Swamp. At the same time, Barlow, in the corps's center, was to fall back to Livesay's house and prepare to advance along Brainerd's freshly cut road. Birney, holding the southern end of the line, was to slide his northernmost brigades to the left and rear of the rest of his division. "The picket line will be strengthened," Hancock directed, "and a few reliable regiments left in the advanced rifle pits until the greater part of the division is withdrawn." [19]

Once Barlow had concentrated his division at the Livesay farm, the second stage of the 2nd Corps's evacuation was to begin. Barlow was to leave first, following Brainerd's trail through the woods to the Wicker farm, turn south to Dispatch Station Road at the Higgins place, then head east toward Long Bridge behind Cutler's and Griffin's 5th Corps divisions. Gibbon meanwhile was to leave the reserve line near Elder Swamp and follow in Barlow's wake. Birney was to assign a staff officer to alert him when Barlow reached the Higgins place, which would be his signal to start east along Dispatch Station Road, taking position at the tail of the 2nd Corps's column behind Gibbon. The pickets, supervised by Lieutenant Colonel John S. Hammell of the 66th New York, were to assemble behind Birney and form the column's rearguard, gathering Griffin's and Cutler's pickets as they marched east along Dispatch Station Road. "Division commanders are requested to adopt measures to prevent the men from falling in rear of the column and into the hands of the enemy, as happened in the last night march," Assistant Adjutant General Walker cautioned. [20]

While the 2nd Corps marched to join them, Warren's two prongs were to merge at Long Bridge, cross the Chickahominy behind Chapman's cavalry, and extend feelers west toward Richmond on Long Bridge Road to screen the army's advance. "It was expected that such a movement by General Warren would deceive Lee," Chief of Staff Humphreys later stressed, "and give him the impression that the Army of the Potomac was advancing upon Richmond, or, if intending to cross the James, that it would do so near Malvern Hill, at City Point, or above." [21]

Passing just south of where the 5th Corps was projected to cross the Chickahominy, Long Bridge Road angled southwest to skirt the southern edge of White Oak Swamp. After marching some five miles, Warren's detachment would reach White Oak Bridge Road, which pierced the swamp to the north and continued up to Bottom's Bridge. After blocking this possible avenue for an enemy attack, Warren's troops were to continue west another mile to the important intersection at Riddell's Shop, where Long Bridge Road, Charles City Road, and Willis Church Road came together. These were the routes that Lee would likely try to use to strike the Union army as it marched south, and it was Warren's job to hold that critical road junction. After Hancock's corps had passed safely by, the 5th Corps was to withdraw and follow it to the James. [22]

Hancock's soldiers would have more than thirty miles to cover; Warren's troops only slightly less. The opportunity to outfox Lee, however, promised to make the long march worthwhile.

While Warren's and Hancock's corps coalesced into a column marching south across Long Bridge, Wright's and Burnside's corps were slated to merge into a second Union column at Jones's Bridge. The logistics of choreographing the 6th and 9th Corps' movements were every bit as complex as those governing the 2nd and 5th Corps' advance. In short, when the 6th Corps disengaged from Cold Harbor after dark on June 12, it was to shift into the reserve line of entrenchments. After the road cleared, the corps was to evacuate the battlefield through Old Cold Harbor, Russell's division leading, with the divisions of Neill and Ricketts following in that order. The 6th Corps's pickets were to remain behind, leaving only after the 2nd and 18th Corps pickets on either side of them had retired. After passing through Old Cold Harbor, the 6th Corps was to march east to the Parsley home, turn south, pass by Hopkins Mill, and come out at Moody's place, which Warren should have vacated several hours earlier. From there, Wright's soldiers were to march east through Emmaus Church to Jones's Bridge and a junction with Burnside.[23]

Wright's task was daunting. Sandwiched into a relatively short battle line between Hancock and Smith, the 6th Corps commander had to coordinate his withdrawal with two adjacent corps—the 2nd and 18th—and make a timely rendezvous with the 9th Corps at a location twenty miles distant. Complicating Wright's assignment was Hancock's request that he cover the northern portion of the 2nd Corps's line when Gibbon withdrew. During the evening of June 10, Hancock, Wright, and Gibbon met at Grant's headquarters and formulated the joint movement's details. It was decided that Neill's 6th Corps division would extend northward to occupy Ricketts's earthworks and its own entrenchments, freeing Ricketts to pass south behind Neill and Russell and occupy "as much of Gibbons' line as he can, forming double lines of battle." Ricketts, Wright warned, must "exercise great caution in relieving the Second Corps, waiting probably till after the moon has set."

At 2:00 A.M. on June 11, Wright began rearranging his divisions according to plan. While Neill slid portions of his division into Ricketts's entrenchments, Ricketts withdrew and marched south, passing behind the 6th Corps's earthworks. The sun was already rising by the time his men reached Gibbon's stretch of line, so the tired troops set up camp there. After nightfall on the eleventh, they completed their assignment, relieving the troops in the northernmost part of Gibbon's formation.[24]

Changes during the week had left Burnside's 9th Corps in disarray. Not only had Thomas Crittenden, commanding one of its three divisions, resigned, but his replacement was James Ledlie, the inebriated brigade commander who had rashly attacked the Confederate fortifications at Ox Ford. And then, on June 11, headquarters informed Burnside that it was assigning the 9th Corps's veteran regular U.S. regiments to Warren. "Please say to the commanding general I am sorry that he has found it necessary to take away from this corps some of its best troops upon the eve of an important movement, a portion of which forms the provost guard of the corps, which is so necessary in a march," Burnside complained to Meade's aide Seth Williams. "I have now fewer men present for duty by several thousand than any other corps in the army."[25]

Adding to these woes, Meade assigned the 9th Corps the longest trek. Like his fellow corps heads, Burnside was slated to withdraw as soon after dark on June 12 "as practicable." He would not, however, follow a direct route to the Chickahominy. Instead he was to angle northeast past Allen's Mill, skim along Matadequin Creek's southern branch, detour through Clopton's, and continue on to Tunstall's Station on the Richmond and York River Railroad, Ledlie's division leading, followed by Potter and Willcox. If the 18th Corps—the third column of advance, moving on a direct route to White House Landing—happened to be passing through Tunstall's Station at the same time, Burnside was to yield until Smith had cleared the road, then continue on to Jones's Bridge by way of Baltimore Cross-Roads and Emmaus Church, "taking care not to interfere with routes of other corps." After uniting with the 6th Corps three miles from Jones's Bridge, the combined 6th and 9th Corps column was to press south to Charles City Court House.[26]

The army's wagon train—another column of advance, consisting of thousands of supply and baggage wagons, ambulances, and a herd of cattle—folded more complexity into the mix. Ferrero's two brigades of U.S. Colored Troops were to proceed from their camps at Old Church to Tunstall's Station, where they were to join the army's ponderous trains. To help minimize congestion and protect the cumbersome wagons, the train and Ferrero's troops were to travel well east of the infantry and cross the Chickahominy at Windsor Shades, near the river's highest navigable point. McIntosh's cavalry would serve as the Army of the Potomac's rear guard, remaining at Old Church until the movement was well underway, then riding to Long Bridge on the Chickahominy.

While the Army of the Potomac rolled south, Smith's troops—minus their wagons and artillery, which were to join the army's supply train—were to march to White House Landing and board transports bound for Bermuda Hundred. Smith's route from Cold Harbor to White House passed through Parsley's

Mill, Prospect Church, Hopewell Church, and Tunstall's Station, where it intersected Burnside's route. From the landing, the 18th Corps would proceed down the Pamunkey to the York, round Point Comfort by Fortress Monroe, and head up the James to rejoin Butler.[27]

Importantly, while Grant had suggested to Butler that Smith's arrival at Bermuda Hundred might enable his corps to immediately attack Petersburg, Grant gave no such instructions to Smith. His written orders were simply to march the 18th Corps to White House Landing, board transports, and rejoin the Army of the James. As Smith later explained, he received "no intimation" that upon reaching Bermuda Hundred, he would be expected to lead an offensive against Petersburg.[28]

At two o'clock on the morning of June 12, Comstock and Porter appeared at Grant's headquarters. Six days had passed since they had left to find an optimal point for the Army of the Potomac to cross the James. "Pleasant sail up James by Harrison's Landing," Comstock wrote in his diary on June 8, "looking as green and beautiful as if we had never spent two miserable months there." They stayed at Bermuda Hundred until the tenth, then retraced their route to Cold Harbor, arriving in the middle of the night, with Comstock ill and Porter grousing over the late hour. "I reached White House at ten o'clock at night, got a horse and rode 15 miles through pine forest and dark as pitch, reaching headquarters after mid-night," Porter later wrote his wife.[29]

The two road-worn travelers went immediately to Grant's tent and spent nearly an hour detailing their findings. Fort Powhatan, they reported, was ten miles downriver from City Point and fully satisfied the general's requirements for a crossing. The army could access the river's northern bank by several good roads from Charles City Court House, and roads on the southern bank ran to City Point and Petersburg. Nearby, Coggins's Point offered excellent grazing land for horses and cattle. Most importantly, the river narrowed somewhat between Willcox Landing on the north bank and Windmill Point on the south.[30]

Spreading out maps they had acquired on their trip, the staffers reviewed their recommendation. Grant seemed unusually anxious and nervous, puffing on a cigar, taking it from his mouth, resting it on the table, letting the embers go out, relighting the tip, and puffing anew. "In giving him the information he desired," Porter recollected, "we could hardly get the words out of our mouths fast enough to suit him." The general interjected, "Yes, yes!" and spoke with visible animation. "This would not have been noticed by persons unfamiliar with his habit," Porter explained, "but to us it was evident that he was wrought up to an intensity of thought and action which he seldom displayed."[31]

Grant's excitement was understandable. The aides had confirmed that his proposed movement—already far beyond the mere planning stages—would bring the Army of the Potomac to the ideal crossing point. For days, Assistant Secretary of War Dana had chronicled the general's anxiety over the staffers' absence—"Grant is waiting for report of Lieutenant Colonel Comstock and Lieutenant Colonel Porter, the officers sent Tuesday to General Butler," he repeated in his numerous reports to Washington. Now the waiting was over.[32]

Communications flew between headquarters and the departments responsible for logistics. Mindful that bridges and transports had to be in place by the time the army reached the James, Grant dispatched Lieutenant Colonel Frederick T. Dent of his staff to communicate the necessary orders to Benham and Butler, who were, as Dana understood it, "to throw a bridge and corduroy the marsh at [the James River opposite Fort Powhatan]." From White House Landing, Abercrombie reported that the hospital could be ready to close by noon on the twelfth, the repair depot could pack up in five hours, the water transport services needed twenty-four-hours' notice, the ordnance officer could be ready in two hours, and the commissary needed eight hours. Notice went out to Quartermaster General Meigs that ships for 16,000 troops—Smith's corps—had to reach White House Landing the next morning. "The movement is very important," headquarters stressed, "and it is necessary that all vessels suitable for transporting troops, which have been sent from this place to Washington and Alexandria, be returned at once, together with such vessels as can be spared."[33]

The task of overseeing preparations for the pontoon bridge across the James fell to Butler's chief engineer, Brigadier General Godfrey Weitzel. A "curious man," the war correspondent Charles Page wrote of him, "endowed with wonderful *nous,* located in a big head, set on a long neck, atop of a long body, swung along by pendulum legs, he is—Godfrey Weitzel, and there is none other. Would there were, for the sake of the country, and every one a brigadier general." Lyman concurred in Page's assessment, terming Weitzel "an intelligent, Saxon looking man with light eyes and beard."[34]

Immediately downriver from Charles City Court House, the James bends sharply south, flows past Fort Powhatan, then curves northeast. The flat, fertile peninsula formed by these meanderings was called Weyanoke. Butler's engineers, in consultation with Comstock and Porter, had identified this broad point as the best site for constructing a pontoon bridge to span the river and reach the southern bank at or near Fort Powhatan. Located some eight river miles below City Point and Bermuda Hundred, the crossing at Weyanoke would be safe from observation by the Confederates, an important requirement for keeping the massive troop movement concealed from Lee.

Where precisely to construct the floating bridge, however, was not yet clear. The trick was to find a location with the least marsh to cross and the shortest expanse of river to span. The James narrows as it turns south along Weyanoke's western shore, which suggested placing the bridge as near to the peninsula's tip as possible. The lower portion of the peninsula, however, was rimmed with marsh, which necessitated a long causeway to access the span.

In response to Grant's request, Weitzel assigned Lieutenant Peter S. Michie—"a young man of great intelligence and most pleasing manners"—to select the optimal location for the pontoon bridge. Michie identified three potential sites. The first was near the tip of Weyanoke Point, where the river is only 1,250 feet wide. The drawback to this first option was marshy terrain on the Weyanoke side, which Michie estimated would require a reinforced causeway about a thousand yards long; its advantage was the location of Fort Powhatan directly across the James, where a road had already been cut up the bluffs leading to the stronghold. Michie located a second site a quarter of a mile upriver. The James is wider here—approximately 1,570 feet across—but the marsh narrower by some two hundred yards, requiring a causeway of only eight hundred yards. The engineer also identified a third site another half mile upstream. Here the river is 1,992 feet wide, but the adjacent marsh only a few hundred feet. Its drawback was difficult access to the far bank, which has steep bluffs. Farm roads already gave access up the bluff across from the first two Weyanoke sites, but the terminus for the third site—the easiest to construct on the Weyanoke side because of the short stretch of marshland—required cutting a road up the south shore's steep incline.[35]

In Michie's opinion the third, or upriver, option was the best choice since constructing a causeway across the marshy approaches to the pontoon bridge was the most onerous and time-consuming part of the operation. Acting on this recommendation, Weitzel telegraphed Comstock, "if the passage was to be made here I would only require, at the farthest, previous notice of thirty-six hours to have the approaches to the bridge ready."[36]

The operation's grand sweep was not lost on Grant's aide Adam Badeau, who had joined the general's staff in early 1864. In his opinion the movement "transcended in difficulty and danger any that [Grant] had attempted during the campaign." Listing the challenges that lay ahead, he observed that Grant intended to "withdraw an army from within forty yards of the enemy's line, and to march through the difficult swamps of the Chickahominy bottom, to positions where that stream could be crossed without interruption from the rebels; then, to advance to the James, a great and tidal river, at a point seven hundred yards across; to effect a passage with all the munitions and supplies of a hundred thousand soldiers, changing his base, at the same time, from White House to City Point, a hundred and fifty miles apart; to effect a combination of Meade's force with that of the James; and finally, advance, with his double army, against Petersburg." The risks were daunting. "Not only was the movement liable to interruption from Lee on the northern side, but Grant's long and circuitous route would compel him to be several days on the march, while the distance from Richmond to Petersburg is only twenty miles, and Lee's camp was within five or six hours of the Army of the James."[37]

The Overland Campaign's next grand maneuver was ready to begin. "Today we commence a flank march, to unite with Butler on the James," Meade wrote his wife. "If it is successful, as I think it will be, it will bring us to the last act of the Richmond drama, which I trust will have but few scenes in it, and will end fortunately and victoriously for us." The soldiers who would be doing the fighting, however, predicted a long road ahead. "I don't think we are going to finish the campaign for some time yet," Major Charles J. Mills wrote his mother. "I suppose we are to make for James River, and then go to work, with the help of gunboats and spades and siege-guns, on our last hard task, and I think we shall do it, too, but it will take a good while. I hope some of us will be left to reap the benefits."[38]

"Hold the corps in readiness to move to the Shenandoah Valley."

Richmond's citizens followed developments across Virginia with interest, but their attention understandably focused primarily on the big armies at their doorstep. "The storm of battle which raged so furiously last week in the immediate vicinity of Richmond has been succeeded by a comparative calm, and matters are now almost as quiet as when the contending armies were seventy miles away," the *Richmond Daily Dispatch* reported. "Grant has evidently become tired of 'butting' against the rebel fortifications, and what he failed to effect by brute force he now essays to accomplish by strategy. Consequently we find him stealthily moving away from our front, and sliding down the south side of the Chickahominy," the newspaper surmised, "endeavoring, if possible, to reach the James, with a view of cooperating with Butler, who is still pent up between that river and the Appomattox."[39]

The *Daily Dispatch* also saw reason to suspect that the Union commander might renew his attacks at Cold Harbor now that Lincoln had won renomination. Grant, the newspaper speculated, "doubtless feared to risk another fight until that purpose was consummated, for a decisive victory for the Confederates would have destroyed Lincoln's prospects completely. The convention over, and the renomination effected, it is not impossible that active hostilities may be immediately resumed."[40]

"I do not like the appearance things have taken on in the last week," Robert Garlick Hill Kean of the Confederate War Bureau wrote in his diary. Hunter had occupied Staunton and Lexington, he noted, and Sheridan's cavalry, "aided by Hunter, [Brigadier General William W.] Averill [sic, Averell], and Crook, ravage all the state and cut communications of Richmond with the West and South." Grant in the meantime was pressing Lee's defenses with small but regular steps. "He evidently intends to take his time," Kean predicted, "burrow up to a key point, [and] attempt to take it by assault."[41]

Breckinridge sent dire news from the Valley. He had only 5,023 infantrymen at his disposal, he reported on June 10, some of them reserves and dismounted infantry, and he expected 4,000 cavalrymen under Brigadier Generals John McCausland and John B. Imboden to join him. Hunter, he estimated, had at least 10,000 infantry and 3,500 cavalry and appeared to be heading toward Lexington. "It seems to me very important that this force of the enemy should be expelled from the Valley," Bragg wrote on Breckinridge's dispatch before forwarding the document to Lee, adding, "If it could be crushed, Washington would be open to the few we might then employ."[42]

Lee replied with a thoughtful exposition of his dilemma. "I acknowledge the advantage of expelling enemy from the Valley," he wrote. "The only difficulty with me is the means." He estimated that the task would require detaching a corps from the Army of Northern Virginia and sending it to the Valley, seriously weakening his ability to defend Richmond. "I think this is what the enemy would desire," he noted, adding that a different tack—"a victory over General Grant"—would also solve the immediate problem. But assailing Grant in his fortified line, Lee observed, would have little chance of success and even "run great risk to the safety of the army." He, however, believed that the Federals were preparing to march, which might afford the Confederates an opportunity to pounce on them while in motion, assuming the Army of Northern Virginia had sufficient troops to venture an offensive. "Think [Grant] is strengthening his defenses to withdraw a portion of his force," Lee deduced, "and with the other move to the James River."[43]

Beauregard's insistence that Lee send soldiers to help defend Petersburg magnified his concern about releasing troops from Cold Harbor to fight in the Valley. Early on June 11, Lee received confirmation that Gracie's brigade at Chaffin's Bluff was on its way to the Howlett Line and that Ransom stood ready to abandon the Chickahominy defenses for Chaffin's. Locked behind earthworks in front of Richmond, the Army of Northern Virginia risked being bled dry to reinforce other, more active theaters.[44]

As the week progressed, Richmond's newspapers voiced diminishing concern that the Army of the Potomac posed a significant threat. "There is no news of interest from Lee's army," the *Daily Dispatch* announced the morning of June 11. "Grant is reported still to be busily engaged in fortifying in our front, and evidently does not design to accept or offer battle again until he is reinforced; even then opinions differ as to whether he will fight in his present position, or attempt to make his way to James River, where he would have the cooperation of the gunboats and Butler's forces on the Southside." Under either scenario, the newspaper was certain of the outcome. "Whatever may be his intention, our army is ready today to enter into a general engagement, with the utmost confidence as to the result."[45]

All Saturday, intelligence poured into Lee's headquarters confirming that Grant was girding for a major movement. "At the White House there are signs of an evacuation," reported Sergeant F. Roscoe Burke, commanding the 9th Virginia Cavalry's scouts. Workers were tearing up the Richmond and York River Railroad and shipping off the iron, Burke noted, and transports were passing up and down the Pamunkey. Cavalry commander Chambliss forwarded this report to Lee's headquarters. "This report is reliable," he stressed, "and I hasten to send it on." Chambliss added that Union sutlers were gone and the "general talk is that Grant is going to James River in a few days."[46]

Confederates stationed on the Chickahominy also spotted signs that something was afoot. Enemy pickets along the river seemed to have doubled, and drums sounding tattoo suggested troop concentrations in that sector. Dense foliage, however, made it difficult for the southerners to see across the river. "We have tried from every prominent point to ascertain what is doing north of Chickahominy, but the trees are not high enough to give a sufficient command," Ransom reported.[47]

Early's division commander Ramseur summed up the army's sense of Grant's probable intentions in a letter to his wife. "We have been very quiet for a few days," he wrote home on June 11. "I expect Grant is endeavouring to throw a force to the South bank of the James. Gen'l Lee is watching him."[48]

On Sunday, June 12, news arrived from the Valley that ratcheted concern in Richmond to a fever pitch. Hunter was pressing toward Lexington, placing the town's fate in doubt and imperiling the entire upper Valley. "If he should threaten Lynchburg," Breckinridge wrote, "and Imboden cannot stop him, I hope some troops can be thrown there to detain him twenty-four hours." From Lynchburg came an urgent plea. "Can you send me reinforcements?" inquired

Brigadier General Francis T. Nicholls, who was defending the town with a scratch force in part composed of patients from local hospitals and inmates from the prison.[49]

Lee faced a difficult decision. Could he pull enough soldiers from Cold Harbor to save Lynchburg without so weakening the Army of Northern Virginia that it could not contain Grant? He had already sent off five of his seven cavalry brigades and Breckinridge's entire division, severely limiting his ability to keep watch on the Federals and man his own defenses. Rescuing Lynchburg would take a substantial body of troops, and Early's 2nd Corps, numbering about 8,250 soldiers, was the logical choice for the job. Recently withdrawn from the northern end of the Confederate line, most of these soldiers were camped in reserve near Gaines's Mill and were well rested.[50]

While Early would be sorely missed at Cold Harbor, Lee calculated that the fall of Lynchburg and the permanent disruption of supplies from the Valley were disasters that he could not survive.

And so on the afternoon of June 12, Lee summoned Early to his headquarters and told him, as the lieutenant general later recalled, "to hold the corps, with two of the battalions of artillery attached to it, in readiness to move to the Shenandoah Valley." After dark he issued Early written instructions that were even more ambitious than his oral directive. The 2nd Corps was to leave for the Valley at 3:00 the next morning, travel by way of Louisa Court House and Charlottesville, coordinate with Breckinridge to defeat Hunter, and then advance north through the Valley, passing through either Leesburg or Harpers Ferry to threaten Washington. Early's venture would serve two purposes. Not only would he rescue Lynchburg, but he also would excite Lincoln's concern for the safety of Washington, hopefully inducing the president to pull troops from Grant to protect the Union's capital. Caught in a desperate situation, Lee had devised a risky but ingenious solution for disrupting his enemy's plans.[51]

Lee, however, faced far greater risks than he imagined. Early's foray could not possible yield positive results for days or even weeks. And unknown to the Confederate commander, Grant was preparing to initiate an ambitious turning movement that very night that would take the Army of the Potomac across the Chickahominy and James Rivers while the Army of the James—at least Smith's augmented 18th Corps—assailed Petersburg. If Grant succeeded in capturing the Cockade City, he would sever the Army of Northern Virginia's supply lines to Richmond from the south, compel Lee to abandon his Cold Harbor fortress, and enable the Army of the Potomac to renew its campaign with overwhelming advantage.

On the eve of Grant's most ambitious maneuver, Lee was sending away an entire corps of veteran infantry under his most aggressive subordinate, unwittingly gutting his ability to respond. With Breckinridge's Division and Early's corps gone, the Army of Northern Virginia could marshal only some 35,000 men to thwart the Union offensive. At Spotsylvania Court House on May 11, Lee had misread Grant's intentions and withdrawn artillery from the Mule Shoe, weakening the very sector of line that his opponent had targeted. He had corrected his mistake at Spotsylvania with a dazzling display of innovative generalship. Whether he could match that performance on this occasion remained to be seen.[52]

After the war the Confederate artillerist Alexander stressed that "it was of immense, of vital importance to Gen. Lee to strike his hardest blow in the progress of Grant's next move. His most obvious move was to seek the connection with Butler between Deep Bottom [on the James] and City Point." He continued: "This would have been the shortest, and this was evidently the move which Gen. Lee anticipated he would make. . . . But Grant had devised a piece of strategy all his own, which seems to me the most brilliant stroke in all the Federal campaigns of the entire war. It was, by some roundabout roads, but entirely out of our observation, to precipitate his whole army upon Petersburg. If he succeeded in capturing it a speedy evacuation of Richmond would follow, and he would be in a position to make the retreat a disastrous one."[53]

"We hailed the announcement of our withdrawal from this awful place."

At 3:00 P.M. on Sunday, June 12, Grant, Meade, and their staffs left their "dusty, dirty, foul smelling camp" near Old Cold Harbor and rode to Warren's headquarters at the Moody place—"a little house, as it were, on skids, like a corn barn," Meade's aide Lyman noted, "and with several pleasant catalpas around it." They arrived there around 5:30, just as Warren was striking his tents. Grant had shaved his beard and mustache close to his face, which mellowed his appearance. Traveling with the headquarters cavalcade, Lyman pegged the commanding general as the quintessential American. "He talks bad grammar, but he talks it naturally, as much as to say, 'I was so brought up and, if I try fine phrases, I shall only appear silly,'" Lyman reflected. "Then his writing, though very terse and well expressed, is full of horrible spelling. In fact, he has such an easy and straightforward way that you almost think that he must be right and you wrong, in these little matters of elegance."[54]

Correspondent Charles Page remarked on the two generals' contrasting appearance. Grant—"the small man on a small black horse"—sat his mount, Jeff

Davis, "with uncommon grace, controls him with one small gauntleted hand, and never once regards the torrent of horsemen that follow, looks neither right nor left, but never fails to acknowledge with a quick gesture the salutes of the soldiers—all-absorbed, all observant, silent, inscrutable, he controls and moves armies as he does his horse." Nearby rode Meade. The Pennsylvanian's mount "is the ideal war horse, tall and powerful, and horse and rider look like a picture of helmeted knight of old, gaunt, tall, grizzled, with the large Roman nose of will and power, and wearing a slouched hat, the wide brim bent down all around, but not concealing the lightning glance of eyes that are terrible in anger—such is Geo. G. Meade, noblest roman of them all."[55]

Union soldiers were aware that the army was preparing to move, but precisely where they were headed remained a mystery. While Grant's and Meade's aides settled into camp, the troops debated their destination. "The whole camp puzzling their brains as to our exact whereabouts and where we go from here," an artillerist wrote home from Moody's.[56]

The evening was unseasonably chilly, prompting the staffers to build a campfire and pull on their greatcoats. "Boxes and boards are made into seats, or rubber blankets are thrown upon the ground to lie on, and all gather close to the crackling rail fire," the newsman Page reported. A pressing topic involved headquarters' supply wagons, which had suffered a mishap while crossing a narrow dam. Assistant War Secretary Dana strode anxiously in front of the fire; Congressman Washburne, on a brief visit from Washington, fell asleep with his feet to the flames; Brigadier General Henry J. Hunt, in charge of the artillery reserve, discussed guns with the engineer Barnard; and Quartermaster General Ingalls fretted about the supply train's holdup. On learning that a few wagons had capsized, Dana cursed the delay—which also postponed his dinner—as "a piece of damn folly." Meade's adjutant Seth Williams was also disgusted, as the spill had left his files of dispatches "in a sopping condition." Stepping toward the fire, Grant put the incident into perspective. "If we have nothing worse than this—," he began, stopping midsentence to let his listeners contemplate the very real risks inherent in their undertaking. Stoking the embers, the general in chief stretched out on a board, slid a bag under his head, and fell fast asleep. "We passed a supperless night under a brilliant moon," an officer recalled.[57]

During the afternoon, Warren's aide Roebling reconnoitered the roads leading to Long Bridge, where the 5th Corps was slated to cross the Chickahominy River. His goal was to find routes for the command's two wings— one marching south from Moody's, the other extending along the Chickahominy from

Hancock's left flank to Bottom's Bridge—to reach the span without being spotted by the Confederates and without interfering with each other's progress. The approach to the bridge ran along a "narrow slip of land with a swamp on each side," the major noted, and only a few rebel cavalrymen patrolled the far shore. Returning to Moody's by way of Emmaus Church, Roebling reported his findings to Warren.

That evening, as Grant, Meade, and their headquarters staffs whiled away the time at Moody's, the two wings of Warren's corps wound their way toward Long Bridge, where they were scheduled to converge. Workers had repaired the road from Moody's, and at 6:00 P.M. Ayres's division got underway, followed by Crawford's division. Warren, who accompanied Ayres's troops, seemed "in a good humor today," according to Colonel Wainwright, and was "quite conversable." The artillerist remarked on the "great charm in moving on such a beautiful clear night through the quiet country, and on good roads."[58]

Warren and his entourage reached Long Bridge soon after dark. "The sky was enameled with wakeful stars, and a new moon toiled slowly through the clouds," a newsman observed. Wilson was already there with Chapman, whose five cavalry regiments—the 3rd Indiana, 8th New York, 1st Vermont, and the newly arrived 22nd New York and 1st New Hampshire—were preparing to force their way across the Chickahominy. Ayres's and Crawford's troops settled beside the road to rest while the cavalrymen cleared the way.[59]

A few miles west the other half of Warren's corps—Griffin's and Cutler's divisions—evacuated their posts along the Chickahominy, filtered back to Dispatch Station Road, and headed southeast toward Long Bridge. Their route passed the site of a cavalry fight from several days earlier. "The very air was rotten," a colonel from New York recorded of the march through stacks of bloated horse carcasses, "the wretched distillations settling down, in the still damp night air, to the bottom of the valley." A soldier in Griffin's division remembered passing "in the rear of the main Union entrenchments at Cold Harbor, at some points so closely as to be able to discern their outline through the flickering light shed by the campfires of the troops occupying them." The men, he thought, "seated about the fires or moving to and fro lent a fantastic appearance to the scene as we hurried by through the darkness of the night."[60]

The Chickahominy at Long Bridge was a sluggish stream bordered by a broad floodplain. "Fancy a wide ditch, partly choked with rotten logs, and full of brown, tepid sickly-looking water, whose slow current would scarcely carry a straw along," Lyman wrote home of the scene. "From the banks of dark mould rises a black and luxuriant vegetation; cypress of immense size, willow oaks, and swamp magnolias, remind you that you are within the limits of a sub-tropical climate, and so does the unhealthy and peculiar smell of decaying leaves and stagnant water." A drawing of Long Bridge, the lieutenant colonel thought, "might pass as the incarnation of malaria and swamp fever." Waiting to cross, Warren's soldiers "shivered and shook," a Pennsylvanian reported, "our teeth rattled together, and we felt as if we were about to freeze."[61]

Tempers flared at Long Bridge. The approaches were in good condition, but the span no longer existed. Major Ford's engineers were on hand to build a pontoon bridge, but Barringer's dismounted Confederate cavalrymen occupied rifle pits along the far bank, and Warren and Wilson seemed unable to cooperate in driving them away. The two generals had sparred a few days earlier over the cavalryman's failure to protect the infantry's flank at Bethesda Church, and Wilson was in no mood to humor Warren's impatience. After an uneasy hour of inaction, he wrote the 5th Corps commander that the advance would remain stalled until Warren saw to it that the engineers could work in safety. Warren ignored the communication and paid no attention to a second note that the cavalryman wrote him a little after 9:00. Rankled by these snubs, Wilson sent a young aide to investigate the cause of the intransigence. The staffer returned visibly upset. Warren had cursed him, he reported, and had instructed him to "tell General Wilson if he can't lay that bridge to get out of the way with his damned cavalry and I'll lay it." Rising to the challenge, Wilson ordered his staff to see to it that the Confederates were chased from the far bank.[62]

It was soon evident that the division commander faced an obstacle more serious than Warren's barbs—Barringer's 1st, 2nd, and 5th North Carolina Cavalry. This battle-hardened outfit had started the campaign under Brigadier General James B. Gordon, and following his mortal wounding on May 13 had served under temporary commanders until the recent appointment of Colonel Barringer. Brother-in-law to Stonewall Jackson and Daniel Hill, Barringer was a fiery North Carolina lawyer bearing scars from a prewar duel and from a shot in the mouth sustained during the Battle of Brandy Station in 1863.

As Chapman's troopers and Ford's engineers manhandled the pontoons into place, Barringer's Tar Heels offered "brisk" resistance from rifle pits on the opposite bank. Rather than force a passage, Chapman decided to send the 8th New York Cavalry two miles downriver to Pollard's Ford, as Warren had earlier recommended, where he hoped to find an unobstructed crossing. Barringer, however, had stationed pickets there, and they greeted the New Yorkers with a blaze of carbine fire. Led by Major Edmund M. Pope, the Union horsemen dismounted and crossed the stream on fallen trees. "It was rather amusing to see officers and men astride of the logs, hitching themselves across as fast as possible, at the same time endeavoring to keep their feet and firearms out of the water," a New Yorker related. "I could not help thinking, with something of a sportsman's instinct, what a beautiful raking shot could have been had upon us, when twenty or thirty of us would be crossing on the same log." Gaining the southern bank, Pope's troopers dispersed the pickets, who fled after squeezing off a few parting shots. Assembling on the south side of the river, the men of the 8th New York painstakingly worked their way upstream along the marshy bank toward Long Bridge.[63]

Warren's staff had assured Major Ford and his engineers that the Chickahominy comprised a single stream at the bridge site, but no one had actually inspected the ground. Ford, who was responsible for the project, insisted on examining the crossing himself. "The night was very dark," Wilson later reported, "the difficulties to be overcome by no means trifling, and the enemy's strength by no means uncertain." Under mounting pressure to clear the way quickly, Chapman decided against waiting for the 8th New York Cavalry and directed the 22nd New York Cavalry to force its way across. Assembling fifty yards above the bridge site, the New Yorkers made their way over, some wading, some swimming, and some clambering across "by the means of fallen trees and overhanging limbs," according to a witness. The Confederates kept up a steady fire that sounded to one participant "like shaking a pepper box." While the New Yorkers splashed through the swampy bottomland to the bridgehead, Ford and a squad from the 3rd Indiana Cavalry rowed across in a pontoon boat under "sharp fire." Together, the New Yorkers and Hoosiers—reinforced by another pontoon-load of Chapman's cavalrymen—drove the rebels from their rifle pits and secured a hold on the Chickahominy's southern bank. Union casualties amounted to one engineer killed.[64]

Shielded by Chapman's cavalrymen, Ford's engineers—directed by Captain James H. McDonald, described by one of his men as "an old and experienced hand at bridge building *under difficulties*"—began laying the pontoon bridge. The work was more arduous than they had anticipated. The stream's main course was 100 feet wide and, as Ford had suspected, was divided by a 250-foot-wide island, with a 60-foot-wide channel on the south. "Extensive swamps bordered the approaches," the major later reported, "the river was filled with sunken piles and timber, the available passage was very narrow, the debris of the old bridge had to be cleared away, and the abutments cut down." At 11:15 P.M. Wilson informed Humphreys that the bridge could not be completed before midnight. In fact, not until one clock on the morning of the thirteenth, after two and a half hours of labor, were the pontoons afloat and the bridging securely in place. The rest of Chapman's troopers came over, bringing with them Lieutenant Charles L. Fitzhugh's Batteries C and E, 4th U.S. Artillery. On reaching the southern shore the cavalrymen headed west along Long Bridge Road, engaging in sporadic firefights with Barringer's retreating horsemen.[65]

Near daylight, Warren's infantrymen tramped over the bridge and fanned into the extensive bottomland south of the Chickahominy. "The soldier steps more thoughtfully over this sluggish Rubicon, as its chill and pestigerous vapors salute his cheek, and as memories of the old Peninsula fights throng upon him," mused a newsman traveling with the army. "Giant cypresses and swamp oaks, ringed at their bases with slime, look down in the moonlight upon you with an oppressive weight of foliage. The flash of torches neutralizes the dense green and lights up the archways of the branches with a strange parlor."[66]

The 5th Corps's assignment was to plug Long Bridge Road from the west, screening the army's movement to the James from Lee's eyes. Crawford's division crossed the floodplain onto high ground overlooking the river near the home of a Mrs. Maddox. Warren established his headquarters across the road from the Maddox place, about a mile and a half from Long Bridge, near where the road from Turner's Ford joined Long Bridge Road. His staff lounged under locust trees in the Maddox garden while Ayres's, Cutler's, and Griffin's troops bivouacked on the floodplain near Long Bridge. "All felt glad that they were leaving the hated peninsula," a surgeon reflected as he gazed into the Chickahominy's fetid waters.[67]

During the afternoon of June 12, while Warren's soldiers marched toward Long Bridge, the rest of the Potomac army's infantrymen prepared to leave the entrenchments that had been their home for almost two weeks. No one was sorry to leave. "Even by comparison with other military fields of Virginia, the present locality is a dreary one," a northerner observed. Wagons had been rolling from the front toward White House Landing for two days, and "their thousands of wheels plowing through the soft and dry roads have covered the country with a pall of gray dust," a newsman noted, "hiding everything and choking everybody." Trees were shredded by artillery shells, and the roads were "strewn, almost paved, with carcasses of horses and mules, most of which were destroyed by hard army usage," a soldier related. "At first unburied, they are now partially covered with loose dirt, in little mounds, which dot the roadside. But their bodies are not all concealed, and when they are, the hoofs and legs protrude, and flies gather and fatten, and the air is poison, and on passing one rider or footman involuntarily shrinks from the foul blow which will strike his senses."[68]

By 3:00 P.M. workers had dismantled the army's field hospitals and tucked sick and wounded men into wagons for the eighteen-mile ride to White House

Landing. The remaining troops acted as though nothing had changed. "Wonder if it is a bluff," a soldier in the 10th Vermont scrawled in his diary.[69]

It was a bluff, and as darkness fell, soldiers began slipping to the rear. Silence was the watchword. "Every man had his tin cup tied fast and his tin plate, if he was rich enough to have one, safely stowed in his haversack, so when the movement was begun there was not a rattle or a jingle to be heard," a man recalled. In places troops crept away on their hands and knees. Pickets maintained a slow patter of musketry well into the night, and regimental bands kept playing, following a routine established days earlier. So far as the Confederates could tell, the Yankees were settling down for another night in their trenches.[70]

Hancock's 2nd Corps, on the southern end of the Federal position, left in stages as planned. Gibbon's division pulled back into the newly constructed reserve line, occupying the entrenchments from Old Cold Harbor to Elder Swamp; Birney's men filtered onto the Livesay grounds; and Barlow's soldiers prepared to press east along Dispatch Station Road, following behind Griffin's and Cutler's 5th Corps troops. Artillery battalions traveled with their divisions, and caissons and reserve batteries gathered on the Livesay farm under Major John G. Hazard's charge. "The night was clear and calm," an officer in the 8th New Jersey remembered. "To drown the noise of the tramp of men, and as a means to counteract any suspicion of the movement, the band played while the brigade was executing the movement, and followed out in rear of it." Chaplain Ezra D. Simons of the 125th New York considered the withdrawal "a marvel of a move. Right from under the faces of the enemy, at one point only a few yards distant, passed out our troops."[71]

The 2nd Corps's pickets, supervised by Colonel Hammell, remained behind to foster the illusion that the fortifications were fully occupied. By 11:00 P.M. the entire corps was on the move. Barlow's division led, followed by Gibbon's and Birney's divisions. "The moon was full; it was a beautiful night, but very cold, and the roads were dry and dirty," a soldier in the 26th Michigan wrote home. "We took by-roads, across fields and through tangled and dark woods along the famous Chickahominy River." Another soldier recalled the "thrill of pleasure" that rippled through Hancock's ranks as the troops realized they were finally leaving Cold Harbor. When they judged they were too far from the enemy to be heard, they broke into song, "swinging along hour after hour, forgetting the fatigue and hardship," a soldier recounted. No one expressed disappointment over leaving. The departure, Hancock's aide-de-camp William G. Mitchell noted, was "very agreeable to all of us, as there seems to be no hope of breaking the enemy's lines here, they are so strong and powerfully garrisoned."[72]

Marching along "too tired to talk," a soldier from Nantucket was startled from his reveries by a loud roar that sounded like a tornado. Assuming that Confederate cavalry was approaching, he and his companions jumped off the roadway and waited as the roar dissipated behind them. "We afterwards learned that an officer's horse at the head of the column became frightened and jumped back on the line of men behind them and they in turn springing out of the way and so on until the end of the line was reached."[73]

North of Hancock, Wright's soldiers slipped into the newly constructed reserve entrenchments running from Gibbon's right flank near Old Cold Harbor to Allen's Mill Pond. Pickets kept up "continuous fire" to drown the noise of the withdrawal, and artillery wheels were muffled to reduce the rumble as the pieces rolled away. The soldiers remained in the reserve works until shortly after midnight, when they headed east toward Prospect Church. Wright's rearmost element—Upton's brigade of Russell's division—guarded the 6th Corps artillery trains until two in the morning, when the pickets also left. During the evacuation, Wright's troops became entangled with some of Gibbon's men who had taken the wrong road and inadvertently stumbled into the 6th Corps's route east of Burnett's Tavern. The traffic jam took a while to sort out, but by 2:00 A.M. Wright's column was off again. "We hailed, almost with acclamations, the announcement of our withdrawal from this awful place," a New Jersey soldier remembered. "No words can adequately describe the horrors of the twelve days we had spent there, and the sufferings we had endured."[74]

Wright's aide Thomas Hyde summed up the prevailing sentiment years later. "It is very interesting to revisit the battlefields of the war, but I never heard anyone who was engaged there express a wish to see Cold Harbor again," he wrote. "Gladly we turned our backs on it."[75]

Smith's corps, adjoining Wright's to the north, disengaged without a hitch. Around noon Smith had dispatched his rearmost elements to White House and had forwarded Captain Samuel S. Elder's artillery to Tunstall's Station, where it was to join the Army of the Potomac's wagon train. Most of his troops, however, were too close to the enemy to leave until after dark. A rumor circulated that they were slated to remain until everyone else had gotten safely away, leading suspicious souls to speculate that the 18th Corps was "to be sacrificed for the salvation of the Army of the Potomac." The concern proved unfounded, much to the relief of the men, who moved out in tandem with the 6th Corps. Ames's division started the evacuation at 8:00 P.M., followed by Brooks's division, then Martindale's. Colonel Guy Henry remained behind to supervise the withdrawal of the pickets, who left at 3:00 A.M. on the thirteenth.[76]

The 18th Corps had suffered horrific losses at Cold Harbor, and emotion welled as the survivors strode in silence along the moonlit roads. "They were happy as they moved away from the trenches of Cold Harbor," one of Stannard's soldiers recalled. Overcome by their good fortune at escaping alive, men broke down and wept.[77]

The 9th Corps, holding the northern end of the Union line, crept from its works soon after dark, leaving campfires burning to conceal its disappearance. "So well was this accomplished that the enemy did not know for an hour after the departure of the corps that our pickets had been withdrawn," a soldier recollected, "and during this time they kept up their firing, by both artillery and musketry." Writing Burnside the next morning, Willcox reported that Hartranft had come in with the pickets, who withdrew "without suspicion." The Confederates, he noted, were still maintaining a "brisk fire" at Fletcher's Redoubt.[78]

Ferrero's division of U.S. Colored Troops left Old Church and wended its way toward Tunstall's Station. The march's chief excitement, Lieutenant Freeman S. Bowley later wrote, occurred when a mule's packsaddle slipped under the animal and sent the panicked beast on a wild and noisy dash up the moonlit road. "A lot of mess pans and kettles were attached to the saddle, and the animal's iron shoes, striking them, made the clatter and the sparks," Bowley explained. "Some pieces of shelter-tent attached to the pack, streaming and flapping, gave the appearance of white wings." Startled by the apparition, the soldiers scattered, and it took their officers over an hour to restore order. Finally, around 3:00 A.M. on the thirteenth, Ferrero's exhausted warriors reached Tunstall's Station and camped along the roadway with the army's huge wagon train.[79]

Grant's turning movement, anticipated for several days by the soldiers of both armies, was now underway. Having abandoned its entrenchments, the Army of the Potomac would remain vulnerable until it crossed the Chickahominy and put a river between itself and the Army of Northern Virginia. Grant's latest gambit, a newsman reflected, "is considered a bold stroke on his part, but one which will be fully justified by the necessities of the case, and if he succeeds the country will ring with praise of his military genius. If he fails and loses his army, the dreadful tidings will fall like a pall over the land, and that which is an almost mid-day brightness will turn to the blackness of midnight."[80]

For the Army of the Potomac, June 13 would rank among its most anxious days.

VII

JUNE 13, 1864

The Army of the Potomac Crosses the Chickahominy

"The hardest fight we have had for a long time."

SHORTLY AFTER SUNRISE ON June 13, Chapman's Union troopers pressed west along Long Bridge Road from Maddox's place, driving back Barringer's Confederate cavalrymen. "We would march a short distance," a man in the 1st Vermont Cavalry remembered of the rolling fight, "run into some rebels, and while the advance was getting ready to drive them away, we would come into line, dismount, and just as we would get to dozing in good shape, would mount up and move forward again." At 6:00 A.M. Wilson, who accompanied Chapman, informed headquarters that Barringer's rebels had delayed him "considerably" by barricading the road at several points.[1]

An hour of sparring brought Chapman's riders to the junction where White Oak Bridge Road forked off to the north. Clattering across White Oak Bridge, Barringer's horsemen deployed in the remains of a three-sided earthen fortification north of the stream, constructed during the Peninsula Campaign in 1862, that dominated the crossing. As Chapman's troopers approached the bridge, the fort's guns—Chapman estimated that the Confederates had six pieces—and cannon from Captain William M. McGregor's horse artillery opened fire. Dismounting, the 3rd Indiana spread out in skirmish formation and repulsed Barringer's pickets, only to be driven back in turn by the artillery. Major Pope, commanding the 8th New York, threw his 3rd Battalion into the fray, stabilizing Chapman's front while Fitzhugh's Battery E provided a counterweight to the Confederate ordnance. "A lively artillery duel ensued," Chapman reported, in which Fitzhugh lost heavily in men and horses.[2]

As combat heated around White Oak Bridge, Warren dispatched Crawford's division to support Chapman. The Pennsylvania infantryman's performance thus far in the campaign had been lackluster, and his troops felt uneasy about him. "We didn't think too much of Crawford," a soldier recently transferred to the division noted. "He was a tall, chesty, glowering man, with heavy eyes, a big nose, and bushy whiskers; and he wore habitually a turn-out-the-guard expression, which was, as we knew, fairly indicative of his military character." This day, however, Crawford would prove himself an aggressive leader, shuttling troops where they were most needed.[3]

At 8:00 A.M. Crawford's 2nd Brigade, under Colonel Bates and containing regiments from Massachusetts, New York, and Pennsylvania, reached White Oak Bridge along with two batteries—Captain Almont Barnes's Battery C, 1st New York Light, and Captain Patrick Hart's 15th New York Light Artillery. Charging up the road, Bates's 94th New York and 12th Massachusetts deployed as skirmishers and came under heavy fire from the Confederate ordnance. "Formed line of battle under a severe shell fire," one of Bates's men recalled. Unable to advance, the Union soldiers dug in, sealing the approaches across White Oak Swamp. Facing them was a "formidable line" of Confederates, who dug in about three hundred yards from the bridge and threw up breastworks. "We lay close to a little ravine that held some of the largest black snakes I ever saw," a Massachusetts man remembered. "We killed four or five of these old residents, and we saw crossing the path that ran from the road to the swamp, a dozen more." Despite persistent rebel artillery fire, Union losses were relatively light, amounting to a handful of deaths and fewer than twenty men wounded. The chief casualty was Captain George B. Rhodes, commanding the 88th Pennsylvania, who was sliced nearly in half by a solid shot. At 8:30 A.M. Wilson informed headquarters that Chapman had "driven the enemy's cavalry across White Oak Swamp and hold[s] the ridge commanding the crossing." A single corps, he added, would suffice to protect the position "against almost any force."[4]

Leaving the job of plugging White Oak Bridge Road to Crawford, Chapman pulled his cavalrymen back to Long Bridge Road and continued west toward Riddell's Shop. A few of Barringer's rebels contested Chapman's advance but retired under superior Union numbers. Help for the Confederates, however, was near at hand in the form of Martin Gary's newly constituted brigade of South Carolina cavalry. Gary was an aggressive, gray-eyed lawyer aptly described as "the strongest of friends and the hardest of haters." Camped near Malvern Hill a few miles south of the Chickahominy, Gary's brigade consisted of the 7th South Carolina Cavalry, the Hampton Legion, and the 24th Virginia Cavalry. Some of these troopers had fought on this same ground two years earlier. "I saw a great many men's bones bleaching the earth, that fell in that day's fight,"

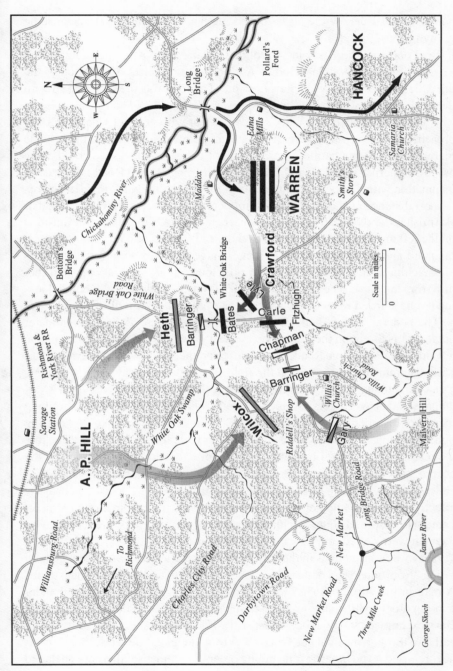

Battle of Riddell's Shop, June 13

one of Gary's riders wrote home, observing that "they might have been some of my friends."[5]

Soldiers from the 7th South Carolina Cavalry were picketing Long Bridge Road near Riddell's Shop. "Dolph, just look at the Yanks," Tom Wood of the 7th called to his friend, Adolphus E. Fant. "The road was literally packed with them," Fant later wrote. "We counted several flags."[6]

A courier pounded into Gary's encampment with news of Chapman's approach, and the troopers were off. The Hampton Legion leading, the brigade marched west to the hamlet of Newmarket "as fast as our horses could carry us," a southerner recalled, and then followed Long Bridge Road northeast to its junction with Charles City Road and Willis Church Road at Riddell's Shop. A short distance farther east, Gary's troopers dismounted, threw out a cloud of skirmishers, and formed a battle line in a belt of woods, the 7th South Carolina on the left and the Hampton Legion on the right. The 24th Virginia remained mounted and explored east along Long Bridge Road, looking for Chapman's approaching Federals. When a Union rider loomed into view, a Virginian shot him from his horse. The rest of Chapman's troopers arrived close behind, looking to one startled rebel as though they had "come up out of the ground."[7]

The Federals found their way blocked "with obstinacy," as Chapman later put it. At his direction the 3rd Indiana Cavalry dismounted and lined up on the left side of Long Bridge Road, facing west, and the 8th New York Cavalry likewise dismounted and formed on the right side of the roadway. Gary's cavalrymen charged and pierced Chapman's skirmish line, only to be repulsed as Indianans and New Yorkers "swept in upon them like a pair of shears, throwing them into disorder and forcing them back, killing a large number." A "rattling fight" ensued as Chapman thrust his entire brigade forward on foot. "The dismounted men advanced in front of the enemy," a Vermonter recalled of the charge, "while the 8th New York flanked them and the battery shelled them." Union artillery, aiming low to disable the 24th Virginia's horses, was brutally effective. "Most of [the horses] had their legs broken," a Confederate remembered. "It was a sad sight to witness, the struggle of the poor brutes. Many of the men were pulled down by the maimed horses."[8]

Gary was conspicuous in the fray. A soldier recalled the flamboyant general riding "from end to end of the line, encouraging us to make every bullet count." A man in the 7th South Carolina left a vivid description of his commander barking orders while balls whizzed past his head. When a staff officer ducked, Gary exclaimed, "Damn you, sir, be still while receiving orders!" But when a ball tore through his own hat, Gary reflexively dodged. "General," the staff officer retorted, "you be still while giving orders." Another southerner concluded that "there was never a braver man in the Confederate war. He did not say, 'Go on, boys'; he went ahead and said, 'Come on, boys,' with his hat in his hand."[9]

Lieutenant Colonel Thomas M. Logan, commanding the Hampton Legion, lacked Gary's good fortune. When a bullet struck his horse, Logan dismounted to examine the injury and was remounting when a bullet passed through his shoulder, grazed his spine, and passed through the other shoulder, making four wounds in all. Logan managed to remount, but with both arms paralyzed, he could not control the animal and was led to an ambulance by an aide.[10]

Seriously outgunned, Gary's brigade retreated west through Riddell's Shop. "It was astonishing to see what a perfect line we kept under such destructive fire of shot and shell," a Confederate recalled: "The trees were riddled with bullets." A Yankee remembered things somewhat differently, claiming that "in a very short time the Johnnies had gone to the rear double quick." A soldier in the 7th South Carolina admitted that the Federals "crowded us, flanked [us] on both sides, [and] there was no alternative but for us to retreat," while a Confederate lieutenant confirmed that the troopers "made a splendid stand but were forced back or rather ordered back to another stand, after the loss of the best men in my company." According to another southerner, he and his companions "walked back to our horses, as the enemy did not follow us."[11]

Still full of fight, Gary's men formed a new line a quarter mile or so west of Riddell's Shop on Charles City Road, taking cover behind a creek.

It was now 11:00 A.M. Under orders to hold the Riddell's Shop intersection, Chapman arranged his veteran 1st Vermont, 3rd Indiana, and 8th New York in a line, the left end resting on Willis Church Road and the right wing covering Charles City Road. Fitzhugh's artillery and the relatively inexperienced 1st New Hampshire and 22nd New York formed a second line in the rear. To better defend the intersection, the troopers piled fence rails and dirt into makeshift breastworks. Chapman's object was to hold the intersection to screen the army's movement across Long Bridge. "Having accomplished his mission, and finding it impracticable to advance further with the force under his command, Colonel Chapman merely advanced a strong skirmish line, and lay in front of the enemy for two hours," a war correspondent observed. "In the interim, our wounded were attended to and our dead buried, as well as the killed of the enemy that fell into our hands." Writing headquarters, Wilson explained that the brigade was still advancing—most likely referring to ongoing reconnaissances to feel out Gary's new position—and that Crawford held the road through White Oak Swamp.[12]

Well into early afternoon, Chapman's skirmishers probed the line that Gary's dismounted horsemen had thrown up behind the little creek. Wilson, who remained to supervise the Union effort, described the deadly screening action as "a period of extraordinary anxiety and hard work, during which much ammunition was expended and much noise made." A Hoosier remembered the daylong running battle as "the hardest fight we have had for a long time." Little did he suspect that veteran Confederate infantry was on the way, and that the day's combat was about to escalate in earnest.[13]

"May he be hung, drawn, and quartered."

Under the protective cover of Chapman's and Crawford's screening actions, the rest of the Union army marched unimpeded along its assigned routes, the 5th and 2nd Corps crossing at Long Bridge, and the 6th and 9th Corps pursuing separate routes toward Jones's Bridge.

Near sunrise on June 13, Hancock's lead elements strode into St. James's Church, a mile short of Dispatch Station on the Richmond and York River Railroad. Soldiers packed the small wooden structure and covered its walls with graffiti. "May he be hung, drawn, and quartered," a man wrote of General Grant, then went on to explain what he meant: "Hung with the laurels of victory, drawn in the chariot of peace, and quartered in the White House at Washington." After resting at the church grounds for two hours, the 2nd Corps resumed its march. Still leading, Barlow reached Long Bridge at 9:30 A.M. Gibbon's troops arrived about 11:00 and halted to eat and boil coffee while Birney's soldiers marched past, tramped over the pontoon bridge, and stopped on the south shore for lunch.[14]

Grant, Meade, and their staffs had left their encampment at Moody's around 5:30 that morning and caught up with the 2nd Corps near the river. They found Hancock sitting on the grass, pouring water from a canteen onto the thigh wound he had received at Gettysburg. He had ridden with his troops from Cold Harbor, but around 1:00 A.M. a surgeon had insisted that he continue in an ambulance. The wound had reopened and, according to Lyman, was causing the general considerable pain. The headquarters entourage waited near Long Bridge while Warren's and Hancock's troops crossed. "For several hours we killed time industriously," one of their number recalled. Francis C. Long of the *New York Herald* thought that the Chickahominy more resembled a Louisiana bayou than a river. The countryside around Long Bridge seemed "almost as dense as an Indian jungle" and was infested with "venomous reptiles, particularly water moccasins, several of which went hissing and writhing across the road as we passed."[15]

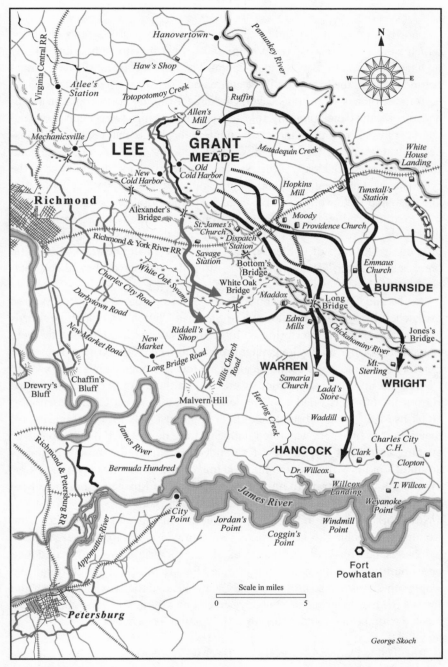

Movements of the armies, June 13

Shortly after noon, the 2nd Corps continued south past Warren's bivouacs, which were spread across the bottomland below the Chickahominy. Birney now led, followed by Barlow and Gibbon. The 5th New Hampshire remained behind to guard the bridge until the entire 2nd Corps was safely underway. By 3:00 P.M. Colonel McIntosh's cavalry brigade, bringing up the column's rear, had crossed the Chickahominy, the New Hampshire men were safely over, and engineers were busy dismantling the pontoon bridge so that it could be transported to the James. The day had warmed, and dust filled the air. A sergeant in the 7th New York Heavy Artillery remembered soldiers "all prostrate in the boiling sun—faces begrimed and features pinched, clothes stained with sweat and dust, and feet swollen and blistered." Another Yankee gazed back from a hilltop, transfixed by the "vibrating movements of that living column," as he later wrote. "It resembled the rippling waters of the restless ocean, or the undulated appearance of endless grain fields, ripe in the head, in the gentle breezes of summer." The panorama, he insisted, was "one of the greatest incidents of my life."[16]

As the 2nd Corps tramped south, the 5th Corps prepared to follow. Warren dispatched Roebling to find a route to Samaria Church "by which our corps could march without interfering with the troops of the 2nd Corps, who were crossing the bridge all day long, their trains following." The existing maps were unreliable, but the major found an alternate route through Smith's Store.[17]

Wright's and Burnside's troops were also on the move. After leaving Cold Harbor the 6th Corps had advanced east through Prospect Church and on to Hopkins Mill. "It was a bright moonlight night, just right for marching, except that the air everywhere was filled with chocking dust, which the dampness of evening could not lay," a New Englander remembered. Marshy lowlands around Hopkins Mill rendered the road impassible for wagons and guns, forcing the 6th Corps's train to retrace its route back to Prospect Church and cut over on another path to Dispatch Station Road. The going was "very tiresome," a New Yorker entered in his diary, "as we not only have to hold our load but we are also troubled to keep awake." No rain had fallen for a week, and the parched, sandy roads resembled "beds of ashes." Wright's infantry continued on to Summit Station, halted ten minutes for breakfast, passed through the empty 5th Corps camps around Moody's, and headed for Emmaus Church and Jones's Bridge. After sunrise the day heated quickly, and the men almost "suffocated with the dust, which hung over the column like a huge cloud," a marcher recalled.[18]

Burnside's troops, also assigned to cross the Chickahominy at Jones's

Bridge, had suffered through an aggravating day of fits and starts. Slipping east past Allen's Mill, they had marched north of Matadequin Creek's south fork, passed by Turner's Store, and finally reached Tunstall's Station on the Richmond and York River Railroad near daybreak, having covered some eighteen miles. Wagon trains packed the roads around the station, and after waiting impatiently several hours for the way to clear, Burnside sent an irate note to headquarters. "The delay would not have been so great had these trains traveled all night as our troops did, but instead of that they hauled out by side of the road and took a good night's rest," he complained. "They were just starting out as I arrived here, and the last of the Second Corps ambulances are just now leaving this place. The road is very narrow and completely blocked, so that my command cannot pass until they are out of the way."[19]

Burnside's winded soldiers, however, viewed the extended halt differently. "Here, fortunately for the comfort of the men, the roads were blocked by the wagon trains of the army, and the weary troops got a few hours welcome rest by the wayside," one recounted. A man from Rhode Island remarked with pleasure that he and his compatriots had "changed our resting place from a wide waste of drifting sand to a bright green valley, between whose shaded hills flowed a tiny stream." Finally around 11:00 A.M., the 9th Corps resumed its march and "struggled onward," an officer recalled, "between and around the long lines of white-topped wagons which crowded the roads." All day Burnside's soldiers labored on, passing by way of Baltimore Cross Roads and Emmaus Church on the road to Jones's Bridge. "We expected the enemy all day on our rear and right flank," a Michigan man wrote in his diary, "but none came."[20]

The engineer Major Edmund O. Beers joined the 6th Corps at Emmaus Church with bridging material for the last leg of the jaunt to the Chickahominy. It was 3:30 P.M. when Wright's lead elements reached Jones's Bridge—or Forge Bridge, as the crossing was sometimes called. "Have just heard that head of General Burnside's column was at Olivet Church, five miles from here, I think, at 2:20 P.M.," Wright informed headquarters. "My men are much exhausted, as the march has been a long one," he added, "much longer than I had supposed from the maps." Rather than pushing ahead, the general proposed resting for the night and resuming the march to Charles City Court House early the next morning.[21]

The Chickahominy at Jones's Bridge was deep, sluggish, and narrow, "lined with deep swamps thickly covered with underbrush and emitting a miasm more disagreeable if possible than that of the Yazoo," a soldier claimed. An 800-foot-wide island divided the watercourse into two streams, and an abandoned Confederate earthwork stood on the southern bank. After clearing away flood wood and shards from the old bridge, Beers's engineers assembled two canvas and two wooden pontoon bridges. Wright's soldiers started over at 5:00 P.M. and bivouacked in fields a mile south at Mount Sterling, near the Jerdone family home—mistakenly called "Verdon" in Union reports. The large meadow of tall grass, an artillerist discovered, was so filled with snakes that the ground seemed "alive, squirming and crawling around." Troops armed with spades, clubs, and sabers fanned across the clearing, killing the serpents and stacking them into mounds. Wright's soldiers were "completely tired out and foot-sore," a marcher noted in his diary. "Never felt any worse," another man agreed. "Those last miles were doled out in suffering by inches," a Vermonter concurred. "If a man wants to know what it is to have every bone in his body ache with fatigue, every muscle sore and exhausted, and his whole body ready to sink to the ground, let him diet on a common soldier's fare till he has only the strength that imparts, and then let him shoulder his knapsack, haversack, gun, and equipments, and make one of our forced marches." [22]

The 6th Corps had covered approximately twenty-two miles since leaving Cold Harbor, the 9th Corps, twenty miles. A guideboard at a nearby crossroads read: "To New Kent C.H., 10 miles. To Charles City C.H., 6 miles." Wright informed Burnside that he expected to start at four the next morning and advised the 9th Corps commander, "as you take the same road as myself, you can decide when to start so as not to be delayed by me. Three hours is not too much time to allow me for drawing out on the road." [23]

Approaching Jones's Bridge around 10:00 P.M., well after Wright had crossed, Burnside decided to camp three miles north of the river. His troops continued arriving until well after midnight. Before retiring, the general directed his division commanders to resume their march to the James at 4:00 A.M., Willcox's division leading, followed by Ledlie and Potter. [24]

The Army of the Potomac's massive wagon train made a late start from Tunstall's Station. Accompanied by Ferrero's U.S. Colored Troops, the wagons inched toward the Chickahominy crossing at Windsor Shades. Also with the wagons were two pontoon trains under Captains Personius and Middleton. Lieutenant Colonel Spaulding, charged with overseeing the various river crossings, rode ahead, examined the Windsor Shades site, and concluded that extensive swamps and marshes on the southwest shore rendered the place impractical. Coles Ferry, eight miles downriver, appeared more suitable, so Spaulding directed that the wagons reroute to there. Yet when Personius and Middleton reached Coles Ferry late on the thirteenth, they discovered that the Chickahominy was wider than they had expected and that their bridging material was insufficient. Canceling the crossing for the day, they sent a message to Spaulding requesting more pontoons.[25]

Of the Union columns, Smith's 18th Corps had the shortest, but not necessarily the easiest, distance to cover. The troops left Cold Harbor through fields littered with bloated horse carcasses and at Tunstall Station wove around "a hundred acres of wagons," a soldier estimated—the same wagons that caused Burnside so much grief. The morning's high point was a boy by the roadside selling lemons, which men "at once purchased, distributed, and [ate] down like apples, peel and all," a soldier recalled.[26]

At the end of their eighteen-mile trek, clusters of Smith's troops dotted the fields around White House Landing by the Pamunkey. "Some crawled on their hands and knees to the river bank, two or three rods away, and drank like so many animals," a New Englander reported. "They were completely exhausted." Sanitary Commission workers at the landing provoked bitter criticism when they offered canned goods to officers but not to enlisted men. "This creates much ill-feeling," a New Hampshire soldier complained, "and threats of mobbing the concern are freely indulged in." A newsman reported that some "panic-stricken sutlers proceeded to strike tents without delay, while the more knowing ones, with an unbroken confidence in Grant, still kept open house and largely increased their personal property by supplying the ravenously hungry command of Baldy Smith with canned meats and strong cheese."[27]

Orders arrived from Grant underscoring the urgency of Smith's movement. "Send forward your troops to Bermuda Hundred as fast as they embark without waiting for divisions," the general in chief directed in a dispatch from Moody's, "the object being to get them to Bermuda Hundred at the earliest possible moment." The document was silent, however, concerning what Smith and his soldiers were to do once they reached their destination.[28]

Midmorning, the 18th Corps began boarding transports for the hundred-and-fifty-odd-mile journey to Bermuda Hundred. "She had room enough, but was dirty, and had no accommodations," a soldier in Stannard's brigade remarked of the propeller ship *J. Devenny*. The 115th New York, Barton's brigade, climbed on board a cattle ship named *Salvor*. The decks were "filthy," the accommodations "the meanest," and the captain so incompetent that the craft grounded on sandbars twice during the first half-dozen miles. Around 10:00 A.M. Smith and his staff assembled on the little steamer *Metamora,* seamen hoisted the flag, and the lead portion of the 18th Corps—Brooks's division—was off. Martindale's transports were not ready until midafternoon, but by 4:00 P.M. his division was also underway. By evening most of the fleet—except for Ames's division, which remained at White House Landing until dawn on June 14—had navigated the Pamunkey and York Rivers to Fortress Monroe at Port Comfort and had anchored for the night.[29]

Ensconced in his cabin on the *Metamora,* Smith penned a note to his wife. "I am once more away from the Army of the Potomac, and Meade is, I suppose, as glad as I am," he wrote. "I once more go to Butler under the old system, and that is very unpleasant, but there is always an air of brains about Butler." By Smith's reckoning the Army of the Potomac could not do anything right: it was a "straggling, disorderly set, compared to the 18th Corps," he observed. "The trains and the men of the 2nd, 9th, and 6th Corps were all over my road and in my way," Smith continued, and advised his wife in closing that he was "trying to make up today, by sleeping, for a terrible night of headache and unrest."[30]

"Enemy left our front last night."

The Army of the Potomac's disappearance from Cold Harbor caught Lee by surprise. During the night of June 12–13, pickets in front of Anderson's 1st Corps detected heightened activity behind Union lines. "Could plainly hear the Yanks talking in front of us and later we thought we detected the movement of wagons," a soldier in Pickett's Division recorded. Near dawn all became quiet. Stealing cautiously to the enemy earthworks, the Confederates discovered that only a few blue-clad troops remained. Discarded tattered uniforms lay in heaps behind Baldy Smith's entrenchments, suggesting that new uniforms had recently been issued. Powell Hill's Confederates discovered a similar situation on their front. "We found at daylight that Grant had eloped in the night," observed Brigadier General James Conner, commanding McGowan's South Carolina brigade. The Army of the Potomac had disappeared, and no one could say precisely where it had gone. A Federal soldier still in the 18th Corps's works said the troops had moved off to White House Landing, while other prisoners told a sharpshooter from Georgia that Grant was heading to Harrison's Landing on the James.[31]

"Enemy left our front last night," one of Mahone's Confederates noted in his diary. "Scouts and skirmishers sent forward a mile or more have returned and reported none within that distance." The entire Union army seemed to have evaporated into thin air. "Even Marse Robert, who knew everything knowable, did not appear to know what his old enemy proposed to do or where he would be most likely to find him," concluded artillerist Major Robert Stiles.[32]

Sounds of combat from escalating firefights near Long Bridge on the Chickahominy gave clues to what had happened. "A rumor was soon in circulation that Grant was moving his whole army toward the James," a correspondent for the *Richmond Dispatch* reported, "and abandoning his position near Cold Harbor, which he had taken so much pain to fortify and render impregnable."[33]

Concrete information hinting at Grant's whereabouts soon arrived at Lee's headquarters. Shortly before midnight on June 12, Barringer informed his division commander, Rooney Lee, that Federals had driven his pickets from Long Bridge and were reportedly laying pontoons across the Chickahominy. The major general forwarded this report to General Lee's headquarters near Gaines's Mill, where it would have arrived near daybreak.[34]

Barringer's intelligence that Federals were crossing at Long Bridge solved at least part of the mystery. Bluecoats were pouring across the Chickahominy, and elements of the Union force—Chapman's and Crawford's men—were advancing toward Richmond on Long Bridge Road. But whether Grant meant to swing west and head for the capital below the Chickahominy or intended to continue south and cross the James was not at all clear. One point, however, was certain. Riddell's Shop intersection, and with it the direct routes to Richmond, must remain in southern hands.

Reductions in Lee's manpower during the previous week—Breckinridge's Division, two cavalry divisions, and Early's entire infantry corps were now gone—severely curtailed the Confederate commander's ability to react to Grant's move. To meet the Union shift toward the James, Lee could muster only Anderson's and Hill's infantry corps, Hoke's Division and Ransom's Brigade recently borrowed from the Petersburg defenses, and three cavalry brigades, totaling approximately 35,000 men. With most of his cavalry absent, he lacked the horsemen necessary to reconnoiter Grant's position. Assuming that Chapman's and Crawford's advance out Long Bridge Road presaged a Union offensive along that axis, Lee directed Hill's corps, which held the southern end of the Confederate entrenchments at Turkey Hill, to cross the Chickahominy and hurry to Riddell's Shop. Confederate engineers had prepared Alexander's Bridge immediately below Turkey Hill, and orders went immediately to Wilcox, whose division was close by, to cross there, strike "the York River Railway near Savage Station, and to continue, following country roads, till the Charles City Road was reached, and then advance on this toward the Chickahominy, to Riddle's Shop and there, halt and entrench."[35]

Wilcox's men were underway by 5:00 A.M., followed by Heth's and Mahone's Divisions. Not all of the Confederates were happy to be on the march. Captain William H. Brunson, commanding the sharpshooter battalion in McGowan's Brigade, had just relieved his men from duty to wash their shirts for the first time in five weeks. "They had about gotten their washing under good headway when they were ordered to assemble and prepare to move at once," a sharpshooter grumbled.[36]

At 8:00 A.M. Anderson's 1st Corps withdrew and trailed behind Hill, Kershaw's Division first, followed by Pickett's and Field's Divisions. Anderson directed his men to proceed across the Chickahominy "by the first Federal bridge below New Bridge, and thence on toward Riddle's Shop," and instructed his wagons and artillery to pass across New Bridge. Hoke's men filed out last. Aside from a scattering of pickets, orderlies, and cavalrymen, the Confederate entrenchments at Cold Harbor stood empty, looking across at the vacant Union lines.[37]

The Army of Northern Virginia marched at a blistering gait. "The day was intensely hot," a South Carolinian recalled, "so that it required unusual vigilance in officers, and unusual exertion in the men, to execute the frequently repeated order to close up and keep in four ranks." Soldiers straggled, but Wilcox, still in the lead, maintained a feverish pace. Crossing the Richmond and York River Railroad near Savage Station, the column pressed on toward Charles City Road.[38]

Wilcox had passed a mile beyond Savage Station when a courier from Gary appeared. Federals, the man reported, had driven the general's cavalrymen from Riddell's Shop and now held the intersection. Increasing his men's stride—a participant called the advance a "forced march"—Wilcox struck Charles City Road two miles west of Riddell's Shop and turned left. More cavalrymen met him there and confirmed the courier's report, adding that the enemy holding Riddell's Shop consisted of cavalry, infantry, and artillery. Hurrying on, Wilcox reached Gary's position west of the shop and halted, posting sharpshooters from Scales's and McGowan's Brigades in front and directing them to scout ahead while he deployed the rest of the division to attack. McGowan's Brigade under Conner formed on the right of Charles City Road, supported by Lane's Brigade, while Scales's Brigade moved into place on the left, supported by Thomas's Brigade.[39]

It was now 2:00 P.M. Connor directed Captain Brunson's sharpshooter battalion to lead the advance, taking care not to stray beyond supporting distance of his brigade, which was to follow in line of battle. Backed by a company from the 14th South Carolina, Brunson pressed on, scattering Chapman's pickets. "The sharpshooters behaved with their usual intrepidity," a witness confirmed, "advancing rapidly and in perfect order through the heavy timber, cheering lustily, and driving the Federal dismounted cavalry before them." Scales's North Carolina infantry pitched in as well, herding the Federals "through the woods and into an open field, and were making a dash to capture a rifle gun which had been shelling [them] when General Wilcox galloped up and ordered [them] to fall back into the pines, where [they] formed line." The South Carolina brigade's historian reported that Confederate skirmishers drove the Federals "so easily and continuously that the line-of-battle had only to follow up and keep in readiness."[40]

Surprised by Wilcox's sudden appearance, Chapman's scouts scampered back to Riddell's Shop with tales of Confederate infantry approaching along Charles City Road. Soon rebel sharpshooters came into view, backed by Wilcox's veteran infantry. "My ammunition being nearly exhausted, and the enemy showing vastly superior numbers, I deemed it prudent to retire to the position held by my second line, which was done in good order," the Federal cavalry commander later reported. Confederate participants, however, insisted that their sharpshooters slipped around Chapman's flank, turned his troopers out of their breastworks, and drove them back in disarray. "We held them as long as we could," a man in the 1st Vermont Cavalry conceded, "and then fell back in 'middling good order' without much loss to the edge of the woods where we drove them from, and then to our horses in the open field, where we mounted up expeditiously as possible, and drew saber."[41]

While Wilcox pounded Chapman at Riddell's Shop—it was now about 4:00 in the afternoon, and Wilson and his staff were enjoying a "first class dinner" in the woods—another of Hill's divisions under Heth joined Barringer's cavalryman at White Oak Swamp and escalated the pressure against Bates's Federals entrenched south of the stream. One of Heth's men proclaimed the Confederate line along the swamp "about the best position we had seen during the campaign." Another observed that "having learned the art and necessity of having good breastworks, we put the theory into practice."[42]

Reacting swiftly to the appearance of rebel infantry, Crawford thrust two more brigades into the fray. Colonel Carle's command, consisting of the 190th and 191st Pennsylvania—newly formed from the former Pennsylvania Reserves—marched out Long Bridge Road to assist the beleaguered troopers. Part of the 190th joined Chapman's horsemen, the remainder of the regiment waiting in reserve in a shallow depression, while the 191st deployed out of sight in woods south of the road. At the same time, Colonel Lyle's brigade rushed to assist Bates. Approaching White Oak Bridge, Lyle's troops came under fire from the rebel fort. "The first shell struck the road before it reached our column," an officer in the 39th Massachusetts recalled. "The men opened to the right and left, and the shell ricocheted down between them." The brigade's left wing fell back, uncovering Bates's 107th Pennsylvania. In the nick of time, Lyle sent the 13th and 39th Massachusetts to plug the gap. Half an hour later Heth's men charged again, and again Lyle and Bates drove them back. Neither side could dislodge the other, and combat along White Oak Swamp settled into a long-range shooting match across the stream.[43]

Sparring at Riddell's Shop, however, was far from over. While the South Carolina sharpshooters held the ground that they had gained, Wilcox directed the rest of his brigades into position. Near dark the rebels attacked again. "So close was the fighting that, viewed from a distance, the contending lines seemed to merge," a Confederate observed. When an infantry regiment on Chapman's right gave way, endangering the cavalry line, the colonel ordered his horsemen to retreat through Carle's Pennsylvanians. "Some difficulty, occasioned by getting the horses through a line of battle formed in our rear by General Crawford's division, created a show of confusion and scare upon the part of the cavalry which did not in reality prevail," as Chapman later explained the fiasco. "The cavalry broke and ran through our infantry," observed Warren's staffer Roebling, who watched in horror as the riders stampeded past, pursued by Wilcox's rebels. "Get your cavalry out of the way or we will fire into them," Crawford cried out. "Get your infantry out of the way or we will run over them," Wilson hollered back.[44]

Crawford's infantry supports, including the 190th Pennsylvania, commanded by Lieutenant Colonel J. B. Pattee, now faced Wilcox's Confederates alone. Pattee's horse was shot from under him, but the lieutenant colonel rallied his skirmishers on his main line. Fitzhugh's guns saved the day for the northerners, sweeping Wilcox's ranks "with grape and canister," a Federal recalled, and driving the rebels back. Particularly hard hit was Scales's Brigade, which charged over a piece of high ground that had been cleared for artillery during the Battle of Frazier's Farm two years earlier. They received the "full fire" of Fitzhugh's gunners and, according to the 22nd North Carolina's historian, "lost heavily."[45]

As the rattle of combat escalated around Riddell's Shop, Bates's and Lyle's infantrymen at White Oak Bridge feared that Chapman and Carle might collapse, enabling Wilcox's Confederates to cut them off from Long Bridge Road. Sandwiched between Heth's and Wilcox's Divisions, the two Union brigades risked destruction. At the height of the battle, Lyle sent his 13th Massachusetts to buttress Carle, but the regiment arrived only after Fitzhugh's artillery and darkness had ended the danger. In the waning daylight Heth's soldiers ventured a final charge across White Oak Swamp but were repulsed by a concerted volley from Lyle's riflemen.[46]

With night closing in, Wilcox's Confederates and Carle's Yankees dug entrenchments, facing off four or five hundred yards east of the Riddell's Shop intersection. Heth's Division, guarding White Oak Bridge, linked with Wilcox's left flank, and Mahone's Division deployed on Wilcox's right, extending south toward Willis Church. "The way our men build fortifications beats the world," Brigadier General Conner wrote his wife. "In three hours we had a capital line of works." Anderson's corps camped in fields south of Hill's men toward Malvern Hill, where the troops reminisced about their exploits on this same ground two years earlier. Gary's troopers returned to their Malvern Hill encampments, bringing their injured comrades with them. "John Thomas was wounded in the leg," a soldier in the 7th South Carolina Cavalry recalled. "[He] appealed to me to help him off the field; he placed his arm around my neck. His boot [was] filling with blood; it squirted on my pants and made me think I was shot. I labored under this impression for some time." The wounded Confederates, the cavalryman observed, "as a general thing, were terribly mangled, [the] result of grape and canister."[47]

Wilcox's advance left Colonel Lyle, who was helping Bates keep Heth at bay, surrounded by Confederates. After dark Lyle summoned his officers and outlined a plan to break out at midnight. "He also told us to tell our men of our position," Lieutenant John H. Dusseault of the 39th Massachusetts remembered, "also that no orders above a whisper should be given, and, that if we heard so much as a tin dipper jingling upon a man's haversack, to cut it off." At the appointed hour, Lyle's troops stole quietly through a field of tall grain. "The men," an officer recalled, "knowing our position and being anxious to get out, kept increasing their pace and rattling the grain, so that it was necessary to halt them and to start them again from time to time until we had cleared the grain field." Lieutenant James B. Thomas of the 107th Pennsylvania declared the movement "the most successfully done [withdrawal] of any line I ever saw."[48]

By midnight Crawford and Chapman were marching to rejoin the 5th Corps. They had performed to perfection their mission of safeguarding the army's passage and promoting the façade of an offensive north of the James. "It was necessary that some small portion of the army should make this demonstration and occupy the attention of the enemy while the chief part of it should be crossing to the Petersburg side of the James," Lieutenant Dusseault reflected. "It was thought to be our turn to take the risk which attended it. General Warren is said to have remarked that he never expected to see us again."[49]

Compared to the previous month's bloodlettings and the slaughter to come, the actions at Riddell's Shop and White Oak Bridge were but minor skirmishes.

Wilcox estimated his casualties at slightly more than a hundred men, most of them in Scales's Brigade, and Heth's losses were likely less. Crawford's subtractions were about fifty, as were Chapman's—the 8th New York Cavalry reportedly lost nine men, the 3rd Indiana, sixteen. The Confederate cavalry engaged at Riddell's Shop never submitted an official tally, but their losses probably approximated those of their Union counterparts.[50]

Strategically, however, the engagements played an important role in screening Grant's movement south. The Army of the Potomac would complete its march to the James undisturbed, and Lee would remain in the dark about his enemy's plans. The 1st Corps's artillery commander later observed that Warren's isolated position had afforded Lee an excellent opportunity to crush a detached portion of the Federal army. "The only trouble was that we were entirely ignorant of the fact that it was isolated," Alexander wrote. "On the contrary, by a well devised piece of strategy (the suggestion of Gen. Humphreys), Warren's Corps had taken up its line so near to Riddell's Shop as to give us the idea that it was the advance corps of Grant's whole army pushing toward Richmond on the road from Long Bridge."[51]

So while the Union juggernaut continued toward the James River, the Army of Northern Virginia took up a new line stretching from a point below the Chickahominy almost to the James, blocking the approaches to Richmond. "Our troops were put in a position to meet any advance of the enemy," a correspondent for the *Richmond Sentinal* observed, "the left being near White Oak Swamp Bridge, and the right near Malvern Hill, which we hold. The line crosses the Charles City Road at right angles, and runs almost parallel to and only a few hundred yards east of the Willis Church Road." Lee had constructed a superb barrier against a Union offense north of the James, should Grant decide to come that way. Grant, however, had a very different maneuver in mind.[52]

"Steady by jerks."

While Warren and Wilson held the Army of Northern Virginia at bay, Hancock's corps, accompanied by Grant and Meade, continued south toward the James. Meade's aides, riding behind Barlow's division, entertained themselves by studying the efficiency of Barlow's provost guards as they rounded up stragglers and prodded laggard troops at bayonet point. "Their tempers do not improve with heat and hard marching," Lieutenant Colonel Lyman observed of the tired men. Meade became concerned that Barlow was pushing his soldiers too hard and asked Lyman to instruct Barlow to treat them more gently. Riding ahead, the aide found Barlow perched in a cherry tree. "By jove," the general called down from the branches. "I knew I should not be here long before Meade's staff would be up. How do you do, Theodore, won't you come up and take a few cherries?"[53]

The column wound past Edna Mills to Samaria Church—often called St. Mary's Church in Union reports—and on through Ladd's Store, Ware's, Walker's, and Wadill's farms, reaching the James River Road around 5:30 P.M. near John J. Clarke's plantation. Willcox Landing was only a short distance away. The road-worn soldiers stared in awe at the broad river, surrounded by fields of wheat, oats, and clover. "To appreciate such a spectacle you must pass five weeks in an almost unbroken wilderness, with no sights but weary, dusty troops, endless wagon-trains, convoys of poor wounded men, and hot, uncomfortable camps," Lyman wrote. "Here was a noble river, a mile wide, with high green banks, studded with large plantation houses. In the distance, opposite, was Fort Powhatan, below which lay two steamers; and, what seemed strangest of all, not a Rebel soldier to be seen anywhere!" A signal officer went onto the remains of the wharf at Willcox Landing and waved a flag to alert the steamers that the Army of the Potomac had arrived.[54]

"The country around Charles City Court House [is] very good," a man traveling with Meade's headquarters observed. "Some fine fields of grain. They will suffer tonight," he predicted. Sergeant John D. Bloodgood of the 141st Pennsylvania reflected that "the march had been a very severe one, but was much preferable to scaling rebel fortifications or lying in front of the rebel line on picket." The 126th New York's Lieutenant Henry Lee wrote his mother that his "feet were blistered worse than they ever was before."[55]

The landscape was indeed impressive, but Charles City Court House left much to be desired. The settlement consisted of "a court house and jail, both unoccupied and in a dilapidated situation," the correspondent E. A. Paul noted. "The only other building in the 'city' was vacated a few days ago by its occupant, who was kind enough to leave for our horses a large quantity of corn; he also left nearly all of his housekeeping goods."[56]

As the 2nd Corps poured into Clarke's fields, Warren's troops bade farewell to the Chickahominy. Major Ford left his pontoons in place at Long Bridge until McIntosh's rearguard cavalry had crossed, then dismantled the span. After dark, when Warren judged that Crawford and Chapman would no longer need assistance from the rest of the 5th Corps, Cutler's division, accompanied by McIntosh and the 5th Corps's wagon train, led the way to Samaria Church, followed by Ayres and Griffin. Chapman lingered until Crawford's division was safely underway, then slipped into the column's rear. "After a hasty feed for ourselves and our horses," a trooper in the 8th New York Cavalry remembered, "we followed in the direction of the main body, guarding the rear and halting for a few hours' rest."[57]

McIntosh's troopers were exhausted. They had left Old Church at 2:00 A.M. and ridden to Allen's Mill, wending their way "through woods and fields, over deserted camps and fortifications, making but a short halt for breakfast." Passing through Hopkins Mill, they crossed the Richmond and York River Railroad between Dispatch and Summit Stations and finally reached the Chickahominy near sundown. Assigned to protect the 5th Corps's train, the weary riders endured an interminable succession of stops and starts. "To relieve the tired horses, when a halt occurred, some men would dismount, and sinking to the ground through exhaustion, would quickly fall asleep," a man in the 5th New York Cavalry later recalled. "Others slept in their saddles, either leaning forward on the pommel of the saddle, or sitting quite erect, with an occasional bow forward, or to the right or left, like the swaying of the flag on a signal station."[58]

The 5th Corps staff reached Samaria Church near midnight and went into camp. At one point Major Roebling thought they were being attacked but discovered that the noise "resulted from the cavalry throwing their cartridges into the fire." Warren, of course, blamed the cavalrymen for his infantry's slow progress. The rest of his soldiers trailed McIntosh and the wagon train, "which was continually getting stuck and wearing out our patience," a weary marcher recalled. Warren's men had suffered through their share of night marches under Grant, and this trek proved every bit as tedious as its predecessors. "You cannot imagine how exhausting night marching is, and we have had a great deal of it," wrote William Fowler of the 146th New York, who had the good fortune to be mounted. "It tells most just after midnight," he observed, "and then the entire of what little mind is left must be concentrated upon keeping the saddle." A soldier in Sweitzer's brigade christened the pace "'steady by jerks,' wearisome and painful." A surgeon remembered the progress as "very tedious, mostly through long lanes of trees flanked by swamps." Soldiers lighting cook fires set the undergrowth aflame, which gave a "species of purgatorial grandeur to the scenes on this night march," the surgeon remarked. Colonel Spear, commanding the 20th Maine, remembered the swamp magnolia and how its scent filled the damp night air. "The men trudged on, patiently, but in the silence of weariness," he observed.[59]

The 2nd Corps camped half a mile north of the James and a mile or so west of Charles City Court House at Clarke's plantation and on Dr. James Willcox's adjacent plantation, called River Edge. A Federal deemed the doctor's yard a "very comfortable place, the prettiest thing about it being a splendid bush of variegated roses." The corps's officers dismounted and "cooled ourselves on the porch of the house overlooking the river, while the signal officers had already put themselves in communication with Fort Powhatan, plainly in sight some few miles below." Hancock, still suffering from his unhealed wound, strolled around the encampment on foot, bareheaded and in shirtsleeves. "He is a curious man, will fret and scold and swear he 'has not a staff officer who will carry an order properly, and return, though all are supposed to be intelligent and educated gentlemen,'" a witness noted that evening. "Everybody listens to this talk with the most careless indifference, but when he gives an order of course it is obeyed."[60]

Concerned that Confederates might overwhelm the army's rearguard at White Oak Swamp and swoop down on Hancock's dozing warriors, the engineer Nathaniel Michler, escorted by the 6th Pennsylvania Cavalry, laid out a defensive line facing north. The upriver portion of these defenses anchored on Herring Creek and arched eastward, covering Swynyard's and Willcox Landing, Charles City Court House, and the Weyanoke Neck, terminating downriver at Tyler's Mill.[61]

Even though Hancock's troops had marched twenty-seven miles since leaving Cold Harbor twenty-four hours before, they immediately entrenched from habit. "Of course everyone is out of humor," a surgeon with Birney's division observed, "and a good deal of grumbling and no little swearing is the consequence." Tired as they were after a month of fighting Lee, a Pennsylvanian commented, they were "never too weary to get under cover." A newsman observed that in the war's early days, "before having learned the value of a line of earthworks, men, when they heard 'Assembly' sounded, would inquire if they had time to make coffee before marching; now they desire to know if they can make rifle pits." To everyone's relief, headquarters decided that digging was unnecessary and ordered it suspended.[62]

The 4th Maine of Birney's division, homeward bound in two days, was an exception. "Though they were told that it would not be necessary to dig rifle pits, the men did so anyway," the regiment's historian reported. "With the end of their term of service just hours away, nobody wanted it to end in tragedy."[63]

Hancock's soldiers reveled in their proximity to the James. "This was the first opportunity for a bath which had been offered since the campaign opened, and soon the water was alive with dirty and tired men," a sharpshooter from Vermont observed, "their hands and faces of bronze contrasting strangely with the Saxon fairness or their sinewy bodies, as they laughingly dashed the water at each other, playing even as they did when they were school boys in Vermont."[64]

Meade located his headquarters in a field near the deceased president John Tyler's family home, Sherwood Forest, close to Charles City Court House. "The mansion though quite pretentious, was considerably dilapidated," a soldier thought. Grant meanwhile settled into camp on Clarke's plantation. Signal officers had opened communication with Fort Powhatan and Wilson's Wharf, connecting Grant with Butler, and the general in chief immediately sent a message to Bermuda Hundred. "Head of column has just reached this place," he wrote the Army of the James's chief. "Will be at Fort Powhatan to commence crossing by 10:00 A.M. tomorrow. Communicate with me if infantry can be transferred rapidly from Wilcox's Wharf. If so, please direct quartermaster to make all necessary preparations immediately." Grant also informed Halleck of his progress. "The advance of our troops have just reached this place," he wrote. "Will commence crossing the James tomorrow. Wilson's cavalry and Warren's corps moved from Long Bridge to White Oak Swamp to cover the crossing of the balance of the army. No fighting has been reported except a little cavalry skirmishing. Smith's corps went around by water and will commence arriving at City Point tonight."[65]

In point of fact, Grant was mistaken about Smith's progress and destination. The 18th Corps's transports were in fact collecting around Fortress Monroe, where they were slated to spend the night and then continue up the James the next morning, arriving at Bermuda Hundred during the afternoon and evening of June 14.

Grant's staff was still debating where the Army of the Potomac should cross the James, either near Charles City Court House, where the scattered units were now concentrating, or farther upriver and to the west, nearer to Butler's encampments at Bermuda Hundred. Adam Badeau later wrote that Grant "was now strongly urged, by someone in his confidence, to move up the north bank of the James and cross at City Point." The aide did not identify who recommended this change in plan, noting only that the general rejected it. Grant was likely concerned that from Malvern Hill, Lee's army was ideally situated to attack the Potomac army's marching column if it advanced upriver along the James's northern bank.[66]

Determined to cross near Charles City Court House, Grant delegated the maneuvers' logistics to Meade, instructing him to reconnoiter Fort Powhatan and neighboring Hill Carter plantation early the next morning to determine the best place to cross. He was also to probe west toward Malvern Hill with cavalry to scout out Lee's position. For his part, Grant would coordinate Butler's and Meade's armies. "I will direct General Butler to turn over to the engineers and quartermasters you designate all transportation, bridging, etc., to be used under their direction until the army is crossed," he promised, instructing Meade to put the Army of the Potomac into camp "at the nearest suitable place on the south side of James River to where they cross, until further orders." Grant's chief of staff, John Rawlins, instructed Butler to "immediately cause the boats you have loaded with stone to be sunk so as to obstruct navigation at a point in the James River above where our gun-boats run, but within reach of their protection, that they may prevent the enemy's removing them should he attempt to do so."[67]

Butler promptly answered Grant's query about the condition of Willcox's Wharf. "Owing to the burning of the wharves it may take a little time to be ready to transfer troops from Wilcox's Wharf to Windmill Point, which is directly opposite," the Massachusetts general advised, adding that he had ordered barges, landing material, and water transportation to Grant's vicinity. His engineer Godfrey Weitzel was already at Fort Powhatan, Butler added, and ought to have a bridge ready by ten the next morning. He also expected Benham's pontoon train from Fortress Monroe to reach Fort Powhatan that night. Once across the James, Butler noted, the Army of the Potomac would be a mere fourteen miles from Petersburg, which was defended by no more than 2,000 troops, most of them militia. "I can, by 3 o'clock tomorrow, have 3,000 well mounted cavalry ready to cooperate with you against Petersburg," he promised, and closed with an invitation for Grant to visit him at Bermuda Hundred.[68]

At 6:45 P.M. Lieutenant Colonel Edward S. Jones of the 3rd Pennsylvania Cavalry reported that he had reconnoitered upriver to Westover Church without encountering Confederates. A native informed him that South Carolina soldiers—doubtless Gary's Brigade—had camped at Crew's plantation on Malvern Hill and had picketed to Salem Church. Captain Adams of the 1st Massachusetts Cavalry, Jones added, was reconnoitering toward Malvern Hill and expected to reach the former battlefield before dark.[69]

Butler had his own worries, chief of which revolved around Lee's probable reaction to Grant's shift south. Now that the Federals had left Cold Harbor, the Army of Northern Virginia was free to descend on Butler's thinly held defenses and overwhelm the Army of the James. Grant, of course, had considered that contingency and gambled that he could keep Lee in the dark long enough to advance Meade within supporting distance of Butler. But the next twenty-four hours promised to be anxious ones for the Army of the James. "General Grant's movements are such that may cause Lee to detach a large force from his army and move it to our front," Butler's chief of staff, Colonel John W. Shaffer, warned Brigadier General Gillmore, whose depleted 10th Corps was holding the Bermuda Hundred line, to "take all possible precaution against surprise and prepare to resist an attack."[70]

Butler's concern deepened during the evening when a Confederate craft appeared on the James near Dutch Gap and fired on a Union gunboat. "Grant has reached the river at Wilcox's Wharf," Shaffer reminded Gillmore and cautioned that "Lee has undoubtedly anticipated Grant's move. The gun-boats coming down looks like a combined attack. General Butler thinks that we may be attacked tonight or in the morning." Gillmore replied that he was aware of the incident but noted that the Confederate vessel "was a kind of tug-boat, and I attach no special importance to her movements." Butler, however, even after receiving a direct order from Grant's headquarters, still refrained from sinking the rock-filled schooners to prevent rebel craft from approaching; saving face in his standoff with Admiral Lee, it seems, made such a move temperamentally impossible. He did, however, order his troops to man the parapets and stand to their guns in the defensive line across Bermuda Hundred. "These redoubts are to be held at all hazards," he instructed.[71]

A newsman with the Army of the James reported its camps buzzing with rumors. "We heard it whisper on the air that General Grant was coming, with the glorious old Army of the Potomac at his back," he wrote. "Another breath of camp night wind said the rebels were gathering on our front in strong force and would attack us during the night. Our pickets were strengthened and General Butler and staff slept in their boots, with horses ready saddled."[72]

At Grant's headquarters Badeau reflected on the unfolding campaign. "The whole plan of the national commander at this juncture assumed magnificent proportions," he later wrote. "Sherman was advancing towards Atlanta and the sea, and [Brigadier General Edward] Canby had been ordered to begin the attack toward Mobile, to meet him, so that the rebel forces west of the mountains were all engaged; Hunter was moving up the Valley of Virginia, Crook and Averill [sic] were converging from the west and south-west, to cut off entirely the supplies reaching Richmond from those directions; Sheridan was advancing to complete the destruction and isolation on the north, while Grant himself moved with the bulk of his forces against Petersburg and the southern railroads, and was ordering cavalry to be sent to cut the canal and the Danville road." Concluded the staffer: "The rebel capital was surrounded by a terrible circle of fire, gradually drawing closer and closer, while the army and commander that guarded it must turn in every direction against the converging and contracting lines."[73]

* * *

While the Union high command laid its plans, Lee and his staff settled into tents near Riddell's Shop. On their way there they had ridden past Parker's Battery, where a "simple witted fellow named 'Possum,'" according to a witness, planted himself in the roadway, grinned at the general, and announced, "Howdy do, dad?" Lee responded, "Howdy do, my man," and continued on.[74]

The Army of Northern Virginia was now fully below the Chickahominy and arrayed in a strong defensive line extending from White Oak Swamp to Malvern Hill. Powell Hill's 3rd Corps manned the northern portion of the Confederate position, stretching southwest across the road junction at Riddell's Shop. Anderson's 1st Corps continued the line south to Malvern Hill, and Hoke's Division encamped a short distance to the west behind Anderson. Several miles north Chambliss's cavalry brigade kept watch over the abandoned Cold Harbor sector. "I have established my line from Grapevine Bridge [on the Chickahominy] to Old Church and Pamunkey River and scouting to the front," Chambliss informed headquarters. His patrols confirmed that Ferrero and McIntosh had abandoned Old Church, and captured stragglers disclosed that Burnside had passed through Tunstall's Station. It was "currently reported among the citizens recently within the enemy's lines," the general wrote, "that their troops are en route for Harrison's Landing" on the James.[75]

At ten o'clock that evening, Lee penned a report to War Secretary Seddon. News from Hampton's expedition sent to thwart Sheridan was "encouraging," he wrote, and a dispatch had just arrived reporting Sheridan's defeat near Trevilian Station. "The enemy retreated in confusion, apparently by the route he came," Lee added, "leaving his dead and wounded on the field." Developments at Cold Harbor, however, were not so clear-cut. "At daybreak this morning it was discovered that the army of General Grant had left our front," the general wrote. "Our skirmishers were advanced between one and two miles, but failing to discover the enemy were withdrawn, and the army was moved to conform to the route taken by him. He advanced a body of cavalry and some infantry from Long Bridge to Riddell's Shop, which were driven back this evening nearly two miles, after some sharp skirmishing."[76]

Although Lee still declined to speculate about Grant's probable route of march, Richmond's newspapers were quick to report every rumor. The *Dispatch* posited that Grant was "moving his whole army towards the James, and abandoning his position near Cold Harbor, which he had taken much pains to fortify and render impregnable." Although sources thought that Grant intended to cross the James, the newspaper believed it "more likely that he will make another effort this side of the James and the Chickahominy."[77]

The *Dispatch*'s uncertainty mirrored Lee's quandary. The Confederate commander had hoped to catch the Union army as it withdrew from Cold Harbor, but hamstrung by the absence of much of his cavalry, he had failed to detect its departure until the movement was well underway. Warren's screening action, assisted by cavalry, had thwarted the diminished Confederate army's attempts to break through to the marching Union columns.

Having failed in his primary objective of catching the Federals astride the Chickahominy while divided and on the march, Lee remained uncertain about what to do next. Grant's rapid southward progress suggested that the Federals contemplated a thrust toward Petersburg. The strong Union cavalry and infantry probe at Riddell's Shop, on the other hand, made a movement against Richmond north of the James equally likely. Uncertain about his opponent's true objective, Lee remained immobile near Riddell's Shop. Stretching from White Oak Swamp to Malvern Hill, the Army of Northern Virginia was ideally positioned to shield Richmond from an attack. At the same time, if Grant forwarded troops across the James, Lee was poised to shift all or part of his army across the river at Chaffin's and Drewry's Bluffs and to rush to Petersburg.

Once again, as had happened so frequently during the campaign, the Confederate commander had no choice but to forfeit the initiative to his opponent.

VIII

JUNE 14, 1864

The Army of the Potomac Starts across the James

"Like a translation from Hades to Paradise."

MONDAY MORNING, JUNE 14, witnessed the Army of the Potomac's infantry concentrating in the countryside around Charles City Court House along the defensive line that the engineer Major Michler had delineated the previous day. Hancock's 2nd Corps was camped on the Clarke and Willcox properties, above Willcox Landing; Warren's 5th Corps was starting out from Samaria Church, a little over six miles northwest of Charles City Court House; Wright's 6th Corps was preparing to march from Mount Sterling plantation, just south of Jones's Bridge and also about six miles away; and Burnside's 9th Corps was stirring near Providence Forge, a mile or so north of Jones's Bridge, prepared to follow behind Wright's men. Several miles east at Coles Ferry, the army's supply trains were congregating, waiting for additional pontoons to bridge the Chickahominy. Northwest of Charles City Court House, Wilson's two cavalry brigades under Chapman and McIntosh patrolled the roads and trails fanning toward the Army of Northern Virginia, which had taken up a formidable line extending from White Oak Swamp to Malvern Hill.

If everything proceeded according to schedule, the massive Union force was poised to coalesce around Charles City Court House by noon, ready to cross the James and initiate its grand maneuver designed to flank Lee out of his strongly entrenched position. "The people seemed to be taken by surprise," a war correspondent observed, "not expecting ever to see so large an army in their vicinity again after the departure of General McClellan's army from the Peninsula."[1]

Meade's chief of staff, Brigadier General Humphreys, was satisfied with the Union army's evacuation of Cold Harbor and its march to the James. Many in the ranks, however, were bewildered by this latest maneuver. "When will wonders cease?" Lieutenant Elisha Hunt Rhodes wrote in his diary. "Thirty six hours ago the Army of the Potomac was within nine miles of Richmond, and now we are forty miles distant." The army was now "a good deal farther from Rich[mond] than we were at Cold Harbor," Lieutenant Henry Lee informed his mother, adding that he and his fellow soldiers "hardly know what we made this move for."[2]

All morning the elements of Humphreys's carefully choreographed plan clicked into place with clocklike precision. Roused from their slumber before sunrise in the fields around Samaria Church, Warren's 5th Corps troops were on the road by 6:00 A.M. Their route took them through Ladd's Store, Georgetown, and on toward Charles City Court House. "The day was insufferably hot, the roads deep with blinding, suffocating dust, and the strain was terrible upon our staggering column," a man in Griffin's division remembered.[3]

Discipline crumbled as the blue-clad host marched past a seemingly endless array of well-appointed plantations. In an effort to reduce straggling and protect private property, Provost Marshal Patrick assigned soldiers to patrol behind the column. One such rearguard, C. D. Bibbins, spied troops swarming into a three-story plantation house and rushed to drive them out. Inside he confronted a soldier threatening to beat a young girl unless she gave him the key to a cabinet. "He was about to carry some of his many threats into execution when I stepped in and ordered him out," Bibbins later wrote, "at the same time trying to shame him for such conduct, and begged [the child's mother's] pardon for him, and assured her that we were not all like him." Half a mile farther on, Bibbins spied another mansion, cleared "a crowd of soldiers" from the house, and rescued the family's milk cow.[4]

Major Abner R. Small of the 16th Maine recalled that the regiment's commander, Colonel Charles W. Tilden, "would wink at a reasonable amount of vandalism, when the health and comfort of his men were concerned, but there was a limit, as in the case of a poor woman who lost her all." Troops burned the woman's rail fence, stripped the boards from her outbuildings, killed her last calf, and even took her teakettle. When she told Colonel Tilden what had happened, he berated his officers and paid for the calf out of his own wallet. "I have often thought of that poor old woman, gray, wrinkled, and worn, bent with the cares of many years, alone on the edge of a clearing hardly large enough, if all cultivated, to bear food for three months," wrote Small, "perhaps awaiting the return of a husband or son, and daily hoping against hope for the presence of either to shield her from insult, and keep her from starvation. Visited by first one army and then the other, who trampled into the earth her little all, alternating betwixt hope and despair, what a life she must have led!"[5]

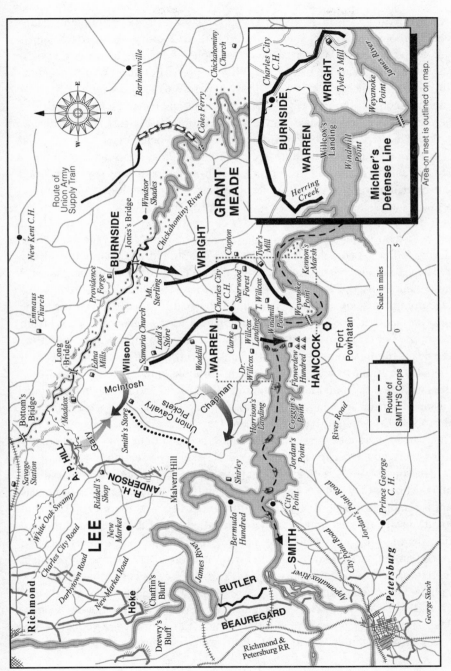

Position of the opposing forces, June 14

At noon Warren's lead elements reached the 2nd Corps encampments. Hancock's troops had already started toward Willcox Landing to board transports across the James, so Warren's soldiers occupied the vacant campsites, two divisions moving onto the Clarke and Willcox properties and two others camping nearer to Charles City Court House along Court House Creek. "We drew rations, and had a good wash in a brook nearby, and recruited up generally," a soldier wrote home to Massachusetts. The artillerist Charles Wainwright set up headquarters in Willcox's yard under a stand of locust trees. "For Virginia, it is a good house, and in quite decent order inside and around," the colonel scrawled in his diary. "I have not been in it myself, though they say the doctor's daughter, a married woman, is quite agreeable." Noted a soldier from Pennsylvania, "I must say I never seen a more beautiful place."[6]

Fifth Corps soldiers found Clarke's cherry trees so enticing that Warren posted a guard with instructions to shoot anyone climbing after the fruit. "One daring fellow sat complacently on the limb of a tree filling his mouth with the red, ripe luscious cherries, and heeding not the expostulations of the guard," a newsman reported. Pandemonium erupted when the guard shot the man in his leg, prompting a horde of soldiers to attack the guard, who fled for his life. "The next moment the tree was covered with blue uniforms—groups emerged from the house with shad and bacon in their hands," the newsman wrote. "In a trice the beautiful mansion was dismantled and everything edible carried off." Soldiers in the 16th Maine, the regiment's historian later recounted, "had a weakness for fence rails, and notwithstanding the ground had been canvassed, occasionally struck a bonanza." According to one warrior, "the people here say that when [McClellan's] army was here they made a heap of money but this time our soldiers take everything they have got, and I guess it is about so. Almost every house where an army goes is cleaned out of eatibles."[7]

The troops were struck by the contrast between their present surroundings and the horror they had left behind at Cold Harbor. "Where we bivouacked was a most delightful part of Virginia, almost a garden, and the most fertile and luxuriant we had seen," an infantryman recalled. An officer recorded his emotions as the 5th Corps went into camp. "No frowning battlements there to storm; no marshalled hosts in battle array stood ready to dispute its passage; no roar of guns to tell of deadly fray; no gleam of bayonets glinting in the sunlight on the fatal charge," he wrote. "All was peace and harmony. Animals luxuriated in the verdant pastures. Men bathed, or dabbled in the flowing waters. Many weary days of marching, intrenching, and fighting were yet before the Army of the Potomac. All thought of this were [sic] thrown aside for the moment, and each enjoyed in his own way this halcyon time. One sad thought, however, crept into the minds of many, and that was the remembrance of the brave comrades they had left lying on the bloody fields all the way from the Rapidan to the James."[8]

Soon after sunrise, Wright's 6th Corps started "at a dog trot" from its camps south of Jones's Bridge. "Having experienced all the disagreeable features of the Wilderness, and still more recently the uninviting region of Cold Harbor, and marching through the marshes and swamps of the Chickahominy, these open and fertile sections of Virginia were welcomed by our senses," a Vermonter wrote. "Comfortable farm houses and patriarchal mansions, situated in clean little villages of cabins surrounded with ornamental trees and festooned with the rare tracery of the Virginia creeper, verdant fields and scented groves and wild flowers in great profusion, filling the air with fragrance."[9]

Near noon the 6th Corps emerged onto a shallow ridge. "Before us in the distance the James River, famed in our country's earliest history and in Indian tradition, lay like a silver scarf stretched across the landscape," a soldier effused. Another man thought that "coming suddenly upon such a peaceful scene, from the torrid battle-scarred region two days behind us might seem like a translation from Hades to Paradise." Surgeon George T. Stevens was moved to eloquence. "A magnificent prospect opened before us," he wrote. "The river in the distance bordered by green fields, one undulating slope four or five miles wide, and twice as long, presenting a scene of surpassing beauty. There were large fields of grain already yellow and nearly ripe for the harvest, green meadows lay in the beautiful valleys, the gentle breeze dallied with the tassels of the long rows of corn, which gave rich promise of an abundant harvest; fine groves upon the hillside, in the valleys and upon the plain, gave a charming diversity to the scene, and the old mansions, embosomed in vines and trees, and surrounded by colonies of outhouses, reminded us of the ease and comfort which had reigned here before the ravages of war had desolated Virginia."[10]

As they approached Charles City Court House—"a little cluster of houses," according to Dr. Stevens—Wright's troops turned southeast along roads leading to Tyler's Mill, on the eastern side of the Weyanoke Peninsula. Wheaton's brigade advanced to the James, forming the right wing of the 6th Corps's portion of Michler's defensive line, facing north. General Wright established headquarters near Sherwood Forest plantation. The stately structure, a soldier noted, "had been visited by marauders and stripped of almost everything." Another man confirmed that this "once delightful home, through the visits of the soldiers, had become a scene of desolation; books and papers strewed the floors, and many a bit of crockery from the china shelves found its way northward as a souvenir of that day's tarrying near the home of a former dweller in the White House."[11]

Settling into camp, Wright's soldiers availed themselves of Virginia's riches with an abandon that rivaled that in Warren's nearby camps. "As soon as we had stacked arms I went out and got all the [cherries] I could eat after which I killed [a] pig and took 1/2 of it to camp," a hungry campaigner recorded. Provost Marshal Patrick found the troops "ravaging the whole country and killing cattle, sheep, etc., with perfect abandon, while the houses are burning with the 5th Corps headquarters in hailing distance." Some, however, were too exhausted to cause mischief. "The men are used up by the intense heat and fatigue of the past week," Lieutenant Rhodes wrote in his diary. "As soon as my tent was pitched I lay down and slept for four hours." Retiring for the evening, John H. Merrill of the 1st Ohio Light Artillery noted in his diary that "everything looks as though we might stay here a day or two."[12]

Burnside followed closely behind Wright. At 7:20 A.M. the 9th Corps commander informed Humphreys that his lead elements had started across the Chickahominy at Jones's Bridge. "As soon as General Wright gets out of the way we will follow him," he promised, "but it looks now as if it would be some hours before we can move." In fact, Burnside's men were on the march by midmorning. "The weather was hot and getting hotter, and the dusty roads were crowded with troops on the move through the finest farming country these 'farmers' sons' had seen in Virginia," a Pennsylvanian wrote home. "Those in authority made the gesture of placing guards to protect the fruit, [but] the precaution was useless, because they had to clear the roads to let the artillery, the cavalry, and the wagons pass, and the infantry had to move into the fields at the roadside." Like Wright's men before them, Burnside's soldiers thought they had entered paradise. "The elegant mansions and well-tilled lands presented a beautiful contrast to the battle-scarred and fortified fields of Cold Harbor," a New Englander recollected. "The noble forests had not yielded to the axes of the engineers, and the blight and desolation of war was nowhere visible."[13]

At noon Burnside's headquarters entourage stopped at Judge Clopton's house, where Mrs. Clopton greeted them "with all the dignity of a high born lady." Mrs. Clopton, whose husband was in a Union prison camp, explained that "if she had known we were coming she would have 'made her toillete,'" Captain Larned noted. With her was Miss Tyler, niece of President Tyler, who lived nearby at Sherwood Forest. Miss Tyler complained that "Negro troops" had sacked her home and asked Burnside to make the plantation his headquarters to protect it. The general promised to do so but soon received orders to proceed to Weyanoke Peninsula and camp on Thomas Willcox's North Bend plantation. "Some of us rode over to Sherwood and the place was a wreck, furniture smashed and bureaus turned upside down; beds ripped open; Library upside down; books and papers mutilated," the staff officer wrote. "Placed a guard and left for [Willcox's home].[14]

All afternoon Burnside's troops collected around North Bend. "The road was shaded by cherry and mulberry trees, which, when we halted, became alive with blue jackets, gathering their fill of the pleasant fruits," a New Englander recalled. "As we approached the James the masts of transports could be seen above the trees upon the right, enlivening the hearts of the men who were tired of the endless pine forests we had been traversing." Another soldier felt that the river "seemed to put us again in communication with the world, after the weeks spent wandering amidst the pine forests and deserted plantations of desolate, war-ravaged Virginia."[15]

The 9th Corps camped behind Michler's line, its right resting near the Jones house on a tributary of the James and the remainder of the corps reaching northwest to link with the 6th Corps. Willcox's home at North Bend "was a rather ordinary house, and very shiftlessly fitted up and furnished like all Virginia houses, but most situated and surrounded by magnificent trees, etc.," the staffer Major Charles J. Mills observed. "Gen Potter of our 2nd division and General Wright of the 6th Corps had their headquarters at the same place and the three staffs coalesce[d] and jollified together."[16]

By evening on June 14, blue-clad troops had fully occupied Michler's defensive line protecting the Weyanoke bridgehead. Warren's 5th Corps held the upriver segment, anchored at Herring Creek; Wright's 6th Corps occupied the middle stretch through Charles City Court House; and Burnside's 9th Corps secured the downriver portion, reaching through Tyler's Mill to the James. "The men were gathered in groups around piles of blazing rails, busily cooking their evening meal," a New Englander recalled. "The bands were discoursing patriotic music, and the whole scene was one of the most striking and magnificent of war." Many units, however, had outstripped their supply wagons. "We stacked arms in line of battle, and just as we did so a quail flew up," Stephen M. Weld of the 9th Corps wrote in his diary. "The men had broken ranks, and they gave chase and caught him." Supplemented with roasted box turtle and hardtack, the quail provided a perfect end to a strenuous day.[17]

War correspondent Sylvanus Cadwallader visited the 36th Wisconsin's encampment, which was filled with soldiers who had joined the Army of the Potomac during the North Anna operations and had been fighting and marching ever since, sustaining severe losses at Totopotomoy Creek and in the big attack at Cold Harbor on June 3. They had yet to change clothes and were "literally encrusted in mud, dirt, dust, perspiration, and blood—unwashed, unkept, unfed, for rations had not always reached them as needed," Cadwallader recorded. The regiment's colonel, John A. Savage, sprawled on the ground, "a picture of suffering, emaciation and exhaustion, never to be forgotten."

Cadwallader had just received fresh rations and directed his cook, who had formerly served as a chef at Willard's Hotel in Washington, to prepare a meal for himself and the colonel. While Savage napped on the correspondent's cot, the cook improvised a sumptuous meal of potatoes, tomatoes, onions, canned fruit, imported sauces and pickles, cream cheese, sausage, canned oysters and lobster, pudding, and pie. On awakening, Savage gorged on the repast, washed down with a "judicious admixture of *spiritus frumenti* and condensed milk, sweetened and spiced to taste, known in army circles by the complimentary name of milk punch." After the feast Savage slept on Cadwallader's cot for an hour, then left, his pockets stuffed with cigars and his canteen filled with whiskey.[18]

In his tent near the Tyler plantation, Chief of Staff Humphreys reflected on the campaign. "I perceive by extracts from foreign papers that the *London Times* and the French Papers give the two American armies the credit of fighting more desperately for a longer time and with more carnage than any nation before them," he wrote home. "That never in the histories of the wars of the Old World, nor in history of man, were so many and such desperate battles fought in so short a time, and that it is difficult to understand how the strain and exhaustion could have been supported."[19]

Not everything, however, was proceeding as planned. While the Army of the Potomac's infantry assembled around Charles City Court House, the army's wagon trains remained stymied north of the Chickahominy at Coles Ferry.

News that the available pontoons were insufficient to bridge the river at Coles Ferry had not reached Lieutenant Colonel Spaulding until the morning of June 14. The engineer immediately ordered the army's other pontoon trains—the ones still at Jones's Bridge and those from Long Bridge, which were now almost to Charles City Court House—to hurry to Coles Ferry. Then he rushed to Coles himself, where he met Captain Personius, who was struggling to bridge the Chickahominy with the resources at hand. The enterprising engineer had built wharves on each bank and had managed to float a few wagons across on a raft made from pontoons. Floating the entire wagon train over, however, was manifestly impossible. "I also found the width of the river was such that with all our pontoon material we could not span the river without extensive timber and corduroy approaches," Spaulding concluded after inspecting Personius's handiwork. Ferrero, whose U.S. Colored Troops were guarding the wagon train, assigned several hundred soldiers to help build a 250-foot timbered approach on the north bank for use when the rest of the pontoons appeared. "I went a fishing—got two bull heads, 1 eel, 4 sunfish, and a mud turtle," Elbert Corbin of Battery B, 1st New York Light Artillery, wrote in his diary as he waited for the bridge's completion. "Had fish for supper."[20]

At 1:00 P.M. Major Beers arrived from Jones's Bridge with his pontoons and bridging material. Four hours later Major Ford appeared with the Long Bridge pontoons. Now all of the Potomac army's pontoons, except those with Sheridan's raiders, were available to bridge the Chickahominy. As night fell on June 14, Ferrero's soldiers completed a raised corduroy approach on the north shore. After dark Personius floated pontoons into the river from each bank, assembling the bridge from each side toward the middle. "It was a pretty heavy job to corduroy the marsh, which was fully half a mile wide and quite deep," observed Assistant War Secretary Dana, who monitored the project. "It was a sleepy moonlight night, but hazy, so that no stars appeared," a man with the 50th New York Engineers recalled. "Every breath of the heavy atmosphere acted as a soporific."[21]

To Spaulding's horror, when the supply of pontoons was exhausted, a 30-foot gap still separated the two wings. To correct this deficiency, engineers detached the pontoons from the north shore, drifted them across the Chickahominy, and fastened them onto the bridge's southern section, eliminating the gap between the two sections but creating a new opening with the north shore. Engineers then laboriously extended the causeway into the river, which "caused considerable delay in the completion of the bridge," Spaulding observed, "but it was finally ready for use about three hours after midnight." Altogether, the timbered and corduroyed approaches amounted to 450 feet, and the bridge itself, 1,240 feet.[22]

Spaulding had done an exemplary job curing an error that advance reconnaissance and planning would have prevented. At long last, during the early morning hours of June 15, the Potomac army's wagon trains began lumbering across the Chickahominy on their way to Charles City Court House, twelve miles distant.

The delay meant that the pontoons were unavailable on June 14 for use in constructing the bridge across the James. Warren's staffer Roebling later reflected on the consequences. Since "the pontoon bridge for the wagon train over the Chickahominy at Coles' Ferry was too short by half its length, a pontoon train under Major Ford was sent down," he wrote. "Our army lost a day by that. In other words, rather than run the very remote risk of losing a wagon train, they run the very positive risk of losing Petersburg, as the success of the whole movement depended on one day."[23]

"Expedition in crossing [the James River] is what is wanted," Grant reminded Meade early on June 14, "and to secure this you can cross from different points or all from one place, as you deem best." Taking these instructions to heart, the army commander at 8:30 A.M. directed Hancock to ferry his troops from Willcox Landing "at once" directly across the river to Windmill Point, where they were to camp on "suitable ground."[24]

Hancock ordered Birney's division to cross first, followed by Gibbon and Barlow. "The scene on the arrival at the river, and especially during the crossing, was very picturesque," observed Lieutenant Colonel Charles H. Banes, who reminisced about his visit to this same region two years earlier with General McClellan. "The similarity did not extend, however, to the morale or physical appearance of the men," he noted. "At the former period they were discouraged and depressed after a campaign without apparent result, and prostrated in body from the effects of the Chickahominy swamps. Now the troops appeared cheerful and full of hope for the future, in their bronzed faces flushed with health and in their firm step, of ability to make still greater sacrifices."[25]

Three steamboats—the *Monohauset,* the *General Hooker,* and the *Eliza Hancox*—stood anchored at Willcox Landing to take Hancock's soldiers across the river. The wharf, however, was ill suited to handle the 2nd Corps's entire complement of troops and accouterments. "There are no conveniences for loading artillery or wagons here now," Hancock's aide Lieutenant Colonel Morgan reported, nor were there boats or barges for horses. "All that can be done is to send the infantry down as needed," Morgan concluded, directing that the corps's artillery, wagons, and horses cross later, either on the anticipated pontoon bridge or after the wharves were improved.[26]

Birney's lead elements boarded the *Eliza Hancox* shortly before 11:00 A.M. and were ferried across to Wind Mill Point. From there they marched to nearby Flowerdew Hundred plantation—also owned by members of the Willcox family—and bivouacked in a clover field, where they "harvested" the owner's vegetables and tore down a barn for firewood. "We cannot cook the stuff raw," a volunteer from Maine explained; "we have already perpetrated outrages enough on our stomachs." Other soldiers stripped cherries from trees, bathed in the river, and feasted on hoecakes eagerly sold by the Willcox family's slaves. Encountering troops near the Flowerdew Hundred plantation house hunting eggs and pigs, Birney, who considered the looting intolerable, "flew into a rage and charged down on the boys, drawing his sabre," recollected Sergeant Wyman S. White of the 2nd U.S. Sharpshooters. According to White, the general refrained from striking anyone but "used some very strong profanity and overbearing language and lost the respect of some of his men."[27]

The river crossing was "slow going," Brigadier General Robert McAllister wrote his wife, since the ferries had to board soldiers at Willcox Landing, cross the river, discharge their passengers at Windmill Point, then steam back for the next load. The cruise across the James, however, raised everyone's spirits. "Our hearts were filled with new hope," a soldier from New Jersey remembered, "for we had bidden farewell to the swamp and the miasmata of the Chickahominy, to the long line of graves that stretched not only across the peninsula, but across the hills, and valleys, and streams, and through the fertile fields and tangled swamps of Virginia up to the Rapidan." A Pennsylvanian thought that "every heart beat high with hope, and every man looked forward to what he believed would be the speedy downfall of the rebellion."[28]

At 1:00 P.M.—three more hours would pass before all of Birney's men were across—Hancock issued a circular. Once Birney was over, his division was to "take up suitable ground for the defense, covering the landing." Gibbon's and Barlow's divisions were to cross next, deploy on Birney's left, and entrench, taking care to leave no intervals in their line.[29]

Waiting their turn, Barlow's troops passed the time resting, bathing, and fishing. "All the hardships and fighting of the past two weeks were forgotten in the hunt for fishing tackle and bait," a soldier in the 116th Pennsylvania remembered, "and the fish caught were a treat, for the commissary was very low."[30]

Someone decided that it would be a good idea to let cattle accompanying the 2nd Corps swim across the James. The experiment started without incident, but a few animals panicked two-thirds of the way across and turned back, spooking the rest. The herdsmen, rowing alongside the cattle in small boats, pulled for their lives as the frenzied creatures tried to clamber aboard. "Some of the boats were upset but no lives were lost except perhaps some of the cattle," an onlooker reported.[31]

The addition of three more boats, nudging the total up to six, helped expedite the crossing of Hancock's artillery, horses, and trains. The additional vessels, however, created new problems, as the landing site was too constricted to accommodate the traffic. Hancock decided to construct a permanent wharf at Windmill Point, and shortly after 7:00 P.M. Colonel Brainerd and 230 workers from the 50th New York Engineers arrived on two tugboats. Locating Birney, Brainerd asked the general to provide him a thousand soldiers to dismantle barns and salvage wood for a pier. "Soon the material born upon the shoulders of the men began to arrive," the colonel wrote. The work, however, took longer than the engineer had anticipated. "The night was cloudy and dark, the country strange," Brainerd recalled. Around three in the morning of the fifteenth, a tugboat brought him half a dozen pontoons, enabling him to complete "a passable and quite permanent landing" before daylight.[32]

All told, ferrying Hancock's troops across the James consumed almost eighteen hours. The process began at 11:00 A.M. on the fourteen: Birney's division was not entirely across until 5:00 P.M., Gibbon's men completed the crossing around 10:00 P.M., and the last of Barlow's troops did not reach the river's southern shore until 5:00 A.M. on the fifteenth. "The James River presented an entrancing sight with moonbeams dancing on the waters, and the steamers plying busily to and fro in the river, with their human freight," a soldier on one of the late-night voyages remembered. "Every heart beat high with hope," a Pennsylvanian recollected, "and every man looked forward to what he believed would be the speedy downfall of the rebellion."[33]

While Meade's infantry moved into position around Charles City Court House and Hancock's corps initiated the movement across the James, Wilson's cavalry—Chapman's and McIntosh's brigades—screened the Potomac army's location from the rebels. "[Samaria] Church and its vicinity were for the next forty-eight hours the scene of about as much active cavalry work as took place in so contracted a space at any time during the war," Wilson later wrote, "and it was doubtless on account of that activity that Lee, with his cavalry following Sheridan, completely lost touch with Grant's army, and failed for two days at least to detect his plans or to foresee his destination."[34]

At dawn on June 14, after four hours of rest, Wilson's troopers downed breakfast at Samaria Church and set off for Charles City Court House to the south. Arriving at Willcox's home around 10:00 A.M., they dismounted and relaxed for several hours, "grooming horses, and issuing rations in the meantime," according to Wilson. A man in the 18th Pennsylvania Cavalry recorded that he "at once went to the river for much needed bathing and washing of shirts, etc.; others led their horses into the river and washed and bathed their galled backs."[35]

Toward evening, a bugler sounded "Boots and Saddles," and the two Union cavalry brigades rode out to patrol the roads toward the Army of Northern Virginia. McIntosh's horsemen retraced their morning's route back to Samaria Church, passing through Warren's infantrymen, who loudly cheered them. Nearing the church, they ran headlong into the Hampton Legion of Gary's Bri-

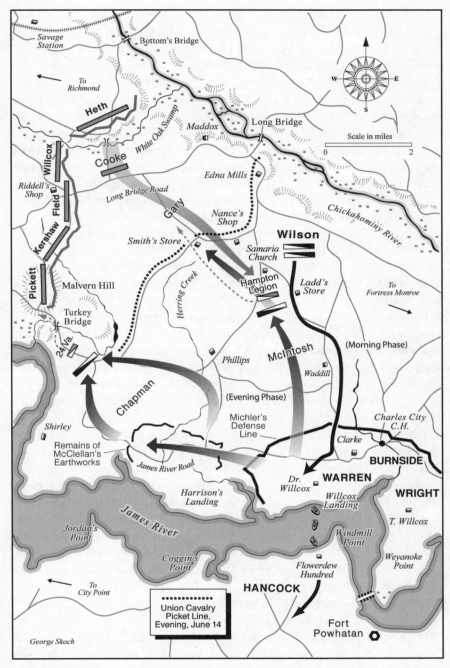

Cavalry operations, June 14–15

gade, which was scouting toward the James in search of the Army of the Potomac. "Skirmishing with the enemy the entire distance, and driving him before me," McIntosh reported to Wilson. Reaching Samaria Church around 8:00
P.M., the Union brigade settled in for the night, pickets advanced on the main
road running north toward Long Bridge and out a side road that passed west
through Nance's Shop to Smith's Store, where it intersected a north–south road
from Harrison's Landing to Long Bridge Road near White Oak Swamp. "The
regiment halted shortly before midnight," a soldier in the 18th Pennsylvania
remembered. "No fires were allowed to be built, nor horses to be unsaddled; a
heavy line of pickets were placed in front." A New Yorker complained that
Confederate pickets were so close that cooking fires were forbidden, which
meant that "the boys ate their supper without the usual coffee." Two squadrons
from the 1st Connecticut ventured north to Long Bridge Road to sound the
alarm if more Confederates approached from that direction.[36]

Chapman's brigade meanwhile rode upriver along the James's northern
bank, heading toward the southern terminus of General Lee's Malvern Hill defenses. Admiral Lee's Union gunboats had been shelling Malvern Hill all afternoon, and judging from Confederate accounts, made life miserable for the
southerners. "9 and 11 inch shells are very ugly things should they explode in
your neighborhood and go making a most terrible and deafening noise and
scattering many fragments of iron and bullets very promiscuously and liber-
ally around and over a great area," one of Pickett's soldiers complained, "and
so making that neighborhood for the time exceedingly unhealthy and undesir-
able to those who value life and limb." The explosions, the soldier noted, "affect the drum of my ear and tend to make me nervous and to wish I was in any
other locality on this earth."[37]

Reaching Harrison's Landing, Chapman's men rode into the remains of
earthworks built by McClellan's soldiers two years earlier. "We halted upon an
extensive field near the river, which was covered by a rich growth of clover," a
New Yorker recalled, "when we unsaddled our weary horses and prepared to
enjoy a few hours' rest and draw some much needed rations for man and beast."
No sooner had the troopers settled in, however, when orders came to saddle up
again. The brigade's pickets were under attack, and a large Confederate force
was rumored to be approaching.[38]

Chapman's troopers rushed to meet the interlopers, who to their relief comprised only a small detachment of Confederate cavalry. After shooing away the
rebels, they returned to Harrison's Landing and extended pickets northward,
connecting with McIntosh's pickets below Smith's Store. Union cavalry now
firmly held the routes leading from Lee's army to Meade's.[39]

*"I fear that the delay with the completion of the bridge
will enable Lee to make Petersburg safe."*

On June 12 Lieutenant Michie had recommended a site for a pontoon bridge across the James, reaching from Weyanoke to a point on the river's southern bank near Fort Powhatan. Butler's chief engineer, Brigadier General Weitzel, forwarded Michie's suggestion to Comstock and the next morning, without waiting for the lieutenant colonel's reply, directed Michie to prepare approaches to the proposed bridge site. Michie's first step was to cut timber to construct a wooden "corduroy" causeway across the peninsula's marshy fringe firm enough to support the army's massive wagon train. Assembling a team of 150 workers, Michie had them slice 1,200 feet of timber into sticks averaging six inches in diameter and 20 feet long. A second team harvested 3,000 feet of timber from the river's southern shore and brought the pieces to a creek above Fort Powhatan, ready to be rafted across to Weyanoke.[40]

At 3:00 P.M. on June 13, Grant informed Weitzel that the Potomac army would reach the Weyanoke bridgehead by 10:00 A.M. on the fourteenth and instructed him to prepare approaches "at once" at the locations Michie had designated. That evening Meade directed Benham to bring all of the pontoons and bridge material from Fortress Monroe "immediately" to Fort Powhatan.[41]

Weitzel's engineers labored all night. Assisted by the 4th New York Heavy Artillery, they improved the road from Tyler's Mill to the upper Weyanoke, removed and rebuilt an aging wharf, and carved a road down the bluff to the river on the south shore. In constructing the approach on the Weyanoke side, they felled massive cypresses, some measuring four feet in diameter, sliced them into smaller pieces, and piled the surplus wood beside the road. After clearing brush they prepared a firm causeway by laying a roadbed of sand, then corduroyed the approach by positioning boards sideways across the bed. The completed causeway crossed five hundred feet of marsh and was strong enough to carry the weight of the massive Union army and its supply wagons, artillery, and cattle. Weitzel had finished the approaches on both sides of the river by 9:45 A.M. on June 14, a quarter of an hour before the time that Grant had set for the army to reach the bridgehead.[42]

Weitzel and Michie had performed their assignment to perfection. The pontoons and other material necessary to build the bridge, however, were nowhere to be seen. In a perfect storm of ineptitude, bad planning, and faulty coordination, the pontoons traveling with the Army of the Potomac were still at Coles Ferry, twelve miles away on the Chickahominy. And the transports with the pontoons that Benham had collected at Fortress Monroe were peacefully at anchor some forty miles downriver, the captain in charge fast asleep.

What had happened was this. On June 4, while formulating his plans for the movement across the James, Grant had instructed Benham to collect bridging material and to "hold it in readiness to be moved at short notice." Most of the available pontoons were at Bermuda Hundred, but by June 12 Butler had sent to Fortress Monroe everything not required for his floating bridge across the Appomattox. Benham now possessed 155 pontoons, sufficient to build 3,100 feet of bridge, and planking for a bridge 2,600 feet long. Since the James River was only 1,992 feet wide at the site selected by Michie, the resources at Fortress Monroe seemed more than sufficient for the task at hand.[43]

The designation of Fortress Monroe as the depot for material to construct a floating bridge at Weyanoke Peninsula, however, was shortsighted. The post was sixty miles downriver from the projected bridge site, while Bermuda Hundred was only eight miles away, and upriver to boot, making it by far the better staging site. From Bermuda Hundred or City Point, bridging material could be quickly transported downriver to Weyanoke; from Fortress Monroe, however, the pontoons, stringers, and chess had to be carried almost eighty miles upriver, against the current. As often happens in war, everything that could go wrong, did go wrong.

On June 12 Grant wrote the 18th Corps's quartermaster, Colonel Herman Biggs, at Fortress Monroe to "forward up the James River all things within your charge and request the engineering officer at Fort Monroe (Benham) for me, to send all the pontoon bridge material he may have on hand" to Fort Powhatan. At 9:30 A.M. on June 13, Benham informed Meade's aide Seth Williams that he was sending the 155 pontoons and related material to Fort Powhatan "immediately." Captain Robbins, who had just hauled most of this material from Bermuda Hundred to Fortress Monroe the previous day, was now to place it all back on the transports and retrace his route sixty miles upriver. One can only imagine the captain's musings about the inanity of his superiors.[44]

Loading the bridging material onto barges to be towed by steamships to Fort Powhatan consumed several hours. Finally, around 2:00 P.M. on June 13, Captain Robbins set off with the flotilla. After steaming approximately eighteen miles upriver, he decided to anchor for the night.[45]

Why Robbins stopped before completing his mission has never been satisfactorily explained. Weitzel, who was waiting impatiently at Weyanoke for the pontoons, blamed the delay on the captain's "inexcusable tardiness" and "more than culpable neglect of duty." This vituperative attack was unduly harsh. Robbins, it will be recalled, had taken the pontoons to Bermuda Hundred in early

June, had brought them back to Fortress Monroe a few days later, and now after less than twenty-four hours, was instructed to take them upriver again. No surviving communications suggest that he was told that the current movement of the pontoons was any less routine than the previous trips, that there was need for haste, or that the pontoons had to reach Weyanoke and Fort Powhatan in time to construct a pontoon bridge to carry the Army of the Potomac across the James midmorning on the fourteenth.[46]

As the morning wore on with no sign of Robbins, Weitzel became increasingly agitated. "So anxious was I that there should be no delay that I sent a dispatch boat for the pontoons down the river, with orders to go until they were found and hurry them up," he wrote in his official report of the affair. Weitzel's emissary located Robbins and the transports anchored below Jamestown, the captain still fast asleep. His discussion with Robbins is unknown, but the flotilla was soon underway. Sometime after noon the ships, with their barges in tow, steamed up to Fort Powhatan and began unloading their cargo of pontoons and bridging material.[47]

Major Duane, the Potomac army's chief engineer, soon arrived with the Regular Engineer Battalion and joined Weitzel, who was still at Weyanoke with several companies of the 1st U.S. Volunteer Engineers. "Nothing had been done, however, toward commencement of the bridge," wrote Gilbert Thompson, an officer in the regular engineers. "The flooring material looked as though it had been struck by a cyclone; the [pontoons] were scattered in confusion over the low, marshy ground along the shore, and the officer of the volunteers was unable to make his men go into the mud and slime and bring the [pontoons] ashore." At Duane's command men from the Regular Engineer Battalion, their noncommissioned officers leading, "jumped into the mud and water almost to their necks and by commendable, but unrewarded, zeal and energy succeeded in one hour in building a bridge abutment about 150 feet long that reached the water proper." The battalion then went to the opposite shore, and the 15th New York Volunteer Engineers, who had arrived from Fortress Monroe with the pontoons, helped them prepare the southern approaches as well.[48]

David F. Ritchie, commanding a New York battery, rode over to watch the bridge construction. "The evening was magnificent and the river, here over a mile wide, was thickly covered with transports of every kind," he remarked, "while the bank was lined with all the paraphernalia of a grand army, marching troops, horses and batteries, and over everything could be heard the strains of martial music from the bands as the vessels moved out toward the opposite bank." Everything connected with the movement, he mused, "has been man-

aged with the most consummate skill and celerity, so far as my observation has
extended. There is no unaccountable delay, no waiting for trains or transports
or pontoon bridges. Secession must begin to feel nervous about this earnest
warrior, this modern Ulysses."[49]

Not everyone shared Ritchie's optimism. Agitated over delays in constructing the pontoon bridge, Grant sent his aide Comstock to "look after progress
of bridge corduroying etc." opposite Fort Powhatan. "Things not going fast,"
Comstock noted in his diary. "Hurried them up a little." Mirroring Grant's concern, the 5th Corps's artillery commander, Colonel Wainwright, scrawled in
his diary his "fear that the delay with the completion of the bridge will enable
Lee to make Petersburg safe."[50]

At 4:00 P.M. on June 14, the engineers finally began assembling the span,
working simultaneously from both shores toward the center. The obstacles
were daunting. Not only did the tide rise and fall four feet in this section of the
James but also the change reversed the flow's direction. To stabilize the floating bridge above the eighty-five-foot-deep main channel, engineers anchored
three schooners on the upriver side of the bridge and three downriver. Because
ships needed to pass through the bridge to reach Butler's army at Bermuda
Hundred and to stock the depot at City Point, the engineers created a one-
hundred-foot section of rafts in the middle of the structure that could be floated
to the side to open a passage.

During the afternoon, Benham arrived from Fortress Monroe and took over
from Duane. The corpulent general, according to Lyman, was in his "usual
condition of active muddle" but fortunately appeared "too late to seriously im-
pede the work." Lyman noted that Benham "carried off all the credit, to the
great rage of Duane."[51]

Shortly before 11:00 P.M. Benham informed headquarters that the final pontoon was in place and that the gap for boats could be closed in fifteen minutes,
if Meade so wished. "Complete the bridge," Meade responded half an hour
later. Burnside, he ordered, was to start his artillery and trains across the bridge
right away, to be followed by the 6th Corps's artillery and trains.[52]

The floating bridge was completed by midnight, seven hours after work on
it had commenced. It was two thousand feet long, ten feet wide, and rested on
101 wooden pontoons spaced twenty feet apart, from center to center, and anchored in place. "The flooring system provided a wearing surface of chess,
wooden planks 12 inches wide by 1 1/2 inches thick, laid on 5 'balks' (stringers) 5 inches square," an engineer reported. A newsman estimated that the
bridge's floor floated two feet above the water and was sufficiently wide for

twelve men or five horses to cross abreast. It was the longest bridge of its type built to date. Assistant War Secretary Dana considered the bridge "unprecedented in military annals, except, perhaps, by that of Xerxes, being nearly seven hundred yards long." Lyman surmised that "in civil life, if a bridge of this length were to be built over a river with a swift current and having a maximum depth of eighty-five feet, they would allow two or three months for the making of plans and collecting of material. Then not less than a year to build it."[53]

"No plan was formulated for me to follow."

Late in the morning of June 14, while Weitzel paced Weyanoke Peninsula's marshy fringe waiting for pontoons, Grant, Rawlins, and several of the general in chief's other aides boarded a boat for Bermuda Hundred to meet with Butler and give him "the necessary orders for the immediate capture of Petersburg." The ship steamed up the James past an imposing array of grand plantations. Eight miles later—it was now 12:30 P.M.—the distinguished party pulled up to the wharf at Bermuda Hundred.[54]

Riding the short distance to the headquarters of the Army of the James, Grant dismounted, handed his reins to an orderly, and strode toward Butler's tent. Seeing Grant approaching, cigar in hand, Butler stepped out and greeted him. It was the first time the two generals had talked face to face since their planning sessions in April, before the campaign began. Chatting cordially, they retired to Butler's tent, where they ate lunch and discussed the impending campaign.[55]

According to Grant in his official report, he gave Butler "verbal" instructions "to send General Smith [to Petersburg] immediately, that night, with all the troops he could give him" without endangering the Bermuda Hundred defenses. "I told him," the general in chief wrote, "that I would return at once to the Army of the Potomac, hasten its crossing, and throw it forward to Petersburg by divisions as rapidly as it could be done; that we could reinforce our armies more rapidly there than the enemy could bring troops against us." In his deathbed memoir decades later, Grant gave a similar recounting of the meeting. "General Butler was ordered to send Smith with his troops reinforced, so far as that could be conveniently done, from other parts of the Army of the James," he wrote. "Smith was to move under cover of night, up close to the enemy's works, and assault as soon as he could after daylight. . . . While there I informed General Butler that Hancock's corps would cross the river and move to Petersburg to support Smith in case the latter was successful, and that I could reinforce there more rapidly than Lee could reinforce from his position."[56]

Butler's recollection of the meeting comported in important particulars with Grant's memory. Smith was to undertake the attack, while elements from the Army of the Potomac would be available to assist if needed. Butler later wrote that he had estimated the entire collection of Confederate troops in Petersburg—including the second-class militia, reserves, penitents, and convalescents—numbered no more than two thousand men, while Smith could muster a force in the range of eighteen thousand. "The only anxiety General Grant had about such an attack," he recalled, "was lest Lee, knowing Grant had crossed the James, and having the shorter line and the railroad from Richmond to Petersburg, should move directly to Petersburg, and that when Smith got there, he should find the city occupied by Lee's veterans." Butler, however, felt that Grant's apprehension was unwarranted, as his own lookouts had detected no movement on Lee's part.[57]

After lunch Grant requested a tour of the Bermuda Hundred defenses. Horses were saddled, and accompanied by Butler and their staffs, he rode to the front. Butler pointed out the sights, including an imposing signal tower near his headquarters, and led Grant down a steep ravine to the Appomattox River. After a whirlwind examination of the fortifications, the entourage clattered back to headquarters. Satisfied with what he had seen, Grant sent a dispatch to Halleck. "Our forces will commence crossing the James today," he wrote at 1:30 P.M. "The enemy show no signs yet of having brought troops to the south side of Richmond. I will have Petersburg secured, if possible, before they get there in much force. Our movement from Cold Harbor to the James River has been made with great celerity and so far without loss or accident."[58]

Grant's appearance at Bermuda Hundred, brief as it was, caused quite a stir. "As he rode along the men ran out of their tents and across the fields to have a look at the 'little man on the gray horse,'" a newsman recorded. "They seemed to look on him with a feeling of awe. But the General was perfectly oblivious of the excitement his presence had created. He chatted with General Butler and puffed away at his cigar. When one was smoked out he took another from his breast pocket, and, lighting it from the old butt, puffed away again." The reporter thought that Grant's presence indicated "strength, firmness and decision, and from what I saw and heard to-day, the men have unbounded confidence in him."[59]

Midafternoon, Grant returned to Charles City Court House. He later claimed that he briefed Meade about his meeting with Butler. He may well have done so, but he failed to make clear the Potomac army's role in his overall plan. In a memorandum prepared two weeks later, Meade firmly denied that Grant ever informed him "of the contemplated movement against Petersburg, and the necessity of [Hancock's] cooperation." To Meade's understanding, Hancock's assignment was to finish ferrying his troops across the James and then to push his men "forward in the morning to Petersburg; halting them, however, at a designated point until they could hear from Smith." Grant also neglected to express Hancock's need to move with expedition, instead authorizing the corps commander to wait for the delivery of rations before setting off. Grant's failure to clearly communicate his grand plan for the approaching operation—Smith was to attack Petersburg while Hancock was to remain ready to support him if necessary—was to profoundly influence the outcome of the offensive.[60]

The soldiers needed rations, and the army's huge wagon train was still at Coles Ferry, waiting to cross the Chickahominy. So as not to delay Hancock, Grant directed Butler to send the 2nd Corps 60,000 rations from Bermuda Hundred. At ten that evening Meade gave Hancock his marching orders. "General Butler has been ordered to send to you at Windmill Point 60,000 rations," he informed the 2nd Corps commander. "Soon as these are received and issued you will move your corps by the most direct road to Petersburg, taking up a position where the City Point railroad crosses Harrison's Creek where we now have a work. After Barlow has crossed, you will cross as much of your artillery and ammunition train as possible up to the moment you are ready to move, and if all is quiet at that time the ferriage of the rest can be continued, and they can join you."[61]

Relying on Meade's directions, Hancock promulgated orders for the morning's advance. At 10:00 A.M., or as soon as rations were distributed, Birney was to march out on the direct road to Petersburg and halt where City Point Railroad crossed Harrison's Creek. Gibbon and Barlow were to follow in that order and deploy on Birney's right, extending toward the mouth of Harrison's Creek. Two batteries would accompany each division. The 4th New York Heavy Artillery would remain behind until the corps's wagons had crossed, then escort the train to the new location.[62]

Also that evening, Grant sent a detailed dispatch to Butler reiterating the oral instructions that he had imparted during his visit. Lee, he began, held a line from White Oak Swamp to Malvern Hill, which placed him too far away to interfere with Smith's projected morning assault on Petersburg. Hancock's corps, which Grant generously estimated at 28,000 men, was expected to be fully across the James by daylight on the fifteenth and would "march in the morning direct to Petersburg, with directions, however, to halt at the point on

that road nearest City Point, unless he receives further orders." While not contemplating Hancock taking an active role in Smith's offensive, he instructed
Butler that "if the force going into Petersburg find reinforcements necessary,
by sending back to General Hancock he will push forward." To ensure that the
2nd Corps was ready to march, Grant formally instructed Butler to "please direct your commissary to send down by boat to Windmill Point tonight 60,000
rations to issue to them. Without this precaution the services of this corps cannot be had for an emergency tomorrow."[63]

The transports carrying Smith's 18th Corps started up the James from Point
Comfort early on the morning of June 14. Before leaving Fortress Monroe,
Smith visited General Butler's wife and resumed his diatribe. "He is thoroughly
disgusted with what they have made him do, and the conduct of the war generally in the details, which he puts upon Meade," Mrs. Butler informed her
husband in a letter. "He is inclined to shield Grant somewhat, but he evidently
looks upon it from the beginning as a desperate butchery for us with comparatively little loss for the rebels." She concluded that she "would rather be a toad,
and feed upon the vapors of a dungeon, than [be] in Meade's place now."[64]

Near noon the 18th Corps passed Weyanoke, where Weitzel was anxiously
awaiting the arrival of pontoons to construct the bridge across the river. Smith,
riding in the lead vessel, *Metamora,* noted that the 2nd Corps was already partially across the river.[65]

Smith reached Bermuda Hundred near sunset, well after Grant had left. Reporting to Butler, he received oral instructions to move at daylight on Petersburg. This was his first intimation, he later claimed, that Petersburg was his
intended objective. Grant, who was responsible for coordinating the various
forces, had never informed Smith of his role in the impending operation against
Petersburg, and Butler gave him no particulars about how he was to proceed.
"No plan was formulated for me to follow," Smith later insisted, "and I at once
set about the study of the maps and giving the orders for the movement."

The intelligence that Smith garnered on short notice was sketchy but encouraging. Butler assured him that the works surrounding Petersburg were "not
at all formidable" and that no Confederate force of consequence occupied the
Cockade City; a horse, he insisted, could jump over the fortifications. Smith
had scant faith in Butler's military prowess—"as helpless as a child on the field
of battle and as visionary as an opium eater in council," he assessed the Massachusetts lawyer and politician—but he accepted the general's representations
as accurate. To augment his two divisions, Smith received Kautz's cavalry division and the infantry division of black troops commanded by Hinks, both of

which had participated in the abortive offensive against Petersburg the previous week. Conferring with Kautz, who spoke from firsthand knowledge, he received further assurances that the rebel works were so inconsequential that his own small cavalry force had been able to ride over them on June 9 with little resistance.[66]

The attack, Butler added, had to be made by daylight the next morning. Nothing, Smith later insisted, was said to him about the availability of reinforcements from the Army of the Potomac.[67]

To execute his assignment, Smith was to lead a collection of units already under his command and others that were new to him. Martindale's and Brooks's 18th Corps divisions, exhausted from their sojourn at Cold Harbor and the trip to Bermuda Hundred, were to accompany him, along with the 10th Corps brigades of Colonels Newton M. Curtis and Louis Bell, which had also been with him at Cold Harbor. Hinks's division of U.S. Colored Troops—two brigades under Colonels John H. Holman and Samuel A. Duncan—were to join him as well, along with Kautz's two cavalry brigades under Colonels Simon H. Mix and Samuel P. Spear. Smith was never certain of his command's precise size: he later estimated his infantry component at less than 10,000 soldiers, although modern estimates place it closer to 14,000, augmented by Kautz's 2,500 horsemen for a total force in excess of 16,000 men in all.[68]

Smith's task was daunting. Fresh off the boat from Cold Harbor, he was expected to organize a force composed in significant part of troops he had never commanded, march them across eight miles of country that he had never seen, and attack a fortified position, also unseen by him, by sunup the next day. The general's abysmal health complicated the assignment even more. The 18th Corps's headquarters at Cold Harbor had been under constant bombardment from Confederate artillery, jangling Smith's nerves and leaving him utterly exhausted. "In addition to this," he recounted, "I was seriously affected by the swamp water we had been obliged to drink at Cold Harbor which causes in me great fever and weakness." He later claimed to be so ill that the trip from White House Landing to the James seemed only a blur.[69]

Smith nonetheless gamely formulated a plan. Holman's brigade was already south of the Appomattox River at City Point, and Duncan's brigade was at Point of Rocks, where Butler's engineers had constructed a pontoon bridge across the Appomattox to Broadway Landing. The rest of Smith's command, however, was scattered in camps north of the river all the way back to Bermuda Hundred Landing. The Broadway pontoon bridge provided the logical crossing point, and Smith decided to funnel his men over the river there. Orders went out for Kautz to start across the pontoon bridge at 1:00 A.M., followed by the two 18th

Corps divisions under Brooks and Martindale. In the meantime Hinks's men were to shift to a road junction called Cope's, close to Broadway Landing and familiar to them from their adventures on June 9, and join the rest of the command when it regrouped south of the river. Once the troops had concentrated at Broadway Landing, they would be positioned to begin an eight-mile advance against the Dimmock Line protecting Petersburg. By Smith's reckoning his entire command should be united on the south side of the Appomattox and ready to start operations by 3:30 A.M., enabling him to meet the early morning deadline that Butler had prescribed for his attack.[70]

Studying the maps provided by Butler, Smith decided to fan his force along a front defined by three roads and two railroads. Forming the right edge of the Union advance was River Road—or Spring Hill Road, as it was sometimes called—which roughly paralleled the Appomattox River's right bank toward Petersburg. Martindale's division, composing Smith's rightmost column, was to proceed along River Road and attack the sector of rebel line closest to the Appomattox. A second road, called City Point Road, ran parallel to River Road a few miles east of it, more or less following the tracks of the City Point Railway to Petersburg. Brooks's division, in the center of Smith's deployment, was to move in tandem with Martindale, keeping roughly to City Point Road and striking the rebel entrenchments next to his sector. A third route, Jordan's Point Road, angled toward Petersburg east of City Point Road. Starting off along City Point Road, Hinks's division was to cut over to Jordan's Point Road and serve as the left wing of Smith's assault, attacking in concert with Brooks.

A short distance beyond Hinks's left ran the Norfolk and Petersburg Railroad, whose tracks defined the lower edge of Smith's fan-shaped formation. After clearing the infantry's route of rebels, Kautz's horsemen were to collect along this railroad to protect the lower Union flank. Once the deployment was completed, Smith's force would stand arrayed in a three-mile line facing the rebel entrenchments, with Martindale on the right by the river, Brooks and Hinks stringing to the south, and Kautz on the far left. Kautz understood that he was to "participate very much the same as with Gillmore, except that I was not expected to do more than to make a demonstration, and try to make the enemy believe that I contemplated going in as we did on the ninth."[71]

Smith's plan made sense on paper, but circumstances complicated its execution. In all, the general later estimated that he had some 10,000 troops at his disposal, although as noted the actual number probably approximated 16,000, which gave him a manpower edge somewhere between four to seven times the number of Confederates guarding Petersburg. It was dark by the time Smith finished meeting with Butler and Kautz, however, and the transports were already depositing his troops at different locations, some of them uncomfortably remote from Broadway Landing. Stedman's brigade, for example, unloaded at Bermuda Hundred Landing, some five miles away. Smith later complained that much of this confusion could have been avoided if he had been alerted of his assignment in advance. Forewarned, he would have "arranged my troops in steamers so that the best commanders would have followed me closely and have debarked rapidly," he wrote.[72]

Making the best of a bad situation, Smith directed the transports carrying Stannard's brigade of Martindale's division to continue on to Point of Rocks, where the troops could disembark near their morning staging area. Ships carrying two of Brooks's brigades—those of Marston and Burnham—were also diverted to Point of Rocks, but Henry's brigade offloaded at Bermuda Hundred Landing, and confusion was inevitable. "The transports were arriving all night," Smith later explained, "and, with the exception of the commands of Generals Hinks and Kautz, it was impossible for any general to tell what troops he had or would have with him." A correspondent watching Smith's soldiers stream toward Broadway Landing noticed that a "thick miasmatic mist commenced rising about nine o'clock, through which the distant campfires faintly beam. Everything appeared weird and ghostlike."[73]

Hinks too had to juggle his two brigades to meet Smith's troops when they came across at Broadway Landing. Holman's brigade was at City Point, south of the Appomattox, but Duncan's was north of the river near Point of Rocks. Hinks's solution was to bring Duncan's brigade across the Appomattox right away. Threading roads already crammed with 18th Corps troops fresh from their transports, Duncan's soldiers crossed the river on the Broadway pontoon bridge around 11:00 P.M. and bivouacked on the south shore.[74]

Smith's chief comfort lay in Butler's and Kautz's repeated assurances that the morning's offensive would be virtually unopposed. "From the information gained at headquarters, from the general commanding, and from refugees, I was lead [sic] to believe that we should encounter no line of works till we reached the main line near Jordan's Hill, that there was but a small force opposed to us, and that my right flank on the Appomattox would entirely command the position of the enemy there," he later wrote.[75]

In the days following Butler's June 9 offensive against Petersburg, Beauregard—headquartered at the Dunlop place on Swift Run, midway between Petersburg and the southern end of the Howlett Line—relentlessly lobbied for reinforcements. Gracie's arrival on June 11 helped by freeing Wise's 26th, 34th, 46th, and 59th Virginia to join the local militia in Petersburg. Wise, charged with defending the city, now had his own brigade; Brigadier General Dearing's brigade, made up of the 7th Confederate Cavalry, the 4th North Carolina Cavalry, 8th Georgia Cavalry, Barham's Virginia Cavalry Battalion, and the Petersburg Virginia Cavalry; the local militia units of Major F. H. Archer's Petersburg Militia; Company F, 24th South Carolina Infantry; Major W. H. Wood's 3rd Battalion Virginia Reserves; the 44th Virginia Infantry Battalion; and some twenty-two artillery pieces in Sturdivant's and Young's Virginia Batteries. In total, Wise calculated that he mustered about 2,200 soldiers, very near the number that Butler had estimated. A modern count, however, places the rebel force closer to 4,250 men.[76]

Wise arrayed his force to defend the portion of the Dimmock Line most vulnerable to attack—the same sector that Butler had targeted in his June 9 offensive. These were the fortifications that began on the Appomattox River downstream from Petersburg and arched three miles to Jerusalem Plank Road. Given the paucity of troops, Wise's coverage averaged one man for every four and a half yards of fortifications. The rest of the Dimmock Line remained undefended.[77]

At 7:15 A.M. on June 14, Beauregard telegraphed Bragg that Grant's movement across the Chickahominy and an apparent increase in the size of Butler's force seriously imperiled his ability to man both the Howlett Line and the Petersburg defenses. "With my present force I cannot answer for consequences," he informed Bragg. "Cannot my troops sent to General Lee be returned at once?" he asked, referring to Hoke's Division and Ransom's Brigade. Three hours later Beauregard telegraphed Lee directly. "Petersburg cannot be reinforced from my small force in lines of Bermuda Hundred Neck without abandoning that position," he warned. "Reinforcements should first reach there before detaching these troops, which possessing local knowledge, should be preferably retained where they are. Should you not have a pontoon bridge below Chaffin's Bluff?"[78]

Shortly after noon, Lee informed President Davis that he thought the Federals "must be preparing to move south of the James." While he knew that part of the Army of the Potomac had crossed the Chickahominy, he could not confirm that all of it had done so, as Wilson's cavalry had successfully screened Grant's movement. "Presuming that this force was either the advance of his army or the cover behind which it would move to James River," wrote Lee, "I prepared to attack it again this morning, but it disappeared from us during the night, and as far as we can judge from the statements of prisoners, it has gone to Harrison's Landing."[79]

Lee weighed his next move. If Grant meant to occupy McClellan's former fortifications at Harrison's Landing, he saw no point in attacking him there, since Union gunboats controlled the adjacent reaches of the James. Lee was also aware that a significant body of Union troops had embarked from White House Landing. He did not know, however, whether those soldiers were leaving because their terms of service had expired or were steaming "up the James River with the view of getting possession of Petersburg before we can reinforce it." Lee recommended remaining "extremely watchful and guarded." Unless he received contrary information by evening, he intended to shift Hoke's Division to Chaffin's Bluff, where it could cross the James behind the Confederate lines and rush to join Beauregard if needed in that quarter. "The rest of the Army can follow should circumstances require it," he closed.[80]

Three hours later Lee updated Davis on developments. "From my present information Gen. Grant crossed his army at several points below Long Bridge, and moved directly toward James River, sending a force in this direction to guard the roads so as to make it impracticable for us to reach him." Lee now believed that the Army of the Potomac was centered near Westover, with elements stationed a short distance downriver at Willcox Landing. "I see no indications of his attacking me on this side of the river," the general wrote, "though of course I cannot know positively." Accordingly Lee felt comfortable sending Hoke to a point near the first pontoon bridge above Drewry's Bluff. "I cannot judge now whether he should move at once to the other side of the river," he noted of Hoke, "but think it prudent that he should be in position to do so when required."[81]

Lee then informed Bragg of his intentions. Judging from recent intelligence, he thought it "probable" that Grant would cross the James. "He shows no indication of operating on this side," Lee observed, "and has broken up his depot at the White House."[82]

At 5:00 P.M. Hoke received instructions to march and set off immediately, alerting Beauregard that he expected to camp "half a mile from Drewry's Bluff, on river road." Lee was not ready, however, to commit the rest of his army—six divisions under Anderson and Hill—to defend Petersburg. Even though he believed that Grant meant to cross the James, he felt uncomfortable moving until he was certain of his opponent's intentions: after all, Grant might send only part of his force to Petersburg and assail Richmond with the rest of the Potomac army. Beauregard had loaned Hoke to Lee during the Cold Harbor operations, so he had no qualms returning the division during Petersburg's moment of need. But with the Army of Northern Virginia reduced to two infantry corps and a single cavalry division, Lee could ill afford more subtractions. Until Grant definitively showed his hand, he saw no option but to remain firmly between the Army of the Potomac and the Confederate capital.[83]

Shortly before dark, Beauregard reported that the 10th and 18th Corps had reinforced Butler at Bermuda Hundred. Bragg further confirmed that Grant had abandoned his White House depot and had advanced to the James somewhere near Harrison's Landing. Lee, Bragg advised Beauregard, remained posted from White Oak Swamp to Malvern Hill, and Hoke was on his way to Drewry's Bluff "with a view to reinforce you in case Petersburg is threatened."[84]

Robert Kean of the Confederate War Department voiced his own estimate of Grant's designs. "He will probably shift to the south side [of the James River] and operate against the Southern railroads; that is greatly the most dangerous part of our system of defense." The *Richmond Daily Enquirer* was of the same mind—"The whole of Grant's army is said to be in motion, and the destination of the best part was the Southside"—but the newspaper also suspected that the Potomac army might attempt a secondary movement. "One of Grant's objectives is to get possession of Malvern Hill, to secure the strong point for future operations on this side of the river, and be within safe distance of his gunboats at Turkey Bend," it writers suggested. From there the Union chief might advance along the river's northern bank to Shirley Plantation, across from City Point, where the troops who had embarked at White House Landing could join him.[85]

Speculation was rife in the Confederate capital, but the time for speculation was almost over. The next day would reveal exactly what Grant had in mind.

IX

JUNE 15, 1864

Smith and Hancock Advance on Petersburg

"A number of dead Negroes are lying about."

JUNE 15, 1864, DAWNED as a day of opportunity for Union arms. Petersburg was lightly defended, the Army of Northern Virginia was too distant to reach the city in time to save it, and the Cockade City's capture would cut the Weldon and South Side Railroads, choking off Lee's supplies. "The Army of the Potomac had reached the James River on June 14th, General Grant having consummated his masterly flank movement to the left and outmaneuvered General Lee in a brilliant manner," New York's state historian observed several years later. "Grant was convinced Petersburg could be captured by a coup. If ever an occasion demanded promptness in decision and celerity in movement, this was one." Unfortunately for the Union cause, promptness of decision and celerity in movement were not readily available this fateful Wednesday.[1]

Baldy Smith's offensive, scheduled to begin at 3:00 A.M., got off to a promising start. Hinks executed his assignment to perfection. At 11:00 P.M. on the night of the fourteenth, Duncan's brigade struck tents at its Point of Rocks bivouac and crossed the pontoon bridge over the Appomattox River at Broadway Landing. Holman's brigade meanwhile left its encampment near City Point and marched to join Duncan. Smith appeared in person at Broadway Landing around 2:00 A.M. and helped mass his division of U.S. Colored Troops, some 3,700 strong, near the Cope property during the next hour. His men were ready to start toward Petersburg well before daylight but could not begin until the veteran 18th Corps troops and Kautz's cavalry arrived to lead the way.[2]

Three o'clock came and went, but Smith's soldiers, fatigued by their journey from Cold Harbor, were nowhere to be seen. Some of the transports bringing these troops from White House Landing unloaded at Bermuda Hundred and others at Point of Rocks, near Broadway Landing. Other steamers ran aground in the shallow Appomattox, leaving their passengers to splash ashore and find

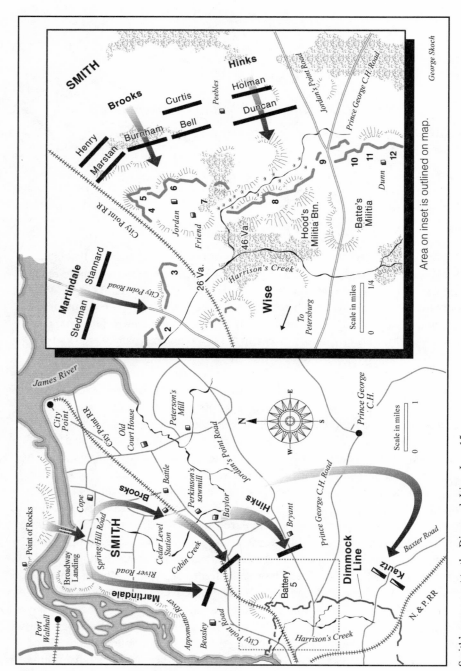

George Skoch

Area on inset is outlined on map.

Smith's movement to the Dimmock Line, June 15

their way to the assembly point. Much of Smith's night was consumed locating far-flung units, collecting his weary troops near the pontoon bridges, and directing them to prepare to march in a few hours. "One would suppose such an order to be unsatisfactory, coming direct upon the heels of a hard two weeks' fighting, and an uncomfortable trip upon a crowded steamer," a correspondent wrote, "but the Eighteenth [Corps] boys are made of stern stuff."[3]

Reveille sounded in Smith's infantry camps, prying the soldiers from the ground and scattering them in search of wood and water. "A thousand kettles for coffee and meat soon hang over the blazing fire, and the cavalry and artillery horses are soon eating from their hanging nose-bags the forage of oats and corn," a New Yorker in Marston's brigade reported. Soldiers packed their tents and baggage and hauled their belongings to central locations for safekeeping. Another call from headquarters sent the troops into formation. "Orderlies and staff-officers riding recklessly in the greatest haste, scatter over the fields and through the woods and openings, and designate the order of march," the New Yorker related. "The men laugh and joke and sing, as if a hunt were up."[4]

The first blush of dawn appeared around 3:30 A.M., with sunrise at 4:38 A.M. As the sun imparted a cheery glow to the early morning sky, Smith's soldiers, Brooks's division leading and Martindale's coming behind, crossed the Appomattox at Broadway Landing "noiselessly on the hay carpeting" that had been spread on the pontoon bridge. "The crossing . . . , first by the light of fires built on either shore, and of lanterns along the bridge, then by the gray streaks of morning light, succeeded by the rosy hues that foretold the rising sun, was very picturesque," a correspondent noted. "Long lines of infantry (Brooks's division) first showed themselves, solemnly issuing out of the mist, and streaming over the hay-covered pontoon bridge, which muffled the noise of their march." Soldiers playfully crossed in "cadence-step" as though marching to music, causing some of them to lose balance and plunge headlong into the river. Their comrades shouted catcalls at the dripping forms emerging from the muck. "As we ascended the right bank of the river, a wide prospect of fine, well-tilled farmlands lay before us," a New Yorker noted, "and the morn, in russet mantle clad, walked over the dew of the eastward hills." Another soldier remarked that the "rapid change of base, revealed to all, that we were running a race with the enemy, with Petersburg as our object." By all appearances, June 15 seemed a fine day for campaigning.[5]

Kautz was also behind schedule. Leaving their Bermuda Hundred encampment around 1:00 A.M. as Smith had directed, his 2,500 cavalrymen—composed of the 11th and 5th Pennsylvania Cavalry, 3rd New York Cavalry, 1st District of Columbia Cavalry, 1st New York Mounted Rifles, and Captain

George B. Easterly's section of the 4th Battery, Wisconsin Light—wound along roadways crowded with infantry. Smith had expected Kautz to lead the 18th Corps across the pontoon bridge, but Brooks's division was already crossing by the time the cavalry reached the span, forcing Kautz to wait before crossing in front of Martindale's division. The last of the riders thundered over the bridge near 4:00 A.M., mist swirling around their horses' hooves. Another hour passed while they meandered through Hinks's assembled infantrymen at the Cope House and turned onto City Point Road, ready to lead the way south.[6]

Smith and his staff waited on the Appomattox's south shore, directing troops into position as they appeared. At 5:00 A.M.—two hours late—the advance on Petersburg could finally begin. Kautz's cavalry shifted left and cantered down City Point Road, following, an officer reflected, "the same road on which we had travelled in Gillmore's expedition a few days before." Hinks's division came behind, followed by Brooks's division and Guy Henry's brigade. "We had gone but a short distance before we came upon the ambulance train," one of Hicks's soldiers remarked, "then I knew that some of us were not coming back again." Martindale's two brigades under Stannard and Stedman turned right and started south along Spring Hill Road. Artillery moved with the division to which it was assigned, field trains and ambulances trailing behind. Troops talked, sang, and carried their muskets at will, wondering what adventures the day would bring. Their objective—Petersburg—was a mere eight miles away.[7]

Adventure came quickly to Martindale's column. A West Point graduate, lawyer, and native New Yorker, Martindale had impressed Lieutenant Colonel Lyman as a "black haired talkative man, full of great plans to do great things." Stannard's brigade led the advance, with the 89th New York fanned out as skirmishers. Following the fight of June 9, Confederates had strewn River Road with dense slashings of timber, which delayed the division's progress. A mile and a half past Broadway Landing, the New Yorkers encountered rebel pickets, but Martindale, who was riding near the head of the column, directed Stannard to deploy his brigade and press on. A small Confederate force impeded the advance by ambushing the Federals, then retiring to new positions before Stannard could attack. Lacking cavalry, the brigade felt its way gingerly, using skirmishers instead of horsemen as scouts. "The enemy, supported by artillery, but in small force, opposed our advance at every advantageous cover of the woods," Martindale later reported.[8]

Three miles south of the Cope House, City Point Railroad angled across Broadway Road at Cedar Level Station. A little farther on stood Perkinson's sawmill,

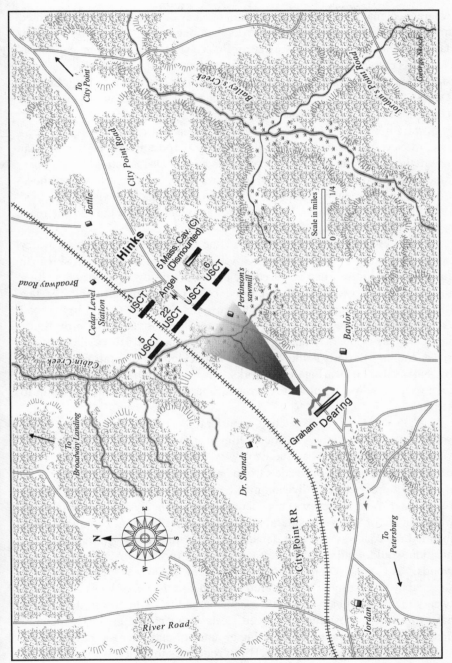

Battle of Baylor's Farm, June 15

where elements from Dearing's Confederate cavalry brigade had dismounted and thrown up temporary breastworks fashioned from fence rails. Captain James I. Mitchell of the 4th North Carolina Cavalry—"a brave and gallant officer," his colonel later termed him—was in charge of the pickets. Farther back stood Dearing's main line, consisting of some four hundred men from Colonel Dennis D. Ferebee's 4th North Carolina Cavalry supported by two guns from Graham's Petersburg Light Artillery.[9]

Riding in the fore of Kautz's advance, Lieutenant Colonel George E. Lewis's 3rd New York Cavalry reached Mitchell's outpost around 6:00 A.M., near where the City Point and Broadway Roads joined. Dismounting, Lewis's carbineers charged Mitchell's pickets and drove them from their advanced position. Mitchell's men, according to a Tar Heel, "fell back slowly and in good order to the entrenchments." Union losses amounted to two horses; one rebel was killed, and one was captured.[10]

While Lewis's New Yorkers reformed, the 1st District of Columbia Cavalry swept forward along both sides of City Point Road in an extended skirmish line. Dearing himself had just arrived, and Graham's two guns began pelting the Yankees, who sought cover in a ravine. To protect his left flank, Ferebee directed Captain Demosthenes Bell to move his Company G over to the road from Broadway. Judging the rebel position too strong to take by storm, Kautz instructed his troopers to hunker down in the ravine until Hinks's infantry arrived. Captain Easterly's 4th Wisconsin Battery pulled up, unlimbered close by, and opened on Dearing's earthworks. The Union gunners got off only fourteen rounds before accurate fire from Graham's two pieces forced them to retire.[11]

At 7:35 A.M. Dearing dispatched a courier to Petersburg to alert Wise of developments. Union forces confronted him in strength and were reportedly advancing "in heavy force" on the Broadway Road. A prisoner reported—erroneously—that some of Burnside's troops were involved in the offensive.[12]

In short order Hinks's division marched up, and the general rode ahead to reconnoiter. What he saw was not encouraging. Ferebee's Carolinians held entrenchments of "very considerable strength," and Graham's gunners commanded the roadway where it debauched from the woods. Approaching the position would require Hinks's troops to march through "exceeding difficult woods," as Colonel Duncan observed, much of which was "marshy and obstructed by fallen timber and covered with a dense thicket of vines and bushes twenty feet high." Once the northerners emerged from the forest, they would have to charge across three hundred yards of open field against an enemy posted on "the crest of a rapidly rising ground" oriented across the roadway.[13]

Completing his reconnaissance, Hinks rode back to Smith, who had arrived with Brooks's division, and received instructions to clear the rebels from the road without delay. Thrusting untried black troops into combat was a risky proposition, but Smith wanted to preserve Brooks's veterans for the main assault against the Dimmock Line, which lay a few miles ahead. According to the aide Livermore, the corps commander directed Hinks "to push on without delay and clear the enemy from our front." While Hinks rode off to prepare for the advance, Smith ordered Kautz to disengage and shift left to make room for the infantry. "In taking the resolution to advance as directly and rapidly as possible against this force," Livermore later observed, "General Smith evinced the determination to reach the enemy's main works at Petersburg as soon as possible, and, although this resolution to attack here as he did involved the loss of several hundred men which might have been avoided by a reconnaissance and a flank attack which would thereby have been made possible and which the enemy could not have withstood for a moment, yet it saved time, which was then of more importance than the sacrifice of men."[14]

Anxious to make a good impression, Hinks galloped to the head of his column and spurred his horse over a ditch. The animal stumbled, pitching the general to the ground. Hinks had been severely injured in 1862 when a rebel bullet pierced his intestines, and the fall wrenched the wound, inflicting excruciating pain. He managed to remount his horse, but his injury soon left him seriously disabled. "His pluck would not permit him to leave the front," an aide remembered, "so he lay there and gave his orders and saw the field through us." Colonel Duncan, commanding the lead brigade, took charge of the advance.[15]

While Hinks's soldiers moved up, Kautz withdrew his cavalrymen and sidled southeast along a farm road to Jordan's Point Road. Confederate gunners redoubled their efforts, hurling shells into the 11th Pennsylvania Cavalry, which the general had left to hold the ravine until the infantry arrived. Soon Duncan's brigade appeared, and opposing battle lines formed across the Baylor family farm. The impending fight would give the Union soldiers their first taste of combat; it would also stand as the first major offensive operation undertaken in Virginia by black troops.[16]

As Kautz rode off, Hinks deployed near Perkinson's sawmill. His route of advance was difficult. Not only would his greenhorns have to navigate the swampy forest around narrow Cabin Creek, but to hit the Confederates head-on they also had to angle slightly to the right and cross City Point Road and City Point Railroad at a diagonal cant. Gouged deeply into the earth, the road and tracks were certain to disrupt Hinks's advance. And once his troops emerged from the forest, they faced a daunting charge across a quarter mile of open field against an enemy entrenched on high ground.[17]

The task was manifestly difficult for experienced soldiers. How Hinks's novices would fare was anyone's guess. "The result of the charge was waited for with great anxiety," the correspondent J. A. Brady observed. "The majority of the Whites expected that the Colored troops would run."[18]

Under Hinks's direction, Colonel Duncan formed his brigade into a front line, Colonel James W. Conine's 5th U.S. Colored Troops (USCT) on the right and Colonel Joseph B. Kiddoo's 22nd USCT, Lieutenant Colonel George Rogers's 4th USCT, and Colonel John W. Ames's 6th USCT ranging to the left in that order across City Point Road. Colonel Holman arrayed his brigade a hundred yards to the rear, the 1st USCT on the right and the 5th Massachusetts Cavalry (Colored) on the left, backed by Captain James R. Angel's Battery E, 3rd New York Light Artillery. The soldiers were to advance without a skirmish line, as Smith's orders called for haste and Kautz's cavalry had presumably cleared the way.[19]

Duncan, a former schoolteacher from New Hampshire who had never commanded troops in combat, directed his regimental commanders to open a "heavy fire" after they had passed through the woods, then to reform with "all possible dispatch" and await the order to charge. An aide noted the "rather pale but determined face with which [Duncan] received and set about executing the order." Confusion in the 5th Massachusetts Cavalry delayed the movement considerably. Dismounted before it had been sent south, the outfit—the only black cavalry unit from Massachusetts, commanded by Colonel Henry S. Russell—seemed at a loss. "The underbrush was so thick in the woods that we could not form a line of battle, but we got into line as soon as we could, and waited to see what the first line of battle would accomplish," a soldier in the 5th Massachusetts Cavalry wrote. The regiment, Hinks later noted, displayed "awkwardness in maneuver, it being composed of new recruits, and drilled only in Cooke's single rank cavalry formation, which entirely unfitted it to act as infantry in line."[20]

At Hinks's command Duncan started forward. It was 8:00 A.M., and the advance through the woods proved as chaotic as the officers expected. Men sloshed through swampy ground around Cabin Creek, knee deep in mud, and rebel shells tore through the trees, raining branches and debris onto the advancing Union force. "Furiously assailed with spherical case, canister, and musketry along the whole line," Hinks narrated in his official report. Colonel Kiddoo's 22nd USCT, in the middle of the first line, lost contact with the units on either side, and the 6th USCT foundered in the swamp.[21]

The 4th USCT emerged from the forest first, and its center companies started across the clearing without waiting for orders. Lieutenant Colonel Rogers directed the troops to fall back, but his instructions came too late. Aiming at the approaching blue uniforms, Graham's Confederate artillerists opened on the isolated cluster of Federals, pouring "heavy enfilading fire" into their right flank. More men from the 4th USCT ventured into the clearing only to be cut down by southern musketry and artillery fire. Captain William V. King of the regiment was killed and three other captains fell wounded. Within minutes, 120 of the 4th's soldiers lay dead or injured.[22]

Colonel Ames's 6th Regiment slogged out of the swamp and into the 4th's rear. Pressing into the clearing with its line askew, Ames's outfit, drawn mainly from Pennsylvania, came under galling rebel musketry that scoured the left end of its line. The 5th Massachusetts Cavalry, advancing on foot through the woods behind the 4th and 6th USCT, fired blindly ahead, shooting into the rear of its sister regiments. The 4th's officers began "madly gesticulating" and calling for the soldiers to stop. Buffeted by rebel bullets and friendly fire, the 4th and 6th pulled back into the woods to reform. Unnerved, the 5th Massachusetts cavalrymen concluded that a retreat was underway and fled "in great confusion," along with elements from the 6th USCT. "We had great charity for the 5th Massachusetts Cavalry," an aide later wrote. "It was officered by a gallant set of men, but was indifferently drilled for foot service and was discontented and spiritless because it was not mounted."[23]

Duncan's right wing had a better time of it. While Ferebee's Confederates concentrated their fire on the 4th and 6th USCT, the 5th and 22nd Regiments formed a coherent battle line. A Confederate officer riding a white horse loudly exhorting his men drew everyone's attention. "We could see him plainly riding up and down the rebel lines to stand, that they had only niggers to contend with," recalled Milton M. Holland of the 5th USCT. "This peculiar personage seemed possessed with supernatural talent," thought Holland. "He would sometimes ride his horse with almost lightning speed, up and down his lines amid the most terrific fire of shot and shell."[24]

Twenty-seven-year-old Colonel Kiddoo ordered his men ahead—"the effect with which the enemy's artillery was playing upon my line was the strongest inducement for me to give this order," he later conceded. Still fresh in his soldiers' minds were reports that Confederates had slaughtered black troops at Fort Pillow in Tennessee six weeks earlier, and they ran forward shouting, "Remember Fort Pillow," mindful that they might meet a similar fate. A correspondent for the *New York Herald* related that the 22nd USCT advanced "with a wild yell that must certainly have struck terror into the hearts of their foe."[25]

Charging across the clearing, Kiddoo's troops overran Dearing's works near the guns and planted their colors on the rebel entrenchments. The Confederates fled after scarcely a fight. "Our major and Colonel Russell were wounded, and several men fell—to advance seemed almost impossible," Charles Torry Beman of the 5th Massachusetts Cavalry wrote his father a few days later, "but we rallied, and after a terrible charge amidst pieces of barbarous iron solid shot and shell, we drove the desperate greybacks from their fortifications and gave three cheers for our victory." Graham's rebels managed to haul off one of their artillery pieces, but Kiddoo's gleeful troops swarmed over the other twelve-pounder howitzer. "The work was beautifully accomplished," a Union officer effused.[26]

Riding to the front, Hinks was pleasantly surprised to find the rebel works crawling with black troops. "What has become of the Johnnies?" he inquired of a jubilant warrior. "Well, suh," came the answer, "they just done it out; didn't care to make close acquaintance." The 4th North Carolina Cavalry reported two men killed and four wounded.[27]

The skirmish was scarcely over when Smith directed Brooks's lead elements—the 13th New Hampshire of Burnham's brigade—onto the Baylor farm battlefield. "A number of dead Negroes are lying about," a New Englander recounted, "and a dead Negro is the most ghastly corpse ever seen; and their wounded are coming back shot in all sorts of ways, in legs, arms, heads, and bodies, but hobbling along and bringing their guns with them." Black soldiers, he thought, "will keep on their feet, and move on, with wounds that would utterly lay out white men, and they stick like death to their guns. A white man severely wounded throws his gun away." Smith was impressed with Hinks's attack but was disturbed by the black soldiers' unrestrained glee. "Their success destroyed their organization," he later wrote, "as they huddled around and kissed the pieces of artillery which had fallen into their hands, and shared their delight as children might have done."[28]

Baylor's Farm, as the battle became called, cost Hinks dearly. The 5th Massachusetts Cavalry reported three men killed and nineteen officers and men wounded, including the regiment's commander and two battalion heads. The 4th USCT sustained some 120 casualties. Losses for the other black regiments were not reported, although they were doubtlessly high, particularly in the 22nd USCT, which spearheaded the assault that broke Dearing's line.[29]

Despite their losses, morale in Hinks's division was palpable. A New Yorker advancing through the ambulances and hobbling wounded soldiers was impressed. "Tell you boys, we made um get," a black warrior called out. "We druv em." Noted the New Yorker: "On that occasion, those who were politically the most conservative, suddenly experienced an accession of respect for the chattel on this discovery of its 'equal' value in a possible emergency." Baylor's Farm had been a small engagement in the scale of 1864 battles, but it stood as an important one in the history of black troops.[30]

Smith had won the little action at Baylor's Farm by driving the Confederates from the field. Ferebee's regiment and Graham's two guns, however, had scored a significant tactical victory by stymieing the main Union infantry column, several divisions strong, for two or more hours and driving a stake through Smith's chances of achieving Grant's goal of an early morning assault against the Dimmock Line. Ferebee's bold stand also shook Smith's confidence in the assurances that Butler had given him the previous evening. The move on Petersburg would not be the cakewalk he had been lead to expect. Clearly the rebels had sufficient troops to send out a force from their works to greet him. And the element of surprise was gone. "At a most unexpected place I had been called upon to develop my force and make an assault," Smith observed, "and this fact leaving not of question the time lost in the operation caused me at once to cease to take anything for granted that had been asserted [to him by Butler]."[31]

Grant's planned offensive against Petersburg had an important second component: the Army of the Potomac, or at least part of it, was to move simultaneously with Smith and stand ready to reinforce the 18th Corps if so requested. While Smith pressed toward Petersburg, Hancock's 2nd Corps was to start from its camps at Flowerdew Hundred and sidle southwest, aiming to support the offensive if needed. Hancock's route to Petersburg was more than twice as long as Smith's march—eighteen miles as opposed to eight—but the 2nd Corps was unlikely to encounter rebel opposition unless it joined Smith in front of the Petersburg entrenchments.

No one, however, had asked Hancock to hurry, had clarified precisely where he was to go, or had even described to him Grant's overall strategy. A major sticking point involved food. Two hours before midnight on June 14, Meade telegraphed the 2nd Corps commander to expect 60,000 rations from Butler. As soon as the victuals arrived, Hancock was to march "by the most direct route to Petersburg, taking up a position where the City Point Railroad crosses Harrison's Creek where we now have a work." Meade said nothing, however, about how long the corps commander should wait for the provisions or when he must begin marching if the rations failed to materialize. More critically, this directive said nothing about Hancock's ultimate assignment and the purpose for his march—to be in position to support Smith. Meade's silence on those points was in turn a consequence of Grant's failure to inform Meade of his plan for taking Petersburg.[32]

Another problem was the map provided by headquarters, which bore no relation to the reality on the ground. Hancock's stated objective—the place where City Point Railroad crossed Harrison's Creek—was actually well behind the Dimmock Line, but at this stage no one at headquarters understood this important geographic fact. The run labeled "Harrison's Creek" on Hancock's map was a different stream—Cabin Creek—that crossed City Point Railway near the Baylor farm and emptied into the Appomattox near Broadway Landing. In his instructions Meade alluded to a Union "work" where Harrison's Creek entered the Appomattox; indeed, Butler had constructed a small fort at Broadway Landing near where Cabin Creek discharged into the Appomattox. Humphreys later speculated that the mix-up about the location of Harrison Creek originated at Butler's headquarters and was passed on to Meade, who blindly repeated it out of ignorance of the topography.[33]

While Hinks's greenhorns received their initiation into combat at Mr. Baylor's farm, Hancock's battle-wise veterans waited at Flowerdew Hundred for their rations. A simple promise to deliver food had become unexpectedly complex. Near midnight on June 14, on receiving word that Butler was forwarding rations from Bermuda Hundred, Hancock's chief of staff, Lieutenant Colonel Morgan, dispatched quartermaster and commissary officers to Windmill Point's upper wharf to receive the food and distribute it. At 2:00 A.M. Morgan went to Willcox Landing to oversee the delivery. Ninety minutes later Hancock informed headquarters that his infantry had completed crossing to the south shore and that his artillery had started over. The illusive rations, however, had yet to appear, causing the general to fret that when they did arrive, the paucity of wagons would make it difficult to distribute the food to the troops. Three hours later he forwarded an update to Meade: "No rations received yet."[34]

Shortly before 7:00 A.M., Colonel Brainerd, who had been repairing docking facilities on the James's south shore, was approached by the 2nd Corps's chief quartermaster, Colonel Richard N. Batchelder. Noting that Brainerd was making ready to cross to the north bank, Batchelder asked the engineer to inform Morgan that he believed the rations were on the way, as he had seen a steamer coming from the direction of Bermuda Hundred. According to Brainerd, who penned his account more than five years later, he crossed the river, delivered the message to Morgan, and then watched with the chief of staff as the steamer continued past the wharf, indicating that it was not carrying the long-awaited victuals.[35]

Morgan's account, written only ten days after the events, differs from Brainerd's narration in important respects. According to Morgan, the engineer informed him that the transport carrying the supplies had arrived. The lieutenant colonel added that he saw the vessel docked at the south shore and watched it "for a length of time sufficient to allow of it being unloaded," after which it motored off. Persuaded that the rations had arrived, Morgan informed Hancock that the rations were being issued, and the general immediately wired Meade's headquarters of this development.[36]

"You will not wait for the rations, but move immediately to the position assigned to you the last evening," Meade responded, instructing Hancock to leave an officer at the wharf to direct the boat with the rations to divert to City Point or wherever else the corps commander considered appropriate. "It is important that you should move," Meade stressed, but then added an important qualifier: "Exercise your judgment as to which will be best—to issue rations now or send them as directed [in previous communications]."[37]

Hancock decided to distribute the promised rations before setting off. Years later his adjutant Francis Walker explained his commander's reasoning. "General Hancock had not been informed that General Smith was to make an attack on Petersburg and that great results might depend on his reaching his destination an hour earlier or later," Walker wrote. "He had been simply told to move toward Petersburg, and there take up a position. As any good commander would, General Hancock preferred to march with his troops rationed; and not knowing—what General Meade himself did not know—that Petersburg was to be assaulted, he took advantage of the alternative offered him."[38]

Hancock scarcely had time to ponder Meade's missive, however, when he received a disconcerting note from his aide William Mitchell. "The rations have not arrived at all," the staffer reported. Morgan, it developed, had been mistaken; whatever the transport had been unloading, it was not food. This new intelligence changed the calculus for Hancock. Impressed by Meade's insistence that he move quickly, the general directed his troops to start toward Petersburg. The rations would just have to wait.[39]

It was now after nine o'clock in the morning. To ensure an immediate start, Hancock telegraphed Birney, who was to lead the march, to "put your column in motion at once" and dispatched Morgan to deliver the order in person. The telegraph, however, "miscarried," as Hancock later put it, and the boat that his aide caught to ferry him across the James ran aground, delaying him for half an hour. Nothing seemed to be going right for the 2nd Corps this morning.[40]

Not until sometime between 10:30 and 11:00 A.M.—battle smoke had long cleared from the Baylor farm—did Hancock's lead elements finally get underway, guided by Morgan. The general, who was still on the James's northern bank, penned another note to Meade. "I have been deceived about the rations," he explained. "It turns out now that no rations have arrived, and I have started the command and left directions that if rations come they shall be taken to City Point." Meade approved this action and again expressed his wish that Hancock "push forward to the position designated for your command, leaving someone to bring up the artillery and wagons."[41]

Ironically, the rations arrived at Windmill Point just as Hancock's men were setting off. The schooner carrying them, it turned out, drew eleven feet of water and could not have landed earlier, as the tide had not yet risen.[42]

The missing rations delayed the 2nd Corps's march by five hours, and the consequences would be enormous. Equally fateful was the erroneous map, which set Hancock off in the wrong direction. Instead of heading toward a junction with Smith, the 2nd Corps angled toward Broadway Landing, several miles north of the impending battle site, and prepared to camp along Cabin Creek, identified on the map as Harrison's Creek. "My orders were based on incorrect information," Hancock later complained, "and the position I was ordered to take did not exist as it was described on my instructions; Harrison's Creek proved to be inside the enemy's lines and not within miles of where it was laid down on the map with which I was furnished to guide me."[43]

Hancock's instructions from headquarters, his misleading map, and Grant's failure to inform Meade and Hancock of Smith's objective or of the necessity for haste all but ensured that the 2nd Corps would be unavailable to assist. "Sent wrong by these orders, his line of march increased several miles, after his time of starting had been delayed several hours, Hancock led forward the corps without an intimation that his presence was to be imperatively required at Petersburg," Walker later wrote. "So far as he had any reason to think, it would be sufficient if he brought up his corps, in good condition, in season to go fairly into camp by nightfall."[44]

"All goes on like a miracle."

While Smith marched toward Petersburg and Hancock's troops prepared to leave Flowerdew Hundred, the rest of the Army of the Potomac moved into position to cross the James. Warren's 5th Corps waited in fields near Dr. Willcox's home, ready to board ferries at Willcox's Wharf, and Burnside's 9th Corps, camped on Weyanoke Peninsula, prepared to march across the pontoon bridge once the artillery and supply wagons traveling with the army had jangled over. Wright's 6th Corps occupied a shorter defensive line laid out by the engineer Michler along a "commanding ridge" across Weyanoke's neck, stretching from Tyler's Mill on the right to the mouth of Queen's Creek on the left. Marching past fine plantation homes, a soldier in the 10th Massachusetts reflected on "the ease and comfort in which the planters had lived, while the array of squalid huts, clustered near, told of the curse of slavery on account of which these thousands of men were so many miles from their own abodes." A soldier from Maine stopped at a hut and bought a bowl of bacon soup from an aged black man whose leg was swollen from a snakebite.[45]

By sunrise the air hung thick with dust and campfire smoke. "The open plain on the north side of the river, and far back into the woods and through the opening which like a large gateway permitted the column to pass, was crowded with the armed host preparing to form in line," a New Englander recalled. "The regimental wagons in seemingly inextricable confusion were running hither and thither, the ambulances and Sanitary Commission wagons were finding their proper places; companies and regiments were marching and counter-marching; batteries were mounting and forming in line; and cavalry regiments were marching and wheeling to their respective brigades and divisions." The view from the shore was "grand," a New Yorker effused. "Here was an army of immense strength fresh from fields black with smoke and red with blood, marching with flying banners and bright hopeful faces 'on to Richmond.'"[46]

Supply wagons traveling with the army rolled along the causeway and onto the pontoon bridge. "From beneath the soiled and dusty wagon covers penetrated the tent poles and their tacking, the buckets and camp kettles, and in nearly every wagon, as an appropriate and component part of the mass of camp material, was a young contraband with soiled cap and broken visor, with haversack around his neck, and his half-covered legs dangling over the tail board," a correspondent noted. Next came commissary wagons, packed with stores and drawn by mules. Then came covered ambulance wagons, followed by wagons of the Sanitary Commission and by an interminable procession of cows. Artillery started across next—"from the plain, down the bank, across the bridge they came, horses and drivers, guns, limbers, and caissons, steadily on, and up the hill from sight into the woods," the correspondent wrote.[47]

"All goes on like a miracle," Assistant War Secretary Dana informed Stanton at 8:00 A.M. The pontoon bridge had been completed, he reported, and artillery trains were thundering across. Hancock's corps had been ferried to the southern shore and was expected to move out "instantly" for Petersburg to support Smith's attack, which was supposed to have been made by daylight. Warren's corps was to be ferried across next, followed by Burnside and Wright. There had been a few glitches—most notably, the army's massive wagon train had not yet arrived from Coles Ferry—but these were minor matters. As for the Confederates, Wilson's cavalry pickets reported that Lee's infantry was still entrenched from White Oak Swamp to Malvern Hill. "Lee appears to have no idea of our crossing the James River," Dana noted in closing. "General Grant moves his headquarters to City Point this morning. Weather Splendid."[48]

Grant also finally intervened to break the impasse between Butler and Admiral Lee over obstructing the James River to prevent Confederate ironclads from interfering with the crossing. "I am directed by General Grant to sink the obstructing vessels in such place as I can protect them by my guns," Butler wrote the admiral. "I should be glad if you would aid in doing so, upon conference with my Chief engineer, General Weitzel, designating the spot which will afford the best aid to your fleet." Brigadier General Barnard supervised the project and identified a suitable location near Trent's Reach. Moored fore and aft and connected with strong chains, Barnard's engineers sunk four schooners in the river's left channel and another in the smaller right channel, "thus leaving no aperture that a vessel of more than ten feet draught could pass through," he later wrote. A forest of booms made from masts and connected by anchor chains obstructed the shallow water between the channels. Writing Navy Secretary Welles that night, Admiral Lee gloated that the schooners had been sunk "under the directions of the army engineers" and not by the navy.[49]

Before leaving for City Point, Grant strolled onto a bluff above the James and watched the panorama unfold before him. His aide Horace Porter later penned a dramatic portrait of the general. "His cigar had been thrown aside, his hands were clasped behind him, and he seemed lost in the contemplation of the spectacle," Porter wrote. "The approaches to the river on both banks were covered with masses of troops moving briskly to their positions or waiting patiently their turn to cross. At the two improvised ferries steamboats were gliding back and forth with the regularity of weavers' shuttles. A fleet of transports covered the surface of the water below the bridge, and gunboats floated lazily upon the stream, guarding the river above. Drums were beating the march, bands were playing stirring quicksteps," he continued, "and mingled with these sounds were the cheers of the sailors, the shouting of the troops, the rumbling of wheels, and the shrieks of steam-whistles."[50]

The scene also transfixed Adam Badeau. "The long procession of men and boats, the masses of white-covered wagons, contrasting with the rich green foliage that reached to the shore, the shinning cannon, the brilliant banners, the aides-de-camp riding rapidly to and fro, the mules tugging their heavy burdens; the surging crowd, the incessant motion, the varying color—all seen under the dazzling sky of June, and reflected back from the blue waters of the James— made a panorama of peculiar and exciting splendor; whilst the idea that the great river was reached at last, that after four long years of toil and combat, the

goal of so many campaigns was in sight; that the evolutions displayed on land
and water, the approach of the army on the northern bank, the passage of one
corps by ferry boats, and of another by the wonderful bridge which spanned
the James, the movement of Hancock from the southern shore, and the departure of Smith sailing up to join him in front of Petersburg—were all conceived
and combined by a single man, for a single purpose—gave significance and
moral grandeur to the scene."[51]

"This is the first time I have seen anything like an army cross a pontoon
bridge and I can assure you it is well worth seeing," John H. Westervelt of the
1st New York Volunteer Engineer Corps scrawled in his diary. "From sunrise
until 12M it was one steady stream tramp tramp and a roar like a R road train
all the time." The profusion of boats was a popular topic of conversation.
"There were craft of all descriptions," a Pennsylvanian observed. "Vessels of
burden, steamers for passage, transports and luggers, ferry-boats, schooners,
sloops, and the high wooden walls of great river boats that had often borne gay
and joyous crowds on many a summer journey." Meade's staffer Lyman was
amused to see the former Confederate ironclad *Atlanta,* now pressed into
Union service, "lying there, like a big mud-turtle, with only its back exposed."
He continued: "The group was completed by two or three gunboats and several
steamers anchored nearby. It was funny to run against the marine in this inland
region, and to see the naval officers, all so smug and well-brushed in their clean
uniforms." A reporter for the *New York World* remarked that "various naval
vessels in the vicinity were crowded with sailors, who looked on in no little
astonishment at the novel proceeding of an army crossing a stream where not
the slightest semblance of a bridge existed the day before."[52]

Reflected Porter: "It was a matchless pageant that could not fail to inspire
all beholders with the grandeur of achievement and the majesty of military
power. The man whose genius had conceived and whose skill had executed this
masterly movement stood watching the spectacle in profound silence. Whether
his mind was occupied with the contemplation of its magnitude and success,
or was busied with maturing plans for the future, no one can tell."[53]

"Awfulest place for a fight we were ever in."

Wilson's Union cavalry was charged with concealing the Army of the Potomac
from Lee. Shortly after daylight on June 15, McIntosh's brigade set out from
Samaria Church, following a route that wound west through Nance's Shop. A
short distance beyond, the Union riders collided again with Confederate

cavalrymen from the Hampton Legion of Gary's Brigade. Driving the rebels back to the intersection at Smith's Store, McIntosh's men turned north toward Long Bridge Road. Leading was Colonel Bryan's 18th Pennsylvania Cavalry, followed by the 2nd Ohio Cavalry and 5th New York Cavalry.[54]

A few miles later the 18th Pennsylvania struck Long Bridge Road east of White Oak Bridge Road. Pushing west, Bryan's troopers drove the Hampton Legion's horsemen before them. "Cavalry still report the enemy steadily advancing," A. P. Hill, whose 3rd Corps occupied the defenses covering White Oak Swamp and Riddell's Shop, reported to Lee's headquarters at 9:00 A.M. "Nothing but cavalry been seen that I can hear of. General Heth has sent [Brigadier General John R.] Cooke's brigade down the road to try and ascertain what is the truth."[55]

Dropping back slowly, the rebel cavalrymen bought time for sharpshooters from Cooke's North Carolina brigade to deploy in woods along the roadway. "Hidden entirely from view," a correspondent noted, Cooke's sharpshooters "poured a deadly fire into the 18th Pennsylvania, killing and wounding several almost at the first discharge." The Pennsylvanians braced for a fight. "The order to dismount, fasten our sabres to our saddles was at once given," one later recalled. "The horses were sent to the rear; the dismounted men formed in line."[56]

The Pennsylvanians soon found themselves in a brutal shooting match with Confederate infantry. "This was the beginning of one of the most stubborn, as well as one of the most discouraging engagements, in which the regiment was engaged during its service," a Union man confessed. "Awfulest place for a fight we were ever in," a Pennsylvanian scrawled in his diary. "Very thick pine brush and few trees. Woods on fire and smoke almost intolerable." Cooke's North Carolinians kept up the pressure, advancing through "dense smoke, burning leaves and brush," according to a southerner.[57]

Overpowered, Bryan's Federals retreated toward Smith's Store, holding off the larger Confederate force with their breech-loading carbines. "Our men took advantage of every object or tree that afforded protection from the fire of the enemy," a Pennsylvanian remembered, "but we were compelled to slowly retire, however stubbornly contesting every foot of ground." John Wilson Phillips of the 18th Pennsylvania recalled that the troopers battled the Confederates "for about four hours unaided in a piece of woods." After giving ground for a mile and a half, the lone regiment was joined by the rest of McIntosh's brigade and Battery E, 1st U.S. Artillery. Lieutenant Colonel George A. Purrington directed his 2nd Ohio Cavalry to dismount and deployed two squadrons in underbrush along each side of the road and a squadron in an open field bisected by the road. "The enemy, being behind a row of fallen timber, had a superior advantage," an Ohio man recalled, "and had we not kept up a continual firing that kept them down and obscured us in a cloud of smoke we would have been a splendid target for them." By noon McIntosh had formed a strong defensive line, the 1st Connecticut positioned to the left of the 5th New York.[58]

As Cooke's Confederates crowded toward this new position, the Union horse artillerists, backed by the 3rd New Jersey Cavalry, opened with canister, driving the southerners back. Determined to break through, Cooke brought up his entire infantry brigade. At about 3:30 P.M. his troops charged into McIntosh's fortified line "at a run and with yells," according to the general. "They fired one volley into our ranks, killing and wounding several," another Confederate recounted, "but we pressed forward, and they broke and ran." Overwhelmed by sheer numbers, McIntosh's troopers retired another quarter mile, formed a new line, held that position for a while, then dropped back to yet another position. "Deliberately and carefully, as a chess player might withdraw knights and bishops from the presence of queens and castles, he maneuvered back, fighting, bringing prisoners, and losing none captured," the correspondent Charles Page observed of McIntosh's tenacious delaying action.[59]

Wilson was intimately involved in coordinating the day's actions from his headquarters at Samaria Church. "His cavalry have been the fingers to feel for, the eyes to see, the enemy," noted Page. "He must watch a front of ten miles. To his headquarters orderlies and officers report—riding up on foaming horses—every few minutes, then speed away on paths diverging like the ribs of a fan. The squadron on that road is to fall back; that battalion to advance on that other road. This officer must vigilantly patrol between his command and another's. Ascertain if the rebels are in such a quarter! Drive them at all hazards from such a locality! You must send in some prisoners! I must have information! Are you secure on your right flank? Am afraid the enemy may penetrate what you report to be a swamp. Communicate, if possible, with Colonel so and so on your left. Rations are on the way. Have you sufficient ammunition?"[60]

By 4:00 P.M. the lines had stabilized again near Smith's Store. Learning that Rooney Lee planned to pull cavalry from Malvern Hill to "take the enemy in the rear," Heth dispatched Davis's Brigade to reinforce Cooke's infantry and Gary's cavalrymen facing McIntosh. The expected troops, however, failed to materialize, and around 6:30 P.M. Heth called off the contest and withdrew to White Oak Swamp. As night came on, McIntosh's men retired to Samaria Church, which they were using as a field hospital, and threw up a defensive barricade made from fence rails. Part of Major Nettleton's battalion of Ohioans under Captain Ulrey remained behind to picket the crossroads near Smith's

Store. Attacked by an overwhelming swarm of Confederates, Ulrey managed to slip away and follow a circuitous route to rejoin his unit near Samaria Church.[61]

McIntosh's Federals had done an excellent job screening the northern approaches to the Potomac army at the cost of some forty-six casualties, thirty-two of them in the 18th Pennsylvania. "During the day we cheered and yelled because we were ordered to do so," one Pennsylvanian recounted. "The yelling would begin at the right and then extend along the whole line of the regiment. We had no other reason to cheer, for, in fact, we were being driven back all day long, and the killed and wounded were numerous in the regiment. We learned afterwards that this was a part of the attempt to deceive the enemy, to make him believe and think that the whole army was on the north side of the James River, and would attempt to reach Richmond from that direction."[62]

That evening Hill reported to Lee's adjutant Walter Taylor that Cooke had captured prisoners from seven regiments in the fight against Wilson. "I have taken a new line," he added, "with my left resting so as to cover the White Oak Swamp Bridge, with a regiment and battery on the other side, and my right covering the Willis Church Road." The position, he assured headquarters, "is a very defensible one."[63]

While McIntosh barricaded the roads leading to Samaria Church, Chapman took a portion of his cavalry brigade—the 1st Vermont, 8th New York, and 22nd New York Cavalry Regiments and a section of Fitzhugh's battery—to reconnoiter the southern end of the Confederate position at Malvern Hill. The rest of his brigade—the 3rd Indiana and 1st New Hampshire Cavalry—remained near Harrison's Landing. Chapman's force advanced in two columns, the right branch passing by the Phillips house to the north and the left following Turkey Creek Road nearer to the river. Supported by a gunboat, the columns joined near Turkey Creek and repulsed Colonel William T. Robbins's 24th Virginia Cavalry, which Gary had assigned to keep watch over the Confederate line's lower sector. The 8th New York and 1st Vermont then dismounted and marched to Turkey Island Creek, which curves around Malvern Hill's base. Crossing the creek, the Federals deployed in skirmish formation and pressed onto Malvern Hill, where they encountered Pickett's infantrymen. "A perfect furor of excitement was raised in the rebel camps when Chapman's brigade arrived at Malvern Hill," a newsman reported. "Immense clouds of dust suddenly commenced rising in every direction, showing plainly that heavy bodies of troops had been put in motion." Prudence trumped valor, however, and the heavily outnumbered Union cavalrymen dropped back, pursued by

Robbins's Virginians and Barringer's North Carolina horsemen. "They drove us this morning," a trooper in the 8th New York Cavalry wrote in his diary, "and the gunboats helped us by shelling them a little."[64]

Chapman's three regiments, supported by artillery, made a bold stand at Turkey Island Creek, where they fought dismounted, firing "by volley, infantry style." As the afternoon advanced, the Federals retired toward their previous night's bivouac near the Phillips house, north of Harrison's Landing. Exhausted from their day's exertions, the Vermonters settled into camp around the Phillips property. "We had an alarm during the night," a Vermonter recalled, "which I remember particularly from the fact that about that time I found myself in the saddle very suddenly, although it was said to be nothing more than John Woodard firing at a hog." The rest of Chapman's men enjoyed a quiet evening at Harrison's Landing. "We have just had a nice dinner, luxuri[ous] as well as substantial," a trooper in the 3rd Indiana Cavalry scrawled in his diary. "Cannonading towards Richmond. Gunboats shelling Malvern Hill."[65]

Chapman's excursion yielded important information. "I took a prisoner belonging to Pickett's division at his house," the colonel reported to Wilson. "He says he left his division this morning about a mile from Malvern, and that they were under orders to move to Drewry's Bluff." Three more prisoners—one from Pickett's Division and two from Gary's cavalry brigade—were also captured and interviewed by Wilson. "Their troops appear to have remained in position all day yesterday and to have marched this morning, in whole or in part, to Chaffin's and Drewry's Bluff, and probably Richmond," the general informed Humphreys at 9:40 that evening. "No disturbance of any kind at St. Mary's or vicinity. No enemy moving in any direction that [McIntosh] can discover."[66]

Wilson's cavalry had performed to perfection its job of screening the Army of the Potomac and of ferreting out Lee's position, which still extended from the upper part of White Oak Swamp toward the James. "This would indicate that [the Confederates] had not penetrated Grant's design of flinging his whole force beyond the James," the newsman Page noted, "but expected him to creep up the left bank under shadow of the gunboats!" Wilson concurred, noting, "my observations satisfied me that Lee was moving not so much to interpose between Grant and the river as to cover Richmond."[67]

"They had our exact range."

The Battle of Baylor's Farm was over by about 8:00 A.M. It took a while to for the Federals to regroup—Smith attributed the delay to Hinks's black soldiers, who were ebullient over their victory and slow to "get back into some kind of order and consistency"—but within an hour, the offensive was rolling south toward Petersburg in three columns, marching roughly abreast. Martindale's division strode cautiously along River Road, its right flank near the Appomattox; Brooks's division marched across Baylor's farm and continued down City Point Railroad and the adjacent wagon road, throwing out a strong line of skirmishes to maintain contact with Martindale; and Hinks's division slipped leftward to Jordan's Point Road along the route it had taken on June 9 and turned toward Petersburg once again, comprising the left wing of the advancing Federal infantry formation. Farther to the left, out of sight of the infantrymen, Kautz's cavalry rode onto the Norfolk and Petersburg Railroad and cantered along the tracks toward the rebel fortifications.[68]

Smith intended for Brooks's division to bear the brunt of the impending offensive. Brooks had served under Smith on multiple occasions and had joined him in openly criticizing Burnside after the Fredericksburg fiasco. Lyman, who described the brigadier general as a "tall strong man, with a heavy, rather sullen face," reported that he "has a great reputation as a valiant man and steady soldier, but seems to quarrel plentifully." Burnham's brigade led Brooks's advance on City Point Road, followed by Henry's and Marston's brigades. Bringing up the rear were Bell's and Curtis's brigades, borrowed from the 10th Corps and temporarily assigned to Brooks. The 13th New Hampshire, commanded by Colonel Aaron F. Stevens, fanned out in advance of the column, connecting with Hinks's pickets on their left.[69]

Two miles of sparring with Dearing's troopers brought Brooks's foremost elements to the edge of a clearing. Several hundred yards ahead stood the Friend family home, and on its right loomed the Dimmock Line's Battery 5, occupied by Captain Sturdivant's Albemarle Battery of five guns. Battery 5 was an imposing structure, made even more formidable by a deep ravine that started near the front of the fort and knifed off to the north, forming a natural moat. To reach the battery, Brooks's troops would have to charge across a quarter mile of open ground, overrun an entrenched rebel picket line, continue another two hundred yards to the ravine, traverse the ditch, then scale the fortress's steep walls, all the while under fire. For soldiers who had recently experienced the killing power of rebel earthworks firsthand at Cold Harbor, the prospects of assailing this imposing fortification seemed daunting indeed.[70]

A Confederate gunner and his companions in Battery 5 were devouring their breakfast of ham and eggs when the Federals appeared. As the rebel later recalled that moment, he and his friends were "congratulating ourselves on the epicurean dish [when] the roar of small arms commenced in the woods a half mile east of where our guns were located." Then, he recounted, "our pickets were seen slowly falling back, and the Yankee infantry were seen spreading out over the broad river bottom and taking the ditches in single file." At that juncture "stern reality burst upon us," he remembered, and "the tempting breakfast was entirely forgotten."[71]

Pressing south along River Road, Martindale's division reached the junction with City Point Road around noon. Smith's aides met the troops there and directed them to continue on and link up with the right end of Brooks's line. The Appomattox River's broad floodplain extended about a mile on their right to the banks. On the far side of the river, a prominent rise called Archer's Hill overlooked the fields stretching toward Petersburg.

Martindale's left-most brigade, under Stannard, tracked along City Point Railroad until Battery 5, crowning high ground to the left, came into view. Continuing farther was perilous, as the position dominated the open floodplain and made it a killing field. After connecting his left with Brooks's right, Stannard directed his men to seek cover from the rebels by hunkering low in a cornfield. There they came under deadly fire from Battery 3, which stood straight ahead and somewhat to their right. "They had our exact range, and we had one man killed and eighteen wounded in a few minutes," a Massachusetts soldier remembered. A shell exploded next to Captain Francis E. Goodwin of the 25th Massachusetts, knocking out his eye, and another shot wounded Lieutenant M. B. Bessey of Stannard's staff. Moving forward at the double quick another hundred yards, the New Englanders sought cover behind a gentle rise of ground. "All day long we were in this corn field under a scorching sun, with no protection save what we obtained pulling up the corn, which was about two feet high, and covering our heads with it," a soldier recollected. "It was provoking to lay there as we did," he reminisced, "hour after hour, and hardly fire a shot in reply to the rebels, who were blazing away at us all the time." Rebel sharpshooters proved so accurate that Captain V. P. Parkhurst, commanding the 25th Massachusetts, was forced to move his headquarters to the rear.[72]

In an attempt to relieve Stannard, Martindale advanced his other brigade, under Stedman, nearer to Batteries 2 and 3 and directed the colonel to extend skirmishers to the Appomattox on his right. This maneuver's folly became painfully apparent when rebel artillery rolled onto Archer's Hill across the river and began firing into the brigade's rear. Lacking protection, Stedman retired to his initial position, leaving only a small reconnoitering party in his front, much of which was swooped up in a sortie by the 26th Virginia.[73]

Meanwhile Hinks's troops, marching along Jordan's Point Road, crossed tiny Baylor's Creek, brushed aside Dearing's pickets, and advanced to the main

Confederate earthworks. The 5th USCT of Duncan's brigade deployed as skirmishers on the left side of the road and bushwhacked through dense thickets to a skirt of woods in front of Batteries 9 and 10. "It was hoped that the fire of these skirmishers would seriously annoy if not entirely silence the guns in these works, which held a very commanding position relative to the works opposite our right and against which the main attack was intended," Duncan later wrote. "But the distance from the edge of the woods to the redoubts against which the regiment was operating was so great—fully 600 yards—that they accomplished little, save to distract the enemy's attention." While the 5th USCT inched ahead, Hinks deployed the rest of the brigade in a line running from Battery 7 on the north, by Peebles's house, to Battery 10 on the south, at the junction of the Jordan's Point and Suffolk Stage Roads.[74]

Unable to inflict damage with his infantry, Duncan tried bringing up artillery. A field behind the 5th USCT seemed a promising place to position the guns, but the commanders of Battery B, 2nd U.S. Colored Artillery, and Battery K, 3rd New York Light Artillery, concluded that the clearing was dangerously exposed to Confederate ordnance. "Every part of the field was so thoroughly commanded by a direct, an oblique, and an enfilading fire from the enemy's guns that prudence dictated the withdrawal of the batteries," was how the colonel later put it. By one o'clock in the afternoon, Hinks decided that the 5th USCT had suffered enough and ordered it withdrawn, leaving two companies to keep the rebels in Batteries 9 and 10 occupied and to guard the brigade's left flank.[75]

Captain Sturdivant's gunners in Battery 5 spied Federal officers congregating near the Beasley home, about a mile down the river. Excited by the opportunity, Sturdivant directed Lieutenant Ferguson to fire upon the cluster of bluecoats. "So as soon as the smoke cleared up we all stood out to see the effect of the shot," a gunner related, "but if any were killed we could not tell, but such scampering into Beasley's house you never saw." The captain then directed Ferguson to shoot through Beasley's house, which he did, but a grove around the building prevented him from gauging the results. Later in the day a Confederate colonel stationed north of the river reported that the ball "passed right through the house and exploded in the back yard where the Yankees had been congregating all the morning." It was, he claimed, "the most beautiful shot he had ever seen."[76]

Hinks next set about arranging Duncan and Holman into two lines for the impending assault, facing Batteries 6 through 10. Under severe fire from the rebel batteries, Duncan formed a first line with the 4th Regiment on the right and the 22nd Regiment on the left and a second line with the 5th on the right and the 6th on the left. Holman arranged his small brigade on Duncan's left, the 1st USCT in front. Once the troops were in position, Hinks advanced them to a crest facing the rebel works, Duncan's lead right regiment—the 4th USCT—joining the left of Brooks's skirmish line. "This was a work of great difficulty," the colonel later noted, "owing to the triple fire of the enemy which had previously prevented the planting of our batteries, and which was now directed with increased rapidity and with great accuracy upon all our movements."[77]

The division was finally in place, stretching from Jordan's Point Road north to the home of the Peebles family. "Here we lay five hours," Duncan recalled, "suffering much from the well-directed fire of the enemy, which he never remitted."[78]

With their flanks now secure—Martindale's division on their right, Hinks's division on the left—Brooks's skirmishers sidled into a ravine immediately inside the wood line. "We spring forward from stump to stump, and from log to log," a New Hampshire man recalled, "drawing the enemy's fire and then gaining ground before he can reload." It was deadly business, made even more lethal by small pockets of rebels occupying rifle pits in the woods. Uncertain whether Hinks's black troops on his left would hold, Brooks directed Burnham to extend his skirmish line's left end rearward to protect his flank in case they fell back. Stevens's 13th New Hampshire, comprising the leftmost element of Burnham's skirmish line, reached south as directed and fastened onto Hinks's rightmost skirmishers.[79]

Brooks's remaining brigades formed in support of Burnham and Marston. Guy Henry's men deployed behind Marston, the right edge of their formation anchored on the Petersburg and City Point Railroad. Bell's brigade, backstopped by Curtis's brigade, moved onto Burnham's left, next to Hinks's troops and across from Battery 6. Situated left of City Point Road, these soldiers sought cover "of a wood and sprout clearings, which skirted the open fields before the enemy's works, across which the range was unobstructed." Their support—Battery C, 3rd Rhode Island Light Artillery—opened a "well-directed fire" toward the Confederate earthworks. The brigade commanders deployed their troops "in line of battle by regiments" and awaited the fateful command to charge.[80]

August Kautz cut an impressive figure. A Petersburg lawyer described the German-born cavalryman as "five feet ten inches high [with] a swarthy complexion, a square massive German head, wears his hair and beard cut close, speaks slowly and thoughtfully, and has the breeding of a gentleman." While Smith's infantry huddled along the Dimmock Line's northeastern face, Kautz aimed his cavalry for a point farther south, where Baxter Road penetrated the rebel entrenchments. He was familiar with the terrain, having traversed much of the same ground during the abortive foray against Petersburg less than a week earlier. His assignment was to "make as much show of force as we could, to draw away as many troops from the real point that had been selected for Smith to assault," the general later wrote. "I was not required to report to General Smith, and did not receive my orders from him, and was subsequently directed to make my report to General Butler."[81]

After leaving Baylor's farm, Kautz's troopers had followed a plantation road to Jordan's Point Road. A small Confederate force tried to block the way, but a dismounted charge quickly removed that obstacle. Continuing along the plantation road, the Union riders crossed Prince George Court House Road, cantered on to the Norfolk and Petersburg Railroad, and then veered onto the Baxter Road and headed directly toward Petersburg. They encountered a stray Confederate patrol, but a squadron from the 11th Pennsylvania Cavalry pushed these rebels aside. By noon Kautz's men came within sight of the Dimmock Line.[82]

A long-distance artillery duel flared as the 4th Wisconsin Battery unlimbered and opened on the rebel works. Confederate artillery replied, and Captain Easterly boldly ran a second gun closer to the enemy and blazed away. Kautz meanwhile scouted the terrain. The land toward the Confederate works was "comparatively level," he later wrote, and provided no cover for an attacking force. Although five rebel forts took part in the artillery duel, Kautz concluded that only a token body of troops occupied the defenses. At 3:00 P.M. he decided to "make a demonstration and if possible, to get through the line."[83]

Penetrating the Confederate earthworks, however, was easier said than done. Deploying Spear's brigade on the left side of Baxter Road and Mix's brigade on the right, Kautz ordered an advance. Captain Easterly rolled his guns into position to support the attack as the rebel artillery bombardment intensified. Kautz's skirmishers started across a field laced with briars and vines and pressed to within five hundred yards of the Confederate position. There the charge fell apart. Mix's skirmishers came under a withering enfilading fire from rebels north of Baxter Road, while one of the supporting Wisconsin artillery pieces jammed. Although the gun was soon back in service, Kautz concluded that he was outnumbered and ordered his men to fall back, which they did, taking up a new line a hundred yards or so in front of their former position. Mortally wounded in the futile charge was Colonel Mix, who was left lying in front of the Confederate works. "As only a portion of the men were armed with carbines, and so many men are required to take care of the horses," Kautz later explained, "our line was really weaker than the enemy's in men, and the skirmishers could not be advanced any farther."[84]

For the next two hours, Kautz's cavalrymen hunkered in the field, pelted by Confederate artillery. "The weather was hot, and a burning sun poured its heat down on the men," the general later wrote. So far as he could tell, Smith's infantry had hunkered down in front of the Dimmock Line and was doing nothing, just as Gillmore's troops had behaved on the ninth. "We believed ourselves again deserted," Kautz later wrote. Flustered, at 5:30 P.M. he ordered his troopers to withdraw to Jordan's Point Road, "having come to the conclusion that Smith had abandoned the assault, as Gillmore had done, and returned to Bermuda Hundred."[85]

"Hold on at all hazards."

Henry Wise had done his best to strengthen the Dimmock Line, but he faced a nearly impossible task. Since the Union threat was expected to come from the direction of City Point, he had concentrated his limited resources in the portion of line downriver from Petersburg, manning the Dimmock Line from Battery 1 on the Appomattox to Battery 40 near Butterworth's Bridge, a distance of some three miles. Even then his troops were stretched thin, be they the 2,200 soldiers of Wise's estimate or the 4,000-odd troops of modern calculations. The remaining five miles of line from Butterworth's Bridge to the Appomattox south and west of town remained unprotected save for a few small cavalry detachments. Wise assigned Colonel Powhatan R. Page to cover the sector from the Appomattox River to Battery 14 with his own 26th Virginia and the 46th Virginia, Major Peter V. Batte's militia battalion, William H. Hood's militia battalion, and Sturdivant's artillery. Wise himself commanded the troops from Battery 14 to Battery 23, which included Colonel John T. Goode's 34th Virginia and Captain C. S. Slaten's Macon Light Artillery Battery. The remainder of the Dimmock Line to Battery 40 was held by the 64th Georgia Battalion, Archer's militia, and a company of the 23rd South Carolina, all under Brigadier General Colston's command. Elements from Dearing's cavalry patrolled the remaining five miles of line arcing back to the Appomattox west of town "merely to give warning of the enemy's approach."[86]

The critical sector of line was Battery 5, occupied by soldiers from the 26th Virginia and Sturdivant's Albemarle Battery. This imposing three-sided redoubt overlooked City Point Railroad and City Point Road, each of which rep-

resented probable avenues of approach by the enemy. Wise considered the redoubts and parapets from the river to Battery 5 "very defective" and "especially
badly laid off" around Battery 5 itself. "There," he explained, "[the line] made
a sharp angle, inwards and acute, and thence gradually curved outwards again,
with a hill and curtilage of Peebles's house on the right, under cover of which
assailants might get strong vantage ground against not only the rifle pits in
front but against the redoubts and breastworks themselves." Put simply, Battery
5 was improvidently located "where the worst constructed line of the war made
a sharp salient angle, leaving the most commanding ground outside of our line
in front." Beauregard later described the position as "ineffably and contempt-
ibly weak."[87]

While Wise fretted, Richmond's newspapers maintained a bold front.
"Grant is reported to have gone to Westover, full thirty miles from Richmond
by the road, in Charles City County," the *Daily Dispatch* assured its readers.
"This is near the point to which McClellan retreated after he was whipped
away from the front of Richmond. The reports of the demoralization of the
Federal army are apparently well grounded, and it may be that he has sought
this locality which, under the protection of his gunboats, he can recuperate his
shattered strength, and get the courage of his men up to the fighting point;
though the more probable supposition is that he designs to cross to the southside, somewhere in the vicinity of City Point."[88]

Beauregard began June 15 as he had ended June 14—petitioning Richmond
for reinforcements. Messages streamed from his headquarters north of the Appomattox to President Davis's military advisor Braxton Bragg. "Return of Butler's forces sent to Grant and arrival of latter at Harrison's Landing renders my
position more critical than ever," he wrote Bragg at 7:00 A.M. "If not re-enforced immediately enemy could force my lines at Bermuda Hundred Neck,
capture Battery Dantzler, now nearly ready, or take Petersburg, before any
troops from Lee's army or Drewry's Bluff could arrive in time. Can anything
be done in the matter?"[89]

After his drubbing by Hinks's novices, Dearing had hurried back to Petersburg and alerted Wise that three Federal brigades had overrun his position at
Baylor's farm. So far as he could tell, Union infantry and cavalry were heading
for the Baxter and Jerusalem Plank Roads. Wise thanked the general for the
intelligence and commended him for delaying the Union offensive long enough
for Petersburg's defenders to prepare.[90]

Forwarding Dearing's information to Beauregard, Wise requested reinforcements. Beauregard in turn forwarded the request to Bragg, along with
Dearing's report that Federal troops were "advancing in heavy force on Broad-

way Road." A prisoner, he added, claimed that some of Burnside's soldiers were among the approaching forces. "If so," noted Beauregard, "it is very im= portant." At 9:30 A.M. he related that Union infantry and cavalry had attacked Dearing's outposts "in force," warning, "They say it is an 'on to Petersburg,' [sic] and more force behind."[91]

Desperate for reinforcements, Beauregard directed Hoke's Division to leave its camps near Drewry's Bluff and start toward Petersburg. At 11:20 A.M. Hoke reported that his troops were "on the march." Beauregard also petitioned Bragg to send Ransom's Brigade back as well. At 11:45 A.M. the Louisianan became even more insistent. "General Wise reports General Dearing's cavalry driven back on Petersburg, with loss of one piece of artillery," he wrote Richmond. "Enemy reported three brigades of infantry and considerable force cavalry, apparently moving toward Baxter and Jerusalem Plank roads. He calls for re-enforcements on his whole line. We must now elect between lines of Bermuda Neck and Petersburg," Beauregard warned. "We cannot hold both. Please answer at once."[92]

Bragg replied immediately. Hoke, he wrote, had been directed to report to Beauregard "early this morning." At 11:30 A.M.—Smith's infantry was now deploying in front of the Dimmock Line—he reported that the division was crossing the James and that Beauregard was best situated to determine where these troops should be deployed. Beauregard's response—timed 1:45 P.M.—was terse. "I did not ask advice with regard to the movement of troops," he wrote, "but wished to know preference of War Department between Petersburg and lines across Bermuda Hundred Neck, for my guidance, as I fear my present force may prove unequal to hold both."[93]

Beauregard hoped that Hoke would afford Wise sufficient reinforcements to safeguard Petersburg. Telegraphing Bragg, he promised to hold the Bermuda Hundred line as long as possible. If Smith broke through, however, he saw no choice but to pull troops from the Howlett Line to reinforce Wise. The Army of Northern Virginia, he suggested, should forward a "strong division" to Port Walthall Junction as a reserve that he could draw on if needed.[94]

Wise fretfully bided his time as increasing numbers of Federals materialized in his front. To deal with Kautz's threat on Baxter Road, he directed Colston's mix of local militia, Georgians, and South Carolinians to join the 34th Virginia there. Responding to Brooks's capture of rifle pits in front of Battery 6, Wise summoned Archer's 3rd Battalion, Virginia Reserves, to reinforce Page and shifted part of Goode's 34th Virginia to the left as well. His relief was palpable when Beauregard informed him that Hoke was on his way to Petersburg. The fresh troops, Beauregard promised, "would be in time to save the

day, if our men could stand their ordeal, hard as it was, a little while longer."
Wise replied: "I will hold on to the last ditch, but the enemy are overwhelming
and reinforcements must be hastened up."[95]

Like Beauregard, Lee juggled priorities across several fronts all morning.
Union cavalry—Wilson's men—seemed unusually aggressive, one arm pressing through Smith's Store toward White Oak Swamp and another toward Malvern Hill. The purpose of these dual probes was not clear. Were the Federal
horsemen simply safeguarding the approaches toward the Army of the Potomac, or were they opening the way for a Union offensive toward Richmond?

Early that morning Beauregard had dispatched his aide Colonel Samuel R.
Paul to visit Lee, explain to him the general's tenuous situation, and inquire
into Lee's plans. Beauregard also instructed Paul to advise that a "large force
of the enemy which had already crossed the James had evidently no other purpose than to commence immediately operations against Petersburg; and that it
was of utmost importance that all the troops taken from my command to re-en-
force the Army of Northern Virginia be ordered back to me with the least possible delay, adding to them such others as could be spared at the time."[96]

Lee's response, Beauregard later wrote, "was not encouraging." According
to Paul's postwar account of the meeting, the Virginian remarked that Beauregard must be mistaken "in supposing that the enemy had thrown any troops to
the south side of James River; that a few of Smith's corps had come back to
[Beauregard's] front—nothing more—and that it was probable the enemy
would cross the James, though, he reiterated, no part of his force had done so
yet, because he could do nothing else, unless to withdraw altogether, as had
been done by McClellan, which he did not believe General Grant thought of."
Paul added that Lee had already ordered Hoke's troops to join Beauregard, and
that if the Louisianan were "seriously threatened," he would send aid and even
come himself. Soon after Paul left, Lee informed Bragg of the visit, noting that
the aide had represented that Beauregard "was of the opinion that if he had his
original force, he would be able to hold his present lines in front of Genl Butler and at Petersburg." To restore Beauregard to his former strength, Lee agreed
to send him Ransom's Brigade, adding that he had "determined to move this
army back near the exterior line of defences near Richmond, but from the
movements of the enemy's cavalry this morning, I do not wish to draw too far
back. Unless therefore I am better satisfied, I shall remain where I am today,
as the enemy's plans do not seem to be settled."[97]

Porter Alexander, the 1st Corps's artillery chief, watched the conference between Lee and Paul from a distance. "I could not hear the conversation, but I
was told of his errand, and Gen. Lee's air and attitude seemed to me so sug-

gestive of hostility that I drew a mental inference that he, for some cause, disliked either the message or the messenger, or perhaps both," he later wrote. "And I imagined a new military precept, to be taught in the schools, that 'persona gratas' should always be selected for messengers who are sent with verbal communications."[98]

Near noon Lee received copies of the various dispatches Beauregard had sent to Bragg. The appearance of Federal troops in front of Petersburg was disturbing, although the source of the invaders was still not evident from these communications. Since Beauregard's reports neglected to identify the units massing in front of the Dimmock Line, Lee had no way of knowing whether they belonged to the Army of the Potomac or if Butler was simply reprising his failed offensive of June 9. In any event, Lee informed Bragg, he had directed Hoke that morning to report to Beauregard and recommended that Ransom be sent forward as well.[99]

Lacking definitive information, Lee saw no choice but to stay put and bar Grant's access to Richmond. The disparity between Grant's and Lee's numbers was daunting. Reduced now to two corps—Anderson's and Hill's—and one cavalry division, the Army of Northern Virginia could marshal at most 30,000 soldiers. If the offensive against Petersburg involved Butler and Smith alone, Grant retained the capacity to hurl four army corps, numbering at least 100,000 troops, against Richmond. For Lee to hold them at bay, he had to remain firmly entrenched in his present line from White Oak Swamp to Malvern Hill. Indeed, even if Grant sent an army corps across the James to assist Butler, Lee's calculus could not change.[100]

"My best chance of success was to trust to a very heavy skirmish line."

Baldy Smith studied the fortifications in front of him. His two weeks at Cold Harbor had taught him a brutal lesson in the killing power of well-sited entrenchments. The situation here gave cause for reflection. After all, Lee's men had built their Cold Harbor fortifications in a matter of hours; the Dimmock Line had been constructed more than a year and a half ago and seemed expertly sited to ward off the very attack that he planned to launch. In addition, Butler's and Kautz's promises of lightly defended Confederate defenses were not bearing out. "Butler's information which he had imparted to me was wrong," Smith later wrote. The general was by no means timid. So far this day he had acted with "great promptness and spirit," as one of Hinks's officers later wrote, having "marched five or six miles, fought a considerable engagement, and driven in the enemy's skirmishers so far as fully to develop their main line." But Smith was not rash either. The last thing he wanted was another Cold Harbor.[101]

The more Smith contemplated the situation, the worse it seemed. "In place of a weak line of works, I found them very strong," he later explained. "In place of a small force, I judged, from the number of guns and the pertinacity of the skirmishers in holding on outside, that the works must be at least tolerably well manned. The artillery fire on the extreme left where Kautz was told me that he had not been able to repeat his feat of riding over the lines. The hills occupied by Martindale were too far off to be said, with our calibers, to command the works in his front running to the Appomattox. They were also lower than the others. All the information given to me the night before was erroneous," he concluded, "and I was obliged to discard it utterly, and get by a reconnaissance correct information for myself." [102]

Lacking an engineering officer, Smith decided to reconnoiter the Dimmock Line himself. His precarious health complicated the task. The ordeal at Cold Harbor had left him with a "serious attack of dysentery, which was raging on the 15th of June, such that I could scarcely sit on my horse," he later recorded, and the "condition of my head was such that I could not remain in the sun for two minutes without an intense headache." [103]

Before setting off, Smith sent a dispatch to Butler. "The fight at Baylor's house broke up my arrangements, so that I have not been able to straighten my line," he advised. "But this, however, will be done at once." He also reported sounds from the direction of Petersburg and inquired whether trains were bringing Confederate reinforcements. Georgia troops, he observed, were in front of part of his line.[104]

Over the next several hours, Smith methodically examined the Dimmock Line. He had scouted the entrenchments in front of Hinks and Brooks by 3:00 and consumed another hour analyzing the fortifications facing Martindale. At 5:00 he returned to his command center with Brooks, satisfied that he fully understood the situation.

What Smith found confirmed his fears. "General Martindale had come up and in his front was a low valley perfectly swept by the enemy's fire of artillery, and cut up by deep ditches and ravines, while a strong line of works, open in the rear and connected by heavily profiled rifle pits, were occupied by the enemy," he observed. "General Brooks's command was at the salient of the line, which consisted of a strongly profiled work heavily flanked on our left by redoubts and rifle-pits en echelon, their flanking works also fronting the line of General Hinks." One of Hinks's aides described the rebel works as presenting "a very formidable aspect to the troops." The entrenchments, he noted, "were situated on commanding crests, and the forest was felled in their front so as to expose advancing lines to the fire for half a mile or more. Numerous pieces of artillery swept the field of fire rapidly and with precision, and a strong line of skirmishers in secure rifle-pits, well advanced in front of the works, kept up a spirited and effective fusillade." In sum, Smith was aghast to discover that he had come up against, not the weak line of entrenchments that Butler and Kautz had described, but a powerful bastion bristling with artillery.[105]

Smith made some rapid calculations. His soldiers were spread along three miles of line. By his own estimate he faced at least a score of cannon and some three thousand Confederates. "Taking therefore any estimate founded on any military rules of which I am cognizant," he later wrote, "I had not the superiority to lead me to anything approaching rashness in presence of such works and such an artillery fire."[106]

But the personal reconnaissance also revealed a fatal weakness in the enemy lines. While Confederate artillery appeared formidable, the entrenchments were thinly manned. The threat to an attacking force came from cannon fire, not from musketry. A densely packed body of assaulting troops would take severe losses, but troops loosely arrayed in a skirmish line stood a fair chance of success. Artillery would pass harmlessly through their formation, and the scant rebel defenders would be unable to generate sheets of musketry that were so destructive of an attacking force. So Smith decided to concentrate his artillery near Brooks's center, open a heavy bombardment to suppress rebel fire, and attack with a double line of skirmishers. Once these men had overrun the works, the rest of his troops were to follow and consolidate the gains. As Smith later articulated his reasoning, "my best chance of success was to trust to a very heavy skirmish line which would not of itself attract much artillery fire and which yet would be sufficient to do the work if the enemy was not very strong in infantry."[107]

Smith's scouting expedition also showed him where to focus his attack. Several ravines sliced in front of Batteries 5 through 7, providing relatively safe approaches to the enemy position. By funneling troops down these broad gullies, the general could launch his offensive close to the Confederate earthworks, minimizing the distance and the time that his men would be under fire. The large ravine in front of Battery 5 was especially attractive. From there, skirmishers could pin down the rebel gunners while the main body of troops charged the fortifications. As Brooks later wrote, Smith determined "to throw forward his line of skirmishers (Burnham's) if possible to the ravine just in front of the enemy's line, from which position it was supposed they might keep down the artillery fire while the main column would cross the opening in our front." [108]

Shortly after 4:00 P.M. Smith sent word to Hinks that there was "but little infantry in the works, and that as artillery could not tear up the line of skirmishers as it could a line of battle, he could take the place with a skirmish line if he could at all." He directed Hinks to form a "very heavy" skirmish line at once, which was to lead the attack, followed by a line of battle if successful. Hinks was to launch his assault either when he received orders from Smith or when Brooks moved forward. [109]

Hancock's soldiers were having a frustrating day. Delayed by the fiasco involving the phantom rations, Birney led the 2nd Corps procession from Flowerdew Hundred around 11:00 A.M. Gibbon got underway at noon, and Barlow's division, bringing up the rear, set off at 1:00 P.M. The soldiers trudged drearily along with empty stomachs under an unforgiving Virginia sun. "Day intensely hot and road dusty," the staffer William Mitchell wrote in his journal. "The men suffering terribly for water during the march, many of them giving out along the road." A New Yorker claimed that his "tongue actually hung out and was covered with dust" and that he "could spit cotton without exaggeration." A Vermont sharpshooter, however, observed that the more enterprising soldiers managed to find something to eat. "A hungry soldier is greatly given to reconnaissances on private account, he has an interrogation point in each eye as well as one in his empty stomach," he noted. "Chickens, most carefully concealed in the darkest cellars, are unearthed by these patient seekers, pigs and cows driven far away to the most sequestered valleys are brought to light; bacon and hams turn up in the most unexpected places, and on the whole, the soldier on the march fares not badly when left to his own devices for a day or so." Now quite skillful in locating hidden food supplies, the sharpshooters, he wryly noted, "managed to sustain life." [110]

Stopping at a deserted house, Mitchell spotted a straggler in the library tearing up books and throwing the shredded pages on the floor. "I struck him with my saber and ordered him to his regiment, when he seized his musket from the corner of the room, bayonet fixed, and plunged right at me," the staff officer recounted. "I knocked his musket to one side and gave him a slash with my saber, opening his head and knocking him clear down a flight of stairs, musket and all, and before I could get down to him he scrambled up and made off toward the column, and I could not overtake him." [111]

Crossing over from the north bank of the James, Hancock finally caught up

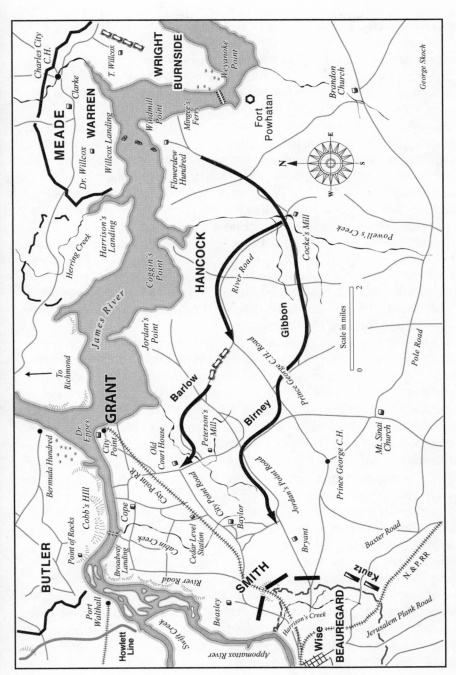

Hancock's route of advance, June 15

with the column. He was exhausted, and his Gettysburg injury was acting up. An officer noted that "the general's wound has given him a great deal of pain and worry all day, and his want of rest and something proper to eat and drink has been very trying." Nonetheless, Hancock insisted on riding at the head of the troops "most of the time, and sharing the same fare—hard tack, muddy warm water, and fat bacon."[112]

Errors in the chart provided by headquarters were becoming painfully apparent. "The map was found to be utterly useless," Hancock later reported, "the only roads laid down on it being widely out of the way." Chief of Staff Morgan, who remained with Birney in the corps's van, tried to steer the marching column toward Harrison's Creek, depicted on the map as entering the Appomattox River four miles downstream from Petersburg. Puzzled by glaring discrepancies between the road that he was traveling and the route as drawn, he sought guidance from local inhabitants. "I have found some guides and have ceased traveling by the map," Hancock informed headquarters in a note to Humphreys at 3:30 P.M. "Firing of two or three hours' duration has been heard since we started," he added. "A negro with us thinks it is on the Prince George Court House Road, one mile and a half this side. I hear of no enemy near Prince George Court House or Old Court House."[113]

On his new guide's recommendation, Hancock turned his column northward from Prince George Court House Road and headed toward Old Court House, where he hoped to strike a crossroad to Harrison's Creek as depicted on the map. To hedge his bets—this part of Virginia remained a mystery to him, and neither the map nor the guides offered much edification—the general directed Birney and Gibbon to follow a side road slanting off to the right, which he marked with dotted lines on a map that he sent to them. Barlow, still in the column's rear, was to take another parallel route toward Old Court House, near City Point, followed by the corps's trains. "A Negro familiar with the road is sent to you," Hancock informed Barlow.[114]

The corps commander still had no inkling that he was expected to move into position to support Smith's assault on the Dimmock Line. Indeed, the 2nd Corps, now divided into two segments, was veering northwestward, heading more toward City Point than toward Petersburg. "Sent wrong [by his initial orders]," Hancock's aide Francis Walker later observed, "his line of march increased by several miles, after his time of starting had been delayed several hours, Hancock led forward the corps without an intimation that his presence was to be imperatively required at Petersburg. So far as he had any reason to think, it would be sufficient if he brought up his corps, in good condition, in season to go fairly into camp by nightfall."[115]

X

JUNE 15, 1864

Grant Loses a Sterling Opportunity

"I hold the key to Petersburg."

NEAR NOON GRANT STARTED toward City Point, where he could better oversee the operation against Petersburg. Meade and his staff remained behind to supervise the rest of the Potomac army's movement across the James. After crossing the river on a ferry, Grant rode toward City Point. A small steamer came by; hailing the ship, Grant, his aide Ely Parker, and a few other staffers traveled the rest of the way to City Point on the boat. Porter and the remainder of the entourage went by land "so as to take some instructions to Hancock's Corps and to familiarize ourselves with that part of the country," Porter later wrote. Grant's aide Orville Babcock and Assistant Secretary of War Dana lost their way and ran into four Confederate soldiers, resulting in "a mutual rapid retreat of which they give an amusing account," staffer Comstock recorded in his diary.[1]

On reaching City Point, Grant established headquarters in Dr. Richard Eppes's yard. The place was strategically located for overseeing both the Army of the Potomac and the Army of the James. Perched on a high bluff at the junction of the James and Appomattox Rivers and at the terminus of the City Point Railroad, Grant could readily communicate with Butler and Meade and had easy access to the evolving battle front.

Much to Grant's relief, summer clothing for himself and his staff was waiting at City Point. For the general was a new flannel dark-blue blouse, single-breasted with four regulation brass buttons in front. "It was substantially the coat of a private soldier," Porter later wrote, "with nothing to indicate the rank of an officer except the three gold stars of a lieutenant general on the shoulder straps." Grant remained oblivious to the condition of his clothes and whether they even fit properly. "I like to put on a suit of clothes when I get up in the morning, and wear it until I go to bed, unless I have to make a change in my dress to meet company," he remarked. "I have been in the habit of getting one coat at a time, putting it on and wearing it every day as long as it looked respectable, instead of using a best and a second best." The general also received a pair of calfskin boots, which he liked so much that he wore them most of the time afterward, donning his heavy top boots only when it rained.[2]

Having heard nothing all morning from Butler, Hancock, or Smith, Grant telegraphed the James commander soon after arriving at City Point. "Have you any news from Petersburg?" he asked, noting that the 2nd Corps had not yet received its rations. Butler was visiting his lookout tower when the message arrived, but his chief of staff, Colonel Shaffer, answered for him. "Nothing heard here from Smith," Shaffer replied. "Rations were sent down the river to Hancock. Will forward more to him at once by land." In response Grant asked the colonel to inform Butler that "as fast as General Meade's army crosses the river they will march up to Harrison's Creek." When the rest of the Potomac army would be available to assist Baldy Smith's operation, however, was not yet clear. The pontoon bridge across the James had been completed shortly after midnight, Grant added, but nothing had crossed yet except "wagons and artillery, and will not until they are all over unless there should be a necessity."[3]

At 3:30 P.M., having still heard nothing from the emerging battle front, Grant wrote Butler again. Hancock, he began, had orders to march toward Petersburg, stopping at Harrison's Creek unless directed otherwise. "I have not yet heard a word of the result of the expedition against Petersburg, but still firing in that direction, and seeing indications of the enemy moving from the north to the south side of James River, I have sent back orders to hurry up this corps," Grant added. "If you require it, send back to General Hancock, under cover to General Gibbon, with directions for him to read, and the corps will push forward with all speed."[4]

Ten minutes later Grant's aide Lieutenant Colonel Dent wrote Butler inquiring if he had heard from Smith. Butler replied that he had heard nothing, but that he had sent two aides with a cavalry squadron to communicate with the expeditionary force. He also informed the general in chief that there had been "pretty sharp" fighting at Petersburg, and from his lookout tower he could see Smith advancing and the enemy falling back. Nothing had passed down the railroad or the Richmond–Petersburg Turnpike, he added, so he doubted that Confederate reinforcements had reached the city. A cloud of dust was visible, however, between Chaffin's farm and Richmond, suggesting that the rebels might be marching to cross the river. Butler was confident that Smith's force, which he placed at 15,000 men, was sufficient to take Petersburg. "I cannot conceive of any more force being needed," he assured Grant, "but if Hancock advances to Harrison's Creek, if I understand the place being the creek that enters into the Appomattox above Port Walthall, he will be within one mile of Smith's point of attack and can afford aid."[5]

Still hearing nothing from Hancock, Grant penned a message to Gibbon, whom he believed was leading the move. "Some of my staff who came up from Fort Powhatan report not having seen the Second Corps marching as they passed," he wrote. "Orders were sent for the corps to march early this morning and General Hancock reported that the orders were sent at 6 A.M. Use all haste in getting up," Grant urged. "Smith carried the outer works at Petersburg today"—referring to the Baylor's Farm fight—"and might need your assistance. This order is intended for the whole Second Corps and is directed to you, supposing you have the advance. Communicate it to all the division commanders and to General Hancock, and push forward as rapidly as possible."[6]

As fortune would have it, Grant's staff officer carrying the message for Gibbon met Smith on City Point Road, informed the general that the 2nd Corps was approaching from Windmill Point, and showed him the note. Smith immediately addressed a companion missive to "Hancock or Gibbon" requesting assistance and dispatched his aide Livermore to find Hancock and deliver it to him. "General Grant has authorized me to call on you to hurry forward to Petersburg to aid in its capture," Smith's message began. "I do not suppose at present there is much infantry over there, but the wide open spaces along my entire front, and the heavy artillery fire of the enemy, have prevented me from attempting any assault and also preventing me from getting any artillery into position to do any service. If the Second Corps can come up in time to make an assault tonight after dark in vicinity of Norfolk and Petersburg Railroad I think we may be successful. But tonight is the last night, as General Lee is reported crossing at Chaffin's Bluff." In closing, he asked Hancock to advise him when the 2nd Corps could be expected and noted that his line's left end rested on Jordan's Point Road. Accompanied by half a dozen cavalrymen, Livermore rode off to find the general and deliver the message to him.[7]

Smith was anxious to attack, but Grant's letter alerting him to Hancock's proximity induced him to wait. His troops had been deployed in front of the Dimmock Line for six hours now, pelted by continuous artillery fire. Waiting another hour or two would be excruciating, but the gain could be enormous. If the 2nd Corps joined him in time for the assault, victory would be certain. And so Smith decided to bide his time.[8]

Soon after shifting onto his new route, Barlow met the orderly carrying Grant's message to "use all haste in getting up" to Smith's position. Barlow gave the man a note to take back to Grant describing the 2nd Corps's location—as accurately as he could estimate it—and dispatched a staff officer of his own to find Hancock. At 5:25 P.M. the aide located Hancock and gave him Grant's message. Thirty minutes later Captain Livermore met the general some seven miles from the front, "riding in a wagon on account of trouble which his Gettysburg wound was giving him," and handed him Smith's message requesting assistance.[9]

According to Hancock, these were the "first and only intimations I had that Petersburg was to be attacked that day. Up to that hour I had not been notified from any source that I was to assist General Smith in assaulting that city."[10]

Alerted now to the true nature of his mission—support for Smith's offensive against Petersburg—the 2nd Corps commander sprang into action. "Everything was at once bent to this end," wrote the aide Francis Walker. The search "for the apocryphal 'Harrison's Creek' was abandoned," he recounted, and Hancock immediately ordered Birney to take his division, followed by Gibbon's, toward the emerging battle front. Hancock also dispatched his chief of staff, Lieutenant Colonel Morgan, to notify Smith of his whereabouts and assure him that the 2nd Corps was marching to his assistance with all due haste. "Fortunately these dispatches were received just when the head of Birney's division was passing a country road leading directly toward Petersburg, and the column (Birney's and Gibbon's troops) was turned in that direction," Hancock later wrote. Morgan recalled, "we could now hear the artillery at Petersburg and the men stepped out briskly."[11]

Accompanied by Livermore, Morgan delivered Hancock's response to Smith. "I reported to him on the field," Morgan later wrote, "I think as early as 6:30 P.M., informing him of the exact position of the corps, and asking him where, under the circumstances, the troops ought to go." According to the lieutenant colonel, Smith told him to put the 2nd Corps on his left "but neither indicated to me where his left was nor sent his staff officer" to show him the way. Instead, the general instructed Morgan to find Hinks and obtain more precise instructions from him. While riding off in the general direction indicated in search of Hinks, he met one of Birney's staff officers on his way to report to Smith. "On my advice he returned at once," Morgan later wrote, "to conduct the head of column to such point as General Hinks might advise."[12]

Sometime before 7:00, Birney, having learned that Smith wished the 2nd Corps to form on Hinks's left, located the division commander and asked for directions. Hinks responded that he had seen an order from Grant directing the 2nd Corps to move toward his left on the Norfolk Road. Assisted by one of Hinks's staff officers, Birney started in that direction, reached the Bryant house, and encountered the head of Kautz's cavalry column. The enemy were in "great force," Kautz warned, and noted that he had been "hanging all day by the eyelids."[13]

Barlow, whose division was still marching on a different road than the rest of the 2nd Corps, was unaware that his fellow divisions were now hurrying toward Petersburg. Still under orders to meet Birney and Gibbon at Old Court House, Barlow dispatched an officer to the hamlet to let them know that he was close by. The aide found Old Court House empty, and no one could inform him of Birney's or Gibbon's whereabouts.

Uncertain what to do next, Barlow sent the engineer Captain Charles Bird to find the rest of the 2nd Corps. Riding south, Bird encountered Morgan on a byroad. According to the captain, Morgan instructed him that Barlow was to "move straight on, cross the railroad, and then take the road to the left; and that he [Lieutenant Colonel Morgan] would meet me near the railroad." Morgan, however, later claimed that he had asked Bird "if he had noticed any roads between us and Old Court House towards Petersburg or to the left, and was answered in the affirmative. I then asked Captain Bird to request Gen. Barlow to take the road from Old Court House to Petersburg, to the left of the railroad, and pointed it out on the map."[14]

Riding back to Barlow, Bird related his conversation with Morgan as he understood it, then headed off to scout the local road network. The general continued into Old Court House at the head of his column, spotted a road bearing left toward the distant musketry and cannon fire, concluded that it must be the road to Petersburg that Bird had mentioned, and turned his column down it. Barlow's troops had progressed but a short way when the captain returned. He had ridden farther out the road that they were previously on, had crossed the railroad, and had found another road that bore to the left and otherwise fit Morgan's description. "He was sure of it," Barlow later wrote. Persuaded by Bird that the road that he had selected was not the road that Morgan intended, the division commander turned his column around, went back to Old Court House, and headed left along the continuation of his original route. After crossing the railroad he turned left again as the captain suggested.[15]

Bird, it developed, had misunderstood Morgan's instructions. Morgan meant for Barlow to take the left fork at Old Court House, which the general had done until dissuaded by Bird. In a memorandum prepared a few weeks later, Barlow explained that he "supposed that Col. Morgan desired me not to take the left hand road [from the Old Court House, as Barlow had originally done] either because I should interfere with other troops, or because the enemy might be there." He added as another reason for his choice of routes Bird's insistence "that Col. Morgan had told him to 'cross the railroad,' whereas the road to the left from Old Court House does not cross the railroad on any map that I have."[16]

At this juncture Barlow was entirely in the dark, relying on oral instructions that Bird had received from Morgan. His troops were exhausted—they had "pushed on as rapidly as possible, making only one short halt"—and he was lost. "I had no means, whatsoever, of knowing where were the 'outer works,' which Gen. Smith had captured, or where Smith's lines were," he later wrote.[17]

Concerned over Barlow's absence, Hancock again dispatched Morgan to find him. Riding to Old Court House, Morgan located the tail of Barlow's column passing through the settlement, directed the corps's wagon train out the correct road—the left fork that Barlow had previously taken and then abandoned—and cantered back to join the division commander. Barlow meanwhile had halted to let his men rest—they were "very tired," according to Morgan—and to get directions from Hancock about where to deploy. According to a memorandum that Morgan prepared two weeks later, "General Barlow stated to me then, what he hardly alludes to now, that he thought the road to the left was the right one, and the principal reason he did not take it was that he thought he might interfere with the other divisions, and that Captain Bird was very confident about his having secured a positive order, through me, to take the road on which I found him." The general, however, insisted that the lieutenant colonel was "entirely mistaken in his recollection of what I stated to be my principal reason for not taking the road to the left. Nearly all my staff officers know that my advanced guard had marched some distance down this road, and they were present at the conversation with Captain Bird which induced me to change the route, and know that it was upon the sole ground that Colonel Morgan had ordered it."[18]

"It seemed like a desperate undertaking."

While Hancock's divided corps groped toward Petersburg, Smith completed the groundwork for his offensive. Burnham's skirmishers advanced to the edge of the woods in front of Battery 5 in preparation for the assault, and the remainder of his brigade crowded close behind. Exhausted from the morning's march and the afternoon's incessant hail of artillery shells, the troops lounged behind logs and stumps. "We are so near Battery 5, that we can occasionally when the wind serves, distinctly hear the [rebel] commandant's orders, 'Load,' 'Fire,' and can look right into the muzzles of his guns, as they are run up to the embrasures and fired straight at us, 'puff,—bang'; sometimes singly, sometimes

all at once," a New Hampshire man recalled. Rebel marksmen in the Friend
and Jordan homes shot at anyone who moved. Even Smith and his staff came
under attack. "A shell burst in a group of staff horses to the right, another cut
a large tree in twain just in front, a solid shot bounded over the back of one of
the horses to the rear, and two spires of dirt shot up into the air on the left, and
we 'changed our base,'" a man at headquarters related.[19]

Hinks also made ready to charge. He was to move forward, Smith instructed,
"as soon as General Brooks's line commenced to advance." In preparation for
the assault, Hinks directed Duncan and Holman to strengthened their skirmish
lines and make sure that they were "advanced to gain the most favorable position [to] drive the enemy's sharpshooters."[20]

Duncan accordingly augmented his skirmish line with three companies
from the 4th USCT and four companies from the 22nd USCT. Spaced at one-
pace intervals, the troops strode cautiously through a stretch of plowed land
planted in fruit trees in front of the Friend house. Confederate artillery responded, and fountains of dirt exploded skyward as shells plowed into the dry
soil. A soldier in the 13th New Hampshire noted that the black troops were
"having a hard time of it." Fully exposed in the dusty field, "they rush forward,
and are then driven back; and then try again, and again; but without success,
and quite a number of them are stretched out on the ground, dead." Battery 5,
he observed, "shells them severely, and they and the shells drive up a great deal
of dust." He concluded that "the Negroes are doing wretched skirmishing."
Colors flying and drums banging, the 4th USCT's main body moved into the
field behind the skirmishers. "In a moment Battery 5 gives them—over our
heads—three or four shells right in their faces," the New Hampshire soldier
noted. "Snap—and back go they like wild men."[21]

To buttress Burnham's left flank, Brooks instructed Bell to insert part of his
brigade between Burnham and Hinks, facing the rebel entrenchments between
Batteries 5 and 6. Captain William J. Hunt of the 117th New York placed approximately a hundred skirmishers into the gap, spaced two paces apart. "Our
position was across a field where the timber had been cut and vines and briers
had grown as they grow only in Virginia," one of Hunt's soldiers wrote home.
By 6:00 P.M. two companies from the 8th Connecticut carrying Sharps rifles
had exhausted their ammunition and were relieved by two companies from the
118th New York. The 92nd New York of Henry's brigade also moved up to reinforce the skirmishers.[22]

As his troops formed to charge, Smith received another surprise. His plan
called for artillery to pound the Dimmock Line around Battery 5 to provide
cover for his skirmishers. Unknown to the general, his artillery chief, Captain

Frederick M. Follett, had ordered his artillerists to take their guns to the rear and water their horses. Follett's decision to withdraw his pieces, Smith later remarked, was made "without consultation and on his own responsibility." The flustered general had no choice but to delay the attack once more.[23]

As time passed and no sound of an offensive reached his ears, Butler grew increasingly concerned. For one thing, he worried that Hancock might not be available to assist. According to Grant's earlier dispatches, the 2nd Corps was heading toward Harrison's Creek, which Butler's map, like Hancock's, showed entering the Appomattox near Broadway Landing. A messenger, however, had informed Butler that the command was at Bailey's Creek, some "five or six miles in the rear of the position on Harrison's Creek." At 7:17 P.M. Butler wrote Grant that he had directed the wagons with Hancock's rations to Bailey's Creek, adding that he would "order Hancock's corps to advance to Smith, whom I have just heard has not been able yet to carry the interior line of the enemy's work." The corps had to move up to Smith's position immediately, he urged, "in view of the possible re-enforcement of the enemy during the night."[24]

A few minutes later Butler sent Smith a dispatch timed 7:20 P.M. "I grieve for the delays," he wrote. "Time is the essence of this movement. I doubt not the delays were necessary, but now push and get the Appomattox between you and Lee. Nothing has passed down the railroad to harm you yet."[25]

It is unclear when this message reached Smith, but there can be no doubt that the directive arrived too late to play any part in his decision to attack. With nightfall approaching, Smith decided on his own to assail the Dimmock Line without waiting for the 2nd Corps. Soon after 7:00 P.M. Smith's division and brigade heads sprang into action. "Don't be afraid," Marston assured his troops. "We are ten to one of the enemy." Burnham gathered his regimental commanders behind the skirmish line and gave directions for the impending assault. During the conference, a cannonball ricocheted into Major Charles E. Pruyn of the 118th New York, tearing a hole through his chest and killing him instantly. Bringing the conference to an abrupt close, the officers returned to their units. The division's skirmish line was to spearhead the attack, each man five paces from his closest companion, while the remainder of the brigades followed close behind. "It was a dare-devil piece of work at best," an officer recalled. "It seemed like a desperate undertaking," admitted another.[26]

Three Union batteries, sixteen guns in all, opened with a roar. "Forward," officers screamed in an attempt to make themselves heard over the whoosh of shells passing overhead. Burnham's skirmishers—the 13th New Hampshire, eight companies from the 8th Connecticut, and elements from the 92nd and

118th New York—stepped into the clearing. Confederate riflemen opened fire, and rebel cannon—the guns of Battery 5, directly across from the New Hampshire men, and of Batteries 6 and 7 to the south—focused on the advancing blue line. "Their path lay across a wide open plain," one of Burnham's officers later wrote of the assault, "and a tremendous fire of shot, shell, and Minnie bullets was poured into them as they advanced, mowing them down by scores and thinning their ranks terribly."[27]

A Confederate in Battery 5 termed the Union artillery response "one of the most sublime sights witnessed during the war. With a bomb bursting overhead every second, it was as if ten thousand lightning bugs were in the air, with an incessant bum, bum, bum. They were shooting a little high, else there would have been none left of us."[28]

The 13th New Hampshire, moving directly toward Battery 5 in a long, thin skirmish line, overran the Confederate rifle pits in the middle of the field, captured about a hundred rebels, and sent them to the rear. Men in blue began falling—Lieutenant S. Millet Thompson, commanding the flankers on the left of the New Hampshire regiment, tumbled from a shot in his left ankle—but the line pressed on. Several New Hampshire troops descended into the ravine at the foot of Battery 5, whose walls rose sharply forty feet to the top of the fort. "If we follow this thing right up now, we can take this battery," Captain Nathan D. Stoodley shouted. "Then we will take it," replied Captain George N. Julian. Joined by Captain Enoch W. Goss and a dozen other soldiers, Stoodley and Julian scampered up the face of the fort—"some straight up over the front walls," an officer recounted, "others up the north side, on bayonets stuck in the sand, grasping grass and weeds to assist in climbing, striking their boots into the gravel—anyhow so it be the quickest way in." An onlooker recalled that Captain Goss's men "with wild cheers swarmed up the hill like bees."[29]

While the New Hampshire men executed their courageous dash, Captain Hunt's skirmishers from Bell's brigade, charging on Burnham's left, ventured an equally daring foray toward the thinly protected interval between Batteries 6 and 7. "We carried the rifle pits near Battery 6 [and] the rebs fell back to a house by the side of the works," a soldier in the 117th New York later reported. "When we came to them there they gave us a volley that made terrible work." Undeterred, Hunt's hundred or so men from the 117th New York, backed by elements from the 3rd New York, pushed on—with "yells that might raise the dead," a participant reported—and found themselves behind the two forts. Exploiting their unexpected advantage, the New Yorkers fired into Battery 5's open rear. At the same time, the New Hampshire troops reached the fort's lip and peered down into the jumbled mass of Confederates milling inside.[30]

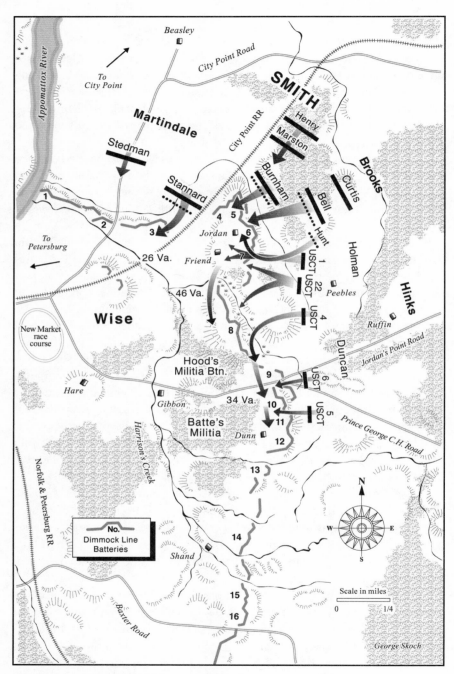

Smith overruns the Dimmock Line, June 15

Leaping into the stunned rebels, Union officers demanded their immediate surrender. "You never saw such a crazy crowd of men as those who captured the fort," an officer from Connecticut later wrote home. "Men were running all around." When Confederates began escaping through the work's open rear, Captain Stoodley turned a captured cannon on them only to discover that the fuses were missing. Stoodley demanded that Captain Sturdivant give him the fuses, but Sturdivant replied that he did not "want to be a party in the matter." A sergeant, however, found the fuses, and Corporal John H. Mawby led a team firing parting shots into the fleeing gray coats. A Confederate recollected one of his companions "wriggling along like a quail shot in the back" before falling to the ground. "Not realizing his condition, I remember—mirabile dictu—breaking out into a big ha! ha!" the southerner recalled.[31]

Victorious Federals rounded up prisoners, including Lieutenant Colonel James C. Councill of the 26th Virginia, who surrendered his sword to Captain Hunt. Captured in the battery were five cannon—four brass twelve-pounder howitzers and an iron gun—211 prisoners, and the 26th Virginia's battle flag. Losses in the 13th New Hampshire totaled four men killed and five officers and forty-four men wounded.[32]

Some Union troops, not comprehending that Battery 5 had fallen, kept shooting at the fort. To stop the firing, Captain Goss tied a white handkerchief to his sword, leapt onto the parapet, and waved the makeshift flag. Sturdivant was surprised to discover the paucity of the force that had captured his battery. "Here are my guns double-shotted for infantry," he muttered, "and all of us captured by a damned Yankee skirmish line!"[33]

The New Hampshire and New York soldiers in Battery 5 spent anxious minutes worrying that the rebels might return in force. Then Brooks's second line—the main body of Henry's brigade—advanced into the field. A man from New Hampshire recalled the stirring scene as the "Union troops marching in one line of battle, apparently a mile long, with all colors unfurled and every officer and man in position, emerged from the woods through which we had advanced before charging across the field upon the Battery and bore across the open field rapidly to the front, in support of the Thirteenth and other troops on the skirmish line; they came up near to the captured Battery 5 and the rebel works flanking it and halted—then we felt secure, and that no force which the enemy had hereabout could move us from our position." Recollected another Federal: "No men were ever so wild as ours were after the capture, and pretty soon three lines of our troops came up, out of the woods, and gave us three cheers for the Thirteenth New Hampshire regiment."[34]

Brooks's soldiers quickly consolidated their stunning victory. The 8th Con-

necticut occupied a hill behind Battery 5 and entrenched, men from the 92nd
New York joined to help, and Colonel Stevens gathered up his New Hampshire
troops and posted them above the steep bluff immediately west of the Friend
house. Henry's brigade deployed to their right and dug in along a road leading
toward Petersburg. "The cheering and enthusiasm all along the line, as the
onset was made and after it proved successful, was thrilling, making one live
a lifetime in a minute," a correspondent reported. "Wounded men waved their
gory arms and shouted their gladness from blood-choked mouths."[35]

Martindale's soldiers, on low ground to Brooks's right, watched the attack
with enthusiasm. "Our regiment cheered enough to split their throats," a Bay
Stater recalled. Emboldened by the fall of Battery 5, Martindale ordered his
division ahead, Stannard along the railroad and Stedman on City Point Road.
It was almost dark before the troops could get moving. Stiffening his skirmish
line with two companies from the 25th Massachusetts, Stannard sent his soldiers swarming over Battery 3. To their surprise, the fort was deserted. "It had
evidently been vacated but a few minutes, and in a great hurry," an orderly sergeant in the 25th Massachusetts noted, "for blankets, clothing, and equipment
were scattered around, and a supper already prepared was left untouched." Two
more brass Napoleons fell to the Federals. Stedman, advancing on Stannard's
right, pushed up to Batteries 1 and 2 but decided the positions were too strong
to storm. With nightfall imminent, Martindale withdrew both brigades to support Brooks's division, leaving an extended skirmish line consisting of the 25th
Massachusetts and 55th Pennsylvania to confront the two batteries closest to
the river. He reported his losses at 13 men killed, 133 wounded, and 38
missing.[36]

The Confederate line's collapse on Brooks's left was also precipitous. Bell's
headlong advance, supported by Captain Martin S. James's Battery C, 3rd
Rhode Island Artillery, had rendered Battery 6 untenable, and elements from
his command quickly secured the fort. At the same time, elements from Lieutenant Colonel Elias Wright's 1st USCT, Colonel Kiddoo's 22nd USCT, and
Colonel Rogers's 4th USCT charged ahead and poured over Battery 6's parapets, sharing in the capture. To the Federals' surprise, many of the Confederate
defenders wore civilian clothing, having rushed from their jobs to man the
Dimmock Line. When a Confederate attempted to surrender to one of Hinks's
men, the black soldier exclaimed, "God Damn you! I will kill you anyway, you
have killed a heap of our good men today." Recollected the Confederate: "I
could see the cap shining on his gun, yet I asked no quarter, expecting the bullet to pass through me instantly; but for some reason, his gun did not go off, so

he lunged at me with his bayonet, and leaping to one side, he kept right on down the hill, thinking no doubt that he had killed me."[37]

Meanwhile, Colonel Kiddoo's 22nd USCT headed toward Battery 7. Braving heavy fire, four companies under Major John B. Cook charged the battery at a run. "I beheld one of the grandest and most awful sights I ever saw," a drummer boy from Maine recalled. "Those colored troops started on a double quick, and as they descended the hill, the fort poured volley after volley into them. The men seemed to fall like blades of grass before a machine, but it did not stop them; they rallied and moved on; it was only the work of a few minutes."[38]

On reaching Battery 7, Kiddoo's men pressed tightly against the fort's outer wall, where they were safe from the Confederates above trying in vain to depress their cannon low enough to hit the attackers. "Break to the right and left," Cook hollered above the din, and his troops obeyed, forming two wings that eased around the fort's opposite walls until they reached the open rear. While the Union men poured into the bastion from behind, soldiers from the 1st and 4th USCT attacked from the front, clambering over the parapet. Surrounded, the defenders of Battery 7 surrendered, forfeiting two howitzers and an iron gun to the Federals. "They scaled the fort, and the enemy, becoming panic-stricken, ran like deer," as an officer of the 1st USCT recalled the capture.[39]

Battery 8—"a strong work advantageously posted on a considerable elevation behind a difficult ravine," according to a Union officer—was Hinks's next target. Leading a detachment of his 1st USCT from Battery 6, Lieutenant Colonel Wright charged south past Battery 7. Heavy fire from Battery 8, however, forced him to seek cover in a lunette between Batteries 7 and 8. Kiddoo meanwhile took his 22nd USCT from Battery 7 and joined Wright, proposing that they combine their commands and attack Battery 8 together. Wright declined, offering instead to support Kiddoo. "I immediately formed a column of companies," the colonel later wrote, "left a few of my men on the parapet of the lunette to engage the gunners on Battery No. 8, which were in easy range, and who were playing with some effect upon my men as they were forming for the charge." As Kiddoo led his soldiers across a steep ravine and through a swamp, rebel defenders lined the crest of Battery 8 and fired down into them. "My men wavered at first under the hot fire of the enemy," he recollected, "but soon, on seeing their colors on the opposite side of the ravine, pushed rapidly up and passed the rifle pits and fort." Wright pitched in as he had promised and together with Kiddoo overpowered the defenders, securing the fort and its howitzer. Union losses amounted to eleven dead and forty-three wounded.[40]

Several of Battery 8's defenders escaped to Battery 9, near where the Prince

George Court House and Jordan's Point Roads merged. There they regrouped and launched a counterattack to retake Battery 8. Kiddoo and Wright repelled the assault, although combat raged so fiercely that his men expended most of their ammunition. Some of Kiddoo's soldiers familiar with artillery manned the captured howitzer and turned it on the attackers. The rebels dropped back to Battery 9, but the men of the 1st and 22nd USCT lacked the firepower to pursue. Battery 9, some five hundred yards to the south, dominated Battery 8 and made life miserable for the Federals who had taken the fort.[41]

Lieutenant Colonel Rogers, not realizing that Battery 8 was now in Union hands, charged into the redoubt with his 4th USCT. Discovering that Kiddoo and Wright were already there, he then turned his attention to Battery 9. Joining him in the endeavor were two companies from the 1st USCT personally led by brigade commander Holman. Brush and timber that the rebels had felled as obstacles slowed their advance, but Rogers's men continued under severe fire along a deep ravine leading to Battery 9. Heavily outnumbered, the rebel defenders fled to Battery 10. Rogers followed in hot pursuit, and his troops stormed that redoubt, driving off the defenders and capturing another piece of ordnance. Battery 11, a short distance away, was now untenable for the Confederates, and they abandoned it to the Federals as well.[42]

Hinks's second line of regiments—the 5th and 6th USCT—stepped off in the gathering darkness toward Batteries 9, 10, and 11, unaware that their fellow soldiers had just captured that segment of the Dimmock Line. Guided by flashes of musketry from the forts, they stumbled through stumps, fallen timber, bushes, and pools of water and charged the walls of the redoubts. "A man would run his bayonet into the side of the parapet, and another would use it as a step-ladder to climb up," Major John McMurray of the 6th USCT recalled. "As we were ascending, I was wondering why the Johnnies behind the parapet were so quiet," he wrote. To his relief, the Confederates had fled, leaving behind the corpse of a seventeen-year-old "fair-haired rebel soldier."[43]

It was now after 9:00 P.M. and almost dark. More than a mile and a half of the fortified Confederate line—Batteries 3 through 11—was in Union hands. The black troops had proven their worth, but at a steep price. Duncan, whose brigade was most heavily engaged, estimated his losses for the day at 378 men; Holman's 1st USCT's casualties alone amounted to 184. Humphreys later wrote that Hinks figured his division lost an aggregate of 507 killed and wounded. "Well, my boy, I see that you have lost a leg for glory," an officer remarked to one of Hinks's wounded warriors. "No, sir," he responded. "I have not lost it for glory, but for the elevation of my race."[44]

Reports circulated that the black troops had exacted the revenge threatened by their battle cry of "Remember Fort Pillow." Writing home five days later, Major Albert F. Brooker of the 1st Connecticut Heavy Artillery, stationed at Bermuda Hundred, informed his mother: "It's said that a Brigade of Nigars charged the Johnies[. As] they went in the rebs said give the *black sons* of bitches no quarter give them *h* &c. I am told that it's just what the nigars did to them," he added, "they took no prisoners but 2 and [I am] told bayoneted every one that was in the rifle pits." Hermon Clark, a soldier in the 117th New York, wrote his father about witnessing a black soldier murder a prisoner captured during the assault against Battery 6. "A great bushy Nigger came up to [the prisoner], knocked him down, and ran his bayonet through his heart. Our boys turned on the Niggers and kept them back." Given the paucity of eyewitness accounts, it is impossible to determine the extent of such killings.[45]

Hinks "was enthusiastic in his praise of the darkies," a surgeon who talked with the general shortly afterward recalled, "and in fact they did very well, though it appears the works were manned by raw troops, who ran away with very little fighting. Men were taken from the streets and put in the works, hands from the factories, school boys, anybody." Smith also expressed satisfaction with the "splendid conduct" of the U.S. Colored Troops to a *New York Times* reporter, noting that he intended to make "special mention of them in his official report." Meade's aide Lyman wrote home that he would "never forget meeting, on the City Point Road, five Confederate soldiers, under guard of nigs! . . . Three of the prisoners looked as if they could have taken off a tenpenny nail, at a snap. The other two seemed to take a ludicrous view of the matter and were smiling sheepishly. As to the negroes, they were all teeth, so to speak, teeth with a black frame."[46]

Satisfied that Brooks and Martindale had their fronts well in hand, Smith visited Hinks's sector—"on horseback with one pantaloons leg in his boot, and wearing a straw hat," according to one of Captain Angel's gunners—where he found the troops "busily engaged in eating their supper without pickets or even sentinels in their front," he later wrote. They appeared "intoxicated by their success," he noted, "and could hardly be kept in order." After directing Hinks to "get his command in order and await events," Smith examined the road to Petersburg, which descended into a narrow valley. "I knew that no fortifications stood between me and Petersburg and that the bridges across the Appomattox were commanded by high ground on the Richmond side, [and] that to hold them I must hold the left bank," he later wrote, adding that he had received "a telegram from Butler informing me that [Confederate] reinforcements were already pouring into the town and I determined to hold what I had, if possible, till the Army of the Potomac came up."[47]

Butler's signal station at Cobb's Hill near Point of Rocks had indeed been reporting Confederate reinforcements streaming toward the Cockade City. "A train of fourteen cars loaded with troops just passed toward Petersburg," a signal officer warned at 6:50 P.M. "The enemy also appears to be sending troops on the roads west of Petersburg. Another train of twenty-two cars has just passed toward Petersburg loaded with troops." At 7:30 P.M. the signal station advised that thirteen train cars had just passed toward Petersburg and that the turnpike was "full of rising dust." An hour later two more trains were spotted approaching the town.[48]

In an untimed message dated simply "In the Field, June 15, 1864," Butler informed Grant that Lieutenant Davenport had just returned with news that Smith held a five-mile line from the Appomattox to a point two miles west of Jordan's Point Road and had captured thirteen guns and 260 prisoners. Hancock had probably joined with Smith, he thought, but rebels seemed to be arriving as well. "We have reason to believe that the enemy in this front has been re-enforced," Butler wrote, "and we have made every disposition to hold our own here." Grant answered an hour later. "Order Hancock up as you suggest," he wrote. "I have ordered General Meade to cross another army corps and to direct them to march all night toward Petersburg." Fresh troops, he predicted, should reach Smith by 10:00 the next morning.[49]

At 8:45 P.M. Butler telegraphed Grant that Smith had carried the enemy works at Jordan's and was pushing toward the river. "These are believed to be the only line of defenses to Petersburg, at least they were so ten days ago." He had forwarded a message to Hancock, he added, directing him to move up at once to Smith's aid.[50]

There is some evidence that persistent reports of Confederates reinforcing Petersburg might have persuaded Butler to order Smith to suspend his attack and dig in. "Sent message to Gen Smith to entrench at once and hold his position," signalman Maurice S. Lamprey wrote in his diary for June 15. "Guess Gen B[utler] is getting rattled over the dust that the rebs are kicking up." Another signalman placed the timing of the directive at seven or eight o'clock in the evening.[51]

Oddly Smith never mentioned Butler's directive to entrench until 1900, when he wrote that he had received a letter from Thomas S. Baird, a former Signal Corps sergeant who claimed to have sent him the order. He also did not recall having received it but blamed his forgetfulness on his ill health that day. The directive has never been found, and there are sound reasons to question whether it actually existed. As late as 9:40 P.M. Butler was inquiring of Smith whether he had made the "contemplated attack" and with what result. And at midnight Smith informed him that "it is impossible for me to go farther to-night." Neither of those communications are consistent with Butler having instructed his subordinate to halt and entrench sometime before 8:00 P.M.[52]

In his official communications explaining his decision not to push into Petersburg, Smith took full responsibility for his actions. In a report to Butler the next day, he pled that "darkness had set in, and having learned some time before that re-enforcements were rapidly coming in from Richmond, and deeming that I held important points of the enemy's line of works, I thought it prudent to make no further advance, and made my dispositions to hold what I already had." Two months later, in his official report of the campaign, Smith asserted that he "deemed it wiser to hold what we had than by attempting to reach the bridges [in Petersburg across the Appomattox] to lose what we had gained, and having the troops meet with a disaster." He added that he "knew also that some portion of the Army of the Potomac was coming to aid us, and therefore the troops were placed so as to occupy the commanding position and wait for daylight." In December 1887, when addressing the Military Historical Society of Massachusetts, Smith blamed darkness, reports of Confederate reinforcements, his bad health, and the exhaustion of his troops. In an 1893 publication he explained that he had "every reason to believe that the enemy's force equaled or exceeded my own," that he knew "nothing of the country in front," that his "white troops were exhausted by marching day and night, and by fighting most of the day in the excessive heat," and that his "colored troops, who had fought bravely, were intoxicated by their success, and could hardly be kept in order." In 1897 he claimed that he would have been "reckless to have plunged into the woods, in an unknown country, at ten o'clock at night, to meet such a force as was reported by Butler and his signal officers, besides having to attack, before reaching the Appomattox, a town where every house was a fortification, and all this in the middle of the night."[53]

In a letter written in February 1878, Hinks recounted the reasons Smith had articulated at the time for calling off the offensive. "General Smith appeared on our line . . . between nine and ten o'clock in the evening," he wrote. "I then suggested to him that we could easily move forward and capture the town. He replied that Beauregard was marching upon Petersburg with a larger force than he had at his command, and would probably enter the town before we could possibly reach it, and that the risk of losing all that we had gained was too great to warrant any further movement that night, and that we should do well if we succeeded in holding all we had gained."[54]

* * *

At about the same time Smith launched his attack against the Dimmock Line, Birney's lead elements reached the Bryant house on Bailey's Creek, a mile or so behind Hinks. Soon afterward Hancock, accompanied by Major Mitchell, rode out to find Smith. Reaching the Bryant house around 7:40 P.M.—Smith's offensive was now in full swing—Hancock met Birney, who was still trying to locate the left end of Hinks's line. He confirmed that the division was forming on Hinks's left, then rode off in search of Smith.[55]

The 2nd Corps commander found Smith "in the field," where he, Hancock wrote, "described to me as well as he could in the dusk of the evening the positions of the enemy's lines he had carried." Hancock did not mention the time of this meeting, but it clearly occurred after the attack had concluded. Smith thought the meeting took place at about 9:30 P.M., "after my return from the front."[56]

According to Hancock, he informed Smith that "two divisions of my troops were close at hand [Birney and Gibbon, at the Bryant place] and ready for any further movements which in his judgment and knowledge of the field should be made. General Smith requested me to relieve his troops in the front line of works which he had carried, so that the enemy should encounter fresh troops should they attempt their recapture." The general's concern, Hancock noted, was that the enemy had been reinforced during the evening. Smith later confirmed that he told Hancock that he "thought any further advance that night involved more hazard than was warranted by any hope of success to be gained, and that if he could relieve my tired command in the front, I thought it was all and the best that could be done." Explaining his reasoning, Smith wrote of having "made up my mind that my force could not succeed in reaching Petersburg that night, and therefore I could not advise Hancock to take his divisions and follow up the success, though it was entirely within my province to give that advice had I believed in it."[57]

The general later claimed: "This interview with Hancock was the first intimation I had had that his troops were in my vicinity, although General Hinks says he saw Birney about eight o'clock, and urged him to go in on our left."[58]

Suffering from his Gettysburg wound and clearly frustrated by the day's confusion, Hancock directed Birney and Gibbon to occupy the captured works. Riding back to locate his command's scattered elements, the general encountered Gibbon and lit into the unfortunate subordinate. "Whilst halting [near Smith's entrenchments, waiting for Smith's troops to clear out of the way], I met Gen. Hancock who had just returned from an interview with Gen. Smith,"

Gibbon recalled of the meeting. "For some reason, which I could not clearly understand, he appeared irritable, out of temper, calling me sharply to account for non-compliance with a general order issued at the commencement of the campaign, requiring troops when halted on the march to form at least one brigade in each division in line of battle, of course, against a possible attack." Gibbon explained that he had neglected the standard precaution because Smith's troops held the road in front of him, but Hancock was not satisfied with the answer. "I returned to my command in a very bad humor," Gibbon recorded, "and soon after receiving orders to advance reached Gen. Smith's position after dark."[59]

Birney's day was also going from bad to worse. His instructions were to form on Hinks's left, but the aides he had dispatched to locate that flank had not returned. Flustered, he decided to march his division down a wooded road that seemed to lead in the right direction. He had proceeded as far as the Prince George or Jordan's Point Road and turned toward Petersburg when an aide arrived from Hancock with instructions to return and occupy the entrenchments that Smith had recently captured. Shortly another officer from the corps commander appeared with contrary orders: "if I held any important road, etc., not to return, but that General Gibbon's division would be on my right, and that one of General Smith's staff would show me the position." That staffer brought Birney and his bedraggled troops to the Dunn house around 10:00 P.M., behind Hinks's division. "I took position in front of them," Birney later wrote, "and a staff officer of General Smith's indicating where his left would be and the position he wished the division of General Gibbon and myself to occupy, I relieved the colored troops on [the] left of the Prince George Court-House Road and General Gibbon on the right to the point indicated."[60]

It seemed to Birney's exhausted troops that they had wasted hours "stumbl[ing] and blunder[ing] around . . . without any aim. We marched and countermarched until we began to think we would pass the entire night in this way." Their commander's temper was completely frayed. At one point Captain Livermore brought Birney a map depicting Hinks's location, but the general refused to look at it and declined an offer to show him the way to Hinks, instead directing Livermore to show one of his staff officers the way. According to Hinks, "shortly after the final assault the division was joined on the left by General Birney's division, of the Second Corps of the Army of the Potomac, with whom it occupied the works during the night." Gibbon's right rested on Battery 5, and Birney's left terminated at the Dunn house, to the left of Prince George Court House Road. Barlow's soldiers would not arrive until daylight on the sixteenth. "By the time the movement was completed it was 11:00," Hancock later wrote, "too late and dark for any immediate advance."[61]

A few minutes after 11:00 P.M., Hancock received a message from Grant suggesting that he do what he had already done. "If requested by General Butler or Smith to move up to where Smith now is do so," the general in chief wrote. "The enemy are now seen to be reinforcing Petersburg by rail and by troops marching." A companion message from Butler confirmed that Confederates were "crowding down troops from Richmond" and requested Hancock to "please move up at once to the aid of Smith and put the Appomattox between you and Lee's army." He added that provisions were on the way and offered to send Hancock "a couple of batteries of artillery."[62]

Hancock responded that he had put two divisions on Smith's left and intended to hold Barlow in reserve. Having reached the front after dark, he explained, "I can determine little about the features of the country, and I cannot tell what the morning will bring forth; but I think we cover all of the commanding points in front of Petersburg." Thanking Butler for the promised rations, Hancock declined the proffered artillery and asked Butler to forward his response to Grant.[63]

Smith's men were relieved that their ordeal was over. "The moon, nearly at its full, cast a mellow light over the scene," a Massachusetts soldier recalled, "while the early evening dews and the cooler night air was refreshing to men who had been prostrated all day under the burning rays of a hot June sun." A warrior in the 118th New York later remembered the "lovely moonlight night. The roofs and spires of Petersburg could be plainly seen a couple of miles away, and to our right and rear the lights of the Bermuda Hundred camps were visible." Another New Yorker recalled how on the "evening of the 15th of June, we stood on the heights, and, by the light of a brilliant moon, contemplated the silent valley, and beheld the nearly defenceless city. Why we did not then go down and possess them, is the question which occurred and recurred times innumerable, during the months of carnage which followed on that line."[64]

Help for Wise's beleaguered Confederates was indeed on the way, although whether the reinforcements would arrive in time or with sufficient strength to contain Smith remained an open question.

Hoke's Division crossed the James on a pontoon bridge near Drewry's Bluff around 11:00 that morning and marched down the pike toward Petersburg. On reaching Chester Station, some eighteen miles from the city, Hoke learned that rail transportation was severely limited. He decided to send Hagood's brigade of South Carolina troops to Petersburg immediately by rail, to be followed by

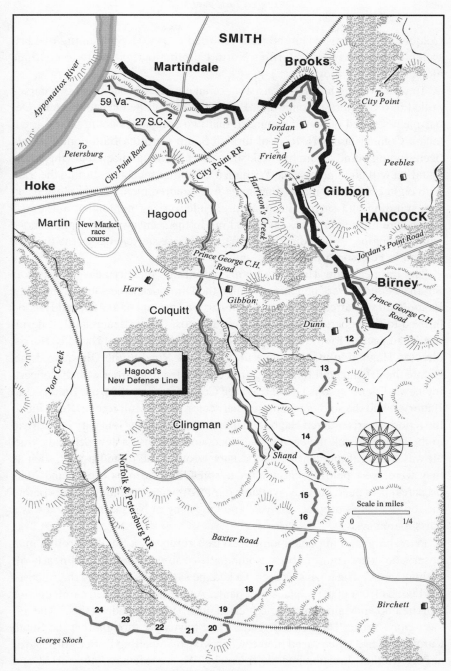

Hancock and Hoke arrive at the Petersburg front

Colquitt's Georgians when the train returned empty. His remaining two brigades—Clingman's and Martin's North Carolina outfits—were to continue
along the Pike by foot.[65]

Toward evening a train—consisting of an engine, a tender, and two cars—
pulled into Chester Station. Major Edward Willis of the Quartermaster's Department stepped out and announced that two companies could board. Lieutenant Colonel James H. Rion of the 7th South Carolina Battalion, who had
been sipping brandy from his flask since morning, announced that "the whole
battalion will go," and his aide William M. Thomas set about stuffing the train
with eight companies numbering some five hundred men. "It was close pack-
ing, standing and sitting, inside and outside, on engine, tender, and cars,"
Thomas reminisced. "I was on top taking in the scenery and the pine smoke
from the engine. I was a dirty white man before we started, but by the time we
arrived in Petersburg I was black."[66]

The train carrying Hagood's troops puffed into the city near dark, just as
Smith's Federals were punching through the Dimmock Line a few miles away.
Beauregard was already in town, having arrived around 6:00 P.M., and Hagood
hurried to the general's headquarters at the post office. Beauregard, it developed, had just left for the front, but his chief engineer, Colonel David B. Harris,
directed Hagood to march out Jerusalem Plank Road to the Dimmock Line.
Before the general could start, a courier arrived from the front with disconcerting news. Enemy troops had carried the Confederate works from Battery 3 to
Battery 7, and the soldiers manning that sector were in full retreat. Reacting to
the report, Harris ordered Hagood to march "immediately" out City Point Road
to the breach, check the enemy's advance, and establish a new defensive line.
"It was a critical moment," Hagood later wrote. "The routed troops, such as
they were, were pouring into the town, spreading alarm on every hand." His
brigade represented the only available reinforcements; it would be hours before
the rest of Hoke's brigades arrived, and the Army of Northern Virginia was a
day's march away.[67]

Petersburg was in pandemonium. Wise's refugees, a South Carolina man
observed, "were running back, some hatless, some shoeless, and nearly all
without guns." The town's women packed the sidewalks, carrying their household goods from place to place in a panic. As the newly arrived Confederates
marched down Main Street, voices cried out, "What brigade is this." The answer came back: "Hagood's Brigade." The townsfolk thought that the South
Carolinians had twice saved their town in May by repelling Butler's offensives
at Port Walthall Junction and Swift Creek. "We are safe now," they cried, and

according to a soldier, "they went down on their knees on the pavements."[68]

Locals volunteered to show Hagood the way to the front, but their directions proved "confused and contradictory." Halting at the New Market race course, the general placed Colonel Charles H. Simonton in command of the brigade and rode ahead with two staffers to reconnoiter. When they reached Harrison's Creek, a wounded Confederate warned that enemy pickets were nearby. Turning his horse, Hagood crossed a field to City Point Road, where he met a courier from Harris. The man had a map, a tallow candle, and matches.

Studying the map by candlelight, Hagood decided to establish a new line on high ground along the Petersburg side of Harrison's Creek; the left rested on the Appomattox River at Battery 1. Elements of Colonel William B. Tabb's 59th Virginia had arrived in Petersburg with Hoke and were assigned, along with the 27th South Carolina, to help hold Batteries 1 and 2. The rest of the new line wound southward along Harrison's Creek's main branch, then veered along its western branch to a point near Battery 15, "having very good command over the cleared and cultivated valley in its front," according to Hagood. Once the line was laid out, the men constructed earthworks, digging, one of them recalled, with "bayonets, swords, tin plates, etc."[69]

The breach had been sealed, at least for the time being. Before long the train carrying Colquitt's Brigade arrived, and soon the Georgians were deploying on Hagood's left, extending the new line across Prince George Court House Road. Near midnight Hoke reached Petersburg with Clingman's and Martin's Brigades. The soldiers had marched fourteen miles since midday, following "the shortest cut, through fields and dusty roads," according to one of Martin's officers. Clingman's troops deployed on Colquitt's right, and Martin's soldiers marched out City Point Road and bivouacked behind Hagood, supporting his South Carolinians. According to one of their number, they "fell asleep on the ground from sheer exhaustion." The division's artillery unlimbered on Hare's Hill.[70]

Having witnessed the Dimmock Line's collapse firsthand, Beauregard made the decision he had been postponing all day. He would withdraw Johnson's Division from the Howlett Line and rush those troops to Petersburg, abandoning Bermuda Hundred in favor of the Cockade City. Lee, he informed the War Department, would have to defend the lines across Bermuda Neck and do so quickly. In a terse message to the Virginian, Beauregard advised him of having "abandoned my lines on Bermuda Neck to concentrate all of my forces here; skirmishers and pickets will leave there at daylight. Cannot these lines be occupied by your troops?" He concluded: "The safety of our communications

requires it." At 10:20 P.M. Johnson's Division received instructions to start toward Petersburg. The arrival of those troops the next morning would swell the
force defending Petersburg to approximately 10,000 men.[71]

At midnight Smith updated Butler. "It is impossible for me to go farther tonight," he wrote, "but, unless I misapprehend the topography, I hold the key to
Petersburg." For the rest of that night, however, the key would remain unturned,
and by morning on the sixteenth, veteran Confederate troops occupied a new
defensive line. "The most bloodcurdling blasphemy I ever listened to, I heard
that night, uttered by men who knew they were to be sacrificed on the morrow,"
one of Hancock's troops reminisced.[72]

*"I do not think there is any doubt that Petersburg itself
could have been carried without much loss."*

Responsibility for the Union failure to capture Petersburg on June 15 began at
the top. Grant's operational objective was to snip Lee's supply lines, compelling the Army of Northern Virginia to abandon Richmond and its powerful
entrenched position at Cold Harbor. With Lee on the run, Grant hoped to seize
the Confederate capital and seek battle with the rebel army outside of its earthworks. It is interesting to ask whether the plan that the general in chief adopted—sending Smith's reinforced 18th Corps to capture Petersburg—was the
optimal maneuver to achieve that goal, and whether he exerted sufficient fore-
sight and leadership to ensure its success.

There can be little quarrel with the fact that the Union movement from Cold
Harbor to the James River was executed with skill and precision. Captain Livermore later proclaimed the operation "one of the boldest and most brilliant
[maneuvers] of modern wars. Two divisions voyaged a hundred and fifty miles
by water from White House to Bermuda Hundred, the remainder of the army
crossed a broad navigable river within twenty miles of the enemy, the two columns arrived at the point of crossing at the same time, and the advance reached
the enemy's pickets without experiencing even a hostile demonstration by the
enemy." A Union artillerist wrote his wife from Willcox Landing on June 15
that "such maneuvering, such gigantic, magnificent generalship as Grant is dis-
playing I think has never been equaled in the history of the world. McClellan's
operations look puny as child's play compared with the movements we are now
witnessing daily. We have marched around, over and through the Chickahominy swamp, fought, entrenched, and fortified in one week more than McClellan

did in all summer. Now we have more than surpassed his famous flank movement to the banks of the James."[73]

The movement to the James, however, must be evaluated relative to the objective that it was designed to achieve—destroying the rebel army's source of supplies and turning Lee out of his formidable entrenchments. Since the supplies cascading into Petersburg along a multitude of rail lines and roads all funneled to the Confederate capital along the Richmond and Petersburg Railroad, cutting that single track at any point along its twenty-mile route between the two cities would have secured Grant's purpose. There was no need for Grant to capture Petersburg, which required overrunning the Dimmock Line; he could have achieved the same result with more certainty and less risk by reinforcing Butler—perhaps with Smith and a corps from the Army of the Potomac—and hurling them against Beauregard's single division manning the entire Howlett Line.

Grant's goal was not only to starve Lee out of Cold Harbor but also to flank him out of that strong position. After taking Petersburg he planned for the Potomac army to swing north toward Richmond, putting the Federal force in Lee's rear. It was not necessary for Grant to capture Petersburg to achieve even this second objective. By marching directly from Cold Harbor to Bermuda Hundred, Meade would have been ideally positioned to advance north along the rail line toward Richmond, leaving Wise to harmlessly while away his time in the Dimmock Line. The maneuver would have rendered Petersburg irrelevant to the campaign's success.

The perspective gained from 150 years of hindsight suggests that Grant would have done better to simply leave part of the Potomac army at Cold Harbor to pin Lee in place while the remainder reinforced Butler, cut the Richmond and Petersburg Railroad, and swarmed north toward the Confederate capital and Lee's rear. In its depleted condition—Early's entire 2nd Corps was gone, as was Breckinridge's Division and most of the army's cavalry—Lee would have been unable to attack the Federal host confronting him at Cold Harbor. The Federals too would have been ideally situated to pursue Lee as he retreated when he learned of the new threat boiling up from the south. In sum, it is fair to question the wisdom of Grant's decision to withdraw his entire force from Cold Harbor, cross it to the south side of the James River, and trust that Baldy Smith would successfully overrun the Dimmock Line, capture Petersburg, and hold the town before Lee could move to retake it. By leaving the Virginian unopposed at Cold Harbor, Grant gambled with the Army of the James's security—Lee, after all, was but a few miles in Butler's rear—and freed him to reinforce Beauregard, either by buttressing the Howlett Line or manning the battlements in front of Petersburg.

Grant's operation as conceived rested on the assumption that Smith's augmented force was sufficient to capture Petersburg. As Livermore later observed, "Upon the question whether this force was sufficient hangs the need of praise or the merit of blame." According to Butler's intelligence, Smith's force seemed more than adequate to overrun the lightly held Dimmock Line, press into Petersburg, and close that Confederate supply terminal. But events on the ground frequently frustrate even the best-laid plans, and Smith's strike against Petersburg is a poster child for that military axiom. A tardy start, unexpected resistance at Baylor's farm, more-fearsome earthworks than expected, and the possibility of reinforcements caused Smith to delay his assault until late in the day; concern over reported Confederate reinforcements and nightfall convinced him to halt once he had captured a portion of the line. While Smith clearly held a numerical advantage over the Confederates protecting Petersburg, events unfolded in a way that prevented him from completing his assignment.[74]

Grant unquestionably envisioned that some portion of Meade's army—Hancock, as it developed—would be readily available to support Smith if required. Yet Meade, Hancock, and Smith all denied that the general in chief shared his vision with them, and their behavior on June 15 supports their denials. During the previous month of campaigning, relations between Grant and Meade had become so strained that by mid-June it appears that the two generals were scarcely speaking with one another. And while Grant informed Butler that Hancock would be available to support Smith, Butler clearly failed to pass that information on to Smith—a casualty, most likely, of strained relations between those two headstrong men.

In July 1864 Meade candidly wrote Grant that if "Major-General Hancock and myself [had] been apprised in time of the contemplated movement against Petersburg, and the necessity of [Hancock's] cooperation, I am of the opinion [Hancock] could have been pushed much earlier to the scene of operations." In reply Grant conceded that he was "very much mistaken if you were not informed of the contemplated movement against Petersburg as soon as I returned to Wilcox's Landing from Bermuda Hundred." The cost of the lost opportunity was apparent to all. "If General Hancock's orders of the 15th had been communicated to him, that officer, with his usual promptness, would have undoubtedly been upon the ground around Petersburg as early as four o'clock in the afternoon of the 15th," Grant admitted in his *Memoirs,* adding, "I do not think there is any doubt that Petersburg itself could have been carried without much loss."[75]

An equally fatal lapse was Grant's failure to timely inform Smith that he was to command the offensive against Petersburg. First told of his assignment when he arrived at Bermuda Hundred late on the afternoon of June 14, Smith had no realistic possibility of meeting Grant's expectations of assailing the Dimmock Line early on the morning of the fifteenth. The logistics of assembling soldiers disembarking from transports and integrating them into a unified command with troops from other units inevitably consumed the entire night.

Hindsight leaves little doubt that a joint attack by Hancock and Smith during the afternoon or evening of June 15 would have overrun the Dimmock Line and Petersburg as well, achieving the mission's objective of severing Lee's supply line. While it is true that Confederate reinforcements were streaming toward the Cockade City, none of those troops reached the town until near dark, and no semblance of organized resistance was in place until midnight. If Hancock had been instructed on the evening of June 14 to advance with all haste toward the rebel defenses and to move into position to support Smith, he would doubtlessly have left Flowerdew Hundred without waiting for rations and would have reached Smith by midafternoon. Not only would Hancock's presence have enabled Smith to launch his offense well before dark, affording him ample daylight to complete the movement into Petersburg, but Hancock's participation—even if only two of his three divisions were available—would have given the offensive irresistible strength and confidence to push into town, sever the rail line, and hold the Appomattox River bridge against Hoke's Confederates.

As Smith later noted: "During the whole afternoon of the 15th of June, while I was anxiously marshaling my scanty forces, so as to break through the long lines of the enemy's fortifications, there was wandering aimlessly about, within about an hour's march of me, one of the most brilliant corps commanders in our army, with more than 20,000 veteran soldiers. General Hancock knew nothing of my operations, and I did not know of the presence of his troops until later in the day."[76]

The Union advance was also unnecessarily delayed by the faulty management of bridging material. Weitzel had completed the approaches for the pontoon bridge across the James by 10:00 A.M. on June 14, but the pontoons did not arrive until that evening, delaying the construction of the bridge for seven or eight critical hours. One set of pontoons—those that had been commandeered to span the Chickahominy—had been diverted to Coles Ferry, while the remaining pontoons were sequestered at Fortress Monroe, inconveniently downstream from where they were needed. Moreover, once the bridge was completed, no troops crossed over it for another eighteen hours. From midnight on June 14 until 6:00 P.M. on June 15, when Meade ordered Burnside's 9th Corps to march to Smith's and Hancock's assistance, the pontoon bridge served as a conduit for the army's massive supply train rather than as a means for rushing troops to the emerging battle front. Coordination from the top—Grant's responsibility—was again severely lacking.

Grant's apparent lack of concern about developments on the ground is difficult to fathom. June 15 represented the culmination of his grand maneuver from Cold Harbor and offered an excellent opportunity to strike a blow calculated to bring the war to a speedy conclusion. The Union general in chief, however, spent much of the morning watching wagon trains cross the pontoon bridge over the James, then hitchhiked a steamboat ride to City Point, where he settled in. He had relegated oversight of Smith to Butler, though not until the afternoon did he attempt to learn what progress he was making. Butler, however, had no idea where things stood, as Smith had not yet communicated with him, and the James commander had sent no one to find out. Coordination from the top—once again, Grant's responsibility—was nonexistent.

Clearly the most important Union command role on June 15 was ensuring that Smith had at his disposal the resources necessary to achieve his objective and that the disparate elements of the offensive were meshing as planned. Astoundingly Grant neither assumed that role himself—he was, after all, only a few miles from the front—nor assigned anyone else to coordinate Smith and Hancock. In hindsight his detachment on June 15, compounded by his failure to designate someone to oversee the offensive on the ground, stands as his most significant lapse during the entire campaign from the Rapidan to Petersburg. And it was a lapse that came at the campaign's culmination, literally denying Union arms the objective they had fought so mightily to achieve during the previous forty-five days.

How are we to judge Smith's performance? Because Smith learned that he was to lead an offensive against Petersburg only a few hours before the attack was slated to begin, he can hardly be faulted for his tardy start. And once underway, he managed the advance to Petersburg with skill, brushing aside Confederate cavalry at Baylor's farm and pushing his columns to the Dimmock Line by late morning.

Smith's delay in launching his evening offensive is also understandable. So far as he knew, his troops were unsupported, and the fortifications that he faced bristled with artillery. Although Butler had promised that the Dimmock Line was thinly manned, Smith found himself confronting a formidable obstacle that gave him good reason to question the accuracy of his superior's information. He can hardly be faulted for conducting a careful reconnaissance—a survey, by the way, that guided him to the Dimmock Line's weak point at Battery 5 and that inspired him to adopt an unorthodox but highly effective mode of attacking the fortifications with a skirmish line. The time consumed in reconnoitering was time well spent, for it enabled Smith to achieve a stunning result with minimal casualties.

The chief criticism of the Union general turns on his failure to press across the final two miles to Petersburg after breaching the Confederate defenses. At that juncture no organized defensive force stood between him and the town. Even if Wise had brought order into his retreating troops, Smith still outnumbered them by a factor of at least four to one. Hoke's lead elements were just reaching Petersburg and might have put up a semblance of resistance, but the numbers were stacked in Smith's favor. Moreover, with Hancock's 2nd Corps in support—or at least Birney's and Gibbon's divisions of the corps, which were close at hand when the Dimmock Line fell—a Federal push into the town would have been well-neigh irresistible.

Smith's aide Livermore later questioned whether taking Petersburg the night of June 15 would have advanced the Union cause, but his explanation rings hollow. "I have no doubt that with prompt movement and the cooperation of Birney we could easily have entered Petersburg at any time before twelve o'clock on the night of the fifteenth of June," the captain admitted. "But could we have gained the works north of the town on the left bank of the Appomattox? Without possession of these works could we have resisted the advance of Lee's army or held the town? Would the mere occupation of the town for a few hours, and the possible destruction of a mile or two of railroad track, have been of any permanent advantage to the Union armies commensurate with the risk and loss? These I think are fairly debatable questions," he declared, concluding that he "believe[d] that nothing was lost by Smith's caution. A brilliant dash would have won *eclat* for him and his officers, but would probably have resulted in no permanent benefit to the cause of the Republic."[77]

To the contrary, storming into Petersburg offered Smith an excellent chance of closing the main Confederate supply artery to Richmond and to Lee's army; remaining in the captured portion of the Dimmock Line risked forfeiting that opportunity and afforded the Confederates the entire night to bring up reinforcements and fortify a new defensive position. Yet Smith elected to hold the Dimmock Line and busied himself girding to stave off an imagined Confederate counteroffensive. "In war there is a critical instant—a night—perhaps only a half hour, when everything culminates," Lyman wrote of Smith's decision. "He is the military genius who recognizes this instant and acts upon it, neither precipitating nor postponing the critical moment." By his reckoning,

Smith failed the test. His soldiers were exhausted, Meade's staffer observed: "But, oh! That they had attacked at once. Petersburg would have gone like a rotten branch."[78]

During the weeks following the June 15 offensive, Smith's superiors showered the general with praise. "I went over the conquered lines with Grant and the engineer officers," Assistant War Secretary Dana wired Washington on June 16. "The works are the very strongest kind, more difficult even to take than was Missionary Ridge at Chattanooga." Dana concluded that Smith's success "was of the most important character [and] gives us perfect command of the city and railroad." Conferring with Meade on the sixteenth, Grant remarked, "Smith has taken a line of works stronger than anything we have seen this campaign." And on July 1 he wrote Army Chief of Staff Halleck that Smith was "really one of the most efficient officers in service, readiest in expedients, and most skillful in the management of troops in action." These were hardly the words Grant would have employed had he considered Smith responsible for missing a sterling opportunity to shorten the war.[79]

As time passed, Grant's relations with Smith soured, and the Union commander took a decidedly less favorable view of Smith's June 15 performance. In July 1865 Grant stressed that between the Dimmock Line and Petersburg on the fifteenth, "there were no other works, and there was no evidence that the enemy had re-enforced Petersburg with a single brigade from any source." That night, Grant recalled, had been "clear, the moon shining brightly, and favorable to further operations." Hancock, he added, reached Smith with two divisions just after dark and offered him the service of his troops. "But instead of taking these troops, and pushing at once into Petersburg, he requested General Hancock to relieve a part of his line in the captured works, which was done before midnight. By the time I arrived the next morning the enemy was up in force." Had Smith acted with dispatch, concluded Grant, the Federals would have controlled the Weldon and South Side Railroads and gained "greatly the advantage in the long siege which ensued." Grant's aide Adam Badeau called Smith's failure to continue on to Petersburg "the greatest mistake of the campaign."[80]

Smith's staffer Livermore blamed his commander's "cautious disposition which led him to halt in the moment of victory, fearing that he should lose what he had gained; but I can see no justification for this, for it would have been but little loss if his corps had been driven back to its starting-point, and it was better to risk it against all the chances than to give the enemy a chance to reinforce Petersburg, which General Smith must have known he would do that night according to the rules of strategy as applied every day." Wrote Livermore: "This unfortunate delay cost us ten months of fighting in front of Petersburg." Echoing this theme, a Confederate veteran remarked after the war that Smith "was not endowed with that intuitive sagacity which swiftly discerns the chances of the moment, and thus halting on the very threshold of decisive victory, contented himself with partial success."[81]

Hancock also received his share of criticism, much of it unfair. On June 21, 1864, the *New York Times* faulted the general for having failed to press into Petersburg. "Had I arrived before dark, and been able to have seen the ground myself, I should have taken decisive action," Hancock wrote in response to the charges; "but not knowing anything of the locality, nor what portion of the works General Smith had carried (for at the time of my arrival he did not know precisely himself what portion of the enemy's works were occupied by his troops), and relying upon his judgment, and desiring not to interfere with his honors, as he was directed to take the place, I offered my advanced troops to him, to use according to his knowledge and discretion, he having seen the position in daylight." Smith, he added, believed the enemy had been reinforced and wanted the 2nd Corps to relieve his men "to prevent an attempt to retake the works by the enemy."[82]

Hancock's superiors jumped to his defense. "Had Major-General Hancock or myself been apprised in time of the contemplated movement against Petersburg, and the necessity of his cooperation, I am of the opinion he could have been pushed much earlier to the scene of operations, but as matter occurred and with our knowledge of them I do not see how any censure can be attached to General Hancock and his corps," Meade wrote. In declining Hancock's request for a formal investigation into his conduct, Grant stressed that "the reputation of the Second Corps and its commander is so high, both with the public and in the army, that an investigation could not add to it." That reputation, he added, "cannot be tarnished by newspaper articles or scribblers."[83]

After the war Union veterans, their recollections doubtlessly influenced by the ten months of brutal combat that followed, wrote of their misgivings during the night of June 15–16. "All night long we could hear the trains rumbling along on the other side of the Appomattox River," a drummer boy from Maine reminisced. "Lee had been outwitted. We had stolen a march on him. We had arrived in front of defenseless Petersburg, and could have gone right in and on to Richmond without a struggle. But that fatal order to halt gave him all night to hurry his forces from Cold Harbor, and in the morning we found plenty of determined rebels in front of us, and thereby the war was prolonged months and hundreds and thousands of lives lost. I swore all night. I kicked and condemned every general there was in the army for the blunder I saw they were making. I only wished I could be the general commanding for one hour. But it was no use; I couldn't be."[84]

As the ensuing days, weeks, and months demonstrated, June 15 marked the end of the campaign of maneuver that had started a little over six weeks before with the crossing of the Rapidan River. The Overland Campaign had reached its conclusion, and the Petersburg Campaign was about to begin.

Epilogue

THE OVERLAND CAMPAIGN IN REVIEW

GENERAL MEADE SPENT the afternoon of June 15 watching the Potomac army's supply trains rumble across the pontoon bridge and gather in fields near the James River's southern bank. "The General in a sharp humor, though things seemed moving well enough," Lyman recorded in his diary. At one point Admiral Lee joined Meade and his staff and bitterly decried his rocky relations with Butler. "He spoke of the sinking of the stone vessels," the lieutenant colonel wrote, "and spoke of it as a slur on the navy, as if it could not keep back the rebel war-ships."[1]

That evening, after Meade and his aides settled down for dinner, Grant's staffer Orville Babcock arrived from City Point with news that Smith had engaged the enemy at 5:00 A.M. and was successfully advancing on Petersburg. Grant, Babcock stressed, wanted the general to forward troops immediately to the battlefront. Shortly after 6:00 P.M. Meade directed Burnside to bring his corps "down to the bridge and cross the river immediately, and move up to Harrison's Creek and form on Hancock's left." Hancock was now supporting Smith, he added, and "the commanding general directs that you do the same." Burnside replied that his men had just received their rations and inquired whether they could eat first. "The commanding general says move at once," Humphreys responded. "Take your rations with you in the wagons."[2]

Over the next three days, Union troops rushed to join Smith and Hancock at the front. Meade took command on June 16, joined by Burnside's 9th Corps and the next day by Warren's 5th Corps. Beauregard strengthened his new defensive line during the night of June 15–16 and successfully repulsed concerted assaults by Smith, Hancock, and Burnside on the sixteenth. June 17 saw a series of poorly coordinated, disjointed Union attacks, predominantly by the 9th Corps, that met with some local success. Beauregard, however, barred Meade's way behind strongly manned earthworks closer to Petersburg. Lee, now comfortable that Grant was concentrating his entire force against Petersburg, dispatched portions of Anderson's 1st Corps to the beleaguered town and went there himself. Renewed Federal assaults on the eighteenth proved no more successful than the earlier attempts, and after a final bloody evening attack, Grant called off the offensive. The arrival of Hill's 3rd Corps and part of Wright's 6th Corps in effect transferred the Cold Harbor standoff to Petersburg, with the Confederates holding a stronger line than ever. Four days of futile attempts to take the city added another 11,000 men to the Union casualty toll.[3]

Grant's failure to capture Petersburg was a consequence of poor leadership at the top and sheer exhaustion at the bottom, not to mention inspired fighting by Confederates ensconced in well-chosen defensive positions. Aside from short visits to the front, Grant remained at City Point, seemingly disengaged from the combat raging only a few miles away. Meade commanded at the front but proved unable to orchestrate a coordinated offensive. Complicating his task was the combat attrition among Union officers. "Hancock's Corps has lost twenty brigade commanders [since May 4], and the rest of the army is similarly situated," Meade wrote his wife. "We cannot replace the officers lost with experienced men, and there is no time for reorganization or careful selection." The campaign's hard marches, brutal combat, and unspeakable deprivations had taken a severe physical and psychological toll on the soldiers of both armies. The Army of the Potomac—like the Army of Northern Virginia—was a shadow of its former self.

Controversy over Grant's and Lee's respective performances during the Overland Campaign began before the shooting stopped and continues to this day. Lee's biographer Douglas Southall Freeman framed the discussion by claiming that the operations from the Rapidan to the James were "on the one side an example of the costliness but ultimate success of the methods of attrition when unflinchingly applied by a superior force, and, on the other side, an even more impressive lesson in what resourcefulness, sound logistics, and careful fortification can accomplish in making prolonged resistance possible, even on a limited field of maneuver, by an army that faces oppressive odds."[4]

Grant's critics have derided the general as a "butcher" who eschewed maneuver in favor of direct and costly assaults. Some have compared him unfavorably to McClellan, who brought this same army to the James River two years earlier by ship without a battle. "If it has been a part of [Grant's] original design to make . . .the lower James his base of operations," the southern newspaper correspondent Peter W. Alexander remarked, "then he has committed a great blunder in marching across the country from Culpeper at a cost of forty or fifty thousand men, when by following McClellan's route he might have reached the same destination without the loss of a single man." Alexander's criticism, of course, misapprehended Grant's objective, which was not primarily the capture of Richmond but the destruction of Lee's army.[5]

After the war the Virginia newspaperman Edward Pollard opined that Grant "contained no spark of military genius; his idea of war was to the last degree rude—no strategy, the mere application of the *vis inertia;* he had none of that quick perception on the field of action which decides it by sudden strokes; he had no conception of battle beyond the momentum of numbers." Northern historians also took up the cry. Grant, John C. Ropes informed the Military Historical Society of Massachusetts, suffered from a "burning, persistent desire to fight, to attack, in season and out of season, against entrenchments, natural obstacles, what not." Concluded Ropes: "[Grant's campaigning] was so wasteful, so thoughtless of men's lives, that it required large reinforcements, an adversary numerically much weaker, and very patient and much enduring soldiers." More recently, the historian Joseph Rose has offered scathing criticism of Grant's generalship throughout the war, including his performance during the Overland Campaign.[6]

Wholesale denunciations of Grant's management of the campaign from the Rapidan to the James go too far. The general's primary goal was to defeat Lee's army and nullify it as an effective force. To achieve this aim he assembled an impressive concentration of Federal might. Multiple armies were to move against Lee, with Meade's Army of the Potomac directly engaging the Confederates, Sigel marching south through the Shenandoah Valley, Crook wrecking railroads in southwestern Virginia, and Butler advancing up the James toward Richmond. Grant's multifaceted offensive was intended to disrupt the Army of Northern Virginia's supply lines, threaten it with potential attacks from several directions, close off its retreat routes, and compel it to reduce its fighting capacity by reinforcing Confederate armies in the Valley and before Richmond. In sum, Grant's overall strategy in Virginia was excellent.

Contrary to his critics' arguments, the general in chief employed a judicious mixture of maneuvers and attacks to achieve his purpose. At no point was his goal simply to win by "attrition"—rather, he strove to defeat Lee on the battlefield, removing the Army of Northern Virginia as a factor in the war. His style of warring was opportunistic, for there could be no certainty about Lee's reaction once Grant set his multiple forces in motion. Lee would likely retreat toward Richmond, though he might flee instead toward Lynchburg and the Shenandoah Valley. Grant's plan had the flexibility to cover those contingencies.

For the main Union effort—the Army of the Potomac's direct offensive against Lee—Grant brought up the 9th Corps and fresh troops from garrisons in the North, swelling the army to almost double the size of Lee's force. Wise to the vulnerability of roads and railways passing through Confederate territory, he adopted a novel system of "flying depots," using ships to transport supplies from Alexandria down the Potomac River and up the tidal rivers nearest to the army. As the Federal juggernaut pressed south, the "flying depots" moved south as well. Hence Grant's source of supplies was safe from Confederate raiders and readily adaptable to the Potomac army's movements.

From the start Grant understood the importance of seizing the initiative and holding tight to his offensive advantage to keep Lee off balance and to prevent the rebel commander from assuming the offensive himself. The very nature of this assignment guaranteed hard fighting and severe casualties, consequences that generally inure to the party pressing the offensive. Mistakes there were, and failures as well, frequently caused by the fractious command structure dictated by Grant's presence and by his untidy division of labor with Meade. The facts, however, do not support the caricature of Grant as a general who avoided maneuver in favor of headlong assaults and needlessly sacrificed his men. Overall his strategic decisions were sound. Their execution—largely the responsibility of Meade and his subordinates—often left much to be desired.

A review of the Overland Campaign focusing on Grant's tactical decisions displays the general in a more favorable light than his detractors admit. Rather than attacking Lee head on across the Rapidan, the Potomac army stole a march under cover of night, slipped downriver in two columns, and crossed at lightly guarded fords, aiming to turn Lee out of his strongly fortified position. An ill-conceived decision to halt for a day to allow supply wagons to catch up, fast marching by Lee's infantry, and poor reconnaissance by Sheridan's cavalry brought Grant's offensive to a bloody halt in the Wilderness. Fought to impasse during the first day of combat, Grant moved to concentrate overwhelming force against Powell Hill's isolated corps on the Orange Plank Road while pinning the rest of Lee's army in place. But poor coordination among the Union corps, the wooded terrain's disorienting nature, and Longstreet's timely and unexpected appearance won the day for the Confederates. May 6 ended with Lee holding a formidable position in the Wilderness.

Instead of blindly hurling his soldiers against the entrenched Confederates, Grant again resorted to maneuver, sliding Meade south toward Spotsylvania Court House in an attempt to draw Lee from his defensible ground and fight him on favorable terrain. This maneuver, like the attempt to turn the Rapidan defenses, was a sound plan. It failed because Confederate cavalry delayed the

Union advance, enabling the 1st Corps to intercept the Federals. Over the next ten days, Grant tried a variety of tactics to pry Lee from his works. Late on May 9 most of Hancock's 2nd Corps attempted to turn the Confederate left flank, but nightfall stalled the maneuver. When Lee tried to capture this isolated force, Grant surmised that the he must have weakened some part of his line and ordered an attack against the entire rebel position. Coordination, however, again eluded Union commanders, and the grand assault degenerated into disjointed localized offensives that Lee's warriors repelled with comparative ease. Grant then marshaled overwhelming force against a discrete, vulnerable sector of the defenses. At first successful, the May 12 offensive against the Mule Shoe ultimately failed because of a determined Confederate counterattack and the absence of a strong guiding hand at the front to coordinate the disparate Union elements.

Grant, however, had no intention of letting up and cast about for ways to retain the initiative. He advanced part of the Potomac army south along Lee's right flank, hoping to strike an unsuspecting portion of the rebel line. Rain slowed the movement, however, and concerned that Lee had shifted troops to counter him, Grant called off the assault. Reckoning that his opponent had weakened the Mule Shoe sector, Grant orchestrated a surprise attack across that blood-soaked field on May 18 only to be repulsed by cleverly sited Confederate artillery.

Concluding that it was "impractical to make any further attack upon the enemy at Spotsylvania Court House," Grant looked again to maneuver, this time feigning south toward the North Anna River. He set a trap by sending Hancock on a twenty-mile march southeast along the Mattaponi River to Milford Station, hoping the lone Union corps would pose too great a temptation for Lee to resist. The plan, like most of Grant's designs in Virginia, was a good one, but it too unraveled in execution, enabling Lee to abandon Spotsylvania Court House and assume a new defensive line below the North Anna.

Again Grant maneuvered, advancing along multiples routes to the North Anna River and securing a bridgehead at Jericho Mills, on the rebels' left flank. Lee thwarted Grant once more by deploying his army into an invulnerable wedge-shaped formation below the river, splitting the Union force. Grant, however, broke the impasse by withdrawing under cover of darkness and marching downriver to Hanovertown. Once again he had chosen maneuver over blind attacks against formidable rebel positions.

After crossing the Pamunkey, the Union host confronted Lee along Totopotomoy Creek. Grant extended leftward, feeling for openings, and Lee countered, provoking heated engagements along Totopotomoy Creek, Matadequin

Creek, and at Bethesda Church. These maneuvers forced Lee to stretch his line for six miles, leaving him no troops to spare. Summoning Smith's 18th Corps from Bermuda Hundred, Grant aimed to send a substantial force below the rebel flank, breaking the stalemate and threatening the Confederate capital. Once again an intelligent plan failed in execution when Smith and Wright's combined assault at Cold Harbor met stiff resistance from Hoke's recently arrived division. Grant planned to renew the offensive the next day, but the Potomac army was unable to reorient before evening, enabling Lee to rush reinforcements to Cold Harbor and strengthen his defenses.

Even though Grant had lost a day, he reckoned that the Army of Northern Virginia had reached its breaking point and that a frontal attack at Cold Harbor stood a reasonable chance of success. The offensive of June 3, however, was another disjointed affair among the Union corps. Reconnaissance was woefully lax, and the cumulative effect of battle weariness and attrition took a devastating toll on the Federals. After futile attempts to renew the offensive, Grant called off the operation.

At this juncture the general in chief reconsidered his options. Since direct attacks against Lee's entrenchments were clearly ineffective, the trick was to compel the rebels to abandon their fortifications. Denying Lee's army food and military supplies seemed productive, so Grant embarked on the plan that this book examines. The initial stages involved Sheridan and Hunter attempting to close off the main Confederate supply routes north of Richmond. The second stage, which evolved over the subsequent week, saw the Army of the Potomac concentrating toward the Chickahominy River, then sidling south to cooperate with the Army of the James in severing Lee's supply routes through Petersburg. The final act was to be a Federal advance north toward Richmond, turning Beauregard out of the Howlett Line and forcing Lee to abandon Cold Harbor.

Grant's plan began well. Sheridan's horsemen clattered toward Charlottesville, aiming to wreck the Virginia Central Railroad, and Hunter's Federals headed toward Lynchburg, terminus of the James River and Kanawha Canal. Once again Lee had no choice but to dance to Grant's tune, dispatching two-thirds of his cavalry to intercept the mounted raiders and sending Breckinridge's Division—and then Early's entire 2nd Corps—to salvage Confederate fortunes in the Valley. During the night of June 12, the Army of the Potomac disengaged from the rebels at Cold Harbor, Warren's 5th Corps screening the march southward and Smith's 18th Corps taking the river route to Bermuda Hundred. Daylight showed Lee that Grant had left, but it was not immediately apparent where his troops had gone. Fearing that the Federals might glide past his right flank and attack Richmond, he deployed across the roads leading to the Confederate capital. The rebel commander also suspected that Grant might be preparing to move against Petersburg, but with most of his own cavalry gone, Lee could do little more than wait until he knew for certain. Grant's plan was working to perfection; by leaving Lee in the dark over whether he intended to attack Richmond or move on Petersburg, he had frozen the Army of Northern Virginia in place.

Grant meanwhile put the next phase of his plan into action, with Smith marching to capture Petersburg and the Army of the Potomac starting across the James River. "I think it pretty well to get across a great river, and come up here and attack Lee in his rear before he is ready for us," the general in chief boasted. The Confederate artillerist Alexander later termed Grant's movement to the James "the most brilliant stroke in all the Federal campaigns of the whole war. It was," he noted, "by somewhat roundabout roads, but entirely out of our observation, to precipitate his whole army on Petersburg, which was held by scarcely 6,000 men. If he succeeded in capturing it a speedy evacuation of Richmond would follow, and he would be in position to make the retreat a disastrous one."[7]

Early on June 15 President Lincoln penned a message to Grant. "I begin to see it," the president wrote. "You will succeed."[8]

But Grant did not succeed. His plan—"brilliant in conception," according to Alexander—failed in large measure because of his own mistakes and oversights. Permitting Butler to launch a feeble, unsupported offensive against Petersburg on June 9 only served to put Beauregard on notice of Union intentions and to alert the town's defenders to prepare for the potential onslaught. Neglecting to inform Smith of his central role in the June 15 offensive and to give him time to reconnoiter and prepare undermined the operation, as did Grant's failure to inform Meade and Hancock of his overall plan and their respective roles in it. Equally responsible was the general's failure to either position himself or someone else at the battlefront to coordinate Smith and Hancock and ensure that they acted in concert to achieve the objective.

Grant's strength was unwavering adherence to his strategic objective. He treated reverses in the Wilderness, at Spotsylvania Court House, on the North Anna River, and at Cold Harbor as tactical setbacks, not defeats. Lee masterfully parried each Union thrust, but Grant broke each impasse and maneuvered, each time threatening Richmond and forcing Lee to resume his defensive posture. No Union general in the eastern theater had displayed such persistence; instead the invariable pattern had been to retreat following reverses comparable to those suffered in the Overland Campaign's major battles. But Grant kept his eye on the ultimate goal. Mistakes there were, but the overall pattern of his operations was that of an innovative general employing thoughtful combinations of maneuver and force to bring a difficult adversary to bay. "For the great and bloody campaign from the Rapidan to Petersburg had now ended in something closely akin to what Lee had most desired to avoid," the Virginian's eminent biographer Freeman conceded. "He could not have forgotten . . . what he had told Early: If Grant reached [the] James River, 'it will become a siege, and then it will be a mere question of time.'" Lee would shortly find himself in that very predicament, locked into the fastness of the Richmond and Petersburg entrenchments, unable to maneuver—and he would remain so until the end of the war, which as he accurately predicted, was now only a question of time.[9]

Grant's chief shortcoming was his failure to develop rapport with Meade and his generals necessary for success. His opportunistic style sat poorly with the Potomac army's commanders, who frequently failed to act with the élan that Grant's strategies required. Grant also initiated major operations without educating Meade and his subordinates about his own designs or allowing them sufficient time to prepare. In retrospect the general in chief should have demarcated more clearly responsibility between himself and Meade, either insisting that the Pennsylvanian take charge of tactical details or taking charge of those details himself.[10]

How did the Army of the Potomac's generals fare during the Overland Campaign? Meade found himself in an impossible position. Although Grant promised to let him manage the army's battles, he broke that oath during the first day of combat in the Wilderness. Thereafter Grant increasingly dictated the army's movements, treating Meade as his de facto chief of staff. "At first I had maneuvered the army, but gradually, and from the very nature of things, Grant had taken control," as Meade characterized their evolving relationship. By the time the armies reached the North Anna River, the two men were barely on speaking terms. Writing home to his wife, Meade admitted that if he could find "any honorable way of retiring from my present false position, I should undoubtedly adopt it, but there is none and all I can do is patiently submit and bear with resignation the humiliation." Grant agreed that Meade's position "proved embarrassing to me if not to him." His failure to keep Meade abreast of his intended movement on Petersburg and the supporting role he expected the Potomac army to play in that exercise accounts in large part for the offensive's failure.[11]

None of Meade's corps commanders distinguished themselves in the campaign. Hancock, generally considered the most talented of the lot, left his flank exposed in the Wilderness, failed to exploit his breakthroughs at the Mule Shoe and at Cold Harbor, and wandered aimlessly during most of June 15—this likely cost the Federals the occupation of Petersburg but cannot fairly be blamed on Hancock, who had no idea he was expected to backstop Smith. As for the 6th Corps, Sedgwick left his flank vulnerable to Gordon's attack in the Wilderness, and his successor Wright, who assumed command when Sedgwick died on May 9, spent the rest of the campaign learning his new job. Warren proved intelligent but irascible—his running disputes with Burnside and Sheridan come to mind—and he seemed incapable, as Meade noted, of executing an order without modifying it. He performed well during the North Anna operations by repelling Hill at Jericho Mills but did nothing exceptional at Cold Harbor. His most significant contribution during the campaign was his successful screening operation during the withdrawal from Cold Harbor. Burnside, whose 9th Corps was finally incorporated into the Potomac army at the North Anna, accepted his diminished status with grace but did nothing to improve his lackluster reputation. Sheridan, whom Grant brought from the West, got off to a rocky start, neglecting to screen the army's movement into the Wilderness or to ferret out Lee's location, then afterward launching his full mounted complement on a major raid toward Richmond that left Grant virtually blind at Spotsylvania Court House. Sheridan's cavalrymen received a boost with Stuart's defeat at Yellow Tavern and performed well at Cold Harbor, where they achieved the unheard-of accomplishment of repelling a Confederate infantry charge. Dispatched to sever the Virginia Central Railroad, Sheridan suffered an embarrassing reverse at Trevilian Station. A bright spot for Union cavalry was Wilson's division, which cooperated seamlessly with Warren during the movement to the James and drew an impenetrable curtain between Lee and the Army of the Potomac while the Federal troops crossed the river.

In sum, Grant brought much-needed energy, persistence, and focus to the Union war effort in Virginia. Particulars of his generalship are open to criticism, but his aggressive, relentless style of warfare put northern arms in a stronger position than any general had achieved in the past. The Potomac army's difficulty adapting to his fast-paced, opportunistic mode of campaigning—and conversely Grant's failure to better mesh with that army's military culture—accounted in significant part for many of the campaign's setbacks. Grant excelled after the stalemates in the Wilderness, at Spotsylvania Court House, and at the North Anna River, when he devised innovative maneuvers that turned apparent defeats into opportunities to regain the initiative. Unfortunately, when the campaign's ultimate goal was finally within his grasp, he neglected to communicate his designs with clarity to his subordinates. Lulled into overconfidence by Butler's assurances that the Dimmock Line would quickly collapse, he overestimated Smith's capacity to exercise independent command and dedicated too few resources to achieve the critical objective of capturing Petersburg. The price in blood over the next ten months would be enormous.

Lee's performance during the Overland Campaign has been rightfully praised. The Virginian began the campaign under serious handicaps. His direct opponent, the Army of the Potomac, outnumbered him two to one and was much better provisioned; Union armies threatened the Shenandoah Valley and Richmond; his ability to draw reinforcements from other quarters was severely limited; he was in questionable health during much of the campaign; and his obligation to protect Richmond hampered his ability to maneuver. Although he received reinforcements—primarily Breckinridge's, Hoke's, and Ransom's infantry and Butler's cavalry—by the end of his stay at Cold Harbor, he had lost considerably more soldiers than he had received. The campaign's attrition was crippling, including not only some 33,000 casualties but also more than twenty general officers killed, wounded, or captured. By June 15 Lee's corps leadership was in shambles, with Stuart killed, Longstreet seriously wounded, Ewell gone, and Hill debilitated by sickness.[12]

Despite these handicaps, Lee not only avoided defeat but also consistently fought Grant to impasse. Innovative use of fieldworks played an important role in his successes, as carefully sited entrenchments increased the Army of Northern Virginia's defensive capacity several fold. In Grant, however, Lee encountered a foe unlike any he had ever met; after each Confederate checkmate, the Union commander maneuvered to fight anew. Lee frequently misjudged his opponent, but he possessed a remarkable ability to rescue his army from seemingly irredeemable predicaments and turn unfavorable situations to his advantage.

During the weeks preceding the Overland Campaign, Lee expected the Army of the Potomac to attack but was uncertain where the blow would fall. Immobilized by Grant's deployment of multiple armies, he forfeited the initiative to his opponent. But once Grant showed his hand and advanced into the Wilderness, Lee seized the initiative. Risking all by dividing his smaller army into three elements separated by several miles of intractable woodland, he fought the Potomac army to a stalemate on the battle's first day and regained the offensive edge on the second day. In the Wilderness the Virginian achieved a victory as complete as any he had won in the past.

But unlike Lee's former opponents, Grant did not withdraw, leaving the rebel commander to puzzle whether his new adversary would retreat across the

Rapidan as Hooker had done a year before after the Battle of Chancellorsville or would march south toward Richmond. Uncertain about Grant's intentions, Lee dispatched his 1st Corps under its new head, Richard Anderson, toward Spotsylvania Court House but held the rest of his army in the Wilderness, awaiting the Federals' move. By a stroke of luck Anderson left before his appointed time and fortuitously blocked Grant's approach to Spotsylvania. Lee's uncertainty about Grant's intention almost cost him the campaign, for if Anderson had followed his instructions and waited, Grant would have won the race to the courthouse town.

Lee's engineers laid out impressive earthworks at Spotsylvania Court House. The vulnerable point was the Mule Shoe, which Grant targeted for attack. While Union troops marched into position during the rainy night of May 11–12, Lee pondered the meaning of the enemy movements. Persuaded that Grant was withdrawing and anxious to pursue, he directed his artillery chief to remove the Confederate guns protecting the salient to major roads well to the rear. Never had Lee made a more egregious miscalculation. Grant was not retreating but had targeted the very segment of fortifications that the Virginian was weakening. Early on May 12 a concentrated Union offensive overran the Mule Shoe and brought Lee's army to the verge of destruction. Union disorganization and a fierce Confederate counterattack, however, saved the day for the southerners.[13]

The Federals left Spotsylvania Court House in stages, affording Lee an excellent opportunity to attack the divided enemy force. While Wright and Burnside remained entrenched in front of the rebel lines, Warren was marching several miles to the east, while Hancock was settling into camp twenty miles away at Milford Station. "Lee now had a superb opportunity to take the initiative either by attacking Wright and Burnside alone or by following the Telegraph Road and striking Hancock's and Warren's corps, or even Hancock's alone, before reinforcements could come up," Grant later conceded. His aide Badeau agreed that "if Lee ever meant to assume the offensive, this was the moment, with Grant on the arc of the circle of which he held the chord; one national corps at Milford, another at Guinea, and two at Spotsylvania, and all in motion by different roads with which they were unacquainted, while the rebels knew every plantation path and every ford, and every inhabitant was a friendly guide for them and a spy on Grant." But unaware of the opportunity to strike a telling blow, he let the moment pass.[14]

Lee's puzzlement over Grant's intentions continued after the Army of Northern Virginia crossed the North Anna River. While his troops spread along the Virginia Central Railroad, the general informed President Davis that he was uncertain of the Union army's whereabouts. His best estimate was that Grant intended to make a dash for Richmond and would stay on the far side of the Mattaponi River. In fact Grant was marching directly toward Lee. Even when Hancock's corps materialized at Chesterfield Bridge on the North Anna, Lee refused to believe what his eyes told him. "This is nothing but a feint," an artillerist heard him remark. "The enemy is preparing to cross below," referring to the Pamunkey River crossings some twenty miles away. This miscalculation enabled Grant to breach the North Anna line with hardly a fight.[15]

Lee stopped Grant with his famous "inverted V" formation, but the Federals slipped away undetected only to emerge downriver at Hanovertown. Lee skillfully chose his lines along Totopotomoy Creek and at Cold Harbor and shifted his forces adroitly to counter Grant's moves. He searched for opportunities to attack, but his offensive attempts—Early's Bethesda Church debacle and Colonel Keitt's encounter with Sheridan at Cold Harbor—ended badly. Adverse developments in the Shenandoah Valley and Beauregard's concern about Petersburg's security compelled him to send off Breckinridge, Early, Hoke, and Ransom, further depleting his outnumbered force confronting Grant.

The Confederate mapmaker Captain Oscar Hinrichs detected concern in southern ranks during the final days at Cold Harbor. "Lee seems to be afraid of Grant who seems only fooling and playing with him," Hinrichs wrote on June 9. Two days later, as Hunter moved victoriously up the Valley, the captain saw the situation as "pretty dark." Lee, he observed, "does not seem disposed to crowd Grant away from his position, and Grant is gradually forcing him to detach men to support other points and with them force him into the fortifications of Richmond, where it becomes merely a question of time whether the enemy get possession [of the city] or not."[16]

Although Lee anticipated that Grant would likely cross the Chickahominy and perhaps the James, the Union evacuation of Cold Harbor caught him by surprise. His options were limited, and he took the most reasonable course open to him—crossing the Chickahominy and barring the approaches to Richmond. Responding to Beauregard's calls of alarm by returning the troops the Louisianan had forwarded to him, Lee found himself commanding an army less than half the size of the force he had led at the campaign's outset.

Lee has been severely criticized for his decision to hold his line from White Oak Swamp to Malvern Hill during the initial days of fighting at Petersburg. "Grant had gotten away from *US* completely and was fighting *Beauregard*," the artillerist Alexander later complained. "The Army of Northern Virginia had lost him, and was sucking its thumbs by the roadside 25 miles away, and wondering where he could be!!!"[17]

In fact on June 14 Lee was fairly certain that the Potomac army was located somewhere along the approximately six-mile stretch of river from Charles City Court House to Harrison's Landing. The next day he learned that enemy forces were attacking Petersburg. What he did not know, however, because Beauregard did not inform him, was the source of the attacking troops. Were they from Butler's Army of the James, which had attempted to take the town on June 9, or did they include some or all of the Army of the Potomac?

Grant's ingenious deployment left Lee no option but to protect the roads leading from the Potomac army's encampments to Richmond. So long as Grant stationed a force north of the James capable of attacking the city, Lee had to stay put or risk sacrificing the Confederacy's capital. Even when some of Meade's elements appeared before Petersburg—one of Dearing's reports erroneously claimed that Burnside's troops were involved—he was still not free to move because Grant might have left a significant Union presence north of the James. "Grant's strategy was working perfectly—Lee was frozen north of the James," a student of the Petersburg Campaign's opening battles has observed. "Rather than anticipating and acting pre-emptively on Federal actions, Lee was uncharacteristically awaiting Grant's moves."[18]

The Overland Campaign had decimated Lee's corps leadership. Longstreet was disabled by a wound in the Wilderness, Ewell was no longer with the army, Hill was in questionable health, and Stuart was dead. The new guard presented mixed quality. Early, now heading the 2nd Corps, displayed a welcome streak of aggressiveness but stumbled badly when attempting to coordinate with Anderson at Bethesda Church and in the June 6–7 operations against Burnside. For his part Anderson successfully thwarted the Union advance to Spotsylvania Court House but failed to distinguish himself afterward. The standouts were Lee's cavalry heads. Stuart kept his commander fully informed of Grant's deployment in the Wilderness and slowed the Union advance to Spotsylvania Court House. His death at Yellow Tavern was a blow to Confederate morale, but Wade Hampton stepped into Stuart's boots and restored much of the mounted corps' confidence with a command performance at Haw's Shop. Under Hampton's guidance southern horsemen performed admirably at Cold Harbor and then, leaving a division behind to screen and reconnoiter, rushed to block Sheridan's railroad-cutting raid and soundly defeated the mounted Federals at Trevilian Station.

How did Lee fare in the Overland Campaign? Like Grant, his performance was mixed. In each key engagement he blocked the enemy's advance. Yet after each battle Grant maneuvered inexorably southward, renewing the fight ever nearer to Richmond. Grant's final movement shifted the center of gravity toward Petersburg and left Lee in his most vulnerable position of the campaign. Confederate success at this juncture required stalemating Grant in front of the Petersburg defenses. Ironically, this definition of success required Lee to accept the very situation that had represented his greatest fear at the campaign's outset.

The Army of Northern Virginia excelled in defending against daunting odds, but its ability to launch its trademark forays and flanking maneuvers diminished sharply as the campaign progressed. In the Wilderness Lee rolled up the Union left with Longstreet and the Union right with Gordon, thwarting Grant's opening offensive. But Lee's two aggressive plays at Spotsylvania Court House—the May 10 attempt to bag Hancock's 2nd Corps and the May 19 engagement at Harris Farm—failed to achieve significant success, and his only offensive at the North Anna River—Hill's attack against Warren at Jericho Mills—failed completely. Equally futile were Anderson's and Early's offensives at Bethesda Church and Keitt's attack against Sheridan at Old Cold Harbor. Early's and Anderson's probes on June 6 and 7 amounted to little more than exploratory gestures. By the end of the Overland Campaign, attrition had gutted the Army of Northern Virginia's vaunted offensive capacity.

Who won the Overland Campaign? The historian Mark Grimsley accurately observed that the ten-month deadlock at Petersburg that followed has colored our perceptions of those intense six weeks of combat. If the campaign had ended with the capture of Petersburg, the severance of Lee's supply lines, the fall of Richmond, and the flight of the Army of Northern Virginia, Grant's performance would be universally hailed as a masterpiece of the military art. Its disappointing finale—at least for the North—led, as Grimsley correctly noted, to declining Union morale, a doubling of the price of gold, and Lincoln's renewed concern about his political fortunes. Moreover, Lee's dogged defensive tactics and his ability to stave off defeat in the face of overwhelming odds, when viewed in conjunction with Grant's prolonged stalemate after the conclusion of the campaign, added additional luster to the Virginian's performance.[19]

The answer to who won the Overland Campaign lies in how one defines winning. One matrix is to consider casualties. Grant lost approximately 55,000 soldiers in forty-two days, almost as many men as Lee had in his army at the beginning of May. Lee, however, lost about 33,000 troops during the same period. While Grant's subtractions were numerically greater than Lee's, his percentage of loss was smaller. Union losses amounted to about 45 percent of the force that crossed the Rapidan, while Confederate casualties reached slightly over 50 percent. And while Grant could draw on a deep manpower pool for re-inforcements, Lee's potential was limited. In addition, Lee had to send off much of his army to help repel other Union offensives. In the game of numbers, Grant was coming out ahead: he was losing soldiers at a lower percentage than was his adversary and had a greater capacity to replace them.[20]

Although Grant's relentless fighting produced a steady stream of casualties, in some respects the general was less reckless with soldiers' lives than his pre-decessors had been. His forces fought major engagements on May 5 and 6 (the Wilderness), May 7 (Todd's Tavern), May 8 (Laurel Hill), May 10 (Po River, Laurel Hill, and Upton's charge), May 11 (Yellow Tavern), May 12 (Bloody Angle), May 18 (second Mule Shoe attack), May 19 (Harris Farm), May 23–24 (Jericho Mills, Henagan's Redoubt, Ox Ford, and Doswell's Farm), May 28 (Haw's Shop), May 31 (Bethesda Church), and June 1 and 3 (Cold Harbor). To those battles must be added the steady attrition on days when no major combat was in progress, especially at Spotsylvania Court House, Totopotomoy Creek, and Cold Harbor. No single day under Grant, however, saw the magnitude of Union casualties that McClellan incurred in one day at Antietam, and no three consecutive days under Grant proved as costly to the Union as Meade's three days at Gettysburg. In round numbers the Peninsula Campaign generated 15,800 Union casualties; Second Manassas 10,000; Antietam 13,000; Freder-icksburg 12,600; Chancellorsville 17,000; and Gettysburg 23,000. The total for these seventeen days of combat before Grant's appearance in Virginia—not counting losses in the numerous smaller engagements during 1862 and 1863— was 91,400 Union casualties. During the Overland Campaign, Grant waged several successive battles, one after the other. But unlike his predecessors, who disengaged after their battles and left Lee to repair his losses, Grant followed up his fights with a vengeance. Not only were his subtractions less than those of his predecessors, but he also had something to show for these sacrifices. Comparing casualties in Virginia before Grant's arrival with those incurred under his command, Assistant War Secretary Dana noted, "Grant in eleven months secured the prize with less loss than his predecessors suffered in fail-ing to win it during a struggle of three years."[21]

If commanders are scored by tactical success, much as one might score box-ers in a match, Lee holds the edge, though not by much. Although consistently outnumbered, he achieved victories, or at least stalemates, at the Wilderness, Spotsylvania Court House, the North Anna River, Totopotomoy Creek, and Cold Harbor, thwarting Grant in each battle. His performance during the cam-paign's last phase—Grant's movement toward Petersburg—started poorly but ended in another stalemate. As commander of an army fending off an enemy double the size of his own, Lee did extraordinarily well. Grant, however, also deserves credit. He consistently disengaged from Lee after each battle, without further loss and in secrecy, and often left the Virginian baffled over precisely where he had gone and what his next move might be. And he successfully exploited Lee's solicitation for Richmond by maneuvering in ways that forced his opponent to abandon his impregnable defensive positions.

If the campaign is viewed in terms of which general came closest to realizing his overall strategic goal, Grant comes out ahead. The rebel commander's grand objective was to hold the Rapidan line, and in this he failed. His secondary goal was to avoid being pinned in the Richmond and Petersburg defenses, and he failed in that objective as well. Grant's goal was to negate Lee's army as an effective fighting force, and in that he largely succeeded. At the campaign's outset the Army of Northern Virginia held much the same line that it had defended for the previous two years. Antietam, Chancellorsville, Gettysburg, and all the other battles of 1862 and 1863 had taken a serious toll on the rebel force, but it remained a formidable military machine. An army of 65,000 Confederates waited along the Rapidan River, confident as ever of victory. In little over a month, Grant broke Lee's offensive capacity and locked the Army of Northern Virginia in the fortifications protecting Richmond and Petersburg, materially changing the battlefield of Virginia in the Union's favor.

The coming months would tell whether Grant could exploit that advantage, or if Lee would once again find a way to elude his grasp.

Appendix 1
The Union Order of Battle

ARMY OF THE POTOMAC
Major General George G. Meade

PROVOST GUARD
Brigadier General Marsena R. Patrick
80th New York
68th Pennsylvania
114th Pennsylvania
1st Massachusetts Cavalry, Companies C and D
3rd Pennsylvania Cavalry

ARTILLERY
Brigadier General Henry J. Hunt

VOLUNTEER ENGINEER BRIGADE
Brigadier General Henry W. Benham

50TH NEW YORK ENGINEERS
Lieutenant Colonel Ira Spaulding
15th New York Engineers

BATTALION U.S. ENGINEERS
Captain George H. Mendell

2ND ARMY CORPS

Major General Winfield S. Hancock
1st Vermont Cavalry, Company M

1ST DIVISION
Brigadier General Francis C. Barlow

1st Brigade
Colonel Nelson A. Miles
26th Michigan
5th New Hampshire
2nd New York Heavy Artillery
61st New York
81st Pennsylvania
140th Pennsylvania
183rd Pennsylvania

2nd Brigade
Colonel Patrick Kelly
28th Massachusetts
63rd New York
69th New York
88th New York
116th Pennsylvania

3rd Brigade
Colonel Clinton D. McDougall
39th New York
52nd New York
57th New York
111th New York
125th New York
126th New York

2ND DIVISION
Brigadier General John Gibbon

1st Brigade
Brigadier General Byron R. Pierce
19th Maine
1st Company Massachusetts Sharpshooters
15th Massachusetts
19th Massachusetts
20th Massachusetts
7th Michigan
42nd New York
59th New York
82nd New York (2nd Militia)
184th Pennsylvania
36th Wisconsin

2nd Brigade
Brigadier General Joshua T. Owen
152nd New York
69th Pennsylvania
71st Pennsylvania
72nd Pennsylvania
106th Pennsylvania

3rd Brigade
Colonel Thomas A. Smyth
14th Connecticut
1st Delaware
14th Indiana

3RD DIVISION
Major General David B. Birney

1st Brigade
Colonel Thomas W. Egan
20th Indiana
3rd Maine
40th New York
86th New York
124th New York
99th Pennsylvania
110th Pennsylvania
141st Pennsylvania
2nd U.S. Sharpshooters

2nd Brigade
Colonel Thomas R. Tannatt
4th Maine
17th Maine
1st Massachusetts Heavy Artillery
3rd Michigan
5th Michigan
93rd New York
57th Pennsylvania
63rd Pennsylvania
105th Pennsylvania
1st U.S. Sharpshooters

3rd Brigade
Brigadier General Gershom Mott
1st Maine Heavy Artillery

4th Brigade
Colonel James A. Beaver[a]
2nd Delaware
7th New York Heavy Artillery
64th New York
66th New York
53rd Pennsylvania
145th Pennsylvania
148th Pennsylvania

12th New Jersey
108th New York
4th Ohio
8th Ohio
7th West Virginia
10th New York Battalion

4th Brigade
Colonel James P. McIvor[b]
8th New York Heavy Artillery
155th New York
164th New York
170th New York
182nd New York

16th Massachusetts
5th New Jersey
6th New Jersey
7th New Jersey
8th New Jersey
11th New Jersey
115th Pennsylvania

4th Brigade
Colonel William R. Brewster
11th Massachusetts
71st New York
72nd New York
73rd New York
74th New York
120th New York
84th Pennsylvania

Artillery Brigade
Colonel John C. Tidball
Maine Light, 6th Battery (F)
Massachusetts Light, 10th Battery
New Hampshire Light, 1st Battery
1st New Jersey Light Battery (B)
1st New York Light, Battery G
4th New York Heavy, 3rd Battalion
New York Light, 11th Battery
New York Light, 12th Battery
1st Pennsylvania Light, Battery F
1st Rhode Island Light, Battery A
1st Rhode Island Light, Battery B
4th United States, Battery K
5th United States, Batteries C and I

[a] Colonel Lewis O. Morris was killed on June 4, replaced by Colonel Beaver.
[b] Replaced by Brigadier General Robert O. Tyler on June 7.

5TH ARMY CORPS[a]

Major General Gouverneur K. Warren

12th New York Battalion

1ST DIVISION
Brigadier General Charles Griffin

1st Brigade
Colonel Joshua L. Chamberlain
121st Pennsylvania
142nd Pennsylvania
143rd Pennsylvania
149th Pennsylvania
150th Pennsylvania

2nd Brigade
Colonel Jacob B. Sweitzer
9th Massachusetts
22nd Massachusetts
32nd Massachusetts
4th Michigan
62nd Pennsylvania

3rd Brigade
Brigadier General Joseph J. Bartlett
20th Maine
18th Massachusetts
1st Michigan
16th Michigan
44th New York
83rd Pennsylvania
118th Pennsylvania

2ND DIVISION
Brigadier General Romeyn Ayres

1st Brigade
Colonel Edgar M. Gregory
5th New York
140th New York
146th New York
21st Pennsylvania Dismounted Cavalry
91st Pennsylvania
155th Pennsylvania
2nd United States, Companies B, C, F, H, I, and K
11th United States, 1st Battalion, Companies B, C, D, E, F, and G
12th United States, 1st Battalion, Companies A, B, C, D, and G
12th United States, 2nd Battalion, Companies A, C, D, G, and H
14th United States, 1st Battalion
17th United States, 1st Battalion, Companies A, C, D, G, and H
17th United States, 2nd Battalion, Companies A, B, and C

2nd Brigade
Colonel Nathan D. Dushane
1st Maryland
4th Maryland
7th Maryland

3RD DIVISION
Brigadier General Samuel W. Crawford

1st Brigade
Colonel Peter Lyle
16th Maine
13th Massachusetts
39th Massachusetts
104th New York
90th Pennsylvania
107th Pennsylvania

2nd Brigade
Colonel James L. Bates
12th Massachusetts
83rd New York
97th New York
11th Pennsylvania
88th Pennsylvania

3rd Brigade
Colonel James Carle
190th Pennsylvania
191st Pennsylvania

4TH DIVISION
Brigadier General Lysander Cutler

1st Brigade
Colonel William W. Robinson[b]
7th Indiana
19th Indiana
24th Michigan
1st Battalion, New York Sharpshooters
2nd Wisconsin
6th Wisconsin
7th Wisconsin

2nd Brigade
Colonel J. William Hofmann
3rd Delaware
4th Delaware
46th New York
76th New York
95th New York
147th New York
56th Pennsylvania
157th Pennsylvania

Artillery Brigade
Colonel Charles S. Wainwright
Massachusetts Light, 3rd Battery (C)
Massachusetts Light, 5th Battery (E)
Massachusetts Light, 9th Battery
1st New York Light, Battery B
1st New York Light, Battery C

8th Maryland
Purnell (Maryland) Legion

3rd Brigade
Colonel G. Howard Kitching
6th New York Heavy Artillery
15th New York Heavy Artillery

1st New York Light, Battery D
1st New York Light, Batteries E and L
1st New York Light, Battery H
New York Light, 5th Battery
New York Light, 15th Battery
1st Pennsylvania Light, Battery B
4th United States, Battery B
5th United States, Battery D

---

[a] This reflects the 5th Corps's composition after it was reorganized on June 5, 1864. See General Orders, *OR*, vol. 36, pt. 3, pp. 613–14.

[b] Replaced by Brigadier General Edward S. Bragg on June 7.

6TH ARMY CORPS
Major General Horatio G. Wright
8th Pennsylvania Cavalry, Company A

1ST DIVISION
Brigadier General David A. Russell

1st Brigade
Colonel William H. Penrose
1st New Jersey
2nd New Jersey
3rd New Jersey
4th New Jersey
10th New Jersey
15th New Jersey

2nd Brigade
Brigadier General Emory Upton
2nd Connecticut Heavy Artillery
5th Maine
121st New York
95th Pennsylvania
96th Pennsylvania

3rd Brigade
Brigadier General Henry L. Eustis[a]
6th Maine
49th Pennsylvania
119th Pennsylvania
5th Wisconsin

4th Brigade
Colonel Nelson Cross
65th New York
67th New York

2ND DIVISION
Brigadier General Thomas H. Neill

1st Brigade
Brigadier General Frank Wheaton
62nd New York
93rd Pennsylvania
98th Pennsylvania
102nd Pennsylvania
139th Pennsylvania

2nd Brigade
Brigadier General Lewis A. Grant
1st Vermont Heavy Artillery
2nd Vermont
3rd Vermont
4th Vermont
5th Vermont
6th Vermont

3rd Brigade
Colonel Daniel D. Bidwell
7th Maine
43rd New York
49th New York
77th New York
61st Pennsylvania

3RD DIVISION
Brigadier General James B. Ricketts

1st Brigade
Colonel William S. Truex
14th New Jersey
106th New York
151st New York
87th Pennsylvania
10th Vermont

2nd Brigade
Colonel Benjamin F. Smith
6th Maryland
9th New York Heavy Artillery, 1st Battalion
9th New York Heavy Artillery, 3rd Battalion
110th Ohio
122nd Ohio
126th Ohio
67th Pennsylvania
138th Pennsylvania

Artillery Brigade
Colonel Charles H. Tompkins
Maine Light, 4th Battery (D)
Maine Light, 5th Battery (E)
Massachusetts Light, 1st Battery (A)
New Jersey Light, 1st Battery (A)

122nd New York
23rd Pennsylvania
82nd Pennsylvania

4th Brigade
Colonel Oliver Edwards
7th Massachusetts
10th Massachusetts
37th Massachusetts
2nd Rhode Island

9th New York Heavy Artillery, 2nd
   Battalion
New York Light, 1st Battery
New York Light, 3rd Battery
1st Ohio Light, Battery H
1st Rhode Island Light, Battery C
1st Rhode Island Light, Battery E
1st Rhode Island Light, Battery G
5th United States, Battery E
5th United States, Battery M

[a] Replaced by Lieutenant Colonel Gideon Clark on June 12.

9TH ARMY CORPS
Major General Ambrose E. Burnside
8th United States

1ST DIVISION
Major General Thomas L. Crittenden[a]
35th Massachusetts (Acting Division Engineers)

1st Brigade
Brigadier General James H. Ledlie[b]
56th Massachusetts
57th Massachusetts
59th Massachusetts
4th United States[c]
10th United States

2nd Brigade
Colonel Joseph M. Sudsburg
3rd Maryland
21st Massachusetts
100th Pennsylvania

Provisional Brigade
Colonel Elisha G. Marshall
2nd New York Mounted Rifles (Dismounted)
14th New York Heavy Artillery
24th New York Cavalry (Dismounted)
2nd Pennsylvania Provisional Heavy Artillery

Artillery
2nd Maine Light Battery (B)
14th Massachusetts Battery

2ND DIVISION
Brigadier General Robert B. Potter
51st New York (Acting Division Engineers)

1st Brigade
Colonel John I. Curtin
36th Massachusetts
58th Massachusetts
45th Pennsylvania
48th Pennsylvania
7th Rhode Island

2nd Brigade
Colonel Simon G. Griffin
31st Maine
32nd Maine
2nd Maryland
6th New Hampshire
9th New Hampshire
11th New Hampshire
17th Vermont

Artillery
11th Massachusetts Battery
19th New York Battery

3RD DIVISION
Brigadier General Orlando B. Willcox
17th Michigan (Acting Division Engineers)

1st Brigade
Colonel John F. Hartranft
2nd Michigan
8th Michigan
27th Michigan
109th New York
51st Pennsylvania

2nd Brigade
Colonel Benjamin C. Christ
1st Michigan Sharpshooters
20th Michigan
60th Ohio
50th Pennsylvania

Artillery
7th Maine, Battery G
34th New York Battery

4TH DIVISION
Brigadier General Edward Ferrero

1st Brigade
Colonel Joshua K. Sigfried
27th United States Colored Troops
30th United States Colored Troops
39th United States Colored Troops
43rd United States Colored Troops

2nd Brigade
Colonel Henry G. Thomas
19th United States Colored Troops
23rd United States Colored Troops
31st United States Colored Troops

Artillery
Pennsylvania Independent Battery D
3rd Vermont Battery

---

[a] Resigned June 7, replaced June 9 by Brigadier General James Ledlie.
[b] Replaced by Colonel J. F. Gould on June 9.
[c] The U.S. regiments of the 1st Brigade, 1st Division, 9th Corps were assigned to the 1st Brigade, 2nd Division, 5th Corps on June 11.

CAVALRY CORPS
Major General Philip H. Sheridan

1st DIVISION
Brigadier General Alfred T. A. Torbert

1st Brigade
Brigadier General George A. Custer
1st Michigan
5th Michigan
6th Michigan
7th Michigan

2nd Brigade
Colonel Thomas C. Devin
4th New York
6th New York
9th New York
17th Pennsylvania

Reserve Brigade
Brigadier General Wesley Merritt
19th New York (1st Dragoons)
6th Pennsylvania
1st United States
2nd United States
5th United States

2ND DIVISION
Brigadier General David McM. Gregg

1st Brigade
Brigadier General Henry E. Davies Jr.
1st Massachusetts
1st New Jersey
10th New York
6th Ohio
1st Pennsylvania

2nd Brigade
Colonel J. Irvin Gregg
1st Maine
2nd Pennsylvania
4th Pennsylvania
8th Pennsylvania
13th Pennsylvania
16th Pennsylvania

3RD DIVISION
Brigadier General James H. Wilson

1st Brigade
Colonel John B. McIntosh
1st Connecticut
3rd New Jersey
2nd New York
5th New York
2nd Ohio
18th Pennsylvania

2nd Brigade
Colonel George H. Chapman
3rd Indiana
1st New Hampshire
8th New York
22nd New York
1st Vermont

HORSE ARTILLERY

1st Brigade Horse Artillery
Captain James M. Robertson
6th New York Battery
2nd United States, Batteries B and L
2nd United States, Battery D
2nd United States, Battery M
4th United States, Battery A
4th United States, Batteries C and E

2nd Brigade Horse Artillery
Captain Dunbar R. Ransom
1st United States, Batteries E and G
1st United States, Batteries H and I
1st United States, Battery K
2nd United States, Battery A

18TH ARMY CORPS
Major General William F. Smith

1ST DIVISION
Brigadier General William T. H. Brooks

1st Brigade
Brigadier General Gilman Marston
81st New York
96th New York
98th New York
139th New York

2nd Brigade
Brigadier General Hiram Burnham
8th Connecticut
10th New Hampshire
13th New Hampshire
118th New York

3rd Brigade
Colonel Guy V. Henry
21st Connecticut
40th Massachusetts
92nd New York
58th Pennsylvania
188th Pennsylvania

Artillery Brigade
Captain Samuel S. Elder
1st United States, Battery B
4th United States, Battery L
5th United States, Battery A

2ND DIVISION
Brigadier General John H. Martindale

1st Brigade
Brigadier General George J. Stannard
23rd Massachusetts
25th Massachusetts
27th Massachusetts
9th New Jersey
55th Pennsylvania

2nd Brigade
Colonel Griffin A. Stedman Jr.
11th Connecticut
8th Maine
2nd New Hampshire
12th New Hampshire
148th New York
19th Wisconsin

3RD DIVISION
Brigadier General Charles Devens Jr. [a]

1st Brigade
Colonel William B. Barton
47th New York
48th New York
115th New York
76th Pennsylvania

2nd Brigade
Lieutenant Colonel Zina H. Robinson [b]
13th Indiana
9th Maine
112th New York
169th New York

3rd Brigade
Brigadier General Adelbert Ames [c]
4th New Hampshire
3rd New York
117th New York
142nd New York
97th Pennsylvania

---

[a] Relieved June 3, replaced by Brigadier General Adelbert Ames.
[b] Replaced by Colonel Alexander Piper on June 5. Piper replaced by Colonel Newton M. Curtis on June 9.
[c] Replaced by Colonel Henry R. Guess on June 4. Guess replaced by Colonel Louis Bell on June 9.

Army of the James Units
Involved in the June 15 Offensive

Hinks's Division
Brigadier General Edward W. Hinks

1st Brigade
Colonel John H. Holman
5th Massachusetts (Colored) Cavalry (Dismounted)
1st United States Colored Troops
10th United States Colored Troops

2nd Brigade
Colonel Samuel A. Duncan
4th United States Colored Troops
5th United States Colored Troops
6th United States Colored Troops
22nd United States Colored Troops

Artillery Brigade
Captain Frederick M. Follett
3rd New York, Battery B
3rd New York, Battery K
3rd New York, Battery M
New York Light, 7th Battery
New York Light, 16th Battery
1st Rhode Island Light, Battery F
Wisconsin Light, 4th Battery
1st United States, Battery B
4th United States, Battery L
5th United States, Battery A
2nd United States Colored, Battery B

Cavalry Division
Brigadier General August V. Kautz

1st Brigade
Colonel Simon H. Mix
3rd New York
5th Pennsylvania

2nd Brigade
Colonel Samuel P. Spear
1st District of Columbia
11th Pennsylvania

Appendix 2
The Confederate Order of Battle

Army of Northern Virginia
General Robert E. Lee

1st Army Corps
Lieutenant General Richard H. Anderson[a]

Kershaw's Division
Major General Joseph B. Kershaw

Kershaw's Brigade
Colonel John W. Henagan
2nd South Carolina
3rd South Carolina
7th South Carolina
8th South Carolina
15th South Carolina
20th South Carolina
3rd South Carolina Battalion

Humphreys's Brigade
Brigadier General Benjamin G. Humphreys
13th Mississippi
17th Mississippi
18th Mississippi
21st Mississippi

Wofford's Brigade
Brigadier General William T. Wofford
16th Georgia
18th Georgia
24th Georgia
Cobb's (Georgia) Legion
Phillips (Georgia) Legion
3rd Georgia Battalion Sharpshooters

Field's Division
Major General Charles W. Field

Jenkins's Brigade
Colonel John Bratton[c]
1st South Carolina
5th South Carolina
6th South Carolina
2nd South Carolina Rifles
Palmetto Sharpshooters

Gregg's Brigade
Brigadier General John Gregg
3rd Arkansas
1st Texas
4th Texas
5th Texas

Law's Brigade
Brigadier General Evander McIver Law
4th Alabama
15th Alabama
44th Alabama
47th Alabama
48th Alabama

Anderson's Brigade
Brigadier General George T. Anderson
7th Georgia

Pickett's Division
Major General George E. Pickett

Kemper's Brigade
Brigadier General William R. Terry
1st Virginia
3rd Virginia
7th Virginia
11th Virginia
24th Virginia

Hunton's Brigade
Brigadier General Eppa Hunton
8th Virginia
18th Virginia
19th Virginia
28th Virginia
56th Virginia

Barton's Brigade
Brigadier General Seth M. Barton
9th Virginia
14th Virginia
38th Virginia
53rd Virginia
57th Virginia

Artillery
Brigadier General E. Porter Alexander

Haskell's Battalion
Major John C. Haskell
Flanner's (North Carolina) Battery
Garden's (South Carolina) Battery
Lamkin's (Virginia) Battery
Ramsay's (North Carolina) Battery

Huger's Battalion
Lieutenant Colonel Frank Huger
Fickling's (South Carolina) Battery
Moody's (Louisiana) Battery
Parker's (Virginia) Battery
Smith's (Virginia) Battery
Taylor's (Virginia) Battery
Woolfolk's (Virginia) Battery

Cabell's Battalion
Colonel Henry C. Cabell
Callaway's (Georgia) Battery
Carlton's (Georgia) Battery
McCarthy's (Virginia) Battery
Manly's (North Carolina) Battery

Bryan's Brigade
Brigadier General Goode Bryan [b]
10th Georgia
50th Georgia
51st Georgia
53rd Georgia

8th Georgia
9th Georgia
11th Georgia
59th Georgia

Benning's Brigade
Colonel Dudley M. DuBose
2nd Georgia
15th Georgia
17th Georgia
20th Georgia

Corse's Brigade
Brigadier General Montgomery D. Corse
15th Virginia
17th Virginia
29th Virginia
30th Virginia
32nd Virginia

[a] Promoted to lieutenant general on May 31.
[b] Reported sick on June 6, replaced by Colonel James P. Simms.
[c] Promoted to brigadier general on June 9.

2ND ARMY CORPS

Lieutenant General Jubal A. Early[a]

RAMSEUR'S DIVISION
Major General Stephen D. Ramseur

Pegram's Brigade
Brigadier General Robert D. Lilley
13th Virginia
31st Virginia
49th Virginia
52nd Virginia
58th Virginia

Johnston's Brigade
Colonel Thomas F. Toon
5th North Carolina
12th North Carolina
20th North Carolina
23rd North Carolina

Hoke's Brigade
Brigadier General William G. Lewis
6th North Carolina
21st North Carolina
54th North Carolina
57th North Carolina
1st Battalion, North Carolina Sharp-
    shooters

GORDON'S DIVISION
Major General John B. Gordon

Evans's Brigade
Brigadier General Clement A. Evans
13th Georgia
26th Georgia
31st Georgia
38th Georgia
60th Georgia
61st Georgia
12th Georgia Battalion

Louisiana Brigade
Colonel Zebulon York
1st Louisiana
2nd Louisiana
5th Louisiana
6th Louisiana
7th Louisiana
8th Louisiana
9th Louisiana
10th Louisiana
14th Louisiana
15th Louisiana

Terry's Brigade
Brigadier General William Terry
2nd Virginia
4th Virginia
5th Virginia
10th Virginia

RODES'S DIVISION
Major General Robert E. Rodes

Daniel's Brigade
Brigadier General Bryan Grimes
32nd North Carolina
43rd North Carolina
45th North Carolina
53rd North Carolina
2nd North Carolina Battalion

Ramseur's Brigade
Brigadier General William R. Cox
1st North Carolina
2nd North Carolina
3rd North Carolina
4th North Carolina
14th North Carolina
30th North Carolina

Battle's Brigade
Brigadier General Cullen A. Battle
3rd Alabama
5th Alabama
6th Alabama
12th Alabama
61st Alabama

Doles's Brigade
Colonel Philip Cook
4th Georgia
12th Georgia

ARTILLERY
Brigadier General Armistead L. Long

Braxton's Battalion
Lieutenant Colonel Carter M. Braxton
Carpenter's (Virginia) Battery
Cooper's (Virginia) Battery
Hardwicke's (Virginia) Battery

Nelson's Battalion
Lieutenant Colonel William Nelson
Kirkpatrick's (Virginia) Battery
Massie's (Virginia) Battery
Milledge's (Georgia) Battery

Page's Battalion
Major Richard C. M. Page
Carter's (Virginia) Battery
Fry's (Virginia) Battery
Page's (Virginia) Battery
Reese's (Alabama) Battery

Cutshaw's Battalion
Major Wilfred E. Cutshaw
Carrington's (Virginia) Battery
Garber's (Virginia) Battery
Tanner's (Virginia) Battery

Hardaway's Battalion
Lieutenant Colonel Robert A. Hardaway
Dance's (Virginia) Battery

21st Virginia
23rd Virginia
25th Virginia
27th Virginia
33rd Virginia
37th Virginia
42nd Virginia
44th Virginia
48th Virginia
50th Virginia

21st Georgia
44th Georgia

Graham's (Virginia) Battery
Griffin's (Virginia) Battery
Jones's (Virginia) Battery
Smith's (Virginia) Battery

[a] Promoted to lieutenant general on May 31.

3RD ARMY CORPS
Lieutenant General Ambrose P. Hill

MAHONE'S DIVISION
Brigadier General William Mahone

Sanders's Brigade
Colonel John C. C. Sanders
8th Alabama
9th Alabama
10th Alabama
11th Alabama
14th Alabama

Mahone's Brigade
Colonel David A. Weisiger
6th Virginia
12th Virginia
16th Virginia
41st Virginia
61st Virginia

Harris's Brigade
Brigadier General Nathaniel H. Harris
12th Mississippi
16th Mississippi
19th Mississippi
48th Mississippi

Finegan's Brigade
Brigadier General Joseph Finegan
2nd Florida
5th Florida
8th Florida
9th Florida

HETH'S DIVISION
Major General Henry Heth

Davis's Brigade
Brigadier General Joseph R. Davis
2nd Mississippi
11th Mississippi
26th Mississippi
42nd Mississippi
55th North Carolina
1st Confederate Battalion

Cooke's Brigade
Brigadier General John R. Cooke
15th North Carolina
27th North Carolina
46th North Carolina
48th North Carolina

Walker's Brigade
Brigadier General Birkett D. Fry
13th Alabama
1st Tennessee (Provisional)
7th Tennessee
14th Tennessee
40th Virginia
47th Virginia
55th Virginia
22nd Virginia Battalion

Kirkland's Brigade
Colonel George H. Faribault

WILCOX'S DIVISION
Major General Cadmus M. Wilcox

Lane's Brigade
Colonel John D. Barry
7th North Carolina
18th North Carolina
28th North Carolina
33rd North Carolina
37th North Carolina

McGowan's Brigade
Lieutenant Colonel J. F. Hunt
1st South Carolina (Provisional)
12th South Carolina
13th South Carolina
14th South Carolina
1st South Carolina (Orr's) Rifles

Scales's Brigade
Colonel William L. Lowrance
13th North Carolina
16th North Carolina
22nd North Carolina
34th North Carolina
38th North Carolina

Thomas's Brigade
Brigadier General Edward L. Thomas
14th Georgia
35th Georgia
45th Georgia
49th Georgia

ARTILLERY
Colonel R. Lindsay Walker

Poague's Battalion
Lieutenant Colonel William T. Poague
Richard's (Mississippi) Battery
Utterback's (Virginia) Battery
Williams's (North Carolina) Battery
Wyatt's (Virginia) Battery

Pegram's Battalion
Lieutenant Colonel William J. Pegram
Brander's (Virginia) Battery
Cayce's (Virginia) Battery
Ellett's (Virginia) Battery
Marye's (Virginia) Battery
Zimmerman's (South Carolina) Battery

McIntosh's Battalion
Lieutenant Colonel David G. McIntosh
Clutter's (Virginia) Battery
Donald's (Virginia) Battery
Hurt's (Alabama) Battery
Price's (Virginia) Battery

Richardson's Battalion
Lieutenant Colonel Charles Richardson
Grandy's (Virginia) Battery
Landry's (Louisiana) Battery
Moore's (Virginia) Battery
Penick's (Virginia) Battery

10th Florida
11th Florida

Wright's Brigade
Brigadier General Ambrose R. Wright
3rd Georgia
22nd Georgia
48th Georgia
2nd Georgia Battalion
10th Georgia Battalion

11th North Carolina
26th North Carolina
44th North Carolina
47th North Carolina
52nd North Carolina

Cutt's Battalion
Colonel Allen S. Cutts
Patterson's (Georgia) Battery
Ross's (Georgia) Battery
Wingfield's (Georgia) Battery

CAVALRY CORPS
Major General Wade Hampton[a]

HAMPTON'S DIVISION
Major General Wade Hampton

Young's Brigade
Colonel Gilbert J. Wright
7th Georgia
Cobb's (Georgia) Legion
Jeff Davis (Mississippi) Legion
Phillips (Georgia) Legion
20th Georgia Battalion

Rosser's Brigade
Brigadier General Thomas L. Rosser
7th Virginia
11th Virginia
12th Virginia
35th Virginia Battalion

Butler's Brigade
Brigadier General Matthew C. Butler
4th South Carolina
5th South Carolina
6th South Carolina

FITZHUGH LEE'S DIVISION
Major General Fitzhugh Lee

Lomax's Brigade
Brigadier General Lunsford L. Lomax
1st Maryland Cavalry
5th Virginia
6th Virginia
15th Virginia

Wickham's Brigade
Brigadier General Williams C. Wickham
1st Virginia
2nd Virginia
3rd Virginia
4th Virginia

WILLIAM H. F. LEE'S DIVISION
Major General William H. F. Lee

Chambliss's Brigade
Brigadier General John R. Chambliss
9th Virginia
10th Virginia
13th Virginia

Gordon's Brigade
Colonel Rufus Barringer
1st North Carolina
2nd North Carolina
3rd North Carolina
5th North Carolina

Gary's Brigade[b]
Brigadier General Martin W. Gary
7th South Carolina Cavalry
24th Virginia Cavalry
Hampton (South Carolina) Legion

HORSE ARTILLERY
Major R. Preston Chew

Breathed's Battalion
Major James Breathed
Hart's (South Carolina) Battery
Johnston's (Virginia) Battery
McGregor's (Virginia) Battery
Shoemaker's (Virginia) Battery
Thomson's (Virginia) Battery

---

[a] Following Major General J. E. B. Stuart's death on May 12, 1864, General Robert E. Lee left the top position in his cavalry corps unfilled. Hampton was the senior division commander and thus also acted as corps commander.

[b] Assigned to the Department of Richmond but operated in tandem with William H. F. Lee's Division.

BRECKINRIDGE'S DIVISION
Major General John C. Breckinridge

Echols's Brigade
Brigadier General John Echols[a]
22nd Virginia
23rd Virginia Battalion
26th Virginia Battalion

Wharton's Brigade
Brigadier General Gabriel C. Wharton
51st Virginia
62nd Virginia Mounted (Dismounted)
30th Virginia Battalion

McLaughlin's Artillery Battalion
Major William McLaughlin
Chapman's (Virginia) Battery
Jackson's (Virginia) Battery

Maryland Line
Colonel Bradley T. Johnson
2nd Maryland
1st Maryland Battery
2nd Maryland Battery
4th Maryland Battery

---

[a] Ill during much of the campaign, temporarily replaced by Colonel George S. Patton.

Department of North Carolina and Southern Virginia
General Pierre G. T. Beauregard

Johnson's Division
Major General Bushrod R. Johnson

Elliott's Brigade
Brigadier General Stephen Elliott
17th South Carolina
18th South Carolina
22nd South Carolina
23rd South Carolina
26th South Carolina
Holcombe (South Carolina) Legion

Johnson's Brigade
Colonel John S. Fulton
17th Tennessee
23rd Tennessee
25th Tennessee
44th Tennessee
63rd Tennessee

Wise's Brigade
Colonel Powhatan Robertson Page
26th Virginia
34th Virginia
46th Virginia
59th Virginia

Gracie's Brigade
Brigadier General Archibald Gracie
41st Alabama
43rd Alabama
59th Alabama

Hoke's Division
Major General Robert F. Hoke

Martin's Brigade
Brigadier General James G. Martin
17th North Carolina
42nd North Carolina
66th North Carolina

Clingman's Brigade
Brigadier General Thomas L. Clingman
8th North Carolina
31st North Carolina
51st North Carolina
61st North Carolina

Hagood's Brigade
Brigadier General Johnson Hagood
11th South Carolina
21st South Carolina
25th South Carolina
27th South Carolina
7th South Carolina Battalion

Colquitt's Brigade
Brigadier General Alfred H. Colquitt
6th Georgia
19th Georgia
23rd Georgia
27th Georgia
28th Georgia

First Military District
Brigadier General Henry A. Wise

Dimmock Line Garrison
Brigadier General Raleigh Colston
64th Georgia Infantry
Colonel John W. Evans
44th Virginia Militia Battalion (Petersburg City Battalion)
Major Peter V. Batte
Archer's Petersburg Militia
Major Fletcher H. Archer
Hood's Militia Battalion
Major Thomas H. Bond

Dearing's Cavalry Brigade
Brigadier General James Dearing
7th Confederate
4th North Carolina
6th North Carolina
62nd Georgia Mounted Infantry
Barham's Virginia Battalion
Graham's Virginia Light Artillery Battery

Boggs's Artillery Battalion
Major Francis J. Boggs
Martin's (Virginia) Battery
Sturdivant's (Virginia) Battery

60th Alabama
23rd Alabama Battalion

Ransom's Brigade
Brigadier General Matthew W. Ransom

24th North Carolina
25th North Carolina
35th North Carolina
49th North Carolina
56th North Carolina

Mosley's Artillery Battalion
Major Edgar F. Mosley
Cumming's (North Carolina) Battery
Miller's (North Carolina) Battery
Slaten's (Georgia) Battery
Young's (Virginia) Battery

Coit's Artillery Battalion
Major James C. Coit
Bradford's (Mississippi) Battery
Kelly's (South Carolina) Battery
Pegram's (Virginia) Battery
Wright's (Virginia) Battery

Read's Artillery Battalion
Major John P. W. Read
Blount's (Virginia) Battery
Caskie's (Virginia) Battery
Macon's (Virginia) Battery
Marshall's (Virginia) Battery

Notes

Abbreviations

B&L	Clarence C. Buel and Robert U. Johnson, eds., *Battles and Leaders of the Civil War,* 4 vols. (New York, 1884–88)
DU	William R. Perkins Library, Duke University, Durham, N.C.
FSNMP	Fredericksburg and Spotsylvania National Military Park
GDAH	Georgia Department of Archives and History, Atlanta
HSP	Historical Society of Pennsylvania, Philadelphia
HU	"Correspondence Relative to the March of Barlow's Division, 2nd Army Corps, from the James River to Petersburg, Va., June 15th 1864," Houghton Library, Harvard University, Cambridge, Mass.
LC	Manuscript Division, Library of Congress
MC	Eleanor S. Brockenbrough Library, Museum of the Confederacy, Richmond
MHS	Massachusetts Historical Society, Boston
ORN	*Official Records of the Union and Confederate Navies in the War of the Rebellion,* 30 vols. (Washington, D.C. 1894–1922).
NYSLA	New York State Library and Archives, Albany
OCHS	Ontario County Historical Society, Canandaigua, N.Y.
OR	*The War of the Rebellion: A Compilation of Official Records of the Union and Confederate Armies,* 130 vols. (Washington, D.C., 1880–1901)
PMHSM	*Papers of the Military Historical Society of Massachusetts,* 14 vols. (Boston, 1881–1918)
PNBP	Petersburg National Battlefield Park
PUSG	John Y. Simon, ed., *The Papers of Ulysses S. Grant,* 20 vols. (Carbondale, Ill., 1967–99)
RNBP	Richmond National Battlefield Park
SHC	Southern Historical Collection, University of North Carolina, Raleigh

SHSP   *Southern Historical Society Papers,* 49 vols. (Richmond, 1876–1944)
USAMHI U.S. Army Military History Institute, Carlisle, Pa.
USC   South Caroliniana Library, University of South Carolina, Columbia
VHS   Virginia Historical Society, Richmond
VSL   Virginia State Library, Richmond

Chapter I

1. Dickert, *History of Kershaw's Brigade,* 375–76; Stocker, *From Huntsville to Appomattox,* 177.

2. Members of the Regiment, *Story of the 21st Regiment, Connecticut Volunteer Infantry,* 245; Walker, *History of the Second Army Corps,* 514; Bartlett, *History of the Twelfth Regiment, New Hampshire Volunteers,* 207; Derby, *Bearing Arms in the Twenty-Seventh Massachusetts,* 306–7; Emmerton, *Record of the Twenty-Third Regiment Massachusetts Volunteer Infantry,* 208–9. Details of the June 3 assault are in Rhea, *Cold Harbor,* 318–64.

3. Stocker, *From Huntsville to Appomattox,* 177.

4. Members of the Regiment, *Story of the 21st Regiment, Connecticut Volunteer Infantry,* 240.

5. Ulysses S. Grant's report, *OR,* vol. 36, pt. 1, pp. 12–13; Grant, *Personal Memoirs,* 2:473.

6. Favill, *Diary of a Young Officer,* 261. See also Hennessy, "I Dread the Spring," 67–70; Schiller, *Autobiography of Major General William F. Smith,* 83; and Sparks, *Inside Lincoln's Army,* 330.

7. Grant's report, *OR,* vol. 36, pt. 1, p. 18.

8. Rufus Ingalls's report, *OR,* vol. 36, pt. 1, pp 276–78; Army of the Potomac's report, Apr. 30, 1864, ibid., vol. 33, p. 1036.

9. Grant to Henry W. Halleck, Jan. 19, 1864, ibid., vol. 33, p. 395.

10. Halleck to Grant, Feb. 17, 1864, ibid., vol. 32, pt. 2, p. 411.

11. Grant to Benjamin F. Butler, Apr. 2, 1864, ibid., vol. 33, pp. 794–95; Grant to Butler, Apr. 16, 1864, ibid., 885–86.

12. Lowe, *Meade's Army,* 187; Longacre, *Army of Amateurs,* 35; Grant to Halleck, 7:00 A.M., May 21, 1864, *OR,* vol. 36, pt. 3, p. 43; Rockwell, "Tenth Army Corps in Virginia," 269. For a fuller sketch of Smith, see Schiller, *Autobiography of Major General William F. Smith.*

13. Grant to William T. Sherman, Apr. 4, 1864, *OR,* vol. 32, pt. 3, p 246; Grant to George G. Meade, Apr. 9, 1864, ibid., vol. 33, p. 828. As Brian Holden Reid points out, Grant's spring campaign was essentially opportunistic in that the coordinated army commanders were to "strive both to seek out and take advantage of opportunities to destroy Lee's army." Reid, "Another Look at Grant's Crossing of the James," 293.

14. *Augusta (Ga.) Constitutionalist,* Jan. 2, 1864; James Longstreet to Alexander Lawton, Mar. 5, 1864, *OR,* vol. 32, pt. 3, p. 588.

15. McCaslin, *Lee in the Shadow of Washington,* 93; Gordon C. Rhea, *In the Footsteps of Grant and Lee* (Baton Rouge, 2007), 9–10.

16. Buck, *With the Old Confeds,* 102. Morale in Lee's army during the Overland Campaign is fully addressed in Power, *Lee's Miserables,* and Gallagher, "Our Hearts Are Full of Hope."

17. Robert E. Lee to Jefferson Davis, Apr. 15, 1864, *OR,* vol. 33, pp. 1282–83.

18. Francis Marion Welchel to family, Apr. 26, 1864, Book 81, FSNMP.

19. Grant, *Personal Memoirs*, 2:151–52. Butler's operations are detailed in Schiller, *Bermuda Hundred Campaign*, and W. Robertson, *Backdoor to Richmond*.

20. Grant to Halleck, May 22, 1864, *OR*, vol. 36, pt. 3, p. 77.

21. Details of Lee's decision to configure his army into a wedge below the North Anna are in Rhea, *To the North Anna River*, 320–24.

22. James C. Biddle to wife, June 5, 1864, George G. Meade Collection, HSP.

23. Grant to Halleck, May 26, 1864, *OR*, vol. 36, pt. 3, pp. 206–7.

24. Porter, *Campaigning with Grant*, 172. Grant's reasons for launching his big attack at Cold Harbor on the morning of June 3 are discussed in Rhea, *Cold Harbor*, 312–17.

25. Agassiz, *Meade's Headquarters*, 100.

26. J. D. Smith, *History of the Nineteenth Regiment of Maine Volunteer Infantry*, 188–89.

27. Muffly, *Story of Our Regiment*, 484; Billings, *History of the Tenth Massachusetts Battery*, 200; Frederick Mather recollections, *Albany (N.Y.) Evening Journal*, Oct. 23, 1895; O. G. Wright letter, June 6, 1864, *Wilmington (N.C.) Daily Journal*, June 20, 1864.

28. Nichols to family, June 6, 1864, *Niagara Falls (N.Y.) Gazette*, Aug. 23, 1938; Armstrong, *Nuggets of Experience*, 50; W. I. Hallock to editor, *National Tribune*, Aug. 24, 1893.

29. Abbott, *Personal Recollections*, 74–75; Hagood, *Memoirs*, 260.

30. Bartlett, *History of the Twelfth Regiment, New Hampshire Volunteers*, 202–3, 208; William C. Oates, *The War between the Union and the Confederacy and Its Lost Opportunities* (New York, 1905), 366–67; Members of the Regiment, *Story of the 21st Regiment, Connecticut Volunteer Infantry*, 238; Rawle, *History of the Third Pennsylvania Cavalry, Sixtieth Regiment Pennsylvania Volunteers*, 433.

31. Nevins, *Diary of Battle*, 405–6.

32. R. Roy, *New York Daily News*, June 23, 1864.

33. Grant, *Personal Memoirs*, 2:272.

34. Lawhon, "Forty-Eighth Regiment," 120; Theodore Lyman to family, June 3, 1864, in Agassiz, *Meade's Headquarters*, 148.

35. Charles S. Venable, "Campaign from the Wilderness to Petersburg," in *SHSP*, 14:536. Casualties on June 3, 1864, are analyzed in Rhea, *Cold Harbor*, 358–62, 385–86.

36. Lyman, "Operations of the Army of the Potomac," 5; Halleck to Grant, June 7, 1864, *OR*, vol. 36, pt. 3, p. 665; Meyers, *Ten Years in the Ranks*, 320.

37. Joseph H. Pierce to Julie, June 9, 1864, Lewis Leigh Collection, USAMHI; Ford, *Cycle of Adams Letters*, 2:140; Martha Derby Perry, comp., *Letters from a Surgeon of the Civil War* (Boston, 1906), 187–88; Malles, *Bridge Building in Wartime*, 234.

38. Emory Upton to Sister, June 5, 1864, in Michie, *Life and Letters of Emory Upton*, 109; Nevins, *Diary of Battle*, 406; Ford, *Cycle of Adams Letters*, 2:142; Silliker, *Rebel Yell and the Yankee Hurrah*, 165.

39. Davis, *Three Years in the Army*, 364.

40. Ford, *Cycle of Adams Letters*, 2:133–34.

41. A. Humphreys, *Virginia Campaign*, 83n1; Meade, *Life and Letters*, 2:201; Theodore Lyman journal, June 4, 1864, Thomas Lyman Letters and Journal, MHS; Biddle to wife, June 5, 1864, George G. Meade Collection, HSP; J. Wilson, *Under the Old Flag*, 1:443–44.

42. J. Wilson, *Under the Old Flag*, 1:443.

43. Ibid., 402, 443; Badeau, *Military History of General Ulysses S. Grant*, 2:186–87; Porter, *Campaigning with Grant*, 115.

44. Meade, *Life and Letters*, 2:200–201.

45. Grant to Nellie, June 4, 1864, in *PUSG,* 11:18.

46. Dana, *Recollections,* 214–15.

47. *Genesee County (N.Y.) Spirit of the Times,* June 11, 1864, quoted in Dunn, *Full Measure of Devotion,* 2:347–48.

48. Lyman, "Operations of the Army of the Potomac," 4; Houston, *Thirty-Second Maine Regiment,* 241–42.

49. Lyman, "Operations of the Army of the Potomac," 5.

50. Duncan, *Lee's Endangered Left,* 258–60.

51. Greene, *Civil War Petersburg,* 4–5.

52. Sumner, *Diary of Cyrus B. Comstock,* 271–72; Biddle to wife, June 5, 1864, George G. Meade Collection, HSP.

53. Halleck's suggestion is described in Porter, *Campaigning with Grant,* 182; and A. Humphreys, *Virginia Campaign,* 194. It is referenced in Grant to Halleck, June 5, 1864, *OR,* vol. 36, pt. 1, p. 11.

54. A. Humphreys, *Virginia Campaign,* 187–88.

55. Grant to Meade, 12:30 P.M., June 3, 1864, *OR,* vol. 36, pt. 3, p. 526.

56. Meade to Grant, and Grant's endorsement, 9:25 P.M., June 3, 1864, ibid., 527.

57. Edward A. T. Nicholson to niece, June 16, 1864, Edward P. Alexander Collection, SHC; James Conner to mother, June 5, 1864, in Moffett, *Letters of General James Conner,* 134.

58. Confederate losses are detailed in Young, *Lee's Army during the Overland Campaign.*

59. Venable, "General Lee in the Wilderness Campaign," 244; Walter H. Taylor to Bettie, June 1, 1864, Taylor Papers, Norfolk Public Library, Va.; Rhea, *To the North Anna River,* 345n55.

60. Ford, *Cycle of Adams Letters,* 2:143.

61. Daniel Boyd to sisters, June 9, 1864, Boyd Family Papers, SHC.

62. John Tyler to Sterling Price, June 7, 1864, *OR,* vol. 51, pt. 2, p. 994.

Chapter II

1. Nathaniel Michler's report, *OR,* vol. 1, pt. 1, p. 302.

2. Special correspondence, June 4, 1864, *Philadelphia Inquirer,* June 8, 1864; Everts, *History of the Ninth Regiment New Jersey Volunteer Infantry,* 120.

3. Walker, *History of the Second Army Corps,* 522–23; Walker, *General Hancock,* 227–29; Hancock's report, *OR,* vol. 36, pt. 1, p. 346; Kreiser, "From Volunteers to Veterans," 243. During the fighting on June 3, the 2nd Corps lost eight colonels, two of whom commanded brigades.

4. Priest, *One Surgeon's Private War,* 107; Thomas Smyth diary, June 4, 1864, Delaware Public Archives, Dover; Armes, *Ups and Downs of an Army Officer,* 97–98; special correspondence, *Philadelphia Inquirer,* June 8, 1864; Walker, *History of the Second Army Corps,* 519.

5. Stewart, *History of the One Hundred and Fortieth Regiment Pennsylvania Volunteers,* 211; Child, *History of the Fifth Regiment, New Hampshire Volunteers,* 254.

6. Miller, *Drum Taps in Dixie,* 110; Stewart, *History of the One Hundred and Fortieth Regiment Pennsylvania Volunteers,* 211; Mulholland, *Story of the 116th Regiment Pennsylvania Volunteers,* 257.

7. Muffly, *Story of Our Regiment,* 131; FCFR letter, *Mobile Advertiser and Register,* June 17, 1864.

8. H. W. Long, "Reminiscence of the Battle of Cold Harbor," RNBP; Hillhouse, *Heavy Artillery and Light Infantry,* 83. A copy of Long's manuscript is also available in United Daughters of the Confederacy Scrapbooks, 12 vols., Florida State Library, Tallahassee, vol. 1.

9. Keating, *Carnival of Blood,* 153; *New York Times,* June 9, 1864. The Confederate sharpshooter who killed Colonel Morris had become known to the Federals as "Broadbrim" because of his distinctive headgear. He was shot in the head later that day.

10. Rhea, *Cold Harbor,* 336; George A. Bowen diary, June 3–4, 1864, FSNMP; Banes, *History of the Philadelphia Brigade,* 274.

11. Robert Gumaer letter, June 4, 1864, *Batavia (N.Y.) Republican Advocate,* June 1864, quoted in Dunn, *Full Measure of Devotion,* 2:318; Bruce, *Twentieth Regiment of Massachusetts Volunteer Infantry,* 394; Aubery, *Thirty-Sixth Wisconsin Volunteer Infantry,* 81; Turino, *Civil War Diary of Lieut. J. E. Hodgkins,* 91–92.

12. Armstrong, *Nuggets of Experience,* 51.

13. Gibbon, *Personal Recollections,* 234–36; John Gibbon to wife, June 4, 1864, Gibbon Collection, Maryland Historical Society; Sumner, *Diary of Cyrus B. Comstock,* 271; *San Francisco Evening Bulletin,* July 5, 1864.

14. Thomas Hyde to mother, June 3, 1864, in J. Hyde, *Civil War Letters by General Thomas Hyde,* 139; Westbrook, *History of the 49th Pennsylvania Volunteers,* 206.

15. Haines, *History of the Fifteenth Regiment New Jersey Volunteers,* 208–9; Charles R. Paul diary, June 4, 1864, Murray J. Smith Collection, USAMHI.

16. Haines, *History of the Fifteenth Regiment New Jersey Volunteers,* 210; Baquet, *History of the First Brigade, New Jersey Volunteers,* 130; Wray, *History of the Twenty-Third Pennsylvania Volunteer Infantry,* 114.

17. John C. Arnold letter, June 5, 1864, Civil War Miscellaneous Collection, USAMHI; Westbrook, *History of the 49th Pennsylvania Volunteers,* 206.

18. Oliver Edwards's report, *OR,* vol. 36, pt. 1, p. 675; Charles A. Whittier reminiscences, Boston Public Library, 14–15.

19. Henry to dear brother, June 3, 1864, *Herkimer County (N.Y.) Journal and Courier,* June 23, 1864; Vaill, *History of the Second Connecticut Volunteer Heavy Artillery,* 67; Best, *History of the 121st New York State Infantry,* 158; "Headquarters, Army of the Potomac, June 4, 8 P.M.," *Philadelphia Inquirer,* June 8, 1864.

20. William S. Truex's report, *OR,* vol. 36, pt. 1, p. 727; John W. Horn's report, ibid., 739.

21. Map in Hazard Stevens to mother, June 6, 1864, Knight Library, University of Oregon; Frank Wheaton's report, *OR,* vol. 36, pt. 1, pp. 689–90.

22. Mark, *Red, White, and Blue Badge,* 273; Bowen, *History of the Thirty-Seventh Regiment Massachusetts Volunteers,* 334; Samuel E. Pingree to Cousin Hunton, June 10, 1864, Vermont Historical Society.

23. Greiner et al., *Surgeon's Civil War,* 196; David A. Stohl to Col. H. C. Eyer, June 5, 1864, Susan Boardman Collection, USAMHI; Page, *Letters of a War Correspondent,* 100.

24. Stevens, *Three Years in the Sixth Corps,* 354; Henry Keiser diary, June 4, 1864, Harrisburg Civil War Round Table Collection, USAMHI; Carleton letter, June 5, 1864, *Boston Evening Journal,* June 9, 1864.

25. Page, *Letters of a War Correspondent,* 94.

26. Guy Henry's report, *OR,* vol. 36, pt. 1, p. 1013; Gilman Marston's report, ibid., 1006; Charles M. Coit's report, ibid., 1010.

27. Bartlett, *History of the Twelfth Regiment, New Hampshire Volunteers,* 209; Derby, "Star Brigade," 134; Everts, *History of the Ninth Regiment New Jersey Volunteer Infantry,* 120; S. Thompson, *Thirteenth Regiment of New Hampshire Volunteer Infantry,* 361.

28. Hiram Burnham's report, *OR,* vol. 36, pt. 1, p 1009; Members of the Regiment, *Story of the 21st Regiment, Connecticut Volunteer Infantry,* 240.

29. Members of the Regiment, *Story of the 21st Regiment, Connecticut Volunteer Infantry,* 244; Bartlett, *History of the Twelfth Regiment, New Hampshire Volunteers,* 209–10; Joseph Waldo Denny, *Address Delivered at Second Reunion K Association, 25th Massachusetts Volunteers, at Worcester, Mass., September 26, 1870* (Boston, 1871), 24.

30. Members of the Regiment, *Story of the 21st Regiment, Connecticut Volunteer Infantry,* 240, 243; Everts, *History of the Ninth Regiment New Jersey Volunteer Infantry,* 120; Bartlett, *History of the Twelfth Regiment, New Hampshire Volunteers,* 212; S. Thompson, *Thirteenth Regiment of New Hampshire Volunteer Infantry,* 362–63.

31. Emmerton, *Record of the Twenty-Third Regiment Massachusetts Volunteer Infantry,* 211.

32. DeForest, *Random Sketches,* 159; S. Thompson, *Thirteenth Regiment of New Hampshire Volunteer Infantry,* 368; Emmerton, *Record of the Twenty-Third Regiment Massachusetts Volunteer Infantry,* 208–9. Stannard received treatment for a leg wound inflicted during the fight. A piece of shell hit the top of his boot, but the thick leather blunted its force, and the fragment scarcely penetrated his skin.

33. Members of the Regiment, *Story of the 21st Regiment, Connecticut Volunteer Infantry,* 244.

34. William F. Smith's report, *OR,* vol. 36, pt. 1, p. 1005; Elias A. Bryant diary, June 3, 1864, USAMHI; Price, *History of the Ninety-Seventh Regiment Pennsylvania Volunteer Infantry,* 287–88.

35. Emmerton, *Record of the Twenty-Third Regiment Massachusetts Volunteer Infantry,* 211.

36. Members of the Regiment, *Story of the 21st Regiment, Connecticut Volunteer Infantry,* 244–45; Guy Henry's report, *OR,* vol. 36, pt. 1, p. 1013; Aaron F. Stevens's report, ibid., 1012; Coit's report, ibid., 1010; Burnham's report, ibid., 1009.

37. Nevins, *Diary of Battle,* 405.

38. Ibid., 406; Daniel Reed Larned to sister, June 5, 1864, Daniel Reed Larned Letters, LC.

39. Grant to Meade, 12:30 P.M., June 3, 1864, *OR,* vol. 36, pt. 3, p. 526; Meade to Grant, 5:45 P.M., June 3, 1864, ibid., 526.

40. Early, *Autobiographical Sketch and Narrative,* 363; Walter H. Taylor to Richard H. Anderson, June 4, 1864, Edward P. Alexander Collection, SHC; Early to Lee, 8:30 P.M., June 3, 1864, *OR,* vol. 51, pt. 1, pp. 245–46; *Our Living and Our Dead,* Apr. 15, 1874; J. A. Lineback diary, June 4, 1864, *Winston-Salem (N.C.) Sentinel,* Jan. 9, 1915; Birkett D. Fry account, in R. Cook, "Last Time I Saw General Lee," 287; Henry Heth's report, MC.

41. Early to Lee, 8:30 P.M., June 3, 1864, *OR,* vol. 51, pt. 1, p. 246.

42. *Sixty-Second Pennsylvania Volunteers,* 28; J. Parker, *Henry Wilson's Regiment,* 463; Tomasak, *Avery Harris Civil War Journal,* 147; Jacob B. Sweitzer to Charles Griffin, 5:00 A.M., June 4, 1864, *OR,* vol. 36, pt. 3, p. 580; Gouverneur K. Warren to Andrew A. Humphreys, 6:45 A.M., June 4, 1864, ibid., 576.

43. Ambrose Burnside to George G. Meade, 6:05 A.M., June 4, 1864, *OR,* vol. 36, pt. 3, p. 583; Hopkins, *Seventh Regiment Rhode Island Volunteers,* 186–87; William C. Beck, "Washington to Petersburg with the Ninth Army Corps," read at the reunion of the 19th New York Battery,

Oct. 27, 1891, Niagara County Historian's Office, Lockport, N.Y., 5; Page, *Letters of a War Correspondent,* 100.

44. Stone, *Personal Recollections,* 172–73.

45. Meade to Warren, 7:45 A.M., June 4, 1864, *OR,* vol. 36, pt. 3, p. 576.

46. Seth Williams circular, 7:15 A.M., June 4, 1864, ibid., 570–71.

47. Sweitzer to Griffin, 5:00 A.M., June 4, 1864, ibid., 580; Burnside to Meade, 6:05 A.M., June 4, 1864, ibid., 583; Warren to Humphreys, 6:40 A.M., June 4, 1864, ibid., 576; Humphreys to Warren, 7:30 A.M., June 4, 1864, ibid.; Meade to Warren, 7:45 A.M., June 4, 1864, ibid., 576; Smith to Humphreys, received 8:30 A.M., June 4, 1864, ibid., 588; Humphreys to Smith, 9:20 A.M., June 4, 1864, ibid.

48. Agassiz, *Meade's Headquarters,* 240. Washington Roebling's father, John A. Roebling, had constructed the Niagara Railway suspension bridge before the war, and Washington went on after the war to complete the Brooklyn Bridge, the longest suspension bridge in the world at the time. His fiancé and later wife was Emily Warren, General Warren's sister.

49. Roebling's report, June 4, 1864, Gouverneur K. Warren Collection, NYSLA; Warren to Meade, 10:00 A.M., June 4, 1864, *OR,* vol. 36, pt. 3, p. 577; Meade to Warren, 11:00 A.M., June 4, 1864, ibid.; Burnside's general order, June 4, 1864, ibid., 587.

50. Humphreys to Meade, 2:45 P.M., June 4, 1864, *OR,* vol. 36, pt. 3, p. 585.

51. Meade and Sheridan's disagreement during the movement to Spotsylvania Court House is described in Rhea, *Battles for Spotsylvania Court House,* 67–69. See also George G. Meade to wife, May 19, 1864, Meade Collection, HSP.

52. Myers, *The Comanches,* 291; Gamma letter, May 26, 1864, *Mobile Daily Advertiser and Register,* June 2, 1864; Special Orders 126, May 14, 1864, *OR,* vol. 36, pt. 2, p. 1001.

53. Page, *Letters of a War Correspondent,* 123; George M. Gilchrist to mother, June 4, 1864, LC.

54. J. Wilson, *Under the Old Flag,* 1:434.

55. Humphreys to Sheridan, June 3, 10:00 P.M., *OR,* vol. 36, pt. 3, pp. 558–59; Humphreys to Wilson, June 3, 10:15 P.M., ibid., 562. Hoping to get a full account of his day's work to Meade, Wilson dispatched his engineer, Capt. H. A. Ulffers, to army headquarters. Ulffers, however, lost his way and apparently rode instead into General Lee's headquarters. He was captured and taken to Lee but revealed, according to Wilson, "only what he thought would add to the night's confusion." The captain was sent off to prison the next day. Ultimately he escaped and joined Sherman's army near Savannah. J. Wilson, *Under the Old Flag,* 1:434–36.

56. Wilson to Humphreys, June 4, 7:00 A.M., *OR,* vol. 36, pt. 3, p. 591; J. Wilson, *Under the Old Flag,* 1:438–39.

57. W. H. Arehart diary, *Rockingham (N.C.) Recorder,* June 3, 4, 1864; Myers, *The Comanches,* 293; McDonald, *History of the Laurel Brigade,* 248–49; M. Thompson, "From the Ranks to Brigade Commander," 301; Tenney, *War Diary,* 118; George Purrington's report, *OR,* vol. 36, pt.1, p. 896; James H. Wilson diary, June 4, 1864, LC.

58. Wells, *Sketch of the Charleston Light Dragoons,* 56–57; John Cumming to "My Dear Carry", June 6, 7, 1864, John Cumming Letters, DU.

59. Robert E. Lee to Pierre G. T. Beauregard, 4:00 P.M., June 1, 1864, *OR,* vol. 36, pt. 3, p. 865.

60. Beauregard to Braxton Bragg, ibid., 870; Graham, "Fifty-Sixth Regiment," 358.

61. Bragg to Beauregard, 9:00 P.M., June 3, 1864, *OR,* vol. 36, pt. 3, p. 871; Beauregard to

Bragg, June 3, 1864, ibid., 871–72; Beauregard to Bragg, June 4, 1864, ibid., 874; William N. Pendleton's report, *OR,* vol. 36, pt. 1, p. 1051.

62. Well A. Bushnell memoirs, Palmer Regimental Papers, Western Reserve Historical Society, Cleveland, 280; Pyne, *Ride to War,* 215; Preston, *History of the Tenth Regiment of Cavalry, New York State Volunteers,* 194.

63. Robert Ransom to Taylor, 5:30 P.M., June 4, 1864, *OR,* vol. 51, pt. 2, p. 986; Ransom to Bragg, 10:30 P.M., June 4, 1864, ibid., 987; Fitzhugh Lee's report, MC; J. D. Ferguson memoranda, DU.

64. Lyman, "Operations of the Army of the Potomac," 3.

65. Agassiz, *Meade's Headquarters,* 148–49; Theodore Lyman journal, June 4, 1864, Thomas Lyman Letters and Journal, MHS; Lyman, "Operations of the Army of the Potomac," 10.

66. Burnside's report, *OR,* vol. 36, pt. 1, p. 914; Potter's report, ibid., 930; Burnside to Meade, 2:30 P.M., June 4, 1864, ibid., pt. 3, p. 585; Jackman and Hadley, *History of the Sixth New Hampshire Regiment,* 279.

67. Agassiz, *Meade's Headquarters,* 149; Larned to sister, June 5, 1864, Daniel Reed Larned Letters, LC.

68. Larned to sister, June 9, 1864, ibid.; Jackman and Hadley, *History of the Sixth New Hampshire Regiment,* 278.

69. Cheek and Pointon, *History of the Salk County Riflemen,* 107–8; Curtis, *History of the Twenty-Fourth Michigan,* 257.

70. Warren to Humphreys, 9:30 P.M., June 4, 1864, *OR,* vol. 36, pt. 3, p. 678; Warren to Lysander Cutler, 11:00 P.M., June 4, 1864, ibid., 581–82.

71. Humphreys to Warren, 7:00 P.M., June 4, 1864, ibid., 578; Warren to Humphreys, 9:30 P.M., June 4, 1864, ibid.; Miers, *Wash Roebling's War,* 25–26.

72. Humphreys to Hancock, 4:30 P.M., June 4, 1864, *OR,* vol. 36, pt. 3, p. 572; 2nd Corps circular, June 4, 1864, ibid., 574; Wright to Ricketts, 6:30 P.M., June 4, 1864, ibid., 583; Warren to Humphreys, 9:30 P.M., June 4, 1864, ibid., 578; special correspondence, *Philadelphia Inquirer,* June 10, 1864.

73. Locke, *Story of the Regiment,* 348.

74. Howe, *Touched with Fire,* 139–40; Morse, *Personal Experiences in the War,* 103–4.

75. Members of the Regiment, *Story of the 21st Regiment, Connecticut Volunteer Infantry,* 245–46.

76. Wilbur Fisk diary, June 4, 1864, LC.

77. Gibbon, *Personal Recollections,* 238; Luther A. Rose diary, June 4, 1864, LC. "The rebels attacked the 2nd Corps and a portion of the 6th Corps Saturday evening, but were handsomely repulsed," one newspaper reported. "They advanced to the attack several times and each time their lines were cut to pieces in their attempt to reach our works." "An Attack by the Rebels Saturday Night," *Springfield (Mass.) Daily Republican,* June 8, 1864.

78. Members of the Regiment, *Story of the 21st Regiment, Connecticut Volunteer Infantry,* 245; Burnside to Meade, 2:00 A.M., June 5, 1864, *OR,* vol. 36, pt. 3, p. 617; Smith to Burnside, 4:10 A.M., June 5, 1864, ibid., 618; Meade to Smith, 5:30 P.M., June 4, 1864, ibid., 589.

79. Daniel Larned to sister, June 5, 1864, Daniel Reed Larned Letters, LC; Roebling to Emily, June 5, 1864, in Miers, *Wash Roebling's War,* 26.

80. Grant to Meade, 8:20 P.M., June 4, 1864, *OR,* vol. 36, pt. 3, p. 570; Meade to Grant, 8:30 P.M., June 4, 1864, ibid.; Humphreys circular, 9:40 P.M., June 4, 1864, ibid., 571; Wright to

Hancock, June 4, 1864, ibid., 573; Hancock to Wright, 10:50 P.M., June 4, 1864, ibid.; Charles H. Morgan to John C. Tidball, June 4, 1864, ibid., 573; Wright to Humphreys, 11:38 P.M., June 4, 1864, ibid., 582.

81. J. Wilson, *Under the Old Flag,* 1:439; James H. Wilson diary, June 4, 1864, LC.

82. Andrew Humphreys letter, June 4, 1864, in H. Humphreys, *Andrew Atkinson Humphreys,* 226–27.

83. Circular, June 3, 1864, in Dowdey, *Wartime Papers of R. E. Lee,* 762–63; circular, June 3, 1864, *OR,* vol. 36, pt. 3, pp. 869–70; H. W. Long, "Reminiscence of the Battle of Cold Harbor," RNBP; Hillhouse, *Heavy Artillery and Light Infantry,* 83; A.F.G. to Friend Rogero, June 7, 1864, Mss. Box 79, P. K. Yonge Library of Florida History, University of Florida, Gainesville.

84. Newsome et al., *Civil War Talks,* 232. While some Florida sources reference the destruction of Breckinridge's salient, a postwar map by Nathan Michler shows part of the work still standing, as does Hancock's map reproduced in the endpapers of Keating, *Carnival of Blood.*

85. Early to Lee, June 4, 1864, *OR,* vol. 51, pt. 1, p. 246; Early to Lee, 7:00 P.M., June 4, 1864, ibid., pt. 2, pp. 984–85.

86. Lee to Anderson, 6:00 P.M., June 4, 1864, in Dowdey, *Wartime Papers of R. E. Lee,* 765.

87. In 1864 accounts the span is sometimes referred to as McClellan's Bridge. It was the primary route of the Union retreat after the Battle of Gaines's Mill in 1862.

Chapter III

1. Lewis H. Steiner diary, June 4, 1864, Maryland Historical Society; Ford, *Cycle of Adams Letters,* 2:141.

2. Dana on the fourth outlined for Stanton the operational plan that Grant detailed in his dispatch to Halleck the next day. Dana to Stanton, 7:00 P.M. June 4, 1864, *OR,* vol. 36, pt. 1, p. 89. See Grant's report, ibid., 22; and Grant to Halleck, ibid., pt. 3, p. 598.

3. Grant to Halleck, ibid., 598; *PUSG,* 9:13. Several historians have pointed out that Grant's claim that he intended to shift the Army of the Potomac south of the James River "from the start" contains a "degree of retrospective justification." See, e.g., Reid, "Another Look at Grant's Crossing of the James," 297. None of Grant's existing contemporaneous communications during the weeks leading up to the campaign express his objective as driving Lee back to Richmond and then crossing the James. Years later Horace Porter described a dramatic conference before the campaign in which Grant "rose from his seat, stepped up to a map hanging on the wall, and with a sweep of his forefinger indicated a line around Richmond and Petersburg, and remarked, 'When my troops are there, Richmond is mine. Lee must retreat or surrender." Porter, *Campaigning with Grant,* 37. Porter's dramatic description, however, is likely hyperbole, as is much of his memoir.

4. Grant to Halleck, June 5, 1864, *OR,* vol. 36, pt. 3, p. 598.

5. A. Humphreys, *Virginia Campaign,* 198.

6. Grant's report, *OR,* vol. 36, pt. 1, p. 22.

7. Grant to Meade, June 5, 1864, ibid., pt. 3, p. 599.

8. Ibid.

9. Badeau, *Military History of General Ulysses S. Grant,* 2:346.

10. Grant, *Personal Memoirs,* 2:280–81.

11. Ibid., 281.

12. Warren to Humphreys, 1:00 A.M., June 5, 1864, *OR,* vol. 36, pt. 3, p. 609.

13. Humphreys to Sheridan, 1:40 A.M., June 5, 1864, ibid., 627; Humphreys to Warren, 1:50 A.M., June 5, 1864, ibid., 609; Wilson to Warren, 3:30 A.M., June 5, 1864, ibid., 610.

14. Sheridan to Humphreys, June 5, 1864, ibid., 628; Humphreys to Sheridan, 8:30 A.M., June 5, 1864, ibid., 628.

15. James H. Wilson diary, June 5, 1864, LC.

16. Burnside to Meade, 2:00 A.M., June 5, 1864, *OR,* vol. 36, pt. 3, p. 617; Meade to Burnside, 3:30 A.M., June 5, 1864, ibid., 618.

17. Smith to Burnside, June 5, 1864, ibid., 618; Burnside to Smith, 8:00 A.M., June 5, 1864, ibid., 624.

18. Hancock to Williams, 7:45 A.M., June 5, 1864, ibid., 603; Warren to Williams, 7:45 A.M., June 5, 1864, ibid., 610; Wright to Humphreys, June 5, 1864, ibid., 616; Nevins, *Diary of Battle,* 411; Page, *Letters of a War Correspondent,* 97.

19. Hancock to Humphreys, 5:00 P.M., June 5, 1864, *OR,* vol. 36, pt. 3, p. 606; Williams to Hancock, 6:00 P.M., June 5, 1864, ibid., 607.

20. Armes, *Ups and Downs of an Army Officer,* 99. Armes, in a letter dated June 6, 1864, placed McCune's death on June 5. Francis A. Walker, writing years later, placed it on June 7 and had McCune killed while standing in front of Hancock's tent. Walker, *History of the Second Army Corps,* 519–20; Walker, *General Hancock,* 226.

21. Page, *Letters of a War Correspondent,* 6.

22. Newell, *Ours: Annals of 10th Regiment, Massachusetts Volunteers,* 279.

23. Porter, *Campaigning with Grant,* 183–84; Lord, *History of the Ninth Regiment, New Hampshire Volunteers,* 431–32; John Hoffman diary, June 5, 1864, RNBP.

24. James A. Beaver diary, June 5–6, 1864, James Beaver Papers, Pennsylvania Historical and Museum Commission; G. Thompson, *Engineer Battalion in the Civil War,* 66–67; McIntosh, "Sketch of the Military Career of David G. McIntosh."

25. Malles, *Bridge Building in Wartime,* 237–39.

26. Kreutzer, *Notes and Observations,* 203–5.

27. Humphreys to Warren, 11:45 A.M., June 5, 1864, *OR,* vol. 36, pt. 3, p. 610; Humphreys to Burnside, 10:50 A.M., June 5, 1864, ibid., 619; orders, 4:00 P.M., June 5, 1864, ibid., 603.

28. Burnside to Humphreys, 4:30 P.M., June 5, 1864, ibid., 620; Humphreys to Burnside, 5:15 P.M., June 5, 1864, ibid., 621; Humphreys to Burnside, 7:35 P.M., June 5, 1864, ibid., 622.

29. Crawford to Warren, June 5, 1864, ibid., 615; Warren to Burnside, 1:45 P.M., June 5, 1864, ibid., 611; Burnside to Warren, 4:20 P.M., June 5, 1864, ibid., 612; Warren to Humphreys, 5:00 P.M., June 5, 1864, ibid., 612; Humphreys to Burnside, 6:35 P.M., June 5, 1864, ibid., 621.

30. Roemer, *Reminiscences,* 213–14; Nevins, *Diary of Battle,* 406.

31. William S. Tilton's report, *OR,* vol. 36, pt. 1, p. 566; Mason Burt's report, ibid., 569; J. Parker, *Henry Wilson's Regiment,* 463–64; Bennett, *Musket and Sword,* 266–68.

32. Page, *Letters of a War Correspondent,* 99.

33. Humphreys to Warren, 1:30 P.M., June 5, 1864, *OR,* vol. 36, pt. 3, p. 611; Tomasak, *Avery Harris Civil War Journal,* 146; Roebling's report, June 5, 1864, Gouverneur K. Warren Collection, NYSLA.

34. Daniel Reed Larned Journal, June 9, 1864, Daniel Reed Larned Letters, LC.

35. Carter, *Four Brothers in Blue,* 426; Tomasak, *Avery Harris Civil War Journal,* 146.

36. Warren to Humphreys, 4:30 A.M., June 6, 1864, *OR,* vol. 36, pt. 3, p. 649.

37. Itinerary of the 3rd Division, 2nd Army Corps, *ibid.,* pt. 1, p. 468; P. Regis de Trobriand's

report, ibid., 472; Robert McAllister to family, June 6, 1864, in J. Robertson, *Civil War Letters of Robert McAllister,* 433–34; Silliker, *Rebel Yell and the Yankee Hurrah,* 166; Marbaker, *History of the Eleventh New Jersey Volunteers,* 189; Birney to Hancock, *OR,* vol. 36, pt. 3, p. 649.

38. Special dispatch, June 5, 1864, *New York Times,* June 8, 1864; Dwight Kilbourn diary, June 6, 1864, Civil War Diaries and Journals Collection, Rutgers University; National Tribune *Scrap Book,* 82.

39. Henry Lee to mother, June 7, 1864, Henry Lee Manuscripts, OCHS.

40. Special dispatch, June 5, 1864, *New York Times,* June 8, 1864; *Philadelphia Inquirer,* June 8, 1864; Ward, *History of the One Hundred and Sixth Regiment Pennsylvania Volunteers,* 269; Banes, *History of the Philadelphia Brigade,* 274.

41. Dana to Stanton, 7:00 A.M., June 6, 1864, *OR,* vol. 36, pt. 1, p. 91; Luther A. Rose diary, June 5, 1864, LC. Lt. Henry Clay Christiancy of Humphreys's staff noted in his diary: "The enemy attacked Russell's division, 6th Corps, about 8:15 P.M., and also along the whole 2nd Corps, but after steady musketry fighting for twenty minutes were everywhere repulsed." Henry Clay Christiancy diary, June 5, 1864, Pickett-Christiancy Papers, LC.

42. Swank, *Stonewall Jackson's Foot Cavalry,* 61.

43. Wright to Humphreys, 9:30 A.M., June 6, 1864, *OR,* vol. 36, pt. 3, p. 652; Gibbon to Walker, June 6, 1864, ibid., 647; Barlow to Walker, ibid., 646; Bartlett, *History of the Twelfth Regiment, New Hampshire Volunteers,* 213.

44. Sheridan to Humphreys, 8:15 P.M., June 5, 1864, *OR,* vol. 36, pt. 3, pp. 629–30; Wilson to Humphreys, 9:15 P.M., June 5, 1864, ibid., 632; Dana to Stanton, 6:00 P.M., June 5, 1864, ibid., pt. 1, p. 90.

45. Carleton, "Our Army Correspondence, June 5, 1864," *Boston Evening Journal,* June 9, 1864.

46. Early to Lee, 5:30 P.M., June 5, 1864, *OR,* vol. 51, pt. 1, pp. 246–47; Dowdey, *Wartime Papers of R. E. Lee,* 765.

47. Younger, *Inside the Confederate Government,* 154; D. Freeman, *Lee's Dispatches,* 216–18.

48. Dowdey, *Wartime Papers of R. E. Lee,* 767.

49. Ibid., 767–68.

50. Grant to Hunter, June 6, 1864, *OR,* vol. 37, pt. 1, p. 598; Grant, *Personal Memoirs,* 2:282–83.

51. Porter, *Campaigning with Grant,* 188; A. Humphreys, *Virginia Campaign,* 199.

52. Grant's plan and the risks inherent in it are discussed in Grant to Halleck, June 5, 1864, *OR,* vol. 36, pt. 3, p. 598; Grant, *Personal Memoirs,* 2:279–81; Badeau, *Military History of General Ulysses S. Grant,* 2:339–42; and A. Humphreys, *Virginia Campaign,* 199.

53. Porter, *Campaigning with Grant,* 187–88. Comstock noted on June 7 that Grant had instructed him and Porter to also determine whether "Butler's line is strong enough and with troops enough to hold it against any force Lee may send till we meet him." Sumner, *Diary of Cyrus B. Comstock,* 272.

54. Grant to Butler, June 6, 1864, *OR,* vol. 36, pt. 3, p. 662.

55. "The Siege of Richmond," *Philadelphia Inquirer,* June 10, 1864; Warren to Humphreys, 4:30 A.M., June 6, 1864, *OR,* vol. 36, pt. 3, p. 649; Spear, *Civil War Recollections of General Ellis Spear,* 120; J. L. Smith, *History of the Corn Exchange Regiment,* 466–67.

56. Burnside to Meade, 6:15 A.M., June 6, 1864, *OR,* vol. 36, pt. 3, p. 653; Committee of the

Regiment, *History of the Thirty-Fifth Regiment Massachusetts Volunteers*, 247. The 1st Michigan and 83rd Pennsylvania picketed between the 9th Corps and the cavalry. William A. Throop's report, *OR*, vol. 36, pt. 1, p. 583.

57. Jackman and Hadley, *History of the Sixth New Hampshire Regiment*, 279.

58. Hancock to Williams, June 6, 1864, *OR*, vol. 36, pt. 3, p. 644.

59. Jackman and Hadley, *History of the Sixth New Hampshire Regiment*, 280.

60. Lewis H. Steiner diary, June 6, 1864, Maryland Historical Society; Gaff, *On Many a Bloody Field*, 358; Roe, *Thirty-Ninth Regiment Massachusetts Volunteers*, 213–14; Nevins, *Diary of Battle*, 407; C. Davis, *Three Years in the Army*, 364; *Annual Circular of the Secretary of the Regimental Association, (Twelfth Webster Regiment)*, 9.

61. Fifth Corps general order, June 5, 1864, *OR*, vol. 36, pt. 3, pp. 613–14. Brig. Gen. Edward S. Bragg replaced Robinson in command of the Iron Brigade on June 7.

62. Lord, *History of the Ninth Regiment, New Hampshire Volunteers*, 431–32.

63. *Richmond Daily Dispatch*, June 9, 1864; Dana, *Recollections*, 214; Cadwallader dispatch, June 16, 1864, *New York Herald*, June 17, 1864.

64. Lyman, "Operations of the Army of the Potomac," 18; Bartlett, *History of the Twelfth Regiment, New Hampshire Volunteers*, 214; Ward, *History of the One Hundred and Sixth Regiment Pennsylvania Volunteers*, 269; "From the Sixth Corps—Interesting Incidents," *Providence (R.I.) Daily Journal*, June 20, 1864.

65. S. Thompson, *Thirteenth Regiment of New Hampshire Volunteer Infantry*, 366; Grant to Julia, June 7, 1864, in *PUSG*, 11:30.

66. Haines, *History of the Fifteenth Regiment New Jersey Volunteers*, 214.

67. James McGinnis letter, June 21, 1864, *Lockport (N.Y.) Daily Journal and Courier*, June 29, 1864; Arthur B. Wyman to sister, June 5, 1864, Civil War Miscellaneous Collection, US-AMHI.

68. Emmerton, *Record of the Twenty-Third Regiment Massachusetts Volunteer Infantry*, 211; J. Robertson, *Civil War Letters of Robert McAllister*, 437; S. Thompson, *Thirteenth Regiment of New Hampshire Volunteer Infantry*, 369; "Near Headquarters Army, Three Miles from Cold Harbor, June 6, 1864," *Philadelphia Inquirer*, June 10, 1864.

69. Roback, *Veteran Volunteers of Herkimer and Otsego Counties*, 96.

70. Ward, *History of the One Hundred and Sixth Regiment Pennsylvania Volunteers*, 270; Turino, *Civil War Diary of Lieut. J. E. Hodgkins*, 92; Mulholland, *Story of the 116th Regiment Pennsylvania Volunteers*, 261; Adams, *Reminiscences of the Nineteenth Massachusetts Regiment*, 101.

71. Lyman, "Operations of the Army of the Potomac," 18.

72. *Detroit Advertiser and Tribune*, June 15, 1864; Stewart, *History of the One Hundred and Fortieth Regiment Pennsylvania Volunteers*, 214.

73. John S. Anglia to parents, June 4, 1864, LC; William Drayton Rutherford to "My Own Beloved," June 5, 1864, FSNMP; Thomas Jackson Strayhorn to sister, June 12, 1864, in Wagstaff, "Letters of Thomas Jackson Strayhorn," 316–17; J. J. Herd to brother and sister, June 9, 1864, RNBP.

74. Charles W. Trueheart to Minnie, June 6, 1864, in Williams, *Rebel Brothers*, 93; John P. Lockhart to mother and sister, June 9, 1864, Hugh Conway Browning Papers, DU; John Bratton to wife, June 5, 1864, in Austin, *General John Bratton*, 213–14.

75. A. B. Mulligan to family, June 5, 1864, in Hutchinson, *"My Dear Mother and Sisters,"*

122; J. J. Herd to brother and sister, June 9, 1864, RNBP; W. A. Hunter to "Dear Wife," June 5, 1864, Gary L. Loderhose Private Collection, copy in author's possession.

76. Gallagher, *Fighting for the Confederacy,* 410; Stiles, *Four Years under Marse Robert,* 290; Melish M. Lindsey to "Friend," June 11, 1864, Special Collections, Alderman Library, University of Virginia, Charlottesville. For an excellent analysis of Confederate entrenchments at Cold Harbor, see Hess, *Trench Warfare under Grant and Lee,* and Keith S. Bohannon, "Breastworks Are Good Things to Have on Battlefields: Confederate Engineering Operations and Field Fortifications at Cold Harbor," RNBP.

77. FCFR letter, *Mobile Advertiser and Register,* June 17, 1864; "From Captain Manly's Battery, June 6, 1864," *Raleigh Daily Confederate,* June 10, 1864.

78. Charles Trueheart to Minnie, June 6, 1864, in Williams, *Rebel Brothers,* 93.

79. Stiles, *Four Years under Marse Roberts,* 277.

80. "From Captain Manly's Battery, June 6, 1864," *Raleigh Daily Confederate,* June 10, 1864; Dame, *From the Rapidan to Richmond,* 209; Wallace, *Richmond Howitzers,* 129.

81. Hancock to Williams, 3:20 P.M., June 6, 1864, *OR,* vol. 36, pt. 3, p. 643; Barlow to Walker, June 6, 1864, ibid., 646–47; Gibbon to Walker, 11:40 A.M., June 6, 1864, ibid., 647–48.

82. Wright to Humphreys, June 6, 1864, ibid., 653; Smith to Meade, 11:25 A.M., June 5, 1864, ibid., 660; Burnside to Humphreys, 7:15 P.M., June 6, 1864, ibid., 656.

83. Circular, 1:30 P.M., June 6, 1864, ibid., 640.

84. Alexander A. Yard diary, June 6, 1864, http://3rdnjcavalry.com/DiaryYard5.html (site discontinued).

85. Joseph P. Fuller diary, June 6, 1864, GDAH; Anderson to Lee, 6:30 A.M., June 6, 1864, *OR,* vol. 51, pt. 2, p. 991; circular, June 6, 1864, ibid., vol. 36, pt. 3, p. 877.

86. Lee to Davis, 7:30 A.M., June 6, 1864, in Dowdey, *Wartime Papers of R. E. Lee,* 767; Lee to Anderson, June 6, 1864, Edward P. Alexander Collection, SHC.

87. Gordon, *Reminiscences,* 317–19; G. Sorrel, *Recollections,* 260.

88. Sorrel circular, June 6, 1864, *OR,* vol. 36, pt. 3, p. 877; Early to Lee, 10:20 A.M., June 6, 1864, ibid., vol. 51, pt. 1, p. 247.

89. Early to Lee, 1:30 P.M., June 6, 1864, ibid., 247–48; Lee to Davis, 3:00 P.M., June 6, 1864, in D. Freeman, *Lee's Dispatches,* 219–20.

90. "General Lee's Army," *Richmond Examiner,* June 8, 1864.

91. Ibid.; Park, *Sketch of the Twelfth Alabama,* 69.

92. Bobbyshell, *48th in the War,* 155; *Richmond Daily Dispatch,* June 8, 1864; Howe, *Touched with Fire,* 141; Committee of the Regiment, *History of the Thirty-Sixth Regiment Massachusetts Volunteers,* 197.

93. Burnside to Humphreys, 5:10 P.M., June 6, 1864, *OR,* vol. 36, pt. 3, p. 655; Roebling's report, June 6, 1864, Warren Collection, NYSLA; Humphreys to Warren, 5:30 P.M., June 6, 1864, *OR,* vol. 36, pt. 3, p. 650; Marvin to Crawford, June 6, 1864, ibid., 652; William A. Throop's report, ibid., pt. 1, p. 583.

94. Cowper, *Extract of Letters of Major-General Bryan Grimes to His Wife,* 55; Park, *Sketch of the Twelfth Alabama,* 69; "General Lee's Army," *Richmond Examiner,* June 8, 1864.

95. Swank, *Stonewall Jackson's Foot Cavalry,* 61.

96. Early, *Autobiographical Sketch and Narrative,* 363–64; T. J. Watkins memoir, FSNMP; *Richmond Dispatch,* June 8, 1864; Cowper, *Extracts of Letters of Major-General Bryan Grimes to His Wife,* 55. A soldier in Benning's brigade of Anderson's corps reported, "a line 2 1/2 miles

long was formed perpendicular to our breastworks—lay there an hour—after which we returned to our former position (behind the works)." Joseph P. Fuller diary, June 6, 1864, GDAH.

97. Clark, *Iron Hearted Regiment*, 128.

98. Hancock to Williams, June 6, 1864, *OR*, vol. 36, pt. 3, p. 643; Page, *Letters of a War Correspondent*, 102; Harris to Mahone, June 6, 1864, William Mahone Collection, VSL; Bernard, *Civil War Talks*, 232.

99. Houston, *Thirty-Second Maine Regiment*, 238–39. Charles Dana noted that there "was an onslaught on Burnside just after midnight, which was successfully repulsed." Dana, *Recollections*, 214.

100. Moore, *Civil War Letters of Lt. Cornelius L. Moore*, 182. The 57th New York joined MacDougall's brigade at Cold Harbor on June 4.

101. Humphreys to Warren, 9:45 P.M., June 6, 1864, *OR*, vol. 36, pt. 3, p. 650; circular, ibid., 651.

102. Grant to Julia, June 5, 1864, in *PUSG*, 11:25.

103. Meade to wife, June 6, 1864, in Meade, *Life and Letters*, 2:201–2.

Chapter IV

1. Sheridan, *Personal Memoirs*, 1:417; Longacre, *Custer and His Wolverines*, 227; Pyne, *Ride to War*, 217.

2. For an excellent description of preparations for the march and estimates of the number of troopers in the Union column, see Wittenberg, *Glory Enough for All*, 23–37.

3. Sheridan, *Personal Memoirs*, 1:417–18; Sheridan's report, *OR*, vol. 36, pt. 1, p. 795.

4. Pyne, *Ride to War*, 218; J. Hall, "Army of Devils," 24.

5. Cheek and Pointon, *History of the Sauk County Riflemen*, 109. Nevins, *Diary of Battle*, 409; Sparks, *Inside Lincoln's Army*, 381.

6. Benjamin F. Meservey's report, *OR*, vol. 36, pt. 1, p. 579; Hancock to Williams, ibid., pt. 3, p. 671; Warren to Humphreys, and Grant endorsement, June 7, 1864, ibid., 675. Grant might well have had in mind the events of May 31, when Warren found himself isolated from the rest of the Union army after crossing Totopotomoy Creek.

7. J. L. Smith, *History of the Corn Exchange Regiment*, 469; Bennett, *Musket and Sword*, 270; Tomasak, *Avery Harris Civil War Journal*, 147.

8. Ritchie, *Four Years in the New York Light Artillery*, 170.

9. Gerrish, *Army Life*, 195; Tomasak, *Avery Harris Civil War Journal*, 147.

10. A. Smith, *History of the Seventy-Sixth Regiment, New York Volunteers*, 302–3; Hofmann's report, *OR*, vol. 36, pt. 1, p. 628; Fowler, *Memorials of William Fowler*, 87–90; George Hugunin diary, June 7, 1864, http://members.nbci.com/cathy_wilson/Julius.html (site discontinued); "Army of the Potomac," *Washington (D.C.) Daily Morning Chronicle*, June 11, 1864.

11. Lyman, "Operations of the Army of the Potomac," 17; special correspondence, *Philadelphia Inquirer*, June 11, 1864; "Our Movements near the Chickahominy," ibid.

12. Roebling to Emily, June 7, 1864, Roebling Collection, Rutgers University Library.

13. William Stokes letter, June 7, 1864, in Halliburton, *Saddle Soldiers*, 145.

14. Circular, 7:00 A.M., June 7, 1864, *OR*, vol. 36, pt. 3, p. 668; Hancock to Williams, 9:10 P.M., June 7, 1864, ibid., 671; Barlow to Walker, June 7, 1864, ibid., 672–73; Moore, *Civil War Let-*

ters of Lt. Cornelius L. Moore, 182; Gibbon to Walker, June 7, 1864, *OR,* vol. 36, pt. 3, p. 673; circular and endorsement, June 7, 1864, ibid., 672.

15. Wright to Humphreys, 8:30 A.M., June 7, 1864, *OR,* vol. 36, pt. 3, p. 678; Smith to Humphreys, 8:10 A.M., ibid.

16. Circular, June 7, 1864, ibid., 669.

17. Early, *Autobiographical Sketch and Narrative,* 464; [Wingfield], "Diary," 41: Robert S. Chew to Captain Symington, June 7, 1864, Edward P. Alexander Collection, SHC; John Bratton to wife, June 8, 1864, in Austin, *General John Bratton,* 215.

18. Albert, *History of the Forty-Fifth Regiment Pennsylvania Volunteer Infantry,* 137–38.

19. Ramseur to wife, June 7, 1864, in Kundahl, *Bravest of the Brave,* 234; Early, *Autobiographical Sketch and Narrative,* 364; Martin P. Avery's report, *OR,* vol. 36, pt. 1, p. 981; William G. Lewis, "Sketch of the Life," North Carolina Department of Archives and History, Raleigh, 25; Potter to Burnside, 12:45 [P.M.], June 7, 1864, *OR,* vol. 36, pt. 3, p. 685.

20. Lord, *History of the Ninth Regiment, New Hampshire Volunteers,* 432–33.

21. Burnside to Humphreys, 10:00 A.M., June 7, 1864, *OR,* vol. 36, pt. 3, p. 681; Humphreys to Burnside, June 7, 1864, ibid.; Willcox to Burnside, ibid.; Burnside to Humphreys, June 7, 1864, ibid., 682; Humphreys to Burnside, 11:45 A.M., June 7, 1864, ibid.; Weld, *War Diary and Letters,* 306–7.

22. Potter to Burnside, *OR,* 36, pt. 3, p. 685.

23. Roemer, *Reminiscences,* 214–16. After the war Roemer met some former Confederates who had attacked the redoubt and identified them as South Carolinians. Ibid., 217n.

24. Early, *Autobiographical Sketch and Narrative,* 364.

25. Frank Huger to Maj. Pickett, AAG, June 7, 1864, Edward P. Alexander Collection, SHC; Sorrel diary, June 7, 1864, MC; Loeher, *War History of the Old First Virginia Infantry Regiment,* 51.

26. Potter to Burnside, 3:30 P.M., June 7, 1864, *OR,* vol. 36, pt. 3, p. 686; Committee of the Regiment, *History of the Thirty-Sixth Regiment Massachusetts Volunteers,* 198.

27. Potter's report, *OR,* vol. 36, pt. 1, pp. 930–31; Argus, *New York Daily News,* June 13, 1864; Potter to Burnside, 12:30 A.M., June 8, *OR,* vol. 36, pt. 3, p. 699.

28. Swank, *Stonewall Jackson's Foot Cavalry,* 62.

29. Sharpe to Humphreys, and enclosure, June 7, 1864, *OR,* vol. 36, pt. 3, p. 668; Humphreys to Burnside, 9:00 P.M., June 7, 1864, ibid., 684; Jane Bowles's statement, June 8, 1864, ibid., pp. 695–96; Sharpe to Humphreys, June 8, 1864, ibid., 696–97.

30. Potter to Burnside, 6:30 A.M., June 8, 1864, ibid., 700; Laboda, *From Selma to Appomattox,* 234; diary of Creed T. Davis, in McCarthy, *Contributions to a History of the Richmond Howitzer Battalion,* 14.

31. Lee to Seddon, 7:00 P.M., June 7, 1864, *OR,* vol. 36, pt. 3, p. 877; [Wingfield], "Diary," 41.

32. *New Orleans Daily Picayune,* Apr. 7, 1865; *Cincinnati Daily Commercial,* Mar. 31, 1865; Pickett to Sorrel, June 7, 1864, Edward P. Alexander Collection, SHC.

33. Swank, *Stonewall Jackson's Foot Cavalry,* 62.

34. *Richmond Sentinel,* June 10, 1864.

35. Dana to Stanton, 7:00 P.M., June 7, 1864, *OR,* vol. 36, pt. 1, p. 92.

36. Ibid.; Coco, *Through Blood and Fire,* 101–2.

37. Dispatch of June 7, 1864, 4:40 P.M., *Richmond Dispatch,* June 8, 1864; Weisiger to Mahone, June 7, 1864, *OR,* vol. 51, pt. 2, p. 992.

38. Beauregard to Bragg, 3:30 P.M., June 7, 1864, ibid., vol. 36, pt. 3, pp. 878–79.

39. John Tyler to Sterling Price, June 7, 1864, ibid., vol. 51, pt. 2, p. 994.

40. Best, *History of the 121st New York State Infantry,* 158–59; Cockrell and Ballard, *Mississippi Rebel,* 277.

41. Thomas A. McParlin's report, *OR,* vol. 36, pt. 1, p. 210.

42. Bartlett, *History of the Twelfth Regiment, New Hampshire Volunteers,* 211; documents collected in Dunn, *Full Measure of Devotion,* 2:327–30; Gibbon to Hancock, 3:00 P.M., June 4, 1864, *OR,* vol. 36, pt. 3, pp. 574–75; report, James M. Hudnut to the 59th Reunion of the Members of the 8th Heavy Artillery Association, Aug. 22, 1823, in Dunn, *Full Measure of Devotion,* 2,329; John R. Cooper, letter to the editor, *Batavia (N.Y.) Republican Advocate,* June 22, 1864.

43. E. D. W. Breneman to Thomas A. McParlin, May 17, 1864, *OR,* vol. 36, pt. 2, p. 841; Thomas A. McParlin's report, ibid., pt. 1, p. 221. See the analysis of these events in Rose, *Grant under Fire,* 411.

44. Winfield S. Hancock to Seth Williams, 1:00 P.M., June 5, 1864, *OR,* vol. 36, pt. 2, p. 603; George G. Meade's endorsement, ibid., 604.

45. John C. Pemberton to Grant, and Grant to Pemberton, both May 25, 1863, ibid., vol. 21, pt. 1, pp. 276–77.

46. Grant's endorsement, June 5, 1864, ibid., vol. 36, pt. 2, p. 604; Meade to Grant, 1:30 P.M., June 5, 1864, ibid., 599.

47. Grant to Lee, June 5, 1864, ibid., 600.

48. Lyman's account of his adventures delivering the flag of truce is from his letter of June 5, 1864, reproduced in part in Agassiz, *Meade's Headquarters,* 149–53, and from Lyman, "Operations of the Army of the Potomac, June 5 — 15, 1864," 11–15.

49. A vivid description of Major Wooten appears in McLaurin, "Eighteenth Regiment," 59.

50. Lee to Grant, June 5, 1864, *OR,* vol. 36, pt. 2, p. 600.

51. Grant to Lee, June 6, 1864, ibid., 638; Army of the Potomac circular, 9:00 A.M., June 6, 1864, ibid., 640.

52. Lee to Grant, June 6, 1864, ibid., 638.

53. Grant to Lee, ibid., 638–39.

54. William Smith diary, June 6, 1864, Zack C. Waters Private Collection, copy in author's possession; J. D. Smith, *History of the Nineteenth Regiment of Maine Volunteer Infantry,* 193–94; Hancock to Humphreys, June 6, 1864, *OR,* vol. 36, pt. 2, pp. 643–44; David B. Birney to Francis A. Walker, June 6, 1864, ibid., 648–49.

55. Craft, *History of the One Hundred Forty-First Regiment, Pennsylvania Volunteers,* 210.

56. William F. Smith to Meade, June 7, 1864, *OR,* vol. 36, p. 2, pp. 687–88.

57. Horatio G. Wright to Meade, 11:05 A.M., June 7, 1864, ibid., 679; DeMay, *Civil War Diary of Berea M. Willsey,* 154.

58. Lee to Grant, June 7, 1864, *OR,* vol. 36, pt. 2, p. 639.

59. *Richmond Daily Dispatch,* June 6, 1864.

60. Grant to Lee, 10:30 A.M., June 7, 1864, *OR,* vol. 36, pt. 2, p. 666.

61. Lee to Grant, 2:00 P.M., June 7, 1864, ibid., 667.

62. Bernard, *Civil War Talks,* 233.

63. Grant's endorsement, June 7, 1864, *OR,* vol. 36, pt. 2, p. 667; Army of the Potomac circular, June 7, 1864, ibid., 669–70.

64. Grant to Lee, 5:30 P.M., June 7, 1864, ibid., 667.

65. "Morgan Narrative," in Walker, *History of the Second Army Corps,* 518; Badeau, *Mili-*

tary History of General Ulysses S. Grant, 2:310n; Ropes, "Battle of Cold Harbor," 360; Livermore, "Truce for Collecting the Wounded at Cold Harbor," 459; Foote, *Civil War,* 3:296; Waldemer, *Triumph at the James,* 266. For a modern analysis critical of Grant's handling of the "Flag of Truce" affair, see Rose, *Grant under Fire,* 411–15.

66. Simpson, *Ulysses S. Grant,* 329.

67. Emmerton, *Record of the Twenty-Third Regiment Massachusetts Volunteer Infantry,* 212; Maier, *Rough and Regular,* 232; Lutz, *Letters of George E. Chamberlin,* 334.

68. Haines, *History of the Fifteenth Regiment New Jersey Volunteers,* 212; Rhodes, *All for the Union,* 161; Haynes, *History of the Tenth Regiment, Vermont Volunteers,* 82; L. Wilson, *Confederate Soldier,* 179; Grant David Carter to brother and mother, June 11, 1864, in Georgia Division, United Daughters of the Confederacy, *Confederate Reminiscences and Letters,* 271.

69. T. C. Gray dispatch, *New York Daily Tribune,* June 11, 1864.

70. Agassiz, *Meade's Headquarters,* 154.

71. Greiner et al., *Surgeon's Civil War,* 201–2.

72. Ibid., 201; Gibbon, *Personal Recollections,* 233; Walker, *History of the Second Army Corps,* 518; William S. Pike diary, June 7, 1864, Niagara County Historian's Office, Lockport, N.Y.; Washburn, *History of the Old 108th New York Veteran Volunteers,* 80.

73. J. R. Cooper to "Friend Waite," June 8, 1864, *Batavia (N.Y.) Republican Advocate,* June 21, 1864; Emmerton, *Record of the Twenty-Third Regiment Massachusetts Volunteer Infantry,* 212; Washington L. Dunn diary, June 7, 1864, Book 23, RNBP.

74. "A Flag of Truce," *Philadelphia Inquirer,* June 11, 1864; Dana to Stanton, June 9, 1864, *OR,* vol. 36, pt. 1, p. 94. Grant in his memoirs also mentioned two survivors, apparently relying on Dana's number. See Grant, *Personal Memoirs* 2:276.

75. Fleming, *Memoir of C. Seton Fleming,* 85.

76. Wright to Marsena R. Patrick, 7:40 P.M., June 7, 1864, *OR,* vol. 36, pt. 2, p. 680.

77. T. Hyde, *Following the Greek Cross,* 212.

78. Hyde to mother, June 8, 1864, in J. Hyde, *Civil War Letters by General Thomas W. Hyde,* 140–41.

79. Ibid.

80. T. Hyde, *Following the Greek Cross,* 213; Hyde to mother, June 8, 1864, in J. Hyde, *Civil War Letters by General Thomas W. Hyde,* 141.

81. Meade to Margaret, June 6, 9, 1864, in Meade, *Life and Letters,* 2:201–2.

82. *Philadelphia Inquirer,* June 2, 1864.

83. Meade to Margaret, June 9, 1864, in Meade, *Life and Letters,* 2:202.

84. Ibid., 202–3; Porter, *Campaigning with Grant,* 190–91.

85. Sparks, *Inside Lincoln's Army,* 381; B. Thomas, *Three Years with Grant,* 207; Rawle, *History of the Third Pennsylvania Cavalry, Sixtieth Regiment Pennsylvania Volunteers,* 433; order, *OR,* vol. 36, pt. 3, p. 670. According to the reporter Cadwallader, Cropsey "always denied having confessed to the falsity of his charge against Gen. Meade." Thomas, *Three Years with Grant,* 209.

86. Nevins, *Diary of Battle,* 409.

87. Gibbon, *Personal Recollections,* 239–40.

88. Thomas, *Three Years with Grant,* 208–9; S. Cadwallader to Charles E. Cadwallader, Apr. 5, 1894, in Pennypacker, *General Meade,* 318.

89. Dana to Stanton, 4:00 P.M., June 9, 1864, *OR,* vol. 36, pt. 1, p. 94; Stanton to Dana, 11:00 P.M., June 10, 1864, ibid., pt. 3, p. 722.

90. Furgurson, *Not War but Murder*, 222; Meade to wife, June 12, 1864, in Meade, *Life and Letters*, 2:203.

91. *New York Times*, June 7, 1864; Burnside to Meade, 6:30 P.M., June 11, 1864, *OR*, vol. 36, pt. 3, p. 751; Grant, *Personal Memoirs*, 2:143–45. An account of the Swinton affair appears in Thomas, *Three Years with Grant*, 210–13. See also William Marvel, *Burnside* (Chapel Hill, N.C., 1991), 381.

Chapter V

1. Haines, *History of the Fifteenth Regiment New Jersey Volunteers*, 213; Westbrook, *History of the 49th Pennsylvania Volunteers*, 207; Britton and Reed, *To My Beloved Wife*, 237.

2. J. R. Cooper to "Friend Waite," June 8, 1864, *Batavia (N.Y.) Republican Advocate*, June 21, 1864.

3. John Russell Winterbotham to "dear folks at home," June 10, 1864, in O'Beirne, "Our Boys Stood Up Like Heroes."

4. Ward, *History of the One Hundred and Sixth Regiment Pennsylvania Volunteers*, 268; Banes, *History of the Philadelphia Brigade*, 275.

5. Special Orders 157, *OR*, vol. 36, pt. 3, p. 711.

6. Ward, *History of the One Hundred and Sixth Regiment Pennsylvania Volunteers*, 268; Banes, *History of the Philadelphia Brigade*, 275; H. S. Campbell to mother, June 7, 1864, Anna B. Campbell Papers, DU.

7. Burnside to Humphreys, 8:30 P.M., June 7, 1864, *OR*, vol. 36, pt. 3, p. 684.

8. Burnside to Larned, 8:00 A.M., June 8, 1864, ibid., 698.

9. Ibid.; Potter to Burnside, 1:00 P.M., June 8, 1864, ibid., 700; Potter to Burnside, June 8, 1864, ibid., 700–701.

10. Potter to Burnside, 5:00 P.M., June 8, 1864, ibid., 701–2.

11. "Headquarters Army of the Potomac, Cold Harbor, June 8, 1864 night," *Philadelphia Inquirer*, June 10, 1864.

12. Bloodgood, *Personal Reminiscences*, 279–80; Craft, *History of the One Hundred Forty-First Regiment, Pennsylvania Volunteers*, 210.

13. Hagood, *Memoirs*, 304.

14. Wade Hampton's report, July 9, 1864, USC. Barringer assumed command of the North Carolina brigade on June 6.

15. Wells, *Sketch of the Charleston Light Dragoons*, 58–59.

16. Ransom to Taylor, 7:00 A.M., June 8, 1864, *OR*, vol. 51, pt. 2, p. 996; Beauregard to Bragg, 10:00 A.M., ibid., 996; *Richmond Daily Dispatch*, June 8, 1864.

17. Davis to Lee, June 9, 1864, *OR*, vol. 52, pt. 2, p. 996.

18. Lee to Seddon, 8:00 P.M., June 8, 1864, in Dowdey, *Wartime Papers of R. E. Lee*, 769.

19. Sorrel to Kershaw, and Sorrel to Gregg, both at 8:00 P.M., June 8, 1864, *OR*, vol. 36, pt. 3, p. 880; Joseph P. Fuller diary, June 8, 1864, GDAH.

20. G. Moxley Sorrel journal, June 8–9, MC; Richard H. Anderson's report, DU; Early to Lee, 4:30 P.M., June 9, 1864, *OR*, vol. 51, pt. 2, p. 997.

21. Wells, *Sketch of the Charleston Light Dragoons*, 59; Charles P. Hansell, "History of the 20th Georgia Battalion Cavalry," GDAH, 11; Fitzhugh Lee to R. E. Lee, June 9, 1864, *OR*, vol. 51, pt. 2, p. 998.

22. W. H. F. Lee to W. H. Taylor, June 9, 1864, ibid., 997–98; Chambliss to W. H. Taylor, June 9, 1864, ibid., 998.

23. Lee to Davis, June 9, 1864, in D. Freeman, *Lee's Dispatches*, 222–23.

24. Ibid., 223.

25. Davis to Lee, June 9, 1864, *OR,* vol. 51, pt. 2, p. 996.

26. Several sources describe the June 9 offensive against Petersburg. For the contemporaneous reports and correspondence, including the vituperative exchanges between Butler and Gillmore, see *OR,* 36, pt. 2, pp. 273–319. The standard treatise on the operation is W. Robertson, *Petersburg Campaign*. Other accounts are in Longacre, *Army of Amateurs,* and Bearss and Suderow, *Petersburg Campaign*.

27. Butler to Gillmore, June 11, 1864, *OR,* vol. 36, pt. 2, pp. 275–78. Hinks contributed some 1,200 men, Hawley about 2,000, and Kautz, 1,300. W. Robertson, *Petersburg Campaign,* 24.

28. Sumner, *Diary of Cyrus B. Comstock,* 272; Porter, *Campaigning with Grant,* 187–88.

29. Butler to Gillmore, June 11, 1864, *OR,* vol. 36, pt. 2, pp. 278–79.

30. Gillmore's report, June 10, 1864, ibid., 288–89.

31. Kautz's report, June 11, 1864, ibid., 308; Archer, "Defense of Petersburg," 116.

32. Archer, "Defense of Petersburg," 132–35.

33. Longacre, *Army of Amateurs,* 135.

34. Raleigh D. Colston's report, *OR,* vol. 36, pt. 2, p. 318.

35. Beauregard to Bragg, 10:45 A.M., June 9, 1864, ibid., pt. 3, p. 884; Beauregard to Bragg, 1 P.M., June 9, 1864, ibid., 885; Beauregard to Bragg, 3:00 P.M., ibid.

36. Lee to Bragg, 2:30 P.M., June 9, 1864, in Dowdey, *Wartime Papers of R. E. Lee,* 770.

37. G. H. Terrett to Beauregard, 10:30 P.M., June 9, 1864, *OR,* vol. 36, pt. 3, p. 887; Bragg to Lee, 11:12 P.M., June 9, 1864, ibid., vol. 51, pt. 2, p. 997.

38. Davis to Beauregard, 4:00 P.M., June 9, 1864, ibid., vol. 51, pt. 2, p. 997.

39. Beauregard to Bragg, June 9, 1864, 11:15 P.M., ibid., vol. 36, pt. 3, p. 885; Bragg to Lee, June 9, 1864, 11:12 P.M., ibid., vol. 51, pt. 2, p. 997.

40. Beauregard to Bragg, June 9, 1864, ibid., vol. 36, pt. 3, p. 886.

41. Hill to Beauregard, June 11, 1864, and Beauregard's endorsement, ibid., 896. Hill was appointed lieutenant general on July 11, 1863, but Davis never submitted the nomination to the Confederate Senate for confirmation.

42. Lee to the Secretary of War, 9:30 P.M., June 9, 1864, ibid., 883; "Historical Sketch," *Our Living and Our Dead,* Apr. 22, 1874.

43. Wright to Humphreys, 9:00 A.M., June 9, 1864, *OR,* vol. 36, pt. 3, p. 714; P. M. Lydic to Burnside, June 9, 1864, ibid.; William F. Smith to Humphreys, 8:45 A.M., June 9, 1864, ibid.; Chapman to Siebert, June 9, 1864, ibid., 716; James A. Beaver to Hancock, 7:20 P.M., June 9, 1864, ibid., 711.

44. Roebling to Emily, June 10, 1864, Roebling Collection, Rutgers University Library; Chamberlin, *Letters,* 335.

45. S. Thompson, *Thirteenth Regiment of New Hampshire Volunteer Infantry,* 366.

46. Lord, *History of the Ninth Regiment, New Hampshire Volunteers,* 432–33.

47. Houston, *Thirty-Second Maine Regiment,* 240–41.

48. Sallada, *Silver Sheaves,* 97.

49. Soldat, June 12, 1864, *Richmond Sentinel,* June 13, 1864; John R. Zimmerman diary, June 11, 1864, Lloyd House, Alexandria, Va.; Loving, *Civil War Letters of George Washington Whitman,* 121.

50. Haines, *History of the Fifteenth Regiment New Jersey Volunteers,* 214–15.

51. Joseph H. Pierce to Julie, June 9, 1864, in Lewis Leigh Collection, USAMHI.

52. Arthur Benjamin Simms to mother, June 9, 1864, in Peacock, "Georgian's View of War in Virginia," 109.

53. H.J.W, *New York Times,* June 14, 1864.

54. Lyman, "Operations of the Army of the Potomac," 16.

55. Ibid., 17.

56. Soldat, June 9, 1864, *Richmond Sentinel,* June 10, 1864; Thomas E. Reed to Cynthia Reed, June 8, 1864, in Spies, *Yours Only,* 149–50.

57. Luther A. Rose diary, June 9, 1864, LC.

58. Blackford, *Letters from Lee's Army,* 231–32.

59. Edward Porter Alexander to wife, June 10, 1864, Alexander Collection, SHC.

60. Waugh, *Reelecting Lincoln,* 202.

61. Greenleaf, *Letters to Eliza,* 104.

62. Butler to Stanton, 7:00 P.M., June 9, 1864, *OR,* vol. 36, pt. 3, p. 717.

63. Kent, *Three Years with Company K,* 281; Lee to Seddon, June 10, 1864, *OR,* vol. 36, pt. 3, p. 888.

64. McIntosh's report, *OR,* vol. 40, pt. 1, p. 889; George O. Marcy's report, ibid., vol. 36, pt. 1, p. 890; [Phillips], "Civil War Diary," 105

65. R. Beale, *History of the 9th Virginia Cavalry,* 126; G. Beale, *Lieutenant of Cavalry in Lee's Army,* 154; Rodgers, "Cavalry's Bold Move."

66. Ibid.; G. Beale, *Lieutenant of Cavalry in Lee's Army,* 155. "Captain Backus was only twenty-three years old, and was one of the most promising officers in the regiment to which he was attached. The fatal bullet went clear through his breast." "An Unsuccessful Dash Made on Our Right," *New York Times,* June 17, 1864.

67. Rodgers, "Cavalry's Bold Move"; G. Beale, *Lieutenant of Cavalry in Lee's Army,* 155.

68. Rodgers, "Cavalry's Bold Move"; R. Beale, *History of the 9th Virginia Cavalry,* 127.

69. G. Beale, *Lieutenant of Cavalry in Lee's Army,* 155.

70. T. Smith, *Reminiscences of Major General Zenal R. Bliss,* 359; [Phillips], "Civil War Diary," 105; Boudrye, *Historic Records of the Fifth New York Cavalry,* 139.

71. Wilson to Humphreys, 2:30 P.M., June 10, 1864, *OR,* vol. 36, pt. 3, p. 736; Humphreys to Wilson, June 10, 9:00 P.M., ibid.

72. Fisher to Humphreys, June 10, 1864, ibid., 726; George H. Sharpe to Humphreys, June 10, 1864, ibid., 725. Chapman reported "no serious disturbance along my line." Ibid., 736.

73. Lee to Seddon, ibid., 887; Beauregard to Bragg, 10:10 P.M., June 10, 1864, ibid., 889; Special Orders 21, Headquarters Department of N.C. and S. Va., June 10, 1864, ibid., 890.

74. Dana to Stanton, 9:00 A.M., June 12, 1864, ibid., pt. 1, p. 95.

75. Halleck to Grant, May 31, 1864, ibid., pt. 3, pp. 375–76; A. Humphreys, *Virginia Campaign,* 196; Special Order 28, June 5, 1864, *OR,* vol. 36, pt. 3, p. 600; Special Order 31, June 9, 1864, ibid., 710; Lowe, *Meade's Army,* 31–32; Stanton to Dana, June 1, 1864, in *PUSG,* 11:32n.

76. Order, 6:30 A.M., June 11, 1864, *OR,* vol. 36, pt. 3, p. 750; Grant to Meade, June 8, 1864, ibid., 695; Michler's report, ibid., pt. 1, p. 302; Lyman, "Operations of the Army of the Potomac," 18.

77. Dana to Stanton, 9:00 A.M., June 7, 1864, *OR,* vol. 36, pt. 1, p. 91; Grant to Abercrombie, June 7, 1864, ibid., pt. 3, p. 691; Rawlins to Abercrombie, June 7, 1864, in *PUSG,* 11:29n; Abercrombie to Rawlins, June 12, 1864, *OR,* vol. 36, pt. 3, p. 768.

78. Thomas McParlin's report, *OR,* vol. 36, pt. 1, p. 263; Meyers, *Ten Years in the Ranks,* 319.

79. S. Williams to G. H. Mendell, June 10, 1864, *OR,* vol. 36, pt. 3, p. 722; Edmund Schriver to Williams, June 10, 1864, ibid., 722–23.

80. P. P. Pitkin to Daniel H. Rucker, 11:00 P.M., June 10, 1864, ibid., 737; Pitkin to E. S. Allen, June 10, 1864, ibid.

81. Ingalls to Williams, June 10, 1864, ibid., 724; Meade to Ingalls, June 10, 1864, ibid., 725; Grant to Meade, June 11, 1864, ibid., 745.

82. Ingalls to Williams, June 10, 1864, ibid., 724.

83. Grant to Halleck, ibid., 709; Rawlins to Abercrombie, ibid., 716; Medical Director's report, ibid., pt. 1, pp. 249–51.

84. Ira Spaulding's report, ibid., 304, 316.

85. Williams to Benham, June 4, 1864, 12M., ibid., pt. 3, p. 593; Williams to Benham, 7:15 A.M., June 4, 1864, ibid., 592; Benham to Williams, June 4, 1864, ibid., 593; Williams to Benham, 6:10 P.M., June 4, 1864, ibid., 594; Benham to Butler, June 6, 1864, ibid., 662; H. V. Slossen to Davis, June 6, 1864, ibid. Benham received conflicting orders from Meade and Halleck with respect to the New York bridging and the bridging from Port Royal. See Benham to Williams, June 5, 1864, ibid., 632; and Benham to Butler, June 5, 1864, ibid., 633. Benham's Volunteer Engineer Brigade consisted of the 15th New York Engineers and the 50th New York Engineers.

86. Williams to Benham, 12:00 A.M., June 4, 1864, ibid., 593.

87. Grant to Halleck, June 10, 1864, ibid., 722; J. Paine order, June 10, 1864, ibid., 740; Weitzel to Benham, ibid.; James L. Robbins's report, June 12, 1864, ibid., 772; Benham to Williams, June 12, 1864, 8:00 P.M., ibid. The record is ambiguous concerning whether Grant directed that the bridging material be concentrated at Fortress Monroe or whether sending the material there from Bermuda Hundred was Butler's idea. The sources cited above comprise the record on that subject and can be read either way.

88. Grant to Halleck, June 5, 1864, ibid., 598; Halleck to Grant, June 7, 1864, ibid., 665; *PUSG,* 11:20n.

89. The saga of Butler's testy relations with Acting Rear Admiral Lee is expertly canvassed in Craig L. Symonds, "Grant Moves South: Combined Operations on the James River, 1864," in Symonds, *Union Combined Operations in the Civil War.*

90. S. P. Lee to Gideon Welles, June 7, 1864, *ORN,* vol. 10, p. 129; S. P. Lee to Butler, May 30, 1864, *OR,* vol. 36, pt. 3, p. 368; Butler to S. P. Lee, May 30, 1864, ibid.; S. P. Lee to Butler, June 1, 1864, ibid., 476; S. P. Butler to Fuller, June 1, 1864, ibid.; Butler to S. P. Lee, June 3, 1864, ibid., 565; Butler to S. P. Lee, June 2, 1864, ibid., 514–15. See also Symonds, "Grant Moves South."

91. S. P. Lee to Welles, June 7, 1864, *ORN,* vol. 10, pp. 129–30.

92. Butler to S. P. Lee, June 7, 1864, *OR,* vol. 36, pt. 3, p. 692; Welles to Lee, June 11, 1864, *ORN,* vol. 10, p. 140; Reid, "Another Look at Grant's Crossing of the James," 306–8.

Chapter VI

1. McIntosh's report, *OR,* vol. 40, pt. 1, p. 889; Wilson to Humphreys, 8:00 A.M., June 11, 1864, ibid., vol. 36, pt. 3, p. 752.

2. McIntosh's report, ibid., vol. 40, pt. 1, p. 889; Wilson to Humphreys, 8:00 A.M., June 11, 1864, ibid., vol. 36, pt. 3, p. 752; Soldat, June 12, 1864, *Richmond Sentinel,* June 13, 1864.

3. Wilson to Humphreys, 8:30 A.M., June 11, *OR,* vol. 36, pt. 3, p. 753; Boudrye, *Historic Records of the Fifth New York Cavalry,* 139; Christ to Richards, June 11, 1864, *OR,* vol. 36, pt. 3, p. 753; Joseph P. Fuller diary, June 11, 1864, GDAH.

4. Thomas Ward, "Sketch of Left Section of Battery K," in Haskin, *History of the First Regiment of Artillery,* 525–27; Smith to Humphreys, 9:00 A.M., June 11, 1864, *OR,* vol. 36, pt. 3, p. 752; Christ to Richards, June 11, 1864, ibid.; Rowley to Washburne, June 11, 1864, Elihu B. Washburne Papers, LC.

5. Dana, *Recollections,* 218.

6. Grant to Washburne, June 9, 1864, in *PUSG,* 11:32.

7. Grant to Meade, June 11, 1864, *OR,* vol. 36, pt. 3, pp. 745–46.

8. Grant to Butler, June 11, 1864, ibid., 754–55.

9. Grant's report, ibid., pt. 1, p. 21.

10. Lyman, "Operations of the Army of the Potomac," 4.

11. Livermore, "Failure to Take Petersburg," 37–38; Grimsley, *And Keep Moving On,* 222.

12. Page, *Letters of a War Correspondent,* 107.

13. Humphreys to Warren, 7:30 P.M., June 10, 1864, *OR,* vol. 36, pt. 3, p. 731; orders, ibid.

14. Roebling's report, June 11, 1864, Gouverneur K. Warren Collection, NYSLA; order, June 10, 1864, *OR,* vol. 36, pt. 3, p. 731; Warren to Humphreys, 6:30 P.M., June 11, 1864, ibid., 750.

15. Order, 5:14 P.M., June 12, 1864, ibid., 762–63; Warren to Griffin, June 12, 1864, ibid., 763.

16. Warren to Humphreys, 2:45 P.M., June 12, 1864, ibid., 762.

17. Meade to Williams, June 10, 1864, ibid., 278–79; Williams to Hancock, 12:35 P.M., June 10, 1864, ibid., 729; Wright to Williams, ibid., 730; Ward, *History of the One Hundred and Sixth Regiment Pennsylvania Volunteers,* 270; Morgan to Birney, June 10, 1864, *OR,* vol. 36, pt. 3, p. 730.

18. Malles, *Bridge Building in Wartime,* 242.

19. Circular, 8:30 A.M., June 12, 1864, *OR,* vol. 36, pt. 3, p. 758; circular, June 12, 1864, ibid., 759–60.

20. Circular, June 12, 1864, ibid., 759–60. In a later circular 2nd Corps headquarters advanced the possibility of Barlow and Gibbon continuing past Wickers to other roads that struck Dispatch Station Road farther east. Whether Barlow and Gibbon continued onto this alternative route is not apparent. Circular, June 12, 1864, ibid., 760.

21. A. Humphreys, *Virginia Campaign,* 201–2.

22. Order, June 11, 1864, *OR,* vol. 6, pt. 3, pp. 747–49.

23. Order, June 12, 1864, ibid., 764.

24. Armes, *Ups and Downs of an Army Officer,* 101; order, *OR,* vol. 36, pt. 3, p. 732; Keifer's report, ibid., pt. 1, p. 735; Horn's report, ibid., 740; Ebright's report, ibid., 750–51.

25. Weld, *War Diary and Letters,* 308; Burnside to Williams, June 11, 1864, *OR,* vol. 36, pt. 3, p. 751.

26. Order, June 12, 1864, *OR,* vol. 36, pt. 3, p. 747–49.

27. Ibid.; Grant to Butler, June 11, 1864, postscript, ibid., 755.

28. W. Smith, "Movement against Petersburg," 79–80.

29. Dana to Stanton, 8:00 A.M., June 12, 1864, *OR,* vol. 36, pt. 1, p. 95; Sumner, *Diary of*

Cyrus B. Comstock, 272–73; Horace Porter to wife, June 14, 1864, Horace Porter Letters, LC.

30. Porter, *Campaigning with Grant,* 189.

31. Ibid., 189–90.

32. Dana to Stanton, June 8, 1864, *OR,* vol. 36, pt. 1, p. 92; Dana to Stanton, June 10, 9:00 A.M., ibid., 94–96; Dana to Stanton, June 11, 4:00 P.M., ibid., 95.

33. Grant to Biggs, June 12, 1864, ibid., pt. 3, p. 769; Abercrombie to Rawlins, June 12, 1864, ibid., 768; P. P. Pitkin to Montgomery C. Meigs, June 12, 1864, ibid., 769.

34. Page, *Letters of a War Correspondent,* 132–33; Lowe, *Meade's Army,* 299,

35. Weitzel's report, *OR,* vol. 40, pt. 1, p. 676; Lowe, *Meade's Army,* 299.

36. Weitzel's report, *OR,* vol. 40, pt. 1, p. 676; Lowe, *Meade's Army,* 299.

37. Badeau, *Military History of General Ulysses S. Grant,* 2:346.

38. Meade, *Life and Letters,* 2:204; Weld to mother, June 11, 1864, in Coco, *Through Blood and Fire,* 102.

39. *Richmond Daily Dispatch,* June 9, 1864.

40. Ibid.

41. Younger, *Inside the Confederate Government,* 155.

42. Breckinridge to Bragg, June 10, 1864, and Bragg endorsement, *OR,* vol. 51, pt. 2, pp. 1002–3.

43. Lee endorsement, June 11, 1864, ibid.

44. Ransom to Taylor, June 11, 1864, ibid., 1003–4.

45. *Richmond Daily Dispatch,* June 11, 1864.

46. Burke to Christian, June 11, 1864, and Chambliss endorsement, *OR,* vol. 51, pt. 2, p. 1004.

47. Ransom to Taylor, 8:00 A.M., June 12, 1864, ibid., 1006–7.

48. Ramseur to wife, June 11, 1864, in Kundahl, *Bravest of the Brave,* 235.

49. Breckinridge telegraph, June 12, 1864, forwarded by Hampton to Bragg, *OR,* vol. 51, pt. 3, p. 1007; Nicholls to Bragg, June 12, ibid., 1008. See the excellent recounting of these events in Duncan, *Lee's Endangered Left.*

50. Estimated strength of Early's corps on June 12 is from Young, *Lee's Army during the Overland Campaign,* 241.

51. Early, *Autobiographical Sketch and Narrative,* 371. Lee's written order has not been found.

52. Young, *Lee's Army during the Overland Campaign,* 247.

53. Gallagher, *Fighting for the Confederacy,* 418–19.

54. Ford, *Cycle of Adams Letters,* 2:149; Agassiz, *Meade's Headquarters,* 156; Lowe, *Meade's Army,* 201.

55. Charles Page, "Grant, Meade, and Other Celebrities," *New York Daily Tribune,* June 20, 1864.

56. Campbell, *Grand Terrible Drama,* 227; Charles W. Reed diary, June 12, 1864, John Reed Papers, LC.

57. Page, *Letters of a War Correspondent,* 111; Agassiz, *Meade's Headquarters,* 156; Lyman, "Operations of the Army of the Potomac," 18–19; Ford, *Cycle of Adams Letters,* 2:149.

58. Nevins, *Diary of Battle,* 414–15.

59. The 22nd New York joined Chapman's brigade on June 5, and the 1st New Hampshire Cavalry arrived on June 9. Chapman's report, *OR,* vol. 36, pt. 1, p. 901; R. H. McBride's report, June 15, 1864, *Washington (D.C.) Daily Morning Chronicle,* June 18, 1864.

60. Roebling's report, June 12, 1864, Warren Collection, NYSLA; Spear, *Civil War Recol-*

lections of General Ellis Spear, 121; Brainard, *Campaigns of the One Hundred and Forty Sixth Regiment New York State Volunteers,* 222.

61. Agassiz, *Meade's Headquarters,* 157; D. Marshall, *History of Company K, 155th Pennsylvania Volunteer Zouaves,* 171.

62. J. Wilson, *Under the Old Flag,* 1:398–99; Roebling's report, June 12, 1864, Warren Collection, NYSLA. In his memoirs Wilson claims that he saw Warren the next day and was surprised to learn that the corps commander did not remember the incident. Wilson wrote that he later told Grant of Warren's rudeness, and that the general in chief replied, "Well, I'll take care of Warren anyhow." Ibid., 401. In his biography of Warren, David Jordan questions whether the incident ever occurred. Jordan, *Happiness Is Not My Companion.* But in his diary Wilson notes, "Intolerance of Warren." James H. Wilson diary, June 12, 1864, LC.

63. "From the Eighth Cavalry, near Harrison's Landing, June 16, 1864," *Rochester Daily Union and Advertiser,* June 23, 1864; "From the Eighth New York Cavalry, near Prince George Court House Virginia, June 20, 1864," *Seneca (N.Y.) County Courier,* June 30, 1864. For the identity of the Confederate cavalry contesting the crossing, see Means, "Additional Sketch Sixty-Third Regiment," 609.

64. Wilson's report, *OR,* vol. 36, pt. 1, p. 883; Chapman's report, ibid., 901–2; Spaulding's report, ibid., vol. 40, pt. 1, p. 296. The newsman Page claimed that twenty Union cavalrymen died storming the Confederate rifle pits, but his account was secondhand and unsubstantiated. Page, *Letters of a War Correspondent,* 120–21. For a contrary description of the action, see "The Crossing of the Chickahominy," *Rochester Daily Union and Advertiser,* July 6, 1864. This article was penned by one of Ford's engineers, who discounted the cavalrymen's assistance and claimed that graphic descriptions of the fight were overblown.

65. Chapman's report, *OR,* vol. 36, pt. 1, p. 902; Spaulding's report, ibid., vol. 40, pt. 1, p. 296; Wilson to Humphreys, 11:15 P.M., June 12, 1864, ibid., vol. 36, pt. 3, p. 767; "The Crossing of the Chickahominy," *Rochester Daily Union and Advertiser,* July 6, 1864.

66. CMT dispatch, June 14, 1864, *Boston Evening Journal,* June 20, 1864.

67. Roebling's report, June 13, 1864, Warren Collection, NYSLA; Tilney, *My Life in the Army,* 93–94; *New York Daily Tribune,* June 18, 1864.

68. "A Gossipy Letter," June 10, 1864, *New York Daily Tribune,* June 15, 1864; H.J.W., *New York Times,* June 17, 1864.

69. Abbott, *Personal Recollections,* 80.

70. Mulholland, *Story of the 116th Regiment Pennsylvania Volunteers,* 263; Keating, *Carnival of Blood,* 168.

71. John Ramsey's report, *OR,* vol. 36, pt. 1, p. 461; Tidball's report, ibid., vol. 40, pt. 1, p. 422. Dwight was already in position with Dow; McKnight and Clark were assigned to Gibbon, Roder and Burton to Barlow, and Gillis and Dwight to Birney. Simons, *History of the One Hundred and Twenty-Fifth New York State Volunteers,* 220.

72. Mulholland, *Story of the 116th Regiment Pennsylvania Volunteers,* 263; Lafayette Church to dear family, June 21, 1864, transcribed by Bob Bowman and Janet Kondziela, Clarke Historical Library, Central Michigan University; Keating, *Carnival of Blood,* 162; Mitchell's daily memoranda, *OR,* vol. 40, pt. 1, p. 316.

73. Miller and Mooney, *Civil War: The Nantucket Experience,* 108–9.

74. Vaill, *History of the Second Connecticut Volunteer Heavy Artillery,* 70; Best, *History of the 121st New York State Infantry,* 160; Lewis Bissell to father, June 18, 1864, in Olcott, *Civil War Letters of Lewis Bissell,* 260; Haines, *History of the Fifteenth Regiment New Jersey Volun-*

teers, 214–15; Read, "Diary of Movements of the 3rd Division 6th Army Corps," June 12, 1864, James B. Ricketts Papers, Manassas National Battlefield Park.

75. T. Hyde, *Following the Greek Cross,* 214.

76. Nicolas Bowen to Samuel S. Elder, *OR,* vol. 36, pt. 3, pp. 766–67; Stannard's report, ibid., vol. 51, pt. 1, 1262–65; Palmer, *History of the Forty-Eighth Regiment, New York State Volunteers,* 153; Longacre, *Army of Amateurs,* 140.

77. Denny, *Wearing the Blue in the Twenty-Fifth Mass. Volunteer Infantry,* 342; Emmerton, *Record of the Twenty-Third Regiment Massachusetts Volunteer Infantry,* 215; Putnam, *Story of Company A, Twenty-Fifth Regiment Mass. Volunteers,* 294–95.

78. L. O. Merriam, "Personal Recollections of the War for the Union," FSNMP, 47; Cogswell, *History of the Eleventh New Hampshire Regiment Volunteer Infantry,* 375–76; Eden, *Sword and Gun,* 17; Willcox to Burnside, 9:00 A.M., June 13, 1864, *OR,* vol. 40, pt., 2, pp. 10–11.

79. Bowley, *Boy Lieutenant,* 77–78.

80. "General Grant's Movement Reviewed," *New York World,* June 16, 1864.

Chapter VII

1. Hoffman, *History of the First Vermont Cavalry,* 180; "Barringer's North Carolina Brigade of Cavalry," *Raleigh Daily Confederate,* Feb. 22, 1865; Wilson to Humphreys, 6:00 A.M., June 13, 1864, *OR,* vol. 40, pt. 2, p. 8.

2. "From the Eighth Cavalry, near Harrison's Landing, June 16, 1864," *Rochester Daily Union and Advertiser,* June 23, 1864; "From the Eight New York Cavalry, near Prince George Court House Virginia, June 20, 1864," *Seneca (N.Y.) County Courier,* June 30, 1864; James H. Wilson diary, June 13, 1864, LC; Trout, *Galloping Thunder,* 504–5.

3. H. Small, *Road to Richmond,* 149.

4. B. Cook, *History of the Twelfth Massachusetts Volunteers,* 135; *Annual Circular of the Secretary of the Regimental Association (Twelfth Webster Regiment),* 10; *Annual Report of the Adjutant-General of the Commonwealth of Massachusetts, for the Year ending December 31, 1864,* 403; I. Hall, *History of the Ninety-Seventh Regiment New York Volunteers,* 200; Kent, *Three Years with Company K,* 282; Vautier, *History of the 88th Pennsylvania Volunteers,* 189; Wilson to Humphreys, 8:30 A.M., June 13, 1864, *OR,* vol. 40, pt. 2, p. 10.

5. "A Rebel General Dead," *New York Times,* Apr. 10, 1881; Waring, "Diary of William G. Hinson," June 6, 1864; David Ballenger to Nancy, June 12, 1864, David Ballenger Collection, USC. The special order constituting Gary's new brigade was promulgated on June 13, 1864. *OR,* vol. 40, pt. 2, pp. 645–46.

6. Chapman's report, *OR,* vol. 40, pt. 1, p. 644; West, *Found among the Privates,* 80.

7. Cureton, "Reminisces," 200; Morrison, "Story without a Hero," 58; Chapman's report, *OR,* vol. 40, pt. 1, p. 644. The deployment of Gary's Brigade is variously described; I have followed the deployment listed in West, *Found among the Privates,* 80–81.

8. West, *Found among the Privates,* 80–81; Chapman's report, *OR,* vol. 40, pt. 1, p. 644; Galloway, "Sixty-Third Regiment," 609; *New York Times,* June 18, 1864, p. 1; "8th New York Cavalry Regiment," *Seneca (N.Y.) County Courier,* June 30, 1864; Hoffman, *History of the First Vermont Cavalry,* 180; *Charleston (S.C.) Mercury,* June 21, 1864. A Confederate at Riddell's Shop reported, "The rule was, before an engagement for the company to count off by fours and the fourth man was to take charge of the three [*sic*] horses of his squad." Edward Octavious Hall,

"Some Recollections," Ellen Pickney Brown Collection, South Carolina Historical Society, Charleston.

9. West, *Found among the Privates,* 72; Cureton, "Reminisces," 201.

10. Morrill, *Builder of the New South,* 54–55; Morrill, *My Confederate Girlhood,* 64–65. Logan was taken to Richmond and ultimately to Clover Hill in Chesterfield County, where he convalesced for three months.

11. West, *Found among the Privates,* 80; Morrison, "Story without a Hero," 58; Chapman's report, *OR,* vol. 40, pt. 1, p. 644; Hoffman, *History of the First Vermont Cavalry,* 180; Stephen Elliott to "Mother and Sisters," June 19, 1864, in John Michael Priest, ed., *Stephen Elliott Welch of the Hampton Legion* (Shippensburg, Pa., 1994), 33; "An Error Explained," *New York Herald,* June 25, 1864; Waring, "Diary of William G. Hinson," June 6, 1864; Doyle, "Gary's Fight at Riddle's Shop."

12. Crawford's report, *OR,* vol. 36, pt. 1, p. 644; McBride, "The Bucktails," 3; "An Error Explained," *New York Herald,* June 25, 1864; Wilson to Humphreys, 11:00 A.M., June 13, 1864, *OR,* vol. 40, pt. 2, pp. 11–12.

13. J. Wilson, *Under the Old Flag,* 1:452; Benedict, *Vermont in the Civil War,* 2:647–48; Samuel J. B. V. Gilpin diary, June 13, 1864, E. N. Gilpin Papers, LC; Hoffman, *History of the First Vermont Cavalry,* 181.

14. Silliker, *Rebel Yell and the Yankee Hurrah,* 169–70; Houghton, *Campaigns of the Seventeenth Maine,* 198–99; Thomas Smyth diary, May 12–13, 1864, Delaware Public Archives, Dover; Carter, *Four Brothers in Blue,* 431; Child, *History of the Fifth Regiment, New Hampshire Volunteers,* 255; Mitchell's journal, *OR,* vol. 40, pt. 1, p. 316; Banes, *History of the Philadelphia Brigade,* 276.

15. Lyman, "Operations of the Army of the Potomac," 19; Lowe, *Meade's Army,* 100; Ford, *Cycle of Adams Letters,* 2:149; Francis C. Long dispatch, June 13, 1864, *New York World,* June 18, 1864.

16. Keating, *Carnival of Blood,* 171; Armstrong, *Nuggets of Experience,* 55; Gibbon to Hancock, 3:15 P.M., June 13, 1864, *OR,* vol. 40, pt. 2, p. 5.

17. Roebling's report, June 13, 1864, Gouverneur K. Warren Collection, NYSLA.

18. Rosenblatt and Rosenblatt, *Hard Marching Every Day,* 229–30; Britton and Reed, *To My Beloved Wife,* 238; Howe, *Touched by Fire,* 144–45; Stevens, *Three Years in the Sixth Corps,* 355; Bowen, *History of the Thirty-Seventh Regiment Massachusetts Volunteers,* 338.

19. Burnside to Humphreys, 10:30 A.M., June 13, 1864, *OR,* vol. 40, pt. 2, p. 9; Wilkinson, *Mother, May You Never See the Sights I Have Seen,* 161.

20. Walcott, *History of the Twenty-First Regiment Massachusetts Volunteers,* 884; Houston, *Thirty-Second Maine Regiment,* 254; John E. Irwin diary, June 13, 1864, Bentley Historical Library, University of Michigan; Hopkins, *Seventh Regiment Rhode Island Volunteers,* 189.

21. Wright to Meade, 3:30 P.M., June 13, 1864, *OR,* vol. 40, pt. 2, p. 9.

22. Hopkins, *Seventh Regiment Rhode Island Volunteers,* 189–90; Ira Spaulding's report, *OR,* vol. 40, pt. 1, p. 197; Britton and Reed, *To My Beloved Wife,* 239; Haines, *History of the Fifteenth Regiment New Jersey Volunteers,* 216; E. Parker, *From the Rapidan to the James under Grant,* 30–31; Rosenblatt and Rosenblatt, *Hard Marching Every Day,* 229–30; E. K. Russell to mother, June 19, 1864, FSNMP.

23. DeMay, *Civil War Diary of Berea M. Willsey,* 156; Wright to Burnside, 5:45 P.M., June 13, 1864, *OR,* vol. 40, pt. 2, p. 10.

24. Larned circular, *OR,* vol. 40, pt. 2, p. 10; Burnside's report, ibid., pt. 1, pp. 521–22; Houston, *Thirty-Second Maine Regiment,* 254; Weld, *War Diary and Letters,* 309.

25. Spaulding's report, *OR,* vol. 40, pt. 1, pp. 296–97.

26. John A. Brady dispatch, June 14, 1864, *New York Herald,* June 17, 1864.

27. S. Thompson, *Thirteenth Regiment of New Hampshire Volunteer Infantry,* 374–75; Brady dispatch, June 14, 1864, *New York Herald,* June 17, 1864.

28. Rawlins to Smith, June 13, 1864, *OR,* vol. 40, pt. 2, p. 17.

29. Emmerton, *Record of the Twenty-Third Regiment Massachusetts Volunteer Infantry,* 215; 115th New York Scrapbook, Sarasota Springs Public Library, Sarasota Springs, N.Y., 45; Brady dispatch, June 14, 1864, *New York Herald,* June 17, 1864; William Russel to Ames, June 13, 1864, *OR,* vol. 40, pt. 2, p. 17; Martindale's report, ibid., vol. 51, pt. 1, p. 1255; Stannard's report, ibid., 1262; Stedman's report, ibid., 1265.

30. E. Smith, "Movement against Petersburg," 108.

31. Zimmerman diary, June 13, 1864, Lloyd House, Alexandria, Va.; Moffett, *Letters of General James Conner,* 135; Montgomery, *Georgia Sharpshooter,* 53; Evans, *16th Mississippi Infantry,* 270–71.

32. Bernard, *Civil War Talks,* 233; Stiles, *Four Years under Marse Robert,* 308.

33. *Richmond Dispatch,* June 14, 1864.

34. W. H. F. Lee to W. H. Taylor, 1:30 A.M., June 13, 1864, *OR,* vol. 51, pt. 2, p. 1009.

35. Cadmus M. Wilcox's report, Lee Headquarters Papers, VHS.

36. Dunlop, *Lee's Sharpshooters,* 99.

37. E. J. Hale's report, 28th N.C., July 19, 1864, James H. Lane Collection, Auburn University; Zimmerman diary, June 13, 1864, Lloyd House, Alexandria, Va.; Sorrel to division and artillery commanders, June 13, 1864, *OR,* vol. 40, pt. 2, p. 647.

38. Caldwell, *History of a Brigade of South Carolinians,* 159.

39. Wilcox's report, VHS; Caldwell, *History of a Brigade of South Carolinians,* 160; Moffett, *Letters of General James Conner,* 135.

40. Ivanhoe, *Richmond Daily Examiner,* June 15, 1864; special correspondent to the *Richmond Sentinel,* n.d., *Charleston (S.C.) Mercury,* June 18, 1864; Mills, *History of the 16th North Carolina Regiment,* 56; Dunlop, *Lee's Sharpshooters,* 101–2; Wilcox's report, VHS; Caldwell, *History of a Brigade of South Carolinians,* 160.

41. Chapman's report, *OR,* vol. 40, pt. 1, p. 644; Dunlop, *Lee's Sharpshooters,* 101–2; Hoffman, *History of the First Vermont Cavalry,* 180.

42. Thomas J. Luttrell diary, June 13, 1864 FSNMP; Jones, "Historical Sketch, 55th North Carolina," 2; Dunlop, *Lee's Sharpshooters,* 101–2; Wilcox's report, VHS; Chapman's report, *OR,* vol. 40, pt. 1, p. 644.

43. James B. Thomas to Lucy, June 15, 1864, in Thomas and Sauers, *"I Never Want to Witness Such Sights,"* 192–93; Roe, *Thirty-Ninth Regiment Massachusetts Volunteers,* 217; C. Davis, *Three Years in the Army,* 370.

44. Wilcox's report, VHS; Chapman's report, *OR,* vol. 40, pt. 1, p. 644; Hoffman, *History of the First Vermont Cavalry,* 180; Dunlop, *Lee's Sharpshooters,* 101–2; Roebling's report, June 13, 1864, Warren Collection, NYSLA.

45. Chapman's report, *OR,* vol. 40, pt. 1, p. 644; McBride, "The Bucktails"; "From the Eighth Cavalry, near Harrison's Landing, June 16, 1864," in *Rochester Daily Union and Advertiser,* June 23, 1864; "From the Eight New York Cavalry, near Prince George Court House Virginia, June 20, 1864," *Seneca (N.Y.) County Courier,* June 30, 1864; G, Davis, "Twenty-Second Regiment," 173.

46. Sterns, *Three Years with Company K,* 283; Thomas and Sauers, *"I Never Want to Witness Such Sights,"* 193.

47. Wilcox's report, VHS; Moffett, *Letters of General James Conner,* 135; G. Moxley Sorrel journal, June 13, 1864, MC; West, *Found among the Privates,* 81.

48. Roe, *Thirty-Ninth Regiment Massachusetts Volunteers,* 216–17.

49. Ibid., 217; Greenleaf, *Letters to Eliza,* 102.

50. Rhea, "Move to the James," 26; Wilcox's report, VHS; A. Humphreys, *Virginia Campaign,* 202. Confederate casualty returns for the battle are fragmentary. For casualties in the 7th South Carolina Cavalry from June 15 through 18, 1864, see, e.g., *Richmond Daily Enquirer,* July 2, 1864.

51. Gallagher, *Fighting for the Confederacy,* 420.

52. Ivanhoe, *Richmond Daily Examiner,* June 15, 1864.

53. Aggasiz, ed., *Meade's Headquarters,* 158.

54. Ibid.; Lyman, "Operations of the Army of the Potomac," 20–21.

55. Luther A. Rose diary, June 13, 1864, LC; Bloodgood, *Personal Reminiscences,* 282; Henry Lee to mother, June 14, 1864, Henry Lee Manuscripts, OCHS.

56. E. A. Paul, "The Recent Change of Base," *New York Times,* June 17, 1864.

57. Roebling's report, June 13, 1864, Warren Collection, NYSLA; Spaulding's report, *OR,* vol. 40, pt. 1, p. 297; 5th Corps special orders, June 13, 1864, *OR,* vol. 40, pt. 2, p. 8; *Rochester Daily Union and Advertiser,* June 23, 1864.

58. Boudrye, *Historic Records of the Fifth New York Cavalry,* 140.

59. Roebling's report, June 11, 1864, Warren Collection, NYSLA; Warren's journal, June 13, 1864, *OR,* vol. 40, pt. 1, p. 453; Fowler, *Memorials of William Fowler,* 90–91; J. Parker, *Henry Wilson's Regiment,* 466; Lewis H. Steiner diary, June 13, 1864, Maryland Historical Society; Spear, *Civil War Recollections of General Ellis Spear,* 121.

60. Bloodgood, *Personal Reminiscences,* 282; Dyer, *Journal of a Civil War Surgeon,* 168–69; Ford, *Cycle of Adams Letters,* 2:151.

61. Michler's report, *OR,* vol. 40, pt. 1, p. 289.

62. Mulholland, *Story of the 116th Regiment Pennsylvania Volunteers,* 266; R. H. McBride's report, June 15, 1864, *Washington (D.C.) Daily Morning Chronicle,* June 18, 1864; Dyer, *Journal of a Civil War Surgeon,* 168.

63. Dalton, *With Our Faces to the Foe,* 335.

64. Ripley, *Vermont Riflemen,* 182.

65. Hopkins, *Seventh Regiment Rhode Island Volunteers,* 190; J. Brown, *Signal Corps,* 385; Grant to Butler, 4:20 P.M., June 13, 1864, *OR,* vol. 40, pt. 2, p. 4; Grant to Halleck, 4:30 P.M., June 13, 1864, ibid., 3.

66. Badeau, *Military History of General Ulysses S. Grant,* 2:350.

67. Grant to Meade, June 13, 1864, *OR,* vol. 40, pt. 2, p. 3; A. Humphreys, *Virginia Campaign,* 203–4; Rawlins to Butler, June 13, 1864, *OR,* vol. 40, pt. 2, pp. 12–13.

68. Butler to Grant, June 13, 1864, *OR,* vol. 40, pt. 2, p. 12.

69. Edwin S. Jones to Williams, 6:45 P.M., June 13, 1864, ibid., 4.

70. Shaffer to Gillmore, 7:30 P.M., June 13, 1864, ibid., 14.

71. Shaffer to Gillmore, 9:00 P.M., June 13, 1864, ibid., 15; Gillmore to Shaffer, 9:35 P.M., ibid.; orders, 9:50 P.M., June 13, 1864, ibid. As Badeau later observed: "Butler had prepared these stone boats long before, but had refrained from sinking them, lest he should seem to reflect on the navy. The naval officers themselves hardly wished to admit the possibility of their being un-

able to hold the river. This, however, was no time for delicacy; a single vessel from Richmond, finding its way by night as far as City Point, might do infinite damage to stores and depots, and if it reached the position of the army, prevent the passage of the river, for a day. The barest possibility of such a chance was to be avoided." Badeau, *Military History of General Ulysses S. Grant*, 2:351.

72. Charles H. Hamman dispatch, *New York Herald*, June 17, 1864.

73. Badeau, *Military History of General Ulysses S. Grant*, 2:346–47.

74. Figg, *Where Only Men Dare to Go*, 204.

75. Special correspondent of the *Richmond Sentinel*, n.d., *Charleston (S.C.) Mercury*, June 18, 1864; Chambliss to Taylor, 7:20 P.M., June 13, 1864, *OR*, vol. 51, pt. 2, p. 1010; Jeff. Phelps to W. H. F. Lee, June 13, 1864, ibid.

76. Lee to Secretary of War, 10:00 P.M., June 13, 1864, *OR*, vol. 40, pt. 2, p. 645.

77. *Richmond Daily Dispatch*, June 14, 1864.

Chapter VIII

1. Special dispatch, June 13, 1864, *New York World*, June 17, 1864.

2. H. Humphreys, *Andrew Atkinson Humphreys*, 231; Rhodes, *All for the Union*, 161; Henry Lee to mother, June 14, 1864, Henry Lee Manuscripts, OCHS.

3. Crawford's division's itinerary, *OR*, vol. 40, pt. 1, p. 188; Roebling's report, June 14, 1864, Gouverneur K. Warren Collection, NYSLA; J. Parker, *Henry Wilson's Regiment*, 466–67.

4. C. D. Bibbins, "Cut Off and Captured," *Richmond Dispatch*, Aug. 16, 1896.

5. A. Small, *Sixteenth Maine Regiment*, 190–91.

6. Warren Hapgood Freeman to parents, June 26, 1864, in W. Freeman, *Letters from Two Brothers*, 128; Judson, *History of the Eighty-Third Regiment Pennsylvania Volunteers*, 218; Nevins, *Diary of Battle*, 418; Menge, *Civil War Notebook of Daniel Chisolm*, 23.

7. R. H. McBride, "Charles City Cross Roads, June 15, 1864," *Washington (D.C.) Daily Morning Chronicle*, June 18, 1864; Charles W. Reed diary, June 14, 1864, John Reed Papers, LC; A. Small, *Sixteenth Maine Regiment*, 189; Greenleaf, *Letters to Eliza*, 103.

8. Powell, *History of the Fifth Army Corps*, 696.

9. Olcott, *Civil War Letters of Lewis Bissell*, 260; Haynes, *History of the Tenth Regiment, Vermont Volunteers*, 177; Haines, *History of the Fifteenth Regiment New Jersey Volunteers*, 217.

10. Haynes, *History of the Tenth Regiment, Vermont Volunteers*, 177; Abbott, *Personal Recollections*, 178; Stevens, *Three Years in the Sixth Corps*, 356. See also Benedict, *Vermont in the Civil War*, 1:470.

11. Wheaton's report, *OR*, vol. 40, pt. 1, p. 496; Mark, *Red, White, and Blue Badge*, 275; Roe, *Tenth Regiment Massachusetts Volunteer Infantry*, 289; Stevens, *Three Years in the Sixth Corps*, 356.

12. Hartwell, *To My Beloved Wife and Boy at Home*, 239; Sparks, *Inside Lincoln's Army*, 383; Rhodes, *All for the Union*, 161; John H. Merrill diary, June 14, 1864, transcribed by Barbara Linderholm, original in Special Collections 1131, Haines, Evans, and Merrill Families, UCLA Library.

13. Burnside to Humphreys, 7:20 A.M., June 14, 1864, *OR*, vol. 40, pt. 2, p. 33; Roberts, *As They Remembered*, 140; Burrage, *History of Thirty-Sixth Regiment Massachusetts Volunteers*, 200.

14. Daniel Reed Larned to "Sister," June 15, 1864, Daniel Reed Larned Letters, LC.

15. Committee of the Regiment, *History of the Thirty-Fifth Regiment Massachusetts Volunteers*, 252; Burnside's report, *OR*, vol. 40, pt. 1, p. 522; Rogers, *Sketch of the Services of the Nineteenth N.Y. Battery*.

16. Coco, *Through Blood and Fire*, 104.

17. Hannum, "Crossing of the James River," 229–30; Wheaton's report, *OR*, vol. 40, pt. 1, p. 496; Burrage, *History of Thirty-Sixth Regiment Massachusetts Volunteers*, 200; Weld, *War Diary and Letters*, 310.

18. Cadwallader, *Three Years with Grant*, 215–16. Savage was mortally wounded four days later during an assault on the Confederate works at Petersburg.

19. H. Humphreys, *Andrew Atkinson Humphreys*, 231.

20. Spaulding's report, *OR*, vol. 40, pt. 1, p. 298; Elbert Corbin diary, June 14, 1864, RNBP.

21. Elbert Corbin diary, June 14, 1864, RNBP; Dana, *Recollections*, 219; Charles H. Crawford, "With the Pontooneers and Engineers," unidentified newspaper clipping, Book 7, RNBP. Corduroying involved laying logs side by side across a roadway to form a firm surface over marshy ground. The surface resembled the thickly ribbed cloth known as corduroy.

22. Crawford, "With the Pontooneers and Engineers." Beers recorded in his diary the time of completion as 5:50 A.M. W. W. Folwell's notes of E. O. Beers's diary, Box 100, W. W. Folwell Papers, Minnesota Historical Society.

23. Roebling journal, June 14, 1864, Roebling Collection, Rutgers University.

24. Grant to Meade, 9:30 A.M., June 14, 1864, *OR*, vol. 40, pt. 2, p. 19; Williams to Hancock, 8:30 A.M., June 14, 1864, ibid., 24.

25. Banes, *History of the Philadelphia Brigade*, 277–78.

26. C. H. Morgan to Hancock, June 14, 1864, *OR*, vol. 40, pt. 2, p. 25.

27. Ibid.; Silliker, *Rebel Yell and the Yankee Hurrah*, 170; Houghton, *Campaigns of the Seventeenth Maine*, 199; Ripley, *Vermont Riflemen*, 182; Wyman, *Civil War Diary*, 261–62.

28. J. Robertson, *Civil War Letters of Robert McAllister*, 440; Marbaker, *History of the Eleventh New Jersey Volunteers*, 192; Craft, *History of the One Hundred Forty-First Regiment, Pennsylvania Volunteers*, 212.

29. Francis A. Walker circular, 1:00 P.M., June 14, 1864, *OR*, vol. 40, pt. 2, p. 29.

30. Mulholland, *Story of the 116th Regiment, Pennsylvania Volunteers*, 267.

31. Wyman, *Civil War Diary*, 261.

32. Malles, *Bridge Building in Wartime*, 244.

33. Galwey, *Valiant Hours*, 233; Hancock to Williams, 3:30 P.M., *OR*, vol. 40, pt. 2, p. 25; Hancock to Humphreys, 6:00 P.M., June 14, 1864, ibid.; Mitchell's itinerary, *OR*, ibid. pt. 1, p. 316; Craft, *History of the One Hundred Forty-First Regiment, Pennsylvania Volunteers*, 212.

34. J. Wilson, *Under the Old Flag*, 2:452.

35. James H. Wilson diary, June 14, 1864, LC; Boudrye, *Historic Records of the Fifth New York Cavalry*, 141; [Phillips], "Civil War Diary," 105; Hoffman, *History of the First Vermont Cavalry*, 181; Rodenbough, *History of the 18th Regiment of Cavalry Pennsylvania Reserves*, 103.

36. McIntosh's report, *OR*, vol. 36, pt. 1, p. 889; Wilson to Humphreys, 6:20 P.M., June 14, 1864, ibid., vol. 40, pt. 3, p. 37; McIntosh to Siebert, June 14, 1864, ibid., 35–36; George O. Marcy's report, ibid., pt. 1, p. 638; Koempel, *Diary*, 10 (June 14, 1864); Tenney, *War Diary*, 119; Rodenbough, *History of the 18th Regiment of Cavalry Pennsylvania Reserves*, 104; Boudrye, *Historic Records of the Fifth New York Cavalry*, 141.

37. Zimmerman diary, June 14, 1865, Lloyd House, Alexandria, Va.

38. Crawford's report, *OR,* vol. 40, pt. 1, p. 644; "With the Eighth Cavalry, near Harrison's Landing, June 16, 1864," *Rochester Daily Union and Advertiser,* June 23, 1864.

39. "With the Eighth Cavalry, near Harrison's Landing, June 16, 1864"; Chapman's report, *OR,* vol. 40, pt. 1, p. 644; Sharpe to Humphreys, ibid., pt. 2, p. 19. Two squadrons from the 1st Connecticut composed the southern end of McIntosh's picket line and linked with Chapman's pickets below Smith's Store.

40. Weitzel's report, *OR,* vol. 40, pt. 1, p. 676.

41. Humphreys to Benham, 9:00 P.M., June 13, 1864, ibid., pt. 2, p. 4.

42. Ibid.; A. Brown, *Diary of a Line Officer,* 52; True, *Plantation on the James,* 157.

43. Benham to Williams, 8:00 P.M., June 12, 1864, *OR,* vol. 36, pt. 3, p. 772; "James L. Robbins' Estimate of Bridge Material Now at Fort Monroe," June 12, 1864, ibid.

44. Grant to Colonel Biggs, June 12, 1864, ibid., 769; Benham to Williams, 9:00 A.M., June 13, 1864, ibid., vol. 40, pt. 2, p. 5.

45. Weitzel's report, ibid., pt. 1, p. 676; Hannum, "Crossing of the James River," 235.

46. Hannum also notes: "Whether or not due diligence was exercised in completing the journey is indeterminate, as that depends on information not at hand, including the direction and strength of the tidal current during the journey, the number of tows, and the maximum speed of the tow boats. The opposing tidal current may have permitted so little progress upstream that anchorage was made." Hannum, "Crossing of the James River," 235.

47. Grant to Biggs, June 12, 1864, *OR,* vol. 36, pt. 3, p. 769; Benham to Seth Williams, 9:00 A.M., June 13, 1864, ibid., 40, pt. 2, p. 5; Weitzel's report, ibid., pt. 1, p. 676.

48. G. Thompson, *Engineer Battalion,* 68–70; Gilbert Thompson memoirs, June 18, 1864, LC; Hannum, "Crossing of the James River," 235.

49. Ritchie, *Four Years in the 1st New York Light Artillery,* 170–71.

50. Sumner, *Diary of Cyrus B. Comstock,* 273; Nevins, *Diary of Battle,* 418.

51. Lowe, *Meade's Army,* 205; Lyman, "Operations of the Army of the Potomac," 22.

52. Benham to Meade, 10:50 P.M., June 14, 1864, *OR,* vol. 40, pt. 2, p. 24; Meade to Benham, 11:30 P.M., June 14, 1864, ibid.; Meade to Burnside, 11:30 P.M., June 14, 1864, ibid., 34; Meade to Wright, 11:30 P.M., June 14, 1864, ibid., 32.

53. Hannum, "Crossing of the James River," 236; "The Crossing of the James by the Army," *Providence (R.I.) Daily Journal,* June 28, 1864; Dana, *Recollections,* 219; Agassiz, *Meade's Headquarters,* 159.

54. Grant's report, *OR,* vol. 36, pt. 1, p. 21; Charles H. Hammond dispatch, June 14, 1864, *New York Herald,* June 17, 1864.

55. *New York Herald,* June 17, 1864.

56. Grant's report, *OR,* vol. 36, pt. 1, p. 25; Grant, *Personal Memoirs,* 2:293–94.

57. Butler, *Butler's Book,* 685–86.

58. Hammond dispatch, June 14, 1864, *New York Herald,* June 17, 1864; Grant to Halleck, 1:30 P.M., June 14, 1864, *OR,* vol. 40, pt. 2, pp. 18–19.

59. Hammond dispatch, June 14, 1864, *New York Herald,* June 17, 1864.

60. Grant, *Personal Memoirs,* 2:294–95; Meade's endorsement, June 27, 1864, *OR,* vol. 40, pt. 1, p. 315; Grant's endorsement, June 28, 1864, ibid.

61. Meade to Hancock, 10:00 P.M., June 14, 1864, *OR,* vol. 40, pt. 2, p. 29.

62. Circular, Headquarters Second Army Corps, ibid., 61.

63. Grant to Butler, 8:30 P.M., June 14, 1864, ibid., 36.

64. J. Marshall, *Private and Official Correspondence of Gen. Benjamin F. Butler,* 4:364–65.

65. W. Smith, "Movement against Petersburg," 80.

66. Ibid.; Livermore, "Failure to Take Petersburg," 55; Warner, *Generals in Blue,* 463.

67. W. Smith, *From Chattanooga to Petersburg,* 124.

68. Smith's estimates of his troop strength are in Smith's report, *OR,* vol. 40, pt. 1, p. 749; W. Smith, "Movement against Petersburg," 88; and Schiller, *Autobiography of Major General William F. Smith,* 729. A more robust figure is convincingly argued and supported in Joseph Mills Hanson, "A Study of the Attack of June 15, 1864," PNBP. According to Hanson's study, the 18th Corps troops, augmented by elements from the 10th Corps that Smith brought back from Cold Harbor, numbered approximately 10,000 men; Hinks's division contained some 3,747 soldiers; Kautz's cavalry division counted about 2,500 troopers; and the additional four batteries that accompanied Smith's expeditionary force—Battery C, 3rd Rhode Island Artillery; Battery D, 1st U.S. Artillery; Battery D, 4th U.S. Artillery; and the 7th New York Battery—contained another 668 men, yielding a grand total of 16,915 for Smith's offensive.

69. Schiller, *Autobiography of Major General William F. Smith,* 98–99; W. Smith, "Movement against Petersburg," 97.

70. Schiller, *Autobiography of Major General William F. Smith,* 98–99; W. Smith, "Movement against Petersburg," 84, 97.

71. William F. Smith's report, *OR,* vol. 40, pt. 1, p. 749; A. Kautz, "Siege of Petersburg," 401. In subsequent recountings Smith gave slightly different renditions of this general plan. See, e.g., Schiller, *Autobiography of Major General William F. Smith,* 100; and W. Smith, "Movement against Petersburg," 81.

72. Schiller, *Autobiography of Major General William F. Smith,* 97–99.

73. C. E. Fuller to Smith, June 14, 1864, *OR,* vol. 40, pt. 2, p. 43; Stannard's report, ibid., vol. 51, pt. 1, pp. 1262–63. The 2nd Pennsylvania Heavy Artillery and the 9th New Jersey were delayed in transit and did not join Martindale's division until late on June 15. Martindale's report, ibid., 1255–56.

74. Butler to Hinks, June 14, 1864, *OR,* vol. 40, pt. 2, pp. 43–44; Hinks to Duncan, June 14, 1864, ibid., 44; Holman's report, ibid., vol. 51, pt. 1, pp. 263–64.

75. W. Smith, "Movement against Petersburg," 81.

76. Beauregard to Willcox, June 9, 1874, in *PMHSM,* 5:119; Beauregard, "Four Days of Battle at Petersburg," 540; Roman, *Military Operations of General Beauregard,* 2:229; H. Wise, "Career of Wise's Brigade," 12–13; "Wise's Brigade," *Richmond Daily Enquirer,* June 24, 1864. Joseph Hanson made a careful analysis of the numbers reported in a wide range of sources and calculates Wise's strength on June 15 as follows:

Infantry (less militia)	1,650
Militia or Reserve	425
Artillery, field	336
Cavalry, two regiments	820
TOTAL	3,231

During the afternoon, Dearing's two remaining regiments returned to Petersburg, increasing the force available to Wise, by Hanson's estimate, to 4,256 men. Hanson, "Study of the Attack of June 15, 1864," PNBP, 14–19.

77. Roman, *Military Operations of General Beauregard,* 2:229; Beauregard, "Four Days of Battle at Petersburg," 540; Livermore, "Failure to Take Petersburg," 52.

78. Beauregard to Bragg, 7:15 A.M., June 14, 1864, *OR,* vol. 40, pt. 2, p. 652; Beauregard to

Bragg, 10:00 A.M., June 14, 1864, quoting from Beauregard to Lee, ibid., 653. Beauregard's reaction to the emerging threat to Petersburg is perceptively described in Greene, "P. G. T. Beauregard and the Petersburg Campaign."

79. Lee to Davis, 12:10 P.M., June 14, 1864, in D. Freeman, *Lee's Dispatches*, 226–31.

80. Ibid., 231–32.

81. Lee to Davis, 3:45 P.M., June 14, 1864., ibid., 232–33.

82. Lee to Bragg, 4:00 P.M., June 14, 1864, ibid., 234.

83. Barefoot, *General Robert F. Hoke*, 200; Hagood, *Memoirs*, 265; *OR*, vol. 40, pt. 2, p. 654.

84. Beauregard to Lee, 8:10 P.M., June 14, 1864, *OR*, vol. 40, pt. 2, p. 653; Bragg to Beauregard, 9:10 P.M., June 14, 1864, ibid.

85. Younger, *Inside the Confederate Government*, 156; *Richmond Daily Enquirer*, June 14, 1864.

Chapter IX

1. New York State Historian, *Third Annual Report*, 79–80.

2. Hinks's report, *OR*, vol. 40, pt. 1, p. 721; Holman's report, ibid., vol. 51, pt. 1, pp. 263–64; Duncan's report, ibid., 265. Hinks's field returns for the day reported 2,200 men in Duncan's brigade, 1,300 in Holman's brigade, and 247 men in Angel's and Choate's batteries, for an aggregate of 3,747 troops. Hinks's report, ibid., vol. 40, pt. 1, p. 721.

3. Fuller to Shaffer, June 14, 1864, ibid., pt. 2, p. 37; "The Capture of Petersburgh Heights," *New York Times*, June 19, 1864.

4. Kreutzer, *Notes and Observations*, 210; "Return of the 18th Corps—Crossing the Appomattox," *New York Daily Tribune*, June 20, 1864.

5. Hall and Hall, *Cayuga in the Field*, 240; S. Thompson, *Thirteenth Regiment of New Hampshire Volunteer Infantry*, 382; DeForest, *Random Sketches*, 210; Mowris, *History of the One Hundred Seventeenth Regiment New York Volunteers*, 113. Joseph Hanson provides the time of sunrise. See "A Study of the Attack of June 15, 1864," PNMP, 23.

6. Kautz's report, *OR*, vol. 40, pt. 1, pp. 728–29; "The Capture of Petersburgh Heights," *New York Times*, June 19, 1864. Kautz's lead elements began crossing the river as early as 1:00 A.M., but the division's main body crossed later, sandwiched between Brooks and Martindale. Samuel P. Spear's report, *OR*, vol. 40, pt. 1, p. 738. Smith referred to the cavalry's movement as "unavoidably delayed." W. Smith, "Movement against Petersburg," 84.

7. DeForest, *Random Sketches*, 210; "Return of the 18th Corps—Crossing the Appomattox," *New York Daily Tribune*, June 20, 1864; "The Negro Troops at Petersburgh: Letter from a Son of Frederick Douglass," *New York Times*, June 26, 1864; Livermore, *Days and Events*, 355.

8. Lowe, *Meade's Army*, 187; Martindale's report, *OR*, vol. 51, pt. 1, p. 1256; Stannard's report, ibid., 1262; "The Capture of Petersburgh Heights," *New York Times*, June 19, 1864.

9. Dennis D. Ferebee's report to William E. Hinton, June 20, 1864, NCDAH; Raiford, *Fourth North Carolina Cavalry*, 73.

10. Ferebee's report, June 20, 1864, NCDAH; George W. Lewis's report, *OR*, vol. 40, pt. 1, p. 736; Spear's report, ibid., 738.

11. Kautz's report, *OR*, vol. 40, pt. 1, p. 729; Ferebee's report, June 20, 1864, NCDAH; Spear's report, *OR*, vol. 40, pt. 1, p. 738; George B. Easterly's report, ibid., 743.

12. Dearing's report, in Beauregard to Bragg, 9:00 A.M., June 15, 1864, ibid., pt. 2, p. 655.

13. Hinks's report, ibid., pt. 1, pp. 720–21; Duncan's report, *ibid.*, vol. 51, pt. 1, pp. 265–66.

14. Schiller, *Autobiography of Major General William F. Smith*, 101; Livermore, "Failure to Take Petersburg," 50; Livermore, *Days and Events*, 355.

15. Livermore, *Days and Events*, 355, 358–59.

16. Kautz's report, *OR*, vol. 40, pt. 1, p. 729; Spear's report, ibid., 738.

17. Dollard, *Recollections*, 127; Duncan's report, *OR*, vol. 51, pt. 1, p. 265.

18. John A. Brady dispatch, *New York Herald*, June 20, 1864. Descriptions of the ensuing fight at Baylor's farm are in Trudeau, *Like Men of War*, 220–22; and Claxton and Puls, *Uncommon Valor*, 134–39.

19. Hinks's report, *OR*, vol. 40, pt. 1, p. 721; Duncan's report, ibid., vol. 51, pt. 1, p. 265; Livermore, *Days and Events*, 356.

20. Duncan's report, *OR*, vol. 51, pt. 1, pp. 265–66; Holman's report, ibid., 263–64; Livermore, *Days and Events*, 356; "The Negro Troops at Petersburgh: Letter from a Son of Frederick Douglass," *New York Times*, June 26, 1864. Holman also had two regiments of the 4th Massachusetts Cavalry and Capt. Francis C. Choate's battery.

21. Hinks's report, *OR*, vol. 40, pt. 1, p. 721.

22. Duncan's report, ibid., vol. 51, pt. 1, p. 266; Sgt. Maj. Christian A. Fleetwood, *New York Anglo-African*, July 9, 1864. The wounded captains were Sidney J. Mendall, John W. Parrington, and Alfred M. Brigham. For an excellent account of the attack, see LeBarr, *Fifth Massachusetts Colored Cavalry*, 80–85.

23. Duncan's report, *OR*, vol. 51, pt. 1, p. 266; C. A. Fleetwood letter, June 28, 1864, *New York Anglo-African*, July 9, 1864; Livermore, *Days and Events*, 357–58.

24. Claxton and Puls, *Uncommon Valor*, 138.

25. Kiddoo's report, *OR*, vol. 40, pt. 1, p. 724; Charles Torrey Beman to father, June 20, 1864, *New York Anglo-African*, July 7, 1864; Brady dispatch, *New York Herald*, June 20, 1864.

26. Kiddoo's report, *OR*, vol. 40, pt. 1, p. 724; Robert N. Verplanck to mother, June 17, 1864, Robert N. Verplanck Papers, Adriance Library, Poughkepsie, N.Y.; Charles Torry Beman to Rev. Amos B. Beman, June 20, 1864, *New York Anglo-African*, July 9, 1864.

27. Quote from Longacre, *Army of Amateurs*, 147; "Fourth N.C. Cavalry," *Richmond Daily Confederate*, June 21, 1864.

28. S. Thompson, *Thirteenth Regiment of New Hampshire Volunteer Infantry*, 382; Schiller, *Autobiography of Major General William F. Smith*, 101.

29. Duncan's report, *OR*, vol. 51, pt. 1, p. 266. Duncan reported that the 22nd USCT lost 150 men killed, wounded, or missing on June 15, although he aggregates losses in the Baylor Farm combat and in the attack against the Dimmock Line later in the day. Col. Horace N. Wells replaced Russell. Holman's report, *OR*, vol. 51, pt. 1, 264.

30. Mowris, *History of the One Hundred Seventeenth Regiment New York Volunteers*, 114.

31. Schiller, *Autobiography of Major General William F. Smith*, 101.

32. Meade to Hancock, 10:00 P.M., June 14, 1864, *OR*, vol. 40, pt. 2, p. 29. Grant instructed Butler after their meeting at Bermuda Hundred to "please direct your commissary to send down by boat to Wind-Mill Point to-night 60,000 rations." At 2:30 A.M. on June 5, Butler directed his commissary officer to send the rations to Hancock with "great promptness." Grant to Butler, 8:00 P.M., June 14, 1864, ibid., 36; Frederick Martin to Charles Morgan, 2:30 A.M., June 15, 1864, ibid., 76; J. Marshall, *Private and Official Correspondence of Gen. Benjamin F. Butler*, 4:366–67, 373; Grant, *Personal Memoirs*, 2:293.

33. Walker, *History of the Second Army Corps,* 529; Walker, *General Hancock,* 233; Humphreys, *Virginia Campaign,* 212. According to the New York state historian, Hancock was furnished "with the so-called Abbott map, that which had been made in 1861 by the Corps of Engineers of the United States Army, and which, for present purposes, was absolutely worthless. For instance, the map indicated the position of Harrison's Creek as flowing four miles from Petersburg—between that place and City Point. As a matter of fact, Harrison's Creek ran inside the enemy's lines and was not within miles of the position laid down on the map." New York State Historian, *Third Annual Report,* 82–83.

34. Morgan's report, *OR,* vol. 51, pt. 1, pp. 269–70; Hancock to Williams, 3:30 A.M. June 15, 1864, in ibid., vol. 40, pt. 2, p. 56; Hancock to Williams, 3:50 A.M., June 15, 1864, ibid.; Hancock to Meade, 6:30 A.M., June 15, 1864, ibid.

35. Malles, *Bridge Building in Wartime,* 245.

36. Morgan's report, *OR,* vol. 51, pt. 1, p. 270; Hancock to Humphreys, 7:15 A.M., June 15, 1864, ibid., vol. 40, pt. 2, p. 57; Walker, *History of the Second Army Corps,* 526–27. Brainerd's and Morgan's recollections might well have been colored by an article by the correspondent William Swinton that appeared on June 21 entitled "How We Lost Petersburg." Swinton's piece attributed the loss to mistaken information conveyed to headquarters by an engineer officer. "Of course, everyone at Head Quarters knew who the Engineer Officer referred to was and so the joke, for so it was considered then, was on me," Brainerd later wrote. Brainerd asked Hancock to open a court of inquiry to clear his name. The general declined but promised to "fix" Swinton, who was expelled from the army soon afterward. Malles, *Bridge Building in Wartime,* 246–47.

37. Meade to Hancock, 7:30 A.M., June 15, 1864, *OR,* vol. 40, pt. 2, p. 57.

38. Walker, *History of the Second Army Corps,* 527.

39. Williams to Hancock, 8:45 A.M., June 15, 1864, *OR,* vol. 40, pt. 2, p. 57; Hancock to Williams, 9:40 A.M., ibid., 58.

40. Hancock to Birney, 9:15 A.M., ibid., 62; Hancock's report, ibid., pt. 1, p. 303; Walker, *History of the Second Army Corps,* 527–28.

41. Mitchell to Hancock, 8:45 A.M., June 15, 1864, *OR,* vol. 40, pt. 2, p. 57; Hancock to Williams, 9:40 A.M., June 15, 1864, ibid., 58; Williams to Hancock, 9:45 A.M., June 15, 1864, ibid. Colonel Smith was to take the two ships carrying the rations for the 2nd Corps to City Point and arrange for them to be sent from there to Hancock at Harrison's Creek. Joseph S. Smith to Williams, 10:30 A.M., June 15, 1864, ibid., 58.

42. Joseph S. Smith to Williams, 10:30 A.M., June 15, 1864, ibid.

43. Hancock's report, ibid., pt. 1, pp. 303–4.

44. Walker, *History of the Second Army Corps,* 529.

45. Nathaniel Michler's report, *OR,* vol. 40, pt. 1, p. 289; Roe, *Tenth Regiment Massachusetts Volunteer Infantry,* 289; National Tribune *Scrap Book,* 83.

46. "The Crossing of the James by the Army," *Providence (R.I.) Daily Journal,* June 28, 1864; "General Grant's Army," *New York World,* June 18, 1864.

47. "The Crossing of the James by the Army," *Providence (R.I.) Daily Journal,* June 28, 1864.

48. Dana to Stanton, 8:00 A.M., June 15, 1864, *OR,* vol. 40, pt. 1, pp. 19–20.

49. Barnard's report, ibid., 677; Butler to S. P. Lee, June 15, 1864, ibid., pt. 2, p. 77; S. P. Lee to Welles, 11:00 P.M., June 15, 1864, ibid., 77–78.

50. Porter, *Campaigning with Grant,* 199–200.

51. Badeau, *Military History of General Ulysses S. Grant,* 2:356–57.

52. Palladino, *Diary of a Yankee Engineer,* 142; J. L. Smith, *Antietam to Appomattox with the 118th Pennsylvania,* 473; Agassiz, *Meade's Headquarters,* 161; "General Grant's Army," *New York World,* June 18, 1864.

53. Porter, *Campaigning with Grant,* 200.

54. Elliott Welch diary, June 15, 1864, Elliott Welch Papers, DU; George A. Purrington's report, *OR,* vol. 40, pt. 1, p. 641.

55. Hill to Taylor, 9:00 A.M., June 15, 1864, *OR,* vol. 51, pt. 2, p. 1017.

56. "Army of Northern Virginia near Riddle's Shop, June 15, 7:30 P.M.," *Richmond Daily Sentinel,* June 17, 1864; "Army of Northern Virginia, June 16, 6 P.M.," *Richmond Daily Dispatch,* June 17, 1864; "Cavalry Corps, near St. Mary's Church," *New York Herald,* June 20, 1864; George O. Marcy's report, *OR,* vol. 40, pt. 1, p. 638; Rodenbough, *History of the Eighteenth Regiment of Cavalry Pennsylvania Volunteers,* 104. The Hampton Legion of Gary's Brigade fought in support of Cooke's infantry. See "Additional Sketches of Survivors Residing in This County," *Anderson (S.C). Intelligencer,* May 26, 1914.

From existing accounts it is difficult to pinpoint the precise location where Cooke's infantry became involved. Louis Boudrye states, "just beyond Smith's Store, in the edge of the swamps, a strong column of rebel infantry was encountered." *Historic Records of the 5th New York Cavalry,* 141. Placing this account in the context of other authorities cited above, it is likely that the "swamp" referenced was White Oak Swamp, which means that McIntosh's lead elements most likely passed through Smith's Store, reached Long Bridge Road, and started west into the fringes of White Oak.

57. Rodenbough, *History of the Eighteenth Regiment of Cavalry Pennsylvania Volunteers,* 104; Tenney, *War Diary,* 120; Cooke, "27th North Carolina Infantry," 2.

58. Rodenbough, *History of the Eighteenth Regiment of Cavalry Pennsylvania Volunteers,* 104; Phillips, "Civil War Diary," 105; "Army of Northern Virginia near Riddle's Shop, June 15, 7:30 P.M.," *Richmond Daily Sentinel,* June 17, 1864; "Army of Northern Virginia, June 16, 6 P.M.," *Richmond Daily Dispatch,* June 17, 1864; "Cavalry Corps, near St. Mary's Church," *New York Herald,* June 20, 1864; George O. Marcy's report, *OR,* vol. 40, pt. 1, p. 638; Cooke, "27th North Carolina Infantry," 2; Gause, *Four Years with Five Armies,* 273.

59. "Cavalry Corps, near St. Mary's Church," *New York Herald,* June 20, 1864; Charles C. Suydam's report, *OR,* vol. 40, pt. 1, p. 640; George A. Purrington's report, ibid., 41; Cooke, "27th North Carolina Infantry," 2; Joseph Mullen Jr. diary, June 15, 1864, MC; Page, *Letters of a War Correspondent,* 122.

60. Page, *Letters of a War Correspondent,* 123.

61. Hill to Taylor, 6:30 P.M., June 15, 1864, *OR,* vol. 51, pt. 2, p. 1017; "Cavalry Corps, near St. Mary's Church," *New York Herald,* June 20, 1864; Purrington's report, *OR,* vol. 40, pt. 1, p. 641. By this juncture the rest of Gary's Brigade had collected on this front. See W. H. F. Lee to Taylor, 5:00 P.M., June 15, 1864, *OR,* vol. 51, pt. 2, p. 1018; and Tenney, *War Diary,* 120.

62. Rodenbough, *History of the Eighteenth Regiment of Cavalry Pennsylvania Volunteers,* 105. Casualties are reported in Francis C. Long dispatch, June 16, 1864, *New York Herald,* June 20, 1864.

63. Hill to Taylor, 6:30 P.M., June 15, 1864, *OR,* vol. 51, pt. 2, p. 1017.

64. Crawford's report, ibid., vol. 40, pt. 1, p. 64; "Cavalry Corps, near St. Mary's Church," *New York Herald,* June 20, 1864; Henry C. Carr diary, June 15, 1864, Henry C. Carr Papers, Civil War Miscellaneous Collection, USAMHI.

65. Norton, *Deeds of Daring,* 79; Hoffman, *History of the First Vermont Cavalry,* 182; Samuel J. B. V. Gilpin diary, June 15, 1864, E. N. Gilpin Papers, LC.

66. Chapman to Wilson, n.d., in Wilson to Humphreys, 12:30 P.M., June 14, 1864, *OR,* vol. 40, pt. 2, pp. 70–71. Wilson reported that by afternoon Gary's Brigade was on the road from Riddell's to Nance's Shop and that Barringer's Brigade was "pushing the enemy on all roads south of that." Wilson to Humphreys, 9:40 P.M., ibid., pp. 71–72.

67. Page, *Letters of a War Correspondent,* 122; J. Wilson, *Under the Old Flag,* 1:452.

68. Schiller, *Autobiography of Major General William F. Smith,* 101.

69. Lowe, *Meade's Army,* 191; S. Thompson, *Thirteenth Regiment of New Hampshire Volunteer Infantry,* 383–84; Bruce, "Petersburg, June 15—Fort Harrison, September 29," 106–7.

70. The battery faced almost due east and was shaped like a square, with its back open toward Petersburg. The ground behind the position dropped off sharply to Harrison Creek.

71. L. D. Davis to Editor, "The Battle Fought at Battery No. 5," *Richmond Times Dispatch,* Mar. 8, 1908.

72. Putnam, *Story of Company A, Twenty-Fifth Regiment Mass. Volunteers,* 295–97; Denny, *Wearing the Blue in the Twenty-Fifth Mass. Volunteer Infantry,* 245–46; Stannard's report, *OR,* vol. 51, pt. 1, p. 1262.

73. Martindale's report, *OR,* vol. 51, pt. 1, p. 1256.

74. Duncan's report, ibid., 266; Livermore, "Failure to Take Petersburg," 53.

75. Hinks's report, *OR,* vol. 40, pt. 1, pp. 721–22; Duncan's report, ibid., vol. 51, pt. 1, 266–67.

76. L. D. Davis to Editor, "The Battle Fought at Battery No. 5," *Richmond Times Dispatch,* Mar. 8, 1908.

77. Duncan's report, *OR,* vol. 51, pt. 1, p. 267.

78. Ibid.; Hinks's report, ibid., vol. 40, pt. 1, p. 722; Kiddoo's report, ibid., 724–25; Trudeau, *Like Men of War,* 223.

79. S. Thompson, *Thirteenth Regiment of New Hampshire Volunteer Infantry,* 384–85. Lt. Col. Charles M. Coit's 8th Connecticut composed the right wing of Burnham's skirmish line, reinforced by soldiers from the 92nd and 118th New York.

80. Ibid., 384–85; Henry's report, *OR,* vol. 40, pt. 1, p. 714; James F. Brown's report, ibid., 717; N. Martin Curtis's report, ibid., 1246–47; Price, *History of the Ninety-Seventh Regiment Pennsylvania Volunteer Infantry,* 291.

81. Keiley, *In Vinculus,* 32–34; A. Kautz, "Siege of Petersburg," 401. For a sympathetic assessment of Kautz, see L. Kautz, *August Valentine Kautz.*

82. Kautz's report, *OR,* vol. 40, pt. 1, p. 729; George W. Lewis's report, ibid., 736; Samuel P. Spear's report, ibid., 738; Roper, *History of the Eleventh Pennsylvania Volunteer Cavalry,* 123.

83. Kautz's report, *OR,* vol. 40, pt. 1, p. 729.

84. Kautz's report, ibid.; Spear's report, ibid., 738; George B. Easterly's report, ibid., 743; Cruikshank, *Back in the Sixties,* 67–68.

85. A. Kautz, "First Attempts to Capture Petersburg," 535; Kautz, "Siege of Petersburg," 402.

86. Sources disagree on the precise arrangement of the Confederate defenders, and the location of some of the Confederate units, such as Hood's Battalion, changed during the day. H. Wise, "Career of Wise's Brigade," 13; Henry A. Wise, "Manuscript of Brigadier General Henry A. Wise Relative to the Battle of Petersburg Virginia in June 1864," LC, 59; Beauregard, "Four Days of Battle at Petersburg," 540; B. Wise, *Life of Henry A. Wise,* 346, 348; William H. Hood, "The De-

fense of Petersburg," in Newsome et al., *Civil War Talks,* 24; Landon C. Bell, *The Old Free State: A Contribution to the History of Lunenburg County and Southside Virginia,* 2 vols. (Richmond, n.d.,), 1:615–16. Joseph Hanson puts Wise's numbers closer to 4,000. "A Study of the Attack of June 15, 1864," PNMP. See also *Siege Operations: Combat Map No. 1-B, 7:45 P.M., June 15, 1864,* ibid.

87. H. Wise, "Manuscript of Brigadier General Henry A. Wise Relative to the Battle of Petersburg Virginia in June 1864," LC, 59; H. Wise, "Career of Wise's Brigade," 13; Roman, *Military Operations of General Beauregard,* 2:568.

88. "From the Front," *Richmond Dispatch,* June 15, 1864.

89. Beauregard to Bragg, 7:00 A.M., June 15, 1864, *OR,* vol. 40, pt. 2, p. 655.

90. Beauregard to Bragg, 11:45 A.M., June 15, 1864, ibid., 656; Roman, *Military Operations of General Beauregard,* 2:567–68; Beauregard, "Four Days of Battle at Petersburg," 540.

91. Beauregard to Bragg, 9:00 A.M., June 15, 1864, *OR,* vol. 40, pt. 2, p. 655; Beauregard to Bragg, 9:30 A.M., June 15, 1864, ibid.

92. Hoke to Bragg, June 15, 1864, ibid., 658; Beauregard to Bragg, June 15, 1864, ibid., 656.

93. Roman, *Military Operations of General Beauregard,* 2:574; Beauregard to Bragg, 1:45 P.M., June 15, 1864, *OR,* vol. 40, pt. 2, p. 656.

94. Beauregard to Bragg, 1:00 P.M., June 15, 1864, ibid., 656; Beauregard, "Four Days of Battle at Petersburg," 540.

95. Beauregard, "Four Days of Battle at Petersburg," 540; Roman, *Military Operations of General Beauregard,* 2:568; Beauregard, "Battle of Petersburg," 373; H. Wise, "Manuscript of Brigadier General Henry A. Wise Relative to the Battle of Petersburg Virginia in June 1864," 61.

96. Samuel H. Paul to Beauregard, May 18, 1864, in Roman, *Military Operations of General Beauregard,* 2:579; Beauregard, "Battle of Petersburg," 372; Beauregard, "Four Days of Battle at Petersburg," 540.

97. Samuel R. Paul to Beauregard, May 18, 1864, in Roman, *Military Operations of General Beauregard,* 2:579; Beauregard, "Battle of Petersburg," 372; Lee to Bragg, 12:20 P.M., June 15, 1864, in Dowdey, *Wartime Papers of R. E. Lee,* 781. Lee's eminent biographer Douglas Southall Freeman correctly identifies inaccuracies in Paul's account, which the aide wrote ten years after the event, albeit with the assistance of earlier memoranda. Those inaccuracies involve the time of the meeting—Paul placed it at 1:00 P.M., although Lee's dispatch to Bragg describing the meeting was sent at 12:20 P.M.—and his failure to mention that he had told Lee that Beauregard believed that he could hold Petersburg if his original force were returned to him. Freeman, *R. E. Lee,* 3:557–59.

98. Gallagher, *Fighting for the Confederacy,* 421.

99. Ibid.

100. According to Alfred C. Young's painstaking analysis, at the end of the Cold Harbor operations, the 1st Corps contained 14,150 troops, and the 3rd Corps amounted to 15,130. Young, *Lee's Army during the Overland Campaign,* 144, 146.

101. Livermore, "Failure to Take Petersburg," 52; Schiller, *Autobiography of Major General William F. Smith,* 102; W. Smith, "Movement against Petersburg," 88–89.

102. W. Smith, "Movement against Petersburg," 88–89.

103. W. Smith, *From Chattanooga to Petersburg,* 33.

104. Smith to Butler, 1:30 P.M., June 15, 1864, *OR,* vol. 40, pt. 2, p. 83.

105. Ibid., 89; Livermore, "Failure to Take Petersburg," 53.

106. W. Smith, "Movement against Petersburg," 88.

107. Smith's report, *OR,* vol. 40, pt. 1, p. 705; Schiller, *Autobiography of Major General William F. Smith,* 103.

108. Livermore, "Failure to Take Petersburg," 56; W. Smith, "Movement against Petersburg," 83.

109. Livermore, "Failure to Take Petersburg," 56.

110. Morgan's report, *OR,* vol. 51, pt. 1, p. 270; Mitchell's addendum, June 15, 1864, ibid., vol. 40, pt. 1, pp. 316–17; Weygant, *History of the One Hundred Twenty-Fourth Regiment, New York State Volunteers,* 349; Barlow to Hancock, June 26, 1864, HU; J. D. Smith, *History of the Nineteenth Regiment of Maine Volunteer Infantry,* 201; Ripley, *Vermont Riflemen,* 183.

111. Mitchell's Addendum, June 15, 1864, *OR,* vol. 40, pt. 1, pp. 316–17.

112. Armes, *Ups and Downs of an Army Officer,* 101.

113. Hancock to Humphreys, June 15, 3:30 P.M., *OR,* vol. 40, pt. 2, p. 59.

114. Hancock's report, ibid., pt. 1, p. 304; Hancock to Humphreys, June 15, 3:30 P.M., ibid., pt. 2, p. 59; Barlow to Hancock, June 26, 1864, HU. Hancock's orders to Birney and Barlow were later reconstructed from memory by Lt. Col. Charles Morgan at Hancock's request. Morgan to Hancock, June 29, 1864, ibid.

115. Walker, *History of the Second Army Corps,* 529.

Chapter X

1. Porter, *Campaigning with Grant,* 200–201; Agassiz, *Meade's Headquarters,* 162; Sumner, *Diary of Cyrus B. Comstock,* 273.

2. Porter, *Campaigning with Grant,* 203–4.

3. Grant to Butler, June 15, 1864, *OR,* vol. 40, pt. 2, p. 72; Shaffer's endorsement, ibid.; Grant to Shaffer, June 15, 1864, ibid.

4. Grant to Butler or Smith, 3:30 P.M., June 15, 1864, ibid., 73.

5. Dent to Butler, 3:40 P.M., June 15, 1864, ibid.; Butler to Dent, June 15, 1864, ibid.; Butler to Grant, June 15, 1864, ibid.

6. Grant to Gibbon, June 15, 1864, ibid., 63.

7. Smith to Hancock, June 15, 1864, ibid., 59; Livermore, *Days and Events,* 360.

8. As Captain Livermore later put it: "The fear arises that Smith delayed his assault for the arrival of the 2nd Corps." Livermore, "Failure to Take Petersburg," 59.

9. Barlow to Hancock, June 26, 1864, HU (reproduced in *OR,* vol. 40, pt. 2, p. 438); Livermore, "Failure to Take Petersburg," 58; Livermore, *Days and Events,* 360; Mitchell memorandum, *OR,* vol. 40, pt. 1, p. 316.

10. Hancock's report, *OR,* vol. 40, pt. 1, p. 304; Livermore, *Days and Events,* 360.

11. Hancock's report, *OR,* vol. 40, pt. 1, pp. 304–5; Walker, *History of the Second Army Corps,* 529–30; Mitchell memorandum, *OR,* vol. 40, pt. 1, p. 316.

12. Walker, *History of the Second Army Corps,* 530–31.

13. Birney to Walker, June 30, 1864, *OR,* vol. 40, pt. 2, pp. 643–44.

14. Barlow to Hancock, June 26, 1864, HU; Morgan to Hancock, June 27, 1864, ibid.

15. Barlow to Hancock, June 26, 1864, ibid. (reproduced in *OR,* vol. 40, pt. 2, p. 438).

16. Morgan to Hancock, June 27, 1864, ibid.; Barlow to Hancock, June 26, 1864, ibid.

17. Birney to Walker, June 30, 1864, *OR,* vol. 40, pt. 2, pp. 643–44.

18. Barlow to Hancock, June 29, 1864, HU. The question of why Barlow went astray is aired

at length in memoranda by Barlow, Morgan, and Francis Walker. *OR,* vol. 40, pt. 2, pp. 436–44. Ultimately Hancock, as related by his aide Walker on July 3, 1864, blamed Barlow. "It appears that General Barlow got an order from General Grant before reaching Old Court House to march to Petersburg at once, which he did not obey," Walker wrote. "He clearly committed an error of judgment in taking the wrong road, for which he is certainly responsible so far as responsibility may attach to it." Walker's endorsement, ibid., 443–44.

19. S. Thompson, *Thirteenth Regiment of New Hampshire Volunteer Infantry,* 385; "Return of the 18th Corps," *New York Daily Tribune,* June 20, 1864.

20. Hinks's report, *OR,* vol. 40, pt. 1, p. 722.

21. S. Thompson, *Thirteenth Regiment of New Hampshire Volunteer Infantry,* 386–88; Duncan's report, *OR,* vol. 51, pt. 1, p. 267.

22. Louis Bell's report, *OR,* vol. 51, pt. 1, p. 1247; Jackson and O'Donnell, *Back Home in Oneida,* 142; Charles M. Coit's report, *OR,* vol. 40, pt. 1, p. 713; Guy Henry's report, ibid., 714.

23. Smith's report, Aug. 9, 1864, in Schiller, *Autobiography of Major General William F. Smith,* 141–42; A. Humphreys, *Virginia Campaign,* 208.

24. Butler to Grant, 7:15 P.M., June 15, 1864, *OR,* vol. 40, pt. 2, p. 75.

25. Butler to Smith, 7:20 P.M., June 15, 1864, ibid., 83.

26. Cunningham, *Three Years with the Adirondack Regiment,* 132; Charles Clark to wife, June 17, 1864, Andrea Solary Private Collection, copy in author's possession; S. Thompson, *Thirteenth Regiment of New Hampshire Volunteer Infantry,* 393.

27. Charles M. Coit's report, *OR,* vol. 40, pt. 1, pp. 713–14; Guy Henry's report, ibid., 714; "Return of the 18th Corps," *New York Daily Tribune,* June 20, 1864; S. Thompson, *Thirteenth Regiment of New Hampshire Volunteer Infantry,* 386; Charles Clark to wife, June 17, 1864, Solary Private Collection, copy in author's possession.

28. L. D. Davis to Editor, "The Battle Fought at Battery No. 5," *Richmond Times Dispatch,* Mar. 8, 1908.

29. S. Thompson, *Thirteenth Regiment of New Hampshire Volunteer Infantry,* 387–88; Putnam, *Story of Company A, Twenty-Fifth Regiment Mass. Volunteers,* 297.

30. Bell's report, *OR,* vol. 51, pt. 1, p. 1247; Jackson and O'Donnell, *Back Home in Oneida,* 142. Two weeks later, when the *New York Herald* gave Burnham credit for breaking the Confederate line at Petersburg, a correspondent protested: "So far as New Hampshire people are concerned, Colonel Bell's brigade and not General Burnham's (as stated) took the rebel line of works at Petersburg on the afternoon of the 15th. The brigade consisted of the 3rd, 117th, and 142nd New York, the 97th Pennsylvania and the 4th New Hampshire Volunteers. The 3rd New York and a part of the 142nd advanced as skirmishers under a heavy fire and were first in the works followed closely by the whole brigade. Hinks' division were on our left. They charged and took two redoubts and the inverting rifle pits, fighting like veterans." "The Fourth New Hampshire," *Manchester (N.H.) Daily Mirror and American,* June 29, 1864.

31. Cunningham, *Three Years with the Adirondack Regiment,* 132; Charles M. Coit to sister, June 16, 1864, Coit Letters, Yale University; S. Thompson, *Thirteenth Regiment of New Hampshire Volunteer Infantry,* 388–90; L. D. Davis to Editor, "The Battle Fought at Battery No. 5," *Richmond Times Dispatch,* Mar. 8, 1908.

32. Bell's report, *OR,* vol. 51, pt. 1, p. 1247; S. Thompson, *Thirteenth Regiment of New Hampshire Volunteer Infantry,* 388, 394.

33. S. Thompson, *Thirteenth Regiment of New Hampshire Volunteer Infantry,* 388.

34. Ibid., 393, 401.

35. "The Capture of Petersburgh Heights," *New York Times*, June 19, 1864.

36. Stannard's report, *OR*, vol. 51, pt. 1, pp. 1262–63; Putnam, *Story of Company A, Twenty-Fifth Regiment Mass. Volunteers*, 98–99; Martindale's report, *OR*, vol. 51, pt. 1, p. 1256.

37. Guy V. Henry's report, *OR*, vol. 40, pt. 1, p. 714; James F. Brown's report, ibid., 717–18; Hinks's report, ibid., 722; Kiddoo's report, ibid., 725; Holman's report, ibid., vol. 51, pt. 1, p. 267; Bell's report, ibid., 1248; Price, *History of the Ninety-Seventh Regiment Pennsylvania Volunteer Infantry*, 291; Mowris, *History of the One Hundred Seventeenth Regiment New York Volunteers*, 114–16; L. D. Davis to Editor, "The Battle Fought at Battery No. 5," *Richmond Times Dispatch*, Mar. 8, 1908.

38. Kiddoo's report, *OR*, vol. 40, pt. 1, p. 725; Ulmer, *Adventures and Reminiscences of a Volunteer*, 45.

39. Duncan's report, *OR*, vol. 51, pt. 1, p. 266; Kiddoo's report, ibid., vol. 40, pt. 1, 725; Trudeau, *Like Men of War*, 224.

40. Kiddoo's report, *OR*, vol. 40, pt. 1, p. 725.

41. Ibid.

42. Duncan's report, ibid., vol. 51, pt. 1, p. 268.

43. Ibid.; McMurray, *Recollections of a Colored Troop*, 169.

44. Duncan's report, *OR*, vol. 51, pt. 1, p. 269; "Return of Casualties in the Union Forces," ibid., vol. 40, pt. 1, pp. 236–37; A. Humphreys, *Virginia Campaign*, 208n1; Coffin, *Four Years of Fighting*, 362–63.

45. Albert Brooker to "My Dear Mother," June 20, 1864, Book 53, RNBP, typescript; Jackson and O'Donnell, *Back Home in Oneida*, 142.

46. Dyer, *Journal of a Civil War Surgeon*, 172; H.J.W., "Details of Wednesday's Operations," *New York Times*, June 21, 1864; Agassiz, *Meade's Headquarters*, 162.

47. Hall and Hall, *Cayuga in the Field*, 241; Schiller, *Autobiography of Major General William F. Smith*, 104–5.

48. David L. Craft to Lemuel B. Norton, June 15, 1864, *OR*, vol. 40, pt. 2, p. 79; Charles F. Garrett to Norton, June 15, 1864, ibid.

49. Butler to Grant, June 15, 1864, ibid., 74; Grant to Butler, 8:15 P.M., June 15, 1864, ibid., 75.

50. Butler to Grant, 8:45 P.M., June 15, 1864, ibid.

51. Documentation relating to Butler's order for Smith to call off his attack is contained in Schiller, *Autobiography of Major General William F. Smith*, 145–55.

52. See Schiller, *Autobiography of Major General William F. Smith*, 145–55; Butler to Smith, 9:40 P.M., June 15, 1864, *OR*, vol. 40, pt. 2, p. 83; and Smith to Butler, 12M, June 15, 1864, ibid.

53. Smith's report, June 16, 1864, *OR*, vol. 40, pt. 1, p. 705; Smith's report, "Action at Cold Harbor and Petersburg, May 27–June 15, 1864," in Schiller, *Autobiography of Major General William F. Smith*, 142; W. Smith, "Movement against Petersburg," 92–99; W. Smith, "From Chattanooga to Petersburg," 25; W. Smith, "General W. F. Smith at Petersburg," 637.

54. Hinks letter, Feb. 21, 1878, quoted in Livermore, "Failure to Take Petersburg, 68–69.

55. Birney to Walker, June 30, 1864, *OR*, vol. 40, pt. 2, p. 644.

56. Mitchell's report, ibid., pt. 1, p. 317; Hancock's report, ibid., 305; Smith, "Movement against Petersburg," 94–95.

57. Hancock's report, *OR*, vol. 40, pt. 1, pp. 305–6; Mitchell's daily memoranda, June 15, 1864, ibid., 317; W. Smith, "Movement against Petersburg," 94–95; Schiller, *Autobiography of Major General William F. Smith*, 105. In his report of these events dated July 22, 1865, Grant

wrote that Smith had "offered the service of these troops as he (Smith) might wish, waiving rank to the named commander, who he naturally supposed knew best the position of affairs and what to do with the troops." Grant's report, *OR,* vol. 36, pt. 1, p. 25. Smith took umbrage at Grant's intimation that Hancock had waived rank. "The waiving of rank by a soldier would be at once a confession of inferiority, but would in no wise lessen the responsibility of the ranking officer," he wrote. "With such a soldier as was Hancock, the statement becomes simply absurd. . . . After I had fully reported to my superior officer [Hancock] the situation, had he thought differently than myself about the strength of the reinforcements or the danger and uncertainty of a night attack, it was perfectly competent for him to order me forward or to take the advance himself with his two divisions." W. Smith, "Movement against Petersburg," 94.

58. W. Smith, "Movement against Petersburg," 95. When he wrote these words in December 1887, Smith must have forgotten about his encounter with Morgan earlier on the evening on June 15.

59. Gibbon, *Personal Recollections,* 243–44.

60. David Birney to Francis Walker, June 30, 1864, *OR,* vol. 40, pt. 2, pp. 643–44.

61. Silliker, *Rebel Yell and the Yankee Hurrah,* 170; Livermore, *Days and Events,* 361; Hinks's report, *OR,* vol. 40, pt. 1, p. 722; Hancock's report, ibid., 306; Mitchell's report, ibid., 317.

62. Grant to Hancock, 8:30 P.M. [received at 11:12 P.M.], June 15, 1864, *OR,* vol. 40, pt. 2, p. 60; Butler to Hancock, 8:30 P.M., June 15, 1864, ibid.

63. Hancock to Butler, June 15, 1864, ibid., 61.

64. Denny, *Wearing the Blue in the Twenty-Fifth Mass. Volunteer Infantry,* 347; Cunningham, *Three Years with the Adirondack Regiment,* 132; Mowris, *History of the One Hundred Seventeenth Regiment New York Volunteers,* 115.

65. Hagood, *Memoirs,* 265; "Hagood's Brigade," 397–98. A thorough account of the arrival of Hoke's troops in Petersburg is in Barefoot, *General Robert F. Hoke,* 201–5.

66. W. Thomas, "Slaughter at Petersburg," 224.

67. Hagood, *Memoirs,* 265–66; Izlar, *War Record of the Edisto Rifles,* 65.

68. DuBose, *History of Company B, Twenty-First Regiment (Infantry), South Carolina Volunteers* 73; Thomas, "Slaughter at Petersburg," 224–25.

69. Hagood, *Memoirs,* 267; Beauregard, "Battle of Petersburg," 374; Thomas, "Slaughter at Petersburg," 224–25.

70. Hagood, *Memoirs,* 267; Peabody, "Some Observations," 156; Elliott, "Martin's Brigade," 195; Robert M. Stribling, "From Markham to Appomattox with the Fauquier Artillery," in Ramey and Gott, *Years of Anguish,* 195.

71. Beauregard to Lee, 11:15 P.M., June 15, 1864, *OR,* vol. 40, pt. 2, p. 657; Roman, *Military Operations of General Beauregard,* 2:231.

72. Smith to Butler, midnight, June 15, 1864, *OR,* vol. 40, pt. 2, p. 83; Wilkeson, *Recollections of a Private Soldier in the Army of the Potomac,* 162.

73. Livermore, "Failure to Take Petersburg," 46–47; Ritchie, *Four Years in the First New York Light Artillery,* 170.

74. Livermore, "Failure to Take Petersburg," 64.

75. Meade's endorsement, July 27, 1864, *OR,* vol. 40, pt. 1, p. 315; W. Smith, *From Chattanooga to Petersburg,* 126n1; Grant, *Personal Memoirs,* 2:298. Hancock concurred, noting that he could have "joined General Smith by marching directly toward him, at Petersburg, by 4 P.M." Hancock's report, *OR,* vol. 40, pt. 1, p. 304.

76. W. Smith, *From Chattanooga to Petersburg,* 124.

77. Hinks letter, Feb. 21, 1878, in Livermore, "Failure to Take Petersburg," 69.

78. Agassiz, *Meade's Headquarters,* 162.

79. Dana to Stanton, June 16, 1864, *OR,* vol. 40, pt. 1, p. 21; Lowe, *Meade's Army,* 207; Grant to Halleck, July 1, 1864, *OR,* vol. 40, pt. 2, p. 559.

80. Grant's report, *OR,* vol. 36, pt. 1, p. 25; Grant, *Personal Memoirs,* 2:298; Badeau, *Military History of General Ulysses S. Grant,* 2:361.

81. Livermore, *Days and Events,* 362; McCabe, "Defense of Petersburg," 268.

82. Hancock to Williams, June 26, 1864, *OR,* vol. 40, pt. 1, pp. 313–14.

83. Meade's endorsement, June 27, 1864, ibid., 515; Grant's endorsement, June 28, 1864, ibid. Hancock's performance on June 15 is carefully examined in Jordan, *Winfield Scott Hancock,* 142–46.

84. Ulmer, *Adventures and Reminiscences of a Volunteer,* 45–46.

Epilogue

1. Lowe, *Meade's Army,* 205.

2. Ibid.; Agassiz, *Meade's Headquarters,* 161; Humphreys to Burnside, 6:00 P.M., June 15, 1864, *OR,* vol. 40, pt. 2, p. 68; Burnside to Humphreys, ibid, 69; Humphreys to Burnside, 6:45 P.M., ibid.

3. Meade, *Life and Letters,* 2:207. For summaries of the fighting on June 16–18, see Howe, *Petersburg Campaign,* and Bearss and Suderow, *Petersburg Campaign.* A. Wilson Greene's forthcoming publication will be the latest definitive word on those engagements.

4. Freeman, *R. E. Lee,* 3:426.

5. Dispatch, May 27, 1864, *Columbia (S.C.) Daily South Carolinian,* June 3, 1864.

6. Edward A. Pollard, *The Lost Cause* (New York, 1867), 510; Ropes, "Grant's Campaign in Virginia," 404; Rose, *Grant under Fire,* 331–420.

7. Gallagher, *Fighting for the Confederacy,* 419.

8. Lincoln to Grant, 7:00 A.M., June 15, 1864, *OR,* vol. 40, pt. 2, p. 47.

9. Freeman, *R. E. Lee,* 3:425.

10. It is interesting to speculate how the campaign might have progressed if Grant had remained in Washington to supervise overall national strategy and left Meade to battle Lee without his persistent and detailed oversight. As general in chief, Grant's role was to manage the national war effort. By traveling with the Potomac army, he increasingly injected himself into the minutia of its operations, leading participants such as Humphreys to bemoan the problems spawned by a divided command. On the one hand, it can be argued that Grant's presence in the field ensured that Meade and his subordinates remained on the offensive, consistently taking the initiative after each reverse. On the other hand, one might argue that Meade, left to his own devices, would have evolved a strategy more suitable to his and his army's temperament and would have achieved Grant's objective—the destruction or neutralization of Lee's army—while incurring fewer casualties. But considering Meade's cautious approach during the seven months when he controlled the Army of the Potomac—from Gettysburg until the coming of Grant—it is difficult to imagine the latter scenario.

11. Rhea, *Cold Harbor,* 7–10.

12. Douglas Southall Freeman also identifies the attrition in Lee's command structure during the Overland Campaign. *Lee's Lieutenants,* 3:513.

13. Campbell Brown memoir, Ewell-Brown Collection, Tennessee State Library, Nashville; Sorrell journal, May 11, 1864, MC.

14. Grant, *Personal Memoirs,* 2:562–63; Badeau, *Military History of General Ulysses S. Grant,* 2:220.

15. Lee to Davis, May 23, 1864, in Dowdey, ed., *Wartime Papers of R. E. Lee,* 747–48; Lee to wife, May 23, 1864, ibid., 748; George E. Neese, *Three Years in the Confederate Horse Artillery* (New York, 1911), 274–74.

16. Richard Brady Williams, ed., *Stonewall's Prussian Mapmaker: The Journals of Captain Oscar* Hinrichs (Chapel Hill, 2014), 134–35.

17. Gallagher, *Fighting for the Confederacy,* 422.

18. Howe, *Petersburg Campaign,* 39.

19. Grimsley, *And Keep Moving On,* 223–24; James M. McPherson, *Battle Cry of Freedom: The Civil War Era* (New York, 1988), 757, 771.

20. The historian Robert E. L. Krick of the Richmond National Battlefield Park raises a valid concern about comparing Confederate casualties as determined by Alfred C. Young in his recent *Lee's Army during the Overland Campaign* with Grant's losses as reported in the *Official Records.* Young worked from a far more expansive database than was available to the assemblers of the *OR,* and it is not at all clear that either party employed the same definition for casualties. Krick suspects that a modern analysis done with Young's rigor would show that Union casualties were higher than we now believe, which would change not only the absolute numbers but also the percentage comparisons. If he is correct, I (and others) might indeed be guilty of comparing apples to oranges.

21. Dana, *Recollections,* 210–11.

Bibliography

MANUSCRIPTS

Adriance Library, Poughkepsie, N.Y.
    Robert N. Verplanck Papers
Auburn University Library, Auburn, Ala.
    James H. Lane Collection
        E. J. Hale's Report
Boston Public Library
    Charles A. Whittier Reminiscences
Central Michigan University, Clarke Historical Library, Mount Pleasant
    Lafayette Church Letter
Civil War Library and Museum, Philadelphia
    William Brooke Rawle Diary and Letters
Delaware Public Archives, Dover
    Thomas Smyth Diary
Duke University, William R. Perkins Library, Durham, N.C.
    Richard H. Anderson Report
    Anna B. Campbell Papers
    Hugh Conway Browning Papers
        John P. Lockhart Letter
    John N. Cumming Letters
    J. D. Ferguson Memoranda
    Elliott Welch Papers
Fredericksburg and Spotsylvania National Military Park
    George A. Bowen Diary
    Thomas J. Luttrell Diary
    L. O. Merriam, "Personal Recollections of the War for the Union"
    E. K. Russell Letter
    William Drayton Rutherford Letter

T. J. Watkins Memoir
    Francis Marion Welchel Letter
Georgia Department of Archives and History, Atlanta
    Joseph P. Fuller Diary
    Charles P. Hansell, "History of the 20th Georgia Battalion Cavalry" (memorandum)
Harvard University, Houghton Library, Cambridge, Mass.
    "Correspondence Relative to the March of Barlow's Division, 2nd Army Corps, from the James River to Petersburg, Va., June 15th 1864"
Historical Society of Pennsylvania, Philadelphia
    George G. Meade Collection
        James C. Biddle Letters
    Andrew A. Humphreys Collection
        George G. Meade Letters
Library of Congress, Manuscript Division, Washington, D.C.
    John S. Anglia Letter
    Cyrus B. Comstock Diary
    Wilbur Fisk Diary
    George M. Gilchrist Letter
    E. N. Gilpin Papers
        Samuel J. B. V. Gilpin Diary
    Daniel Reed Larned Letters
    Pickett-Christiancy Papers
        Henry Clay Christiancy Diary
    Horace Porter Letters
    John Reed Papers
    Luther A. Rose Diary
    Gilbert Thompson Memoirs
    James H. Wilson Diary
    Elihu B. Washburne Papers
    Henry A. Wise, "Manuscript of Brigadier General Henry A. Wise Relative to the Battle of Petersburg Virginia in June 1864"
Lloyd House, Alexandria, Va.
    John R. Zimmerman Diary
Manassas National Battlefield Park
    James B. Ricketts Papers
        James M. Read, "Diary of Movements of the 3rd Division, 6th Army Corps"
Maryland Historical Society, Baltimore
    Gibbon Collection
    Lewis H. Steiner Diary
Massachusetts Historical Society, Boston
    Theodore Lyman Letters and Journal

Minnesota Historical Society, Saint Paul
    W. W. Folwell Papers
Museum of the Confederacy, Eleanor S. Brockenbrough Library, Richmond
    Henry Heth's Report
    Fitzhugh Lee's Report
    Joseph Mullen Jr. Diary
    G. Moxley Sorrel Journal
New York State Library and Archives, Albany
    Gouverneur K. Warren Collection
        Washington A. Roebling's Report
        Gouverneur K. Warren Diary and Letters
Niagara County Historian's Office, Lockport, N.Y.
    William C. Beck, "Washington to Petersburg with the Ninth Army Corps"
    William S. Pike Diary
Norfolk Public Library, Va.
    Walter H. Taylor Papers
North Carolina Department of Archives and History, Raleigh
    Dennis D. Ferebee's Report
    William G. Lewis, "Sketch of the Life"
Ontario County Historical Society, Canandaigua, N.Y.
    Henry Lee Manuscripts
Pennsylvania Historical and Museum Commission, Harrisburg
    James A. Beaver Papers
        James A. Beaver Diary
Petersburg National Military Park
    Joseph Mills Hanson, "A Study of the Attack of June 15, 1864"
    Siege Operations: Combat Map No. 1-B, 7:45 P.M., June 15, 1864
Private Collections
    Gary L. Loderhose Private Collection
        W. A. Hunter Letter
    Andrea Solary Private Collection
        Charles Clark Letter
    Zack C. Waters Private Collection
        William Smith Diary
Richmond National Battlefield Park
    Keith S. Bohannon, "Breastworks Are Good Things to Have on Battlefields: Confederate Engineering Operations and Field Fortifications at Cold Harbor"
    Albert Brooker Letter
    Elbert Corbin Diary
    Charles H. Crawford, "With the Pontooneers and Engineers"
    Washington L. Dunn Diary
    J. J. Herd Letter

John Hoffman Diary
H. W. Long, "Reminiscence of the Battle of Cold Harbor"
Rutgers University Library, New Brunswick, N.J.
    Roebling Collection
        Washington A. Roebling Journal
        Washington A. Roebling Letters
    Civil War Diaries and Journals Collection
        Dwight Kilbourn Diary
South Carolina Historical Society, Charleston
    Ellen Pickney Brown Collection
        Edward Octavious Hall, "Some Recollections"
Tennessee State Library, Nashville
    Ewell-Brown Collection
        Campbell Brown Memoir
U.S. Army Military History Institute, Carlisle, Pa.
    Elias A. Bryant Diary
    Susan Boardman Collection
        David A. Stohl Letter
    Civil War Miscellaneous Collection
        John C. Arnold Letter
        Henry C. Carr Diary
        Arthur B. Wyman Letter
    Harrisburg Civil War Round Table Collection
        Henry Keiser Diary
    Lewis Leigh Collection
        H. Pierce Letter
    Murray J. Smith Collection
        Charles R. Paul Diary
University of California Los Angeles Library
    John H. Merrill Diary
University of Florida, P. K. Yonge Library of Florida History, Gainesville
    A.F.G. to Friend Rogero (Mss. Box 79)
University of Michigan, Bentley Historical Library, Ann Arbor
    John E. Irwin Diary
University of North Carolina, Southern Historical Collection, Raleigh
    Edward P. Alexander Collection
        Robert S. Chew Letter
        Frank Huger Letter
        Edward A. T. Nicholson Letter
        Walter H. Taylor Letter
    Boyd Family Papers

University of Oregon, Knight Library, Eugene
    Hazard Stevens Letter
University of South Carolina, South Caroliniana Library, Columbia
    David Ballenger Collection
    Wade Hampton's Report
University of Virginia, Alderman Library, Charlottesville
    Melish M. Lindsey Letter
Vermont Historical Society, Barre
    Samuel E. Pingree Letter
Virginia Historical Society, Richmond
    Lee Headquarters Papers
        Cadmus M. Wilcox Report
Virginia State Library, Richmond
    William Mahone Collection
    Nathaniel Harris Letter
Western Reserve Historical Society, Cleveland
    Palmer Regimental Papers
        Well A. Bushnell Memoirs
Yale University Library, New Haven, Conn.
    Charles M. Coit Letters

NEWSPAPERS

Albany (N.Y.) Evening Journal, October 23, 1895
Anderson (S.C.) Intelligencer, May 26, 1914
Augusta (Ga.) Constitutionalist, January 2, 1864
Batavia (N.Y.) Republican Advocate, June 1864
Boston Evening Journal, June 9, 20, 1864
Charleston (S.C.) Mercury, June 18, 21, 1864
Cincinnati Daily Commercial, March 31, 1865
Detroit Advertiser and Tribune, June 15, 1864
Herkimer County (N.Y.) Journal and Courier, June 23, 1864
Lockport (N.Y.) Daily Journal and Courier, June 29, 1864
Manchester (N.H.) Daily Mirror and American, June 29, 1864
Mobile Daily Advertiser and Register, June 2, 17, 1864
New Orleans Daily Picayune, April 7, 1865
New York Anglo-African, July 7, 9, 1864
New York Daily News, June 13, 23, 1864
New York Daily Tribune, June 11, 15, 18, 20, 1864
New York Herald, June 17, 20, 25, 1864

New York Times, June 7, 8, 9, 14, 17, 18, 19, 21, 26, 1864; April 10, 1881
New York World, June 16, 17, 18, 1864
Niagara Falls (N.Y.) Gazette, August 23, 1938
Philadelphia Inquirer, June 2, 8, 10, 11, 1864
Providence (R.I.) Daily Journal, June 20, June 28, 1864
Raleigh Daily Confederate, June 10, 1864; February 22, 1865
Richmond Daily Confederate, June 21, 1864
Richmond Daily Dispatch, June 6, 8, 9, 11, 14, 17, 1864; August 16, 1896
Richmond Daily Enquirer, June 24, July 2, 1864
Richmond Daily Examiner, June 8, 15, 1864
Richmond Daily Sentinel, June 10, 13, 17, 1864
Richmond Times Dispatch, March 8, 1908
Rochester Daily Union and Advertiser, June 23, July 6, 1864
Rockingham (N.C.) Recorder, June 3, 4, 1864
San Francisco Evening Bulletin, July 5, 1864
Seneca (N.Y.) County Courier, June 30, 1864
Springfield (Mass.) Daily Republican, June 8, 1864
Washington (D.C.) Daily Morning Chronicle, June 11, 18, 1864
Wilmington (N.C.) Daily Journal, June 20, 1864
Winston-Salem (N.C.) Sentinel, January 9, 1915

BIOGRAPHIES, MEMOIRS, AND NARRATIVES

Abbott, Lemuel A. *Personal Recollections and Civil War Diary, 1864.* Burlington, Vt., 1908.
Agassiz, George R., ed. *Meade's Headquarters, 1863–1865: Letters of Colonel Theodore Lyman from the Wilderness to Appomattox.* Boston, 1922.
Annual Report of the Adjutant-General of the Commonwealth of Massachusetts, for the Year Ending December 31, 1864. Boston, 1866.
Archer, Fletcher H. "The Defense of Petersburg on the 9th of June, 1864." In *War Talks of Confederate Veterans,* edited by George S. Bernard, 105–49. Petersburg, Va., 1892.
Armes, George A. *Ups and Downs of an Army Officer.* Washington, D.C., 1900.
Armstrong, Nelson. *Nuggets of Experience.* San Bernardino, Calif., 1904.
Austin, J. Luke, ed. *General John Bratton: Sumter to Appomattox, in Letters to His Wife.* Sewanee, Tenn., 2003.
Badeau, Adam. *Military History of General Ulysses S. Grant, from April, 1861, to April, 1865.* 3 vols. New York, 1881.
Barefoot, Daniel W. *General Robert F. Hoke: Lee's Modest Warrior.* Winston-Salem, N.C., 1996.
Beale G. W. *A Lieutenant of Cavalry in Lee's Army.* Boston, 1918.

Beauregard, G. T. "The Battle of Petersburg." *North American Review* 145 (November 1887): 367–77.

———. "Four Days of Battle at Petersburg." In *B&L*, 4:540–44.

Bennett, Edwin Clark. *Musket and Sword; or, The Camp, March, and Firing Line in the Army of the Potomac*. Boston, 1900.

Blackford, Susan Leigh, comp. *Letters from Lee's Army; or, Memoirs of Life in and out of the Army in Virginia during the War between the States*. New York, 1947.

Bloodgood, John D. *Personal Reminiscences of the War*. New York, 1893.

Bowley, Freeman S. *A Boy Lieutenant: The 30th United States Colored Troops*. Fredericksburg, Va., 1997.

Britton, Ann H., and Thomas J. Reed, eds. *To My Beloved Wife: The Letters and Diaries of Orderly Sergeant John F. L. Hartwell*. Teaneck, N.J., 1997.

Brown, Augustus Cleveland. *Diary of a Line Officer*. New York, 1906.

Bruce, George A. "Petersburg, June 15 — Fort Harrison, September 29: A Comparison." In *PMHSM* 14:85–115.

Bryant, Elias A. *The Diary of Elias A. Bryant of Francestown, N.H.: as Written by Him in His More Than Three Years' Service in the U.S. Army in the Civil War*. Bethesda, Md., 1991.

Buck, Samuel D. *With the Old Confeds: Actual Experiences of a Captain in the Line*. Baltimore, 1925.

Butler, Benjamin F. *Butler's Book: A Review of His Legal, Political, and Military Career*. Boston, 1892.

Campbell, Eric A. *A Grand Terrible Drama*. Bronx, N.Y., 2000.

Carter, Robert G., comp. *Four Brothers in Blue; or, Sunshine and Shadows of the War of the Rebellion*. Austin, Tex., 1978.

Claxton, Melvin, and Mark Puls. *Uncommon Valor: A Story of Race, Patriotism, and Glory in the Final Battles of the Civil War*. Hoboken, N.J., 2006.

Cockrell, Thomas D., and Michael B. Ballard, eds. *A Mississippi Rebel in the Army of Northern Virginia*. Baton Rouge, 1995.

Coco, Gregory A., ed. *Through Blood and Fire: The Civil War Letters of General Charles A. Mills, 1862–1865*. Lanham, Md., 1982.

Coffin, Charles Carleton. *Four Years of Fighting: A Volume of Personal Observations with the Army and Navy, from the First Battle of Bull Run to the Fall of Richmond*. Boston, 1866.

Cook, Roy Bird. "Last Time I Saw General Lee." *Confederate Veteran* 6 (1927): 287.

Cowper, Pulaski, comp. *Extract of Letters of Major-General Bryan Grimes to His Wife*. Raleigh, N.C., 1884.

Cureton, Thomas J. "Reminisces of the War." In *Recollections and Reminiscences,* by South Carolina United Daughters of the Confederacy, 1:200. 10 vols. N.p., 1990–98.

Dame, William M. *From the Rapidan to Richmond and the Spotsylvania Campaign*. Baltimore, 1920.

Dana, Charles A. *Recollections of the Civil War.* New York, 1899.

DeForest, Bartholomew S. *Random Sketches and Wandering Thoughts; or, What I Saw in Camp, on the March, the Bivouac, the Battle Field and Hospital, while with the Army in Virginia, North and South Carolina, during the Late Rebellion.* Albany, N.Y., 1866.

DeMay, Jessica H., ed. *The Civil War Diary of Berea M. Willsey.* Bowie, Md., 1995.

Dollard, Robert. *Recollections of the Civil War and Going West to Grow Up with the Country.* Scotland, S.D., 1906.

Dowdey, Clifford, ed. *The Wartime Papers of R. E. Lee* .New York, 1961.

Doyle, W. E. "Gary's Fight at Riddle's Shop." *Confederate Veteran* 39 (January 1931): 19–20.

Dyer, J. Franklin. *The Journal of a Civil War Surgeon.* Edited by Michael B. Chesson. Lincoln, Neb., 2003.

Early, Jubal A. *Autobiographical Sketch and Narrative of the War between the States.* Bloomington, Ind., 1960.

Favill, Josiah M. *The Diary of a Young Officer Serving with the Armies of the United States during the War of the Rebellion.* Chicago, 1909.

Figg, Royall W. *Where Only Men Dare to Go; or, The Story of a Boy Company.* Baton Rouge, 2008.

Fleming, Francis P. *Memoir of C. Seton Fleming, of the Second Florida Infantry, C.S.A.* Jacksonville, Fla., 1881.

Foote, Shelby. *The Civil War—A Narrative.* 3 vols. New York, 1974.

Ford, Worthington Chauncey, ed. *A Cycle of Adams Letters, 1861–1865.* 2 vols. Boston, 1920.

Fowler, Philemon H., comp. *Memorials of William Fowler.* New York, 1875.

Freeman, Douglas Southall, ed. *Lee's Dispatches to Jefferson Davis.* New York, 1957.

———. *Lee's Lieutenants: A Study in Command.* 3 vols. New York, 1942.

———. *R. E. Lee: A Biography.* 4 vols. New York, 1934.

Freeman, Warren Hapgood. *Letters from Two Brothers Serving in the War for the Union to Other Family at Home in West Cambridge, Mass.* Cambridge, Mass., 1871.

Gallagher, Gary W., ed. *Fighting for the Confederacy: The Personal Recollections of General Edward Porter Alexander.* Chapel Hill, N.C., 1989.

———. "Our Hearts Are Full of Hope: The Army of Northern Virginia in the Spring of 1864." In *The Wilderness Campaign,* edited by Gary W. Gallagher, 36–65. Chapel Hill, N.C., 1997.

Galwey, Thomas Francis. *The Valiant Hours: An Irishman in the Civil War.* Harrisburg, Pa., 1961.

Gause, Isaac. *Four Years with Five Armies* (New York, 1908).

Georgia Division, United Daughters of the Confederacy. *Confederate Reminiscences and Letters 1861–1865.* Atlanta, 1996.

Gerrish, Theodore. *Army Life: A Private's Reminiscences of the Civil War.* Portland, Maine, 1882.

Gibbon, John. *Personal Recollections of the Civil War.* New York, 1928.

Gordon, John B. *Reminiscences of the Civil War.* New York, 1904.

Grant, Ulysses S. *The Personal Memoirs of U. S. Grant.* 2 vols. New York, 1885.

Greene, A. Wilson. *Civil War Petersburg: Confederate City in the Crucible of War.* Charlottesville, Va., 2007.

———. "P. G. T. Beauregard and the Petersburg Campaign." In *Lee and His Generals: Essays in Honor of T. Harry Williams,* edited by Lawrence Lee Hewitt and Thomas E. Schott, 153–80. Knoxville, 2012.

Greenleaf, Margery, ed. *Letters to Eliza from a Union Soldier, 1862–1865.* Chicago, 1970.

Greiner, James M., et al., eds. *A Surgeon's Civil War: The Letters and Diary of Daniel M. Holt, M.D.* Kent, Ohio, 1994.

Hagood, Johnson. *Memoirs of the War of Secession.* Columbia, S.C., 1910.

Hall, James O., ed. "An Army of Devils: The Diary of Ella Washington." *Civil War Times Illustrated* (February 1978): 18–25.

Halliburton, Lloyd. *Saddle Soldiers: The Civil War Correspondence of General William Stokes of the 4th South Carolina Cavalry.* Orangeburg, S.C., 1993.

Hannum, Warren T. "The Crossing of the James River in 1864." *Military Engineer* 15 (May–June 1923): 229–37.

Hennessy, John J. "I Dread the Spring: The Army of the Potomac Prepares for the Overland Campaign." In *The Wilderness Campaign,* edited by Gary W. Gallagher, 66–105. Chapel Hill, N.C., 1997.

Hess, Earl J. *In the Trenches at Petersburg: Field Fortifications and Confederate Defeat.* Chapel Hill, N.C., 2009.

———. *Trench Warfare under Grant and Lee: Field Fortifications in the Overland Campaign.* Chapel Hill, N.C., 2007.

"Historical Sketch." *Our Living and Our Dead,* April 22, 1874.

Howe, Mark D., ed. *Touched with Fire: Civil War Letters and Diary of Oliver Wendell Holmes Jr., 1861–1864.* New York, 1969.

Humphreys, Andrew A. *The Virginia Campaign of '64 and '65.* New York, 1883.

Humphreys, Henry H. *Andrew Atkinson Humphreys: A Biography.* Philadelphia, 1924.

Hutchinson, Olin Fulmer, Jr., ed. *"My Dear Mother and Sisters": Civil War Letters of Capt. A. B. Mulligan, Co. B, 5th South Carolina Cavalry—Butler's Division—Hampton's Corps, 1861–1865.* Spartanburg S.C., 1992.

Hyde, John H., ed. *Civil War Letters by General Thomas Hyde.* Privately printed, 1933.

Hyde, Thomas W. *Following the Greek Cross; or, Memories of the Sixth Army Corps.* Boston, 1894.

Jackson, Harry F., and Thomas F. O'Donnell, eds. *Back Home in Oneida: Hermon Clarke and His Letters.* Syracuse, N.Y., 1965.

Jordan, David M. *Happiness Is Not My Companion: The Life of General G. K. Warren.* Bloomington, Ind., 2001.

———. *Winfield Scott Hancock: A Soldier's Life.* Bloomington, Ind., 1988.

Kautz, August V. "First Attempts to Capture Petersburg." In *B&L*, 4:533–37.

——. "The Siege of Petersburg: Two Failures to Capture the 'Cockade City.'" In *Battles and Leaders of the Civil War, Volume 6*, edited by Peter Cozzens, 393–406. Urbana, Ill., 2007.

Kautz, Lawrence G. *August Valentine Kautz, USA: Biography of a Civil War General*. Jefferson, N.C., 2008.

Keiley, Anthony M. *In Vinculus; or, The Prisoner of War, being the Experience of a Rebel in Two Federal Pens, Interspersed with Reminiscences of the Late War, Anecdotes of Southern Generals, Etc*. New York, 1866.

Koempel, Philip. *Phil Koempel's Diary, 1861–1865*. N.p., 1920.

Kundahl, George H., ed. *The Bravest of the Brave: Correspondence of Stephen Dodson Ramseur*. Chapel Hill, N.C., 2014.

Livermore, Thomas L. *Days and Events, 1860–1866*. Boston, 1920.

——. "Failure to Take Petersburg." In *PMHSM*, 5:35–73.

——. "The Truce for Collecting the Wounded at Cold Harbor." In *PMHSM*, 4:457–59.

Longacre, Edward G. *Army of Amateurs: General Benjamin F. Butler and the Army of the James, 1863–1865*. Mechanicsburg, Pa., 1997.

Loving, Jerome M., ed. *Civil War Letters of George Washington Whitman*. Durham, N.C., 1975.

Lowe, David W., ed. *Meade's Army: The Private Notebooks of Lt. Col. Theodore Lyman*. Kent, Ohio, 2007.

Lutz, Caroline Chamberlin, ed. *Letters of George E. Chamberlin*. Springfield, Ill., 1883.

Lyman, Theodore. "Crossing of the James and Advance on Petersburg." In *PMHSM*, 5:25–31.

——. "Operations of the Army of the Potomac, June 5–15, 1864." In *PMHSM*, 5:1–24.

Marshall, Jessie Ames, comp. *Private and Official Correspondence of Gen. Benjamin F. Butler during the Period of the Civil War*. 5 vols. Norwood, Mass., 1917.

McBride, R. E. "The Bucktails." *National Tribune*, February 12, 1885.

McCabe, W. Gordon. "Defense of Petersburg." In *SHSP*, 2:257–306.

McCaslin, Richard B. *Lee in the Shadow of Washington*. Baton Rouge, 2004.

McIntosh, D. G. "Sketch of the Military Career of David G. McIntosh." In *Treasured Reminiscences*, collected by John K. McIver Chapter, UDC, 47–52. Columbia, S.C., 1911.

McMurray, John. *Recollections of a Colored Troop*. Brookville, Pa., 1916.

Meade, George, ed. *Life and Letters of George Gordon Meade*. 2 vols. New York, 1913.

Menge, Springer W., ed. *Civil War Notebook of Daniel Chisolm*. New York, 1989.

Meyers, Augustus. *Ten Years in the Ranks, U.S. Army*. New York, 1979.

Michie, Peter S. ed. *The Life and Letters of Emory Upton, Colonel of the Fourth Regiment of Artillery, and Brevet Major-General, U.S. Army*. New York, 1885.

Miers, Earl S., ed. *Wash Roebling's War.* Newark, 1961.

Miller, Delavan S. *Drum Taps in Dixie: Memoirs of a Drummer Boy, 1861–1865.* Watertown, N.Y., 1905.

Miller, Richard F., and Roger F. Mooney. *The Civil War: The Nantucket Experience.* Nantucket, Mass., 1994.

Moffett, Mary Conner, ed. *Letters of General James Conner.* Columbia, S.C., 1950.

Montgomery, George F., Jr., ed. *Georgia Sharpshooter: The Civil War Diary and Letters of William Rhadamanthus Montgomery, 1839–1906.* Macon, Ga., 1997.

Moore, Gilbert C., Jr., ed. *The Civil War Letters of Lt. Cornelius L. Moore, Co. I, 57th Regiment, New York State Volunteers.* Chattanooga, Tenn., 1989.

Morrill, Lily Logan. *A Builder of the New South: Notes on the Career of Thomas M. Logan.* Boston, 1940.

———, ed. *My Confederate Girlhood: The Memoirs of Kate Virginia Cox Logan.* Richmond, 1932.

Morrison, R. V. "A Story without a Hero." *Confederate Veteran* 27 (January 1919): 57–58.

Morse, F. W. *Personal Experiences in the War of the Great Rebellion, from December, 1862, to July, 1865.* Albany, N.Y., 1866.

The National Tribune *Scrap Book: Stories of the Camp, March, Battle, Hospital, and Prison Told by Comrades.* Washington, D.C., 1909.

Nevins, Allan, ed. *Diary of Battle: The Personal Journals of Colonel Charles S. Wainwright, 1861–1865.* New York, 1962.

Newsome, Hampton, et al., eds. *Civil War Talks: Further Reminiscences of George S. Bernard and His Fellow Veterans.* Charlottesville, Va., 2012.

New York State Historian. *Third Annual Report of the State Historian of the State of New York.* New York, 1898.

O'Beirne, Kevin. "Our Boys Stood Up like Heroes." *Irish Volunteer* 5 (2000): 1.

Olcott, Mark, ed. *The Civil War Letters of Lewis Bissell.* Washington, D.C., 1981.

Page, Charles A. *Letters of a War Correspondent.* Boston, 1899.

Palladino, Anita, ed. *Diary of a Yankee Engineer: The Civil War Story of John H. Westervelt, Engineer, 1st New York Volunteer Engineer Corps.* New York, 1997.

Parker, Ezra K. *From the Rapidan to the James under Grant.* Providence, R.I., 1909.

Peabody, Frank E. "Some Observations Concerning the Opposing Forces at Petersburg on June 15, 1864." In *PMHSM*, 5:147–56.

Peacock, Jane Bonner, ed. "A Georgian's View of War in Virginia." *Atlanta Historical Journal* 23, no. 2 (Atlanta 1979): 91–136.

Pennypacker, Isaac R. *General Meade.* New York, 1901.

[Phillips, John Wilson]. "The Civil War Diary of John Wilson Phillips." *Virginia Magazine of History and Biography* 62, no. 1 (January 1954): 96–123.

Porter, Horace. *Campaigning with Grant.* New York, 1897.

Power, J. Tracy. *Lee's Miserables: Life in the Army of Northern Virginia from the Wilderness to Appomattox.* Chapel Hill, N.C., 1998.

Priest, John Michael, ed. *One Surgeon's Private War: Doctor William W. Potter of the 57th New York*. Shippensburg, Pa., 1996.

Ramey, Emily G., and John K. Gott, comps. *The Years of Anguish: Fauquier County, Virginia*. N.p., 1965.

Reid, Brian Holden. "Another Look at Grant's Crossing of the James, 1864." *Civil War History* 39, no. 4 (December 1993): 291–316.

Rhodes, Robert Hunt, ed. *All for the Union: the Civil War Diary and Letters of Elisha Hunt Rhodes*. New York, 1991.

Ritchie, Norman L., ed. *Four Years in the New York Light Artillery: The Papers of David F. Ritchie*. New York, 1997.

Roberts, Agatha L. *As They Remembered*. New York, 1964.

Robertson, James I., Jr., ed. *The Civil War Letters of Robert McAllister*. New Brunswick, N.J., 1965.

Robertson, William G. *Backdoor to Richmond: The Bermuda Hundred Campaign*. Baton Rouge, 1987.

———. *The Petersburg Campaign: The Battle of Old Men and Young Boys, June 9, 1864*. Lynchburg, Va., 1989.

Rodgers, W. A. "Cavalry's Bold Move." *National Tribune*, May 6, 1897.

Roemer, Jacob. *Reminiscences of the War of the Rebellion*. Flushing, N.Y., 1897.

Roman, Alfred. *Military Operations of General Beauregard in the War between the States, 1861–1865*. New York, 1884.

Rose, Joseph A. *Grant under Fire*. New York, 2015.

Rosenblatt, Emil, and Ruth Rosenblatt, eds. *Hard Marching Every Day: The Civil War Letters of Wilbur Fisk, 1861–1865*. Lawrence, Kans., 1992.

Sallada, William A. *Silver Sheaves: Gathered through Clouds and Sunshine*. Bethesda, Md., 1992.

Schiller, Herbert M., ed., *Autobiography of Major General William F. Smith, 1861–1864*. Dayton, Ohio, 1990.

———. *The Bermuda Hundred Campaign*. Dayton, Ohio, 1988.

Sheridan, Philp H. *Personal Memoirs of P. H. Sheridan*. 2 vols. New York, 1888.

Silliker, Ruth L. ed. *The Rebel Yell and the Yankee Hurrah: The Civil War Journal of a Maine Volunteer, Private John W. Haley, 17th Maine Regiment*. Camden, Maine, 1985.

Simon, John Y., ed. *The Papers of Ulysses S. Grant*. 20 vols. Carbondale, Ill., 1967–99.

Simpson, Brooks D. *Ulysses S. Grant: Triumph over Adversity, 1822–1865*. Boston, 2000.

Small, Harold A., ed. *The Road to Richmond: The Civil War Memoirs of Major Abner R. Small of the 16th Maine Vols.: With His Diary as a Prisoner of War*. Berkeley, Calif., 1957.

Smith, Thomas T., ed. *The Reminiscences of Major General Zenal R. Bliss, 1854–1876*. Austin, Tex., 2007.

Smith, William F. *From Chattanooga to Petersburg under Generals Grant and Butler.* Boston, 1893.

——. "General W. F. Smith at Petersburg." *Century Magazine* 54 (1897).

——. "The Movement against Petersburg, June, 1864." In *PMHSM,* 5:75–116.

Sorrel, G. Moxley. *Recollections of a Confederate Staff Officer.* New York, 1917.

Sparks, David S., ed. *Inside Lincoln's Army: The Diary of Marsena Rudolph Patrick, Provost Marshal General, Army of the Potomac.* New York, 1964.

Spear, Abbot, ed. *Civil War Recollections of General Ellis Spear.* Orono, Maine, 1997.

Spies, Mary-Joy, ed. *Yours Only, Thomas: Letters from a Union Soldier.* Valhalla, N.Y., 1999.

Stevens, George T. *Three Years in the Sixth Corps.* Albany, N.Y., 1866.

Stiles, Robert. *Four Years under Marse Robert.* New York, 1903.

Stone, James M. *Personal Recollections of the Civil War.* Boston, 1918.

Sumner, Merlin E., ed. *The Diary of Cyrus B. Comstock.* Dayton, Ohio, 1987.

Swank, Walbrook D., ed. *Stonewall Jackson's Foot Cavalry: Company A, 13th Virginia Infantry.* Shippensburg, Pa., 2001.

Symonds, Craig L., ed. *Union Combined Operations in the Civil War.* New York, 2013.

Tenney, Luman Harris. *War Diary, 1861–1865.* Cleveland, 1914.

Thomas, Benjamin P., ed. *Three Years with Grant, as Recalled by War Correspondent Sylvanus Cadwallader.* New York, 1961.

Thomas, Mary Warner, and Richard A. Sauers, eds. *"I Never Want to Witness Such Sights": The Civil War Letters of First Lieutenant James B. Thomas, Adjutant, 107th Pennsylvania Volunteers.* Baltimore, 1995.

Thomas, William M. "The Slaughter at Petersburg, June 18, 1864" In *SHSP,* 25:222–30.

Thompson, Magnus S. "From the Ranks to Brigade Commander." *Confederate Veteran* 29 (1921): 301.

Tilney, Robert. *My Life in the Army: Three Years and a Half with the Fifth Army Corps, Army of the Potomac, 1862–1865.* Philadelphia, 1912.

Tomasak, Peter, ed. *Avery Harris Civil War Journal.* N.p., 2000.

Trout, Robert J. *Galloping Thunder: The Stuart Horse Artillery Battalion.* Mechanicsburg, Pa., 2002.

Trudeau, Noah Andre. *Like Men of War: Black Troops in the Civil War, 1862–1865.* Boston, 1998.

True, Ransom Badger. *Plantation on the James: Weyanoke and Her People, 1607–1938.* Privately printed, 1986.

Turino, Kenneth C., ed. *The Civil War Diary of Lieut. J. E. Hodgkins, 19th Massachusetts Volunteers, from August 11, 1862, to June 3, 1865.* Camden, Maine, n.d.

Ulmer, George T. *Adventures and Reminiscences of a Volunteer: A Drummer Boy from Maine.* N.p, 1892.

Venable, Charles S. "General Lee in the Wilderness Campaign." In *B&L,* 4:240–46.

Wagstaff, Henry M., ed. "Letters of Thomas Jackson Strayhorn." *North Carolina Historical Review* 13, no. 4 (October 1936): 311–34.

Walker, Francis A. *General Hancock*. New York, 1895.

Waring, Joseph I., ed. "The Diary of William G. Hinson during the War of Secession." *South Carolina Historical Magazine* 75, no. 1 (January 1974): 14–23.

Warner, Ezra J. *Generals in Blue: Lives of the Union Commanders*. 1964. Reprint, Baton Rouge, 1995.

Waugh, John C. *Reelecting Lincoln: The Battle for the 1864 Presidency*. New York, 1997.

Weld, Stephen M. *War Diary and Letters of Stephen Minot Weld, 1861–1865*. Cambridge, Mass., 1912.

Wells, Edward L. *A Sketch of the Charleston Light Dragoons*. Charleston, S.C., 1888.

Wilkeson, Frank. *Recollections of a Private Soldier in the Army of the Potomac*. New York, 1887.

Williams, Edward B., ed. *Rebel Brothers: The Civil War Letters of the Truehearts*. College Station, Tex., 1995.

Wilson, James H. *Under the Old Flag*. 2 vols. New York, 1912.

Wilson, LeGrand James. *The Confederate Soldier*. Fayetteville, Ark., 1902.

[Wingfield, H. W.] "Diary of Captain H. W. Wingfield." *Bulletin of the Virginia State Library* 16 (July 1927): 27–48.

Wise, Barton H. *The Life of Henry A. Wise*. London, 1899.

Wise, Henry A. "The Career of Wise's Brigade, 1861–1865." In *SHSP*, 25:1–21.

Wittenberg, Eric. *Glory Enough for All: Sheridan's Second Raid and the Battle of Trevilian Station*. Lincoln, Neb., 2007.

Young, Alfred C. *Lee's Army during the Overland Campaign*. Baton Rouge, 2013.

Younger, Edward, ed. *Inside the Confederate Government: The Diary of Robert Garlick Hill Kean*. Baton Rouge, 1993.

UNIT HISTORIES

Adams, John G. B. *Reminiscences of the Nineteenth Massachusetts Regiment*. Boston, 1899.

Albert, Allen D. *History of the Forty-Fifth Regiment Pennsylvania Volunteer Infantry, 1861–1865*. Williamsport, Pa., 1912.

Annual Circular of the Secretary of the Regimental Association (Twelfth Webster Regiment). Number 7. 1902.

Aubery, James M. *The Thirty-Sixth Wisconsin Volunteer Infantry*. Milwaukee, 1900.

Banes, Charles H. *History of the Philadelphia Brigade*. Philadelphia, 1876.

Baquet, Camille A. *History of the First Brigade, New Jersey Volunteers, from 1861 to 1865*. Trenton, N.J., 1910.

Bartlett, Asa W. *History of the Twelfth Regiment, New Hampshire Volunteers, in the War of the Rebellion*. Concord, N.H., 1897.

Beale, Richard L. T. *History of the 9th Virginia Cavalry in the War between the States.* Richmond, 1899.

Benedict, George G. *Vermont in the Civil War: A History of the Part Taken by the Vermont Soldiers and Sailors in the War for the Union, 1861–5.* 2 vols. Burlington, Vt., 1888.

Best, Isaac O. *History of the 121st New York State Infantry.* Chicago, 1921.

Billings, John D. *The History of the Tenth Massachusetts Battery of Light Artillery in the War of the Rebellion.* Boston, 1881.

Bobbyshell, Oliver Christian. *The 48th in the War, being a Narrative of the 48th Regiment Infantry, Pennsylvania Veteran Volunteers, during the War of the Rebellion.* Philadelphia, 1895.

Boudrye, Louis N. *Historic Records of the Fifth New York Cavalry, First Ira Harris Guard.* Albany, N.Y., 1865.

Bowen, James L. *History of the Thirty-Seventh Regiment Massachusetts Volunteers in the Civil War of 1861–1865.* Holyoke, Mass., 1884.

Brainard, Mary G. *Campaigns of the One Hundred and Forty-Sixth Regiment New York State Volunteers.* New York, 1915.

Brown, J. Willard. *The Signal Corps, U.S.A., in the War of the Rebellion.* Boston, 1896.

Bruce, George A. *The Twentieth Regiment of Massachusetts Volunteer Infantry, 1861–1865.* Boston, 1906.

Burrage, Henry S. *History of Thirty-Sixth Regiment Massachusetts Volunteers, 1862–1865.* Boston, 1884.

Caldwell, J. F. J., *The History of a Brigade of South Carolinians, First Known as Gregg's, and Subsequently as McGowan's Brigade.* Philadelphia, 1866.

Cheek, Philip, and Mair Pointon. *History of the Salk County Riflemen, Known as Company A, Sixth Wisconsin Veteran Volunteer Infantry, 1861–1865.* Madison, Wis., 1909.

Child, William. *A History of the Fifth Regiment, New Hampshire Volunteers, in the American Civil War, 1861–1865.* Bristol, N.H., 1893.

Clark, James H. *The Iron Hearted Regiment.* Albany, 1865.

Cogswell, Leander W. *A History of the Eleventh New Hampshire Regiment Volunteer Infantry in the War of the Rebellion.* Concord, N.H., 1891.

Committee of the Regiment. *History of the Thirty-Fifth Regiment Massachusetts Volunteers.* Boston, 1884.

Committee of the Regiment. *History of the Thirty-Sixth Regiment Massachusetts Volunteers.* Boston, 1884.

Cook, Benjamin F. *History of the Twelfth Massachusetts Volunteers.* Boston, 1882.

Cooke, John R. "27th North Carolina Infantry." *Our Living and Our Dead,* January 14, 1874.

Craft, David. *History of the One Hundred Forty-First Regiment, Pennsylvania Volunteers.* Towanda, Pa., 1885.

Cruikshank, George L. *Back in the Sixties: Reminiscences of the Service of Company A, 11th Pennsylvania Regiment.* Fort Dodge, Iowa, 1893.

Cunningham, John L. *Three Years with the Adirondack Regiment: 118th New York Volunteers Infantry.* Norwood, Mass., 1920.

Curtis, O. B. *History of the Twenty-Fourth Michigan of the Iron Brigade.* Detroit, 1891.

Dalton, Peter P. *With Our Faces to the Foe: A History of the 4th Maine Infantry in the War of the Rebellion.* Union, Maine, 1998.

Davis, Charles E. *Three Years in the Army: The Story of the Thirteenth Massachusetts Volunteers from July 16, 1861, to August 1, 1864.* Boston, 1894.

Davis, Graham. "Twenty-Second Regiment." In *Histories of the Several Regiments and Battalions from North Carolina in the Great War, 1861–'65,* edited by Walter Clark, 2:161–80. 5 vols. Goldsboro, N.C., 1901.

Denny, Joseph Waldo. *Wearing the Blue in the Twenty-Fifth Mass. Volunteer Infantry.* Worcester, Mass., 1879.

Derby, William P. *Bearing Arms in the Twenty-Seventh Massachusetts Regiment of Volunteer Infantry during the Civil War.* Boston, 1883.

———. "The Star Brigade." In Carleton, *Stories of Our Soldiers: War Reminiscences by "Carleton" and by Soldiers of New England, Collected from the Series Written Especially for the* Boston Journal. Boston, 1898.

Dickert, D. Augustus. *History of Kershaw's Brigade.* Newberry, S.C., 1899.

DuBose, Henry Kershaw. *The History of Company B, Twenty-First Regiment (Infantry), South Carolina Volunteers.* Columbia, S.C., 1909.

Dunlop, William S. *Lee's Sharpshooters; or, The Forefront of Battle: A Story of Southern Valor That Never Has Been Told.* Little Rock, 1899.

Dunn, Wilbur R. *Full Measure of Devotion: The Eighth New York Volunteer Heavy Artillery.* 2 vols. Kearney, Neb., 1997.

Eden, R. C. *The Sword and Gun: A History of the 37th Wisconsin Volunteer Infantry.* Madison, Wis., 1865.

Elliott, Charles E. "Martin's Brigade, of Hoke's Division, 1863–64." In *SHSP,* 23:189–98.

Emmerton, James A. *Record of the Twenty-Third Regiment Massachusetts Volunteer Infantry in the War of the Rebellion, 1861–1865.* Boston, 1886.

Evans, Robert G., comp. *The 16th Mississippi Infantry: Civil War Letters and Reminiscences.* Jackson, Miss., 2002.

Everts, Hermann. *A Complete and Comprehensive History of the Ninth Regiment New Jersey Volunteer Infantry.* Newark, 1865.

Gaff, Alan D. *On Many a Bloody Field: Four Years in the Iron Brigade.* Bloomington, Ind., 1999.

Galloway, John M. "Sixty-Third Regiment." In *Histories of the Several Regiments and Battalions from North Carolina in the Great War, 1861–'65,* compiled by Walter Clark, 3:529–57. 5 vols. Goldsboro, N.C., 1901.

Graham, Robert D. "Fifty-Sixth Regiment." *Histories of the Several Regiments and*

Battalions from North Carolina in the Great War, 1861–'65, compiled by Walter Clark, 3:313–404. 5 vols. Goldsboro, N.C., 1901.

"Hagood's Brigade: Its Services in the Trenches of Petersburg, Virginia, 1864." In *SHSP,* 16:397–98.

Haines, Alanson A. *History of the Fifteenth Regiment New Jersey Volunteers.* New York, 1883.

Hall, Henry, and James Hall. *Cayuga in the Field: A Record of the 19th New York Volunteers, All the Batteries of the 3rd New York Artillery, and 75th New York Volunteers.* Auburn, N.Y., 1873.

Hall, Isaac. *History of the Ninety-Seventh Regiment New York Volunteers (Conkling Rifles) in the War for the Union.* Utica, N.Y, 1890.

Haskin, William L., comp. *The History of the First Regiment of Artillery, from Its Organization in 1821, to January 1st, 1876.* Portland, Maine, 1879.

Haynes, Edwin M. *A History of the Tenth Regiment, Vermont Volunteers.* Lewiston, Maine, 1870.

Hillhouse, Don. *Heavy Artillery and Light Infantry: A History of the 1st Florida Special Battalion and 10th Infantry Regiment, CSA.* Jacksonville, Fla., 1992.

Hoffman, Elliott W., ed. *History of the First Vermont Cavalry Volunteers in the War of the Great Rebellion.* Baltimore, 2000.

Hopkins, William P. *The Seventh Regiment Rhode Island Volunteers.* Boston, 1903.

Houston, Henry C. *The Thirty-Second Maine Regiment of Infantry Volunteers.* Portland, Maine, 1903.

Izlar, William V. *A Sketch of the War Record of the Edisto Rifles.* Columbia, S.C., 1914.

Jackman, Lyman, and Amos Hadley. *History of the Sixth New Hampshire Regiment in the War for the Union.* Concord, N.H., 1891.

Jones, Charles R. "Historical Sketch, 55th North Carolina." *Our Living and Our Dead,* April 22, 1874.

Judson, Amos M. *History of the Eighty-Third Regiment Pennsylvania Volunteers.* Erie, Pa., 1865.

Keating, Robert. *Carnival of Blood: The Civil War Ordeal of the Seventh New York Heavy Artillery.* Baltimore, 1998.

Kent, Arthur A., ed. *Three Years with Company K: Sergt. Austin C. Stearns, Company K, 13th Massachusetts Infantry.* Rutherford, N.J., 1976.

Kreutzer, William. *Notes and Observations Made during Four Years of Service with the Ninety-Eighth New York Volunteers, in the War of 1861.* Philadelphia, 1878.

Laboda, Lawrence R. *From Selma to Appomattox: The History of the Jeff Davis Artillery.* Oxford, Miss., 1994.

Lawhon, William H. H. "Forty-Eighth Regiment." In *Histories of the Several Regiments and Battalions from North Carolina in the Great War, 1861–'65,* compiled by Walter Clark, 3:113–24. 5 vols. Goldsboro, N.C., 1901.

LeBarr, Steven M. *The Fifth Massachusetts Colored Cavalry in the Civil War.* Jefferson, N.C., 2016.

Locke, William H. *The Story of the Regiment*. Philadelphia, 1868.

Loeher, Charles T. *War History of the Old First Virginia Infantry Regiment, Army of Northern Virginia*. Richmond, 1884.

Longacre, Edward G. *Custer and His Wolverines: The Michigan Cavalry Brigade, 1861–1865*. Boston, 2004.

Lord, Edward O. *History of the Ninth Regiment, New Hampshire Volunteers in the War of the Rebellion*. Concord, N.H., 1895.

Maier, Larry B. *Rough and Regular: A History of Philadelphia's 119th Regiment of Pennsylvania Volunteer Infantry, the Gray Reserves*. Philadelphia, 1997.

Malles, Ed, ed., *Bridge Building in Wartime: Colonel Wesley Brainerd's Memoir of the 50th New York Volunteer Engineers*. Knoxville, Tenn., 1997.

Marbaker, Thomas D. *History of the Eleventh New Jersey Volunteers*. Trenton, N.J., 1898.

Mark, Penrose G. *Red, White, and Blue Badge: Pennsylvania Veteran Volunteers: A History of the 93rd Regiment, Known as the "Lebanon Infantry."* Harrisburg, Pa., 1911.

Marshall, D. P. *History of Company K, 155th Pennsylvania Volunteer Zouaves*. N.p., 1888.

McCarthy, Carlton. *Contributions to a History of the Richmond Howitzer Battalion*. Richmond, 1883–85.

McDonald, William. *A History of the Laurel Brigade, Originally the Ashby Cavalry of the Army of Northern Virginia and Chew's Battery*. Baltimore, 1907.

McLaurin, William H. "Eighteenth Regiment." In *Histories of the Several Regiments and Battalions from North Carolina in the Great War, 1861–'65*, compiled by Walter Clark, 2:15–78. 5 vols. Goldsboro, N.C., 1901.

Means, Paul B. "Additional Sketch Sixty-Third Regiment." In *Histories of the Several Regiments and Battalions from North Carolina in the Great War, 1861–'65*, compiled by Walter Clark, 3:545–658. 5 vols. Goldsboro, N.C., 1901.

Members of the Regiment. *The Story of the 21st Regiment, Connecticut Volunteer Infantry, during the Civil War*. Middletown, Conn., 1900.

Mills, George Henry. *History of the 16th North Carolina Regiment in the Civil War*. Rutherfordton, N.C., 1901.

Mowris, James A. *A History of the One Hundred Seventeenth Regiment New York Volunteers (Fourth Oneida), from the Date of Its Organization, August, 1862, to That of Its Muster Out, June, 1865*. Hartford, Conn., 1866.

Muffly, J. W. *The Story of Our Regiment: A History of the 148th Pennsylvania Volunteers*. Des Moines, 1904.

Mulholland, St. Clair A. *The Story of the 116th Regiment Pennsylvania Volunteers in the War of the Rebellion: The Record of a Gallant Command*. Philadelphia, 1899.

Myers, Frank M. *The Comanches: A History of White's Battalion, Virginia Cavalry, Laurel Brigade, Hampton Division, A.N.V., C.S.A.* Baltimore, 1871.

Newell, Joseph K. *Ours: Annals of 10th Regiment, Massachusetts Volunteers in the Rebellion*. Springfield, Mass., 1875.

Norton, Henry. *Deeds of Daring; or, History of the Eighth New York Volunteer Cavalry*. Norwich, N.Y., 1889.

Palmer, Abraham J. *The History of the Forty-Eighth Regiment, New York State Volunteers*. Brooklyn, N.Y., 1885.

Park, Robert E. *Sketch of the Twelfth Alabama*. Richmond, 1906.

Parker, John L. *Henry Wilson's Regiment: History of the Twenty-Second Massachusetts Infantry, the Second Company Sharpshooters, and the Third Light Battery, in the War of the Rebellion*. Boston, 1887.

Powell, William H. *History of the Fifth Army Corps*. New York, 1896.

Preston, Noble D. *History of the Tenth Regiment of Cavalry, New York State Volunteers*. New York, 1892.

Price, Isaiah. *History of the Ninety-Seventh Regiment Pennsylvania Volunteer Infantry during the War of the Rebellion, 1861–1865*. Philadelphia, 1875.

Putnam, Samuel H. *The Story of Company A, Twenty-Fifth Regiment Mass. Volunteers in the War of the Rebellion*. Worcester, Mass., 1886.

Pyne, Henry R. *Ride to War: The History of the First New Jersey Cavalry*. New Brunswick, N.J., 1961.

Raiford, Neil Hunter. *The Fourth North Carolina Cavalry in the Civil War*. Jefferson, N.C., 2003.

Rawle, William B. *History of the Third Pennsylvania Cavalry, Sixtieth Regiment Pennsylvania Volunteers, in the American Civil War*. Philadelphia, 1905.

Ripley, William Y. W. *Vermont Riflemen in the War for the Union, 1861–1865: A History of Company F, First United States Sharpshooters*. Rutland, Vt., 1883.

Roback, Henry. *The Veteran Volunteers of Herkimer and Otsego Counties in the War of the Rebellion, being a History of the 152nd New York*. Little Falls, N.Y.

Rockwell, Alfred P. "The Tenth Army Corps in Virginia, May, 1864." In *PMHSM*, 9:265–99.

Rodenbough, Theophilus F. *History of the 18th Regiment of Cavalry Pennsylvania Reserves*. New York, 1909.

Roe, Alfred S. *The Tenth Regiment Massachusetts Volunteer Infantry, 1861–1864*. Springfield, Mass, 1909.

———. *The Thirty-Ninth Regiment Massachusetts Volunteers, 1862–1865*. Worcester, Mass., 1914.

Rogers, Edward W. *Sketch of the Services of the Nineteenth N.Y. Battery*. Copied by B. Conrad Bush. Ann Arbor, Mich., n.d.

Roper, John L. *History of the Eleventh Pennsylvania Volunteer Cavalry*. Philadelphia, 1902.

Simons, Ezra D. *A Regimental History of the One Hundred and Twenty-Fifth New York State Volunteers*. New York, 1888.

The Sixty-Second Pennsylvania Volunteers in the War for the Union: Dedicatory Exercises at Gettysburg, September 11, 1889. Bethesda, Md. 1992.

Small, Abner R. *The Sixteenth Maine Regiment in the War of Rebellion, 1861–1865.* Portland, Maine, 1886.

Smith, Abram P. *History of the Seventy-Sixth Regiment, New York Volunteers.* Syracuse, N.Y., 1867.

Smith, John D. *The History of the Nineteenth Regiment of Maine Volunteer Infantry, 1862–1865.* Minneapolis, 1909.

Smith, John L. *Antietam to Appomattox with the 118th Pennsylvania.* N.p., 1892.

————. *History of the Corn Exchange Regiment: 118th Pennsylvania Volunteers, from Their First Engagement at Antietam to Appomattox.* Philadelphia, 1888.

Stewart, Robert L. *History of the One Hundred and Fortieth Regiment Pennsylvania Volunteers.* Philadelphia, 1912.

Stocker, Jeffery D., ed. *From Huntsville to Appomattox: R. T. Coles's History of 4th Regiment, Alabama Volunteer Infantry, C.S.A., Army of Northern Virginia.* Knoxville, Tenn., 1996.

Thompson, Gilbert. *The Engineer Battalion in the Civil War.* Washington, D.C., 1910.

Thompson, S. Millett. *Thirteenth Regiment of New Hampshire Volunteer Infantry in the War of the Rebellion, 1861–1865.* Boston, 1888.

Vaill, Theodore F. *History of the Second Connecticut Volunteer Heavy Artillery, Originally the Nineteenth Connecticut Volunteers.* Winsted, Conn., 1868.

Vautier, John D. *History of the 88th Pennsylvania Volunteers in the War for the Union, 1861–1865.* Philadelphia, 1894.

Walcott, Charles F. *History of the Twenty-First Regiment Massachusetts Volunteers in the War for the Preservation of the Union.* Boston, 1882.

Walker, Francis A. *History of the Second Army Corps in the Army of the Potomac.* New York, 1887.

Wallace, Lee A., Jr. *The Richmond Howitzers.* Lynchburg, Va., 1993.

Ward, Joseph R. C. *History of the One Hundred and Sixth Regiment Pennsylvania Volunteers.* Philadelphia, 1883.

Washburn, George H. *History of the Old 108th New York Veteran Volunteers.* Rochester, N.Y., 1894.

Wilkinson, Warren. *Mother, May You Never See the Sights I Have Seen: The Fifty-Seventh Massachusetts Veteran Volunteers in the Last Year of the Civil War.* New York, 1990.

West, Robert Jerald L. *Found among the Privates: Recollections of Holcomb's Legion, 1861–1864, by James L. Strain and Adolphus E. Fant, Correspondents to the Union County News, Union County, S.C.* Sharon, S.C., 1997.

Westbrook, Robert S. *History of the 49th Pennsylvania Volunteers.* Altoona, Pa., 1898.

Weygant, Charles H. *History of the One Hundred Twenty-Fourth Regiment, New York State Volunteers.* Newburgh, N.Y., 1877.

Wray, William James. *History of the Twenty-Third Pennsylvania Volunteer Infantry, Birney's Zouaves*. Philadelphia, 1904.

Campaign Studies

Baltz, Louis J. *The Battle of Cold Harbor, May 27–June 13, 1864*. Lynchburg, Va., 1994.

Bearss, Edwin C., and Bryce A. Suderow. *The Petersburg Campaign, Vol. I: The Eastern Front Battles, June–August 1864*. El Dorado Hills, Calif., 2012.

Chick, Sean Michael. *The Battle of Petersburg, June 15–18, 1864*. Lincoln, Neb., 2015.

Duncan, Richard R. *Lee's Endangered Left: The Civil War in Western Virginia, Spring of 1864*. Baton Rouge, 1998.

Furgurson, Ernest B. *Not War but Murder: Cold Harbor, 1864*. New York, 2000.

Grimsley, Mark. *And Keep Moving On: The Virginia Campaign, May–June 1864*. Lincoln, Neb., 2002.

Horn, John. *The Petersburg Campaign*. Boston, 1993.

Howe, Thomas J. *The Petersburg Campaign: Wasted Valor, June 15–18, 1864*. Lynchburg, Va., 1988.

Rhea, Gordon C. *The Battle of the Wilderness: May 5–6, 1864*. Baton Rouge, 1994.

———. *The Battles for Spotsylvania Court House and the Road to Yellow Tavern: May 7–12, 1864*. Baton Rouge, 1997.

———. *Cold Harbor: Grant and Lee, May 26–June 3, 1864*. Baton Rouge, 2002.

———. "The Move to the James and the Battle of Riddell's Shop." *North & South* 10, no. 6 (June 2008): 16–28.

———. *To the North Anna River: Grant and Lee, May 13–25, 1864*. Baton Rouge, 2000.

Ropes, John C. "The Battle of Cold Harbor." In *PMHSM*, 4:341–62.

———. "Grant's Campaign in Virginia, 1864." In *PMHSM*, 4:365–405.

Waldemer, Donald E. *Triumph at the James: The Checkmate of General R. E. Lee*. N.p., 1998.

Dissertations

Kreiser, Lawrence A., Jr. "From Volunteers to Veterans: A Social and Military History of the II Corps, Army of the Potomac, 1861–1865." Ph.D. dissertation, University of Alabama, 2001.

Index

and movements, 45, 46; June 6 positions
and movements, 95; June 8 positions and
movements, 143; vs. Sedgwick at Wilderness, 327
Gordonsville, 100
Goss, Capt. Enoch W., 295, 297
Gracie, Brig. Gen. Archibald, 150–51, 161,
185, 247
Graham, Capt. Edward, 149, 256, 259–61
Grant, Brig. Gen. Lewis A., 40
Grant, Lt. Gen. Ulysses S., *129, 135;* Adams's description of, 62; appearance
compared to Meade, 188–89; Barnard
and, 162; Burnside and, 45–46; on Butler,
10; casualties produced by, assessment of,
333; cautions on Petersburg, 173; at City
Point, 319–20; Cold Harbor, 13–14, 16–
22, 26; Eustis and, 39; Fortress Monroe
conference with Butler, 5–6; jokes on initials of, 27; March 10 meeting with
Meade, 3; June 4 operations, 40, 52–53,
59, 60–61; June 5 operations, 69, 78; June
6 operations, 82–83; June 6–7 negotiations and truce to recover dead and
wounded, 113–21; June 7 operations, 99,
103, 110–12; June 8 operations, 142–44;
June 9 operations, 145, 151; June 13 operations, 207, 214, 218–20; June 14 operations, 232, 241–44; June 15 failure to capture Petersburg, 310–18; June 15
operations, 261, 264, 266, 278, 287–89,
302, 320; Lee compared to, 7; Lee on
Richmond and, 154; Lee's strategies and,
187; letters, 20, 86; Lincoln's promotion
of, 2–3; on malingerers, 88; Meade, relationship with, 124–25; Meade compared
to, 3–4; Overland Campaign (overview),
ix–x; Overland Campaign performance,
assessment of, 320–28, 332–34; plans and
logistics for withdrawing from Cold Harbor and crossing the James, 161–69, 171–
84, 188, 238, 240; as quintessential
American, 188; rations jest, 51; reporter
Carleton with, 79; Richmond and New
York River Railroad repairs and, 163;
Sheridan and, 49; on Smith, Hancock,

and waiving rank issue, 402n57; southern
graffiti about, 202; speculation if he had
remained in Washington, 403n10; Spotsylvania and, 188; strategic planning,
4–6, 31, 62–66, 146, 369n3; Swinton–
Burnside affair and, 128; withdrawal
from Cold Harbor, 188–90, 196. *See also*
Army of the James; Army of the Potomac
Grant, Orvil, 37
Grapevine Bridge (Sumner's Upper Bridge),
101, 221
Gregg, Brig. Gen. David McM.: June 4 positions and movements, 52, 53; June 5 positions and movements, 73, 79; June 7 positions and movements, 99
Gregg, Brig. Gen. John, 37, 40, 144
Gregory, Col. Edgar M., 85
Grey, Pvt., 119
Griffin, Brig. Gen. Charles: June 4 positions
and movements, 45–47; June 5 positions
and movements, 75; June 6 positions and
movements, 83–85; June 7 positions and
movements, 100, 101, 103; June 9–10 positions and movements, 156; June 11–12
positions and movements, 176, 178, 190,
193, 194; June 13 positions and movements, 215; June 14 positions and movements, 224
Griffin, Col. Simon G., 55, 56, 95, 108
Griffin, Lt. Charles B., 108
Grimes, Brig. Gen. Bryan, 96
Grimsley, Mark, 174, 332
Guinea, 329

Hagood, Brig. Gen. Johnson, 37–39, 306–9
Haines, Alanson A., 154
Hall, Lt. Caldwell K., 39
Halleck, Maj. Gen. Henry W.: Barnard ap-
pointment, 162; ferries requested by
Grant, 65; Grant on Smith to, 316; James
crossing logistics and, 166–67; June 13
positions and movements, 218; June 14
plans and, 242; strategic planning, 4–5,
62, 63; supply lines plans, 25
Hammell, Lt. Col. John S., 115, 178, 194
Hampton, Maj. Gen. Wade: June 4 positions

ments, 42; June 6 positions and movements, 81; June 14 positions and movements, 250

Union 18th Corps, *138;* casualties of, 17; James crossing logistics and, 238; May positions and movements, 10–11, 13–17; June 4 positions and movements, 41–44, 58–59; June 5 positions and movements, 68; June 6 positions and movements, 81; June 9–10 positions and movements, 153; June 9 positions and movements, 146; June 11–12 positions and movements, 172–73, 179, 181; June 13 positions and movements, 207–8, 218; June 14 positions and movements, 250; June 15 positions and movements, 251, 254, 310; leadership and structure of, 346; Overland Campaign review and assessment, 324–25; Petersburg plans, 187; planning for relocation to Bermuda Hundred, 165; return, to shift power in front of Petersburg, 173; withdrawal from Cold Harbor, 195–96; wounded recovery issue, 113. *See also* Smith, Maj. Gen. William F. "Baldy"

Union Artillery. *See* U.S. Artillery

Union Cavalry Corps, 4, 345. *See also* Gregg, Brig. Gen. David McM.; Sheridan, Maj. Gen. Philip H.; Torbert, Alfred Brig. Gen. T. A.; Wilson, Brig. Gen. James H.

Upton, Brig. Gen. Emory: on Cold Harbor, 18; June 4 positions and movements, 38–39; June 5 positions and movements, 77; June 8 reprieve, 139; June 11–12 positions and movements, 195

Upton's charge, 333

U.S. Artillery: *1st,* Battery E, 268; *4th,* Battery C, 192; *4th,* Battery E, 192, 198

U.S. Colored Troops, *137; 1st,* 258, 275, 298–300; *2nd* Artillery, Battery B, 274; *4th,* 258–60, 275, 293, 298–300; *5th,* 258, 274; *6th,* 258–59; *22nd,* 258–60, 293, 298–300, 394n29; Battle of Baylor's Farm, 258–61; Fort Pillow massacre, 259; June 8–10 positions and movements, 146, 159, 160; June 11–12 positions and movements, 180; June 15 positions and move-

ments, 251, 271–75; *New York Times* praise of, 301. *See also* Ferrero, Brig. Gen. Edward; Hinks, Brig. Gen. Edward W.

U.S. Engineer Battalion, Company A, 70

Van Brocklin, Martin, 166

Vaughn, Brig. Gen. John C., 80–81

Venable, Lt. Col. Charles S., 17, 90

Vermont units: *1st,* 51, 58, 190, 201, 270; *1st* Cavalry, 197; *1st* Heavy Artillery, 152

Virginia and Tennessee Railroad, 5, 22

Virginia Central Railroad: June 3 positions and movements, 24, 25; June 4 positions and movements, 51; June 5 positions and movements, 63, 65, 73, 78, 81–82; June 7 foray against, 99–100, 105; June 8 positions and movements, 142; June 9 positions and movements, 145; Overland Campaign review and assessment, 324, 327, 329

Virginia units: *1st* Company, Richmond Howitzers, 40; *9th* Cavalry, 159, 186; *17th,* 153–54; *24th* Cavalry, 198, 200, 270; *26th,* 247, 277, 297; *34th,* 247, 277, 279; *44th* Infantry Battalion, 248; *46th,* 247, 277; *59th,* 247, 309; Barham's Cavalry Battalion, 248; Petersburg Cavalry, 248; Petersburg Militia, 248; Reserves, 3rd Battalion, 248

Wadill's farm, 215

Wainwright, Col. Charles S.: on Cold Harbor, 18; on Cropsey affair, 126–27; on June 5 siege operations, 68; June 11–12 positions and movements, 176, 190; June 14 positions and movements, 226; on Leary place, 100–101

Walker, Lt. Col. Francis A.: June 3 positions and movements, 33; June 5 positions and movements, 69; June 11–12 positions and movements, 178; June 15 positions and movements, 263, 264, 286, 290, 400n18

Walker's farm, 215

Ward, Joseph R. C., 77

Ware's farm, 215